HISTORY MATTERS

HISTORY

MATTERS

*Essays on Economic Growth,
Technology, and Demographic Change*

EDITED BY

TIMOTHY W. GUINNANE,

WILLIAM A. SUNDSTROM,

AND WARREN WHATLEY

STANFORD UNIVERSITY PRESS
STANFORD, CALIFORNIA 2004

Stanford University Press
Stanford, California

© 2004 by the Board of Trustees of the Leland Stanford Junior University. All rights reserved.

Printed in the United States of America on acid-free, archival-quality paper.

Library of Congress Cataloging-in-Publication Data

Essays on economic growth, technology, and demographic change / edited
by Timothy W. Guinnane, William A. Sundstrom, and Warren Whatley.
p. cm.
"The essays collected in this volume were, with two exceptions,
presented at a conference in honor of Professor Paul A. David, held at
Stanford University on June 2–3, 2000. The conference was sponsored by
the Stanford Institute for Economic Policy Research (SIEPR)"—P. .
ISBN 0-8047-4398-3 (cloth : alk. paper)
1. Economic history—Congresses. 2. Economic
history—Methodology—Congresses. 3. Economic development—Congresses.
4. Technological innovations—Economic aspects—Congresses.
5. Population—Economic aspects—Congresses. I. Guinnane, Timothy II.
Sundstrom, William Andrew. III. Whatley, Warren C.
HC13.E85 2003
330.9—dc21
2003007584

Original Printing 2003

Last figure below indicates year of this printing:

12   11   10   09   08   07   06   05   04   03

Typeset by Interactive Composition Corporation in 10.5/15 Minion

For Paul:
Teacher, scholar, mentor, friend

CONTENTS

LIST OF CONTRIBUTORS

KENNETH J. ARROW is Joan Kenney Professor of Economics, Emeritus, Stanford University.

TIMOTHY BESLEY is Professor of Economics, London School of Economics.

CHARLES W. CALOMIRIS is Paul M. Montrone Professor of Finance and Economics, Graduate School of Business, Columbia University.

SUSAN B. CARTER is Professor of Economics, University of California, Riverside.

STEPHEN COATE is Kiplinger Professor of Public Policy, Cornell University.

CHARLES FEINSTEIN is Chichele Professor of Economic History, Emeritus, and Emeritus Fellow of All Souls College, University of Oxford.

TIMOTHY W. GUINNANE is Professor of Economics, Yale University.

PHILLIP WONHYUK LIM is Research Fellow, Korea Development Institute.

PETER C. MANCALL is Professor of History, University of Southern California.

THOMAS A. MROZ is Professor of Economics, University of North Carolina, Chapel Hill.

TROND E. OLSEN is Professor of Finance and Management Science, Norwegian School of Economics and Business Administration, Bergen.

DOUGLAS J. PUFFERT is Visiting Lecturer in Economics, University of Warwick.

ROGER L. RANSOM is Professor of History, University of California, Riverside.

MELVIN W. REDER is I. and G. J. Brown Professor of Urban and Labor Economics, Emeritus, University of Chicago.

PAUL W. RHODE is Professor of Economics, University of North Carolina, Chapel Hill.

JOSHUA L. ROSENBLOOM is Professor of Economics, University of Kansas.

GEOFFREY ROTHWELL is Senior Lecturer and Director of the Honors Programs, Department of Economics, Stanford University.

WARREN C. SANDERSON is Professor of Economics, SUNY, Stony Brook.

PAUL STONEMAN is Research Professor, Warwick Business School, University of Warwick.

WILLIAM A. SUNDSTROM is Professor of Economics, Santa Clara University.

RICHARD SUTCH is Distinguished Professor of Economics, University of California, Riverside.

PETER TEMIN is Elisha Gray II Professor of Economics, MIT.

MARK THOMAS is Associate Professor of History, University of Virginia.

DAVID F. WEIMAN is Professor of Economics, Barnard College.

DAVID R. WEIR is Senior Research Scientist, Institute for Social Research, University of Michigan.

THOMAS WEISS is Professor of Economics, University of Kansas.

WARREN WHATLEY is Professor of Economics, University of Michigan.

PREFACE

The essays collected in this volume were, with two exceptions, presented at a conference in honor of Professor Paul A. David, held at Stanford University on June 2–3, 2000. The conference was sponsored by the Stanford Institute for Economic Policy Research (SIEPR), which provided generous financial and institutional support. Additional financial support from the Social Science History Institute (SSHI) at Stanford University and the Breetwor Fellowship at Santa Clara University is also gratefully acknowledged.

The editors would like to thank a number of individuals who helped make the conference a success, including Deborah Carvalho, Stephen Haber, Lawrence J. Lau, John Pencavel, John Shoven, and the numerous session chairs and discussants. We are particularly indebted to Dafna Baldwin for her organizational skills and unfailing attention to detail. We also thank Susan B. Carter for her role in initiating plans for the conference and making first contacts with participants and contributors.

Two individuals must be named as having been especially crucial to the success of the conference and the subsequent volume. Gavin Wright served as adviser to the organizers and liaison to Stanford University before, during, and after the conference. And the late Moses Abramovitz offered early encouragement in the planning process as well as an insightful and entertaining address to the conference on the subject of his long collaboration with Paul David. The text of Professor Abramovitz's remarks can be found at the SIEPR web site, http://siepr.stanford.edu/conferences/Abramovitz.pdf.

We are grateful to our editors at Stanford University Press, Judith Hibbard, the late Kenneth MacLeod, Janet Mowery, Norris Pope, and Kate Wahl, for bringing this volume to fruition.

Finally, we are delighted to dedicate this volume to Paul A. David, who has been a personal and an intellectual inspiration to each of the contributors.

HISTORY MATTERS

EDITORS' INTRODUCTION

Timothy W. Guinnane, William A. Sundstrom,
and Warren Whatley

The practice of economic history today reflects an ongoing process of borrowing and integrating from economics, history, and other social sciences. Compared with economic history even thirty years ago the field is now more technical, drawing on advances in economic theory and econometrics, but also more reliant on the historian's techniques of archival research and close source scrutiny. At the same time, the discipline of economics has become more open to taking explicit account of the influence of the past. This fruitful interchange between economics and history reflects an increased awareness, then, that history matters.

No scholar has done more over this period to define the approaches, themes, and standards of economic history than Paul A. David. Furthermore, no scholar has more forcefully and influentially argued the case for making economics a truly historical social science—one that, like evolutionary biology, gives past events a central explanatory role in understanding the present. Like most productive scholars he has a long list of publications, including some classic papers that are read by thousands and will continue to be read for many years to come. Like most productive scholars his influence is also felt through the work of his students, both those who worked formally with him as Ph.D. students and those who collaborated with him in other ways. What sets Paul David apart from most scholars, however, is that certain fundamental ideas and methods are distinctly associated with his work within the economics profession. It is the deepest sort of influence when a scholar alters the way others do research even when the topic has nothing to do with the scholar's own specific interests. The essays in this volume all deal in some way with one or more of the issues or methods that David has helped to define.

Although the essays assembled here cover a considerable range of topics and approaches, three broad themes emerge, themes that might be summarized in three phrases: history matters, context matters, and the facts matter. The authors would no doubt agree that an appreciation of these themes is a principal lesson they have taken away from their interactions with Paul David and his work.

The notion that history matters through strong "path dependence" is an idea closely associated with Paul David. Path dependence means different things to different people and in the hands of some has become little more than a buzzword, straw man, or vague conception that draws together disparate ideas. In David's work the term has specific meaning: namely, path dependence describes processes in which the long-run character of the system depends critically on the history of the system—that is, on the specific sequence of events, some of which may be random in nature. Historical events or accidents are not merely short-term "perturbations" to the system, but may alter the evolution of the system in a fundamental way. As David has written, "In such circumstances 'historical accidents' can neither be ignored, nor neatly quarantined for the purpose of economic analysis; the dynamic process itself takes on an essentially historical character" (David 1985, p. 332). Fundamentally, to take path dependence seriously is to demand a "historical economics." And as some of the essays included here make clear, thinking about path dependence may lead to some startling welfare and policy conclusions, which play no little role in the controversy surrounding the idea.

A second perspective that Paul David has championed is the idea that context matters—that the deep "fundamentals" of economic and social structure, institutions, and even culture, can have strong effects on purely economic matters, and that economic modeling must take explicit account of these fundamentals. The economist who takes this idea seriously will occupy an uncomfortable perch between economists who often sweep such concerns under a rug and those who fully appreciate the complexity of human society and react to it with the intellectually nihilist position that attempts to model the complexity are fruitless. The first generation of new economic historians, epitomized by the Nobel laureates Douglass North and Robert Fogel, reinvigorated the field of economic history by applying rigorous price theory to the past and downplaying the importance of historical and cultural context. Indeed, in his early work, North tried to show that institutions were mere epiphenomena of underlying relative factor prices (North and Thomas 1973). But the work of Paul David and others has shown that what Eugene Hammel in another context called "culturally smart microeconomics" pays enormous dividends.

A third hallmark of David's work pertains to the matter of facts and evidence: an insistence on careful and creative use of the tools of economic theory and econometrics in the task of measuring social and economic phenomena of the past. This approach has not been a worship of technique for its own sake; sometimes the theory is simple and the statistical tools no more sophisticated than weighted means. But this insistence on careful modeling and measurement has paid off in many of David's contributions, and by example has raised the standards for modeling and measurement in many other works.

1. HISTORY MATTERS: PATH DEPENDENCE

An important implication of the standard assumptions of neoclassical economics is that the dynamic evolution of the economy is described by movement toward a unique equilibrium path that can be predicted from certain underlying fundamentals, including tastes, technologies, and endowments. The equilibrium may be a moving target because the underlying tastes and technologies may change, and endowments can be altered by random shocks, but the relationship between those changes and the long-run equilibrium is a continuous one. For this reason, even in the neoclassical world history matters, but in a circumscribed manner: small changes in fundamentals have small effects on long-run outcomes.

The neoclassical approach often implies that the economy can eventually "shake free" of its history, in the sense that deviations from the equilibrium path will diminish in impact over time. A well-known illustration of such a process in economics comes from the standard Solow growth model. Consider an economy in which half the physical capital has been destroyed by war or natural disaster. The resultant reduction in per capita product would be transitory in the sense that capital deepening would eventually cause the economy to converge back toward the equilibrium per capita product implied by its underlying technology, population growth, and savings behavior.

In systems typified by path dependence, history matters in a more fundamental way. As David has defined it, "A path dependent stochastic process is one whose asymptotic distribution evolves as a consequence (function) of the process's own history" (David 2000, p. 5). This is a precise way of saying that the process cannot shake free of its history. Because path dependence implies multiple dynamic equilibria, relatively small historical events, if they lead to the selection of an alternative equilibrium path, can have large and persistent long-run implications. Furthermore, as David (1985) suggests for the case of the QWERTY typewriter keyboard, society might not be indifferent between the alternatives. The possibility of lock-in on an inferior technology cannot be ruled out. Path-dependent growth, *pace* Solow, may exhibit divergence rather than convergence.

It is one thing to assert that path dependence exists and therefore that history matters in this far-reaching way. But economics cannot be satisfied with mere assertion, both on general methodological grounds and because neoclassical economics, as the dominant paradigm, tends to receive the benefit of the doubt among practicing economists (see the essay by Reder in this volume). Hence, a convincing theoretical and empirical case must be made that the assumption of path dependence is appropriate in a given case. A particular virtue of Paul David's work in this area has been his careful specification of the theoretical conditions that are likely to give rise to path dependence. It is then the task of the economic historian or empirical economist to determine for each specific case whether the conditions have plausibly been met. These two strands in the literature on path dependence—its theoretical underpinnings and its empirical applications—are both represented in this volume.

The Theory of Path Dependence

Kenneth Arrow's essay is a good place to start because it presents a lucid overview of the theoretical underpinnings of the literature to date and argues that the idea of path dependence is more general than is often appreciated. Much of the literature on path dependence has stressed the causal role of increasing returns. Network effects are a widely cited example. Suppose, for example, that agents can choose between two competing technologies and that the net benefit of a technology is an increasing function of the number of adopters. Then the sequence of early adoptions can have a powerful impact on the ultimate equilibrium choice of technology (Arthur 1989; David 1985). Adoption of one of the alternatives has a positive feedback effect, encouraging further adoptions. In this case increasing returns take the form of a positive network externality.

But is path dependence always, or even usually, a consequence of increasing returns? Arrow argues that the fundamental source of path dependence is not increasing returns but irreversibility of investment. In his dynamic equilibrium model path dependence arises even with constant returns to scale when capital is infinitely durable (and therefore investments are irreversible). Early investment decisions become a sunk cost, and during subsequent periods agents may find it optimal to continue to use installed capital rather than scrap it, even if it is less productive than an alternative capital good would be. Arrow cites a number of illustrative cases of path dependence, including Thorstein Veblen's classic account of German industrialization and the purported advantages of being a follower. In each case, he argues, irreversibility of investment plays a crucial role.

Paul Stoneman takes another theoretical approach to path dependence and once again shows that it is more general than has been appreciated. Most models of path dependence are built, as Arrow noted, on network externalities or feedback. In his chapter Stoneman constructs a simple intuitive model that has no network features but exhibits path dependence nonetheless. The key feature of his model is what Stoneman calls "legacy" effects. There are two technologies, and the benefits of installing one depend on whether the other has already been installed. If the two technologies exist side by side then the situation is much like a standard production function with positive but declining marginal productivity of capital. A more novel situation arises when one technology is in place and another is new. Then, as Stoneman shows, the pattern of diffusion depends critically on (among other things) which is the new technology. Thus the decision to adopt a new technology at a given time depends not just on prices at that time, but on the path of adoption up to that point. This is the central feature of path dependence, and Stoneman generates this result without externalities of any kind.

Arrow's and Stoneman's chapters share a common feature, which is the demonstration that path dependence, which was originally associated with network externalities and thus thought to be of limited importance in the real economy, can arise in far more general circumstances. Both chapters focus on the nature of investments. Arrow isolates the irreversibility of the investment as the central point. Stoneman's chapter, which uses a different kind of model, can be thought of as deriving a set of conditions under which the cost of reversing an earlier adoption decision might affect the probability of adopting a given technology today. Together these chapters suggest a more expansive view of the role of path dependence in the economy.

To increasing returns and irreversibilities, Douglas Puffert's chapter adds a third factor contributing to path-dependent processes: limited foresight. Puffert notes that, given perfect foresight and complete future markets, increasing returns need not imply path dependence because agents could in principle select the single globally optimal dynamic path from the alternatives. In a sense, the multiple dynamic equilibria of increasing returns would collapse into a single rational-expectations equilibrium. But the real world is characterized by imperfect information and limited foresight, and in such a world path dependence becomes possible as agents make decisions sequentially and myopically. Puffert finds unconvincing the critiques frequently leveled at Paul David and Brian Arthur that fault them for assuming imperfect foresight.

Puffert's essay goes on to examine the implications of *network form* for path dependence. By network form he has in mind the structure of interconnections among users in the network. Puffert notes that many networks have a lumpy structure, in which local subnetworks use common standards, but subnetworks may then be linked in various ways with varying degrees of compatibility. The network effects operate to different degrees within or between these subnetworks. Puffert examines a number of case studies, including railroad gauges, electrical power distribution, telecommunications, and computers. His overview of these cases points to the importance not only of network form, but also of so-called gateway technologies, which help overcome compatibility problems across standards.

Arrow, Stoneman, and Puffert all provide strong theoretical grounds for thinking that path dependence can occur. But how significant is the challenge of path dependence to conventional economic theory and methodology? The view that path dependence plays an important role in the real world is what Melvin Reder terms "strong history" in his contribution to this volume. Using Thomas Kuhn's framework, Reder argues that strong history and strong (neo-classical) economics constitute competing paradigms for economics. The neoclassical paradigm, however, is the incumbent, and "with that goes the default position in allocating the burden of proof." Strong history, as a challenger to orthodoxy, will necessarily be held to a higher standard of empirical support than strong economics.

Reder chooses not to take sides on the empirical debate. But he does identify an additional factor favoring the neoclassical paradigm in the battle for the hearts and minds of economists and economic historians. Namely, the neoclassical model is a powerful tool in empirical work, even of a purely descriptive nature. The neoclassical equilibrium conditions imply relationships among prices, quantities, and underlying technical parameters that permit the researcher to draw broad inferences from limited information. In Reder's view, most economists would be loath to relinquish these tools without overwhelming evidence of their falsity.

Case Studies of Path Dependence

Some of the most interesting discussions of path-dependence literature are found in case studies of specific historical phenomena. Here the challenge is to uncover and document the role of history in the evolution of a specific economic structure without lapsing into generalities about how the past must of course matter. A good example is Charles Calomiris's discussion of post–World War II international monetary institutions. Calomiris argues that the "second thirty-years' war" (the period extending from World War I through World War II) can be thought of as a shock that gave rise to institutions of a specific historical nature: the decline of the gold standard and the spread of regulation. The absence of the gold standard and the new regulations increased the expectation of bailout, trade volatility, and inflation and gave rise to the International Monetary Fund and the World Bank. These institutions continue to evolve and to influence policy today. Given that these institutions emerged in response to historically specific shocks (the world wars and the Great Depression) and continue to influence policy, they can be thought of as path dependent in nature.

Phillip Lim, like Calomiris, applies the concept of path dependence to the evolution of institutions, an application that has been encouraged by David (1994) in his own work. Lim argues that the role of the state in South Korea's economy emerged as a path-dependent adjustment to historical accidents during the postwar period, resulting in a set of institutions that have recently contributed to the country's financial difficulties. In pre-1961 South Korea the United States backed a conservative anticommunist regime that used cronyism to build its political base. After 1961 the anticommunist regime was bent on economic development as a response and counterweight to perceived North Korean communistic success. Lim characterizes the post-1961 policy regime as a risk-guarantee system that was adopted after Korea was forced to acquiesce to IMF and U.S. pressures. These choices had lasting consequences. Under the risk-guarantee regime, the state guaranteed loans to select firms based on their success in the export sector. State action in times of crisis revealed that the state would bail out these companies. As firms came to expect this, moral hazard became institutionalized. The resulting inefficiencies gave rise to financial crises, and the state's bailout during these crises only reinforced the expectation that the state would bail out the private sector the next time. The April 1996 collapse of the semiconductor market is but the most recent cycle in the risk-guarantee regime.

The persistence of an apparently suboptimal economic policy regime is also a central theme of Peter Temin's account of the evolution of federal regulation in the U.S. telecommunications industry. Recounting the debates between the Federal Communications Commission and the firms in the industry beginning in 1959, Temin argues that the FCC has never been able to treat costs consistently in regulating pricing. The reason is that the FCC has consistently favored entrants over the entire forty-plus years of its existence, arguing that the incumbent firm (AT&T through much of the period) should charge high prices when it extends into competitive markets, but should charge low prices to entrants who want access to its network. Although the ostensible regulatory policy is that prices should cover costs, the proper definition of the relevant costs has been repeatedly contested by the FCC and the phone company, with the FCC persistently advocating the definition of cost that most favored entry. Although Temin does not attempt to explain the hysteresis in FCC thinking, what is clear is that the regulator has failed to adapt its regulatory approach to changes in the competitive structure of the industry.

The recent literature on economic growth and economic geography has seen an increased interest in models that are explicitly historical. One important source of path dependence in these models is external economies of scale. The role of external economies in regional and urban economic development is one of the oldest themes in economics, dating back to Adam Smith's *Wealth of Nations* and elaborated upon by subsequent economists, most notably Alfred Marshall. In his work on Chicago, Paul David (1987) demonstrated the importance of such agglomeration economies. These ideas have received renewed interest among economists in the so-called new economic geography (see, for example, Krugman 1993). In his chapter, Paul Rhode applies the related concept of home market effects to understanding the U.S. Pacific Coast economy after World War II.

Home market effects occur when expanding local or regional demand for products facilitates increased productivity locally through external economies or learning. Rhode hypothesizes that the booming wartime home market may have pushed the West Coast economy from a low-level to a high-level equilibrium, defying wartime expectations that the region would suffer serious and potentially long-lasting economic dislocations after the war. To demonstrate the importance of home market effects, Rhode uses a panel of California manufacturing industries to estimate a reduced-form model of industry value added. The key finding is that the size of the California economy, as measured by the (log) ratio of California to national income, affects individual industry manufacturing activity with an elasticity in excess of 1, suggesting powerful positive feedback. Rhode's chapter weds historical description and data analysis to make the case that California's postwar economic growth was indeed a path-dependent process.

The implications of path dependence for decision makers, including government policymakers, continue to be a source of contention. As Geoffrey Rothwell shows in his chapter, policy decisions can offset lock-in effects in path-dependent regimes, but not without cost. Rothwell examines the optimality of China's nuclear power program, applying a model developed jointly with Paul David. In the model there are two generations of nuclear power plants. Choosing a standardized design in generation one offers the opportunity to learn by doing in both generations, reducing operating costs substantially. Alternatively, in generation one planners could choose a diverse menu of plant designs, forgoing learning gains but retaining flexibility in the future and gaining from experimentation with alternative designs. Using plausible parameter values for the Chinese case, Rothwell simulates total power generation costs for different degrees of diversity. He finds that Chinese decision makers, for a variety of reasons, chose greater technological diversity than would have been optimal.

2. CONTEXT MATTERS

Path dependence or strong history is one route to a more historical economics. Another is to make use of historical description to contextualize and enrich the explanatory models of economic theory. A good example of this attention to what we refer to above as deep fundamentals is the chapter by Timothy Besley, Stephen Coate, and Timothy Guinnane on the English Poor Law reform of 1834. The implicit contrast here is to a type of institutional economic history pioneered by Douglass North and his students. North, especially in his earlier work, emphasized the explanatory power of very simple economic models. Given his goals and the nature of the debates in which he was engaged, this simplicity might have been warranted, but more recent institutional economic history has shown that more careful attention to the social and economic context pays ample dividends through a better appreciation of the constraints facing the historical actors in question.[1] Besley, Coate, and Guinnane stress the social and political circumstances that determined the availability of information on the poor to those administering the Poor Law.

Central to the New Poor Law, as implemented under the Poor Law Act of 1834, was the reduction of the power of local authorities and the elimination of outdoor relief for the able-bodied through the use of the workhouse test. The workhouse test was a simple administrative device: when individuals applied for poor relief, officials could make relief conditional on entering the workhouse, and nothing more. By setting a standard for economic relief and psychological stress in the workhouses, self-selection into the poorhouses revealed the true opportunity utility of potential entrants. If the relief standard was set low and the psychological stress level set high, then only the neediest (deserving) poor would enter the poorhouse.

While much of the literature on the New Poor Law emphasizes the low relief level set by the workhouses, Besley, Coate, and Guinnane emphasize how the workhouse test economized on information that had become increasingly unreliable during this time. The workhouse test screened the deserving from the undeserving poor and deterred the kind of behavior that would lead to poverty. The dramatic social and economic change that took place in England starting in the late eighteenth century also broke down the local nature of social ties that had verified information on the poor. The New Poor Law took the form it did, the authors argue, because its architects wanted to reduce the information needed to administer poor relief.

Susan Carter, Roger Ransom, and Richard Sutch's chapter is in many ways the summary of a long and fruitful dialogue with Paul David on the topics of U.S. fertility decline and its relation to broader themes of growth and savings in the nineteenth-century economy. Carter, Ransom, and Sutch disagree with some aspects of David's own contributions on these subjects, but the spirit of their work is very much in keeping with the notion of paying close attention to the cultural and historical trends that shape economic and demographic behavior.

Historians have long appreciated that fertility declined earlier and more rapidly in the United States than it did in much of Western Europe. Estimates that Carter, Ransom, and Sutch discuss show that total fertility rates of whites fell by about half between 1800 and 1900. A long succession of scholars have sought to explain this precocious decline in fertility, usually tying it into other great themes in American economic history such as migration and the availability of cheap land on the frontier. In a well-known contribution to the literature, Richard Easterlin (1976) linked fertility decline to the closing of the frontier by arguing that declining land availability made it increasingly costly for farmers to endow their children with adequate farmland. Unable to meet their target bequests to a large number of children, they reduced their fertility. In contrast, both David (Sundstrom and David 1988) and Carter, Ransom, and Sutch stress the role of children in the provision of old-age support for their parents. Using a bargaining model, Sundstrom and David argued that the key and hitherto underappreciated force was the increase in off-farm opportunities for children. As economic development improved children's off-farm opportunities, the terms of the bargain between the generations tilted in favor of the children; parents responded by reducing the number of children they had and provided for old age in other ways.

Carter, Ransom, and Sutch also see the rise of off-farm opportunities as a key causal factor, although they emphasize the problem of "child default" (children simply leaving) rather than the changes in bargaining power. They make two important contributions to this discussion. The first is a masterful overview and analysis of the available data, improving on previous work by disaggregating to the county level and incorporating a variety of variables and alternative measures. The second is to provide a different twist on the David-Sundstrom argument. Carter, Ransom, and Sutch argue that a major driving force in the decline of fertility was in fact a *cultural* change: the decline of patriarchal family relations and the rise of what they call life-cycle behavior, under which children were increasingly viewed as a consumption good rather than an investment in old-age security. This change in turn had far-reaching implications for such macroeconomic phenomena as savings behavior.

In his chapter, David Weiman explores another dimension of the historical context of economic activity: namely, the spatial and industrial structure of markets and its subtle influence on the development of the organizational structure of business firms. Specifically, he argues that the spatial pattern of wholesale trade influenced the design of the early Bell telephone system. Weiman's method is an analytical rendition of the strategies and insights of key managers and engineers of the newly formed AT&T Company between 1887 and 1914. Weiman reviews the basic technology of early telephone service and Bell's traffic studies, which suggest the affinity between long-distance telephone service and wholesale trade. The essay focuses on the hierarchical organizational structure of long-distance telephone networks and how this is explained by the natural flow of long-distance telephone traffic and ultimately increasing returns to long-distance telephone service.

Another legacy of history that shapes economic action is the structure of political institutions, both national and international. Whether jurisdictions cooperate or compete in setting taxes and other economic policies may have important welfare consequences. In his chapter, Trond Olsen develops a model of competition between national governments for technology investments by large multinational enterprises. Olsen shows that in a setting with asymmetric information, competition between countries to lure direct investment may lead to over- or underinvestment relative to the efficient level, depending in part on the ownership structure of the multinational firm. The analysis suggests a reason that national governments might take an active interest in patterns of equity ownership of investing firms, for reasons not only of distribution but also of efficiency.

3. FACTUAL MATTERS: ECONOMICS AND HISTORICAL MEASUREMENT

Economic history is the field of economics that has perhaps been most concerned with questions of data quality. The limitations of historical data have inspired historians to seek out unusual new data sources and to tease the most information possible out of the available numbers. Careful attention to economic theory is required in order to combine limited data and plausible assumptions to yield useful inferences. Several chapters in this volume apply methods pioneered or inspired by Paul David to do just that.

Estimating economic growth before the advent of modern economic or demographic statistics is a central task of economic history. An important tool in this endeavor is the conjectural estimation methodology championed by David (1967) in his study of U.S. economic growth during the early nineteenth century. Making use of basic growth accounting equations, snippets of historical data, and plausible assumptions about production parameters and the growth of various components of the economy, the researcher arrives at "controlled conjectures" about income and growth.

The chapter by Peter Mancall, Joshua Rosenbloom, and Thomas Weiss employs the conjectural methodology to estimate rates of economic growth in the American Lower South during the eighteenth century. The authors present a "reality check" for those who have asserted that colonial growth rates of per capita product were in the range of 0.3 to 0.5 percent per year. Using plausible assumptions, the authors suggest that the true figures were likely much smaller, closer to 0.1 percent for the period before the American Revolution. An important innovation of Mancall, Rosenbloom, and Weiss's contribution is to offer estimates that include the Native American population. These conjectures are based on scanty evidence, but even so they show how the picture of economic growth must look quite different when Indians are included. Indeed, inclusion of the native population considerably increases the estimates of per capita growth rates. This result arises because by all accounts the per capita income of Native Americans was considerably below that of the colonists, and the dramatic shift in the composition of the population away from the Indians therefore drove overall per capita incomes up.

Economic historians who attempt to estimate economic growth in more modern industrialized economies often have better data to work with, but confront new challenges. Estimating national product and economic growth based on output data for specific industries or sectors of the economy requires estimating the value added of each sector and using appropriate weights to aggregate the components into the national total. Estimating real growth by sector raises the difficult question of how to adjust value added for price changes in both the inputs and the outputs (David 1962, 1966). In their chapter, Mark Thomas and Charles Feinstein provide a careful analytical discussion of the biases inherent in alternative deflation procedures, given incomplete data. They show that the choice of a second-best index to measure real growth in value added involves tradeoffs: which index is least biased may depend on the values of several parameters, such as the share of materials in value added and rates of technological change and relative price changes. Using ranges of values for these parameters appropriate to the nineteenth-century British economy, Thomas and Feinstein provide estimates of the likely magnitudes of the biases. Importantly, they are able to show that some simple and commonly used indicators of real growth, such as the growth of real inputs or of real outputs, may give seriously misleading estimates of growth in value added. But their findings are hardly nihilistic. They show that even with infrequent observations on prices and quantities, one can do much better deflating with an easily calculated Fisher index.

When historical data are not up to modern standards, a fruitful approach can be to devise entirely novel methodologies and measures that can take advantage of whatever data are available. Paul David and Warren Sanderson took this approach to the measurement of fertility decline in historical populations. In some circumstances one has access to tabulations of the number of children ever born to married women, the age at which these women married, and the duration of their marriages. This is very crude information by the standards of modern surveys but in some ways is more detailed than what is usually available historically. David and Sanderson devised a method (CPA, for cohort parity analysis) that amounts to comparing the fertility behavior of two populations and interpreting the differences (see David and Sanderson 1988). The "model" population is one in which there is little or no fertility control, and the "target" population is the one thought to be exhibiting some fertility control. With a few judicious assumptions CPA can yield estimates of the fraction of the population controlling fertility and the number of children born to women who are doing so.

Sanderson's chapter in this volume explores the strengths and limitations of CPA. In part the chapter responds to an earlier critique by Barbara Okun and coauthors, who argued that CPA was not a reliable tool because it was very sensitive to some determinants of fertility that often cannot be measured, given the limitations of historical data. Sanderson defines and discusses three types of bias that might invalidate CPA results and then uses simulations to show how such problems can be identified in specific cases. His "user's guide" suggests some simple tests that can help practitioners avoid the pitfalls of misusing CPA. Based on an application of these techniques to the case of Irish fertility in 1911, Sanderson concludes that earlier findings based on CPA were largely reliable, and that CPA remains a robust and powerful tool for historical demography.

Thomas Mroz and David Weir's chapter represents a different way to use a powerful modeling tool in a concrete historical application. Their chapter focuses on ways to make practical use of explicit economic modeling in a circumstance where full-blown structural models quickly become computationally intractable. In any life-cycle decision (such as fertility) there will arise two fundamental modeling issues. One is unobserved heterogeneity, which if ignored can bias estimates. The other is the complicated dynamics of any forward-looking decision. Most decisions have consequences for both the present and the future. Econometric models that attempt to incorporate the future implications of current decisions must somehow model the agent's decision-making process throughout all relevant future periods. Here the problem is not so much that the data are lacking as that any model that tries to deal with these two fundamental econometric problems will be both impossible to estimate and difficult to interpret. Even a very parsimonious model, one incorporating only three or four choice variables, can imply many thousands of future "states" for each set of decisions. These modeling difficulties have impeded the application of structural approaches in situations such as life-cycle fertility.

Mroz and Weir focus on ways to simplify the model while still capturing the essentials of the problem at hand. Their approach is based on a combination of judicious simplifications. On the one hand, they rely on discrete factor approximations to model unobserved heterogeneity. On the other, they reduce the dimensions of the dynamics by treating each couple's decision problem as a series of two-period optimization problems; rather than model the next twenty periods, Mroz and Weir model "this period" and "everything after." Their two approximations are related in that the simplified dynamics means some intercouple variation will appear as unobserved heterogeneity when it is more formally the consequence of the simplified treatment of consequences. Their model, unlike fully structural models, can be estimated without tying up a supercomputer, and because of its relative simplicity allows the research to incorporate a larger and more complicated set of choice variables. This chapter outlines a remarkable compromise between reduced-form models and full structural models and should help advance econometric modeling of dynamic decision-making processes.

It is our hope and expectation that the reader will bring away from this diverse collection of essays an increased appreciation of the many ways in which history and economics may inform and enrich one another. And if, as we would insist, scholarship is itself subject to path dependence, much like the social and economic phenomena considered here, this volume will also serve to demonstrate the profound and enduring influence of Paul A. David on these disciplines and the scholars who engage in them.

Note

1. In fairness, in his later work North himself has embraced a more nuanced view of the role of institutions and culture (see, e.g., North 1990).

References

Abramovitz, Moses, and Paul A. David. 2000. "American Macroeconomic Growth in the Era of Knowledge-Based Progress: The Long-Run Perspective." In Stanley L. Engerman and Robert E. Gallman, eds., *The Cambridge Economic History of The United States.* Vol. 3. Cambridge, England: Cambridge University Press.

Arthur, W. Brian. 1989. "Competing Technologies, Increasing Returns, and Lock-in by Historical Events." *Economic Journal* 99: 116–31.

David, Paul A. 1962. "The Deflation of Value Added." *Review of Economics and Statistics* 44: 148–55.

———. 1966. "Measuring Real Net Output: A Proposed Index." *Review of Economics and Statistics* 48: 419–25.

———. 1967. "The Growth of Real Product in the United States before 1840: New Evidence, Controlled Conjectures." *Journal of Economic History* 27: 151–97.

———. 1985. "Clio and the Economics of QWERTY." *American Economic Review Papers and Proceedings* 75: 332–37.

———. 1987. "Industrial Labor Market Adjustments in a Region of Recent Settlement: Chicago, 1848–1868." In Peter Kilby, ed., *Quantity and Quiddity: Essays in U.S. Economic History,* pp. 47–97. Middletown, Conn.: Wesleyan University Press.

———. 1994. "Why Are Institutions the 'Carriers of History'? Path Dependence and the Evolution of Conventions, Organizations, and Institutions." *Structural Change and Economic Dynamics* 5: 205–20.

———. 2000. "Path Dependence, Its Critics, and the Quest for 'Historical Economics.'" Working paper subsequently published in Pierre Garrouste and

Stavros Ioannides, eds., *Evolution and Path Dependence in Economic Ideas: Past and Present.* Cheltenham, England: Edward Elgar, 2001.

David, Paul A., and Warren Sanderson. 1988. "Measuring Marital Fertility Control with CPA." *Population Index* 54: 691–713.

Easterlin, Richard A. 1976. "Population Change and Farm Settlement in the Northern United States." *Journal of Economic History* 36: 45–75.

Eichengreen, Barry. 1992. *Golden Fetters: The Gold Standard and the Great Depression, 1919–1939.* New York: Oxford University Press.

Krugman, Paul. 1993. *Geography and Trade.* Cambridge, Mass.: MIT Press.

North, Douglass C. 1990. *Institutions, Institutional Change, and Economic Performance.* Cambridge, England: Cambridge University Press.

North, Douglass C., and Robert Paul Thomas. 1973. *The Rise of the Western World: A New Economic History.* Cambridge, England: Cambridge University Press.

Sundstrom, William A., and Paul A. David. 1988. "Old-Age Security Motives, Labor Markets, and Farm-Family Fertility in Antebellum America," *Explorations in Economic History* 25: 164–97.

I

WHY HISTORY MATTERS: PATH DEPENDENCE AND ECONOMIC THOUGHT

1

PATH DEPENDENCE AND COMPETITIVE EQUILIBRIUM

Kenneth J. Arrow

1. INTRODUCTION

Paul David has been a pioneer and innovator in so many directions that it is hard to keep track of them all. He has moved with ease from specific historical events and episodes to broad generalizations, both theoretical and empirical in nature. The diffusion of the reaper, with close attention to both social interaction and profitability, the need for purchasing-power comparisons to replace foreign-exchange rates in international welfare comparisons, the bias toward labor-saving innovation in explaining the evolution of the distribution of income, the interpretation of Habbakuk's thesis on American economic growth relative to England's, and more recently the comparative roles of science and technology in technical change are merely a few of the many contributions that David has made to the progress of economics and in particular to the analysis of technical change and its economic implications.

I want here to discuss one particular thesis that David has been strongly associated with, the idea of *path dependence*. This is a concept whose general meaning is fairly clear, though a precise definition is not so easy. Roughly speaking, it means that the long-term historical evolution of an economy (or any other system) depends on where it started, or perhaps on some of the disturbances to the system during its history. The critical point is that the effect of these initial conditions or disturbances is essentially permanent; it does not gradually vanish with time.

Many economic theories do not show path dependence, for example, the Solow growth model, which predicts that all economies will converge to the same limiting capital-labor ratio even though they may start with very different ratios. It is a thesis of Paul David and others that real economies display path dependence.[1]

I do not think there is the slightest question that path dependence is a real phenomenon in economic history and development, as it is in biological evolution and in the history of political and social institutions. My purpose in this chapter is to examine one claimed aspect of path dependence, namely, that it arises as a result of increasing returns to scale in some relevant part of the economy. I will argue, by means of an example, that this is not so. Even with constant returns to scale and perfectly competitive equilibrium, path dependence is possible.

My suggestion is that it is the irreversibility of investment, not increasing returns, that is at the root of path dependence. Even though Paul David has emphasized the role of increasing returns in path dependence, my thesis is rooted in one of his papers, that on the failure of Great Britain to adopt the reaper (David 1971). A study of his paper convinced me that the argument there did not depend in any way on increasing returns, and the model of this chapter is loosely suggested by David's analysis.

2. THE FORMAL NOTION OF PATH DEPENDENCE

A. Dynamic Systems in General

In this chapter, I confine myself to deterministic dynamic systems. The evolution of the system is governed by the dynamic relations and the initial conditions. Suppose the system converges for all or some set of initial conditions. There is *path dependence* if the limit depends on the initial conditions—that is, if for different initial conditions the system converges to different limits. The classic case is that of a drop of rain falling on a hill. Once landed, the water's flow is determined by the law of gravity and the particular topography. The rain will eventually go into a valley, but which valley depends on the point of initial contact with the ground.

B. Intertemporal Competitive Equilibrium

The specific dynamic system we want to look at is intertemporal competitive equilibrium with an infinite horizon. The finite-horizon intertemporal equilibrium model was first formulated by Lindahl (1929) and subsequently by Hicks (1939); the infinite-horizon version of a complete general equilibrium was first studied by Bewley (1972). It is now known that such models are capable of extremely complex behavior, even chaotic solutions (Boldrin and Montrucchio 1991). It is perhaps therefore not surprising that path dependence is possible in intertemporal equilibria.

Note that in competitive models, including intertemporal competitive models, we are assuming concavity of the production functions and therefore rejecting increasing returns.

3. SOME EXAMPLES OF PATH DEPENDENCE

A. Path Dependence in General History

Historians, unlike economists, have always been very prone to assume path dependence. Large consequences flow from the idiosyncrasies of kings and other leaders (for example, Henry VIII's love life and the separation of England from the Catholic Church). Blaise Pascal's remark that the history of the world would have been different if Cleopatra's nose were somewhat longer would be compatible with much historical analysis, though Pascal himself was no historian. I ran across the work of the great Dutch historian Pieter Geyl (1961–64) on the separation of the Netherlands from Belgium. He argued that, to begin with, there was little difference between the northern and southern Netherlands, as they then were. Politically, they were a set of fiefs jointly under the effective sovereignty of the Spanish ruler. The resentment of Spanish rule was common. The religious division between Protestants and Catholics was about the same. However, as the Spanish sought to reestablish their control against the revolt, the convoluted seacoasts in the north provided greater refuge for the rebels. As the Spanish regained control in the south, Protestant refugees fled north, changing the religious balance. It was therefore because of geography that the north became the successful point of resistance and also the center of Protestantism, to the point that when independence was ceded to the north, the two areas increasingly diverged in religion and other social attitudes. Two hundred years later, the unity of the Netherlands was reestablished by the decision of the victors over Napoleon but could not be maintained with such divergence of religion and of national sentiment.

B. Veblen on German Economic Development

Thorstein Veblen's (1915) study of the rise of Germany as an industrial power is a prime example of path dependence in economic history. Veblen's rich analysis covers many aspects of German development and still repays study, but the particular point I want to emphasize is his explanation why Germany, a latecomer to industrial development in comparison with Great Britain, managed to surpass it. If we assume the two countries had access to the same technologies in, say, 1870, but Great Britain had accumulated more capital, we would expect according to simple models that Germany would gradually catch up with Great Britain but would always lag behind it. As generally perceived, though, the latecomer actually surpasses its rival.

Veblen's view was that this was not an accident but the natural result of being a follower. His argument was illustrated by the railroad systems and the corresponding freight-handling equipment at the ports. The British started with narrow-gauge railroads and built equipment to transfer freight from railroads to ships that matched. Later technological developments showed that standard-gauge railroads were more efficient. The Germans, building later, followed the later technology. The technological knowledge was equally available to the British, but since they would have had to replace both railways and freight-handling equipment, it was never worthwhile. Hence, though both countries had access to the same technology and both were responding rationally, the Germans would develop higher productivity than the British.

In Veblen's account, there is path dependence because the future course of economic development is determined, even in the long run, by the initial capital configurations around 1870.

C. Urban Agglomeration

It is fairly common to observe that industrial and commercial activity is concentrated in cities rather than spread out uniformly. Further, while some cities clearly have some special locational advantage, such as a fine port, many do not. Many are located on plains where there seems to be no special advantage over many other sites. It is has long been a common argument, already found in Marshall (1920), that there are external economies that explain the structure of cities. This point of view was elaborated in the work on the economics of location; see Christaller (1966); Lösch (1954).

This insight can be given a dynamic interpretation. Given an initial unequal distribution of activity, the locations with denser activities have an advantage that causes new activities to accumulate there, reinforcing the original inequality. This process has been elaborated on by Arthur (1988).

D. Lock-in in Product Development

It has several times been claimed that the specific characteristics of products can be historically determined. An outstanding example is Paul David's argument that the configuration of the typewriter keyboard was determined by historical accident (David 1985). In early typewriters, there were many different assignments of letters to keys. The one now used had as its chief advantage not speed but avoidance of jamming the keys. As the technology improved, this property became irrelevant. But in the meantime there was an accumulation of human capital invested in learning the keyboard, an investment that made it uneconomic to switch to a new keyboard designed for speed, even though such existed.

Arthur (1989) gave a general model in which development of a product in one direction lowered the costs of continuing in that direction, even though an alternative path would ultimately have yielded a greater product. He argued that the development of the videocassette recorder, in choosing between two rival formats, illustrated his model.

E. British Nonuse of the Mechanical Reaper

As I have indicated, interpreting David (1971) has led to this paper. Paul David sought to explain why the mechanical reaper, whose use was so widespread in the United States, was not used by British farmers. He argued that it was due to the plowing practices that were well adapted to an economy with hand-reaping. The furrows were very deep, made more so by centuries of repeated plowing. As a result, the reaper would cut only the grain growing at the tops of the furrows, leaving the rest to be discarded or reaped by hand. Hence, there might be no gain to the farmers from switching to the reaper. Of course, the fields could be replowed to adapt to the mechanical reaper; but this would require a large capital cost that, it might be inferred, would not pay in subsequent labor-saving. The American farmers, starting with virgin soil, had no such capital cost.

F. Is Path Dependence a Consequence of Increasing Returns?

Some of the examples given above certainly assume increasing returns. It seems to be assumed by Paul David, by Brian Arthur, and, I suppose, by many others, that path dependence is intrinsically linked with increasing returns. Actually, the presence or absence of increasing returns in these examples is more subtle than might be thought. In the typewriter keyboard case, for example, the indivisibility (I take for granted that increasing returns always depends on the presence of an indivisibility) is in the acquisition of human capital (the skill of working at a particular keyboard). A similar analysis can be made of the other cases. But in the last example, the nonuse of the mechanical reaper in Great Britain, no increasing returns are present at all. The argument is just as valid on an arbitrarily small piece of land with an arbitrarily small amount of reaper-time.

One aspect is common to all the examples: the durability of the capital. If plowing were renewed each year or if typists had to relearn their keyboards at short intervals, none of the lock-in, path-dependent character of economic history would be present. I will present a simple model to show that even under all of the conditions that characterize competitive equilibrium, including constant returns to scale, path dependence is possible when there is an irreversible element to capital formation.

4. AN ILLUSTRATIVE MODEL

There are three production processes, 0, 1, and 2, with successively increasing labor productivities. Process 0 requires no capital; processes 1 and 2 require specific kinds of capital (not shiftable across processes). Some capital of type 1 exists, none of type 2; process 2 has just been invented. Neither kind of capital depreciates. Each production process has fixed coefficients for labor and for capital. Both kinds of capital are produced by labor alone. There is one consumer product, produced by the three processes; utility is linear in the product. There is one consumer, who maximizes the integral (over infinite time) of discounted consumption, with force of discount (consumption interest rate) equal to ρ.

Let N_i be the total amount of labor used in process i. Let M_i be the amount of labor used to produce capital of type i ($i = 1, 2$). Let v_i be the amount of labor needed to produce one unit of the consumer good by process i ($i = 0$, 1, 2). Let μ_i be the amount of labor needed to produce one unit of capital of type i ($i = 1, 2$). Finally, let capital be so measured that in both processes 1 and 2, one unit of capital is needed to produce one unit of the consumption good.

Let $K_i(t)$ be the amount of capital of type i at time t. $K_1(0)$ is some given positive number, $K_2(0) = 0$.

Given these conditions, an optimum path, which is also a competitive equilibrium in this simple one-person case, is determined. It will be shown that, for a large range of values of the parameters, the optimal path requires full utilization of the existing capital in process 1 forever; the remaining labor force is divided between building up capital in process 2 and producing the consumption good from that process with whatever capital has been built up.

Let the total labor force be normalized at 1, so that, at any time t,

$$\sum_{i=0}^{2} N_i(t) + \sum_{i=1}^{2} M_i(t) = 1. \qquad (1)$$

Total output of the consumption good is

$$C(t) = \sum_{i=0}^{2} (v_i)^{-1} N_i(t). \qquad (2)$$

The consumer (and the economy) maximizes the time integral of (2) discounted by $\exp(-\rho t)$, subject to (1), the capital accumulation equations,

$$dK_i/dt = (\mu_i)^{-1} M_i \quad (i = 1, 2), \qquad (3)$$

and the constraints in processes 1 and 2 that no more labor is applied than can be used in view of the amount of capital available,

$$N_i \le v_i K_i. \qquad (4)$$

Let p_i ($i = 1, 2$) be the costate variables corresponding to the accumulation equations (3), w the Lagrange parameter for the constraint (1), and q_i ($i = 1, 2$) be the Lagrange variables for the constraints (4). Then the current-value Hamiltonian for the optimization problem is

$$H = \sum_{i=0}^{2} (v_i)^{-1} N_i + \sum_{i=1}^{2} p_i (\mu_i)^{-1} M_i + \sum_{i=1}^{2} q_i (v_i K_i - N_i) + w\left(1 - \sum_{i=0}^{2} N_i - \sum_{i=1}^{2} M_i\right).$$

The evolution of the costate variables is then given by

$$dp_i/dt = \rho p_i - v_i q_i \quad (i = 1, 2). \tag{5}$$

The first-order conditions for maximizing H with respect to the variables M_i, N_i are:

$$v_0 w \geq 1 \qquad\qquad [N_0] \tag{6}$$

$$v_i(q_i + w) \geq 1 \qquad\qquad [N_i] \ (i = 1, 2) \tag{7}$$

$$p_i \leq \mu_i w \qquad\qquad [M_i] \ (i = 1, 2). \tag{8}$$

The variable in brackets is zero if the inequality is strict.

I will not go into a taxonomy of all the cases. I want to see if there is a range of parameters for which all new investment takes place in capital for process 2 but capital for process 1 continues to be used fully. Since the system is linear (apart from corners), it turns out that we can confine ourselves to solutions in which the costate variables and Lagrange parameters are constant over time. We will assume this and demonstrate that such a solution exists.

From (5), stationarity of the dual variables implies that

$$\rho p_i = v_i q_i \quad (i = 1, 2). \tag{9}$$

Suppose $M_i > 0$. Then equality holds in (8). In view of (9), this can be written

$$v_i q_i = \rho \mu_i w. \tag{10}$$

Then $q_i > 0$, so that the constraint (4) must hold with equality,

$$N_i = v_i K_i, \tag{11}$$

and therefore $N_i > 0$. Hence, equality holds in (7). Together with (10), there are two equations in q_i and w. In particular,

$$w = (\rho \mu_i + v_i)^{-1}. \tag{12}$$

Clearly, we cannot have both $M_1 > 0$ and $M_2 > 0$, except by coincidence, for (12) would give us two different values for w. If we look for solutions with $M_2 > 0$, then we have in general $M_1 = 0$.

If $M_2 > 0$, then $N_2 = v_2 K_2 > 0$, $M_1 = 0$ (except by chance), and

$$w = (\rho\mu_2 + v_2)^{-1}. \tag{13}$$

The parameters have been chosen to satisfy (7–8) for $i = 2$. To have a solution in which process 1 continues to be used, so that $N_1 > 0$, equality must hold in (7) for $i = 1$. It must also be shown to be possible to satisfy condition (6) and condition (8) for $i = 1$. If we substitute for w from (13) into (7–8) with $i = 1$, we find after a little manipulation,

$$1 - v_1(\rho\mu_2 + v_2)^{-1} = v_1 q_1 \leq \rho\mu_1(\rho\mu_2 + v_2)^{-1}. \tag{14}$$

Will there exist $q_1 > 0$ satisfying (14)? It is necessary and sufficient that the first term be positive and less than or equal to the third. This is equivalent to the following conditions:

$$(v_1 - v_2)/\mu_2 < \rho, \tag{15}$$

$$v_1 - v_2 \geq \rho(\mu_2 - \mu_1). \tag{16}$$

Since $v_1 > v_2$ by assumption, (16) holds either if $\mu_2 \leq \mu_1$ (in which case process 2 dominates process 1 in both inputs) or if

$$\rho \leq (v_1 - v_2)/(\mu_2 - \mu_1). \tag{17}$$

Finally, we have to ensure that (6) is satisfied; this guarantees that process 0 is not accepted. If again we substitute for w from (13), (6) is equivalent to

$$\rho \leq (v_0 - v_2)/\mu_2. \tag{18}$$

If, then, the rate of force of discount is within the range determined by (15), (17), and (18) (with (17) omitted if $\mu_2 \leq \mu_1$), there will be a solution to the first-order conditions for which there is no investment in process 1 but the capital in both processes is fully utilized. The labor force is divided among three activities, producing in process 1 with the existing capital, producing in process 2 fully utilizing existing capital, and building up capital in process 2. Further, no labor is used in process 0. Finally, capital in process 1 is constant.

One easy and yet interesting implication of this characterization may be drawn (I am indebted to the editors for raising this question). The labor balance equation (1) becomes

$$N_1(t) + N_2(t) + M_2(t) = 1 \text{ for all } t.$$

But $N_1(t) = v_1 K_1(0)$, $N_2(t) = v_2 K_2(t)$, and $dK_2/dt = (\mu_2)^{-1} M_2(t)$, so that

$$dK_2/dt = (\mu_2)^{-1}[1 - v_1 K_1(0) - v_2 K_2(t)].$$

Then, $K_2(t)$ approaches a limit, $K_2{}^* = (v_2)^{-1}[1 - v_1 K_1(0)]$, so that consumption, $C(t)$ approaches a limit,

$$C^* = K_1(0) + K_2{}^* = (v_2)^{-1} + [1 - (v_1/v_2)]K_1(0).$$

Since process 2 uses less labor per unit output than process 1, $v_1/v_2 > 1$, the coefficient of $K_1(0)$ is negative. In the long run, the initial holding of process 1 capital is disadvantageous, even though it is optimal when account is taken of the greater consumption in the initial period.

The key point is that the capital and production level in process 1 remains always that in the original period. Thus even in this completely competitive model, with constant returns to scale, the equilibrium is path dependent. The path dependence arises from the irreversibility of the capital invested in process 1.

5. COMMENTS

It seems to me to be an error to attribute path dependence to increasing returns. Rather, it seems to be due to irreversibility. All the examples that seem to imply the indispensability of increasing returns to path dependence also involve irreversibility, sometimes rather subtly, such as the irreversibility of human capital investment in the typewriter keyboard example. This of course is not to deny the importance of increasing returns as a factor in economic analysis and in social policy formation.

The concept of capital and, with that, the definition of irreversibility, must be taken in a broad sense. Consider the following realistically important case, raised to me by the editors. Consider a network of users. At any moment, each can choose among several alternative inputs (for example, software), but the value of each choice depends on the number of others who have made the same choice. Replacements are made at fixed intervals, but individual choices are staggered in time. Hence, if one choice has become predominant, each individual reaching the time of replacement decision will tend to make that choice. This will be true even if new alternatives are being introduced that would improve efficiency if they were adopted by everyone at the same time.

This is certainly a case of path dependence. However, since the input decisions endure for a period of time, they are irreversible in the sense meant here. Hence, this case is in no way a contradiction to the view that irreversibility is an essential feature of all path dependence.

Note

1. I survey some of the history of this concept in Arrow (2000).

References

Arrow, K. J. 2000. "Increasing Returns: Historiographic Issues and Path Dependence." *European Journal of the History of Economic Thought* 7: 171–80.

Arthur, W. B. 1988. "Urban Systems and Historical Path Dependence." In J. H. Ausubel and R. Herman, eds., *Cities and Their Vital Systems,* pp. 85–97. Washington, D.C.: National Academy Press.

———. 1989. "Competing Technologies, Increasing Returns, and Lock-in by Historical Small Events." *Economic Journal* 99: 116–31.

Bewley, T. 1972. "Existence of Equilibria in Economies with Infinitely Many Commodities." *Journal of Economic Theory* 4: 514–40.

Boldrin, M., and L. Montrucchio. 1991. "On the Indeterminacy of Capital Accumulation Paths." In R. Becker and E. Burmeister, eds., *Growth Theory.* Vol. 2: *Optimal Growth Theory.* Aldershot, U.K.: Edward Elgar.

Christaller, W. 1966. *Central Places in Southern Germany.* Englewood Cliffs, N.J.: Prentice-Hall.

David, P. 1971. "The Landscape and the Machine: Technical Interrelatedness, Land Tenure, and the Mechanization of the Corn Harvest in Victorian Britain." Chapter 8 in D. N. McCloskey, ed., *Essays on a Mature Economy: Britain after 1840.* London: Methuen.

———. 1985. "Clio and the Economics of QWERTY." *American Economic Review Papers and Proceedings* 75: 332–37.

Geyl, P. 1961–64. *The Netherlands in the Seventeenth Century.* Revised and enlarged ed. London: E. Benn.

Hicks, J. R. 1939. *Value and Capital.* Oxford: Clarendon Press.

Lindahl, E. 1929. "Prisbildningsproblemets Uppläggning fran Kapitalteorisk synpunkt." *Ekonomisk Tisdsrkift* 31–81. Translated as Chapter III in Lindahl (1939).

———. 1939. *Studies in the Theory of Money and Capital.* London: George Allen and Unwin.

Lösch, A. 1954. *The Economics of Location.* New Haven, Conn.: Yale University Press.

Marshall, A. 1920. *Principles of Economics,* 8th ed. London: Macmillan.

Veblen, T. 1915. *Imperial Germany and the Industrial Revolution.* New York: Macmillan.

2

PATH DEPENDENCE AND RESWITCHING IN A MODEL OF MULTI-TECHNOLOGY ADOPTION

Paul Stoneman

1. INTRODUCTION

This chapter is concerned with two areas of economic analysis to which Paul A. David has made significant contributions. The first is the analysis of technological diffusion, where David (1969) makes the first statement of the probit or rank model of diffusion. The second area is that relating to networks, compatibility, and non-ergodicity in economic systems and the illustration that history matters. Much of the early foundation of this body of analysis was laid out in David (1985) and David and Greenstein (1990).

This chapter explores a simple model of technique choice involving multiple (two) technologies that are partial substitutes for each other. It is first shown that the model exhibits non-ergodicity and thus that history matters. Usually however, path dependence or non-ergodicity is associated with worlds exhibiting (positive) network externalities or feedback (Arthur 1988) such that the payoff to a particular action increases with the number of other economic agents who have also chosen that action. In the model presented here there are no such positive network externalities. There are, however, individual "legacy" effects (with negative feedback). Although it is generally recognized that network externalities may exist, most of economics considers them to be the exception rather than the rule, and the implication is that it is not necessary to be overconcerned about non-ergodicity. However legacy effects as modeled here are shown to be almost synonymous, inter alia, with production functions exhibiting positive but declining marginal productivities. Such production functions are widely accepted as a valid modeling tool within economics and thus, if with such an assumption it can be shown that there is non-ergodicity, the phenomenon may be much more common than had previously been considered, and the variety of worlds in which history matters may be much greater than had been previously thought.

This chapter is largely concerned with the choice of technology by the firm. In macroeconomics especially, and in much of microeconomics, technique choice is usually considered to be the choice of the appropriate capital-labor ratio. However no firm actually chooses a capital stock per se. Firms choose which machines to adopt and how many, and the capital stock results simply through the valuation of the machines purchased. In this chapter, therefore, technique choice is considered in terms of individual machines that incorporate particular technologies. This is a mode of thought that is the basis of most work on technological diffusion. The resulting model, apart from the findings in regard to ergodicity, also shows reswitching; that is, there is not necessarily a monotonic relationship between the rate of interest and the preferred technology choice, and thus capital intensity may in some circumstances increase as the interest rate increases. Reswitching has not been much addressed since the Cambridge Capital Controversies of the late 1960s, and the fact that it reappears here is fascinating. One might note, however, that when first addressed, reswitching was labeled the Ruth Cohen curiosum. It is difficult to decide whether the appearance here is any more than a curiosum.

The work in this chapter has a history. A number of years ago when M. J. Kwon and I were working on the diffusion of multiple technologies, a result arose that has always merited further consideration. The thrust of the result is that if one considers the adoption of two process technologies that are (partial) substitutes for each other then the adoption or diffusion paths of the two technologies will show non-ergodicity, in that where the firm chooses to be in time t depends upon where it was in the previous period (see Stoneman and Kwon 1994). The third contribution of this chapter is to further explore the diffusion of multiple technologies and to draw out the implications for diffusion analysis.

The next section discusses examples of the sorts of technologies with which the chapter is concerned. In section 3 the basic model is constructed and analyzed. In the following sections non-ergodicity, diffusion, and reswitching are explored; conclusions are drawn in the final section.

2. THE TECHNOLOGIES

The interest of this chapter is in technologies that are partial substitutes for each other. Consider two technologies, A and B, where, relative to the profit earned on the previous technology, if used alone technology A will yield an annual gross profit gain (that is, not taking installation costs into account) of $g_A > 0$; if used alone technology B will yield an annual gross profit gain of $g_B > 0$; and if A and B are used jointly the gross profit gain is $g_A + g_B + v$. Technologies A and B are labeled complements if $v \geq 0$, and substitutes if $v < 0$ and thus $g_A + g_B + v < g_A + g_B$.

Within the class of substitute technologies the interest here is in only those that are partial substitutes.[1] These are defined as technologies such that $v < 0$, but not so large in absolute size as to make $g_A + g_B + v$ less than zero; that is, $g_A + g_B > g_A + g_B + v > \max(g_A, g_B)$ and by implication, for such technologies, $g_A + g_B + v > 0$, $g_A + v > 0$, $g_B + v > 0$. For such technologies therefore: (1) use of either technology alone yields a profit gain; (2) the use of both technologies together yields a profit gain greater than using either technology alone; (3) but the profit gain from using both technologies together is less than the sum of the profit gains from the use of the two technologies alone. Thus technology B(A) is a partial substitute for technology A(B) if the gross profit gain from installing technology B(A) is lower when technology A(B) has been previously installed than when it has not, but, even when A(B) has been previously installed, there is still some positive profit gain to be realized from installing technology B(A).

Is partial substitutability as just defined likely to be commonly observed? It is important to note that the definition of substitutability is based upon profit gains. Gross profit gains from adoption will arise partly through the direct impact of the technologies upon the firm's production costs and partly through the indirect impact upon the firm's revenues. To explore whether partial substitutability between two technologies is likely to exist, a two-step approach is taken. First the impact of cost reductions upon the firm's profits is looked at; then the impact upon the firm's costs of introducing the two technologies is explored. To make life simple, it is assumed that the adopting firm is a monopolist.

Define the demand relationship as

$$p = F(Q) \qquad (1)$$

where Q is the output of the firm and p is the price of output. Let the costs of production, ignoring any costs of buying the new technology, be

$$C = (c - e)Q, \qquad (2)$$

where e is the reduction in unit costs generated by the adoption of a technology or technologies. Gross profits may then be defined as

$$\Pi = Q \cdot F(Q) - (c - e)Q, \qquad (3)$$

and at the profit-maximizing level of output

$$\delta\Pi/\delta Q = 0. \qquad (4)$$

Taking the total derivative of (3) and using (4) yields that

$$d\Pi = Qde. \qquad (5)$$

From (5) it is clear that for a given reduction in unit costs (de) the resulting total profit gain ($d\Pi$) will be greater the greater Q is. However as Q is a negative function of unit costs (c), the lower are unit costs the higher will be the profit gain from a further reduction in costs. This profit gain will be greater the larger is (the absolute value of) the firm's (own price) elasticity of demand (in other words, the greater the elasticity of demand, the greater will be the impact of a cost reduction and thus a price reduction on output).

The "revenue effects" as thus modeled imply that if two technologies A and B are independent of each other in their effect on costs, then the profit gains from introducing B(A), given that A(B) had already been installed, would be greater than the sum of the profit gains from introducing both alone (because introduction of the second technology is predicated on a lower cost base once the first has been installed and thus would generate greater gross profit gains). Thus if the cost reduction from introducing technology B(A) is independent of whether technology A(B) has already been introduced, then the two technologies will always show complementarity in the sense defined above and v would always be positive rather than negative (as required in the definition of partial substitutability). This implies that if partial substitutability is to be observed then the technologies must be such that the cost reductions generated by introducing the technologies must be interdependent, and the cost reductions resulting from introducing technology A(B) must be dependent upon whether B(A) has been previously adopted.

To explore this further, allow that there are four possible cost levels: c_0, $c_0 - \alpha$, $c_0 - \beta$, and $c_0 - s$, associated respectively with the use of neither A nor B, the use of A alone, the use of B alone, and the use of both A and B. Measure (de) in (5) by α, β, or s. Representing the increase in profits relative to the state where neither A nor B is used as g_i, where $i =$ A, B, or S—that is, the use of either A or B or both and $Q(i)$ as the associated level of output—then, using (5),

$$g_A = \alpha Q(A) \tag{6}$$

$$g_B = \beta Q(B) \tag{7}$$

$$g_S = g_A + g_B + v = sQ(S) \tag{8}$$

For technologies A and B to be partial substitutes, it is necessary that (1) $g_A > 0$, (2) $g_B > 0$, (3) $g_A + g_B > g_S = g_A + g_B + v$, (4) $g_A + g_B + v > g_A$ and (5) $g_A + g_B + v > g_B$. The first two of these are satisfied as long as the introduction of A alone or B alone reduces costs—that is, if $\alpha > 0$, $\beta > 0$. For the other three conditions to be satisfied requires that:

$$sQ(S) < \alpha Q(A) + \beta Q(B) \tag{9}$$

$$sQ(S) > \alpha Q(A) \tag{10}$$

$$sQ(S) > \beta Q(B). \tag{11}$$

For (10) and (11) to be satisfied it is necessary and sufficient that $s > \alpha$ and that $s > \beta$; that is, the introduction of both technologies reduces costs below those that arise when either technology is introduced alone. Of course if $\alpha > 0$, $\beta > 0$, and $s > \alpha$, $s > \beta$ then $s > 0$. For (9) to be satisfied requires that

$$s < \alpha + \beta + [\alpha(Q(A) - Q(S))/Q(S) + \beta(Q(B) - Q(S))/Q(S)] \quad (12)$$

Given $s > \alpha$ and $s > \beta$, then $Q(A) - Q(S) \leq 0$ and $Q(B) - Q(S) \leq 0$, the absolute value of these latter two terms being dependent on the size of s relative to α and β and the elasticity of demand. For partial substitution to exist it is necessary but not sufficient that $s < \alpha + \beta$. If the elasticity of demand were zero then this would be a sufficient condition for (12) to hold. However as the (absolute value of the) elasticity of demand increases and the term in square brackets in (12) becomes a larger negative, for given α and β, s must become smaller if (12) is to hold. In fact for nonzero values of the elasticity of demand, partial substitutability requires that $s < \alpha + \beta - z$ where $z = \alpha(Q(A) - Q(S))/Q(S) + \beta(Q(B) - Q(S))/Q(S)$ and allows for differences between $Q(A)$ and $Q(S)$ and $Q(B)$ and $Q(S)$, which differences will be the greater the larger is the elasticity of demand.

The conditions for partial substitutability are thus that $s > \alpha > 0$, $s > \beta > 0$, $s < \alpha + \beta - z$. These may be interpreted to mean that, relative to the use of neither technology, (1) the introduction of technology A will reduce unit production costs; (2) the introduction of technology B will reduce unit production costs; (3) the introduction of both technologies will reduce unit production costs by more than the introduction of either technology alone; but (4) the introduction of both technologies will reduce unit production costs by less than the sum of the returns to the introduction of both technologies alone, the size of the required difference being greater the larger is the elasticity of demand.

Partial substitutability between two technologies as defined here thus requires, (1) that the two technologies should be partial technological substitutes in that, given technology A(B) in place the introduction of technology B(A) should reduce costs further but by a lesser amount than if technology A(B) had not already been in place, and (2) some restriction upon the (absolute) size of the elasticity of demand. Low values for the elasticity of demand are not out of the question. If one can thus show that partial technological substitution is reasonably prevalent then partial substitutability with respect to profit gains as defined above can be accepted as not uncommon. The remainder of this section thus discusses whether the requirements on cost reductions are likely to be commonly observed. What is required is that when two technologies are being used, those technologies should show some (but not too much) technological substitutability in the production process; that is, given technology A in place, the introduction of technology B should reduce costs further but by less than if technology A had not already been in place.

In order to explore technological substitutability in costs it is useful to address two scenarios. The first is when the two technologies exist (and have long existed) contemporaneously in the production possibility set. The second is where one of the technologies (say A) is an existing technology and the other technology (say B) is a new technology. The two scenarios are treated separately, the former being dealt with first.

If the two technologies exist side by side in the existing production possibility set then the scenario of partial substitutability may be considered as reflecting the standard assumption of a production function exhibiting a positive but declining marginal productivity of capital. Then, the adoption of A could represent, say, the use of "a" extra units of capital and the adoption of B could represent "b" extra units of capital. The adoption of A and B could represent the adoption of "$a + b$" extra units of capital. Under a standard assumption that the production function exhibits positive but declining marginal productivity of capital, the cost reduction induced by adding $a + b$ is positive, greater than adding a alone or b alone, but less than the sum of the cost reductions induced by adding a alone and b alone.

An example that that may well be appropriate goes back to Joan Robinson. She commonly illustrated declining marginal productivity by considering the case of two men digging a hole, providing them first with one spade and then two spades and then three spades. She argued that the provision of the first and second spades would increase output (the first by more than the second because of congestion effects) but that the third would provide only a small increase in production (there is no third digger to use it). For the multi-technology case being considered here one could change the example slightly and consider the provision of a fork to two men (or one man) digging a hole who already have (or has) a spade, or the provision of a spade to two men (or one man) who already have (has) a fork. The parallel is obvious.

Other particular examples of contemporaneous technologies that might be considered to exhibit partial technological substitutability are: (1) cars and motorbikes, in that the use of either can yield a transport cost reduction relative to neither, but, as the services offered by each are to some degree the same, the ownership of both will yield a somewhat greater cost reduction than having either alone but less than the sum of the cost reductions generated by each individually; (2) cars and commercial vehicles on the same grounds; (3) electricity- and gas-using power sources on similar grounds.

Turn then to consider the case where one of the technologies (say technology B) is new. One approach here is to consider what is almost a dynamic version of the marginal productivity story. There are a number of R&D models (such as Dasgupta and Stiglitz 1980) that allow the impact of R&D spending (x) on the unit production costs of the firm to be modeled as

$$c = c(x) \text{ where } c'(x) > 0, c''(x) < 0. \tag{13}$$

In other words, the marginal product of R&D spending in terms of production costs is positive but declining. One interpretation of this relationship is that, as R&D spending occurs, new technologies are discovered; however the most productive are discovered first. Alternatively, x could be thought of as a technology index or a "stock of technology." As the stock of technology increases so the marginal product of an extra unit is positive but declining. Thus the cost reduction produced by R&D spending of $2x$ will be positive but less than twice the cost reduction produced by R&D spending of x. This is exactly the sort of result required for partial substitutability. If R&D spending of x can be used to produce technology A or B, and the spending of $2x$ produces both A and B, this approach would suggest that having both A and B would reduce costs by more than A or B alone but by less than the sum of A and B alone. However, thinking of the stock of possible technical advances as limited is not necessarily reasonable and there thus may be no reason why additions to the stock of technology should always show declining marginal productivity. It may therefore be preferable to consider particular technological examples more directly.

Examples of partial substitutability in production between new and old technologies are: (1) word processors and typewriters where owning both yields a greater return than having either alone (one cannot easily fill in the blanks on preprinted forms with a word processor), but because the two technologies replicate some functions, owning both yields less than the sum of the returns to owning either alone; (2) technical innovations and organizational innovations in that either may be adopted alone (Milgrom and Roberts 1995) but joint adoption will yield a greater return, although perhaps not as great as the sum of the returns to each individually; (3) letter post and the fax machine, which to some degree replicate functions, but the former allows the communication of materials the latter does not, whereas the latter allows faster communication; (4) mobile phones and fixed lines where the mobile phone provides portability but the land lines provide greater coverage. There are many other examples.

On the cost side, therefore, there may be many examples of technological substitutability. In fact, because such substitutability is little more than arguing that the marginal product of capital is positive and declining, such technological substitutability is commonly assumed to exist in economics. Given that lower values for the elasticity of demand are not out of the question, this finding implies that, with respect to total gross profit gains, partial substitutability is quite feasible in a wide variety of circumstances.

3. THE MODEL

Consider two time periods, t and $(t-1)$, in an implicitly multi-period model. There are two technologies available, A and B; the firm may choose to install one, neither, or both of these technologies. These technologies are such that, over and above the profit on the previous technology, if used alone technology A will yield an annual total gross profit gain of $g_A > 0$ and technology B an annual total gross profit gain of $g_B > 0$. The two technologies are assumed to be partial substitutes as defined above, and thus, if used jointly, the annual total gross profit gain, over and above that on the previous technology, will be $g_A + g_B + v < g_A + g_B$, thus $v < 0$, but $g_A + v > 0$, and $g_B + v > 0$. For simplicity assume that g_A, g_B, and v are constants over time.

Assume also that the firm holds myopic price expectations[2] on the cost of acquiring the technologies and that the costs of acquisition are $P_A(\tau)$ and $P_B(\tau)$ in time τ, $\tau = t - 1, t$. It is simplest if these costs are considered independent of the level of output of the firm. This formulation is very similar to that embodied in David (1969), where it is assumed that the cost of adopting new technology is independent of firm (farm) size. To ensure that investment decisions are irreversible, it is assumed that capital goods have a zero resale price. It is also assumed that technologies are infinitely long-lived (a zero depreciation rate). Define r as the interest/discount rate.

At time τ the firm may be in one of several technology states. It may have installed technology A, technology B, neither technology, or both technologies. Label these states of the world with subscripts A, B, 0, and S respectively. Define $\pi_{ij}(\tau)$ (i = A, B, 0, and S, and j = A, B, 0, and S) as the net present value of the payoffs to the firm from switching from technology state i to state j in time τ. Thus, for example, $\pi_{0B}(\tau)$ is the net present value of the payoff to switching from use of neither technology to the use of technology B in time τ.

A firm that that in time τ has not previously installed either technology has four choices. It may in time τ install technology A alone, technology B alone, neither technology, or both technologies. Given that the present value of an annual profit stream g in perpetuity discounted at rate r is g/r, the net present values of the payoffs to these four strategies are

$$\pi_{00}(\tau) = 0, \tag{14}$$

$$\pi_{0A}(\tau) = g_A/r - P_A(\tau), \tag{15}$$

$$\pi_{0B}(\tau) = g_B/r - P_B(\tau), \text{ and} \tag{16}$$

$$\pi_{0S}(\tau) = g_A/r - P_A(\tau) + g_B/r - P_B(\tau) + v/r. \tag{17}$$

Given that the present value of the payoff to installing neither technology is zero, a profit-maximizing firm will then in time τ:

1. install both technologies A and B if this strategy has a positive present value and this present value is greater than that arising from installing A alone or B alone—that is, iff: $\pi_{0S}(\tau) > 0$; $\pi_{0S}(\tau) > \pi_{0A}(\tau)$; and $\pi_{0S}(\tau) > \pi_{0B}(\tau)$.

2. install technology A alone if this strategy has positive present value and this present value is greater than that arising from installing both technologies or B alone—that is, iff: $\pi_{0A}(\tau) > 0$; $\pi_{0A}(\tau) > \pi_{0S}(\tau)$; and $\pi_{0A}(\tau) > \pi_{0B}(\tau)$.

3. install technology B alone if this strategy has a positive present value and this present value is greater than that arising from installing both technologies or B alone—that is, iff: $\pi_{0B}(\tau) > 0$; $\pi_{0B}(\tau) > \pi_{0S}(\tau)$; and $\pi_{0B}(\tau) > \pi_{0A}(\tau)$.

4. install neither technology if the present value of installing A, B, or both are all negative—that is, iff: $\pi_{0S}(\tau) < 0$; $\pi_{0A}(\tau) < 0$; and $\pi_{0B}(\tau) < 0$.

Figure 2.1 plots a series of curves in (P_A, P_B) space along which, respectively: $\pi_{0S}(\tau) = 0$; that is, where, for a firm that has not previously installed either technology, the net present value of the payoff from installing both technologies

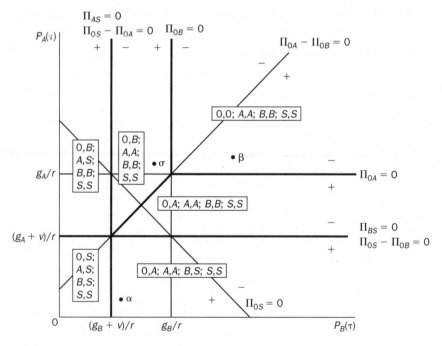

Figure 2.1 Technology choice in time τ

in time t is zero, above which the net present value is positive and below which it is negative; $\pi_{0A}(\tau) = 0$, where the present value of installing A alone is zero, below which the payoff is negative, and above which it is positive; $\pi_{0B}(\tau) = 0$, where the net present value of installing B alone is zero, to the right of which it is negative, and to the left of which it is positive; $\pi_{0B}(\tau) = \pi_{0S}(\tau)$, along which the payoff to installing B alone is the same as installing both A and B, below which it is more profitable to install both, and above which it is more profitable to install B alone; $\pi_{0A}(\tau) = \pi_{0S}(\tau)$, along which it is equally profitable to install A or both A and B, to the left of which it is more profitable to install both, and to the right of which it is more profitable to install A alone; and $\pi_{0B}(\tau) = \pi_{0A}(\tau)$, along which it is equally profitable to install A or B, above which it is more profitable to install A, and below which B. Following the strategy choice arguments detailed above, these curves enable one to split up the (P_A, P_B) space into areas in which in time τ, from an initial position in which neither technology has been installed, technologies A, B, both, or neither will be installed.

The interesting propositions start to arise when firms that installed either technology A or B in a previous period are considered. Consider first a firm that has already installed technology A (and only technology A). The firm then has the choice in time τ to scrap technology A and not install B, scrap A and install B, keep technology A but not install B, or keep technology A and install B. The net present values of the incremental profits (relative to having technology A) from these four strategies are, respectively, $\pi_{A0}(\tau)$, $\pi_{AB}(\tau)$, $\pi_{AA}(\tau)$, and $\pi_{AS}(\tau)$ and given by

$$\pi_{A0}(\tau) = -g_A/r, \tag{18}$$

$$\pi_{AB}(\tau) = -g_A/r + g_B/r - P_B(\tau), \tag{19}$$

$$\pi_{AA}(\tau) = 0, \text{ and} \tag{20}$$

$$\pi_{AS}(\tau) = g_B/r + v/r - P_B(\tau). \tag{21}$$

Given that $(g_A + v)/r > 0$ then $\pi_{AS}(\tau) > \pi_{AB}(\tau)$. Given $g_A > 0$ then $\pi_{AA}(\tau) > \pi_{A0}(\tau)$. Thus the net present value of strategies that involve scrapping technology A are always dominated by strategies that involve keeping technology A, and thus technology A will never be scrapped. The only decision the firm thus has to make is whether to also install technology B alongside technology A. The firm will install technology B if the net present value of the payoff from this is positive, that is, iff

$$\pi_{AS}(\tau) = g_B/r + v/r - P_B(\tau) > 0. \tag{22}$$

Thus if $g_B/r + v/r > P_B(\tau)$, a firm having previously invested in technology A will invest in technology B in time τ and end up with both technologies A and B. In Figure 2.1 the curve along which $\pi_{AS}(\tau) = g_B/r + v/r - P_B(\tau) = 0$ is also plotted in (P_A, P_B) space, that is, where the net present value of the payoff from installing B in time τ given A already installed is zero. To the left of this curve $\pi_{AS}(\tau) > 0$, and to the right of the curve $\pi_{AS}(\tau) < 0$. One may note that this curve is the same as that along which $\pi_{0A}(\tau) = \pi_{0S}(\tau)$.

Following arguments similar to those above, a firm that has already invested in technology B (and only technology B), will in time τ not scrap that technology, but will add technology A iff

$$\pi_{BS}(\tau) = g_A/r + v/r - P_A(\tau) > 0. \tag{23}$$

If $g_A/r + v/r > P_A(\tau)$, a firm already having invested in technology B will invest in technology A in time τ and end up with both technologies A and B. Figure 2.1 plots in (P_A, P_B) space the curve along which $\pi_{BS}(\tau) = g_A/r + v/r - P_A(\tau) = 0$. Below this curve $\pi_{BS}(\tau) > 0$ and above the curve $\pi_{BS}(t\tau) < 0$. One may note that this curve is the same as that along which $\pi_{0B}(\tau) = \pi_{0S}(\tau)$.

Finally, it is clear that $\pi_{S0}(\tau)$, $\pi_{SA}(\tau)$, and $\pi_{SB}(\tau)$ are all negative and because $\pi_{SS}(\tau) = 0$, a firm that has previously installed both A and B will not scrap either A or B or both.

In Figure 2.1 these results are brought together by separating the (P_A, P_B) space into six areas, for each of which a label i, j is used to indicate the optimal technology choice j in time τ given the previous technology state i; for example, B,S indicates both A and B in time t if B is previously installed.

4. NON-ERGODICITY

The essence of non-ergodicity or path dependence is that history matters. One may interpret this in a number of ways. The interpretation used here is that an economy shows path dependence if the economy's equilibrium position in time t is dependent upon the path followed up to time t; that is, today's equilibrium is determined by yesterday's outcome. In the current context the frame of reference is the firm rather than the economy as a whole. The performance or position indicator is the firm's choice of technology. The relevant history is the time path of the prices of acquiring the two technologies, which is modeled as exogenous to the technology choice process. If the firm's choice of technology in time t, given the prices of the technologies in time t, is dependent upon the time path of these prices in periods before t then the economy is said to exhibit non-ergodicity and history matters. If the choice of technologies in time t depends only upon the prices in time t and is independent of prices in previous periods then the system is ergodic and history does not matter. In this section it is shown that the simple model presented above exhibits non-ergodic behavior in that the optimal technology choice for the firm in time t is dependent on the prices in time $t - 1$.

Consider two time periods, t and $t - 1$. Assume that the firm has not installed either technology before time $t - 1$, then from Figure 2.1 it is possible to identify four different strategy choice outcomes in time $t - 1$ depending on prevailing prices in time $t - 1$:

Case 1: If $P_B(t - 1) > g_B/r$ and $P_A(t - 1) > g_A/r$ (that is, $\pi_{0B}(t - 1) < 0$, $\pi_{0A}(t - 1) < 0$), the optimal strategy for the firm in time $t - 1$ is to install neither technology A or B.

Case 2: If $P_A(t - 1) < g_A/r$, $P_B(t - 1) > (g_B + v)/r$ and $(g_A/r - P_A(t - 1) - g_B/r + P_B(t - 1)) > 0$ (i.e., $\pi_{0A}(t - 1) > 0$, $\pi_{0A}(t - 1) > \pi_{0B}(t - 1)$, $\pi_{AS}(t - 1) < 0$), then the firm's optimal strategy in time $t - 1$ is to install technology A alone.

Case 3: If $P_A(t - 1) < (g_A + v)/r$, $P_B(t - 1) < (g_B + v)/r$ (i.e., $\pi_{0S}(t - 1) > 0$, $\pi_{0S}(t - 1) > \pi_{0A}(t - 1)$, $\pi_{0S}(t - 1) > \pi_{0B}(t - 1)$), then in time $t - 1$ the optimal strategy for the firm is to install both A and B.

Case 4: If $P_A(t - 1) > (g_A + v)/r$, $P_B(t - 1) < g_B/r$, $(g_A/r - P_A(t - 1) - g_B/r + P_B(t - 1)) < 0$ (i.e., $\pi_{0A} < 0$, $\pi_{0B} > 0$, $\pi_{BS} < 0$) then in time $t - 1$ the optimal strategy for the firm is to install technology B alone.

In time t, assume that $P_B(t) > (g_B + v)/r$ and $P_A(t) < (g_A + v)/r$, and then from Figure 2.1, the optimal strategy for the firm in terms of technique choice in time t given its technology state in time $t - 1$ is 0A, AA, BS, SS; that is, if the firm has previously installed neither of the technologies it will install technology A in time t, if it has previously installed A it will retain A but not install B, if it has previously installed B it will now install A as well, and if it has previously installed both it will retain both. It is then immediately clear that in time t: for case 1, the firm's optimal choice is to install technology A and have technology A alone; for case 2, the firm will undertake no further investment and thus again will end up with technology A alone; for case 3 the firm will again undertake no further investment and thus retain A and B; and for case 4 the firm will further install technology A, ending up with both technologies A and B. These results are illustrated in Figure 2.2, where, for values of $P_A(t)$ and $P_B(t)$ that satisfy $P_B(t) > (g_B + v)/r$ and $P_A(t) < (g_A + v)/r$, (P_A, P_B) space is divided into areas in which, according to the values of $P_A(t - 1)$ and $P_B(t - 1)$, the optimal technology stock in time t will be technology A or S (i.e., A and B).

It is immediately clear from these results that the optimal technology choice in time t is dependent on the prices in time $t - 1$, and as such path dependence

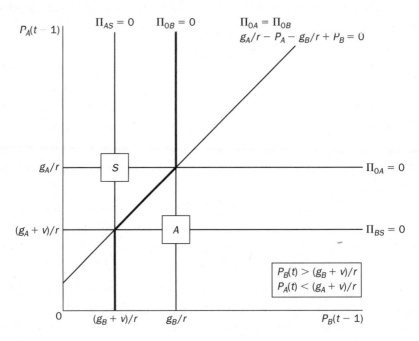

Figure 2.2 Technology choice in time t as a function of $t - 1$ prices

is being shown. It is informative to explore the reasoning behind this result a little further. The main point can be made by asking why it is that for given prices of A and B in time t, if in time $t - 1$ prices lead to the choice of A alone then in time t it is not profitable to also install B, whereas if in time $t - 1$ prices indicate that B alone should be installed then in time t, A should also be adopted. The reasoning is simple. The time t choices depend on incremental profits from actions in time t. The time $t - 1$ choices determine these time t profit increments. Thus time $t - 1$ choices affect time t choices and outcomes. If v were zero and there were no partial substitution effects then the time t profit increments would be independent of the time $t - 1$ choices and there would be no path dependence. It is for this reason that one might label the partial substitution as a legacy effect: past actions have an impact upon current incremental profits.

Figures similar to Figure 2.2 could be produced for other values of $P_A(t)$ and $P_B(t)$ that again illustrate path dependence. In fact, it is also clear from Figure 2.1 that path dependence exists for all combinations of $P_A(t)$ and $P_B(t)$ except when $P_A(t) < (g_A + v)/r$ and $P_B(t) < (g_B + v)/r$ (i.e., where the optimal technology choice in time t is S whatever the state in time $t - 1$) and that the optimal choice of technology in time t is dependent upon the technology adoption decision made in time $t - 1$ and thus on technology prices in time $t - 1$.

There are other ways of illustrating the path dependence result, for example, by trying to draw the demand curves for technologies A and B; however, for what follows the following seems reasonably informative. In Figure 2.1, assume that before $t - 1$ the firm has not adopted either technology (so that P_A and P_B are well into the northeast quadrant), let the price combination (P_A, P_B) in time t be at point α, but let there be two alternative $t - 1$ positions, β and σ. These points are arranged such that between time $t - 1$ and t the prices of both capital goods fall, regardless of which path is followed. At point β, in time $t - 1$ the firm will not install either technology but in time t will install technology A, ending up owning technology A alone. At point σ the firm in time $t - 1$ will install technology B, and then in time t will install technology A, ending up with both technologies A and B. Thus, starting from a position where neither technology is installed, if prices follow one route to end at α, the technology in place in time t with prices α will differ from the technology in place at time t if prices follow a different route to reach α. This is a clear example of path dependence.

5. DIFFUSION ANALYSIS

As stated above, the origins of this analysis lie in an exploration of multi-technology diffusion. In this section that issue is addressed again. For the model to apply to diffusion phenomena it is only necessary to allow that one of the technologies A or B exists before the other (in time $t - 1$) and then the other appears for the first time in time t. Let the prior technology be A. Then the new technology, technology B, appears on the market in time t and is available alongside technology A. Diffusion analysis is then concerned with the pattern of demand for technology B in time t and the determinants of that demand. A usual result would be that the demand for B in time t is a negative function of its own price. In a multi-technology environment one is also interested in how the price of technology A will affect the demand for B. It is that issue that is addressed in this section. For simplicity it is assumed throughout that when technology B is introduced the amount installed is one unit. It is also assumed that before $t - 1$ no installation of technology A has occurred.

To consider the impact of the prices of A and B on the demand for B, define a number of cases.

Case 1: In this case, $P_A(t - 1) < g_A/r$, the firm will introduce technology A in time $t - 1$, and the firm will thus enter time t having already installed technology A. It was shown above that the firm will retain this technology in time t. From Figure 2.1, a firm having already installed technology A will also install technology B in time t iff $P_B(t) < (g_B + v)/r$. The demand curve for B in time t is thus simple in this case. Demand is zero for all $P_B(t) > (g_B + v)/r$, and one for all $P_B(t) < (g_B + v)/r$. Within the confines of the case the demand for B in time t is insensitive to the price of A in time t.

Case 2A: In this case, $P_A(t - 1) > g_A/r$ and $P_A(t) > g_A/r$. Thus in time $t - 1$, when A is the only technology available the firm would not introduce technology A at that time. Nor is it profitable to install A alone in time t. From Figure 2.1, if A has not been installed at time $t - 1$ and $P_A(t) > g_A/r$ then the optimal strategy for the firm in time t is to install technology B alone if $P_B(t) < g_B/r$ and to install neither technology otherwise. The demand curve for technology B in time t is thus simple in this case: that is, if $P_B(t) < g_B/r$ the demand for technology B will be positive (unity); otherwise demand will be zero. Within the confines of the case the demand for B is not sensitive to the price of A in time t.

Case 2B: In this case, $P_A(t-1) > g_A/r$; thus in time $t-1$, when A is the only technology available the firm would not introduce technology A, but in time t, $g_A/r > P_A(t) > (g_A + v)/r$. Thus in time t it is profitable to install technology A alone but not in conjunction with technology B. The demand for B will thus depend on whether it is more profitable to install A alone or B alone. Given $\pi_{0A}(t) = g_A/r - P_A(t)$ and $\pi_{0B}(t) = g_B/r - P_B(t)$ it is more profitable to install B alone iff $g_B/r - g_A/r + P_A(t) > P_B(t)$. Thus if $P_B(t) < g_B/r - g_A/r + P_A(t)$, the demand for B will be unity and if $P_B(t) > g_B/r - g_A/r + P_A(t)$ the demand for B will be zero (and when the inequality is an equality either A or B may be chosen). Defining the threshold value of $P_B(t)$ as $P_B^*(t)$, below which the firm will buy technology B and above which it will not, so that $P_B^*(t) = g_B/r - g_A/r + P_A(t)$, this threshold is a positive function of $P_A(t)$, and thus, within the confines of this case the threshold level $P_B^*(t)$ increases as $P_A(t)$ increases.

Case 2C: In this case, $P_A(t-1) > g_A/r$; thus in time $t-1$, when A is the only technology available the firm would not introduce technology A. But in time t, $P_A(t) < (g_A + v)/r$, and thus in time t it is profitable to introduce technology A either alone or in conjunction with technology B. However it is only profitable to install both technologies rather than technology A alone iff $P_B(t) < (g_A + v)/r$, and thus the demand for B is unity if $P_B(t) < (g_A + v)/r$ and zero if $P_B(t) < (g_A + v)/r$. Within the confines of the case the threshold price for B is independent of $P_A(t)$. In this case the threshold price for B is the same as in Case 1.

In Figure 2.3 these results are presented in (P_A, P_B) space by plotting, as a function of $P_A(t)$, the critical values of $P_B(P_B^*)$ in time t, below which the firm will buy technology B in time t and above which the firm will not buy technology B. In the figure the first curve labeled (1) plots critical values for $P_B(t)$ on the assumption that $P_A(t-1) < g_A/r$—that is, case 1 where technology A

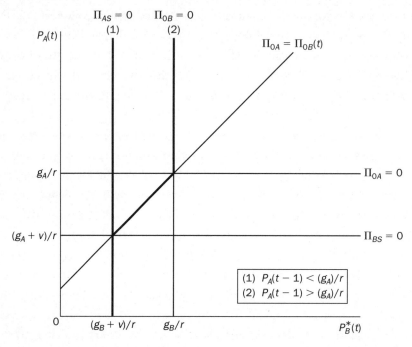

Figure 2.3   Critical values of $P_B(t)$, $P_B{}^*(t)$

is installed in time $t - 1$. The second curve (2) plots critical values of the threshold price on the assumption that $P_A(t - 1) > g_A/r$—that is, cases 2A, 2B, and 2C where technology A is not installed in time $t - 1$. For curve 2, points above $P_A(t) > g_A/r$ relate to case 2A, points where $(g_A+v)/r < P_A(t) < g_A/r$ refer to case 2B, and points where $(g_A + v)/r > P_A(t)$ refer to case 2C. Curve 1 represents critical values of $P_B(t)$ for firms that have previously installed technology A, and curve 2 relates to critical values when the firm has not previously installed the new technology.

The first point that is illustrated by Figure 2.3 is that when technology A has been previously installed $P_B{}^*(t)$ is always less than or equal to $P_B{}^*(t)$ when technology A has not been previously installed. Thus for a given price of technology B, the firm is less likely to install technology B in time t if technology A has been previously installed. Thus, if two firms are identical in all respects except that one has previously installed A and one has not, the latter is more likely to install technology B in time t. This would suggest that prior introduction of technology A would slow the diffusion of technology B. This is, of course, as one would expect of substitute technologies. The legacy arising from prior introduction of technology A reduces the incremental profit from installing technology B.

The second point to make on the basis of Figure 2.3 concerns the impact of $P_A(t)$ on the demand for B in time t. If A has been previously installed (case 1) then $P_A(t)$ has no impact upon the demand for B, and thus the diffusion of B would be unaffected by $P_A(t)$. If A has not been previously installed (cases 2A–2C) for values of $P_A(t)$ such that $(g_A + v)/r > P_A(t)$ and $P_A(t) > g_A/r$, changes in $P_A(t)$ do not affect the threshold price. However, if $(g_A + v)/r < P_A(t) < g_A/r$ (case 2B) then reductions in $P_A(t)$ lead to reductions in the threshold price for B in time t. Reductions in the threshold price make adoption less likely. Thus as the price of A falls there is for a given price of B less likelihood that technology B will be adopted.

The implications of this for diffusion analysis are as follows: for technologies that are partial substitutes in the sense defined here, (1) the lower $P_A(t - 1)$ is, the more likely it is for technology A to have been previously installed, the lower will be the threshold price for B in time t, and thus the slower diffusion will be; (2) for some range of $P_A(t)$, if technology A has not been previously installed, the lower $P_A(t)$ is, the lower will be the threshold price for $P_B(t)$, and thus the slower diffusion will be; and (3) as a result, the modeling of the impact of previous technology adoption decisions and previous and current technology prices on the diffusion path of a new technology is not obvious.

The diffusion story can become even more complex if one allows that the appearance of the new technology B actually affects the price of the old technology A. There is some historical evidence that the appearance of new technologies can lead to reductions in the quality-adjusted price of old technologies. For example, Harley (1973) discusses how wooden ships became cheaper through the appearance of iron ships partly because shipping services were an input into the construction of wooden ships and thus cheaper iron ships helped reduce the cost of wooden ships. Allowing that wooden and iron ships are partial substitutes, then this story, within the current model, could imply a series of events such as follows. With the appearance of iron ships (technology B) those firms who already have wooden ships (technology A) would also install iron ships if their price is low enough—that is, $P_B(t) <$ $(g_A + v)/r$; but any reductions in the price of wooden ships that this usage induces would not affect the decision to buy either iron or wooden ships. For those firms that do not have wooden ships, there is a greater likelihood, compared to owners of wooden ships, that they will buy an iron rather than a wooden ship for a given price of an iron ship, but any reduction in the price of wooden ships that this induces will not affect the decision to buy wood or iron until the price of wooden ships falls below $P_A(t) = g_A/r$. After this point, further reductions in the price of wooden ships would lead them to be less likely to buy iron ships. If the price of wooden ships is dependent on the use of iron ships, this process could slow the fall in the price of wooden ships. If diffusion is to proceed, the price of iron ships must fall, but because this fall induces greater use of iron ships and thus cheaper wooden ships, the diffusion of iron ships would be slower than if this were not the case. However, once a point is reached where the price of wooden ships $P_A(t)$ falls below $(g_A + v)/r$, the firm's demand for iron ships and thus their diffusion is no longer a function of $P_A(t)$, being dependent only on the price of iron ships, and thus the feedback effect no longer affects the diffusion of iron ships.

6. RESWITCHING

Many years ago, as a very new Ph.D. student in Cambridge (UK), I decided that I wanted to work on the Cambridge capital controversy, especially reswitching. After one term I was warned off by Joan Robinson on the grounds that there was nothing interesting left to say on this issue. This model however may have something more to say.

The reswitching phenomenon is basically that, given two technologies, A and B, as the interest rate falls the profit-maximizing choice of technology will change, either as A, B, A or B, A, B. Given that one of A or B can be defined as more capital-intensive, either the A,B or the B,A switch must be in a less capital-intensive direction as opposed to the more capital-intensive direction predicted by neoclassical theory. The Cambridge capital controversy essentially concerned issues of when such a phenomenon can occur. Nowhere in the resulting literature was there any discussion of partial substitution as a cause of reswitching. It is shown here, however, that partial substitution can lead to reswitching.

Assume that technology A is an existing technology available in time $t - 1$ whereas technology B only becomes available in time t. Allow that the interest rate is the same at time t and $t - 1$ and thus that comparisons are being made between worlds with different constant interest rate regimes. Assume also, and this is a vital condition for the results, that $P_A(t - 1)$ is such that $g_B > g_A/P_A(t - 1)$ but $(g_B + v) < g_A/P_A(t - 1)$.

In Figure 2.4, four curves are plotted in (r, P_B) space, as opposed to the (P_A, P_B) space used previously (note that the horizontal origin is unity): (1) $r = g_A/P_A(t - 1)$, above which curve technology A will be installed in time $t - 1$ and below which it will not; (2) $r = g_B/P_B(t)$, below which in time period t it will be profitable for the firm to install technology B alone and above which it will not (and which has been drawn as linear for ease of drawing); (3) $r = (g_B + v)/P_B(t)$, below which it will be profitable for the firm in time t to install technology B in addition to technology A and above which it will not (also drawn as linear for ease of drawing); and (4) a curve along which $g_A/r - P_A(t) = g_B/r - P_B(t)$, above which, if technology A has not already been

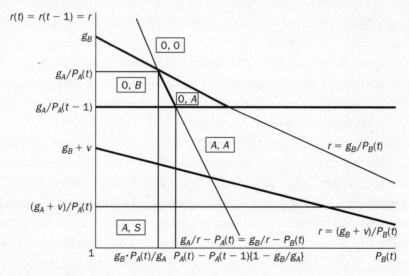

Figure 2.4 Technology choice and the interest rate

installed, it is more profitable to install technology A in time t and below which it is more profitable to install technology B in time t (and which has been drawn as linear for ease of drawing). The figure is plotted as if this curve becomes binding over some range of r, but this is not crucial to the results (this is equivalent to assuming that $P_A(t) < P_A(t-1)$).

The (r, P_B) space is split into areas marked (i, j) where i and $j = 0, A, B, S$, and i indicates the technology installed in time $t - 1$, and j the technology (stock) at time t. The interesting results arise for values of $P_B(t)$ such that $P_B(t) < P_A(t) - P_A(t-1)(1 - (g_B/g_A))$, but for simplicity it is easier to show the result for $P_B(t) < g_B P_A(t)/g_A$, which satisfies the previous condition. The issue of interest is whether the firm will buy the newly available technology B in time t and how this changes with the value of r.

Given $P_B(t) < g_B P_A(t)/g_A$, for values of $r < (g_B + v)/P_B(t)$, the firm will have bought technology A in time $t - 1$ and will buy technology B in time t. For a higher interest rate so that $g_A/P_A(t-1) > r > (g_B + v)/P_B(t)$, the firm will again have bought technology A in time $t - 1$ but will now not buy technology B in time t. For a yet higher interest rate such that $g_A/P_A(t-1) < r < g_B/P_B(t)$ the firm will not have bought technology A in time $t - 1$ but will buy technology B in time t. Finally, for very high interest rates such that $r > g_B/P_B(t)$, the firm will not buy technology A in time $t - 1$ or technology B in time t. Thus in terms of the demand for technology B in time t, the pattern is that for a low interest rate the firm buys technology B, for a slightly higher rate it does not, for a yet higher rate it does so again, and for an even higher rate it does not again. This is an example of reswitching in that the demand for technology B in time t is over some range of r positively related to r and over other ranges negatively related to r[3].

Essentially what is happening in the model is that higher interest rates affect not only the time t but also the time $t - 1$ acquisition decisions. As the interest rate increases (ceteris paribus) the firm is less likely to install technology A in time $t - 1$. The decision to install technology A in time $t - 1$ then affects the profit increments from installing technology B in time t. A low interest rate means that it is profitable to install A in time $t - 1$ and encourages the firm, given A, to also install B in time t. As the interest rate rises, the firm will still install A in time $t - 1$, but the higher rate discourages the firm from also installing B in time t. An even higher rate discourages installation of A in time $t - 1$, but without A the firm can earn higher incremental profit from B in time t and thus again buys B in time t. A very high rate discourages the firm from buying A in time $t - 1$ or B in time t.

As well as illustrating reswitching, these results have a message for the study of diffusion. They suggest that it is necessary to think carefully about the relationship between the adoption of new technology and the interest rate. In a comparison of high interest rate and low interest rate worlds, there is no necessary monotonic relationship between the level of the interest rate and the demand for the new technology.

7. CONCLUSIONS

In this chapter a model of technology adoption has been explored where the two technologies being adopted are partial substitutes in the sense that (1) the adoption of either would increase profits, (2) the adoption of both increases profits by more than the adoption of either alone, but (3) the adoption of both increases profits by less than the sum of the profit gains from the adoption of each alone. The model has been interpreted as relating to situations in which either both technologies have always been available or where one of the technologies is new. This latter view enables a diffusion-based interpretation of the results.

It has been shown that the model exhibits both (1) path dependence—that is, today's optimal outcome is dependent upon the path that the economy has followed in the past and (2) reswitching—that is, the capital intensity of the optimal technology choice is not necessarily monotonically related to the interest rate. With respect to diffusion it was shown that, within the model, the ownership of an old technology can slow down the adoption of a new technology, but the full picture of the role of old technologies in the diffusion of new can be quite complex.

These results rely only upon partial substitutability, and it has been argued that partial substitutability may be the result of a very common assumption in economics. If the firm's own price elasticity of demand is not too large, then a production function exhibiting a positive but declining marginal productivity of capital will generate the required partial substitution characteristics. Because production functions in economics are usually assumed to exhibit such properties, the behavior exhibited by the model may be quite common.

Path dependence and reswitching cause one to rethink a number of fundamental economic issues. The fact that path dependence and reswitching can be shown in a simple model built upon pretty standard assumptions suggests that perhaps there are many economic issues that need rethinking.

Notes

1. I am grateful to Peter Swann for his suggestions on how to make the definitions clearer. The model is restricted to partial substitutes rather than substitutes in general because if technologies A and B are full substitutes such that $g_A + g_B + v < \max(g_A, g_B)$ then the firm not having installed either technology will never wish to install both, and/or the firm having already installed technology A will never wish to install technology B, and/or the firm that has already installed technology B will not wish to install technology A. In essence therefore if A and B are full substitutes then the firm will never own both. In such circumstances the results do not show anything particularly different from what one might expect.

2. The assumption of myopia is not essential but considerably simplifies the presentation. The original attempt to explore this issue (Stoneman and Kwon 1993) did in fact allow for perfect foresight, and the same sort of results arose.

3. One might note that with respect to the stock of capital in time t reswitching can also be shown. For $P_A(t) - P_A(t-1)(1 - g_B/g_A) > P_B(t) > g_B \cdot P_A(t)/g_A$ as r decreases the stock of capital in time t goes through the sequence 0, A, B, A, S with the sequence A, B, A reflecting reswitching.

References

Arthur, W. B. 1989. "Competing Technologies, Increasing Returns and Lock-in by Historical Events." *Economic Journal* 99: 116–31.

Dasgupta, P., and J. Stiglitz. 1980. "Industrial Structure and the Nature of Innovative Activity." *Economic Journal* 90: 266–93.

David, P. A. 1969. *A Contribution to the Theory of Diffusion*. Stanford Center for Research in Economic Growth Memorandum No. 71, Stanford University.

———. 1985. "Clio and the Economics of QWERTY." *American Economic Review* 75: 332–36.

David, P. A., and S. Greenstein. 1990. "The Economics of Compatibility Standards." *Economics of Innovation and New Technology* 1: 3–43.

Harley, C. K. 1973. "On the Persistence of Old Techniques: The Case of North American Wooden Shipbuilding." *Journal of Economic History* 33: 372–98.

Milgrom, P., and J. Roberts. 1995. "Complementarities and Fit: Strategy, Structure and Organisational Change in Manufacturing." *Journal of Accounting and Economics* 19: 179–208.

Stoneman, P., and M. J. Kwon. 1993. "The Diffusion of Multiple Process Technologies." WBS Research Papers No. 88, April.

———. 1994. "The Diffusion of Multiple Process Technologies." *Economic Journal* 104: 420–31.

3

PATH DEPENDENCE, NETWORK FORM, AND TECHNOLOGICAL CHANGE

Douglas J. Puffert

A process of economic allocation is called *path dependent* when the sequence of allocations depends not only on fundamental, a priori determinants—typically listed as technology, factor endowments, preferences, and institutions—but also on particular contingent events. Instead of converging to a determinate, predictable, unique equilibrium, such processes have multiple potential equilibria, and which one is selected depends on the specific history of the process. Positive feedbacks among agents' choices lend persistence and, indeed, increasing impact to particular early choices and other events.

Under what conditions is an allocation process path dependent? I address this question, first, by synthesizing elements of previous answers, focusing on the conditions under which allocation is determined over time rather than at a single moment. Second, I extend my answer by focusing on two issues: first, the form or graphical structure of the explicit or often "virtual" networks that characterize the interdependency of agents' choices and thus the structure of positive feedbacks, and second, the specific characteristics of technology and technological change, which in various ways affect the relative attractiveness of different potential equilibria and the permanence of "lock-in" to a specific path of allocation. My emphasis here, like that of most of the literature, is on path dependence in technology—specifically, in the selection of specific techniques. After developing this theme, I also briefly apply the ideas here to what David (1993) has called the homomorphism of path dependence in technology, institutions, organizations, and other matters.

Paul David (1985, 1987) specified three conditions that may work together to make processes of technological change path dependent: the technical interrelatedness of system components, quasi-irreversibility of investment (or, more generally, switching costs), and positive externalities or increasing returns to scale. These conditions lead agents to coordinate their choices and also lend persistence to the resulting allocation.

W. Brian Arthur (1989, 1994) focused attention on a single condition: increasing returns to adoption that are realized not at a single point in time but rather dynamically. These increasing returns may arise either on the supply side of a market as a result of learning effects (learning by doing or by using) or on the demand side as a result of positive network (or agglomeration) externalities that raise the benefits of a technique, product, or location for each user as the total number of users increases. Either case results in a positive feedback from the macro state of the system to the choices of individual agents, possibly resulting in de facto standardization on a single technique.

By contrast, the most prominent critics of the concept of path dependence, S. J. Liebowitz and Stephen E. Margolis (1994, 1995), called attention to two conditions under which allocation processes are *not* path dependent: first, foresight into the effects of choices, and second, opportunities to coordinate agents' choices through communication, market interactions, and the appropriation and promotion of alternative techniques—in short, actions that internalize the mutual externalities of agents' choices. They argue that purposeful behavior overrides the purposeless mechanisms that they understand to be the basis of path dependence, and that path dependence can therefore affect only aspects of the economy that no agent has an incentive to change—and that neither economic agents nor economists have a reason to care about.

As we will consider, economic agents often act under conditions of limited foresight and limited internalizability, and their purposeful actions show that they both care about and take account of that fact. Because these conditions are both prevalent and interesting, economists should examine explicitly how they affect the nature and outcomes of an economic allocation process.

These considerations of the conditions for path dependence are complementary in ways that I examine in the following section. Even together, however, these considerations do not explain differences in the outcomes of empirical cases that fulfill the conditions. For example, some cases result in a single, "global" de facto standard, others in multiple local or subnetwork standards. Some cases of standardization or lock-in appear permanent, but some have given way to new standards, sometimes showing a tendency to converge to an optimal technique. Externality-internalizing behavior proves fully compatible with path dependence in some cases but not in others. The latter part of this chapter offers a partial accounting for these differences.

1. TOWARD A SYSTEMATIZATION OF THE CONDITIONS FOR PATH DEPENDENCE

Our path toward a fuller characterization of the necessary and sufficient *concrete* conditions for path dependence begins with Paul David's (1999) reflections on the ultimate *abstract* conditions: First, there must exist multiple, *diverging* feasible paths of allocation, each one locally *stable* so that agents are not "led back to a single, globally stable attractor of the kind that characterizes an ergodic dynamical system."[1] Second, the factors or criteria that select among these branching paths must be to some extent "orthogonal" to any system-level economic issues at stake—for example, efficiency. This means, in part, that "the actual path of development must . . . be an emergent system property whose 'selection' was an unintended consequence of the interactions among agents that were not engaged in any conscious collective choice" (David 1999, p. 7). A process for which the path to be taken is itself an object of choice is not path dependent.

The divergence of paths noted under the first condition is, straightforwardly, the result of positive feedbacks, the increasing returns to adoption identified by Arthur. In David's terms, this may be the result of technical interrelatedness combined with increasing returns or positive externalities. As both Arthur (1989) and David (1985) note, positive feedbacks may end if increasing returns are bounded or exhausted at a sufficiently low level.

The local stability of paths is largely the result of quasi-irreversibility of investment—high switching costs. If the decisions that put an allocation process on one path are costlessly reversible (including in terms of information and transactions costs), then the process can always move to the path that is revealed as optimal. Less strictly, if switching costs are positive but still sufficiently low relative to the gains from switching, then a path revealed as suboptimal loses its local stability. As we shall see, both the costs and benefits of switching may vary with the state of technology, and new technology may bring an end to the local stability of a particular path.[2] Furthermore, the private and social costs and benefits of switching depend on transactions costs in internalizing the externalities prevalent in path-dependent processes. These transactions costs may be quite high under conditions of strong technical interrelatedness and institutions that set the interests of different agents against one another, as Scott (2001) showed in a study of Britain's "coal wagon problem." However, the innovation of new internalization mechanisms (generally organizations or institutions) may lower transactions costs and so bring an end to the local stability of a particular path.

The second of David's conditions, the lack of a close link between factors that select among alternative paths and the system-level economic issues at stake, is what gives room for the impact of particular contingent events, that is, events not necessitated by systematic, a priori factors. These contingent events may be either purposeful choices by economic agents—for example, variations in strategy motivated by idiosyncratic beliefs about unproven technologies and unexplored markets—or else "historical accidents" that are exogenous from the point of view of these agents. In either case, such events are the sorts of things that management scholars and the business press cite as reasons for the relative success of different firms, but which are not yet well incorporated into economic theory.

What can cause this divergence between the factors that select among alternative paths and the ultimate economic issues at stake? First, positive externalities. Even in a "path-independent" process, externalities cause a discrete divergence between a theoretical social optimum and a realized equilibrium, a divergence quantifiable in relation to the difference between private and social costs and benefits. In a path-dependent process, externalities can result in the selection of a whole different path, and the original divergence can in a certain sense be greatly magnified. Of course, to the extent that externalities are internalized, as assumed by Liebowitz and Margolis (1994, 1995), this divergence disappears. In practice, however, externalities are rarely if ever fully—or perhaps even mostly—internalizable, and the presumption remains that uninternalized externalities could be a substantial factor in the onset—as well as in the continued local stability—of a path dependent process.[3]

Second, and in most cases more important, the selection among paths may take insufficient account of the issues at stake because agents do not know enough to foresee the consequences of their choices—either the destinations of diverging paths or how their choices can best ensure the realization of desired outcomes. Agents may, for example, have uncertain or mistaken views about the relative advantages of different new techniques or about other agents' interests, or they may not foresee such later emerging factors as the benefits of technical standardization and thus the tendency of a de facto standard to emerge. Importantly, this applies not only to the possible selection of an inefficient rather than (Pareto-)efficient path, but also to the selection among alternative Pareto-efficient paths that generate different payoffs for different agents.

These two factors, especially foresight, distinguish path dependence from the fulfilled-expectations processes that in some models determine allocation when network externalities are present. Let us suppose—quite counterfactually—the existence of perfect, complete intertemporal markets, with complete information about technological possibilities (which may nevertheless be time dependent) and agents' interests and preferences. In this case the optimal path (or set of Pareto-optimal paths) is clear to all agents; furthermore, all externalities can be internalized. Future markets clear at time zero, leaving no deciding role for the dynamics of the process as such, and thus there is no path dependence. When all objects of future choice (and their consequences) are known and thus "present" at the beginning of an allocation process, and when the externalities of agents' choices are internalized, then the path itself becomes an object of choice for the internalizing, optimizing agent—precisely David's (1988, 1997) criterion for what he calls "moderate to mild history," as opposed to the "strong history" of path dependence. There may still be multiple potential Pareto-optimal equilibria as a result of increasing returns, but the selection among these takes place through some process of formation of rational (and subsequently fulfilled) expectations, perhaps assisted by the preemptive actions of (externality-internalizing) agents who have a stake in which Pareto-optimal equilibrium is selected (Katz and Shapiro 1985).

However, a world in which information about the characteristics and uses of new technologies and the interests and strategies of agents is progressively revealed, not foreseen from the beginning, is one in which the path of allocation as such is not an object of choice for any agent, and the end result of an allocation process may be decided by its particular history. Because this is certainly the sort of world in which we live, Paul Krugman (1998) is unwarranted in criticizing Arthur for not basing his models on fulfilled expectations (in contrast to Krugman's own models of increasing returns yielding multiple equilibria).

Fulfilled-expectations processes also involve positive feedbacks and have a certain continuity with path-dependent processes. In fact, those who model such processes implicitly assume a period of uncertainty during the process of expectation formation, a period during which both suppliers and users of competing techniques seek to understand and influence the process (Katz and Shapiro 1994; Besen and Farrell 1994). During this period the process is path dependent, as agents consider various outcomes possible and form their expectations in response to the ensemble of each other's contingent actions.

The consequences of imperfect foresight and imperfect internalizability are similar whether the system-level issue at stake is potential inefficiency or, rather, which of two or more (each Pareto-efficient) proprietary products or techniques will be established as a de facto standard. Under these conditions, future paths as such are not objects of choice at the beginning of the process for interested agents, individually or collectively. The competition is not decided at one point in time by a Katz-Shapiro (1985) mechanism; it is decided over time, path dependently. This does not, of course, rule out strategic behavior—quite the contrary. If the sponsors of the alternative techniques recognize that the allocation process is a path-dependent one with positive feedbacks, they act strategically to influence the early events that have a disproportional impact on the subsequent evolution of the process. They promote their proprietary system "architectures" in the manner described by Morris and Ferguson (1993). Such behavior is pervasive in advanced-technology industries (Shapiro and Varian 1999).[4]

2. A GENERAL ANALYTICAL FRAMEWORK

In order to examine, first, whether particular empirical allocation processes are path dependent, and second, the role of both network form and technological change in path dependence, I propose here an analytical framework with three features: sources of variation in agents' choices, a source of positive feedbacks in their choices, and the possibility, in some but not all cases, of reversal of initial choices. This framework is relatively general and too informal to constitute a model, but it is applicable to a broad range of empirical cases. It builds upon previous rigorous modeling approaches and points the way to new ones.

Adopters or Users of Techniques

There are two types of agents: (1) users and, in some cases, (2) suppliers of alternative products or techniques.[5] A typical potential user chooses the technique $T \in \{T_1, T_2, \ldots\}$ that maximizes either her consumption utility or the net value of a technique in productive activity. Following Arthur (1989) and others, the technique's value (in production or consumption) $V(T)$ is treated as the sum of two terms,

$$V(T) = D(T) + E(T). \tag{1}$$

$D(T)$ represents the user's technical valuation of the technique, based on the user's expectations about how the technique will serve either the particular tastes of the consumer or the particular productive activities of the producer; in productive activity, this term represents (discounted) expected streams of incremental net revenues or profits. This technical valuation function offers, we shall see, several ways to introduce variation into the process, and it is the chief means through which technological change can affect the process as it proceeds. The second term, $E(T)$, reflects the user's expected benefits of using the same technique as other users—the expected present value of network integration benefits or network externalities. This function is the source of positive feedbacks, and the form of this function reflects the form of value-producing network interactions among agents, as I consider in a later section.

David (1993) has called attention to the need to consider reversibility as well as irreversibility of choices, and I propose to do so by stipulating a conversion cost that is not necessarily prohibitive. The value of the technique to which one switches is then

$$V(T) = D(T) + E(T) - C(T), \qquad (2)$$

where $C(T) > 0$ is the cost of conversion to that technique (assumed here to be independent of which other technique was used previously). For a user's current technique, $C(T) = 0$.

It may be noted that $D(T)$ is normalized differently in equation (2) than in equation (1), differing by the sunk costs of adopting technique T. In general, conversion costs may be regarded as the portion of these sunk costs that must be paid out anew when switching from one technique to another. In the case of railway track gauge, for example, the same roadbed substructure and rolling stock can usually be used for track of different gauges, but rails have to be moved, wheel trucks altered, and sometimes locomotives replaced.

Suppliers or Sponsors of Techniques

Although in some cases techniques are inherently nonproprietary—railway track gauges, for example—in many cases they are developed and sponsored by a second class of agents. Their role is to explore new technology, choose the specific features of marketed products or techniques, and then supply and promote their techniques through pricing and marketing. In pursuing research and selecting features, they may need to make guesses both about the potential for further improvements in specific techniques and about what features will best serve user needs in a yet unproven market. In their pricing and marketing behavior, they help form users' expectations both about the value of the specific technique—$D(T)$—and about the future choices of other users and thus the future value of network benefits—$E(T)$ (Katz and Shapiro 1994; Besen and Farrell 1994; Liebowitz and Margolis 1994, 1995). In this, they serve as partial internalizers of the externalities among users.

Solution Concepts

How a model of allocation is solved depends on further assumptions. Given perfect foresight (into both technology and users' interests) and internalizability, as discussed in the previous major section, paths as a whole are objects of choice at the beginning of the process, and it is reasonable to apply models in which rational fulfilled expectations lead to a Pareto-optimal result. Such processes are not path dependent.

More realistically, given imperfect foresight, as new adopters arrive over time and choose the technique that offers the highest expected total value, both $D(T)$ and $E(T)$ may change in ways not perfectly predicted or controlled. Several potential sources of variation could lead to a branching of potential paths of allocation. For one, potential adopters may vary either in the objective suitability of different techniques for their purposes or in their subjective expectations about the suitability of different techniques. Arthur's (1989) well-explored stochastic arrival process considers what happens when such adopters arrive at the market sequentially in unforeseeable random order. Market share evolves, at first, as a random walk, but when one technique gains a sufficient market share, learning or network effects override the preferences of some adopters for minority techniques, causing the process to "lock in" to the technique that had gained the early lead for purely stochastic reasons.

This approach has the weakness that it does not readily lend itself to incorporating either expectations, except in a truncated form, or the sponsorship of techniques and internalization of externalities—points that Liebowitz and Margolis (1995) seized upon. Nevertheless, Arthur's more general analysis of the dynamics of positive feedbacks in market share does not depend on the specific stochastic-arrival mechanism and remains generally valid. Furthermore, I have found the stochastic-arrival mechanism to offer a good explanation for the adoption of specific railway track gauges by the earliest local railways in various regions (Puffert 2000, 2002).

Another reason to look beyond the stochastic-arrival mechanism is that stochastic variations in adopter arrival are likely to be weak in cases where numerous adopters make simultaneous choices—and other potential sources of variation are likely to be much stronger. Most important, I believe, are the contingent aspects of the behavior of suppliers, particularly their decisions concerning what lines of research and development to pursue, what features to include in their products or techniques, and how to market their techniques. As Nelson and Winter (1977) have taught us, firms do not follow known recipes for maximizing profits but rather engage in exploratory behavior, particularly in the context of unproven technology and untested market interest. A range of behavior is possible, some strategies succeed better than others, and, given increasing returns to adoption, variations in behavior may easily be sufficient to set an allocation process on one path rather than another (see Puffert 2003).

Adopters also live in a world of uncertainty, and their expectations may well be influenced both by the contingent actions of suppliers and by "exogenous" events that seem to offer information about the relative technical values and future market shares of different products or techniques. Thus, even the outcome of a single, well-publicized early typing contest may have affected the later course of allocation of keyboard systems (David 1986; cf. Liebowitz and Margolis 1990).

Over time, greater information is revealed about the relative value of different techniques in application, but meanwhile the allocation process has already proceeded along a specific, locally stable path. Even if the technique and path selected are shown to offer less to users than some other that had been available, the new information may offer less incentive than would be needed to overcome the local stability and redirect the process.

3. TECHNOLOGICAL CHANGE AND PATH DEPENDENCE

Technological change may affect the path dependence of an allocation process in several ways. First, again, it is a source of variation. The uncertainty associated with new technology and its potential uses creates room for a variety of contingent beliefs, expectations, and behaviors that together may determine which particular path an allocation process takes. Second, as Cowan (1990) has noted, particular contingent technological advances may encourage development of those advances rather than exploration of other techniques that in some cases would offer greater long-term benefits. Third, technological change may introduce new best techniques. These may be "locked out" because conversion costs (including transaction costs) outweigh possible gains, or they may offer sufficient benefits to induce conversion, rendering the old technique obsolete and ending the previous path-dependent lock-in. In a fourth effect, technological change may lead to a sort of reconvergence of different paths, at least in the sense that a technique evolves to develop features similar to those that might have developed along a different path. In terms of the analytical framework here, these first four effects all work through the technical valuation function $D(T)$.

Fifth, technological change can reduce the level of conversion costs $C(T)$ and thus end the local stability of an established path. Sixth and last, technological change may affect the network benefit or externality function $E(T)$ through the introduction of adapters or "gateways" (David 1987) that offer a substantial degree of network integration even in the absence of a common technique. Adapters are devices that enable products using one technique to function within a system or network that is based on another technique. Gateways are connections among otherwise incompatible networks, formed either by adapters or by the performance of some task that effectively converts a product or service from one technique to another. In railways, for example, rolling stock that crosses a "break of gauge" can shift to the new gauge either through adjustable wheels and axles (an adapter) or through the complete exchange of wheel trucks (a gateway operation).

4. NETWORK FORM AND PATH DEPENDENCE

Models that examine path dependence or, more generally, network externalities often assume that network externalities (or network integration benefits) vary simply with what David (1993) calls the macro state of the system; that is, that $E(T)$ can be expressed simply as $E(N(T))$, $E' > 0$, where $N(T)$ is the number of adopters (or, alternatively, market share) of technique T. As David notes, this is often inappropriate, and he proposes, as an alternative, the assumption that agents have direct value-producing interactions only with their immediate neighbors on a one- or two-dimensional lattice. Here we consider also a larger set of network forms that arise in concrete empirical cases.

In general, the network externalities or network integration benefits for each agent i depend on her specific value-producing interactions with other agents, that is, on both the graph Γ representing these interactions, and perhaps on the agent's position within that graph:

$$E_i(T_i) = E_i(\Gamma(\mathbf{T}_i, T_i)), \tag{3}$$

where T_i is the technique chosen by i and $\mathbf{T}_i$ is the vector of techniques chosen by agents other than i. Both the dynamics of the allocation process and features of its outcomes depend on the specific graphical structure. The various possible network structures may involve either direct interactions among users or interactions through providers of "network services" (Figure 3.1). The

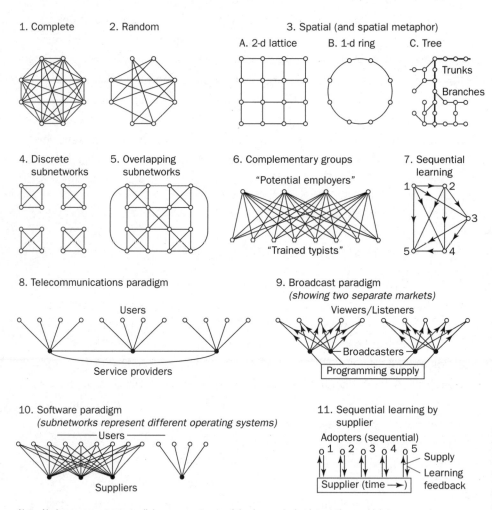

Note: Nodes represent agents; links represent potential value-producing interactions, which are actualized only if agents use a compatible technique—including by means of adapter or gateway, which may reduce the net value of the link.

Figure 3.1 Alternative network forms

following discussion assumes that all potential value-producing interactions are of equal value.

Alternative Forms

Direct interactions among users of a technique may take numerous forms, of which the following are important basic types (see Figure 3.1).

1. A complete network structure features direct interactions (the links or "edges" in a graph) among all users (the nodes in a graph) who adopt a compatible technique. For such networks, if the values of interactions are assumed equal, then $E(T)$ takes the form $E(N(T))$.

2. A *random* network structure involves defined ex ante probabilities of interactions among pairs of users. If these probabilities are equal for all links, then functional form $E(N(T))$ again applies.

3. *Spatial* networks involve direct links only among immediate neighbors, most simply modeled as within a regular lattice. In many empirical examples, there are also economically relevant indirect links with the neighbors' neighbors (and so on), so that the broader "connectivity" of the network is also relevant. For example, local railway lines have an interest in the ability to exchange traffic both with immediate neighbors and indirectly with more distant railways. Because different agents have different neighbors, function $E_i(\Gamma(\mathbf{T}_i, T_i))$ varies among agents and may take a relatively complicated form.

4. When potential interactions occur only within unconnected or *discrete subnetworks,* with complete or random links within the subnetworks, function $E_i(\Gamma(\mathbf{T}_i, T_i))$ depends only on the number of other users within the user's subnetwork that use the same technique. Whether users in other subnetworks use the same technique does not matter.

5. *Overlapping subnetworks* are similar to the foregoing in terms of the structure of each agent's incentives, but agents who potentially interact with each other differ in the sets of other agents with whom they could have interactions. Spatial networks in which only direct

interactions matter are a subset of this network form and offer a simplified modeling approach.

6. *Complementary groups* consist of agents possessing complementary components of some larger production system, each of whom therefore has potential value-producing interactions only with the other group. The paradigm for this network form is the set of trained typists together with the set of firms who buy typewriters and hire typists to use them (David 1985), which may be regarded as a special case of either of two sorts of networks discussed by Economides (1996): first, the supply network of firms or agents in upstream and downstream industries, and second, buyers and sellers in markets where both gain from increasing market "thickness." In different contexts, members of one group may have potential interactions with all or with only some of the members of the complementary group, and the resulting overall form could be either densely interconnected or divided into subnetworks.

7. For each of the foregoing network forms, value-producing interactions could be either reciprocal or one-way. An important example of a one-way effect is a *sequential learning* process in which later adopters of a technique have an opportunity to adopt a less expensive or improved version as a result, respectively, of learning-by-doing in the production of earlier versions or learning-by-using in their application. Each adopter in this case benefits from, or "interacts with," previous adopters only. Arthur (1989) motivated his basic model of path-dependent allocation by considering just such an effect. It is noteworthy here that supply-side learning effects can, like demand-side effects, be modeled in terms of networks.

At least four important network structures are based on *indirect interactions* among users of the technique, where direct interactions are with the suppliers of network services:

8. In the *telecommunications paradigm* (Economides 1996), users are connected directly to service providers who in turn are connected directly both to a set of other users and to other service providers with

connections to further sets of users. Each service-provider network requires use of a common technique (for example, a specific cellular or wireline analog or digital standard), but connection is possible to users of other techniques and other service providers, although often at a greater cost or price. Interconnections among "local" networks are provided by gateways, so that a common user technique is not needed.

9. In the *broadcast paradigm,* network interactions are one-way from service providers to users, whose receivers must be compatible with broadcast signals. Given that users receive signals from multiple broadcasters, it is advantageous that all of these use the same technique. Broadcasters also often gain revenues from having more viewers or listeners.

10. In the *software paradigm,* there is monopolistic competition among suppliers of application software for specific hardware platforms or operating systems—for example, for computers or video players. As a result, both the variety and the price of software improve for each user as the total number of users increases, making the hardware platform or operating system more valuable. The value of network interactions for each user may, for example, take the form $E(M(N(T)))$, where M is the number of software suppliers. This functional form reduces to $E(N(T))$, and the network form itself can therefore be regarded as collapsing to form 1. In cases where different sets of agents use different application software, the network form may collapse to 4 or 5.

The relevant feature of software is that, as pure information content combined with a low-cost distribution medium, it exhibits high fixed costs and low variable costs, giving rise to strong economies of scale. The network externalities in this case are not technological but rather pecuniary in nature, and Liebowitz and Margolis (1994) have asserted and attempted to demonstrate that the externalities therefore have no effect on the nature of the allocation process, based in part on the quixotic assumption that all software-supplier rents can be internalized by the sponsor of a technique (the supplier of the hardware or operating system).[6] However, as Krugman (1991, p. 485) points out, "In competitive general equilibrium, of course, pecuniary externalities have no welfare significance and could not lead to . . . interesting dynamics . . . . In the presence of imperfect competition and increasing returns, pecuniary externalities matter; for example, if one firm's actions affect the demand for the product of another firm whose price exceeds marginal cost, this is as much a 'real' externality as if one firm's research and development spills over into the general knowledge pool."

11. Finally, learning effects may be mediated by the suppliers of techniques that are subject to learning. Nevertheless, the network form can be regarded for some purposes as collapsing to that of form 7.

Implications of Network Form

The main implication of network form for an allocation process is that positive feedbacks are not always based simply on the macro state of the process. Sometimes they are, as for network forms 1, 2, 7, and perhaps 10, and in such cases the choices of new adopters tend to reinforce any asymmetries in total market share. If economically relevant network interactions take place only in discrete subnetworks (form 4), then positive feedbacks take place only within these subnetworks. Indeed, if only a small number of agents are involved and these already directly communicate with each other, then they can simply coordinate their choices by agreement before adopting a technique. Extended families can adopt the same videorecording system in order to exchange home videos, and coauthors can adopt common word-processing software (Liebowitz and Margolis 1994).

Much more often, however, subnetwork interactions take place among overlapping subnetworks, whether spatial (form 3) or otherwise (form 5). In these cases, an interesting dynamic may develop, as I have both modeled and documented empirically in the case of railway track gauge (Puffert 2000, 2002). Early adopters in an allocation process coordinate their choices "locally" (to use the spatial metaphor also for nonspatial cases), but different techniques may be adopted in different locations. Later adopters use the same technique as adjacent established users, leading to the expansion of regional networks of a common technique. Eventually, regions using different techniques run into each other, so that agents on the borders of these regions cannot adopt the same technique as all potential partners in interaction. Local standard techniques emerge, but a "global" (or continental) standard does not. If indirect as well as direct connections among agents matter, as in the case of railways, then all agents pay a price for the resulting diversity. Of course, given perfect foresight and complete internalization of externalities, all agents will coordinate their actions from the start (unless diversity is in fact efficient due to differences among users in which technique suits their needs). Empirically, however, both factors are often missing in the crucial early stages of an allocation process.

The emergence of diversity in a spatial network (or any network of overlapping subnetworks) raises the issue of conversion in a way that does not arise when feedbacks from the macro state of the system lead to global standardization from the start. David (1993) and coauthors (David and Foray 1993; David, Foray, and Dalle 1998) examine the case where agents on the borders among regions of common technique may change their technique randomly to that of one or another neighbor, as might happen when network interactions are random and conversion is costless. This enables them to draw on the extensively developed theory of Markov random fields or interacting particle systems. I examine the case where conversions have a cost and depend deterministically on systematic network interactions. Both approaches show how conversion can yield increasing coordination over time, possibly but not necessarily eliminating early diversity. My approach also demonstrates how various schemes for the internalization of externalities—for sharing the costs of conversion—can contribute to the resolution of diversity, providing that transactions costs are sufficiently low (Puffert 2002). It also demonstrates that permanent or even temporary diversity, and thus unrealized network integration benefits, can be a greater source of inefficiency in an allocation process than selection of a "wrong" technique.

The consideration of network forms also clarifies where adoption of a common technique matters most for the facilitation of network interactions, and where gateways and adapters render complete standardization less important. In both the telecommunications and the broadcast paradigm (forms 8 and 9), users must adopt the same technique as their service provider(s), but not necessarily the same technique as all other users. In telecommunications, network-level gateways enable users of different service providers to interact. Broadcasters can, at relatively low cost, convert programming developed in one format to their own format. Broadcast receivers can also be made for multiple formats, as has long been the case for radios and is increasingly so for televisions, particularly in combining digital satellite and high-definition capabilities with analog. Gateways can also link spatial subnetworks together at costs that may be low enough to effectively unify the networks, as in the case of electric power distribution, or not, as in the case of railway track gauge.

Case Studies

The value of these considerations can be seen concretely in a sampling of empirical cases representing different network forms and different characteristics of technology (Table 3.1, pp. 82–83).

Railways form spatial networks in which standardization of track gauge facilitates the exchange of traffic among companies or state administrations (Puffert 2000, 2002). Early in the history of railways, diversity in gauge emerged in numerous regions in response to uncertainty and changing opinions about optimal gauge and lack of foresight about the later importance of long-distance network integration because early railways usually served strictly local transport needs. Although the diffusion of specific engineering traditions limited the proliferation of gauges, six gauges gained widespread adoption in North America, seven or more became regional standards in Europe, and multiple gauges were introduced on all other continents and in numerous countries. The introduction of specific gauges to specific regions was essentially a stochastic arrival process, as gauges were chosen by engineers and promoters representing random draws from a heterogeneous population.

Nearly all the diversity of gauge in North America and much of that in Europe was later resolved as demand grew for long-distance transport. This was sometimes facilitated by side-payments, interregional system-building, and coordination—practices that internalized the mutual externalities of local railways. Costly diversity remains in Australia, in India, at the border of France with Spain, and in numerous other places. A variety of gateway techniques (such as mixed-gauge track and exchangeable wheel trucks) have offered a degree of network integration despite diversity and have also sometimes facilitated long processes of conversion, providing a "migration path." Most railway engineers regard the common 4'8.5" (1435 mm.) gauge, adapted from the gauge of small coal carts in mines near Newcastle and used today on nearly 60 percent of world railways, as narrower than optimal, but the main source of inefficiency in the process of gauge selection has been the emergence and persistence of diversity.

Adoption of a common technique has mattered less for railway electrification networks (Puffert 1993a, 1994a), because railways have usually preferred to change locomotives at (national or company) borders anyway. Nevertheless, recent efforts to achieve a "Europe without frontiers," particularly in high-speed train service, have increased the cost of diversity. The development of relatively efficient adapters in multi-current locomotives and high-speed trainsets is bringing improvements in network integration.

Early industrial and household electrical power distribution networks were marked by an initially vigorous competition between Edison's direct-current (DC) and Westinghouse's alternating-current (AC) systems, as each promoter's strategy responded both to network effects and to a series of technological innovations (David and Bunn 1988; David 1990). Development of an inexpensive gateway technique, the rotary converter, provided a means to join together local subnetworks of each system, enabling end users to adopt the systems best suited to their needs and facilitating the progressive replacement of DC by AC in the trunk distribution system, where the advantages of AC proved substantial. Technological change broke the allocation process free of its early history, making it path independent—although the persistence of a variety of local-standard AC frequencies and voltages has certainly been path dependent. The process of rationalization was facilitated in the end by externality-internalizing cooperation between Edison's and Westinghouse's firms.

Table 3.1

Features of network technologies

Technology (selected specific techniques)	Form or Graphic Structure	Network Characteristics				Internalization of Externalities
		Interactions		Locus of Adapters / Gateways	Characteristics of Technology and Technological Change	
		Nature or Source	Foreseen?			
Railway track gauge (4'8.5", 5'0", 5'3", 5'6", 750 mm., 1000 mm.)	Spatial (tree)	Traffic (car) exchange	Early: often not	Users (cars) and network	Heterogeneity and change in preferred practice. Variety of gateways	By users; facilitated conversion
Railway electrification (AC 16.67 Hz 15 kV, DC 1500 V, etc.)	Spatial (tree)	Trainset and locomotive exchange	(Not an early issue)	Users (trainsets and locomotives)	Changes in preferred practice. Recent good adapters	Little
Electrical power distribution (AC/DC, 50/60 Hz, 110/230/other voltages)	Spatial (tree)	Power transmission	Relatively early	Network and some users	Heterogeneous users. Very efficient adapter	Supplier cooperation
Color television (NTSC, SECAM, PAL, HiVision, HD-MAC, U.S. and other digital)	Broadcast discrete subnetworks	Signal reception	Yes (to extent that it matters)	Network (broadcasters) and some users	New digital technology renders older obsolete	Cooperation in setting standards
Cellular telephony (AMPS, TACS, NMT, GSM, TDMA, CDMA)	Telecom subnetworks[a] Learning	Signal exchange Learning	Yes (to extent that it matters)	Network, users (for roaming)	Rapid innovation. Digital superseded original analog	Cooperation in setting standards
Internet (data telecom) (TCP/IP versus OSI)	Telecom interlink	Data exchange	Yes	Users and network	Rapid innovation. Evolvable, convergent	Cooperation in setting standards

(Continued)

Table 3.1 (*Continued*)

Technology (selected specific techniques)	Network Characteristics				Characteristics of Technology and Technological Change	Internalization of Externalities
	Form or Graphic Structure	Nature or Source	Foreseen?	Locus of Adapters / Gateways		
		Interactions				
Magnetic and optical recording and reproduction (VHS, Beta, CD[-ROM], DVD, audio cassette, DAT, DCC, MD)	Software complete, Overlapping subnetworks, Learning	Software sale/rental, Media exchange, Learning	Yes or mostly	Users	Series of new products and media, Digital now replacing analog	Promotion, Cooperation in setting standards
Microcomputer operating systems (MS-DOS), Macintosh, Windows, Unix, Linux)[b]	Software subnetworks, Subnetworks	Software market, File exchange	Varied	Users	Rapid technological and market change, Evolvable, convergent	Promotion, User coordination
Nuclear power systems (light water, gas graphite)	Learning	Supplier learning	Some	None	Early uncertainty, High development cost	By system suppliers
Pest (insect) control (pesticides, integrated pest management)	Spatial Learning	Spillover of medium Learning	Yes	None	Changing pest environment (species, resistance)	User coordination
Typewriter keyboards (QWERTY, Ideal, DSK)	Complementary groups[c]	Production system	?	Users (machine)	Neurophysiological habituation of typists, Remappable keyboards	Supplier promotion

[a]Networks overlap to the extent that users "roam" in other local subnetworks.

[b]The case is discussed in a longer version of this chapter, available from the author.

[c]Whether interacting agents form small discrete subnetworks or an interconnected network is disputed.

Television broadcasting has heretofore required local standards so that viewers could readily receive signals from different broadcasters, but broadcasters have been able to use signal converters to adapt programming from different formats. Adapters and multi-system receivers for users can now receive both analog signals and digital signals from satellites and terrestrial high-definition television (HDTV) broadcasters. Standards have been selected by national authorities, in several cases with a view to industrial policy based partly on learning effects. France and Germany introduced the SECAM and PAL color television standards, respectively, rather than adopt the North American NTSC system, in part to reduce the advantage of experienced U.S. equipment manufacturers. Japanese government and equipment manufacturers developed their analog HiVision HDTV system during the 1980s in an effort to take the lead in HDTV, hoping to establish a global standard that they would dominate. Europeans responded with their own system, HD-MAC. Both systems, however, were rendered obsolete during the 1990s by development in the United States of a digital HDTV system. Japan and Europe have subsequently adopted variants of the U.S. standard. Thus technological change overcame efforts to preemptively determine new standards. This new technology may well overcome the historical legacy in much of the world.

Cellular telephony requires a common technique for a given service provider, but network-level gateways offer connections to other cellular and wireline telephone users, and multi-system handsets facilitate user "roaming" in areas of different service providers. Thus there has been no path-dependent obstacle to the introduction of rapidly improving new techniques. There is path dependence, however, in competition among alternative techniques for adoption by service providers and regulators, as learning effects reduce the costs and improve the capabilities of both network equipment and handsets (Puffert 1993b).

The Internet is a network of networks—of numerous local area and wide area electronic data networks that use a variety of architectures and signal protocols. These are linked to the Internet and thus to each other by means of signal-protocol converters or "gateways"—a term first applied to technical standards in this context.[7] The Internet may be regarded as the network interlinking the hub nodes within the telecommunications paradigm (form 8).

After the early development of data-communications networks based on proprietary architectures (primarily those of IBM and DEC), two efforts were undertaken to develop vendor-independent suites of standards. One, based on the Transmission Control Protocol/Internet Protocol (TCP/IP) developed incrementally for the now widespread Internet. Over much the same period, international standards-development organizations sponsored the definition, by computer scientists, of an alternative, much more comprehensive suite of standards known as the Open Systems Interconnection (OSI) model.[8] Although OSI has numerous theoretical advantages over TCP/IP, it has gained little acceptance in the market. Equipment and software suppliers have found it easier to develop and test products within a functioning network and standards environment, while network users have not wished to purchase products based on untested concepts. In the early 1990s, experts debated whether TCP/IP and OSI internets would function in parallel during a period of transition to OSI or whether TCP/IP would evolve by incorporating OSI concepts that extend TCP/IP's capabilities in ways particularly demanded by users ("Great OSI Debate," 1992). The latter has proven to be the case. The capacity of the TCP/IP technique to evolve, and thus converge in some respects with the OSI model, have brought the allocation path to a point, in some but not all dimensions of technology, that might have been reached along other possible paths.

Markets for magnetic and optical recording and reproducing technologies for audio, video, and data involve at least three sorts of network interactions: direct exchange of software among users (within discrete or overlapping subnetworks); software-supply effects both in sales and in rental markets; and learning effects by system-equipment suppliers, giving rise to reduced costs and improved features (Puffert 1994b). Suppliers' foresight about the tendency for competitive exclusion in the setting of de facto standards has led them to unite in supporting common standards for such technologies as first-generation compact discs (CDs and CD-ROMs) and second-generation DVDs (digital versatile discs), forming common expectations and effectively choosing the path of allocation at the outset of the process. DVD equipment has been made backward-compatible for current CDs and CD-ROMs (it has built-in adapters), reducing the cost to consumers of migration to the new technique and eliminating any tendency for the market to remain locked in to the older technique.

Foresight has not always preempted path-dependent allocation processes in this industry. The most celebrated systems competition was that among systems for consumer video recording—primarily Sony's Betamax system and JVC's VHS—from the mid-1970s to mid-1980s. Arthur (1994) explained this as the result of positive feedbacks in the video film rental market, as video rental stores stocked more film titles for the system with a larger user base, and new adopters chose the system for which they could rent more videos. However, Cusumano, Mylonadis, and Rosenbloom (1992) showed that this effect, although important, emerged at only a late stage in the competition, when VHS already had a strong lead. Nevertheless, they argued that the earlier process already had a path-dependent market-share dynamic because an increasing number of manufacturers and distributors supported VHS over Betamax as they came to believe that VHS would emerge as a de facto standard. Three contingent early differences in strategy were crucial. First, Sony proceeded without major cosponsors for its Betamax system, while JVC shared VHS with several major competitors. Second, the VHS consortium quickly installed a large manufacturing capacity. Third, Sony opted for a more compact videocassette, while JVC chose instead a longer playing time for VHS, which proved more important to many customers. The strategic choices of firms were a source of contingent variation that affected the subsequent course of allocation, making the allocation process path dependent.

Learning effects have been the principal source of path dependence in the adoption of nuclear power techniques (Cowan 1990). The dominant "light-water" reactor design appears to be inherently less efficient than potential alternatives, but it was rushed into use because the Cold War political value of peaceful uses for nuclear technology overrode the value of finding the most cost-effective technique. Thereafter, engineering experience for the light-water technique continued to make it the rational choice for new reactors over less well developed alternative designs, although equal development of the alternatives might have made them superior. The principal U.S. suppliers and sponsors of light-water reactors, Westinghouse and General Electric, acted as internalizers of externalities by offering early systems at prices below cost in order to gain experience and offer improved systems to later adopters at higher prices.

Both local positive feedbacks and learning effects have affected farmers' choice between systems of chemical pest control and integrated pest management (IPM) (Cowan and Gunby 1996). IPM relies in part on predatory insects to devour harmful ones, and the drift of chemical pesticides from neighboring fields often makes the use of IPM impossible. Predatory insects also drift among fields, further raising farmers' incentives to use the same techniques as neighbors. To be practical, IPM must be used on the whole set of farms that are in proximity to even one other in the set—that is, the larger network made up of the overlapping subnetworks that are subject to drifting pesticides. Where this set is large, the transactions costs of persuading all farmers to forgo chemical methods are often prohibitive. Adoption of IPM has also depended on learning, both at the global level and locally. The path-dependent local lock-in of both techniques has sometimes been upset by such developments as invasions by new pests and the emergence of resistance to pesticides.

Finally, the disputed case of early typewriter keyboard systems is ripe for further examination in light of issues raised here. David (1985, 1986) argued that typists, their third-party teachers, and their employers each choose systems based on the potential pool of matches in a densely interconnected network (Figure 3.1, form 6), generating marketwide positive feedbacks. By contrast, Liebowitz and Margolis (1990) argue that externality-internalizing typewriter suppliers could have offered in-house training to purchasers of alternative keyboards, and they implicitly deny that typists would have cared about the systems used by other potential employers. They assume a discrete-subnetwork form of interaction. Further research could clarify the relative prevalence of different mechanisms in the early employment market for typists and thus the form of the overall virtual network and the scope and effect of positive feedbacks. Furthermore, Liebowitz and Margolis argue that the purposeful behavior of typewriter suppliers overrode the effects of contingent events. If, however, the existence of positive feedbacks is confirmed, then the relevant question is, rather, how both purposeful behavior and other contingent events interacted with the underlying dynamic of the process. The full story of the emergence of the QWERTY standard is clearly more complicated than either the story thread pursued by David or the mechanism proposed by Liebowitz and Margolis. David's essential explanation is likely more robust, however, to the presence of multiple mechanisms in the employment market.

5. CONCLUDING REMARKS

The positive feedbacks that give rise to path-dependent processes of economic allocation arise because agents derive increasing value from an increasing number of interactions with other agents. These interactions often depend on the adoption of some common technique, and they either arise out of physical networks or can be treated as arising out of virtual networks. Different network forms affect the dynamic of allocation in different ways, giving rise to general standardization or creating diversity among regions or subnetworks.

Technological change may affect either the network-independent values of alternative techniques, or the extent to which value-producing interactions depend on the adoption of a common technique, or the cost of conversion. Each of these possibilities affects how the allocation process evolves and how easily it breaks free of its past. Because new technologies and their uses—as well as the interests and strategies of interacting agents—are revealed progressively over time, allocation processes also evolve progressively rather than being decided in one timeless moment of expectations formation. The economics of path dependence tells us not only how *history* matters in allocation; it also tells us how, even more fundamentally, *time* matters.

The case studies examined here establish two facts that have often been neglected in previous studies. First, allocation processes driven by network integration benefits often lead not to a single "global" standard but rather to multiple regional or subnetwork standards. In the context of some network forms and some technologies, these subnetworks are natural market niches; in other contexts, subnetworks defined by common techniques arise as path-dependent artifacts of contingent events. Second, subnetworks based on different techniques are quite often integrated with each other by means of gateways. In some networks—for example, for telecommunications or electric power supply—this integration is close to perfect; in other networks—based, for example, on common railway gauges or computer operating systems—gateways offer only a relatively imperfect and costly integration.

The persistence of diversity among subnetworks raises new questions regarding efficiency. Might this diversity offer greater scope for development of different techniques, allowing the best technique to emerge, prove itself, and ultimately win the whole market? In cases where one technique does eventually win the whole market, is the selected technique the winner of a market test—or is it the path-dependent result of earlier contingent events? I have shown the latter explanation to be correct in the case of railway track gauge (Puffert 2000, 2002), but further research may identify cases where early diversity facilitated the emergence of a more optimal technique than early standardization would have done.

The case studies also demonstrate the prevalence of behaviors that partially internalize externalities. In cases where early foresight was good—such as the introduction of CDs and DVDs—these behaviors selected outcomes preemptively, short-circuiting any tendency for the emergence of path-dependent competition. In other cases, these behaviors entered into later stages of path-dependent processes, rationalizing the outcomes somewhat but not leading to outcomes that were independent of earlier contingent events and paths.

Paul David's and Brian Arthur's assertions of the importance of path dependence thus withstand the critique of Liebowitz and Margolis, but the positive insights of these critics lead to a fuller understanding of when and how economic allocation is path dependent. Our understanding is also improved through taxonomies, first, of the network forms that characterize the value-producing interactions among agents, and second, of the aspects of technological change that in various ways affect the emergence and stability of alternative paths of allocation. Taking these considerations into account opens up a richer set of dynamic processes affecting economic allocation, showing in new ways how "history matters." More research is needed to gain analytical control over the various possibilities and to see how frequently each arises in the real world.

Path-dependent processes of change in matters other than technology are also, I would hypothesize, the result of value-producing interactions among agents. Institutions, organizations, cultures, and subcultures, for example (David 1994), all consist in interactions—interactions that have particular network forms and that depend on use of common practices or "techniques": languages and jargons, symbols, rules and norms, and more. Like path-dependent technological change, the evolution of institutions, organizations, and cultures surely depends on the pattern of interactions (that is, the form or structure of social networks), the characteristics of innovative practices, foresight, switching costs, possibilities for internalizing external gains from switching, and other matters analogous to those discussed here.

NOTES AND REFERENCES

Notes

1. An ergodic system is one in which the distribution of states that the system can assume becomes independent of particular past states.

2. From another perspective, this is not the end of local stability but rather the reconvergence of different paths.

3. Liebowitz and Margolis's (1994; 1995) general response concerning the role of externalities in path dependence is that any inability to internalize externalities can be characterized as the result of transactions costs, so that the path taken represents the most efficient one known and attainable, once all costs are taken into consideration. Granting the partial validity of this argument, it remains the case that potential paths may differ in their foreseeable relative efficiency by an amount within the range of the perhaps considerable transactions costs required to direct the emergent collective choice to the (expected) most efficient outcome. Furthermore, the argument does not address either the implications of lack of foresight or cases where the issue at stake is not Pareto efficiency but rather the distribution of rewards. What is problematic in Liebowitz and Margolis's discussion of externalities is not their analysis of the impact of transactions costs on behavior but rather their assertion that a process that is not inefficient by their criteria is uninteresting and not at variance with "the neoclassical model of relentlessly rational behavior leading to efficient, and therefore predictable, outcomes" (Liebowitz and Margolis 1995).

4. It is curious that Liebowitz and Margolis regard such purposeful behavior as the antithesis to path dependence rather than as presupposing it. Liebowitz and Margolis argue that purposeful, forward-looking behavior overrides the effects of mere "accidents" or initial conditions—that economic allocation does not evolve mechanistically from the past but is rather steered by interested agents toward desired future ends. In this they surely have a point, but they do not come to terms with the positive feedbacks that interact with purposeful behavior and the limitations that history imposes on what future-oriented behavior can accomplish.

5. I use the term *technique* (where Arthur uses *technology* or *system variant*) to refer to a particular instantiation of a more general technology. Thus computer operating systems in general are a technology, while MS-DOS and Linux are techniques. The system of flanged wheels on fitted rails is a technology, while specific railway track gauges are techniques.

6. Moreover, Liebowitz and Margolis asserted that network externalities are generally pecuniary rather than technological in nature. This is simply false, as the examples in this paper show.

7. According to a standard industry reference (VLSI Research 1988, p. xxi), a gateway is "a particular type of equipment used to connect incompatible networks by means of a protocol translator." David (1987) brought the term into general use for technical standards. The term was also applied to railways in an otherwise unremarkable 1986 seminar paper by the present author.

8. The OSI project received much of its impetus from European firms and governments seeking to reduce the competitive advantage of U.S. firms that promoted their proprietary architectures. The more modest TCP/IP project was designed simply to interconnect networks using different architectures

References

Arthur, W. Brian. 1989. "Competing Technologies, Increasing Returns, and Lock-in by Historical Events." *Economic Journal* 99: 116–31.

———. 1994. *Increasing Returns and Path Dependence in the Economy*. Ann Arbor: University of Michigan Press.

Besen, Stanley M., and Joseph Farrell. 1994. "Choosing How to Compete: Strategies and Tactics in Standardization." *Journal of Economic Perspectives* 8: 117–31.

Cowan, Robin. 1990. "Nuclear Power Reactors: A Study in Technological Lock-in." *Journal of Economic History* 50: 541–67.

Cowan, Robin, and Philip Gunby. 1996. "Sprayed to Death: Path Dependence, Lock-in and Pest Control Strategies." *Economic Journal* 106: 521–42.

Cusumano, Michael A., Yiorgos Mylonadis, and Richard S. Rosenbloom. 1992. "Strategic Maneuvering and Mass-Market Dynamics: The Triumph of VHS over Beta." *Business History Review* 66: 51–94.

David, Paul A. 1985. "Clio and the Economics of QWERTY." *American Economic Review* (Papers and Proceedings) 75: 332–37.

————. 1986. "Understanding the Economics of QWERTY: The Necessity of History." In W. N. Parker, ed., *Economic History and the Modern Economist.* Oxford: Oxford University Press.

————. 1987. "Some New Standards for the Economics of Standardization in the Information Age." In P. Dasgupta and P. Stoneman, eds., *Economic Policy and Technological Performance.* Cambridge, England: Cambridge University Press.

————. 1988. "Path Dependence: Putting the Past into the Future of Economics." Institute for Mathematical Studies in the Social Sciences Technical Report 533, Stanford University.

————. 1990. "Heroes, Herds, and Hysteresis in Technological History: Thomas Edison and the Battle of the Systems Reconsidered." *Journal of Industrial and Corporate Change* 1: 129–80.

————. 1993. "Path-Dependence and Predictability in Dynamic Systems with Local Network Externalities: A Paradigm for Historical Economics." In D. Foray and C. Freeman, eds., *Technology and the Wealth of Nations: The Dynamics of Constructed Advantage.* London: Pinter.

————. 1994. "Why Are Institutions the 'Carriers of History'? Path-Dependence and the Evolution of Conventions, Organizations and Institutions." *Economic Dynamics and Structural Change* 5: 205–20.

————. 1997. "Path Dependence and the Quest for Historical Economics: One More Chorus of the Ballad of QWERTY." University of Oxford Discussion Papers in Economic and Social History, Number 20.

————. 1999. "At Last, a Remedy for Chronic QWERTY-Skepticism!" Stanford University Department of Economics Working Paper No. 99-025 (September).

David, Paul A., and Julie Ann Bunn. 1988. "The Economics of Gateway Technologies and Network Evolution: Lessons from Electricity Supply History." *Information Economics and Policy* 3: 165–202.

David, Paul A., and Dominique Foray. 1993. "Percolation Structures, Markov Random Fields and the Economics of EDI Standards Diffusion." In G. Pogorel, ed., *Global Telecommunication Strategies and Technological Change.* Amsterdam: Elsevier.

David, Paul A., Dominique Foray, and J.-M. Dalle. 1998. "Marshallian Externalities and the Emergence and Spatial Stability of Technological Enclaves." *Economics of Innovation and New Technologies* 6: 147–82.

Economides, Nicholas. 1996. "The Economics of Networks." *International Journal of Industrial Organization* 14: 673–99.

"Great OSI Debate." 1992. Event at Interop 92 Spring Conference, Washington, D.C., May 22, 1992.

Katz, Michael L., and Carl Shapiro. 1985. "Network Externalities, Competition, and Compatibility." *American Economic Review* 75: 424–40.

———. 1994. "Systems Competition and Network Effects." *Journal of Economic Perspectives* 8: 93–115.

Krugman, Paul. 1991. "Increasing Returns and Economic Geography." *Journal of Political Economy* 99: 483–99.

———. 1998. "The Legend of Arthur." *Slate*, January 14, 1998 (www.slate.com).

Liebowitz, S. J., and Stephen E. Margolis. 1990. "The Fable of the Keys." *Journal of Law and Economics* 33: 1–25.

———. 1994. "Network Externality: An Uncommon Tragedy." *Journal of Economic Perspectives* 8: 133–50.

———. 1995. "Path Dependence, Lock-In, and History." *Journal of Law, Economics, and Organization* 11: 204–26.

Morris, Charles R., and Charles H. Ferguson. 1993. "How Architecture Wins Technology Wars." *Harvard Business Review* (March–April): 86–96.

Nelson, Richard R., and Sidney G. Winter. 1977. "In Search of a Useful Theory of Innovation." *Research Policy* 6: 36–76.

Puffert, Douglas J. 1993a. "Technical Diversity and the Integration of the European High-Speed Train Network." In J. Whitelegg, S. Hultén, and T. Flink, eds., *High-Speed Trains: Fast Tracks to the Future*. Hawes, North Yorkshire: Leading Edge.

———. 1993b. "Technical Standards and International Competition: The Case of Cellular Communications." *Industry, Trade, and Technology Review*, U.S. International Trade Commission, October.

———. 1994a. "The Technical Integration of the European Railway Network." In A. Carreras, A. Giuntini, and M. Merger, eds., *European Networks, 19th–20th Centuries*, Proceedings, Eleventh International Economic History Congress. Milan: Universita Bocconi.

———. 1994b. *Industry and Trade Summary: Audio and Video Recording and Reproducing Equipment*. USITC publication 2822.

———. 2000. "The Standardization of Track Gauge on North American Railways, 1830–1890." *Journal of Economic History* 60: 933–60.

————. 2002. "Path Dependence in Spatial Networks: The Standardization of Railway Track Gauge." *Explorations in Economic History* 39: 282–314.

————. 2003. "Entrepreneurship, Innovation, and Path Dependence." Working paper, Department of Economics, University of Warwick.

Scott, Peter. 2001. "Path Dependence and Britain's 'Coal Wagon Problem.'" *Explorations in Economic History* 38: 366–85.

Shapiro, Carl, and Hal R. Varian. 1999. *Information Rules: A Strategic Guide to the Network Economy.* Cambridge, Mass.: Harvard Business School Press.

VLSI Research. 1988. *VLSI Manufacturing Outlook.* San Jose, Calif.: VLSI Research.

4

THE TENSION BETWEEN STRONG HISTORY AND STRONG ECONOMICS

Melvin W. Reder

This essay attempts to describe the sources of the tension named in its title and to discuss some of their causes and consequences. The idea of Strong History is rooted in a preanalytic vision that the content of any historical process is richer than can be encompassed by any theory or model of it; that is, significant features of the process will be excluded by any theory, though some of the excluded features may be retrieved by using appropriate preceding observations of the process as explanatory instruments.[1] In other words, to understand a sequence of events one always needs, in addition to a theory, to make reference to some antecedent events: history always matters. Put differently, Strong History contends that typically the relationship(s) obtaining among a set of variables at any given moment are partially dependent upon the values that these variables have taken at sometime in the past; that is, path dependence is ubiquitous, or almost so.

By contrast with Strong History, the preanalytic vision of "economics" (Strong Economics) is that a historical process is teleological in nature, envisaging the movement of a set of interrelated variables through time as being guided (directed, attracted) by a goal—equilibrium—which is independent of both the initial and all intervening positions of the variables.[2] Although this vision allows disturbances of one kind or another to cause "wobbles" in the recorded time path of the variables, it precludes the possibility that such departures (from the goal-directed path) could change the goal or be characterized as other than noise.[3] One very important consequence of this vision is that it enables those who share it to use a postulated (equilibrium) relationship among a set of variables as a basis for inferring (deriving) unobserved values of some of the variables from observed values of others.

Although "economics" should not be limited to its contemporary neoclassical variant, it is with this variant that Strong History is contending, and the following discussion is structured accordingly. Because the essential characteristics of a neoclassical model are well known, a detailed recapitulation is unnecessary. However, the properties that are most heavily stressed in the following discussion are: (1) market prices are equal to marginal costs of production and, barring strong evidence to the contrary, a measure of either may be used as a valid proxy for a measure of the other; (2) a statement analogous to (1) holds for the relation of the market price of any input to the value of its marginal product; and (3) barring strong evidence to the contrary, the marginal cost of producing anything is the lowest attainable with extant technology.

I

While the point of this essay is quite general, it is convenient to focus upon one leading example, the now famous QWERTY.[4] Briefly, the position of Strong History is that although the QWERTY typewriter keyboard became technically less efficient than a known alternative, nevertheless it remained the "economywide" standard because its initial adoption and early diffusion made the cost of changing to a superior alternative exceed the gain from greater efficiency that would have ensued from making the change. In other words, an initial advantage combined with subsequent network externalities and the cost of retraining existing typists to use a new keyboard caused a "lock-in" of QWERTY and a corresponding "lock-out" of alternative keyboards of which (at least) one was more efficient. For simplicity I accept the implicit premise of the ambient debate that the lock-in of QWERTY was permanent.

For the purpose of discussion, abstract from the complicated details of early keyboard history and imagine that each of a number of competing typewriter makers was assigned one of a set of possible keyboards by a random process. Suppose that in the early history of the industry the perceived differences in efficiency among the various keyboards were not sufficiently salient to influence the marketability of the typewriters in which they were embodied so that the relative success of their manufacturers depended on other factors considered to be "accidents of history." Suppose further that as a result of these accidents, one particular typewriter, A, gained a markedly larger share of the market than its competitors. Then, because of various network externalities, the initial lead in sales made it advantageous for prospective new users to adopt A rather than one of the less popular alternatives. The advantage of adoption—to an individual user—increased with the aggregate number of adoptions so that A, together with its idiosyncratic features (notably its keyboard), became the industry standard and was "locked in."

Once "lock-in" is achieved, the choice of technology becomes (in some degree) impervious to new information about the comparative efficiency of alternative technologies. Unless the gain from changing techniques is sufficiently large as to cover the cost of doing so (in the case of QWERTY, the cost of retraining extant typists and replacing their keyboards), discovery that previously overlooked or newly discovered advantages of an unused technique make it more efficient than the incumbent method will not cause technology to be changed. Thus continued utilization of a prevailing technique despite its inferior efficiency (relative to a currently available alternative) might be the result of "accidents of history" that lead to its early adoption combined with costs of change making for resistance to subsequent innovation. In short, the current choice between QWERTY and alternative keyboards depends on circumstances that prevailed during the period when typewriters were first invented, and cannot be deduced solely from knowledge of the alternative technologies currently available and relative prices.

This is the viewpoint of Strong History, which contrasts with that of neoclassical economics (Strong Economics). The latter assumes that the relations among the variables of its standard model reflect a tropism for an unique equilibrium and exhibit no other systematic characteristics. From this viewpoint there is no possibility of lock-in of a suboptimal technique such as QWERTY or, indeed, even of a historical pattern in which adoption of a sub-optimal technique occurs other than by chance. Although the hypotheses that (1) the history of a technique's utilization can be completely described as (noise-contaminated) movement toward a unique equilibrium and (2) the choice among a plurality of available techniques requires (inter alia) consideration of the history of their utilizations are incompatible, it is possible that each hypothesis might be valid for particular times and circumstances. Since this is admitted by partisans of both hypotheses, it might be supposed that controversies would be limited to decisions about which hypothesis to apply in particular cases. But as anyone familiar with the literature can attest, this is not the case. Looming behind debate on specific applications is a general methodological dispute about the location of the "burden of proof" and "how big an effect is sufficient" to warrant rejection of one hypothesis or the other.

Both of these issues stem from dispute over the strength of the evidence required to establish that path dependence occurred in a particular case. In the case of QWERTY the empirical evidence that Paul David and his coworkers have been able to marshal has failed to persuade neoclassical economists that, because of its early history, the typewriter industry became locked into a technically inferior keyboard despite the emergence of an alternative known to be superior.[5] It is not denied that lock-in *could* have emerged from the circumstances alleged (that is, network externalities that lead to the adoption of a unique industry standard): what is denied is that the evidence is sufficient to establish that lock-in did occur in fact and, a fortiori, that the case made is strong enough to warrant citation of QWERTY as an example of market failure.

Obviously, it would be extremely difficult to measure the magnitude of the efficiency loss associated with the recorded course of economic history instead of a counterfactual alternative, especially when the description of the latter is incomplete. But fortunately, our argument is concerned only with the criteria for appraising measurement procedures, and not with judging the comparative accuracy of measurements actually performed. Liberally interpreted, the neoclassical view of technological development does not preclude network externalities, or even the possibility that such externalities might lead to a "limited amount" of lock-in. What it does preclude is that such lock-in as might occur should be the cause of an "appreciable" loss of efficiency from failure to adopt alternative technologies that are superior. The neoclassical position is that if such loss were appreciable, a way would be found to avoid it.[6] In a nutshell, the neoclassical position is that the forces making for path dependence are weaker than the countervailing tropism for efficiency.

The weasel word in the argument is "appreciable." In empirical application (as distinguished from formal argument) the neoclassical position typically allows for the operation of extraneous forces—for example, those captured in the net of path dependence—that create room for "small" deviations from optimality in a variety of contexts, of which one of the more salient is suggested by the term "transaction cost." But the empirical content of "small" or "appreciable" is not given a generally applicable definition and is left to the arbitrament of ad hoc argument. As the case of QWERTY indicates, this does not always facilitate agreement between partisans of the rival hypotheses. It is my contention that this failure to reach agreement is due to the magnitude of the stakes in the debate about path dependence together with the weakness of the empirical evidence available to support either position.

To make the point, let me quote David (1999, p. 7):

> For economists to accept the contention that path dependence only matters if it is accompanied by market failures would be to cast aside as uninteresting, and hence not worthy of explanatory attention, myriad features of the organization of economic activity, along with numerous issues of long-term economic growth, distribution, and intergenerational equity that lie beyond the narrow purview of well-defined issues concerning allocative efficiency.

This statement is indisputable, and I doubt that many neoclassical economists would disagree with it. However, they would couple agreement with denial that path dependence (often) leads to efficiency losses great enough to warrant use of the term "market failure." I suspect that if it were conceded, however improperly, that path dependence never led to market failure, much—though not all—of the interest that economists take in the subject would disappear.

The concern of economists with the possibility of market failure arises from the central role of (successful) market operation in their preanalytic vision of how the world works. To suggest that markets fail "by much" and/or "very often" is to challenge their way of looking at the world and the competence of their profession—and the value of their credentials as members—to perform its social function, which rests upon this vision. Focusing on this concern suggests a way to "specify" the magnitude of the efficiency loss that is the bone of contention between David and "QWERTY skeptics." The magnitude in question is "the minimum loss that would suffice to induce neoclassical economists to agree that a case in question (for example, QWERTY) constituted a mark against their preanalytic vision." If needed, this magnitude could be scaled in the "oomph" metric, lack of which has prompted an eloquent protest from David (1999, p. 3):[7]

> I suppose this is what soon might catch on as "the new economics of oomph." Unfortunately, despite the many occasions on which the term is invoked, "oomph" itself has yet to be clearly defined, much less subjected to measurement. (Although clearly the concept refers to some cardinal magnitude—since it is something that we don't seem to have enough of—even the appropriate unit of measurement remains unspecified. It is, perhaps, the "oompha"?) From the context, however, one may surmise that this innovation in quantitative rhetoric is a suggested calibration of the persuasive force of an argument. Who, then, is to say whether the level of oompha's are enough, the most skeptical member of the audience?

To find the answer to this question, let us ask another one: who is the object of the attempt at persuasion? While not completely homogeneous, almost certainly a very large part of David's intended audience consists of neoclassical economists. With a few honorable exceptions, outside the field of economics there is very little interest in or comprehension of the intellectual stake in the debate about path dependence. And within economics, the resistance to Strong History comes very largely from neoclassical adherents. Therefore, if the object of the argument is persuasion, it is they—unreasonably skeptical though they may be—who set the level of the oomph standard.

Similarly, it is they who determine the locus of the burden of proof. They will not relinquish their (quite tight) prior that the history of any economic process will conform (albeit approximately) to the realizations of a model approximating Pareto optimality until strong incontrovertible evidence to the contrary compels them to do so. In taking this stance, not all of them adopt a dogmatic prior: for example, the remarks of McCloskey quoted in David (1999) and the discussion of Liebowitz and Margolis (1999, chap. 3) indicate recognition of the possibility that path dependence might sometimes occur while denying that the evidence so far presented establishes that it has appeared sufficiently often, and/or in any of the cited instances has had consequences sufficiently salient as to warrant abandoning their prior. However, the defensiveness manifested in their arguments suggests apprehension that at sometime in the future such evidence might be forthcoming, or even that the evidence already presented might be sufficient to create doubt in some neoclassicals of insufficiently robust conviction.

On the Strong History side, David (1993, p. 38) concedes:

> I believe that any satisfactory development of "historical economics" will eventually have to integrate heterodox insights with the knowledge previously gained about (linear) systems in which random disturbances are always "averaged away", and convergence to the unique equilibrium solution is assured. After all, there are many aspects of economic life where the interactions among agents . . . do not seem to be dominated by perceptible feedback effects. . . .
>
> So, it will continue to be important work to empirically identify those resource allocation processes that are well explained in terms of linear models informed by conventional "convergence" theories, leading to historical narratives of a simpler form in which the influence of initial conditions . . . is quite transient, and thus compatible with long run *ergodic* behavior.

Thus it would seem not hopeless that continued research and discussion might advance mutual understanding and possibly change some minds. However, it is not likely that agreement will be reached about the proper sharing of the burden of proof. To see why this is so, frame the debate (between Strong History and neoclassical economics) as an example of a revolutionary situation in the sense in which Thomas Kuhn speaks of a Scientific Revolution. An established paradigm, loosely called neoclassical economics, is being attacked by a number of anomalies (of which QWERTY is a leading example) presented by Strong Historians. The embattled defenders seek to dispel the anomalies either by defensive modifications of the paradigm (for example, refining the theory) or by disputing the relevance, salience, or both, of the anomalous find-ings. Opinions as to the state of the battle and its probable outcome vary from one combatant to another but are strongly correlated with the side taken by the opiner. However, the neoclassical paradigm is the incumbent, and with that goes the default position in allocating the burden of proof. It is the defenders of the incumbent paradigm who determine when they have had enough.

There are many factors that motivate support of an accepted paradigm or (more generally) idea in the face of a challenge from a rival. Because these are obvious and generally recognized I shall not waste space by reiterating them. But together they imply that the challenger of an established paradigm must choose between (1) denying the status of the paradigm and (2) accepting the burden of proving that the accumulated and undispelled anomalies presented are well enough substantiated and of sufficient salience as to require either "fundamental modification" or outright abandonment of the paradigm. So far as I am aware, David has not yet decided which of these two options he will accept.

In "At Last, a Remedy" he rejects (2) strongly and comes close to (1). Thus he asks, "Where is it written that the burden of showing quantitative impor-tance in this matter belongs only on the shoulders of those who keep finding grounds (in both reason and fact) for disputing the presumption of optimal-ity or near optimality?" (David 1999, p. 4). But elsewhere he recognizes (while deploring) the incumbent status of the neoclassical paradigm. In "Historical Economics in the Longrun" he writes:

> Economic theorists, too, have begun to worry more than they used to do about causation, a condition that became particularly evident in their disaffection with the artificiality of the "tatonment" process imagined in the theory of competitive general equilibrium. . . .
>
> This inattention to causal explanation involving sequential actions, and to the disequilibrium foundations that must underlie any predictively useful theories of economic equilibrium, has impoverished modern economic theory and contributed to the disjuncture between theoretical and empirical programmes of research. Efforts within the profession, finding external encouragement if such is needed, must move us towards acknowledging the possible path-dependence of outcomes. . . .

In short, there has been an alteration of the general climate of thought, which is according new significance to details of historical sequence—a development associated with the growth of interest in non-linear dynamics across many disciplines and the consequent emergence of the so-called "sciences of complexity." This intellectual ferment may be eroding the basis of the former stability of the ahistorical path on which our particular discipline has remained trapped (all too self-contentedly, it should be said) for well over a century. But equally if not more decisive will be the attainment of "critical mass" among the subset working on problems of positive feedback within the discipline of economics. (David 1993, pp. 36–38)

In this last quote, I perceive David as being temporally ambiguous about the status of the incumbent paradigm: such ambiguity is characteristic of the rhetoric of scientific revolutionaries. While recognizing the incumbent status of a paradigm, they wish to rally supporters and attract recruits—as well as strengthen their own convictions—by proclaiming that things are in process of change. Uttered at the right time, such battle cries can alter the status of a paradigm. And this exhortation—or better, these several exhortations—may one day be enshrined in the methodological wing of the pantheon of dog mengeschichte. But whether this will happen is yet to be determined.

It is clear that David believes that the neoclassical paradigm is not only well on the road to obsolescence, but that its coming demise is well deserved and its present incumbent status unmerited. Indeed, he holds that for over a century the improper extension of its influence has had the effect of misdirecting empirical research in economics. But at times he fails to recognize the fictility of the empirical expression of that paradigm. Defenders of the paradigm do not deny that history reveals some examples of monopoly or oligopoly; of event sequences that can usefully be described as adjustments to an (as yet) unachieved equilibrium or as transitory money illusions, etc. I suggest that a good deal of path dependence can—and will—be similarly absorbed in the receptacle of disturbances that always adorns cliometric efforts performed in accordance with the neoclassical paradigm.

For example, as of a quarter-century ago—give or take a few years—the technology for playing recorded music was locked into the 33 rpm LP format by the same type of network externalities that are exhibited in the case of

QWERTY. (And before the LP, the industry standard was the 78 rpm.) But the effect of the CD has been to make it virtually impossible to obtain any new or recently recorded music on a 33 rpm disc (should anyone care to do so). Who knows when a similar fate will overtake QWERTY? Pace Keynes, "In the long-run all locked in positions become open." But to defend the neoclassical paradigm with such arguments is to seek salvation through evisceration. And, at times, neoclassical appeals to the long run have come perilously close to such intellectual suicide.

Thus whether the "quantum of path dependence" found by Strong Historians will prove too much for the (neoclassical) paradigm to accommodate depends not only upon the content of technological innovations, but also upon how fictile the paradigm is allowed to become. That is, it will depend upon how great the perceived deadweight loss associated with particular event sequences must be; how long it must persist; and the number and salience of candidate sequences for anomaly status that are presented, before adherents of the paradigm will concede that in the *typical* case it is necessary "to investigate for the effects of path dependence before applying theorems that require the existence of competitive equilibrium." Since this concession is not likely to come soon, as an interim expedient to facilitate agreement about the role of path dependence in particular cases (like QWERTY) it might be stipulated that recognition of path dependence entails no implications about generalized market failure.

However, it is unlikely that Strong Historians would leave the matter of paradigmatic implications alone. (Nor would I urge that they do so.) A major objective of their research agenda is to alter the presuppositions about history implied by the neoclassical paradigm. It is this objective that makes the conventions of debate (such as the location of the burden of proof) so important, and so much a matter of contention. For example, Mikado-like, David could simply declare that the evidence already presented by economic historians, together with the state of opinion in scientific communities other than economics, constitutes sufficient ground for rejecting the presumption of incumbency claimed by neoclassicals. But the consequence of such a declaration would be to break off debate, leaving the many neoclassicals in all other branches of economics free either to ignore evidence of path dependence, or to interpret it as a reflection of short-run disturbances of one kind or another and affording no basis for rejecting the paradigm.

This would be tantamount to perpetuating the status quo within the economics community. While Strong History would exist, it would be restricted to a disputed corner of the discipline with neoclassical presuppositions continuing to dominate the main parts of the intellectual landscape. Because this is less than David and like-minded cliometricians will settle for, they must continue the debate—albeit under protest—on terms dictated by the history of the subject, and not by considerations of either fairness or efficiency in the pursuit of knowledge.

II

As portrayed in section I, the partisans of Strong History are well defined and unwavering in their commitment to its cause. At times, they certainly sound that way. But in this section, I suggest that this is only part of the story. To a considerable extent the continuing influence of the neoclassical paradigm comes from the need of all economists, including Strong Historians, to make use of it. As in so many battles of ideas, the enemy's fifth column is us.

To see this, it is necessary only to reflect on the implications of inferring an unobserved price (or a relation among unobserved prices) from a relation among observed quantities, or the converse. It is hardly necessary to remind economic historians how often this is done or the main reason—lack of direct observations—for doing it. Even more obvious is the paucity of effort—accompanying such inferences—to allow for the possible influence of factors reflecting path dependence upon the equations used in making the inference.

It would be hard to find a better example of adherents of Strong History using the neoclassical paradigm as support for this practice than the appendix to a recent paper by Moses Abramovitz and Paul David (1999). There, a proposition about a change in relative factor quantities (the capital-labor ratio) is inferred from a change in relative factor shares (of income) by means of an argument involving the elasticity of substitution between the factors. The underlying argument is based on an "augmented Solow model" in which "the respective average factor-shares in gross output over the time interval are taken as approximating the respective input elasticities during that time interval."[8] While the historical component of the ambient analysis of the sources of variation in the growth rate of factor productivity is as strong as one could want (see Abramovitz and David 1999, esp. pp. 107–12), the analysis is kept within the framework of the augmented Solow model. Retaining this framework precludes considering the possibility that changes in the divergence of factor rewards from factor marginal productivities might have resulted from, say, variations in the rents of locked-in positions.

I am entirely in sympathy with the Abramovitz-David approach to growth accounting (1999, Part Two) via refinement of factor concepts (such as distinguishing tangible from intangible capital) and teasing out factor biases in technical progress. But that is not the point: the point is that, in the account they present, they have chosen (felt compelled?) to cling to a neoclassical framework. This framework makes it possible to analyze the sources of growth in a systematic way and use the analysis as a basis for making contact with other stories about one or another aspect of economic growth.[9] Whether it would be possible to conduct such an analysis from a framework (yet to be constructed) of Strong History is not clear. However the failure of Abramovitz-David even to make the attempt is indicative of the persisting affinity of even Strong Historians for an intellectual framework whose influence they decry in other contexts.

But to remark on the pervasive influence of the neoclassical framework is not to claim that the framework is sturdy. In the deft hands of Abramovitz-David the augmented Solow model manages to provide an account of economic growth that remains within the neoclassical shell. But the added complexity associated with the process of augmentation (for example, introducing human capital into the list of inputs, finding complementarities and other interactions between observed and unobserved variables) makes one wonder what new gadgets might be required to enable the model to accommodate the history of the next half-century. Nevertheless, although need for resort to conceptual inventiveness to save a theory will always be a source of embarrassment to its intellectually sensitive adherents, I doubt that the embarrassment will be great enough to cause large-scale abandonment of the neoclassical paradigm.

This is because of the great capability of the paradigm to generate predictions about the direction of the impact of a change in one variable upon one or more other variables, without need for much specification of ambient circumstances. Skill in manipulating the paradigm to such effect is a great part of the economist's stock in trade and, understandably, he or she will not relinquish it easily. Since typically such manipulation requires assuming the absence of (long-run) path dependence, the assumption will be made except where evidence to the contrary has enough oomph to make them ashamed to do so. What is enough oomph depends upon the importance of the results sought, the difficulty of specifying and making satisfactory allowance for possible path dependence, and the (anticipated) sensitivity of the final results to incorporation (in the analysis) of the factors making for path dependence. This means that, for any one of us, the height of the oomph threshold is likely to vary with the problem at hand. QWERTY skeptics tend across the board to set the threshold higher than Strong Historians, though for other problems the difference in settings may be quite small.

Where a problem is framed in terms of game theory, the interaction of the players becomes critical, which makes it difficult to avoid explicit consideration of path dependence in accounting for the effects of learning and the like. But where the problem is to explain the behavior of market-determined prices and quantities, avoiding the complexity that arises all too easily from path dependence provides economists with good reason to stick with neoclassical models as long as they can. Thus for most adherents of either side, the choice between Strong History and Strong Economics is not absolute but varies with the problem at hand. The "irrepressible" methodological debate that arises (as in the case of QWERTY) results primarily from the inadequacy of available empirical evidence to decide essential issues of fact: for example, is QWERTY really less efficient than the Dvorak keyboard, and even if it were, would the efficiency loss be appreciable? Because partisans of both positions can manage to disagree on such matters without complete loss of scientific credibility by either side, appeal is made to the comparative merits of the assumptions made and procedures used in reaching the conflicting conclusions.

Perhaps further empirical study, case by case, can resolve such issues, but the time constraint is binding. Grants need to be obtained and justified, faculty appointments made, thesis writers given procedural guidance, policy makers advised, journalists given unhedged statements for the generation of headlines, and so on. Consequently, minds have to be made up, and fairly quickly. And arguments based upon methodological propriety can be made to lead to unambiguous conclusions, despite the reluctance of the data to confirm them. As we well know, such arguments tend mainly to persuade those who are already convinced. But, as many of us can testify, they also serve to shore up the convictions of those making the arguments, and perhaps this is where the need is greatest.

Hence arguments about "burden of proof" and "how much oomph is enough" will continue with David in the forefront. As of the present writing he refuses to concede the presumption that in the absence of "sufficient reason to the contrary" the default assumption of economic history should be that economic phenomena conform to the neoclassical vision—at least not until "sufficient" is defined to his satisfaction. In methodological writings he urges us not to portray seeming path dependence in terms reconcilable with neoclassical presumptions but instead to seek the best model available from a (much) wider set that deliberately admits nonergodic members.

The effect of what David urges would be to preclude working economists, especially economic historians, from such practices as using measures of factor shares as proxies for the products of marginal factor productivities and factor quantities or vice versa on the maintained assumption that the implications of long-run competitive equilibrium are the best available approximation to observation. To the question of what set of assumptions should be used as a replacement for the (implications of the) neoclassical vision, the answer would be, more or less, as follows: investigate the question at hand without a strong prior drawn from any very abstract vision, and eschew empirical judgments that rest upon the assumption that the conditions of competitive equilibrium are approximately satisfied by the observed state of affairs.

If this answer were accepted, economists would view the world with looser priors than most of them now adopt. Perforce, they would be more hesitant to offer explanations of how the world works, or how to improve it, than at present. While this might help to avoid much misguided advice on policy, it would also dim the vision of the world with which (most) economists operate, thereby lessening the confidence they have in their own collective judgment on issues of public policy and, as a further consequence, the confidence that society at large reposes in that judgment.

Abhorrence of this last consequence makes them reluctant to accept path dependence as the default option when evidence on a point is inconclusive. The critical question is where to set the standard for determining that enough salience-weighted instances of path dependence have been found, and sufficiently confirmed, to warrant displacing consonance with the neoclassical vision as the default option. The history of science suggests that, at any given point in time, the answer to such a question depends critically upon the availability of an acceptable alternative. Because there is not as yet such an alternative, the amount of oomph sufficient to cause neoclassical adherents to abandon their vision remains larger than what can be mustered by those urging them to do so.

Finally, a personal note. I have long been a neoclassical adherent though with doubts and reservations greater than those entertained by most of those who are similarly minded. Consequently, more than most, I have felt and continue to feel the tension expressed in the title of this chapter. For this I thank Paul David who has long been a major contributor to the wellspring that nourishes my negative thoughts. While these thoughts may have made me wiser, I am certain that they have not added to my intellectual comfort; however I doubt that David intended that they should.

Notes

Acknowledgments: This essay benefited greatly from the comments of Moses Abramovitz, William Sundstrom, and Gavin Wright. Often I have heeded their advice and altered the argument; sometimes I have persisted in disagreeing, though with apprehension. In any event I bear sole responsibility for what remains.

1. As used here the notion of a preanalytic vision is an instantiation of Schumpeter's (1954, pp. 41 et seq.) concept bearing the same name.

2. The goal may either be time invariant or follow a specified time path. In the latter case, as of any given moment, the goal will be some particular position on the specified time path.

3. Put differently, goal-directed time paths are ergodic.

4. The classic references to the economics of QWERTY are David (1985, 1986). The leading reference expressing opposition to the Strong History interpretation of QWERTY is Liebowitz and Margolis (1999), which summarizes their earlier work on the same subject.

5. See, for example, Liebowitz and Margolis (1999), chapter 2.

6. A technical question arises at this point: does the neoclassical position contend (1) that if the efficiency loss were "sufficient," knowledge of an existing superior technique would (somehow) get to those who would benefit from having it, or only (2) that if a more efficient technique were known to exist it would displace a less efficient one, providing the efficiency gain was sufficient? I would interpret the spirit of the neoclassical position to imply the former (stronger) assumption, but I am not aware of explicit discussion of this point.

7. Lack of "oomph" is the term introduced by Deirdre McCloskey to rationalize her lack of concern over efficiency losses of the magnitude attributed to QWERTY and other instances of alleged lock-in (see discussion in David 1999).

8. Abramovitz and David (1999), Technical Appendix note 1, p. 2A.

9. For example, see their discussion of private saving behavior (section 2.4).

References

Abramovitz, Moses, and Paul A. David. 1999. "American Macroeconomic Growth in the Era of Knowledge-Based Progress: The Long-Run Perspective." Working Paper, Stanford Institute for Economic Policy Research, Stanford University, Stanford , Calif.

David, Paul A. 1985. "Clio and the Economics of QWERTY." *American Economic Review* 75: 332–37.

———. 1986. "Understanding the Economics of QWERTY: The Necessity of History." In W. N. Parker, ed., *Economic History and the Modern Economist.* London: Basil Blackwell.

———. 1993. "Historical Economics in the Longrun: Some Implications of Path-Dependence." In G. D. Snooks, ed., *Historical Analysis in Economics.* London: Routledge.

———. 1999. "At Last, a Remedy for Chronic QWERTY-Skepticism!" Stanford University Department of Economics Working Paper, Stanford, Calif.

Liebowitz, S. J., and Stephen E. Margolis. 1999. *Winners, Losers, and Microsoft.* Oakland, Calif.: Independent Institute.

Schumpeter, Joseph A. 1954. *History of Economic Analysis.* New York: Oxford University Press.

II

PATH DEPENDENCE IN PRACTICE

5

FINANCIAL HISTORY AND THE LONG REACH OF THE SECOND THIRTY-YEARS' WAR

Charles W. Calomiris

1. INTRODUCTION: APPLYING THE PATH DEPENDENCE PARADIGM TO FINANCIAL HISTORY

This essay is about financial and monetary history, and the role of path dependence in understanding that history—specifically, the extent to which the shocks of the period 1914–44 had a lasting effect on the past five decades of financial and monetary history. In financial and monetary history, path dependence works most potently through the way historical accidents shape the private and public institutions that govern the financial sector—that is, choices about the structure and powers of private and public financial intermediaries, monetary standards, and commercial laws.

The "path dependence paradigm" (PDP) in this context boils down to a point of view with three separate, but related, elements: (1) that historical shocks can precipitate institutional innovation, (2) that the "specific history" of shocks can have lasting importance through its effects on institutional change, and (3) that institutions make a difference for economic outcomes. The first two elements imply that specific history matters for institutional history; the third element implies that specific history matters for important economic outcomes.[1]

One way to "test" path dependence, and these three elements of the PDP, is to specify an "anti-PDP null hypothesis," which evidence about path dependence would reject. The null is that specific history's effects on important institutions does not matter much for very long. In other words, the under-lying structure of preferences, resources, and "technology" (broadly defined to include laws, norms, and institutions, as well as technical knowledge) evolves in a way that is not importantly influenced by the sequence of histori-cal disturbances experienced.

Two different points of view about economic history can underlie the null: (1) that laws, institutions, and norms do not matter much for economic out-comes, per se, so that even if laws, institutions, and norms are affected by spe-cific history, that is not important; or (2) that laws, institutions, and norms do matter, but that they are not influenced for long by specific history.

As a statement about the "immunity" of *all* institutional history to specific shocks in the long run, the second argument implies the existence of a map-ping from a set of exogenous preferences, initial knowledge, and environmen-tal conditions (predetermined by a combination of geological accident and human biology) to a set of derived laws, norms, and institutions. That is, if laws, norms, and institutions matter, but specific history does not, it must be that we never stray very far from the predetermined set of laws, norms, and institutions. Such would be the view of either a Marxist interpretation of financial history (governed ultimately by the history of class struggle), or a pure neoclassical (Darwinian/Panglossian) view that "efficiency" guides all institutional choice.

Anyone familiar with the history of economic development will be able to cite substantial evidence against the view that institutions do not matter for economic outcomes, or the Marxian or Panglossian views that financial insti-tutions evolve along some predetermined path. The history of the past fifty years—particularly the persistence of basic institutional differences among countries, the persistent poverty of many of the world's countries, and the close links that have been identified empirically between the political and in-stitutional weaknesses in many countries and their poor long-run economic performance—makes it clear that institutional history both differs and mat-ters across countries in the long run. Unstable, unwise, corrupt, and ineffective governments have been the rule rather than the exception in scores of countries for many decades.

Nevertheless, rejecting the determinism of a Marxist or Panglossian view of institutional history is not the same as accepting the importance of path dependence in the history of financial institutions. There is an alternative perspective (which I will call political determinism) that views changes in financial institutions as determined in the long run by core social and political institutions, norms, and customs. That view sees those core elements (rather than the shocks that directly affect financial institutions) as the important conditions shaping financial history in the long run. Specific shocks that produce financial institutional change, according to this view, merely accelerate change that would have been produced in any case, as the result of political forces that were moving inexorably toward that end.

Indeed, much of the controversy over the long-run determinants of financial history consists of reasonable disagreement between advocates of path dependence (the view that specific shocks created long-run change in financial institutions) and advocates of political determinism. The version of the null hypothesis that is most difficult to reject typically is some version of political determinism.

Consider, for example, the current controversy over the interpretation to attach to the importance of legal origins as empirical predictors of both financial and economic development. La Porta et al. (1997) and Levine (1997) find that persisting institutional inadequacies in legal systems matter for long-run financial development, and that measures of legal system quality are good instruments in regressions that connect financial development and economic development (in other words, aspects of financial development predicted by legal system attributes—which are plausibly viewed as exogenous to contemporaneous economic growth—have explanatory power for economic growth in cross-sectional regressions of economic growth).

That research also emphasizes the dependence of specific contemporary attributes of the legal system on the initial conditions (the legal tradition) that shaped subsequent legal history. In these and many other studies, not only have researchers identified "bad" commercial laws and "bad" banking regulations that have persisted for many decades in many countries; they have also found that, to a very large extent, *distant historical accidents* (the specific history of a country's legal origins) that determined which of four broad legal heritages a country adopted (British, French, German, or Scandinavian) explain to a large extent the relative efficacy of current legal and institutional arrangements affecting the financial sector, and the economic consequences of the quality of those financial institutional arrangements. In short: distant legal history seems to matter empirically for financial and economic development.

Is this convincing evidence of the importance of path dependence in the long-run development of financial laws and institutions? Did initial choices of legal tradition constrain the long-term legal, financial, and economic development of many countries? Not necessarily. It may be that political factors that influenced the concentration of political power over the past century produced both financial and economic underdevelopment, and that the correlation with legal origins is largely coincidental. Indeed, Rajan and Zingales (1999) make this argument. They show that legal origins were not good predictors of the level of financial or economic development achieved by countries before World War I, and thus question the argument of La Porta et al. (1997) and Levine (1997) that the distant choice of legal traditions determined legal, financial, and economic development. Initial legal origins may have influenced subsequent political development (as suggested by Fohlin 2000), but it is also possible that political history shaped legal and financial institutions, and that legal origins are simply correlated by coincidence with subsequent political history.

The same controversy between political determinism and institutional path dependence emerges repeatedly in the context of the financial institutional changes of the 1914–44 period. To advocates of path dependence, the shocks of World War I, the Great Depression, and World War II set the stage for institutional changes that would not otherwise have occurred, and which had profound consequences. To advocates of political determinism, those changes were inevitable and were merely hastened by the specific history of the "second thirty-years' war." In this essay I try to come to grips with that disagreement.

It is always difficult to argue for or against the importance of the PDP, because doing so requires the construction of a plausible counterfactual. It is easy enough to show that the specific institutions wrought by World War I, the Depression, and World War II would not have come into being at the same time, or with the same names or specific structures, as those that actually arose. But it is harder to show that reasonable facsimiles would not have arisen soon thereafter.

Consider the example of Mexico's 1994–95 financial crisis. Mexico's national deposit insurance system, and the U.S. Exchange Stabilization Fund (ESF) played important roles in the Mexican crisis (the first by encouraging the risks that sunk the Mexican banking system, the second by providing a mechanism for assisting the government during its collapse). Both of these institutions are traceable to the shocks of the Great Depression: Mexican deposit insurance—like all government deposit insurance—followed the 1934 precedent set by the Federal Deposit Insurance Corporation (FDIC), and the Exchange Stabilization Fund (through which $12 billion was lent to the Mexican government by the secretary of the Treasury in 1995 after Congress refused to appropriate funds for that purpose) was established in 1934 as a monetary policy tool for combating the Depression (see Schwartz 1997). In that sense, the Mexican crisis (in its specifics) was a child of the Great Depression. But stating this fact is not the same as showing that Mexico would not have developed deposit insurance without the U.S. example, or that the Mexican bailout would have been substantively different in the absence of the ESF loan.

Chandler's (1972, 1977) opposite judgments about the importance of the specific histories of anthracite coal and railroads provide a model of how to reasonably argue for or against the PDP. After demonstrating how the discovery, mining, and transport of anthracite coal had been a crucial determinant of the locations of manufacturing and the growth of particular towns and cities during the antebellum period, Chandler concludes that the initial reliance on anthracite coal probably did not have an important effect on subsequent economic development.

His view of the effects of railroads on American economic history is quite different. Chandler properly bases his case for or against the PDP on judgments about the historical context in which shocks occur. The reach and speed of railroads fundamentally altered the scale, geographic scope, and structure of firms, with important implications for the organization of production, distribution, and management. Anthracite coal left its footprint in American economic history, but in the context of the broader history of technological change, its specific history was of temporary significance, largely because rail-roads changed the resource and transportation constraints that had made the anthracite mines so important. Without anthracite, railroads still would have been invented, and coal-based industrialization still would have occurred, albeit a few years later. Thus Chandler reasonably concludes that the history of technological progress and industrialization in the United States was perma-nently altered by railroads, but not by anthracite coal.

Reaching firm conclusions about the importance of specific history for financial institutions is harder than for technology because institutional and legal change depends primarily on political processes. Defining counterfactual political history is inherently more difficult than defining technological coun-terfactuals. Yet the task is the same: to use the broader historical context to dis-tinguish between events that matter for the long run and those that do not. In what follows I describe the significant shocks of the 1914–44 period from the perspective of financial and monetary history and try to sort out their relative long-run importance.

2. WHAT WORLD WAR I STOPPED

When Winston Churchill described the period 1914–44 as the "second thirty-years' war" he was making a point about path dependence among the shocks that produced World War I, the Depression, and World War II. World War II grew out of the rise of Nazism, which would have had little hope as a political movement in the absence of the Great Depression (Temin 1989). The shocks that gave rise to the Great Depression (which revolved around global mone-tary policy errors and exchange rate misalignments) were the direct conse-quence of the failed attempt to restore the monetary/exchange rate system that was destroyed by World War I (Eichengreen and Sachs 1985, 1986; Temin 1989; Bernanke and James 1991; Eichengreen 1992).

If World War I had not occurred, the world economy likely would have continued the process of globalization and liberalization that had been under way for several decades, and would have retained the financial and monetary rules on which that process was based. World War I—and the shocks of the Great Depression and World War II that followed in its wake—brought to an end a period that had seen unprecedented success, a success that was based on the globalization of markets in gold, commodities, labor, and capital (Obstfeld and Taylor 1998).

From 1870 to 1913 a truly global system had developed with common basic institutional ingredients across countries. Despite unevenness in economic growth over time and across countries—which coincided with terms of trade shocks, or global deflationary episodes—growth was quite high, particularly among developing economies. Capital and labor flowed to markets where production and export opportunities were high (Argentina is the most striking example). Globalization was a powerful tool for progress, particularly for low wage earners migrating from Europe.

With respect to financial systems, there were three important common elements in the pre–World War I institutional structure, which had been adopted increasingly throughout the world in the four decades before World War I. These were (1) the chartering of privately owned commercial banks operating on a limited-liability basis, (2) openness to international capital flows (financed ultimately by exports), and (3) adherence to the gold standard. Financial systems were managed with very limited government involvement (relative to the post–World War I period) in most countries. Before World War I, central banks existed in some, but not all, countries. No global financial institutions existed to coordinate countries' policies, although central banks did cooperate extensively during crises (for example, by lending reserves to one another) (Eichengreen 1992). Government guarantees of financial institutions were quite limited and in most countries did not exist (see Calomiris 2000b).

Before 1913, there was a well-defined institutional "best practice" for developing countries. Participation in global trade was the means to gain access to global capital markets, which were seen as the necessary means to finance rapid growth. Adherence to the gold standard was a matter of national pride and a commitment to honesty in financial affairs, not just an exchange rate policy (Bordo and Kydland 1995). Similarly, the development of a healthy private domestic banking system was a top priority for most developing economies, and policymakers maintained a firm commitment to market discipline (based on the understanding that government protection promoted undesirable risk-taking by banks). Bank insolvency was rare, and systemwide collapses of banking systems were virtually unknown.

Calomiris (2000b) finds only seven cases of a "significant degree of banking system insolvency" for a large sample of countries from 1870 to 1913. Significant insolvency is defined as a banking system whose failed banks' negative net worth in aggregate exceeds 1 percent of annual GDP. By that measure, Canada, Germany, France, Britain, the United States, Mexico, Russia, Japan, Holland, Denmark, Sweden, and Finland never experienced a significant degree of banking system insolvency. Norway, Italy, Brazil, Argentina, and Australia account for the seven significant crisis episodes (with Brazil accounting for three of the seven). None of these crises produced negative net worth-to-GDP ratios in excess of 10 percent, and the median ratio was 3 percent. This incidence and magnitude of crises appears small by modern standards. Over 100 severe banking crises have occurred in the past two decades, with more than twenty crises resulting in negative net worth-to-GDP ratios in excess of 10 percent (Calomiris 2000b).

I will argue that perhaps the most important legacy of the specific history of 1914–44 for financial policy has been the creation of fragile banking systems, which have been a direct consequence of the willingness of government to protect banks from the consequences of their own risk-taking. In the absence of the shocks of 1914–44, the domestic and international "financial architecture" of government policy that has protected banks was historically unprecedented and, I will argue, unlikely to have arisen in the absence of the shocks of 1914–44.

More generally, the collapse of the global economy after 1913 did not just increase poverty and economic isolation during the chaotic period 1914–44. That collapse also destroyed the institutional base on which the global economy had been built. Global private market capital flows are just now regaining their pre–World War I levels (as a ratio of GDP), and domestic banking privatization and liberalization in emerging market economies are also phenomena of the 1980s and 1990s.

The gold standard was never fully restored after its World War I collapse, and the result has been an international monetary system with higher average inflation and much higher inflation and exchange rate volatility than during the pre–World War I gold standard. After an unsuccessful attempt at restoring the gold standard in the 1920s, and the establishment of fixed exchange rates among industrial countries on a dollar standard after World War II, which ended in 1971–73 (Bordo and Eichengreen 1993), the United States, Japan, and Europe have allowed their exchange rates to float relative to one another. Until recently, emerging market countries have generally pursued pegged exchange rate policies, where currencies were weakly linked in a variety of ways to one of the "hard" currencies of the developed countries. That approach produced historically unprecedented volatility in nominal exchange rates resulting from frequent exchange rate collapses. Developed countries' monetary authorities permitted high levels of inflation during the 1960s and 1970s, and developing countries experienced even higher rates of inflation during those decades. Indeed, before the 1990s, hyperinflations were not uncommon phenomena among developing economies.

Recently, monetary policy has changed in both developed and developing economies. The three central banks that have controlled developed country monetary policy (the Federal Reserve, the Bundesbank/European Central Bank, and the Bank of Japan) all have substantially reduced the levels of inflation in their economies since the 1970s. Beginning in the 1990s, developing economies have also moved away from loose exchange rate pegs and toward new policies of either freely floating rate systems (as in Mexico and East Asia since their crises), or rigidly fixed exchange rates via currency boards or dollarization (as in Argentina, Estonia, Lithuania, and Ecuador). Rates of inflation in developing countries have also fallen substantially from their levels in the 1960s, 1970s, and 1980s, when hyperinflations were not uncommon. Nevertheless, volatility in exchange rates among the three core currencies and those of the peripheries persists, as do market perceptions of the risk of exchange rate collapse even in currency board countries, indicating that the world is still very far away from the uniformity and reliability of exchange rates achieved under the classical gold standard.

Underlying the fifty-year interruption of globalization and its core institutional base was a political environment within emerging market countries—and more broadly an ideological movement around the world—that was hostile to globalization and economic liberalism. The collapse of the global economy during the 1914–44 period, and the increasing use of government control over the economy as a wartime measure in World Wars I and II, did more than destroy trade and capital flows and the institutions of the global economy. These changes also undermined the legitimacy of globalization and the institutions that accompanied it, and pointed increasingly in the direction of state control as a substitute for markets. That was particularly true in developing economies, which had hitched their wagon to the global engine of growth only to see that engine take their economies over the cliff of the Great Depression.

Even in developed economies, the confidence in markets was substantially eroded by the chaos and collapse of the 1914–44 period. The post–World War II world was one where protectionism, socialism, and nationalization of enterprises became respectable policies, justified by a new emphasis on market failures within the economics profession.

3. FINANCIAL INSTITUTION INNOVATIONS OF THE 1914–44 ERA

Innovations in financial institutions during the 1914–44 era reflected these trends. Domestically, the regulation of money and banking changed dramatically. Central banks, which had not existed in many countries under the classical gold standard, became virtually universal. Central banks increasingly took on new powers in the areas of monetary policy, assistance to banks, and control of domestic and international payment systems.

The commercial banking sector became a key instrument of government planning, especially in developing economies, but also in Japan, and to a lesser extent in Europe. In many countries banks were nationalized, and in countries where they remained in private hands their lending typically was controlled by, and subservient to, government plans, and their activities were severely limited by regulations. Even in the United States, government loan assistance for special purposes (mortgage subsidies, farm credit subsidies) became a federal government activity, beginning with the Federal Land Banks (1916), which subsidized farm mortgages. The Federal Home Loan Banks were established in 1932 to promote mortgage lending, and Fannie Mae was chartered in 1938 to provide subsidies through purchases in the secondary mortgage market.

HCl3 .E85

$FeCl_3$

Lofton Makms

Colorado

- why NOT statehood
  increased taxes
    for state offices,
      conscription

- better economy
  in 1870's paved way
  for statehood

Idaho

National government protection of bank liabilities—an American novelty beginning in 1934—soon spread to other countries. Government assistance to weak banks (as opposed to assistance to depositors in those banks) began in the United States in 1932 in the form of the Reconstruction Finance Corporation (RFC), whose powers and resources were significantly expanded under Roosevelt in 1933. By the 1980s, those policies had been widely imitated throughout the world; government protection of failed bank depositors, bond holders, and even stockholders had become standard operating procedure in virtually all countries.

In the United States, the Depression saw the centralization of power within the Federal Reserve (the Fed), and the creation of new monetary powers for the Treasury, which resulted in roughly fifteen years of Treasury dominance over monetary policy (Calomiris and Wheelock 1998). Stripped of the discipline of the gold standard, post–World War II monetary policy, in the United States and worldwide, lost its long-run anchor. For countries other than the United States, the dollar would become that anchor until 1971 (through the Bretton Woods dollar exchange standard). But the supply of dollars was determined by the U.S. authorities (before 1951, that meant the Treasury Department, and after 1951 the Fed; see Calomiris and Wheelock 1998). Ultimately, the absence of the long-run discipline of the gold standard encouraged unprecedented peacetime inflation in the United States, which caused the Bretton Woods system to unravel and left the world with its current tripolar currency system.

The Bretton Woods financial institutions—the International Monetary Fund (IMF) and World Bank (WB)—were another important legacy of the 1914–44 period. These institutions were founded in 1944 as a means of restoring an orderly global financial system. The IMF's role was to restore convertibility on current account in international transactions and assist countries suffering short-term balance-of-payments problems to ensure stability in exchange rates, or make occasional exchange rate adjustments when necessary. The WB's role was to provide long-term international capital flows to substitute for the absence of private capital markets—initially with a focus on financing the rebuilding of Europe, and later, focusing increasingly on developing countries on the periphery.

4. DID THESE INNOVATIONS MATTER?

These changes in financial institutions within the United States, and internationally, were multiple and significant, and seem to have had lasting importance from a variety of perspectives (that is, political, as well as economic). Few legacies of the New Deal have been as far-reaching as the changes wrought in banking regulations and monetary policy (although some of those regulations—notably Regulation Q and the separation of investment and commercial banking, were undone respectively in the 1980s and in 1999; see Calomiris 2000a). The protection of banks offered by deposit insurance, bank bailouts, and central bank lending is now widely faulted for the unprecedented instability suffered by banking systems worldwide in the past two decades (Caprio and Klingabiel 1996; Calomiris 2000b; Beim and Calomiris 2000).

The IMF and the World Bank live on as reminders of post–World War II reconstruction policy, even though the environment in which they were created (one of fixed exchange rates and virtually no private capital flows) has given way to the new world of flexible exchange rates and massive private capital flows. Indeed, in the case of the IMF, its current operations reflect an adaptation to new circumstances that were not envisioned by its charter. Senator Phil Gramm has said that the "IMF is an agency that started out with a mandate . . . and like all government agencies, when that was no longer their mission, they found a new mission" (Drajem 2000). The IMF transformed itself into a crisis manager and long-term lender when the fixed exchange rate system it was charged with supporting collapsed in the 1970s.

The World Bank's loans became a trivial proportion of world capital flows by the 1990s. For example, for the eleven countries that receive 70 percent of the World Bank's loans, lending from the bank (and other multilateral development banks) totaled less than 2 percent of their capital inflows over the past decade. Like the IMF, the World Bank has been adapting to evolving circumstances, moving to help subsidize and guarantee private sector lending, in addition to making subsidized loans to governments, although all of its activities are dwarfed by the size of private capital flows unrelated to World Bank, or other development bank, programs.

Empirical studies suggest that, on average, the economic impact of the IMF and WB have been unimpressive in recent decades. All three studies of IMF programs (including one by its own staff) failed to find evidence of a significant positive effect of IMF programs on economic growth or asset values in recipient countries. The majority of the World Bank's programs are judged (by its own evaluations) as failing to achieve "satisfactory sustainable" results (International Financial Institution Advisory Commission 2000; Calomiris 2000c).

That poor average performance is not to say, however, that these institutions are unimportant. The IMF and WB control substantial resources and are active participants in the formulation of macroeconomic, microeconomic, and debt management policies of developing countries. Their resources may be small as a fraction of global capital, but the subsidies they deliver are large as a fraction of the wealth under the command of the government officials in recipient countries—a metric of greater relevance to understanding the political influence these institutions wield. The debates that have arisen in recent years about their shortcomings and their abuses of power attest to their central role in the economics and politics of developing countries (International Financial Institution Advisory Commission 2000; Calomiris 2000c).

For example, despite the small magnitude of IMF loan subsidies, researchers often argue that the IMF has had important effects (often detrimental effects) on economic performance, either through its ex ante effects on capital flows or its ex post effects on the resolution of sovereign distress. Sachs (1989) argues that IMF support for the delayed restructuring of sovereign debt imposed unnecessary burdens on developing economies. Eichengreen (1999, p. 71) agrees:

> IMF policy through most of the 1980s was to lend to countries that had fallen into arrears on their external debts only after they had reached an agreement in principle with their creditors. The notion was that the Fund should provide assistance only if the banks contributed to burden sharing by at least clearing away the country's arrears. Eventually, however, experience with the debt crisis raised doubts about that approach. The banks, their balance sheets strengthening as they drew down their Latin American exposure, hardened their positions. Rather than the policy providing the IMF with a lever to encourage burden sharing by the banks, the banks realized that they could use [the IMF] as a club in their battle with governments.

The IMF essentially lent to countries to permit them to maintain the fiction that they were meeting their debt service, while in fact, no new flows of capital were being sent to those countries, and IMF assistance resulted in an escalating debt burden over the 1980s. After the resolution of the debt (with substantial effective default on debts under the Brady Plan), capital flows increased almost immediately, suggesting that an earlier debt resolution would have allowed Latin America to share in the growth enjoyed by Asia in the 1980s.

With respect to the ex ante consequences of IMF lending, several critics have noted that IMF support provides an incentive for capital suppliers to make loans to insolvent or risky developing country banks or enterprises—particularly international banks providing short-term, dollar-denominated debts, which are the first to exit with the assistance of IMF protection. The buildup of such debt before the Mexican, Asian, and Russian crises, and the rush for the exits that eventually ensued by these debtholders, is generally viewed as a central contributing influence on the magnitude of exchange rate depreciation and banking collapse (Beim and Calomiris 2000, Chap. 8). In Mexico the cost of banking sector resolution will be roughly 20 percent of annual GDP. In Thailand and Korea estimates place the cost at 30 percent of GDP, and in Indonesia the costs are estimated at a staggering 55 percent of GDP.

According to market participants, the IMF's role in generating these capital inflows was central. Consider the following quotations, which are drawn from emerging market advisory newsletters issued by some of the most influential traders in these markets:

> [December 1997] The massive Asian-crisis-inspired injections of high-powered global money by the IMF will . . . ensure a market in which there is tremendous technical support. Add in the clear moral hazard caused by the IMF bail-outs—two investors last week told me that they were planning to put on large Brazilian positions (even though they were very unhappy with the currency regime) because they were convinced that a Brazilian crisis would result in an immediate IMF bail-out—and it is hard to see why fundamentals should matter. (Calomiris and Meltzer 1999, p. 90)

Within months of this newsletter's publication, Russia's markets had collapsed, and Brazil had devalued.

Argentina, perhaps more than any other country, has depended on IMF conditional lending over the past several years to maintain its access to international markets. It is now widely perceived as on the verge of a public finance meltdown, which many commentators blame, in part, on the IMF and U.S. Treasury. The chronology of policy failure in Argentina is aptly summarized in a recent financial markets newsletter:

[May 2000] Between 1996 and 1999, the IMF and IDB [Interamerican Development Bank] all but led the marketing effort for Argentine bonds. The two institutions voiced strong endorsements each time that there was a confidence crisis in Argentina. The IDB went so far as to dispatch its most senior economist to New York last summer to recommend that U.S. portfolio managers buy Argentine bonds. At the same time, the Street came to realize that the U.S. Treasury was the real force behind the IMF and IDB support for Argentina. It was never clear why there was such unwavering support. The motivation could have been geo-political. Argentina was a staunch supporter of U.S. political policies around the world and across the region. Argentina was also the poster-child of the so-called Washington Consensus. . . . Therefore, the U.S. needed Argentina to succeed. At the beginning of the year, when the Machinea team traveled to Washington to seek a revised Standby Facility, the team met first with the U.S. Treasury before meeting with the IMF and the World Bank. These actions sent clear signals to the market that the country had an implicit guarantee from Washington. Otherwise, it would have been irrational for any creditor to lend so much money to such a leveraged country with such little flexibility. (Calomiris 2000c, p. 89)

Among their political influences, the existence of the multilaterals and the ESF has substantially boosted the powers of the U.S. Treasury (and the other G7 finance ministries) in international policy, often tilting the balance of power within the G7 toward the executive branch and away from the legislative branch of government. The IMF, the WB, and other multilateral agencies can channel assistance where the G7 finance ministers dictate that it go, without the "inconvenience" of legislative debate and approval that would otherwise precede foreign aid.

Fannie Mae and its sister institution, Freddie Mac, also are roundly criticized as ineffectual and undesirable mechanisms from the standpoint of the public interest (Calomiris 2000d; Jaffee 2000; Wallison 2000; Ely and Wallison 2000). Nevertheless, they are very large institutions and are quite influential politically (through their lobbying efforts and campaign contributions in Washington, which many critics regard as their primary area of expertise).

Fannie and Freddie now hold roughly half of the conventional (non-jumbo) mortgages outstanding in the United States and are projected to hold 100 percent of outstanding conventional mortgages by the year 2003 (Ely and Wallison 2000).

The departure from the gold standard may be the single most important change in the financial system since World War I. No substitute for the international gold standard has been established. Historically, the departure from a monetary system based on a specie numeraire typically was a temporary phenomenon, and usually a wartime measure. But the world has yet to restore gold convertibility, indicating an unusually lasting shock to the world financial system. The Fed, the European Central Bank, and the Bank of Japan still lack a long-run nominal anchor to guide monetary policy, and despite the reduction in inflation over the past two decades, inflation remains higher and more volatile than during the pre–World War I era. Empirical evidence indicates that both the higher level and the greater volatility of inflation have been associated with important economic costs in the form of lower real output (Judson and Orphanides 1996).

5. WOULD THESE INSTITUTIONAL CHANGES HAVE HAPPENED ANYWAY?

Even if these financial innovations can be traced to the shocks of the second thirty-years' war, even if they have persisted, and even if they remain important, that does not necessarily imply that they are examples of important path dependence. One must also argue that in the absence of the specific shocks of 1914–44 these institutional changes (or similar ones) would not have occurred.

Would government deposit insurance, bank bailouts, and farm loan and mortgage subsidies have arisen in the absence of the shocks of the 1920s and the Great Depression? Would the gold standard have disappeared even if World War I had not occurred? Would global economic institutions like the World Bank and the IMF have come into existence without the collapse of fixed exchange rates, international trade, and international capital flows that precipitated them in 1944?

Reasonable people can (and do) disagree in their answers to these questions. The most reasonable arguments against the importance of path dependence are based on political determinism. For example, Eichengreen (1996) and Bordo and Eichengreen (1998) take the positions, respectively, that the long-term decline in countries' willingness to maintain credible monetary/exchange rate policies, and the disappearance of gold as the global standard of value, were inevitable. Bordo and Eichengreen (1998) argue that even if the shocks of 1914–44 had not occurred, the physical supply of gold would have eventually made adherence to the gold standard impracticable. Eichengreen (1996) sees the adherence to the gold standard in the decades before World War I as something of a historical aberration and argues that the credibility of the system was fragile and unlikely to have survived for long even if World War I had not occurred. Furthermore, he argues that a decline in adherence to credible exchange rate targets was the inevitable result of the expansion of the democratic franchise throughout the world over the course of the nineteenth and twentieth centuries:

The extension of the franchise and the emergence of political parties representing the "working classes raised the possibility of challenges to the single-minded priority the monetary authorities attached to convertibility. Rising consciousness of unemployment and of trade-offs between internal and external balance politicized monetary policy" (Eichengreen 1996, p. 43).

Eichengreen's argument about the effect of the spread of democracy, and its short-term political pressures, for undermining the commitment to long-term monetary rules is a powerful one. Indeed, it can also be applied to deposit insurance, bank bailouts, and credit subsidies—all policies that appeal to populist pressures for short-term stabilization, with long-run costs to taxpayers that are hard to measure and distant in their incidence, making them particularly attractive to myopic, democratically elected government officials.

Nevertheless, there are weak spots in these lines of argument. The Bordo-Eichengreen view of the necessary collapse of the gold standard is based on a mechanical model of gold reserve adequacy. There are many margins through which the deflationary scarcity of gold reserves could have been avoided: (1) endogenous increases in the supply of gold in response to deflation (as had occurred in the past, according to Rockoff 1984), (2) reductions in the reliance on government-supplied high-powered money (movements into substitutes for paper cash in response to deflationary pressures), and (3) the establishment of bimetalist or symmetalist monetary regimes that would have permitted the substitution of alternatives to gold as reserve assets.

It is implausible to argue that a peacetime collapse of the gold standard would have occurred as the result of diverging growth trends in money demand and gold supply that would have produced gold scarcity, not least of all because there is no evidence that a monetary standard has ever collapsed for this reason. Indeed, there is much contrary evidence that monetary standards have adapted to changes in the relative price of gold or silver. Supplies of precious metals expanded, and token (or bimetallic) currencies were adopted or withdrawn in response to changes in the value of the standard of value. For example, Redish (1994) shows how the decline in the value of gold in the nineteenth century precipitated the movement away from a bimetallic standard, and away from the use of silver token currency, toward a pure gold standard. It seems reasonable to expect that a rise in the value of gold would have reversed that process.

With respect to the question of whether political changes associated with the spread of democracy made exchange rate volatility, deposit insurance, bailouts, and targeted credit subsidies inevitable, it is worth noting that many of the economic trends associated with greater political enfranchisement—including state ownership of firms; government ownership, control, and regulation of banking systems; and high rates of inflation—have been reversed in the past twenty years. Liberalization, deregulation, and disinflation are a worldwide trend of the past twenty years that has spread to developing as well as developed economies. Indeed, as noted above, there is a new movement (of uncertain long-run credibility) to reestablish currency boards (in Hong Kong, Argentina, Estonia, and Lithuania) and to dollarize Latin America (so far, only Ecuador has chosen this option). The recent bank regulatory changes in Chile, Argentina, and Mexico also represent a startling reversal of the safety net policies that had produced bailouts and disastrous losses for taxpayers during those countries' previous financial crises. The central goal of the new regulatory regimes in these countries is the establishment of credible market discipline through a combination of openness to foreign bank entry and credible prudential regulation of banks. In Argentina, the regulatory process heavily relies upon market signals of bank risk (Calomiris and Powell 2000).

These changes are symptoms of the poor fit between global economic liberalism and unstable monetary and bank regulatory policies. The primary force underlying the trend toward privatization, liberalization, deregulation, and disinflation has been globalization. Emerging market economies have increasingly felt the pressure to compete in international markets to reap the rewards of access to export markets and sources of capital. But those rewards are not unconditional. Competition for access to export and capital markets takes place not only at the level of firms and individuals, but also at the level of governments. Governments have been prodded to develop environments more conducive to efficient production of exports and more inviting to foreign capital. And governments that subsidize risk-taking by their domestic banks and other firms, or that otherwise fail to provide a stable financial environment, have found that sudden outflows of capital, and banking and exchange rate collapses, are punishments worth avoiding. The realization by governments of the need to compete produced the privatization, financial liberalization, and disinflation of the 1980s and 1990s, and the lessons of the costs of unstable liberalization have produced the regulatory reform and changes in exchange rate regimes (the movement away from pegging, and toward either firmly fixed or floating exchange rate policies) now under way.

It follows that, absent the demise of global competition for export markets and foreign capital produced by the shocks of 1914–44, the tendency Eichengreen (1996) identifies of democracy to promote statism, inflation, and protection of domestic special interests would have been substantially mitigated. From this perspective, I think it is reasonable to argue that without World War I, and the shocks that followed in its wake, the global economy, the gold standard, and the market discipline that banks faced before World War I would have continued. Individual countries, particularly on the periphery, no doubt would have strayed from global orthodoxy from time to time, but the centripetal forces favoring conformity to global norms should not be underestimated.

In the case of deposit insurance in particular, it would be hard to argue that a different history of shocks would have produced the same institutional innovation. Deposit insurance was a very unpopular idea in the United States as of 1929. It had been attempted in eight states during the early twentieth century and had produced moral hazard and banking system collapse that was widely recognized at the time (Calomiris 1990; Flood 1991; Calomiris and White 1994). Congressional initiatives to sponsor federal deposit insurance were attempted again and again from the 1880s until the 1930s. They were routinely rejected in committee and only once before 1933 reached Congress for a vote (in 1913). Deposit insurance was opposed by Roosevelt, by the Treasury, by the Fed, and by the American Bankers Association. Its victory in 1933 was largely a result of momentary political opportunism, not destiny (Calomiris and White 1994).

It is also noteworthy that the main advocates of deposit insurance—small bankers in agricultural states, who saw deposit insurance as a means of transferring subsidies from taxpayers and large, low-risk banks to small, high-risk banks—were also in retreat economically during the 1920s. Agricultural distress had produced a wave of small-bank failures and the repeal of many states' laws prohibiting branch banking (Calomiris 2000a). Bank consolidation was proceeding rapidly in the 1920s and early 1930s. A similar phenomenon occurred in the wake of the small bank failures of the 1970s and 1980s and led to the repeal of branching limits within and across states from 1980 to 1994. If deposit insurance (which gave a new lease on life to small banks) had not passed because of the specific history of the Great Depression, then (even if the agricultural distress of the 1920s—itself linked to the shocks of World War I—had not occurred) it is likely that the U.S. banking system would have moved rapidly in the direction of consolidation and branching during the 1930s and 1940s. The United States would have developed a much more stable banking system based on large, branching banks at a much earlier date.

Without the U.S. deposit insurance system to imitate, and in the presence of global competition in export markets and capital markets, there is little reason to believe that deposit insurance, and the bank bailout policies engineered initially by the RFC, would have spread to other countries.

Without the shocks of 1914–44, it is also hard to imagine how or why the major industrialized countries would have created the IMF or the World Bank. On this point, Bordo and Eichengreen (1998, pp. 445–46) concur: Initiatives to coordinate macroeconomic policy were hardly pervasive under Bretton Woods, but it is likely that they would have been even less frequent and less successful after World War II had there been no IMF.

The IMF and the World Bank are an excellent example of an asymmetry in political decision-making. The principle behind their continuing survival (as noted by Senator Gramm) was recognized by Alexander Hamilton in the eighteenth century as an important source of path dependence:

> To undo ... requires more enterprise and vigor. ... than not to do. ... This is particularly true where a number of wills is to concur. ... In collective bodies, *votes* are necessary to ACTION; absences may produce INACTION. It often happens that a majority of voices could not be had to a resolution to undo or reverse a thing once done, which there would not be a majority of voices *to do*. (Hamilton 1795)

In a conversation I had with the late former secretary of the Treasury William Simon (an outspoken IMF critic), he expressed regret at not having moved more aggressively to dismantle the IMF during the collapse of the Bretton Woods system, and expressed doubts as to whether the inertia that now protects the IMF and World Bank from reform could ever be overcome.

While the collapse of the gold standard, the creation of the bank safety net, and the founding of the IMF and World Bank are prime examples of the importance of path dependence, other financial institution changes of the 1914–44 period are less clear examples. The long-term trend toward subsidizing particular markets for credit—especially credit toward farmers and mortgagors—probably was not importantly affected by the shocks of 1914–44. Both of these tendencies were apparent during relatively normal times, as well as during episodes of severe shock. Federal Land Banks were created in 1916 during a period of agricultural boom. Freddie Mac (which expanded the mortgage subsidy already provided by Fannie Mae) was created in 1970.

Agricultural credit and mortgage credit subsidies, and the institutions that provide them, appear to be good examples of financial innovations guided by the inevitable forces of political determinism. They illustrate principles that seem to have general predictive power for understanding the relative success of special interests (see Olson 1965; Stigler 1971; Peltzman 1976; Becker 1983,

1985; and Goldin and Libecap 1994): (1) policies that provide significant transfers to a small and well-defined minority with clear common interests are likely to succeed in the political process; and (2) policies that succeed in transferring smaller subsidies to a large proportion of the population are unlikely to have large deadweight costs and are likely to include politically important groups of voters among the recipients of the subsidies. Agricultural subsidies of various kinds, including credit subsidies, are an obvious example of the first principle, while mortgage subsidies targeted to the middle class (toward which Fannie's and Freddie's programs are geared) are an example of the second principle.

6. CONCLUSION

To a great extent, the financial institutions and rules that dominate the domestic and global economies remain influenced by the specific history of the second thirty-years' war. The end of the gold standard, the ensuing volatility of exchange rates, high and volatile rates of inflation, the creation of an aggressive domestic and international safety net for banks, and the creation of powerful international multilateral institutions (the IMF and WB), are long-run consequences of the specific history of 1914–44. Other institutional inventions—including the development of new farm credit and mortgage intermediaries—were important, but their development seems to have been less dependent on the specific history of that period.

Long-run, of course, does not mean permanent. The financial architecture that emerged from the 1914–44 period is subject to change, particularly as new global competition provides motives for institutional innovation. The new interest in currency boards and dollarization is one example of such innovation, as are recent improvements in emerging market bank regulation, and bipartisan movements to reform the IMF and the WB. The new concern about the role of domestic government safety nets for banks and multilateral lenders in promoting excessive risk-taking in global financial markets may also be an early indicator that the return to pre–World War I globalization will bring with it new international competition among governments and new pressures to reform government and multilateral policies. That prospective emphasis on market discipline would constitute a partial return to the financial institutional basis of the pre–World War I economy.

Even Fannie Mae and Freddie Mac are facing a bipartisan movement calling for the elimination of the subsidization of their operations—a movement that brings together officials of the Reagan, Bush, and Clinton administrations, Ralph Nader, and the large commercial banks (Wallison 2000).

The success of all these reform efforts is by no means ensured, and would be contingent on political exigencies that are difficult to define, much less predict. But if successful, those reform movements would be a shock with potentially widespread and long-lived ramifications.

Note

1. For reviews of the role of path dependence in financial institutions, see Calomiris and Hanes (1995); Calomiris and Ramirez (1996); and Calomiris (2000a, 2000e).

References

Becker, Gary S. 1983. "A Theory of Competition among Pressure Groups for Political Influence." *Quarterly Journal of Economics* 98: 371–400.

———. 1985. "Public Policies, Pressure Groups, and Dead Weight Costs." *Journal of Public Economics* 28: 329–47.

Beim, David O., and Charles W. Calomiris. 2000. *Emerging Financial Markets.* Boston: Irwin/McGraw-Hill.

Bernanke, Ben S., and Harold James. 1991. "The Gold Standard, Deflation, and Financial Crisis in the Great Depression: An International Comparison." In R. Glenn Hubbard, ed., *Financial Markets and Financial Crises.* Chicago: University of Chicago Press: 33–68.

Bordo, Michael D., and Barry Eichengreen. 1998. "Implications of the Great Depression for the Development of the International Monetary System." In M. D. Bordo, C. Goldin, and E. N. White, eds., *The Defining Moment: The Great Depression and the American Economy in the Twentieth Century.* Chicago: University of Chicago Press: 403–53.

———. eds. 1993. *A Retrospective on the Bretton Woods System: Lessons for International Monetary Reform.* Chicago: University of Chicago Press.

Bordo, Michael D., and Finn Kydland. 1995. "The Gold Standard as a Rule: An Essay in Explorations." *Explorations in Economic History* 32: 423–64.

Calomiris, Charles W. 1990. "Is Deposit Insurance Necessary?" *Journal of Economic History* 50: 283–95.

———. 2000a. *U.S. Bank Deregulation in Historical Perspective.* Cambridge: Cambridge University Press.

———. 2000b. "Victorian Perspectives on the Banking Collapses of the 1980s and 1990s." Manuscript, Columbia University.

———. 2000c. "When Will Economics Guide IMF and World Bank Reform?" *The CATO Journal* 20 (Spring–Summer): 85–103.

———. 2000d. "Are Fannie and Freddie 'Optimal Mechanisms'? An Economist's Case for GSE Reform." In Peter J. Wallison, ed., *Conflicting Duties at Fannie Mae and Freddie Mac: Public Purposes and Private Interests.* Washington, D.C.: AEI Press.

———. 2000e. "Banks and Banking: A Short History." Manuscript, Columbia University.

Calomiris, Charles W., and Christopher Hanes. 1995. "Historical Macroeconomics and American Macroeconomic History." In Kevin D. Hoover, ed., *Macroeconometrics: Developments, Tensions, and Prospects,* pp. 351–416. Boston: Kluwer Academic Publishers.

Calomiris, Charles W., and Allan H. Meltzer. 1999. "Fixing the IMF." *The National Interest* (Summer): 88–96.

Calomiris, Charles W., and Andrew Powell. 2000. "Can Emerging Market Bank Regulators Establish Credible Discipline? The Case of Argentina, 1992–1999." NBER Working Paper, forthcoming.

Calomiris, Charles W., and Carlos D. Ramirez. 1996. "The Role of Financial Relationships in the History of American Corporate Finance." *Journal of Applied Corporate Finance* (Summer): 52–73.

Calomiris, Charles W., and David C. Wheelock. 1998. "Was the Great Depression a Watershed for American Monetary Policy?" In M. D. Bordo, C. Goldin, and E. N. White, eds., *The Defining Moment: The Great Depression and the American Economy in the Twentieth Century,* pp. 23–65. Chicago: University of Chicago Press.

Calomiris, Charles W., and Eugene N. White. 1994. "The Origins of Federal Deposit Insurance." In Claudia Goldin and Gary D. Libecap, eds., *The Regulated Economy,* pp. 145–88. Chicago: University of Chicago Press.

Caprio, Gerard D., Jr., and Daniela Klingabiel. 1996. "Bank Insolvency: Bad Luck, Bad Policy, or Bad Banking." In Michael Bruno and Boris Pleskovic, eds., *Annual World Bank Conference on Development Economics, 1996.*

Chandler, Alfred D. 1972. "Anthracite Coal and the Beginnings of the Industrial Revolution in the United States." *Business History Review* 46: 142–81.

———. 1977. *The Visible Hand: The Managerial Revolution in American Business.* Cambridge, Mass.: Harvard University Press.

Drajem, Mark. 2000. "IMF Board to Review Lending Policies in Answer to Reform Calls." *Bloomberg News,* May 31, 2000.

Eichengreen, Barry. 1992. *Golden Fetters: The Gold Standard and the Great Depression, 1919–1939.* New York: Oxford University Press.

———. 1996. *Globalizing Capital: A History of the International Monetary System.* Princeton, N.J.: Princeton University Press.

———. 1999. *Toward a New International Financial Architecture: A Practical Post-Asia Agenda.* Washington, D.C.: Institute for International Economics.

Eichengreen, Barry, and Jeffrey D. Sachs. 1985. "Exchange Rates and Economic Recovery in the 1930s." *Journal of Economic History* 45: 925–46.

———. 1986. "Competitive Devaluations in the Great Depression: A Theoretical Reassessment." *Economic Letters* 22: 67–71.

Ely, Bert, and Peter Wallison. 2000. *Nationalizing Mortgage Risk: The Growth of Fannie Mae and Freddie Mac.* Washington, D.C.: AEI Press.

Flood, Mark D. 1991. "The Great Deposit Insurance Debacle." *Federal Reserve Bank of St. Louis Review* 74: 51–77.

Fohlin, Caroline. 2000. "Economic, Political, and Legal Factors in Financial System Development: International Patterns in Historical Perspective." Social Science Working Paper 1089, California Institute of Technology, May.

Goldin, Claudia, and Gary S. Libecap, eds. 1994. *The Regulated Economy.* Chicago: University of Chicago Press.

Hamilton, Alexander. 1795. *Report of the Secretary of the Treasury.*

International Financial Institution Advisory Commission. 2000 [a.k.a. "The Meltzer Report"]. *Report of the International Financial Institution Advisory Commission,* Allan H. Meltzer, Chairman, March.

Jaffee, Dwight. 2000. "The Effects on the Mortgage Markets of Privatizing Fannie Mae and Freddie Mac." Presented at the American Enterprise Institute Conference, "Thinking about the Future of Fannie Mae and Freddie Mac." May 23, 2000.

Judson, Ruth, and Athanasios Orphanides. 1996. "Inflation, Volatility, and Growth." Working Paper 96–19, Federal Reserve Board.

La Porta, R., F. Lopez-De-Salines, A. Shleifer, and R. Vishny. 1997. "Legal Determinants of External Finance." *Journal of Finance* 52: 1131–50.

Levine, Ross. 1997. "Banks and Economic Development: The Legal Determinants of Banking Development and the Impact of Banks on Long-Run Growth." Manuscript, University of Minnesota.

Obstfeld, Maurice, and Alan M. Taylor. 1998. "The Great Depression as a Watershed: International Capital Mobility over the Long Run." In M. D. Bordo, C. Goldin, and E. N. White, eds., *The Defining Moment: The Great Depression and the American Economy in the Twentieth Century,* pp. 353–402. Chicago: University of Chicago Press.

Olson, Mancur. 1965. *The Logic of Collective Action.* Cambridge, Mass.: Harvard University Press.

Peltzman, Sam. 1976. "Toward a More General Theory of Regulation." *Journal of Law and Economics* 19: 211–40.

Rajan, Raghuram, and Luigi Zingales. 1999. "The Politics of Financial Development." Working Paper, University of Chicago.

Redish, Angela. 1994. "The Latin Monetary Union and the Emergence of the International Gold Standard." In M. D. Bordo and F. Capie, eds., *Monetary Regimes in Transition,* pp. 68–85. Cambridge: Cambridge University Press.

Rockoff, Hugh. 1984. "Some Evidence on the Real Price of Gold: Its Costs of Production and Commodity Prices." In M. D. Bordo and A. J. Schwartz, eds., *A Retrospective on the Classical Gold Standard, 1821–1931,* pp. 613–50. Chicago: University of Chicago Press.

Sachs, Jeffrey D., ed. 1989. *Developing Country Debt and the World Economy.* Chicago: University of Chicago Press.

Schwartz, Anna J. 1997. "From Obscurity to Notoriety: A Biography of the Exchange Stabilization Fund." *Journal of Money, Credit, and Banking* 29: 135–53.

Stigler, George J. 1971. "The Theory of Economic Regulation." *Rand Journal of Economics* 2: 1–21.

Temin, Peter. 1989. *Lessons from the Great Depression.* Cambridge, Mass.: MIT Press.

Wallison, Peter J., ed. 2000. *Conflicting Duties at Fannie Mae and Freddie Mac: Public Purposes and Private Interests.* Washington, D.C.: AEI Press.

6 | PATH DEPENDENCE IN ACTION: THE ADOPTION AND PERSISTENCE OF THE KOREAN MODEL OF ECONOMIC DEVELOPMENT

Phillip Wonhyuk Lim

1. INTRODUCTION

Developing countries typically face three interrelated policy challenges: investment, conflict management, and engagement with the outside world. They must formulate effective strategies to accumulate both physical and human capital, cope with social conflicts, and maximize the benefits of "openness" while containing the risks (Rodrik 1999). In the early 1960s, the Republic of Korea (South Korea) addressed these developmental challenges by combining state-led financial resource allocation with export market orientation. The government nationalized banks and assumed a dominant role in financial resource allocation, providing selective guarantees on private sector foreign borrowing. The government in effect formed a risk partnership with large private firms. Replacing the import substitution bias of the 1950s with outward orientation, the government, for the most part, used the performance of firms in competitive export markets as a selection criterion. As for conflict management, successive authoritarian regimes used both the carrot of improving living standards and the stick of ruthless suppression before Korea was democratized in the late 1980s.

As Table 6.1 shows, Korea's economic performance over the three decades before the 1997 Asian economic crisis was truly exceptional. Although the Korean model of economic development has come under heavy criticism since the 1997 crisis, no such criticism would seem convincing without some explanation for its apparent success in the past.

Table 6.1

Comparative growth experience, 1960–1990

(percent per year)

Regions and Countries[a]	Output		Labor: Number of Workers	Physical Capital		Human Capital	
	GDP	GDP per Worker		Total Physical Capital	Physical Capital per Worker	Labor Quality[b]	Years of Schooling
East Asia	7.46	4.71	2.75	10.89	8.14	1.33	1.94
Latin America	3.27	0.85	2.42	4.51	2.09	0.98	1.57
Middle East	5.14	2.71	2.43	6.43	4.00	1.36	2.93
South Asia	4.10	2.02	2.08	5.38	3.30	1.51	3.39
Sub-Saharan Africa	3.42	0.81	2.61	3.64	1.03	0.77	1.83
Developed countries	3.56	2.38	1.17	4.62	3.44	0.63	0.90
Malaysia	6.86	3.71	3.14	9.43	6.29	1.52	2.47
Indonesia	5.92	3.74	2.18	7.91	5.73	1.75	3.62
Philippines	4.11	1.59	2.52	6.10	3.58	1.40	1.64
Singapore	8.17	5.27	2.90	12.93	10.03	0.69	1.03
Korea	8.49	5.93	2.56	11.90	9.34	2.18	2.83
Taiwan	8.31	5.66	2.66	11.87	9.22	1.83	2.41
Thailand	6.97	4.26	2.72	9.75	7.03	0.39	0.89
Japan	6.17	5.03	1.14	9.35	8.22	0.10	0.48

SOURCE: Hahn and Kim (2000).

[a]Regional averages are weighted by each country's average GDP between 1960 and 1990.

[b]The labor quality index is constructed as the weighted average of educational attainment for workers, where the weights are based on the (diminishing) rate of return from each additional level of schooling (primary, secondary, and tertiary).

It is the objective of this paper to shed light on the adoption and evolution of the Korean model of economic development using the concept of path dependence. This paper is organized as follows. Invoking the concept of path dependence, section 2 briefly reviews "the QWERTY paradigm" and discusses how this exemplar of decision-making in a network context can be applied to the adoption of economic systems. Section 3 examines the set of initial conditions that affected the choice of economic systems in Korea in the early stages of development. After Korea was liberated from the Japanese colonial rule in 1945, the reassignment of property rights and the realignment of political forces provided the background of subsequent economic decisions, but what later came to be known as "the Korean model" was not the initial choice. A series of "historical accidents" that led to its adoption in the early 1960s is highlighted. Section 4 looks at the path-dependence mechanism that led to the economic crisis of 1997 in Korea. After a brief analysis of the consolidation of Korea's government-business risk partnership, this section examines how the installed base of economic actors interested in preserving this system prevented Korea from adopting fundamental reforms.

2. THE QWERTY PARADIGM AND COMPETING ECONOMIC SYSTEMS

The essence of the QWERTY paradigm is that the adoption probabilities associated with competing systems depend on their current market shares (network sizes) as well as their stand-alone qualities and extraneous factors. When the adoption probabilities depend positively on the current market shares, the allocation process exhibits increasing returns. Because the expected network size of such an increasing-returns system is positively influenced by the size of the installed base, "historical accidents" in the early stages of the system competition are likely to have a significant effect on the eventual outcome. Moreover, if the adjustment cost is sufficiently high, a local optimum is the best that can be hoped for, and the global optimum may not be obtained (David 1985, 2000; Arthur 1994).

For competing economic systems, the current "market share" associated with a particular economic system would refer to the "influence proportion" of economic players in support of that system, and the parameters of the adoption probability function would reflect the given political economy setting. In such a situation, policymakers advocating one economic system or another must take into account its stand-alone qualities as well as its compatibility with the interests of economic players who have made specific investments. Depending on the level of organization and the payoff structure associated with policy choices, these economic players exert varying degrees of influence on the decision-making process.

The objective function of policymakers may not be efficiency maximization, just as the typewriter manufacturers' objective function is not. Under such conditions, the most efficient economic system may not be adopted even if it can be identified. Furthermore, especially when increasing returns are significant, a system that was once efficient but is no longer so may persist. For example, Dertouzos et al. (1989) argued that the previous success of America's mass production system made it difficult for Americans to adapt to the new world of flexible manufacturing.

3. THE ADOPTION OF THE KOREAN MODEL OF ECONOMIC DEVELOPMENT

Korea achieved national unity and established a centralized rule in the mid-seventh century, a remarkably early date by any standard. A pyramidlike structure, with the central government at the apex, characterized the social organization of Korea for more than a thousand years. In the economic sphere, the central government traditionally allowed little room for merchants or other groups to pursue moneymaking ventures on their own. Thus, in the Korean context, both economic stagnation and economic development had to be state led (Cha and Lim 2000). The elite scholar-officials at the center could easily exploit mass society and engage in factional rent-seeking competition. Alternatively, "the best and the brightest" could take advantage of Korea's homogeneity and centralization to mobilize resources for development. To a large degree, these contrasting possibilities were realized after Korea was liberated from a brief but brutal Japanese colonial rule (1910–45).

The end of the Japanese colonial rule meant that Korea was confronted with the crucial tasks of reassigning property rights and reestablishing the external trade and foreign-exchange regime. The "enemy properties" of the Japanese and their collaborators had to be either nationalized or sold off, and the rules governing trade and foreign exchange had to be modified to deal with the vacuum created by the severing of economic relations with Japan. Furthermore, given the lack of domestic capital and technology, policies designed to attract investment had to be implemented. In this regard, Korea's economic situation after liberation was similar to that of Central and Eastern European countries after the collapse of the socialist bloc. In addressing these policy challenges, Syngman Rhee, the first president of the Republic of Korea, took a rather myopic and politically motivated approach. In fact, Rhee's use of policy instruments to finance elections and other party activities through a close alliance with select private firms played a dominant role in a succession of economic decisions during his presidency (1948–60).

After the outbreak of the Korean War in 1950, the United States reassessed Korea's geostrategic importance and provided generous aid and assistance.[1] The Korean government deposited the local currency equivalent of all U.S. aid into a counterpart fund whose use would be jointly determined by the Americans and the Koreans. The exchange rate became a contentious issue, however, as Rhee insisted on repaying the advances at a rate that significantly undervalued the dollar. The market exchange rate (as approximated by the rate applied to UN soldiers stationed in Korea) was at times nearly three times as high as the official rate. Rhee's reasoning was clear: the possession of foreign exchange and aid goods at less than their market value would create arbitrage opportunities and would allow him to distribute favors to businessmen willing to provide kickbacks to the Liberal Party (Haggard 1990, p. 57).

In the end, what passed for an economic system in Korea in the 1950s was primarily shaped by Rhee's use of policy instruments to secure and sustain his power base. The sale of "enemy properties" resulted in windfall gains for favored businessmen and an undue concentration of economic power. The overvaluation of the Korean currency, designed to maximize arbitrage opportunities, had the effect of severely discouraging exports.

When a student protest in April 1960 finally put an end to the Syngman Rhee government, Korea was in a dismal state. Korea's per capita GDP in 1960 was lower than such Sub-Saharan African countries as Mozambique and Senegal—to say nothing of most countries in Asia and Latin America. In fact, a cross-country study on economic development shows that Korea had a rather unusual economic structure in the early 1960s (Perkins 1997). The share of agriculture and mining in the Korean GNP was close to 50 percent, nearly 15 percentage points higher than the average of other countries of comparable size and per capita income. The share of manufacturing, slightly over 10 percent of GNP, was unusually low, nearly 20 percentage points below the average. Even more remarkable was the extremely low share of exports; it amounted to only 3 percent of GNP when the average was about 15 percent.

This was a dramatic departure from the 1930s and the early 1940s when Korea's exports amounted to about 30 percent of GNP. The Rhee government's myopic policy was largely responsible for turning a trading nation into an aid-dependent near-autarky.

Coming in the wake of the Student Revolution of April 1960, which had put an end to the corruption-prone regime under Syngman Rhee, the "Military Revolution" of May 1961 provided the political background for the adoption of the Korean model of economic development. Upon seizing power through a bloodless coup, General Park Chung Hee and his followers declared that they were determined to "focus all energy into developing capability to confront communism, in order to realize the people's long-standing wish for national unification." Park's overriding concern was the communist regime in North Korea, which had successfully carried out a series of reconstruction and economic development programs after the Korean War (Park 1963).

Although Park and his followers had only rudimentary knowledge of economics, they believed that the state should take a leading role in economic development. In order to centralize economic policymaking, the military government established the Economic Planning Board (EPB) in July 1961. The EPB was charged with the task of formulating and implementing five-year economic development plans based on an "indicative planning" approach. The military government also took several measures to strengthen the role of the state in resource allocation. After the student revolution of April 1960, prominent businessmen were accused of having grown rich through political connections with the previous Syngman Rhee regime. Taking over the task of dealing with these "illicit wealth accumulators," the military government accused them of tax evasion and other illegal business practices and forced them to turn in their equity shares in commercial banks as "fines." This drastic measure paved the way for the government to exert direct control over commercial banks, in effect renationalizing the banks that had been privatized in the late 1950s. In a little more than a year, the military government thus established various levers of control. The question remained, however, what kind of state-led system it would be.

Developing countries around the world at this time were faced with a variety of competing economic systems. The dearth of private entrepreneurs and lack of domestic capital in these countries seemed to imply that the state would have to take the initiative and rely on foreign capital or forced domestic savings to accelerate economic development. Given these conditions, some countries opted for the socialist system while others tinkered with market-based ones. Many Latin American countries pursued import-substituting industrialization supplemented by foreign direct investment, expressing skepticism about the benefits of free trade as primary producers. In Asia, Taiwan was making a transition from import substitution to export-oriented industrialization, promoting state-owned enterprises in intermediate goods industries and private enterprises in the labor-intensive sector.[2] Singapore was about to adopt a state-led development model of its own, relying on state-owned enterprises ("government-linked companies") in infrastructure-related industries and foreign multinationals in the manufacturing sector as twin engines of growth (Low 1991).

Like these developing countries, Korea had to define the role of the state and the market, set the terms of engagement with the outside world, and find a way to gain access to foreign resources to make up for the lack of domestic capital. The military government initially tried to pursue inward-looking industrialization under the principle of "guided capitalism." According to the First Five-Year Plan (1962–66) released by the Supreme Council in July 1961, the government would take charge of investment in manufacturing. Korea would earn hard currency by exporting *primary* products and undertake massive investment projects in such *basic* industries as steel and machinery. Seeking to consolidate political support through populist measures, the military government also expanded public works, granted pay raises to government employees, and guaranteed high prices to farmers (Haggard 1990, pp. 67–68).

Intended or not, these economic policies bore a striking resemblance to those adopted by Latin American countries. In the 1950s, Korea had operated a de facto import-substitution regime, marked more by cronyism than developmentalism. Now, it seemed that Korea was about to adopt a development-oriented import-substitution regime. A series of "historical accidents," however, prevented this outcome and led the military government to switch to an export-oriented system. Strong economic pressure from the United States and decisive reaction from the fiercely nationalistic Korean leaders played a critical role in this dramatic transition.

The U.S. authorities were initially supportive of the development-oriented Park and his followers, but they became increasingly alarmed as the military government pursued an ambitious program of "industrial deepening." The American experts advised the Korean government to invest in infrastructure and make the most of human capital and existing factories instead of carrying out massive projects in heavy industries. The military government, however, pushed ahead with its program, trying to obtain capital for such ambitious projects as an integrated steel mill (Kimiya 1991).

In June 1962 the Korean government even implemented a shocking currency reform program without prior consultation with the United States. Through a compulsory deposit-for-equity swap measure, a certain portion of existing deposits was to be converted into equity shares in a new Industrial Development Corporation, which would then use these captured domestic savings to invest in heavy industries. The military government would guarantee an annual dividend return of 15 percent on these shares. The Americans were not amused. Critical of the antimarket nature of this measure and insulted by the lack of consultation, the U.S. government forced the Park government to lift the freeze on deposits by threatening to postpone economic assistance (C. Kim 1995, pp. 81–95).

The United States also insisted on an economic stabilization program. The military government had precipitated inflation that approached an annual rate of 30 percent in 1962, and the United States was apparently determined to prevent the military government from carrying out inflation-financed investment projects in heavy industries. The U.S. aid leverage was strengthened by a poor harvest and a foreign-exchange crisis in Korea in the second half of 1962. The U.S. officials took full advantage of this to demand major economic reforms and also to press the military leaders to honor their pledge to restore an elected regime by 1963.[3] In order to secure an adequate supply of grain for the coming months, the Korean government had little choice but to acquiesce to these demands (Mason et al. 1980, pp. 196–97). In December 1962 the Korean government decided to revise the First Five-Year Plan to reflect major changes in economic policy,[4] but the lessons were not lost on the Korean policymakers. Reassessing the import-substituting industrialization strategy that they had initially favored, Park and his followers began to search for radically different policies that would save them from ever being trapped in such a vulnerable position again. In the end, the Park government would go far beyond the orthodox economic policies prescribed by the Americans and adopt drastic measures to promote exports and increase economic independence.

The Park government implemented three interrelated sets of economic policies that came to define the Korean model of economic development. First, the government accommodated the U.S. demands and instituted a set of macroeconomic reforms designed to "get the prices right" and stabilize the economy. Second, the government adopted drastic measures to share the investment risks of the private sector, providing, in particular, explicit repayment guarantees to foreign institutions that extended loans to private firms. Third, Park himself spearheaded the effort to boost exports, offering various incentives based on market performance. The resulting government-business risk partnership, for which the export market performance of private firms was primarily used as a selection criterion, defined the core of what later came to be known as "the Korean model."

The macroeconomic reforms ensured that Korea's state-led development model would be a market-based one. Building on the stabilization policies of 1963–64, the government devalued the Korean won from 130 to the dollar to 255 to the dollar in May 1964. Also, in order to protect depositors from inflation and to encourage domestic savings, the government raised the ceiling on the one-year time deposit rate from 15 percent to 30 percent on September 30, 1965 (C. Kim 1995, p. 114).

These orthodox polices, designed to reduce distortions in macroeconomic variables, were accompanied by dirigist measures that deliberately introduced distortions into the microeconomic incentives. The Park government knew that Korea lacked the domestic resources to carry out its ambitious economic development program, but unlike Latin American countries at the time (or Southeast Asian countries in the 1980s), it was not willing to depend on foreign direct investment (FDI). Seeking to tap into foreign capital while limiting the influence of foreign multinationals, the fiercely nationalistic Korean government decided to rely heavily on foreign loans. Because domestic firms at the time lacked the standing in the international capital market, however, the government decided to take up the problem of asymmetric information and allow state-owned banks to issue a repayment guarantee to foreign financial institutions that provided loans to Korean firms.

In taking this measure, the Park government signaled that it was willing to form a risk partnership with business leaders. Although Park Chung Hee and his followers had initially condemned most of these businessmen as "illicit wealth accumulators," they apparently concluded that combining state monitoring with private entrepreneurship would be the most effective means of carrying out the economic development plans. The alternative of using state-owned enterprises (SOEs) to accelerate industrialization, as in Taiwan, was not actively pursued.[5] The government decided to use its credibility to raise capital on the international market and allocate financial resources to private firms, in effect *contracting out* the provision of goods and services to the private sector under a system of government monitoring as well as a guarantee on loans. Through direct monitoring and a market test based on export performance, the government tried to contain the potential costs of moral hazard that state-backed debt financing created. Export performance, in particular, provided the government with a relatively objective criterion for selecting private firms when it made its decision on repayment guarantees.

In order to increase economic independence through export promotion, the government also introduced a number of export incentives. The short-term export credit system was streamlined as early as 1961. The essence of the new system was the automatic approval of loans by commercial banks to those with an export letter of credit. The government also gave exporters various tax deductions, generous wastage allowances, tariff exemptions, and preferential policy loans.[6] In order to monitor export performance according to indicative targets set at the beginning of each year, the president himself chaired monthly export promotion meetings. Strong export performers even received medals and national recognition on Export Day, which was established in 1964 to commemorate the day when Korea's annual exports exceeded 100 million dollars for the first time. Aware of Korea's comparative advantage in the 1960s, the government encouraged private firms to concentrate on labor-intensive industries.[7]

Based on export-led industrialization and state guarantees on private-sector foreign borrowing, the Korean model of economic development proved an efficient choice given Korea's resource endowment at the time. In 1965 the primary and secondary enrollments in Korea were similar to the rates in countries with three times its per capita income (World Bank 1993, pp. 45–46).

Cheap and high-quality labor could be readily employed to produce a high rate of return on investment in physical capital, if Korea could tap into foreign capital and technology to compensate for the shortage of domestic resources and exploit its comparative advantage. The government's decision to issue a selective guarantee on the foreign borrowing of private firms and promote exports was a solution to this developmental challenge. The Korean government thus corrected for capital market imperfections and removed the constraints that had made it very difficult for firms to exploit profitable investment opportunities in the 1950s.

What the Korean government did "right" in the take-off stage was of a different nature than is usually pointed out in the existing literature (Krueger 1979; Amsden 1989; Rodrik 1995). The market failure effectively addressed by the government in the 1960s was due to the imperfections in the international capital market rather than coordination failures involving nontradable goods in the domestic manufacturing sector. Far more important for Korea's economic growth, however, was the Park government's effort to correct for the *government failures* of the past: the policies designed to generate arbitrage opportunities that had made it virtually impossible for firms to exploit Korea's comparative advantage in the 1950s. With the government addressing financing problems as well as macroeconomic imbalances, private firms could now invest and export to take advantage of unexplored profit opportunities. Rapid capital accumulation, combined with learning by exporting, was the key to Korea's economic success.

In the terminology of the QWERTY paradigm, once the "market share" of policymakers attached to Syngman Rhee's crony capitalism was drastically reduced in the wake of the 1960 student protest and the 1961 coup, the adoption of the Korean model of economic development was driven more by "historical accidents" than by foresight and design. Although the evolution of economic systems is typically marked by path dependence due to the influence of the entrenched interests, the corruption-prone system under the Rhee government lost its supporters in the changed political environment, and this provided an opening for competition among alternative economic systems. Initially, the economic policy of the military government was heavily influenced by those who argued for an "industrial deepening" program, in which the government would have carried out massive investment projects in basic industries. In the second half of 1962, however, they lost their influence when the United States used its aid leverage to demand stabilization measures and also to press the military leaders to stick to their commitment to restore an elected regime by 1963. Determined to avoid being trapped in such a vulnerable position again, the military government accepted advice from the technocrats and business-men advocating an export-led growth strategy and went far beyond the ortho-dox economic policies prescribed by the Americans. Incidentally, the new Korean economic system proved a popular choice in political economy terms as well. In this regard, it is important to note that if a nation has a comparative advantage in the labor-intensive sector, as in the case of Korea in the 1960s, ex-port orientation can improve the welfare of workers. An accidental product of strong U.S. pressure and nationalistic Korean response, the system could thus secure wide support.

4. CONSOLIDATION, DELAYED REFORM, AND CRISIS

Korea's economic development model centered on export-led industrializa-tion and government-business risk partnership encouraged rapid capital accumulation and produced spectacular economic growth. Reassured by government guarantees and subsequent economic growth, foreign financial institutions expanded loans to Korean firms and provided the lion's share of necessary capital for investment projects.[8] Korean firms, for their part, dramatically increased their leverage while their profitability actually *declined:* the debt-equity ratio of manufacturing firms, as measured by their total liabil-ities divided by net worth, soared from 92.7 percent in 1965 to 328.4 percent in 1970. While encouraging investment conducive to rapid economic growth, the Korean system thus led to a highly leveraged corporate sector that became extremely vulnerable to shocks.

Although the Korean system was designed to contain idiosyncratic moral hazard by making government support contingent on market performance, it was not prepared to deal with the increased *systemic* risks as manifested in the higher leverage of private firms. Apparently successful firms kept borrowing to expand their business under government guarantees on foreign debt, and neither the government nor the private sector stopped to think seriously about the potential toll that a major economic downturn would take on heavily indebted firms.

When a serious economic slowdown following the investment explosion of the late 1960s threatened to topple the debt-plagued corporate sector in 1972, the Park government decided to bail out the debt-plagued corporate sector and issued the Presidential Emergency Decree for Economic Stability and Growth on August 3, 1972. The Emergency Decree placed an immediate moratorium on the payment of all corporate debt to the curb lenders and called for an extensive rescheduling of bank loans at a reduced interest rate. The moratorium was to last three years, after which all curb funds had to be turned into five-year loans at an annual rate of 16.2 percent—when the prevailing market rate exceeded 40 percent. The August 3 Emergency Decree forced "usurious" curb lenders and disorganized taxpayers to share losses, but left the owners and managers of firms and banks intact.

In retrospect, the August 3 Emergency Decree of 1972 marked a watershed in the evolution of the Korean economy. When the government was forging a risk partnership with private firms in the 1960s by guaranteeing repayment on their foreign borrowing, the government issued a repayment guarantee to foreign financial institutions rather than to Korean firms. Aware of moral hazard created by insurance, the government certainly did not intend to guarantee the governance rights of the incumbent owner-managers (O 1995). The Emergency Decree of 1972, however, established the precedent that the government would take extraordinary measures to relieve financial distress when necessary, *without* holding the management of firms and banks accountable for their previous investment and lending decisions. Moreover, the Emergency Decree seemed to imply that an excessive dependence on debt would not only go unpunished but might actually be rewarded by the government—as long as other companies also depended heavily on debt.

The government could have chosen a more market-oriented solution instead of strengthening the government-business alliance. In a sense, the two alternatives represented competing economic systems at the time. Under a more market-oriented approach, the government would have separated the problem of financial restructuring from that of protecting the governance rights of incumbent owner-managers. For those firms whose going-concern value was deemed to be greater than the liquidation value, creditors would have used a combination of debt forgiveness, debt rescheduling, and debt-equity swaps. These firms would have survived after restructuring, but their owner-managers would have been replaced. The installed base of economic players interested in preserving the government-business risk partnership, however, pushed the government away from adopting a more market-oriented solution. Violating the property rights of the creditors in the informal curb market, the government relieved the debt burden of the private firms it had come to rely on as agents to carry out its ambitious economic development plans. The August 3 Emergency Decree of 1972 thus fundamentally changed the nature of state guarantees and ushered in a new era characterized by the deepening of the government-business risk partnership.

The ensuing heavy and chemical industry (HCI) drive aggravated moral hazard because the government was increasingly trapped in a vicious cycle of intervention (Stern et al. 1995). During the late 1970s, HCIs accounted for almost 80 percent of all fixed investment in the manufacturing sector when their share in the manufacturing sector's output was around 40 percent. The banks as well as the newly established National Investment Fund supported the HCI drive by providing policy-oriented loans at a *negative* real interest rate. In order to minimize time and exploit scale economies in establishing the capital-intensive HCI sector, the government relied on a select group of large family-based business groups and provided them with extremely generous financial support. Known as *chaebol,* they more than doubled their share of GDP during the heyday of the HCI drive from 1973 to 1978.

The HCI drive in the 1970s transformed the government-business risk partnership decidedly in favor of these family-based business groups. Unlike in the 1960s, international competitiveness (that is, "market test") no longer operated as a selection criterion. Although Park Chung Hee might have felt that he could always control the chaebol firms as "quasi-SOEs," he was in fact creating behemoths that would come to dominate the Korean economy. Having channeled massive resources into the chaebol to carry out high-priority investment projects—sometimes over the initial objection of their owner-managers, the government had to take responsibility should these projects turn sour. Moreover, the gigantic size and high leverage of the chaebol strengthened the case for a "too big to fail" argument should a crisis strike.

These developments in the 1970s had a profound impact on Korea's development paradigm. The Emergency Decree of 1972 and the HCI drive consolidated the government-business risk partnership and exacerbated moral hazard. The installed base of business interests with a high debt burden pushed the government to provide financial relief at the expense of curb lenders. Subsequently, the industrial targeting approach adopted during the HCI drive trapped the government in a vicious cycle of intervention, and the massive financial support extended to the top chaebol consolidated the government-business risk partnership.

By the 1980s it had become possible for successful Korean firms to raise capital on their own. It had also become increasingly difficult for the government to identify profitable investment opportunities and monitor the performance of individual firms. Moreover, increased domestic and foreign pressure for liberalization and democratization was beginning to force the government to relinquish some important policy instruments that it had used to motivate and discipline private firms. Given the reduced desirability and effectiveness of government intervention in the economy, policymakers should have fundamentally redefined the role of the government.

In fact, as early as the beginning of the 1980s, many technocrats did advocate a transition to a more market-oriented system (Jones and SaKong 1980). They were clearly aware of the dilemma that the government faced. Since the collapse of a large chaebol would bury the financial system in nonperforming loans, the government was more or less obliged to guarantee the chaebol's stability. This implicit guarantee, however, encouraged the chaebol to undertake excessive investment. Expecting to be bailed out should a crisis strike, they would discount the downside risks and invest wildly—unless restrained by the government. In order to maintain economic stability, the government thus found itself having to intervene in the investment decisions of private firms.

The solution to this apparent dilemma was for the government to let market forces operate and allow a nonviable chaebol to go bankrupt while containing the fallout from its collapse. The government would have to hold the incumbent owner-managers accountable for their previous decisions and refrain from intervening in the investment decisions of private firms in the future. Moreover, autonomous financial institutions, free from the control of the government *and* industrial capitalists, would have to be allowed to make decisions on their own and bear the full consequences of their actions. The government would have to redefine its role and focus on competition policy and prudential regulation rather than allocate financial resources according to its industrial policy objectives. In other words, the government would have to stop providing direction and insurance to private firms, but limit its role to setting and enforcing "the rules of the game" and providing a social safety net. This series of decisive measures would serve as a credible signal that the regime had indeed changed.

Backed by a new political leadership determined to arrest the inflationary spiral in the wake of the second oil shock, the technocrats were able to impose tough stabilization measures and to reorient economic policy away from the industry targeting approach of the HCI drive. They were, however, far less successful in introducing policies designed to enhance the autonomy of the financial sector and to promote competition in the product and capital market. By this time, the Korean economic system had produced a coalition of economic players who were interested in consolidating and maintaining the government-business risk partnership. The politicians and bureaucrats were certainly unwilling to relinquish the levers of control. The state control of the banks continued, and the government took a decidedly bureaucratic approach to competition policy. The chaebol tried to expand their influence in the financial sector through the ownership of nonbank financial institutions, and to limit the presence of foreign multinationals in the domestic market. Although domestic and foreign pressure for liberalization and democratization did lead to the adoption of some market-oriented reforms, the government-business risk partnership continued to dominate.

The lack of fundamental reform proved fatal for the Korean economy. In 1995 the average debt-equity ratio of the top thirty chaebol was 347.5 percent. The lower-ranking groups (numbers eleven to thirty) had been earning a negative average return on assets since 1993. Halla, Jinro, and Sammi, in particular, had a debt-equity ratio of over 2,000 percent as they piled up losses. Financial institutions, however, continued to provide credit to these companies.

In 1996 the average debt-equity ratio of the top thirty chaebol climbed to 386.5 percent, but the financial institutions still propped up the debt-plagued conglomerates. In April 1996, Korea's terms of trade began to decline sharply as the price of semiconductors collapsed. The decline in the terms of trade reached 20 percent by the end of the year, and it turned out to be Korea's biggest terms-of-trade shock since the oil shock. In 1997 the average debt-equity ratio of the top thirty chaebol reached 519.0 percent. Korea was on the brink of yet another debt crisis.

The Korean experience illustrates that once an economic system is well established it is very difficult to introduce fundamental changes because the economic players interested in preserving the existing system tend to be the ones who wield a great deal of influence in the policymaking process. The Korean model of economic development itself was adopted only when the entrenched interests associated with the old corruption-prone system were wiped out in the wake of a student revolution and a military coup. As for the new economic system based on the government-business risk partnership, the chances for fundamental change were smaller than in the case of the old system. It was not just because the new system was far more successful than the old one. In the case of the old system, which was based on crony capitalism, a political upheaval throwing out the entrenched interests would do the trick—if it were followed by an institutional reform designed to reduce rent-seeking in the economy. In the new system, however, a political upheaval replacing one set of policymakers with another would not result in a fundamental change—unless the new politicians and bureaucrats were willing or forced to relinquish their control over the economy. Only in the wake of the economic crisis has Korea begun to make substantial progress in this regard.

Notes

Acknowledgments: The author would like to thank Paul David, Ha Won Jang, Euysung Kim, and Jacob Metzer for helpful comments. Jina Yu provided excellent research assistance. An extended version of this paper (Lim 2000) is available from the author upon request.

1. Foreign aid financed nearly 70 percent of total imports to Korea from 1953 through 1962. It was equal to nearly 80 percent of total fixed capital formation and 8 percent of GNP. Net foreign savings, as measured by the current account deficit of the balance of payments, averaged 9 percent of GNP for this decade (Mason et al. 1980, p. 185).

2. From the perspective of path dependence, it may be worthwhile to elaborate on the reaction of economic players who had vested interests in the import-substitution regime. When import-substitution policies became increasingly ineffective because of market saturation and slowed growth, Taiwanese firms appealed to the Ministry of Economic Affairs to permit them to organize cartels. Technocrats, however, were acutely aware of the limits of import-substituting industrialization given the small market size of Taiwan. Also, the growing problem of corruption under the import-substitution regime reminded political leaders of their past mistakes on the mainland. Overcoming the resistance of protected business interests, the Taiwanese government adopted an export-oriented strategy in the late 1950s (Haggard 1990).

3. The stabilization program pushed by the United States called for curtailing the budget deficit and limiting growth of the money supply to 5 percent in 1963. The following year similar restrictions plus a 50 percent devaluation were imposed as conditions for continued aid.

4. The revised plan advocated a free-market economy, scrapping "guided capitalism" as the basic principle of economic policy. It also emphasized the importance of stabilization policy, scaled down GNP growth targets, and crossed out such investment projects as an integrated steel mill. Last but not least, the revised plan called for a shift in export priorities from primary products to labor-intensive manufactured goods.

5. General Park Chung Hee had once organized communist sympathizers in the Korean Army before he converted to the cause of anticommunism. Drastic nationalization and extensive reliance on SOEs probably would have raised sensitive questions about Park's past as a one-time communist sympathizer.

6. The interest rate on export loans was subsidized heavily from the mid-1960s to the beginning of the 1980s. When the 1965 interest rate reform was implemented, the interest rate on export credit was left untouched. Consequently, the rate differential between export loans and general ordinary loans widened sharply, approaching nearly 20 percentage points (Cho and Kim 1997, pp. 36–37).

7. In 1962, labor-intensive manufactures accounted for less than 15 percent of Korea's total exports of $54.8 million. In 1963, exports increased by $32 million to $86.8 million (a 58.4 percent jump!), and labor-intensive manufactures such as textiles and footwear accounted for more than 80 percent of this increase. Overall, exports increased at an average annual rate of 35 percent in real terms from 1963 to 1969 (Yoo 1996, pp. 8–9).

8. In the First and Second Five-Year Economic Development Plan periods (1962–71), foreign savings accounted for 52.8 percent and 39.4 percent of total investment, respectively. The share of foreign savings in investment remained significant through the 1970s, hovering around 20 percent.

References

Amsden, Alice H. 1989. *Asia's Next Giant: South Korea and Late Industrialization.* New York: Oxford University Press.

Aoki, Masahiko, Hyung-ki Kim, and Masahiro Okuno-Fujiwara, eds. 1997. *The Role of Government in East Asian Economic Development: Comparative Institutional Analysis.* New York: Oxford University Press.

Arthur, W. Brian. 1994. *Increasing Returns and Path Dependence in the Economy.* Ann Arbor: University of Michigan Press.

Cha, Dong-Se, and Phillip Wonhyuk Lim. 2000. "In Search of a New Capitalist Spirit for the Korean Economy." In Kenneth Judd and Young-Ki Lee, eds., *An Agenda for Economic Reform in Korea: International Perspectives,* pp. 449–89. Stanford, Calif.: Hoover Institution Press.

Cho, Yoon Je, and Joon Kyung Kim. 1997. *Credit Policies and the Industrialization of Korea.* Seoul: Korea Development Institute.

David, Paul A. 1985. "Clio and the Economics of QWERTY." *American Economic Review* 75: 332–37.

————. 2000. "Path Dependence, Its Critics and the Quest for 'Historical Economics'" Mimeo, Stanford University.

Dertouzos, Michael L., et al. 1989. *Made in America: Regaining the Productive Edge*. Cambridge, Mass.: MIT Press.

Haggard, Stephan. 1990. *Pathways from the Periphery: The Politics of Growth in the Newly Industrializing Countries*. Ithaca, N.Y.: Cornell University Press.

Hahn, Chin Hee, and Jong-Il Kim. 2000. "Sources of East Asian Growth: Some Evidence from Cross-Country Studies." Paper prepared for the Global Research Project, *Explaining Growth*, initiated by the World Bank.

Jones, Leroy P., and Il SaKong. 1980. *Government, Business, and Entrepreneurship in Economic Development: The Korean Case*. Cambridge, Mass.: Harvard University Press.

Kim, Chung-yum. 1994. *Policymaking on the Front Lines: Memoirs of a Korean Practitioner, 1945–79*. Washington, D.C.: Economic Development Institute of The World Bank.

————. 1995. *A Thirty-Year History of Korean Economic Policy: A Memoir* [in Korean]. Seoul: Joong-Ang Daily News.

Kim, Eun Mee. 1997. *Big Business, Strong State: Collusion and Conflict in South Korean Development, 1960–1990*. Albany, N.Y.: State University of New York Press.

Kimiya, Tadashi. 1991. "The 'Failure' of the Inward-Looking Deepening Strategy in South Korea: The Limits of the State's Structural Autonomy in the 5.16 Military Government." Ph.D. dissertation, Korea University [in Korean].

Krueger, Anne O. 1979. *The Developmental Role of the Foreign Sector and Aid*. Cambridge, Mass.: Harvard University Press.

Lim, Wonhyuk. 2000. *The Origin and Evolution of the Korean Economic System*. Policy Study 2000–03. Seoul: Korea Development Institute.

Low, Linda. 1991. *The Political Economy of Privatisation in Singapore*. Singapore: McGraw-Hill.

Mason, Edward S., Mahn Je Kim, Dwight H. Perkins, Kwang Suk Kim, and David C. Cole. 1980. *The Economic and Social Modernization of the Republic of Korea*. Cambridge: Harvard University Press.

O, Wonchul. 1995. *Korean-Style Economic Building: An Engineering Approach* [in Korean]. Seoul: Kia Economic Research Institute.

Park, Chung Hee. 1963. *The Country, the Revolution and I*. Seoul: Hollym Corporation.

Perkins, Dwight H. 1997. "Structural Transformation and the Role of the State: Korea, 1945–1995." In Dong-Se Cha, Kwang Suk Kim, and Dwight H. Perkins, eds., *The Korean Economy 1945–1995: Performance and Vision for the 21st Century,* pp. 57–98. Seoul: Korea Development Institute.

Rodrik, Dani. 1995. "Getting Interventions Right: How South Korea and Taiwan Grew Rich." NBER Working Paper No. 4964, Cambridge, Mass.

———. 1999. *The New Global Economy and Developing Countries: Making Openness Work.* Washington, D.C.: Overseas Development Council.

Shin, Inseok, ed. 2000. *The Korean Crisis: Before and After.* Seoul: Korea Development Institute.

Stern, Joseph J., Ji-hong Kim, Dwight H. Perkins, and Jung-ho Yoo. 1995. *Industrialization and the State: The Korean Heavy and Chemical Industry Drive.* Cambridge, Mass.: Harvard Institute for International Development.

World Bank. 1993. *The East Asian Miracle: Economic Growth and Public Policy.* New York: Oxford University Press.

Yoo, Jungho. 1996. "Challenges to the Newly Industrialized Countries: A Reinterpretation of Korea's Growth Experience." KDI Working Paper No. 9608, Seoul: Korea Development Institute.

7

CONTINUING CONFUSION: ENTRY PRICES IN TELECOMMUNICATIONS

Peter Temin

The Telecommunications Act of 1996 says that many prices need to be set according to costs. This appears to be a great advance over previous language that required only that prices be nondiscriminatory, just, and reasonable. I want to argue here that the advance is illusory. Regulatory battles over the meaning of costs show that they are no more concrete than the prior standard. The same battles have been going on now for forty years with many changes of language, but little advance in clarity or agreement.

Current debates and political struggles over the price of entry into local service echo the debates of twenty and thirty years ago over the price of entry into private-line and switched interexchange services.[1] The question was posed then as now in terms of costs. But the costs of what? This essay compares the debates about entry into private-line and switched interexchange services in the 1960s and 1970s with current debates about entry into local service. Debates in the 1960s and 1970s revolved around fully distributed costs (FDC) and long-run incremental costs (LRIC). Debates in the 1990s in the implementation of the Telecommunications Act of 1996 revolve around the Efficient Component Pricing Rule (ECPR), Total System LRIC (TSLRIC), and Total Element LRIC (TELRIC). Despite the change in nomenclature, the concepts and arguments are the same, and many *new* prices are far from costs.

The Federal Communications Commission (FCC) has been constant in these forty years in its efforts to promote competition. But its position on pricing standards has changed. This essay tries to identify what has changed and what has not in this ongoing debate. I argue that the issues in question have remained the same—and unresolved—for forty years. The commission's economic analysis has not increased in sophistication over these four decades. I argue this position by analyzing the debates over Telpak in the 1960s, Exchange Network Facilities for Interstate Access (ENFIA) in the 1970s, and the Telecommunications Act of 1996 now. I focus particularly on the first of these because it illustrates the terms of debate clearly and because it reveals that today's issues were current forty years ago. I close by placing current prices for the Internet in older debates.

I

The story of interconnection begins in 1959 when the FCC decided that radio frequencies above 890 megahertz (that is, microwaves) should be made available for private point-to-point communication.[2] AT&T, which owned the entire Bell System at this time (offering both local and interexchange service), had set charges for this service to make it competitive with switched telephone service, known in the trade as message toll service (MTS). The price of MTS in turn was set according to agreements between AT&T and the FCC that implemented a regulatory costing methodology known as the *separations process* in which revenues and expenses were divided between intrastate and interstate jurisdictions. The cost of interstate transmission had been falling rapidly in the years after World War II, and the government asked AT&T to shift more and more of its local access costs into the interstate category. This shift resulted in separations payments from AT&T's Long Lines to the Bell Operating Companies and independent telephone companies, the forerunner of the current interexchange access charge, that kept local service cheap and interstate prices high in 1959 (Temin and Peters 1985). Point-to-point services were not covered by the separations agreement, but AT&T had set high prices for them to protect its market for switched service.

Motorola, the primary supplier of microwave equipment, estimated that after ten years of private microwave systems, AT&T's revenues would fall by less than 3 percent. This loss may have appeared trivial to people observing

AT&T from the outside, but it hardly seemed insignificant within the telephone company. AT&T established a planning group to consider the implications of the FCC's *Above 890* decision and propose a response to it. AT&T's internal planning group recommended a dramatic reduction in AT&T's rates for private-line service to meet the competition from private microwave systems. AT&T's "offering was intended to be a mirror image of the economic characteristics of private microwave."[3] It consequently was based on the cost structure of a hypothetical competitor of AT&T, not on that of AT&T itself.

AT&T's proposed Telpak tariff allowed buyers to choose from a limited number of offered capacities and pay a fixed rate per mile for the capacity, regardless of use. Option A consisted of 12 voice-grade channels; Option B, 24; Option C, 60; and Option D, 240. There also were terminal charges for active channels according to the way and the extent to which the channels were being used. The suggested rates from AT&T approximated the costs that a firm would face if it built its own system. Options A and B reduced prices by about half; Option C by three-quarters; D by seven-eighths.[4]

The regulatory standard of nondiscriminatory, just, and reasonable prices has been interpreted over the years as precluding volume discounts. Value-of-service pricing allowed prices to vary by class of service, but not by the size of customers. No account was taken of the economies of serving large customers; the ideal of treating all customers alike was more powerful than the ideal of varying prices with costs. The Telpak tariff therefore was a sharp break from traditional regulatory pricing. AT&T wanted to vary prices by the costs of serving individual private-line customers, even though it had no desire to make a wholesale switch from value-of-service pricing to prices that would reflect costs throughout the telephone network.

AT&T had opened a Pandora's box by basing a particular price on costs. Given that AT&T's proposed rates did not reflect AT&T's physical facility, but rather the alternative physical facility that would have been employed if AT&T were not supplying the service, the question of what costs to use would lead to enduring controversy. And if the expense of serving private-line customers was to determine the price of their services, why not use the expense of other services to set their prices? The Telpak controversy lasted for fifteen years and revolved around the same issues that are now critical in the implementation of the Telecommunications Act of 1996.

AT&T, as threatened incumbent, was acting then as it does now as an aspiring entrant (into local service). It was championing low prices in order to discourage entry of others as it now champions low prices to promote its own entry. The difference, of course, is that it was on the selling side before, the buying side now. Telpak was not the price charged for interconnection; it was the incumbent company's price for services competing with those of new entrants.

AT&T now supports the use of a theoretical network model in pricing access to the local loop.[5] Like the calculations underlying the Telpak tariff, this model is unrelated to any existing phone company's actual costs. It is a hypothetical cost structure, the cost of an alternate supply of telecommunications services if incumbent firms were not supplying them. This position is easier to maintain as an entrant than as an incumbent. It also is easier to use for a minor source of revenue such as private lines than for a company's main business.

AT&T presented the Telpak tariff to the FCC staff in December 1960. Motorola and Western Union, competitors whose business was being threatened, attacked the Telpak rates as discriminatory, not compensatory—that is, not high enough to cover the Bell System's costs—and designed to destroy competition. These were serious charges; the Communications Act specified that "any unjust or unreasonable discrimination in charges" was unlawful.[6] The commission, attempting to structure the arguments for and against Telpak, defined three possible ways in which Telpak would be lawful. First, Telpak would not be discriminatory if the Telpak service was functionally different from other private-line service. Second, Telpak would be not unreasonably discriminatory if it was functionally the same as other services but the rate differences arose from different costs. Third, Telpak service would be sufficiently dissimilar from other private-line service to justify different rates even if the costs were the same, if non-Telpak customers would benefit from the tariff through retention of otherwise lost income—that is, the surplus of revenues over costs.[7]

AT&T, replying to the FCC's explicit criteria, asserted that Telpak service was indeed different and—even if it wasn't—AT&T's costs of furnishing it were different. The FCC rejected both claims out of hand, although we shall see the FCC employing exactly this reasoning to defend a pricing rule today. The question then boiled down to the third possibility, whether Telpak imposed a burden on the other users of the telephone network. A decade later, this would become known as "the burden test" associated with William Baumol, who was an economic consultant to AT&T after 1966. The FCC did not explicitly adopt this test in 1961, referring to it only as "the principal argument of AT&T," but it still used the burden test in evaluating whether Telpak was discriminatory.[8] Since the income available to pay common costs or to provide income to stock holders was dependent on the costs of services, the FCC's criterion required the calculation of costs.

The burden test now goes by the name Efficient Component Pricing Rule (ECPR), also associated with Baumol (Baumol and Sidak 1994). It is a more severe test than most economists would impose for a test of predatory pricing. For them, the question is whether the price exceeds the relevant costs, that is, whether the rates are compensatory. In the burden test and ECPR, if the service being repriced takes away business from other services furnished by the incumbent that earn a surplus of revenue over costs, then the gain from selling more of the repriced service must outweigh the loss from the other services. The burden test and ECPR both start from the revenue flows that are the focus of rate-of-return regulation. They give the rate payers a property right in the surpluses generated by the existing rate structure, formalizing an enduring characteristic of telephone and other utility prices.

Once the FCC ruled that criteria for the lawfulness of AT&T's Telpak rates depended on their relation to costs, the way in which costs were calculated moved to the center of the regulatory stage. The traditional role of costs in the regulatory process had been to determine the overall rate of return of the telephone system and to separate interstate and intrastate assets. This separation was used to divide revenues and expenses between intrastate and interstate regulatory jurisdiction, generating payments from AT&T's Long Lines to the Bell Operating Companies. The costs were the total costs of the system as a whole or of the interstate and intrastate parts of it. And they were historical; they represented the costs of the existing plant as it had been accumulated over the years (Temin 1987, chap. 1).

AT&T anticipated an expansion of its private-line services at Telpak rates. It therefore would be constructing new equipment to provide these services, a process in which it was continuously engaged but that would be accelerated by the new low rates. To decide whether Telpak was compensatory, AT&T calculated the costs of supplying these services. The company argued that Telpak revenue should be compared with the cost of the new equipment that would be used to provide the new services, reasoning that "so long as the Telpak rates covered the costs of that additional plant, the business we in turn obtained by offering the service would be profitable to the Bell System."[9] Phrased differently, rates calculated on this basis would pass the burden test. In modern terms, they also were forward-looking.

Anticipating possible FCC objections to the use of current costs, AT&T furnished both these costs and "in plant" or historical costs, even though only current costs were used in the initial Telpak filing. AT&T's preferred costs, current or incremental costs, were derived from a study of the actual construction costs by the Bell System in 1958–60, the years immediately before the investigation. The "in plant" costs were calculated from the historical record as represented by the data and methodology used for the separations process. As in the separations process, all costs were distributed among the telecommunications services.

The FCC's response to all of the cost estimates it received was complex. It first applied the burden test. With the aid of several rough assumptions about demand elasticities and cost-price ratios, the FCC concluded that Telpak would generate less net revenue to AT&T than sales at individual private-line rates. In other words, the lower per unit profit under Telpak would reduce profits more than the expansion of sales from these lower rates would increase them.[10] Telpak failed the burden test.

The FCC could have stopped there. If it believed the burden test was the appropriate regulatory standard, it should have ordered AT&T to revise the Telpak rates. But the commission either did not like the burden test or was unwilling to rely on the assumptions used to implement it. It went on to apply the less stringent test proposed by Motorola and Western Union: was Telpak compensatory? This decision would lead the FCC into a new world of cross subsidization.

The commission was faced with several different cost estimates. It had received two sets of costs from AT&T and another set from Motorola, representing the costs of independent microwave systems. The FCC used AT&T's "in plant" (historical) costs to estimate that the overall rate of return on Telpak was 6.5 percent as of October 1, 1961, a reasonable rate in light of AT&T's total allowed interstate rate of return of 7.4 percent. After some manipulation of these data, however, the FCC found that the returns varied for the different categories of Telpak. Telpak A realized 10 percent; B less; C still less; and D actually had a 1 percent loss.[11] Telpak D therefore did not simply flunk the burden test; it was predatory pricing. Because regulatory pricing did not allow quantity discounts, the FCC regarded these categories of Telpak as separate services.

The commission, faced with a choice of cost standards, had opted for those used traditionally in rate-of-return regulation and the separations process. These costs fully distributed AT&T's costs among its many services. The FCC reached back into its regulatory tradition and ignored AT&T's argument that the tradition was becoming irrelevant. The FCC, consistent with its initial estimate that only a tiny portion of the Bell System's network was at risk, argued implicitly through its choice of an average cost standard that AT&T should be considered a protected monopoly. The telephone company, by contrast, argued that it was already a competitive firm. Both positions were overstated.

The FCC compared Telpak A and B to Motorola's estimates of private microwave costs for the appropriate number of channels. It concluded that private microwave systems could not compete with AT&T's normal private-line service for these relatively small capacities. It therefore ruled that Telpak A and B were not justified by competitive necessity.[12] By itself, this was not unwelcome to AT&T since the demand for the smaller options had fallen short of expectations. But it left Telpak C and D, neither of which earned a rate of return even close to AT&T's total rate of return by the FCC's preferred accounting and one of which actually was making losses. As the FCC saw it, there could be no clearer case; Telpak was unlawful in the terms of the Communications Act, and the FCC ordered AT&T in 1964 to file new rates.[13]

Telpak users, as well as AT&T, appealed the decision. Their effort signaled the arrival of a new political force: Telpak users who resisted the commission's efforts to raise AT&T's private-line rates. The burden test would have empowered users of ordinary telephone services. No such calculation was needed for Telpak customers. They quickly had acquired a property right in these low rates.

The FCC gave AT&T until the following September to eliminate Telpak A and B. It deferred action on Telpak C and D, asking AT&T to submit new cost data justifying the two larger options. AT&T appealed to the U.S. Court of Appeals. The court reaffirmed the FCC decision in 1966, but the FCC deadline was put off until August 1, 1967.[14] The original Telpak rates therefore were in force for six years despite the FCC's finding that Telpak A and B were not justified on one basis, and that Telpak C and D were unjustified on another. (Telpak C and D rates did not change even in 1967.) The delay allowed AT&T to continue offering service at rates designed to limit competitive inroads into its private-line business.

While Telpak was in the courts, AT&T's disaggregated cost data were discussed in the context of "The Seven Way Cost Study." The FCC requested that AT&T allocate revenues and *book cost* among a variety of services in 1963 as part of the commission's investigation of domestic telegraph tariffs. The FCC was concerned in this inquiry to protect Western Union from unfair competition, but in light of the other questions before it at the time, the commission broadened its study to all interstate services, divided into seven categories.

AT&T argued that book costs—which distributed costs to services by rules similar to those employed in the separations process—were inappropriate for the questions under consideration. Nevertheless, AT&T complied with the FCC's request: "As a matter of practical necessity the principles of the [separations] manual were used as the basis of the seven-way split."[15] AT&T's new cost study was based on the year ending August 31, 1964, and presented to the FCC in September 1965. The FCC concluded that the overall rate of return for the seven categories of interstate services was 7.5 percent, but the earned rate of return for Telpak was only 0.3 percent.[16] AT&T, it seemed, was not making any profit on Telpak; it was furnishing this service to preempt the competition by discriminatory pricing.

AT&T also computed its own set of costs based on current costs. Telpak earned a 5.5 percent return in AT&T's calculation, near the company's overall interstate return of 7.5 percent. It was lower than the average return because demand was skewed more toward the larger size categories of Telpak than had been anticipated in 1961. If the demand had developed in the proportions forecast in 1961, Telpak's earnings on a current cost basis would have been 9.5 percent.[17] To AT&T, the variation between realized Telpak profit and average interstate profits was well within a normal error. To the FCC, it was out of the ballpark.

The FCC's version of AT&T's rate of return on Telpak, 0.3 percent, would haunt the telephone company for years to come. It appeared to be such a clear signal of the company's predatory practices that it was cited often (Brock 1981, p. 210; Breyer 1982, p. 305). AT&T's demurs about the commission's methodology fell on deaf ears, and its preferred calculations went unnoticed. The company had given the commission the ammunition with which to shoot at it, and the commission had been unable to resist.

It was clear that the rates for Telpak C and D would have to be raised substantially when parts A and B were canceled in order to keep the rates compensatory, even though the FCC and AT&T had not agreed on a costing methodology. AT&T was willing to raise Telpak rates by 1967. The competitive threat from Motorola and its customers had been deflected temporarily, and rising costs made entry unprofitable even with higher Telpak rates. AT&T decided to propose the Telpak rate increase early in 1967, but to defer filing the increase in order to give the customers time to react. The issue by then was not AT&T's desires, but the ability of Telpak users to prevent their rates from going up. The new rates were filed in 1968 and again in 1969 and became effective, after several legal delays and suspensions, on February 1, 1970.[18]

Opposition showed that the property rights of customers were real—whether the users were the consumers of AT&T's traditional services or of its new and innovative ones. Property rights also came into being very quickly. But the property rights of users in specific rates were limited. They were able to delay the rise in Telpak rates for two or three years, not to stop them.

As Telpak rates finally were being raised, Alfred Kahn published his classic, *The Economics of Regulation*. Kahn forcefully advocated the use of marginal or incremental costs in his book, but he was far more careful and cautious than AT&T. He confronted the problem of common costs in a Marshallian analysis.

He concluded that "the economically efficient solution does involve equating the price of each joint product to its marginal *opportunity* cost" (Kahn 1970, vol. I, p. 83, emphasis added).

In other words, the price of each product has to equal the marginal cost of supplying an additional unit of that product, given the existing production of the other products with joint or common costs. If a product is in low demand, so that some of the jointly produced product is being discarded, then the price for that product is simply the marginal cost of retrieving that which was to be discarded. (This was AT&T's position for Telpak.) But if a product is in high demand, so that an increase in demand for it would require additional production of all the joint products, then consumers of this product must pay the entire joint cost. At the margin, the common cost is incurred for the benefit of this product alone; the other jointly produced products are discarded. The marginal opportunity cost includes the common cost.

Marginal opportunity costs therefore can vary from including none of the joint costs to including all of them. It depends on demand. Happily, Kahn's analysis did not generate a knife-edge solution of all or nothing. In many cases, the demands of all jointly produced products are such that they are all demanded (at positive prices) in the relevant range of output. Then the marginal opportunity cost is shared among the products. In economics jargon, the vertical sum of the demand curves for each product equals the marginal cost curve of production—including the joint costs and any other additional costs for individual products—at a point indicating equal consumption of all products at each product's price. Each product's price also equals the marginal opportunity cost at this point. The marginal opportunity cost depends on the location of the demand curve—that is, on the intensity of demand.[19]

Kahn's rule therefore implies that demand considerations affect the applicable cost of any service. The traditional distinction between demand and supply so beloved of economists is not useful here. Employing incremental costs without consideration of joint costs will not cover common costs. And the efficient prices that cover these costs cannot be derived from costs alone; no fully distributed costs of the sort discussed in the Telpak debates will generate the marginal opportunity cost. This opportunity cost can only be derived from an examination of both costs and demands of all jointly produced products or services.

The next few years saw a variety of further cost discussions among Baumol, AT&T representatives, and the FCC staff. No reference was made to Kahn's analysis, just as Telpak was not mentioned in Kahn's book. The regulatory discussions took place in a continuing series of informal meetings in which AT&T's and the FCC's economics experts explored their differences, punctuated by various formal proceedings. Throughout these discussions, AT&T's expert, Baumol, argued for the use of long-run incremental costs (LRIC), as he preferred to label current costs, in the presence of competition. The FCC's expert, William Melody, countered that long-run incremental costs were arbitrary. Since fully distributed costs (FDC) had been accepted and agreed to by both a variety of regulatory jurisdictions and AT&T for the purpose of dividing revenues and costs for separation purposes, they should be used also for rate-making purposes.[20] The discussions clarified the difference between these two points of view, but generated no agreement.

The FCC followed the recommendations of its common carrier bureau chief, Bernard Strassburg, and terminated its Telpak investigations "without opinion on the merits" in 1970. It incorporated the record it had accumulated into a new investigation that Strassburg later regarded as "a waste of time and effort."[21] The FCC did not decide whether to use LRIC or FDC in evaluating rates until 1976, although it did not gather any new information after the hearings pitting Baumol and Melody against each other.

Hearings on costs were held in 1971 that anticipated the arguments these economists would make a decade later in the U.S. antitrust suit against AT&T. Baumol formalized the burden test first mentioned a decade previously and argued strenuously for the use of LRIC. He also reiterated a position articulated by James Bonbright five years earlier that LRIC could not be used for all services when there were large common fixed costs.[22] He therefore was in the position of advocating LRIC for some purposes while agreeing to use fully distributed (historical) costs for other purposes. In particular, Baumol approved the use of FDC for determining the rates of monopoly services that would provide the revenue anticipated under rate-of-return regulation. He was taken to task for this apparent inconsistency in his views five years later when the FCC finally expressed its opinion on the matter of cost methodology.[23]

Entrants advocating the use of incremental costs do not have to worry about the incumbent's common costs. AT&T did not have that luxury in the

1970s as it tried to lower its service prices to deter entry. It has that luxury now as it tries to get the regional Bell operating companies (RBOCs) to lower interconnection prices to encourage entry. Given the level of the regulatory discussions, Kahn's analysis may have been too complex to be used. It nevertheless provides a way to avoid the arbitrary assignment of joint costs to products, and it is simple in comparison with current economic analysis.

The FCC's delay was caused by internal debate. Strassburg had on his desk at the time of his retirement in 1973 a draft decision supporting the use of LRIC.[24] The FCC was not as steadfast in its commitment to average costs as its published opinions in the 1960s and 1970s suggest. The staff of the Common Carrier Bureau had recognized after a decade of debate that the introduction of competition altered the context in which AT&T operated and called for new cost allocation methods. This view, however, was not that of the new chief of the Common Carrier Bureau, Walter Hinchman, who did not send Strassburg's draft up to the commission. He called for a new draft reaffirming the applicability of average costs, and the FCC formally adopted FDC as its cost standard in 1976, fifteen years after the introduction of Telpak created a need for a disaggregated cost standard.[25]

II

At almost the same time that the Telpak debate wound down to its anticlimactic end, MCI moved its offerings and the debate from private lines to switched service; it began to offer its Execunet service, a switched telephone service like AT&T's MTS. The FCC agreed with AT&T that its earlier decisions allowing private-line competition did not extend to MCI's Execunet service. But the court ruled that the FCC had failed explicitly to restrict MCI to private-line services. In the absence of a specific exclusion, the court did not see any regulatory barrier to MCI's new service.[26]

This decision raised the question what rates AT&T would charge MCI for the interconnection needed to operate Execunet service. If MCI were allowed to subscribe to local service at ordinary business rates, it would be doubly favored in its competition with the Bell System. It would receive the local service for rates subsidized by AT&T's long-distance service through the separations process. In addition, it would not be obligated to set prices on its long-distance service to earn a return on part of the local plant, as message toll service by the Bell System was required to do. Using the same equipment as AT&T, MCI's capital costs would be over one-third lower (Temin 1990).

AT&T was not about to let this happen without a struggle. In Telpak, AT&T had charged a low price to retard entry. But now AT&T wanted to charge a high price to retard entry. The different position reflected different circumstances. The controversy over Telpak involved the part of the Bell System that handled interexchange service. This corresponds to AT&T today. The controversy over MCI's Execunet service involved the part of the Bell System that provided local service. This corresponds to the RBOCs today. AT&T acted consistently in seeking to limit entry, but inconsistently in terms of pricing rules. Because it operated an integrated network, it had to adapt its rule to the part of the network under attack. It championed LRIC in the 1960s, FDC in the 1970s.

Recalling the reasoning that led to the separations process, AT&T argued that long-distance service offered by MCI, no less than long-distance service by AT&T, had to pay part of the cost of the local network. The Bell System filed its Exchange Network Facilities for Interstate Access (ENFIA) tariff with the FCC in May 1978. The tariff imposed charges on specialized common carriers like MCI equal to the charges for local interconnection assigned to AT&T's long-distance service by the separations process. It was an early example of what is now called imputation. It also was an application of FDC, newly approved in another context—Telpak—by the FCC.

From the point of view of pricing standards, AT&T and the potential entrants had switched sides. In the debate over private lines, AT&T had championed incremental costs or LRIC while entrants had supported average costs or FDC. Now AT&T wanted to charge FDC to potential entrants. MCI wanted to pay existing consumer prices, without arguing that they were incremental prices or that they fit any other normative standard. The difference between this conflict and Telpak is in the entrants' relation to AT&T's network. In Telpak, entrants were competing with the network; in ENFIA, they were interconnecting. Telpak was the price charged by AT&T to customers choosing between entrants and the Bell System. ENFIA was the price charged by AT&T to its competitors.

Not only did interconnection allow this change of pricing rules; the magnitude of AT&T's message toll service demanded it. Private lines were a small part of the Bell System's business. Long-distance service was its bread and butter. AT&T could charge LRIC for many services, but not for all, as noted above, because it needed to cover its common cost. AT&T could forgo the contribution to common costs from private lines because they were small. But it could not forgo the contribution from MTS. AT&T therefore was consistent in its higher logic, although it was championing different costing standards in separate proceedings.

The FCC was in an anomalous position. It had insisted that AT&T base its prices on FDC as a way of encouraging entry. But if AT&T could use FDC as advocated in its proposed ENFIA tariff, entry into MTS would be discouraged. The commission was not forced to articulate a position about common costs, and it did not have to choose explicitly between competing objectives. The FCC switched sides on this issue without having to make an explicit statement. Only now has the FCC made its new position explicit.

Various pressures forced AT&T to negotiate with its putative competitors in 1978 about the price they would pay for interconnection. AT&T started from its proposed tariff and admitted that some discount might be warranted for the inferior service of the competitors. Customers using Execunet, for starters, had to dial many more digits than users of the Bell System's MTS. MCI and its colleagues acknowledged in turn that they should pay something toward the costs of local networks, but the two parties were still far apart. They eventually agreed that the new entrants would pay 35 percent of the charge paid by the Bell System's MTS for local interconnection until their combined revenues exceeded $110 million. The price would rise to 45 percent until the combined revenues reached $250 million. They would be 55 percent thereafter. AT&T anticipated that the interconnection charge would continue to rise as the entrants' business increased, but this was not spelled out in the agreement.[27]

ENFIA therefore was a compromise with the advantages and disadvantages of all compromises. From a theoretical point of view, ENFIA acknowledged the importance of joint costs and the obligations of interconnectors to contribute to them. Incremental costs were not the cost standard behind ENFIA; some kind of distributed cost was. But the nature of the distributed cost was not set in the compromise. The FCC had debated endless variants of FDC a decade earlier, and the negotiations that produced ENFIA did not advance the discussion. Because the new tariff was a compromise, the questions of how to determine the size of common costs and appropriate contributions to them were swept under the rug.

The principle underlying the compromise was clear, however. All interexchange carriers (long-distance companies) had to contribute something toward the joint costs of the local network. The questions of how much and whether all interexchange carriers should pay the same amount were not addressed in any general way, and theoretical clarity was not sought. But the compromise clearly rejected the LRIC standard. The FCC held to the FDC principle without confronting the problems of its implementation.

III

Everything changed with the 1982 consent decree known as the MFJ and divestiture and again with the Telecommunications Act of 1996. But the cast of characters only has been reshuffled to make the same arguments to each other—rather like *Six Characters in Search of an Author*. The positions today are expressed in new language, but the new terms are simply reruns of familiar concepts. It should be noted that postdivestiture AT&T is only an interexchange carrier like MCI, and its interests diverged from those of predivestiture AT&T representing the whole Bell System.

The Telecommunications Act said that the "just and reasonable rate for the interconnection of facilities and equipment . . . and . . . for network elements . . . (A) shall be (i) based on the cost (determined without reference to a rate-of-return or other rate-based proceeding) of providing the interconnection or network element . . . and (ii) nondiscriminatory, and (B) may include a reasonable profit."[28] This provision clearly breaks with the old rate-of-return process, but substitutes a directive that harks back to the debates under the old standard. All the prices debated in connection with Telpak and ENFIA were based on costs. The question always was what was meant by costs. The 1996 Act was not specific about what alternate process should be used to calculate costs.

The FCC interpreted these directives in two stages. The Notice of Proposed Rulemaking stated the commission's intent to use incremental costs in one of its many variants as its definition of costs. The FCC cited the authority of Alfred Kahn in this interpretation. Their reference carried a 1988 date, but the cited book is only a reprint of the 1970 book discussed above. In the FCC's footnote, Kahn was joined or echoed by other authors, who must be regarded in this context as secondary sources.[29] By basing its current position on a book published in 1970, the FCC implicitly acknowledged that progress on these issues in the past thirty years has been virtually nil. More recent contributions to the academic literature emphasizing incentives and imperfect information were ignored.[30] In addition, no mention was made of Kahn's marginal opportunity cost.

MCI and AT&T proposed to implement the commission's directive by means of a design for a theoretical network that would provide the same services as the existing telecommunications network. Common costs appear seldom if at all in this model. Like Telpak, this theoretical network is a "green field" model—or in the latest version a "scorched node" model—giving the hypothetical costs that a putative entrant would incur.[31] Postdivestiture AT&T and MCI, as entrants into local service, can make this point more easily than the old AT&T could thirty years earlier as the incumbent supplier of private-line services. They do not need to explain the difference between their forward-looking costs and actual current costs because they do not currently have any local operations costs. And they do not need to worry about recovering common costs because the costs in question are the RBOCs', not theirs.

Baumol supported this position on behalf of AT&T as he did thirty years earlier. The question of common costs was disposed of in a footnote claiming, "there are no significant common or shared costs among the groups of network elements." Baumol and his coauthors argued in the text of their affidavit, however, that RBOCs can misallocate costs in anticompetitive manners.[32] It would be hard—though not impossible—to do so if there were not common costs to be allocated.

The RBOCs naturally opposed this initiative and branded the theoretical model as nonsense. They took the position that the old AT&T took in the

ENFIA negotiations, acting then as a supplier of local services, that entrants who interconnect with the telephone network need to contribute to the common costs of maintaining the existing network. They face the same suspicion and hostility at the FCC that the Bell System faced two decades ago. Without the clear evidence of the separations process, however, they now are hard-pressed to identify common costs.

After considering the comments from these various parties, the FCC issued its rules. The commission confirmed its earlier suggestion that forward-looking LRIC was the appropriate basis on which to calculate costs.[33] This was AT&T's position in proposing the Telpak tariff in 1961. The company wanted to use incremental costs based on anticipated investments; the FCC at that time insisted on using historical data and some form of distributed-cost pricing. The FCC today agrees with AT&T's position in 1961. No additional clarity or subtlety appears to have been introduced.

The FCC acknowledged in its rules that there might be common costs.[34] The commission announced that it would be happy with two ways of dealing with common costs. The first was to "allocate common costs using a fixed allocator" like a fixed mark-up on incremental costs. This is a form of FDC, the FCC's approved costing method in the 1960s and 1970s. It has no beneficial efficiency properties, and it will lead to the same kind of controversy I have described above. The second approved costing method is to allocate the common costs to services where competition is pending. Prices for competitive services would be high; for monopoly services, low. This is the opposite of the two-tier pricing scheme proposed by Baumol on behalf of AT&T in the 1970s. It was criticized then as arbitrary. It is arbitrary today as well. And it is hard to see how high prices for competitive services can be maintained.

The FCC went out of its way to reject Ramsey pricing, that is, basing prices on the elasticity of demand as well as costs. This mode of pricing has beneficial efficiency properties, as economists have known since the 1920s. The FCC cited Frank Ramsey's original paper (1927) and then a book by Mitchell and Vogelsang (1991). Their book is distinguished by the disjunction between its two halves on the theory and practice of telecommunications pricing. The FCC cited them for their description of Ramsey pricing, and it effectively turns their description of the industry into a normative rule.

The FCC argued that Ramsey prices for "bottleneck facilities" would be too high to promote competition.[35] This position ignores the question of whether competition is desirable if the facilities in question are truly bottlenecks. It also disregards the progress of technology, which tends to eliminate existing bottlenecks. In the specific case cited by the FCC of the local loop, wireless technology is the obvious candidate. Ramsey pricing, by making it attractive to develop new technologies, may be a good way to promote competition.

The same issues dominate discussion of the pricing rules for Internet service providers. These firms are the successors to the subjects of the FCC's various computer inquiries. Starting in the 1970s, about the same time as the ENFIA controversy, the FCC tried to draw a line between communications (AT&T) and computers (IBM). On one side of the line was the Bell System with its separations process; on the other, data processing that was not part of the telephone network.[36] This line has become ever more blurred—even nonexistent—as computers have become more powerful and versatile and as data have come to be traded back and forth across various networks. Yet the separations process has been transformed into access charges, and the presumed difference between communications and data processing has resulted in no charges being levied for communication between computers. This communication began as point-to-point services—like those involved in the *Above 890* decision—that were part of the federal government's efforts to provide communication between computer centers to save on expensive purchases of computing power. The FCC created a specific exemption from access charges for data services. As computers became cheaper and more widespread, these services evolved gradually into the Internet (Abbate 1999). The initial exemption from access charges continues today as an exemption for Internet service providers for Internet access, Internet telephony, and e-mail.

Internet telephony has been making great strides recently in part because Internet service providers do not have to pay the access charges to local exchange companies that conventional interexchange carriers do. They are in the position MCI aspired to for its Execunet service. The parallel is in fact stronger due to the use of "reciprocal compensation" in which companies pay each other for terminating their calls. An Internet service provider that registers as a competitive local exchange company receives this compensation since it receives calls but does not make any.

Execunet in the 1970s was favored both because it did not have to pay access charges and because it could subscribe to subsidized local service. Internet service providers now are doubly favored because they do not pay access charges and they are paid (by other telephone companies) each time a subscriber dials up. As AT&T did in the 1970s, the RBOCs have protested the Internet service providers' exclusion from the responsibility to pay access charges. The FCC responded that they did not have to be treated like interexchange carriers (long-distance telephone companies) because they were not utilizing the facilities of the local exchange company in the same way or for the same purpose as companies offering plain old telephone service.[37]

This ruling has been affirmed by the court on the grounds that Internet service providers do not utilize the services of the local exchange carrier in the same way as customers "who are assessed per-minute interstate access charges."[38] This statement echoes AT&T's claim of forty years before that its Telpak service was not offered at discriminatory pricing because the service was different from message toll service, even though it used the same facilities. Although the FCC rejected that argument in the early 1960s, it embraced it in the 1980s for Internet service providers and had it confirmed by the court in the late 1990s. This shows once again how durable and unresolved the issues are, enabling various bodies to restate and reverse earlier positions. The court's statement also carries the uncomfortable implication that the Internet exemption to interexchange access charges could vanish if customers were charged on a per minute basis.

The point is not who is right or wrong in these ongoing disputes. It is that the same issues are still being disputed and litigated. The issues were set up approximately forty years ago when AT&T introduced the Telpak tariff. The FCC, then as now, evaluated the tariff by its relation to costs. The issues, then as now, were whether historical or prospective costs should be used, how an allowance for common costs should be included, and when it is discriminatory to charge different prices for the use of the same facilities. These issues were not resolved then and are still open now. Internet users are the beneficiaries. Like the users of Telpak, they now have a property right in free access and e-mail.

IV

Plus ça change, plus ç'est la même chose

The issue of common costs bedevils regulators and legislators trying to introduce competition into previously monopolized markets. Incumbents always say that these costs are large and can be ignored only at the customers' peril. Entrants by contrast say these costs are figments of the incumbents' imagination. The debates—clothed in industry-specific jargon—restate familiar positions over and over again.

The FCC has been very hostile to incumbents for a generation. It was eager to reduce the Bell System's monopoly when the Bell System existed. And it is now eager to reduce the RBOCs' monopoly. The FCC started this task initially by emphasizing the importance and magnitude of these fixed costs. When AT&T wished to reduce the price for private lines to discourage entry, the FCC argued that it was short-changing other customers who had to pay for the fixed cost. The FCC now has changed sides. It urges the RBOCs to charge low prices for telephone interconnection on the basis that joint fixed costs are too small to worry about and approves even lower prices for Internet connections on the basis that this is a different service than telephony.

Other regulatory bodies have not been so sanguine. Electric power is being opened up to competition in a race with telecommunications. Pricing decisions are being made at the state level in that industry, overseen by the Federal Energy Regulatory Commission. In Massachusetts and California, prices are being reduced only slowly so that incumbent utilities can phase out their fixed common costs. In both states, the regulators have created a new actor, the Independent System Operator, who will perform many of the centralized functions formerly provided by the utility. In particular, the Independent System Operator will configure the network, decide on new capacity, and contract for independent supplies. The Federal Energy Regulatory Commission, unlike the FCC, recognizes that there are important common costs in the provision of network services.[39]

Forty years of debate in telecommunications have failed to clarify the issues involved or to remove regulators from the issue of telecommunications pricing. Regulators continue to rehearse traditional arguments as they set prices. They are as insistent today as they were in the early 1960s that incumbent market power requires a heavy regulatory hand. Although relative prices are changing, there is no evidence that regulation decreases as prices approach "costs." We might do well to consider whether a lighter regulatory hand would be more appropriate to increasingly competitive conditions.

Notes

1. Private lines are dedicated lines to specific end points that are not switched by dialing or other means.

2. 27 FCC 359, Docket 11866 (1959).

3. Henry M. Boettinger, "Testimony," *U.S. v. AT&T*, CA 74–1698, T. 24, 896.

4. 38 FCC 373, at 385–86, Docket 14251 (1964).

5. Hatfield Associates, "The Cost of Basic Network Elements: Theory, Modeling and Policy Implications," unpublished document, prepared for MCI, Inc., March 29, 1996.

6. 48 Stat. 1064 (1934), sec. 202(a).

7. 38 FCC 373, at 376 (1964).

8. Ibid.

9. Albert M. Froggatt, "Testimony," *U.S. v. AT&T*, CA 741698, p. 8.

10. 38 FCC 373, at 390 (1964).

11. 38 FCC 373, at 392 (1964).

12. 38 FCC 373, at 386 (1964).

13. 38 FCC 373, at 396 (1964).

14. *American Trucking Association v. FCC*, 126 U.S. App DC 236, 377 F 2d 121 (1966), cert. denied 386 U.S. 943 (1967); 7 FCC 2d 30–31, Docket 16258 (1966).

15. Froggatt, "Testimony," AT&T Exhibit 90, Docket 14650 (1965), p. 5.

16. 9 FCC 2d 30, at 37, Docket 16258 (1967).

17. Froggatt, "Testimony," *U.S. v. AT&T*, p. 29.

18. 20 FCC 2d 393, Docket 18128 (1969); *Associated Press v. FCC*, 148 U.S. App DC 172, 448 F 2d 1095 (1971).

19. The demand curve for each product equals its supply curve at this point, where the supply curve is constructed on the assumption that other products are produced and sold at the same volume. Each supply curve is constructed by examining the demand curve for other products to see how much of the joint costs their consumers would pay at this volume. The supply curve shows in each case how much of the joint costs remains to be paid by the product in question. This is not a normal supply curve for a product, but it is a supply curve in the sense of

showing what must be paid to obtain an additional unit of each product. It shows the marginal opportunity cost at each level of output.

20. See, for example, Baumol, "Testimony," FCC Docket 16258 (1966); William H. Melody, "Testimony," FCC Exhibit 52, Docket 16258 (1968).

21. Bernard Strassburg, "Testimony," *U.S. v. AT&T*, CA 74–1698, T. 23450.

22. James C. Bonbright, "Testimony," AT&T Exhibit 89, Docket 14650 (1965).

23. 61 FCC 2d 587, at 613, 617, 626, Docket 18128 (1976).

24. FCC, Second Draft of Working Group in Docket 18128, Defendant's Exhibit S-2825C, *SPCC v. AT&T*, CA 78–0545.

25. 61 FCC 2d 587, at 589 (1976).

26. *MCI v. FCC*, No. 75–1635, 561 F. 2d 365 (D.C. Cir.), *cert. denied* 434 U.S. 1040, 1978.

27. FCC, *Memorandum Opinion and Order*, FCC CC Docket No. 78–371, April 12, 1979, 71 FCC 2d 440.

28. 1996 Act, sec. 101, para. 252(d)(1).

29. FCC, *Notice of Proposed Rulemaking*, CC Docket No. 96–98, April 19, 1996, p. 43n. Even though one of the cited authors, Stephen Breyer, is now a Supreme Court Justice, he does not aspire to be a professional economist.

30. For example, Laffont and Tirole (1993).

31. Hatfield Associates, "Hatfield Model, Version 2.2, Release 2: Model Description," unpublished document, September 4, 1996.

32. William J. Baumol, Janusz A. Ordover, and Robert D. Willig, "Affidavit," submitted to the FCC in response to the NPRM, April 9, 1996, pp. 3–4.

33. FCC, *First Report and Order*, Docket 96–325, August 1, 1996, sec. 7, paras. 672–78.

34. Ibid., para. 696.

35. The FCC clearly does not think this way. It closed the pricing section of the rules with a strong assertion that any prices dependent on demand—or other factors other than costs—would be discriminatory under the Act. FCC, *First Report and Order*, Docket 96–325, August 1, 1996, sec. 7, paras. 861–62.

36. FCC, *Final Decision*, FCC Docket 20828, May 2, 1980, 77 FCC 2d 384.

37. FCC, *First Report and Order*, Docket 97–158, May 16, 1997, para. 50.

38. U.S. Court of Appeals, Eighth Circuit, No. 97–2618, Southwestern Bell, Petitioner, August 19, 1998.

39. "Ferc Approves Framework for California Restructuring, Defers Tough Details, *Electric Utility Week*, December 2, 1996, p. 7; "Massachusetts Competition

Rule Affirms Rights of Distribution Firms to Franchises," *Electric Utility Week*, January 6, 1997, p. 1; "California Regulators Still Debating Extent of Direct Access Next January," *Electric Utility Week*, April, 28, 1997, p. 10.

References

Abbate, Janet. 1999. *Inventing the Internet.* Cambridge, Mass.: MIT Press.

Baumol, William J., and J. Gregory Sidak. 1994. *Toward Competition in Local Telephony.* Cambridge, Mass.: MIT Press.

Breyer, Stephen. 1982. *Regulation and Its Reform.* Cambridge, Mass.: Harvard University Press.

Brock, Gerald W. 1981. *The Telecommunications Industry.* Cambridge, Mass.: Harvard University Press.

Kahn, Alfred E. 1970. *The Economics of Regulation: Principles and Institutions.* New York: Wiley.

Laffont, Jean-Jacques, and Jean Tirole. 1993. *A Theory of Incentives in Procurement and Regulation.* Cambridge, Mass.: MIT Press.

Mitchell, Bridger M., and Ingo Vogelsang. 1991. *Telecommunications Pricing: Theory and Practice.* Cambridge, England: Cambridge University Press.

Ramsey, Frank P. 1927. "A Contribution to the Theory of Taxation." *Economic Journal* 37 (March): 47–61.

Temin, Peter. 1987. *The Fall of the Bell System.* New York: Cambridge University Press.

———. 1990. "Cross Subsidies in the Telephone Network After Divestiture." *Journal of Regulatory Economics,* 2 (December): 349–62.

Temin, Peter, and Geoffrey Peters. 1986. "Is History Stranger Than Theory? The Origin of Telephone Separations." *American Economic Review, Papers and Proceedings* 75 (May): 324–27; reprinted in William N. Parker, ed., *Economic History and the Modern Economist,* pp. 50–59 (Oxford: Basil Blackwell, 1986).

8

AFTER THE WAR BOOM: RECONVERSION ON THE PACIFIC COAST, 1943–1949

Paul W. Rhode

1. INTRODUCTION

One of the most dramatic changes in twentieth-century American history was the emergence of its Pacific Coast region as a core area of economic activity and innovation. Between 1900 and 1980, the share of the far western states (Alaska, California, Hawaii, Nevada, Oregon, and Washington) in national population more than quadrupled, rising from about 3.2 percent to almost 15.5 percent. Its share of personal income more than tripled, increasing from 5.3 percent to 17.4 percent. By 1980 the leading urban areas of the far western states—Los Angeles, the San Francisco Bay Area, and Seattle—gained world-wide recognition as centers of high technology.

Much of the traditional historiography treats the region's experience during the Second World War as the watershed event in its twentieth-century growth. For example, Gerald Nash's influential work argued that World War II represented a fundamental discontinuity in the West's development and that wartime supply contracts and facility investments were the driving forces in the rapid transformation of the Pacific states from a stagnating economic "colony" of the industrial Northeast into a dynamic pace-setting region (Nash 1990).

The West clearly experienced disproportionately rapid expansion during the early 1940s. Indeed contemporary observers referred to the wartime boom as the region's "second Gold Rush." Civilians migrated west in unprecedented

numbers to fill jobs in the region's burgeoning aircraft and shipbuilding industries. In addition, military facilities in the region were home base for thousands of soldiers and sailors engaged in the Pacific campaign. Between 1940
and 1945, the region's total population increased by 2.7 million persons, or by
over one-quarter. Nor is there much disagreement that the "engine of growth"
was military spending. Between June 1940 and June 1945, the far western
states received $27 billion in federal government spending for war supply
contracts and facility investments. This accounted for about one-eighth of the
national total, roughly twice the region's prewar share in population or manufacturing activity.

Yet there has emerged a vigorous debate about whether the Second World
War represented as fundamental a discontinuity as the Nash thesis suggests.[1]
Recent studies have pointed to evidence of stability in the region's political and
economic structure and to the roots of the region's wartime growth in its prewar
economic development. This essay attempts to advance and, in important ways,
move beyond the continuity vs. discontinuity debate by examining the Pacific
Coast's economic experience in the immediate postwar period (1945–49). I
argue here that the conversion process, which has been unduly neglected in the
recent debate, was crucial for the region's consolidation of the transitory gains
during the war into permanently higher levels of economic activity.

After military spending peaked in 1943, fears spread throughout the West
that the region's postwar economy would not provide sufficient jobs for its
greatly enlarged labor force. Serious economic disruptions were widely foreseen. In California, responsible authorities estimated that 1 million workers—
about one-quarter of the labor force—would be unemployed one year after
demobilization. In response to these challenges, public agencies such as the
California State Reconstruction and Reemployment Commission sought to
plan for orderly conversion to a peacetime economy. In addition, business
groups and local officials lobbied the federal government and eastern firms to
keep the West's new steel complex and other "war winnings" in operation.

The transition proved far easier than most observers had anticipated.
The region's unemployment rate in the immediate postwar period generally
remained in single digits and the expected mass out-migration did not occur.
Instead, the enlarged western market induced a rapid inflow of new branches

of national manufacturing firms, a vigorous expansion of existing operations, and a surge of small local startups. Many war workers and plants shifted quickly to supply civilian markets. The demands for housing, schools, and services, left unfilled during the war, fostered vigorous job growth in construction, trade, and other services. By 1950 the Pacific Coast's employment structure had largely returned to its prewar composition, although on a significantly larger scale.

Drawing inspiration from the New Economic Geography literature, as well as from the traditional historiography of the West, this essay argues that strong "home market effects" account for the relatively easy conversion experience on the Pacific Coast. Based on an empirical investigation of the long-run relationship between manufacturing production and the size of the region's market, this study finds surprising support for the highly speculative claims that the region's economic structure could support multiple equilibria and that the transitory shock of military spending during World War II helped push the Pacific Coast economy from a "low-level" equilibrium to a "higher-level" equilibrium consistent with the same fundamentals.

The next section briefly examines the nature and effects of the war boom on the West Coast economy. Section 3 discusses local conversion planning efforts, with a focus on wartime expectations about the postwar size of the Pacific Coast population, migration flows, employment levels, and unemployment rates. Section 4 details how the actual postwar experience unfolded and explores how the expansion of the home market made the transition easier than anticipated. Section 5 uses a new data set on California manufacturing to put the World War II episode into historical context by examining the long-run relationship between the growth of the region's industrial output and the size of the local market.

2. THE WAR BOOM

There is no question that World War II created an intense economic boom on the U.S. Pacific Coast. Between June 1940 and June 1945, the federal government spent about $23.5 billion in major war supply contracts and $3.5 billion for military and industrial facilities in the region. California led the way, receiving

$19.7 billion, or nearly three-quarters of the region's total expenditures.[2] The West Coast's share of national military spending, 11.8 percent, well exceeded its 1940 share of the nation's resident population, 6.5 percent, and its 1939 share of the nation's manufacturing wage-earners, 5.3 percent. But it is important to note that most of the wartime contracts were for aircraft (roughly $12 billion) and ships (about $9 billion), activities in which the region demonstrated significant comparative advantages before the attack on Pearl Harbor.[3]

The wartime boom led to a 61 percent increase in nonagricultural civilian employment on the Pacific Coast between 1940 and 1944. Table 8.1 (pp. 192–193) offers a picture of the employment trends in the region as a whole and in its largest state, California. The expansion of the manufacturing sector drove job growth in the region. The construction and government sectors tended to keep pace with the overall expansion; most other sectors grew in absolute but not relative terms. During the war, the region's manufacturing sector added about 1 million workers as employment increased from 623,000 workers in the 1939–40 period to 1,615,000 in the 1943–44 period. This two-and-one-half-fold increase in manufacturing employment accounted for over 60 percent of the overall expansion of nonagricultural employment.

Driving this enormous growth in western manufacturing was the military's high demand for the products of the region's aircraft and shipbuilding industries. During the war, Pacific Coast aircraft plants produced 38 percent of the nation's planes; its shipyards built 44 percent of the government's merchant ships.[4] To meet the military's demand, employment in West Coast shipyards soared from less than 7,000 in 1939 to over 515,000 at the peak in the summer of 1943.[5] The number of workers in the region's aircraft plants climbed from 25,000 in 1939 to 315,000 in the summer of 1943. Together these sectors accounted for about one-half of the region's total expansion of nonagricultural employment between 1940 and 1943. Associated with the enormous growth of these high-wage "war industries" were increases in the region's wages relative to the country as a whole. For example, the hourly wage in California manufacturing rose from 114.9 percent of the national average in the 1939–41 period to 120.7 percent in the 1943–45 period (California Division of Labor Statistics and Research 1953, p. 81).

The expansion of employment opportunities resulted in dramatic reductions in unemployment, substantial increases in labor force participation, especially of women, and significant inflows of population. The region's jobless rate, which languished at double-digit levels on the eve of the war, fell to less than 1 percent by 1944. Unfortunately we lack comprehensive monthly data of the level and rate of unemployment in the Pacific Northwest during the war years, but the high-quality series available for California (displayed in Figure 8.1) can serve as a useful proxy for movements in the region as a whole.[6] As the figure shows, the state's unemployment rate fell from 15.2 percent in January 1940 to 8.1 percent in December 1941, and to the incredibly low rate of 0.3 percent in October 1943. This meant that in a labor force of 3,908,000 workers, only 12,000 were without jobs. The region's labor market became so

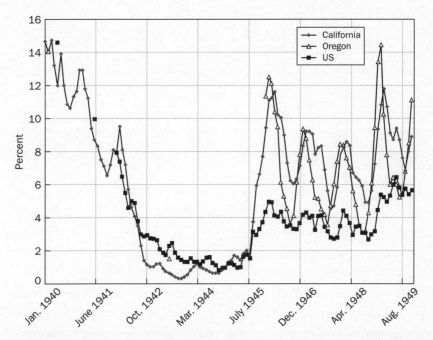

Figure 8.1   Unemployment rates in California, Oregon, and United States, 1940–1949

SOURCES: California Employment Development Department, "California Labor Force, 1940–1982: Monthly Non–Seasonally Adjusted Data," downloaded from http://www.calmis.cahwnet.gov/FILE/LFHIST/CAL$4-8.TXT; Oregon State, Annual Reports of the Oregon Unemployment Compensation Commission, Salem Oregon, various years, 1940–1950; U.S. Bureau of Labor Statistics, *Handbook of Labor Statistics*, 1950 ed., Bulletin 1016 (Washington, D.C.: U.S. Government Printing Office, 1951), p. 35.

Table 8.1
Pacific Coast civilian employment by major sector, 1939–1950

Employment in Thousands

	Total	Mining	Contract Construction	Manufacturing	Transportation and Public Utilities	Trade	Fire	Service	Government
Pacific									
1939	2,501.6	45.6	106.2	588.4	271.3	660.0	121.7	344.4	364.0
1940	2,670.2	46.7	124.1	658.9	282.9	688.9	127.4	354.0	387.3
1941	3,117.8	46.7	184.8	860.8	314.7	750.1	134.0	377.5	449.2
1942	3,722.8	39.7	219.3	1,261.4	335.7	770.0	128.4	412.1	556.2
1943	4,239.1	34.6	201.2	1,648.3	354.7	777.7	125.2	439.2	658.2
1944	4,305.1	34.3	204.0	1,581.5	378.0	805.0	125.3	463.0	714.0
1945	4,052.1	34.4	175.3	1,249.3	390.1	853.6	130.6	476.8	742.0
1946	4,014.8	37.8	223.3	1,001.8	408.4	965.9	158.7	529.0	689.9
1947	4,170.4	38.8	265.7	1,034.9	428.7	1,023.0	170.2	546.4	662.7
1948	4,281.5	40.4	301.6	1,053.1	432.9	1,042.9	179.1	547.5	684.0
1949	4,178.2	38.9	263.6	1,003.2	416.5	1,014.1	180.7	542.8	718.4
1950	4,331.1	36.6	295.1	1,076.3	419.8	1,032.9	194.1	545.5	730.8
Share of growth									
1940–1944	1.00	−0.01	0.05	0.56	0.06	0.07	0.00	0.07	0.20
1944–1950	1.00	0.09	3.50	−19.43	1.61	8.77	2.65	3.17	0.65
1940–1950	1.00	−0.01	0.10	0.25	0.08	0.21	0.04	0.12	0.21

California

1939	1,812.0	40.0	76.4	384.4	185.1	504.7	96.4	274.7	250.3
1940	1,931.8	40.0	89.5	440.2	190.3	524.2	100.9	280.4	266.3
1941	2,264.9	41.1	135.1	593.6	213.0	572.1	105.8	297.4	307.8
1942	2,689.7	33.8	152.3	876.0	233.8	588.0	100.4	321.3	384.1
1943	3,083.5	29.4	137.9	1,165.5	250.8	596.1	97.3	341.5	465.0
1944	3,116.5	29.9	133.1	1,109.7	268.0	614.0	96.0	355.2	510.6
1945	2,960.8	30.6	136.1	860.8	279.5	654.2	100.2	365.7	533.7
1946	2,972.6	33.5	172.3	706.7	295.5	737.1	122.3	405.0	500.2
1947	3,079.9	34.2	202.4	721.8	312.6	774.7	132.3	418.9	483.0
1948	3,162.9	35.6	225.2	734.2	317.9	790.6	139.8	418.7	500.9
1949	3,088.0	34.4	197.7	701.5	306.0	767.2	141.0	415.6	524.6
1950	3,209.5	32.3	225.3	759.7	307.1	783.2	151.8	416.8	533.3

Share of growth

1940–1944	1.00	−0.01	0.04	0.57	0.07	0.08	0.00	0.06	0.21
1944–1950	1.00	0.03	0.99	−3.76	0.42	1.82	0.60	0.66	0.24
1940–1950	1.00	−0.01	0.11	0.25	0.09	0.20	0.04	0.11	0.21

SOURCE: U.S. Bureau of Labor Statistics website.

tight that the war authorities declared Los Angeles, Portland-Vancouver, San Diego, San Francisco–Oakland, and Seattle-Tacoma "congested production areas" and placed restrictions on new procurement activity (Wilcox 1943).

Well before the market became this tight, western employers sought out new sources of labor. Migrants from the Dust Bowl, who had been unwelcome in the 1930s, were now actively recruited (California Division of Labor Statistics and Research 1947). Housewives, students, retirees, and others discouraged from work by a decade of depression were drawn into the labor force. These forces more than offset the region's losses due to military enlistment and conscription. According to the U.S. Bureau of Labor Statistics, the total labor force on the Pacific Coast (including the armed forces) rose from about 4,268,000 in April 1940 to 5,859,000 in April 1945, an increase of 37.3 percent. This compares with a national gain of 20.5 percent. Of the 1,591,000 added workers, natural increase added about 6 percent and the participation of "extra workers" about 41 percent. Interstate migration made up over one-half of the increase, some 847,000 workers. Given 1935–40 migration rates, 410,000 would have been expected, leading the bureau to conclude that "abnormal" migration accounted for 437,000 added workers (Pearlman 1947).

As a result of this surge in migration, World War II was a period of vigorous population growth on the Pacific Coast. Between July 1940 and July 1945, the region's civilian population expanded from 9,678,000 to nearly 11,300,000 residents. The total increase in the civilian population actually understates the migration flow because these figure ignore the withdrawal of the region's residents into military service. Net migration to the region totaled almost 2 million people (1,984,000) over the 1940–45 period. At the peak, more than 600,000 people moved to the Pacific Coast each year (U.S. Department of Commerce 1947, pp. 11–12).

When the war ended, the region's population and labor force were significantly larger than before. In addition, millions of footloose servicemen and women awaited demobilization. But the region's industrial structure, expanded in such a rapid and unbalanced matter during the war, faced serious problems of reconversion. The leading question of the day was, "Where will all these people find jobs if they stay in the West?"

3. CONTEMPORARY EXPECTATIONS

Western business, labor, and political leaders became highly concerned about the region's postwar prospects. In part, this reflected the nationwide apprehension that the depressed conditions of the 1930s would return. But the local leaders had additional reasons to worry. The war boom had attracted so many new workers: workers without strong roots in the region, workers with a history of moving on. If jobs were unavailable in the postwar period, these migrants might either return home or, if they remained, become public charges.

In addition, the war boom had been highly unbalanced, with most of the expansion occurring in a few sectors—aircraft and shipbuilding—that were bound to contract sharply once the war was over. As local observers often noted, "reconversion" was a misnomer on the West Coast. Many of the Pacific Coast factories had not converted from peacetime production to contribute to the war effort but had been constructed as the conflict raged. When the war has over, these plants would either begin to compete in the civilian market for the first time or shut down. Adding to these concerns was the possibility that victory in Europe might precede victory in Japan by many months or even years and that the West Coast would remain on a war footing long after "normalcy" prevailed in the rest of the nation. Manufacturers in the East and Midwest would then be able to capture the postwar civilian markets before the western plants had a chance to convert.

The region began to prepare for peace well before the war was won. The California legislature established the State Reconstruction and Reemployment Commission to address these issues in 1943 (U.S. Senate 1944b, p. 5335). In the Pacific Northwest, the strong regional planning staffs, set up during the New Deal, were themselves converted to plan for postwar development (Puget Sound Regional Planning Commission 1943). The 12th District Federal Reserve Bank also lent a hand.

Up and down the coast, business, academic, and government organizations began to sample, survey, plan, and predict. Among the key issues was how large the region's postwar population and labor force would be. To answer this and other questions, the planners wanted to know how many of the recent entrants into the labor market would remain and how many veterans would return. As an example, in early 1944 the Kaiser interests conducted a massive survey in the Portland area, drawing responses from over 80,000 war workers. They found that about 52 percent of the respondents who had migrated within the previous three years intended to remain in the area after the war. Of these, about 41 percent were definite in their intention to stay, and another 59 percent intended to stay if they found work. Based on this study, Emory Worth of the Oregon State Manpower Commission estimated that roughly 40,000 inmigrant workers, representing about one-eighth of the 1944 labor force, would remain in the Portland-Vancouver area after the war (U.S. Senate 1944b, pp. 5305–7). Glossing the numerous surveys conducted in Washington State, Nathaniel Engle, director of the Bureau of Business Research at the University of Washington, found that "about half" of incoming war workers "definitely want to remain in the State" and that between 44 and 48 percent of working women expected to drop out of the labor force after the war. Adding the state's 115,000 returning veterans, he estimated that Washington's postwar labor force would be larger by 339,000 workers, or 36 percent, than in 1939. (U.S. Senate 1944a, pp. 5005–11)

California authorities were both confident and concerned that the Golden State would keep a larger share of its recent migrants. The State Reconstruction and Reemployment Commission declared in early 1944 that "in no event is the State expected to lose even temporarily more than one-quarter to one-fifth of its wartime migrants, while a net population loss by 1950 is considered highly unlikely" (CSRRC 1944b, pp. 17–19; see also CSRRC 1944a, p. 31). They estimated that in "194X"—the first year after demobilization—California's population would be between 8.35 and 8.75 million and that in 1950 the state would likely have a population of 8.5 to 9 million (CSRRC 1944c, pp. 29–30; CSRRC 1944b, pp. 17–19). O. Wheeler, director of research at the 12th District Federal Reserve Bank, summarized the prospects of the West as follows: "Well over half of the in-migrants intend to remain in the region, at least if they can find jobs . . . . A third or more of the former housewives apparently wish to continue working" (U.S. Senate 1944a, pp. 5342–43).

In early 1945, authorities on the coast received more worrying news: not only did their own veterans plan to return, but unexpectedly large numbers of veterans from other states hoped to join them. The news came from a U.S.

Army study of the postwar migration plans of enlisted men conducted in the summer of 1944. Most enlisted men nationwide (82.7 percent) stated they intended to return to the region from which they came; four-fifths said they would return to the same state. In the national sample, 10.8 percent were undecided about where to locate, and 6.5 percent planned to return to a different division from their prewar residence. Of this 6.5 percent, over one-quarter stated they intended to move to the West Coast. This was a greater share of movers than any other region attracted. Reinforcing this westward flow was the fact that enlisted men from the Pacific region were more likely than those from any other region to be "homeward-bound." Nearly nine out of ten intended to return to the West Coast, and only 3.6 percent planned to move away. According to the authors of the study, the net effect of the movement of servicemen would be "a rapid expansion in the Pacific coast states" (Jaffe and Wolfbein 1945).

This news gave greater impetus to local efforts to gauge the extent of employment and unemployment during the conversion period. The conventional wisdom was that employment in the war industries would fall to less than one-tenth of its wartime peak. For example, a 1944 study of Pacific Coast shipyards by the Federal Reserve Bank of San Francisco indicated that the region's shipbuilders expected to have 40,000 employees in an "ordinary year with good business" and only 16,000 in an "ordinary year with bad business."[7] In 1943 the sector employed 515,000 workers, implying that roughly half a million workers would be laid off in the conversion process.[8]

In combination with the Committee for Economic Development, the bank conducted a more comprehensive survey of Pacific Coast manufacturing firms regarding their "postwar intentions" in the spring and summer of 1944.[9] They asked how much employment the firms were currently providing and how much they would offer in the postwar period under "good economic conditions" and under "bad conditions." Overall, the region's manufacturing firms expected to employ around 780,000 workers if times were "good" and about 500,000 if times were "bad." The former represented an increase of about 40 percent from the actual 1939 level of employment, but a reduction by one-half from the 1943 peak. The latter figure was below even the prewar level. Manufacturers in Oregon and Washington appeared more optimistic than those in California. The most notable sign of this difference was that the manufacturers outside of the aircraft and shipbuilding industries in the Pacific Northwest expected that under "good conditions" they would hire more workers than they did in 1943, whereas those in California expected their employment to decline.

The California State Reconstruction and Reemployment Commission painted an even more pessimistic picture of the state's postwar prospects. It estimated the civilian labor force in "194X" would be between 3.6 and 4 million workers. With "the smoothest readjustment and the highest possible levels of business activity," there would be 3.2 million civilian jobs within a year of demobilization, but with moderately adverse conditions only 2.8 million jobs. In any case, employment would be below the 1943 peak of 3.5 million jobs, and it would take three to four years of normal growth to recover to this level. According to a commission report published in late 1944, unemployment in "194X" California would range between 365,000 and 1.2 million, with the most likely prospect between 450,000 and 800,000 workers (CSRRC 1944d, pp. 12–15).

As the war progressed, responsible authorities in the state became still more pessimistic about the extent of unemployment. In 1945, Samuel May, director of the Bureau of Public Administration at the University of California, estimated that total unemployment in California at the end of the first year of demobilization (assumed in his study to be 1946–47) would range between 905,000 and 1,085,000, levels he found "startling." The main reason for the difference from the State Reconstruction and Reemployment Commission figures was that 200,000 to 350,000 veterans from other states were now expected to move to California after the war. May anticipated that the state's labor force would be higher than in 1943 by 670,000 workers and employment lower by 315,000 to 490,000. Overall, California employment would be in the range of 2,955,000 to 3,130,000 thousand workers, implying that about one-quarter of the labor force would be unemployed.[10]

4. THE POSTWAR EXPERIENCE

What actually happened after the war? How did the experts' predictions measure up? As revealed in the data in Table 8.1, the region's readjustment proved far easier than most of the responsible authorities predicted. Contemporary observers were stuck by two phenomena: (1) overall employment recovered rapidly; as a writer at the Federal Reserve Bank put it in mid-1946, the region experienced a loss of 45 percent of its manufacturing jobs "without collapsing or, indeed, showing any signs of distress"; and (2) the employment structure at a broad (one-digit SIC) level almost immediately returned to its prewar composition—repeating a common refrain, a 1948 Federal Reserve article noted: "The distribution of workers among major industry groups is now not markedly different than before the war. Little trace remains of the wartime pattern of employment."[11]

As many contemporaries noted, the adjustment process began before the conflict ended with employment in the war industries falling gradually from 1943–44 on. Nonetheless, the cutbacks after VJ Day hit the West Coast hard. In the four-week period after August 15, 1945, more than 300,000 workers lost their jobs. Most of the decline resulted from the termination of about 100,000 shipyard workers (out of 385,000 employed) and 75,000 aircraft workers (out of an initial employment of 185,000). Over the next six weeks, another 100,000 workers were laid off, again mostly in the high-paying "war industries." By the end of 1945, total employment in the region's aircraft and shipbuilding industries fell to about 280,000, down from 750,000 at the start on the year.[12]

Unemployment started to climb. By February 1946 the jobless rate in California entered double digits for the first time since 1941 (see Figure 8.1). But the situation quickly improved. Both the number of unemployed persons (485,000) and the jobless rate (11.6 percent) peaked in April 1946. By summer the state's unemployment rate again dropped into single-digit levels and remained in the 5–8 percent range until the 1949–50 recession. I have found comparable monthly figures for unemployment rates in Oregon over the immediate postwar period (which are included in Figure 8.1) but unfortunately none for Washington State. The available information suggests that the unemployment rate in the Pacific Northwest was slightly higher than in California in the last years of the war and was typically slightly lower in the late 1940s. Estimates of unemployment in the three Pacific Coast states from the U.S. Employment Service indicate that the number of unemployed in the region peaked at 725,000 in March 1946 and fell to about 600,000 by May. The latter approximately matched the prewar (April 1940) level, when the labor force was about one-third smaller. Obviously unemployment in the conversion period was substantially higher than the wartime low of around 100,000 (in 1943–44), and the region's unemployment rate remained several percentage points higher than the national average. But joblessness in the postwar period was far below expectations and never threatened to bankrupt the region's unemployment compensation systems as had been feared.[13]

One reason that unemployment was not higher was that the inflow of out-of-state veterans to the West proved to be smaller than most of the wartime studies had predicted. In 1947 the Current Population Survey estimated that about 1,301,000 World War II–era veterans lived in the Pacific region, only about 80,000 more than resided there before entry into active service (U.S. Bureau of the Census 1947). The region continued to receive a positive, albeit smaller, inflow of migrants. Between July 1, 1945, and July 1, 1947, the civilian population of the Pacific Coast increased from 11,700,000 to 13,551,000. Of this increase, migration accounted for about 342,000. The postwar surge in family formation caused the rates of natural increase in the Far West to reach unprecedented levels. The surplus of births over deaths accounts for over four-fifths of the region's population growth.

Overall, nonagricultural employment in the three Pacific Coast states fell by 290,000 workers, or about 7 percent, between 1944 and 1946. But the 1946 level was still 50 percent above the 1940 level. Most of the decline appears to be due to the voluntary withdrawal of the "extra workers"—housewives, students, and retirees—from the labor market. The decline, moreover, was only temporary. By 1950, nonagricultural employment in the region surpassed even the wartime peak.

How could the Pacific Coast's economy sustain its greatly enlarged labor force and population after the war? It is useful to frame the issue in a simple demand and supply model of the labor market. During the Second World War, the Pacific Coast experienced a dramatic increase in labor demand in its war industries, which led to the expansion of its labor force. After 1943 the military demands began to diminish, but employment did not fall as much as predicted. Why did the wartime reallocation of aggregate income and employment "stick"? There are several possible explanations, and I would not like to fall into the trap of insisting that only one is valid.

One possible explanation is that the wartime stimulus did not really end. The emergence and growth of the military-industrial complex during the Cold War period is a familiar theme in the economic history of the recent past. That said, it is important to note that military spending declined sharply after World War II. Between 1945 and 1948, real U.S. military spending (in 1958 dollars) contracted by $127.6 billion, or 92 percent. (By way of contrast, the post–Cold War defense contraction from 1989 to 1996 was only 29 percent; even in absolute terms, the recent drop of $20.9 billion was dwarfed by the 1945–48 decline.)[14] While data on the regional allocation of defense spending for the 1946–50 period are not readily available, it is absolutely certain that spending in the Pacific region was far lower than at the wartime peak.

A reading of the West Coast business press in the immediate postwar period reveals that virtually no one considered military spending a suitable permanent foundation for the region's economy. While there were expressions of concern that the postwar contraction was too rapid, most business writers placed their faith in the private sector. To the extent that the local business community demanded government intervention, it was to combat freight rate discrimination, to help establish western basing points for steel prices, and to sell off war surplus facilities in an orderly manner. Nothing in the experience of West's business leaders suggested that the region's long-term economic growth could be based on military sales, and few realized that defense demand would remain permanently higher until the beginning of the Korean conflict.

Between 1945 and 1947, the region's aircraft industry suffered a severe contraction but soon activity stabilized at a level far above prewar production. By 1948 the Pacific Coast industry was already in the black owing to a resumption of military orders and successful reconversion of a part of the industry to civilian production. One important trend accompanying the postwar contraction of the aircraft industry was its reconcentration on the West Coast. Before Pearl Harbor over half (51 percent) of the floor space was on the West Coast. During the war, the military authorities induced the leading West Coast firms to build and operate large plants in the mid-continent region. Although the share of national aircraft floor space (and production) located on the West Coast fell to about one-quarter (28 percent), the share "managed" by West Coast firms remained roughly constant. After the war, the West Coast firms shut down almost all of their mid-continent branch plants, and the West Coast share climbed back to about half (47 percent) of the national total.[15]

By way of contrast to the aircraft industry, Pacific Coast shipbuilding virtually collapsed after VJ day. By early 1947 the region's private and navy yards split evenly the sector's labor force of 65,000 workers (down from the peak of 594,000 in July 1943 and 376,000 in August 1945). For several years after mid-1947, industry received no orders for new ships and performed only repair work. By early 1950, employment had fallen to about 32,000. Although the industry recovered slightly during the Korean conflict, Pacific Coast shipyard activity never again approached one-tenth of the 1943–44 levels.[16] In summary, military demand in the immediate postwar period, while higher than before the war, was far below the wartime peak.

A second alternative explanation for the continued high employment level is that migration is costly. Once people had made the investment to move west in response to the wartime boom, they would not automatically move back home when the boom ended. The elasticity of labor supply in response to the expansion of demand was higher than that in response to the contraction, implying the temporary boom had a ratchet effect on the region's labor force. This argument has some plausibility. But in combination with a decline in labor demand in the "war industries," it implies that relative wages would have to fall dramatically to sustain employment. The available evidence suggests regional wages did decline, but the movements were surprisingly mild. In California, for example, the hourly manufacturing wage fell from 120.7 of the national average in the 1943–45 period to 114.0 in the 1947–49 period. The latter figure was 0.8 percentage points below the ratio prevailing in the 1939–41 period. Given the conventional estimates of own-price elasticity of demand for labor (say −0.75), this change would account for only a trivial fraction of the relative increase in the state's employment, holding the labor demand constant.[17]

The complete explanation must then include an increase in relative labor demand from a source other than the military. It could be due to an increase in demand for the region's exports, which included principally agricultural and wood products and nonferrous metals. But between 1943 and 1946, aggregate employment in these activities actually declined in both California and the Pacific Northwest.

The second and more promising candidate for an expansion of demand was the region's home market. The wartime boom had increased the real income on the Pacific Coast by almost 77 percent between 1940 and 1945. The region's share of national income rose from 9.7 percent to 11.9 percent and its share of national population rose from 7.4 percent to 8.9 percent (U.S. Department of Commerce 1947, pp. 11–13). But the wartime controls and labor market conditions slowed economic adjustments to meet the enlarged civilian demands.

The robust growth of the national economy in the immediate postwar period is commonly attributed to pent-up demand: the combination of large levels of private savings built up during the war and of small existing stocks of consumer durables and housing following a decade-and-a-half of limited purchases. By most measures, pent-up demand on the West Coast was especially intense. During the early 1940s, the region's per capita income became the highest in the nation, contributing to the rapid accumulation of liquid assets. For example, per capita sales of war bonds on the Pacific Coast were consistently 25–30 percent higher than the national average. Between 1941 and 1945 the region's residents purchased over $4.5 billion Series E savings bonds, accounting for about 11.6 percent of national sales. Other forms of liquid savings also rose dramatically over the war. Between the end of 1939 and the end of 1945, bank deposits on the Pacific Coast rose from $5.2 billion (7.6 percent of the national total) to $17.0 billion (10.3 percent) (U.S. Department of Commerce 1948, pp. 36–38). When this spending power was released, a tremendous boom resulted.

Despite the huge flows of migrants, civilian construction virtually stopped on the West Coast in the war years. By 1943–44, acute housing shortages appeared in most of the leading urban centers. Indeed, as authorities noted, the question of where the enlarged population would find homes in the postwar West was second only to the question of where they would find jobs. When construction controls were lifted after mid-1945, the region enjoyed an extremely vigorous residential construction boom. The real value of authorized construction in urban areas on the Pacific Coast in 1947–48 was roughly three times the 1943–44 level.[18] And as Table 8.1 reveals, over the 1944–48 period, the building sector added 92,000 employees in the Pacific region as a whole, almost all in California.

Even larger and more immediate changes occurred in the trade and service sectors. These activities had not kept pace with the expansion during the war. Indeed, many small retail and wholesale establishments closed because of materials and labor shortages. For example, in California the number of retail stores licensed by the state (to collect sales taxes) declined from 250,000 in 1940 to fewer than 174,000 in 1943. After the war peak, the number bounced back, increasing to 251,000 in 1946 and to 278,000 in 1948 (California State Department of Employment 1949, p. 294). In Washington State, it was reported that 1,500 trade establishments per month were started in late 1945 and early 1946. The West Coast trade sector added nearly 238,000 jobs between 1944 and 1948, and the service sector (including finance, insurance, and real estate) nearly 138,000. The bulk of these increases occurred in California, where employment in the trade expanded by 177,000 and that in services by 108,000 (California State Division of Labor Statistics and Research 1953, pp. 18–20).

Finally, although employment in the manufacturing sector fell sharply in 1945–46, almost all of the contraction was in shipbuilding and aircraft. Many of the other "war industries," such as chemicals, petroleum, rubber tires, and automobiles, recovered quickly after their initial cutbacks. And the growth in the "nonwar industries" offset the decline in the war industries to a far greater extent than was expected. Even excluding aircraft and shipbuilding, the number of manufacturing production workers on the West Coast increased by almost 70 percent between 1939 and 1947. The industrial groups typically associated with larger scale (SIC 28–30, 33–38) generally experienced faster growth.

At a conceptual level, we may distinguish three ways—called here *multiplier, accelerator,* and *threshold* effects—in which local production may depend on the local market. In the first, based on the familiar multiplier mechanism of macroeconomics, the level of local production increases roughly proportionately with the size of local income or population. This relationship appears to characterize trade, much of the service sector, and manufacturing activities such as printing or the processing of perishable foods. In proximate terms, the multiplier relationship probably explains most of the expansion of the Pacific Coast economy after the war. But such growth is "passive" or "induced" and, from first principles, cannot account for the entire increase or explain its fundamental cause.

The second effect, based on the accelerator principle, recognizes that for some activities the size of local demand depends on the change (rather than the level) of local population and income. The construction sector and building-materials industries fall into this category. The vigorous growth of building activity explains another large part of the region's postwar recovery. But this mechanism cannot alone account for why the higher level of economic activity was sustainable. As the discussion of the investment accelerator in any standard macro text points out, the process has self-generating cycles. Once growth begins to slow, sectors characterized by an accelerator relationship will begin to contract, further slowing the economy. To explain the appearance of a permanently high level of economic activity in the region requires something more.

The third type of home market effect—the threshold effect recently highlighted in the New Economic Geography literature—is one possibility. The idea here is that production technologies for some goods involve fixed costs or other forms of increasing returns to scale that make local production unprofitable if the local market is too small. As the market grows, it becomes economical to establish a larger number of plants producing a wider range of goods in the region. In this case, local production will increase more than one-for-one with an increase in the size of the local market. Much of the increase in western manufacturing outside of the war industries appears to fit into this category.

5. MULTIPLE EQUILIBRIA?

The third type of home market effect is especially intriguing in light of the prediction in the New Economic Geography literature that a region might possess more than one equilibrium level of economic activity consistent with the same "fundamentals." Paul Krugman's work has emphasized that three factors—increasing returns to scale (with the accompanying conditions of imperfect competition), labor mobility, and transportation costs—are key for such home market effects to matter significantly. The case of manufacturing on the

Pacific Coast in the mid-twentieth century matches the theoretical requirements well.[19]

In addition, accounts of the West's growth written as the region developed—
the key works here are by Gordon (1954) and Niklason (1930)—stress the role
of home market effects in the growth process. Gordon called the inadequate
size of the western market "the most important factor that has hampered the
growth of manufacturing" in the region. Because of the small market, western
firms could not produce "on a sufficiently large scale" to offset the competitive
advantages of eastern producing centers. These accounts also recognized
the reverse flow from local production to local market size, which made the
process self-reinforcing. Indeed, a reading of the region's business press yields
the impression that the process was self-generating. In particular, many writers
in the 1940s argued the temporary boom during World War II set "the West on
its way."[20]

Did the World War II shock shift the Pacific Coast economy from a low-
level equilibrium to a high-level equilibrium? Were the home market effects
that strong? To address these questions, this section explores in greater detail
the long-run relationship between income and the value of manufacturing
production. As part of a larger project on the economic development of the
region, I have constructed a new panel data set on manufacturing activity in
the United States and California for the period since 1849. Comprehensive
data on four-digit industries were drawn from the Census of Manufacturing
and assembled into consistent time series. (A list of the variables used in
the analysis is provided in Table 8.2. Their summary statistics are reported in
Table 8.3.) Unfortunately the data refer only to California and not to the
Pacific Coast as a whole. But given the state's great importance in the region
and its dominant role in the expansion during World War II, examining the
California experience in detail promises to shed considerable light on the
development process of the region more generally.

To assess the role of home market effects, I predict the level of real manufacturing value added in California using the level (or national share) of
personal income earned in the state as a measure of the size of the home
market.[21] This analysis adopts the following conceptual approach: California
real manufacturing value added is modeled as proportional to national real

Table 8.2
List of variables

Dependent Variable

lcalrva	Log of the value added of manufacturing in California deflated by the national GDP deflator.

Cross-section Variables

lusrva	Log of the value added of manufacturing in the United States deflated by the national GDP deflator.
lusrvest	Log of the value added of manufacturing in the United States deflated by the national GDP deflator and divided by the number of establishments nationally.
lusest	Log of the number of establishments nationally.
lusrwgwe	Log of the census average wage rate of manufacturing in the United States, as captured by the wage bill divided by the number of wage earners/production workers and then deflated by the national GDP deflator.
SIC20–SIC38	Zero/one dummy variables for the standard industrial classification. Categories based on the 1947 manual with SIC39, Misc. Manufacturing, as the omitted category.
export	Dummy variables with one denoting canning and preserving, petroleum refining, aircraft, and shipbuilding.

Time-series Variables

lrfr	Log of an index of real freight rates based on the Southern Pacific's revenues per ton-mile deflated by the GDP deflator.
lrelwage	Log of manufacturing wage rates in California relative to the United States as a whole as captured by the census average wage.
lcalry	Log of California personal income deflated by the national GDP deflator.
lusry	Log of U.S. personal income deflated by the national GDP deflator.
dcalusy	Difference between *lcalry* and *lusry*; orthogonalized higher-order terms also used.
year, yrX	Year effects, year dummies.

manufacturing value added, with the proportion depending on relative demand, $\delta(D_{it})$, and supply, $\sigma(S_{it})$, where D represents the set of demand shifters and S represents supply shifters. This relationship may be written as:

$$CalRVA_{it} = \delta(D_{it})\sigma(S_{it})USRVA_{it}.$$

Relative supply is modeled as a function of establishment scale, human capital requirements, relative wages over time, freight rates over time, and the industry's two-digit category. Relative demand is modeled as a function of the

Table 8.3
Data description and summary statistics

Variable	Observations	Mean	Standard Deviation	Minimum	Maximum
lcalrva	5,174	7.423405	4.020248	0	15.92315
lusrva	5,174	12.35482	1.844457	4.725273	17.88064
lusrvest	5,174	7.194097	1.356098	2.826674	12.92957
lusrwgwe	5,174	2.519553	0.439907	−4.298731	5.156118
lcalry	5,174	15.34731	1.133722	13.27001	17.06468
lusry	5,174	18.10674	0.758972	16.52545	19.28708
dcalusy	5,174	−2.759428	0.384385	−3.345407	−2.222397
ocalusy2	5,174	−0.000909	0.116656	−0.1492343	0.166946
ocalusy3	5,174	0.005191	0.030653	−0.0432281	0.049357
lrelwage	5,174	0.169469	0.083795	0.0769611	0.329304
lrfr	5,174	−4.294594	0.557019	−5.041845	−2.914655
export	5,174	0.020495	0.1417	0	1
SIC20	5,174	0.098415	0.297903	0	1
SIC21	5,174	0.007927	0.08869	0	1
SIC22	5,174	0.079466	0.270491	0	1
SIC23	5,174	0.069606	0.254506	0	1
SIC24	5,174	0.037316	0.189554	0	1
SIC25	5,174	0.022429	0.148087	0	1
SIC26	5,174	0.029002	0.167829	0	1
SIC27	5,174	0.03519	0.184276	0	1
SIC28	5,174	0.092227	0.289375	0	1
SIC29	5,174	0.014308	0.118768	0	1
SIC30	5,174	0.010248	0.10072	0	1
SIC31	5,174	0.031516	0.174724	0	1
SIC32	5,174	0.062838	0.242696	0	1
SIC33	5,174	0.058005	0.233775	0	1
SIC34	5,174	0.07676	0.266235	0	1
SIC35	5,174	0.072119	0.25871	0	1
SIC36	5,174	0.024362	0.154185	0	1
SIC37	5,174	0.031129	0.173684	0	1
SIC38	5,174	0.032289	0.176784	0	1

SOURCES: See text.

California income relative to national income ($\theta_t = CalY_t / USY_t$) and, in some formulations, whether the industry exports. A sample formulation would have θ_t raised to a power η and be stated in logs:

$$\log (CalRVA_{it}) = \eta \log (\theta_t) + \log \sigma(Z_{it}) + \log (USRVA_{it}).$$

In the models run, the coefficient on $\log(USRVA_{it})$ is not constrained to equal unity, reflecting the possibility that $USRVA$ enters in the supply shifters as well.

Following in the spirit of the Davis and Weinstein (1999) interpretation of Krugman's work, the test of the "home market effect" hypothesis has two forms:

$\eta > 0$ "home markets" matter at least weakly (for example, transport costs > 0).

$\eta > 1$ "home markets effects" lead to a greater than one-for-one increase in production in line with the New Economic Geography models.

Table 8.4 presents the results of the Tobit regressions run on the pooled cross section/time series over the 1879–1963 period. Equation 1 predicts the (log of) real value added of each industry in California based on the (log of) industry's national real value added, establishment scale, and wages per wage earner, and time-series variables reflecting the general relative wage in California, an index of real regional freight rate, and California personal income and national personal income.[22] A set of consistent and largely sensible results emerges from the analysis. Industries with large establishment sizes nationally (as captured by the variable *lusrvest*) had lower levels of output in the state, confirming the impression that the region's limited market constrained industrial activity in sectors characterized by increasing returns to scale. Industries with high human capital intensity (reflected in *lusrwgwe*) were more common in the state.

Among the time-series variables, the relative wage variable has a significant negative effect, whereas the freight rates variable proved insignificant. The coefficient on California income has a large positive effect, but that on national income has a large (r) negative effect, which is troubling. Is this due to strong backwash effects? It seems more likely to be the result of the substantial collinearity that exists between state and national incomes. In line with the conceptual approach outlined above, the model may be run using income shares. The standard likelihood ratio test approves of this formulation (but it is interesting that the use of manufacturing output shares—that is, constraining the coefficient of *lusrva* to be unity—is rejected).

Table 8.4

Tobit regressions of pooled cross-section time series.
Dependent variable: *Lcalrva* with two-digit SIC dummies

		Equation					
		1	*2*	*3*	*4*		*5*
					All	*Export*	*Home Only*
lusrva	Coefficient	1.782	1.780	1.783	1.770	−0.552	1.774
	Standard Error	0.033	0.033	0.033	0.033	1.061	0.033
lusrvest	Coefficient	−1.256	−1.258	−1.264	−1.298	1.182	−1.299
	Standard Error	0.046	0.046	0.046	0.047	0.319	0.047
lusrwgwe	Coefficient	1.510	1.511	1.503	1.600	−0.552	1.060
	Standard Error	0.175	0.175	0.182	0.184	1.061	0.186
lrelwage	Coefficient	−1.961	−2.313	−0.911	−0.952	1.151	−0.940
	Standard Error	0.828	0.758	0.946	0.945	6.698	0.959
lrfr	Coefficient	−0.357	0.017	−0.820	−0.176	0.279	−0.181
	Standard Error	0.407	0.085	0.213	0.212	0.739	0.216
lcalry	Coefficient	1.926					
	Standard Error	0.536					
lusry	Coefficient	−2.414					
	Standard Error	0.536					
dcalusy	Coefficient		1.439	1.378	1.341	−1.131	1.334
	Standard Error		0.276	0.277	0.275	0.963	0.281
ocalusy2	Coefficient			−0.348	−0.429	−2.373	−0.431
	Standard Error			0.433	0.434	3.080	0.440
ocalusy3	Coefficient			−4.415	−4.269	3.819	−4.287
	Standard Error			1.652	1.655	11.091	1.678
_se	Coefficient	3.059	3.059	3.057	3.030		3.069
	Standard Error	0.035	0.035	0.035	0.035		0.036
Pseudo R^2		0.1508	0.1507	0.1510	0.1538		0.1497
No. of Observations		5,174	5,174	5,174	5,174		5,068
No. of left-censored Observations		948	948	948	948		948

SOURCES: See text.

Equation 2 reports the results of the income share regression. The coefficient of California's income share (as reflected by *lcalusy*) becomes about 1.44, which implies that a 10 percent increase in the size of the region's market increases its industrial output by about 14 percent. This seems large, but it is not wholly implausible given that the elasticity of national manufacturing output with respect to income was about 1.27 in the sample. What remains implausible is that the effect is constant over all market sizes. Equation 3 addresses this problem by adding (orthogonalized) higher-order terms in the market size variable. Likelihood ratio tests approve of including terms up to the third order. These results suggest an S-shaped and somewhat more damped "home market effect." The exact impact of a given change in the market size depends on what the income share is.

A key problem in the interpretation of these regressions is the issue of omitted variable biases. To control for the possibility that short-run supply shocks (strikes, earthquakes) might be attributed to the California market share, I have included individual-year dummies in the model successively. In no case were the effects statistically significant or the basic results altered. Inclusion of a time trend also proved inconsequential. A further possible problem is that the results may reflect business cycle effects. To control for this effect, I included a measure of the U.S. output gap, specifically the deviation of real GDP from its long-run average. The business cycle coefficient proved statistically insignificant, and again the basic pattern of results was not changed.

There remains the possibility that the measured home market effects are picking up omitted long-run supply shifts. Indeed, the New Economic Geography literature has its own supply-side candidate: labor market pooling effects, which can also lead to a positive feedback relationship. One way to begin to address this issue is to examine a model in which the export and nonexport industries are treated separately. The "home market" and "plant scale" effects are presumably less important for the export industries. If the "home market" effect remains strong, it lends support to the argument that the model is really capturing supply-side instead of demand-side forces.

Equation 4 runs the regression with separate coefficients for the leading export activities, defined to comprise canning, petroleum refining, shipbuilding, and aircraft.[23] The regression includes a new set of variables created by multiplying the existing variables by a one/zero dummy reflecting whether or not the industry falls in the export category. Essentially, these industries are allowed separate slope terms. While the estimates are not highly precise, the separate slope terms wipe out most of the establishment size and home market effects for the export industries. An increase in the region's market size by one percent (using 1939 as a base) *reduces* output in the export industries by 0.6 percent. The absence of a home market effect for exports paradoxically supports the home market hypothesis overall: it is not working where it shouldn't be.[24]

What do these results imply about the possibility of multiple equilibria and the impact of World War II spending? To explore these issues, consider a toy model of the California economy. Let it be made up of three parts: a resource-base or export sector that produces a given output, B, independent of the size of the home market; a service sector where production grows proportionately with the home market, $S = sY$; and the manufacturing sector characterized by the nonlinear production-income relationship estimated above, $M(Y)$. Ignoring the distinction between income and output, aggregate income will equal:

$$Y = B + sY + M(Y) = (B + M(Y))/(1 - s). \qquad (1)$$

Obviously, there may be multiple equilibria in Y supported by the same base, B, if the nonlinear equation 1 has more than one root. This will depend on the strength of the nonlinear production-income relationship embodied in $M(Y)$ relative to the size of B. Even if there are multiple equilibria, they may not be very different if the roots are close.

Let us use this model to analyze the state of the California economy on the eve of World War II. To be concrete, assume the primary sector (farming, agricultural services, and mining) is the base. Over the 1938–40 period, this sector made up 10.5 percent of earnings in California, whereas manufacturing accounted for 16.1 percent of the state's earnings. We will treat the remaining 73.4 percent of earnings as the service sector.[25]

From the regression analysis, we know that holding all other variables (including national income) constant, the $M(Y)$ relationship in 1939 has roughly the following form in the cubic specification:

Percentage increase in California:

Income	5	10	15	20	25	30
Manufacturing value added	9.4	17.0	22.8	26.8	29.0	29.4

A data point of special interest is what would happen if income increased by 21 percent—the percentage change in California's income share over the 1939–47 period. The regression equations indicate that a 21 percent increase in the California home market would have resulted in a 27.3 percent increase in manufacturing value added under the cubic specification. In the model sketched above, would such increases in income have created a sufficiently large market (in the absence in a change in the base) to support itself? Simple calculations suggest not; the effects are powerful, but not quite strong enough. An increase in manufacturing value added of 27.3 percent combined with no change in the base would have increased California income by only about 16.6 percent $(=(0.105 + 1.273 \times 0.161)/0.266) - 1)$.

But the results suggest that an increase in 1939 income by 11 percent would have been self-sustaining. An 11 percent increase would have increased manufacturing output by 18.5 percent, which in turn would have been sufficient to support the initial increase in income. This implies that roughly one-half of the increase in the region's income share over the war might be due to a transition between "low-level" and "high-level" equilibria. Even if the home market effects have been overestimated here, the slope of the output-income relationship shown in equation 1 appears quite steep in the relevant range. This implies that a small change in the base, for example due to the shift in military spending from its low prewar values to its somewhat higher postwar values, could have had a large effect on the level of aggregate activity. Obviously this is just a toy model, but these results offer surprisingly strong support for the rather speculative predictions of the New Economic Geography literature and call for further research.

6. CONCLUDING REMARKS

This essay argues that the experience of the Pacific Coast economy after World War II is consistent with the existence of strong home market effects. The econometric analysis of the long-run relationship between local income and manufacturing production suggests that these effects were not constant across all market sizes. Rather, they first increased and then diminished in strength. This has two interesting historical implications.

First, the home market effects appear strongest not in the immediate post-war period, but in the interwar years. During the 1920s, the Pacific Coast, and especially California, enjoyed a period of vigorous economic growth, which was cut short by the Great Depression. Many aspects of the region's postwar experience—its population growth, the establishment of branch plants by national manufacturing firms, the building boom, and the expansion of the service sector—were also present in the 1920s. It remains an open question whether World War II shocked the Pacific Coast to a level of economic activity that was otherwise unattainable or merely sped the transition to the inevitable long-run equilibrium. I would argue that the continuity vs. discontinuity debate over the impact of World War II in the West should shift to consider this broader issue, which requires giving greater attention to the region's secular development and less to the "four short years" of the war.

Second, the home market effects became far weaker as the region matured. If regional leaders used the late-1940s experience as a guide and downplayed the risk of becoming dependent on military spending in the Cold War period, they were drawing a mistaken historical lesson. When the cutbacks came in the early 1990s, the region's economy appears to have suffered much more than after the larger declines of military spending in the 1945–48 period. There was no great "unfilled" home market waiting in the wings to absorb the displaced aerospace workers and to propel continued growth. Unfortunately, you are only truly young once.

Notes

Acknowledgments: I would like to acknowledge the helpful comments and suggestions of Michael Edelstein, participants at the 1998 Economic History Association meetings at Durham, North Carolina, and the 2000 "History Matters" Conference at Stanford, California, and especially the editors of this volume. They made this a better essay. Any remaining errors are my responsibility.

1. See Lotchin 1992 and the articles in "Special Issue: Fortress California at War," *Pacific Historical Review* 63 (August 1994). For my initial take on this debate, see Rhode 1994.

2. U.S. Bureau of the Census (1947), pp. 7, 77; "Industry's Leaders Outline West's Industrial Prospects," *Pacific Factory* (January 1946), p. 48; California State Chamber of Commerce 1948–49.

3. For this argument, see Rhode (2000).

4. U.S. Civilian Aeronautical Administration 1946; Fisher (1949).

5. Officials at the Federal Reserve Bank of San Francisco noted: "More than any other industry, shipbuilding has been responsible for the vast increase in population and employment on the Pacific Coast since 1940, and its demand for materials and supplies has been the principal factor responsible for the rapid expansion and development of the heavy metals and metal working industries in the (12th) District." *Monthly Review* (May 1944), p. 21.

6. Annual data on the unemployment rate in Washington State indicate that the unemployment rate fell from 14.7 percent in 1940 to 2.5 percent during the 1943–44 period. In the latter period, fewer than 20,000 were unemployed. *Pacific Northwest Business* (Sept. 1955), pp. 28–31. In Oregon the unemployment rate fell from 14.0 percent in March 1940 to 1.5 percent in June 1943. At the latter date, there were only 9,000 unemployed out of a labor force of 602,500. Oregon State, *Eleventh Annual Report of the Unemployment Compensation Commission for the Year 1948*, p. 14.

7. Federal Reserve Bank of San Francisco, *Monthly Review* (December 1944), p. 64. The estimates for postwar employment even under bad conditions were above the 1939 level of 6,500 workers in the West Coast yards.

8. Actually, many workers, understanding the industry's limited postwar prospects, "left early" to seek other employment opportunities. These departures and difficulties in attracting workers to the industry's dead-end jobs added to the shipbuilders' problems of completing work during the war.

9. "Postwar Intentions of Pacific Coast Manufacturers," Federal Reserve Bank of San Francisco, *Monthly Review* (February 1945), pp. 17–20. As the Fed economists noted, the survey covered only existing firms and therefore missed any increase in activity planned by potential new entrants.

10. For various estimates, see U.S. Senate (1946), pp. 4004–57, 9828.

11. Federal Reserve Bank of San Francisco, *Monthly Review* (April–May 1946), p. 19; *Monthly Review* (November 1948), pp. 105–6.

12. Federal Reserve Bank of San Francisco, *Monthly Review* (August–September 1945), pp. 62–63; *Monthly Review* (October–November 1945), p. 77; (January 1946), p. 1.

13. Federal Reserve Bank of San Francisco, *Monthly Review* (June–July 1946), p. 23.

14. Defense spending from "Table 3.1—Outlays by Superfunction and Function: 1940–2006" of http://w3.access.gpo.gov/usbudget/fy2002/hist.html; GNP/GDP deflator from U.S. Bureau of the Census (1975) Series E1, p. 197, linked to post-1970 series from U.S. Council of Economic Advisers 2002, p. 278.

15. Cunningham (1951), pp. 203–15; U.S. Civilian Aeronautical Administration, *Statistical Handbook of Civil Aviation* (1948), p. 54; 1949, p. 54.

16. Federal Reserve Bank of San Francisco, *Monthly Review* (February 1949), p. 20; U.S. Bureau of Labor Statistics, "Employment in the Shipbuilding Industry, 1935–43," *Monthly Labor Review* (May 1944), pp. 951–52; "Employees in the Shipbuilding and Repairing Industry, by Region," in U.S. Bureau of Labor Statistics, *Employment and Pay Rolls: Detailed Report* (various monthly reports, 1946–51).

17. The labor demand estimate is from Ehrenberg and Smith 1991, p. 117.

18. "All Urban Building Construction" reported in U.S. Bureau of Labor Statistics, *Construction*, Bulletins 916, 984, 1047, 1146 deflated by GNP deflator referenced above.

19. See, for example, Fujita, Krugman, and Venables (1999). The work obviously builds on the shoulders of giants such as Adam Smith (1904), esp. chaps. 1–3; and Marshall (1952), esp. Book IV, chap. X.

20. See Gordon (1954), pp. 36, 56–57, 63, 70; Niklason (1930), pp. 398, 404; and CSRRC (1946), esp. chap. IV.

21. Data series based on this general concept are available for 1880, 1900, and 1920 from Easterlin (1957), p. 188; and annually for 1929 on from the U.S. Department of Commerce (1984). Using a methodology similar to Easterlin's, I have developed independent state estimates for 1890 and 1910. The intervening years were filled in by interpolation.

22. One potential difficulty that must give pause is the endogeneity of industrial production and the size of the home market/regional income. Indeed, the feedback from production to the market size is at the heart of the cumulative causation story. Here is where the micro-data help (in addition, to providing standard errors on the magnitude of the effects and a far number of degrees of freedom to test alternative explanations). The typical four-digit industry was very small compared with the total size of the California economy. For example, in 1939 the value added of the median California industry was $577,099, a little over one-tenth of 1 percent of the total personal income of $5.3 billion.

23. Interregional trade data are scanty, but the available information indicates that canning and petroleum accounted for the vast majority of California manufacturing exports. Including aircraft and shipbuilding, these industries account for about 19.5 percent of California manufacturing value added in 1939.

24. The cubic series is quite well behaved within the sample, but it would be problematic to extrapolate it far out of sample because no bounds have been imposed. The underlying series on the market/income share is quite flat until the 1900s and then "takes off"; the stabilization of the income share begins in the late 1950s and early 1960s, at the end of the period under consideration.

25. If the definition of the base is enlarged to include federal government earnings (the extractive sector plus), the share of total income becomes 15.7 percent in 1939. The service share becomes 68.2 percent. Making this change would tend to reduce further the possibility of multiple equilibria.

References

California State Chamber of Commerce. 1948–49. *Postwar Industrial Growth in California, 1945–1948.* Series Report no. 41.

California State Department of Employment. 1949. *Proceedings of the Governor's Conference on Unemployment.* Sacramento, Calif.

California State Division of Labor Statistics and Research. 1947. *Labor in California, 1945–1946.* San Francisco.

———. 1953. *Handbook of California Labor Statistics, 1951–1952.* San Francisco.

CSRRC (California State Reconstruction and Reemployment Commission). 1944a. *Estimates of Population Growth in California, 1940–1950.* Sacramento, Calif.

———. 1944b. *How Many Californians?* Sacramento, Calif.

———. 1944c. *How Much Post-War Income?* Sacramento, Calif.

———. 1944d. *How Many Jobs for Californians?* Sacramento, Calif.

———. 1946. *The Steel and Steel-Using Industries of California.* Sacramento, Calif.: State Printing Office.

Cunningham, William G. 1951. *The Aircraft Industry: A Study in Industrial Location.* Los Angeles: Lorrin Morrison.

Davis, Donald R., and David E. Weinstein. 1999. "Economic Geography and Regional Production Structure: An Empirical Investigation." *European Economic Review* 43: 379–407.

Easterlin, Richard. 1957. "Regional Growth in Income." In Simon Kuznets et al., *Population Redistribution and Economic Growth: United States, 1870–1950,* Vol. III. Philadelphia: American Philosophical Society.

Ehrenberg, Ronald G., and Robert S. Smith. 1991. *Modern Labor Economics: Theory and Public Policy.* 4th ed. New York: Harper Collins.

Federal Reserve Bank of San Francisco. Various years. *Monthly Review.*

Fisher, Gerald J. 1949. *A Statistical Summary of Shipbuilding under the U.S. Maritime Commission During World War II.* Historical Reports of the War Administration, U.S. Maritime Commission, no. 2.

Fujita, Masahisa, Paul Krugman, and Anthony J. Venables. 1999. *The Spatial Economy: Cities, Regions, and International Trade.* Cambridge, Mass.: MIT Press.

Gordon, Margaret. 1954. *Employment Expansion and Population Growth.* Berkeley: University of California Press.

Jaffe, Abram J., and Seymour L. Wolfbein. 1945. "Postwar Migration Plans of Army Enlisted Men." *Annals of the American Academy of Political and Social Science* 238: 18–26.

Lotchin, Roger. 1992. *Fortress California, 1910–1961: From Warfare to Welfare.* New York: Oxford.

Marshall, Alfred. 1952. *Principles of Economics.* London: Macmillan.

Nash, Gerald. 1990. *World War II and the West: Reshaping the Economy.* Lincoln: University of Nebraska Press.

Niklason, C. R. 1930. *Commercial Survey of the Pacific Southwest.* Washington, D.C.: GPO.

Oregon State. Various years. *Annual Reports of the Unemployment Compensation Commission.* Salem, Ore.

Pacific Factory. Various years.

Pacific Northwest Business. Various years.

Pearlman, Lester M. 1947. "Prospective Labor Supply on the West Coast." *Monthly Labor Review* 64: 565–66.

Puget Sound Regional Planning Commission. 1943. *Puget Sound Region War and Postwar Development.* Washington, D.C.: GPO.

Rhode, Paul W. 1994. "The Nash Thesis Revisited: An Economic Historian's View." In "Special Issue: Fortress California at War." *Pacific Historical Review* 63: 363–92.

———. 2000. "The Impact of World War Two Spending on the California Economy." In R. Lotchin, ed., *The Way We Really Were: The Golden State in the Second Great War,* pp. 93–119. Urbana: University of Illinois Press.

Smith, Adam. 1904. *Wealth of Nations.* London: Methuen.

U.S. Bureau of the Census. 1947. *County Data Book: 1947.* Washington, D.C.: GPO.

———. 1947. *Estimated Number of Veterans of World War II in Continental United States by States, April 1, 1947.* Current Population Report, Series P-25, no. 5.

———. 1975. *Historical Statistics of the United States, Colonial Times to 1970.* Washington, D.C.: GPO.

U.S. Bureau of Labor Statistics. *Construction.* Various issues.

U.S. Civilian Aeronautical Administration. 1946. "Aircraft, Engine, and Propeller Production, U.S. Military Acceptances, 1940–45."

———. *Statistical Handbook of Civil Aviation.* Various years.

U.S. Council of Economic Advisers. 1947. *Midyear Economic Report of the President, July 21, 1947.* Washington, D.C.: GPO.

———. 2002. *2002 Economic Report of the President.* Washington, D.C.: GPO.

U.S. Department of Commerce. Office of Domestic Commerce. 1947. *State and Regional Market Indicators, 1939–45.* Economics Series, no. 60. Washington, D.C.: GPO.

———. 1948. *State, Regional, and Local Market Indicators, 1939–46.* Economics Series no. 67. Washington, D.C.: GPO.

U.S. Department of Commerce. 1984. *State Personal Income, 1929–1982.* Washington, D.C.: GPO.

———. 1997. *Statistical Abstract of the United States: 1997.* Washington, D.C.: GPO.

U.S. Senate. 1944a. *Developing the West through Small Business: II, Field Hearings Seattle, Wash., July 26 and 27, 1944.* Hearings before the Special Committee to Study and Survey Problems of Small Business Enterprises, 78th Cong., 2d sess., Pt. 41. Washington, D.C.: GPO.

———. 1944b. *Developing the West through Small Business: III, Field Hearings Portland, Oreg., July 28, 1944.* Hearings before the Special Committee to Study and Survey Problems of Small Business Enterprises, 78th Cong., 2d sess., Pt. 42. Washington, D.C.: GPO.

———. 1946. *California Looks to Its Economic Future: II, Field Hearings Fresno, Calif., Feb. 25, 1946.* Hearings before the Special Committee to Study and Survey Problems of Small Business Enterprises, 79th Cong., 2d sess., Pt. 86. Washington, D.C.: GPO.

Washington State Employment Security Department. *Annual Reports to the Governor.* Various years. Olympia, Wash.

Wilcox, Winifred S. 1943. "West Coast Manpower Program." *Manpower Review* 10: 3–5, 24.

9

STANDARDIZATION, DIVERSITY, AND LEARNING IN CHINA'S NUCLEAR POWER PROGRAM

Geoffrey Rothwell

1. THE CHINESE NUCLEAR POWER PROGRAM DURING THE 1990S

In the 1980s China began constructing two Pressurized Water Reactor (PWR) nuclear power plants (NPPs): Qinshan 1 on the central China coast and Daya Bay 1 and 2 near Hong Kong (see Table 9.1). Qinshan 1 was built by the China National Nuclear Corporation (CNNC) with a nominal capacity of 300 megawatts-electric and a net capacity of 279 MW (net megawatts).[1] Given the high local content, it had a low initial capital cost. However, early operating problems and problems with damaged fuel rods (which caused the plant to close from July 1998 to October 1999) required imported capital additions, increasing the capital cost significantly. On the other hand, the two 944 MW units at Daya Bay were built with expensive foreign equipment and engineering from France and the UK through Framatome (of France) and a joint venture of General Electric Company (of the UK) and Alcatel-Alsthom (of France) with French and British financing. Both plants came into commercial operation in 1994. Both had problems in early operation. These problems were solved by 1995. Both were operating at high capacity factors through 1997 (see Rothwell 1998).

The Chinese and the international nuclear equipment and services suppliers were optimistic about the future of nuclear power in China in 1996 when China published its Ninth Five-Year Plan (1996–2000) (see Suttmeier and Evans 1996). It called for constructing eight units at four sites before the year

Table 9.1
Chinese nuclear power plants

Plant	Province	Cost ($/kW)[a]	Type[b]	Net MW	Date[c]	Utility[d]	NSSS Manufacturers[e]	Turbine-Generator[e]	Architect-Engineer[e]	Constructor[e]
In Operation										
Qinshan 1	Zhejiang	$2,500	PWR	279	1994	Qinshan NPC	CNNC, Japan (Mitsubishi)	CNNC	CNNC	CNNC
Daya Bay 1, Daya Bay 2	Guangdong	2,300	PWR	2 × 944	1994	Guangdong NPJV	France (Framatome)	France and UK (GEC-Alsthom)	France and UK	France, CNNC
Total MW in operation				2,167						
Under Construction										
Qinshan 2-1 Qinshan 2-2	Zhejiang	1,700	PWR	2 × 610	2002 2003	Qinshan NPC	CNNC, Korea, France	US (Westinghouse)	China, France	CNNC
Ling'ao 1 Ling'ao 2	Guangdong	2,000	PWR	2 × 935	2002 2003	Guangdong NPJV	France (Framatome)	France and UK (GEC-Alsthom)	France and UK	CNNC, France, Japan
Qinshan 3-1 Qinshan 3-2	Zhejiang	2,500	PHWR	2 × 665	2002 2003	Qinshan NPC	Canada (AECL)	Japan (Hitachi)	U.S. (Bechtel)	Canada, CNNC, Korea
Tianwan-1 Tianwan-2	Jiangsu	1,700	WWER	2 × 950	2004 2005	Lianyungang NPJV	Russia	Russia	Russia	Russia
Total MW under construction				6,320						

SOURCE: Sinton (1998) and IAEA (2000), updated with information from *Nucleonics Week*.

[a]Cost per kW is approximate.

[b]Types: PHWR = Pressurized Heavy Water Reactor; PWR = Pressurized Water Reactor; WWER = Water (Cooled)–Water (Moderated) Electricity Reactor

[c]Date is commercial operation date.

[d]Abbreviations: NPC = Nuclear Power Corporation; NPJV = Nuclear Power Joint Venture

[e]Abbreviations: NSSS = Nuclear Steam System Supply; AECL = Atomic Energy of Canada Ltd.; CNNC = China National Nuclear Corporation; GEC = General Electric Co. of the UK; GEC-Alsthom = joint venture of GEC and Alcatel-Alsthom (France)

2000. These are (1) Qinshan 2, a follow-on to Qinshan 1 with two 610 MW PWR units; (2) Ling'ao, a follow-on to (and near) Daya Bay with two 935 MW PWR units with French and British technology and financing; (3) Qinshan 3, two Canadian Pressurized Heavy Water Reactors (PHWRs), similar to units in (the Republic of) Korea, with Canadian financing; and (4) Tianwan (between Qinshan and Beijing), two Russian 950 MW WWERs (pressurized Water-cooled and Water-moderated Electricity Reactors) with Russian financing (Sinton 1998).

Further, the CNNC was optimistic that China would build 20,000 MW of nuclear capacity by 2010 and 30,000–40,000 MW by 2020, for example, by finishing eight units with 6,000–8,000 MW every five years from 2000 to 2020. This optimism carried over to the international (Asian and European) community. Although U.S. nuclear equipment suppliers were excluded from the Chinese market because of nonproliferation concerns with the export of U.S. nuclear technology to China, Westinghouse signed an agreement in 1995 to supply turbine generators for the Qinshan 2 plant, and U.S. engineering services supplier Bechtel was awarded the "balance-of-plant" design contract for Qinshan 2 in 1996. In October 1997 the United States and China concluded an agreement that allowed U.S. nuclear steam system supply (NSSS) manufacturers to export nuclear equipment to China on a case-by-case basis. The U.S. nuclear power industry was elated to be able to enter this "$60 billion" market (see Winston and McManamy 1997).[2] However, no major projects have been awarded to U.S. NSSS suppliers.

In early 2000 the Beijing government asked the leading Chinese nuclear industry participants to focus on developing a standardized PWR. However the Tenth Five-Year Plan (2001–05) is vague regarding nuclear power development. According to Premier Zhu Rongji (2001): "While making full use of existing power-generating capacity, we need to develop hydroelectric power and build large-scale thermal power plants near coal mines . . . and moderately develop nuclear power."[3]

It is unlikely that China will be able to begin building a standardized plant by 2005 because (1) none of the plants in the Ninth Plan have been fully completed, (2) demand growth for electricity has slowed as Chinese heavy industry has been restructured, (3) international finance for nuclear power plants has been difficult to obtain, (4) Chinese national policy has shifted attention away from building generating capacity to improving the transmission and distribution system, and (5) the Chinese nuclear licensing and regulatory agency, the National Nuclear Safety Administration (NNSA) is overwhelmed with the diversity of the nuclear technologies under construction (see Hibbs 1999b, 2000a; and Suttmeier and Evans 1996). International optimism regarding a nuclear power boom in China has waned.

Should China have focused earlier on a standardized design, as the French did in 1974? This chapter examines the optimality of China's approach based on David and Rothwell (1996b). The next section discusses standardization and diversity in nuclear power programs. Section 3 parameterizes the Chinese strategy with a model where a central planner attempts to minimize the present value of construction and operation costs by choosing the optimal level of diversity. The model examines the tradeoff between "learning-by-doing" in the construction of standardized nuclear power units and "learning-by-using" many nuclear power technologies to increase the probability of discovering the least costly NSSS design in a particular national context. The model shows that the optimality of diversity depends crucially on the ability of the Chinese nuclear power industry to incorporate learning into a standardized design. The issue of how to maximize learning is discussed in section 4.

2. STANDARDIZATION AND DIVERSITY IN INTERNATIONAL NUCLEAR POWER

Diversity in nuclear power plant design can be examined along at least four dimensions: (1) the nuclear fuel, (2) the moderator of the nuclear reaction, (3) the nuclear reactor coolant, and (4) the method of transforming heat from the reactor into electricity. Although there have been many experimental designs combining these options, current operating designs are (1) Pressurized light Water–cooled and –moderated Reactors using enriched uranium, PWRs, and WWERs (a Soviet-designed, Russian-modified pressurized Water-cooled, Water-moderated Electricity Reactor); (2) Boiling light Water–cooled and –moderated Reactors using enriched uranium (BWRs), and Advanced BWRs (ABWRs); (3) Graphite-moderated Reactors (GRs) of many types, including the early British and French Gas-Cooled Reactors (GCRs), later British

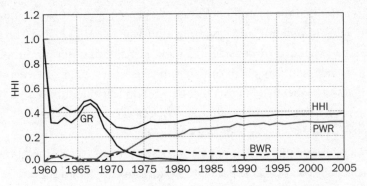

Notes: GR = Graphite-Moderated Reactor; PWR = Pressurized Water Reactor;
BWR = Boiling Water Reactor.

Figure 9.1 Squared market shares and the Herfindahl-Hirschman index for international nuclear power reactors

Advanced Gas Reactors (AGRs) and the Soviet-designed water-cooled RBMK, for example at Chernobyl; (4) Heavy Water–moderated Reactors (HWRs), including the Canadian Pressurized Heavy Water Reactor (PHWR or CANDU), using natural uranium; and (5) Fast Breeder Reactors (FBRs). Current world operating capacity includes PWRs (207 units with 196 GW), BWRs (92 units with 79 GW), WWERs (48 units with 31 GW), GRs (54 units with 27 GW), HWRs (32 units with 16 GW), and FBRs (4 units with 1 GW) (see IAEA 2000).

World nuclear power diversity can be measured with a Herfindahl-Hirschman Index (HHI) used in studies of industrial concentration, as in David and Rothwell (1996a).[4] HHI is the sum of the squared market shares: Σs_j^2, where s_j is the market share (of capacity) of a reactor type j. Figure 9.1 shows changes in the world HHI from 1960 through 2005 (considering nuclear units under active construction). Until the early 1970s the graphite reactor had the largest nuclear power market share. However, during the 1970s the PWRs surpassed GRs, and light water reactors (PWRs, BWRs, and WWERs) now dominate world nuclear power.

3. STANDARDIZATION AND DIVERSITY IN THE CHINESE COMMERCIAL NUCLEAR POWER PROGRAM

To understand China's nuclear power strategy, I apply the model in David and Rothwell (1996b) to China's Ninth and Tenth Five-Year Plans. The primary assumption is that the central nuclear power planner's goal is to minimize the present value of building and operating a nuclear power industry. The problem can be simplified by considering a two-generation program: In the first stage of Generation I, N plants are built. In the second stage of Generation I these plants are operated at costs that depend on learning through standardization. In Generation II, one technology type is selected and X sets of N plants are constructed. What is the optimal level of diversity in Stage 1?

To help answer this question, I simulate the present value of total costs of electricity based on plausible parameter values for the Chinese case. The basic parameters and their posited values are indicated in Table 9.2. Costs are simulated for alternative choices of technological diversity in the first stage, allowing for an explicit calculation of the tradeoff between cost reductions through experimentation with alternative technologies, and cost reductions arising from economies of standardization. In section 3.3, I then explicitly solve for the cost-minimizing degree of diversity and show how it depends on critical scale and learning parameters.

Table 9.2
Parameter values for simulation

Parameter	Definition	Unit	Value
N	Number of units per stage	—	8
k	Construction cost per kW	$/kW	$2,400
γ	Learning in construction	%	10%
W	Capacity of units in MW	MW	900
c	Operating cost	$/MWh	$40
σ	Standard deviation in CS	$/MWh	$4
x	Stages in Generation II	—	4
r	Discount rate	%	7%
CRF	Capital recovery factor	%	8%
τ	Construction time	Years	5
$\tau_2 = \tau_3$	Nuclear power plant lifetime	Years	30
τ_4	Years to Generation II	Years	10
δ_1	Discount factor t = 5	%	70%
$\delta_2 = \delta_3$	Present value of annuity	—	12.10
δ_4	Discount factor t = 10	%	50%
α	Learning in Generation II operation	%	50%
α^*	Where diversity = standard	%	82%

3.1. GENERATION I

Stage 1: Construction

In Stage 1 a total of N nuclear power units are built with n units of M types: $N = n \cdot M$. If the total number of units (N) is given exogenously (for example, by electricity demand), the planner's problem can be characterized as either choosing the optimal number of technology types (M) or, equivalently, choosing the optimal level of diversity, where diversity (d) can be measured as (M/N). Alternatively, standardization can be measured as ($1/M$) and, under the assumption of an equal number of units of all types, it is equal to the HHI. The planner can choose a level of diversity between two extremes: (1) no diversity, that is, complete standardization (following the French example, see David and Rothwell 1996a), where $d = 1/N$, and (2) complete diversity, where $d = 1$. In the simulation presented here, $N = 8$, and costs are simulated for $M = 1, 2, 4$, or 8 different technologies.

To determine the optimal level of diversity, assume that (1) there is an equal number of units of all types $n_j = n$, where $j = 1, \ldots, M$, and (2) first-of-a-kind construction costs (in dollars per net megawatt-electric, MW) are the same for each type ($k_j = k$ for all j), where k *includes* financing costs such as Interest During Construction. For example, k equals \$2,400 per net kW or \$2.4 million (M) per MW. Further, assume all units are built *simultaneously* during the construction period, equal to τ years; for example, $\tau = 5$ years beginning in 1995. Here, learning in construction activity is equivalent to economies of scale in the number of units, so

$$k_n = kn^{-\gamma}, \quad 0 < \gamma \le 1, \tag{1}$$

where k_n is the construction cost per MW (at the end of Stage 1, *including* finance charges during construction) for a set of n units of a single type and γ is a measure of learning. For example, if $\gamma = 0.10$, $k_1 = \$2,400/kW$, $k_2 = \$2,239/kW$, $k_4 = \$2,089/kW$, $k_8 = \$1,949/kW$, etc. (see Table 9.3, line 3). These numbers approximate the experience in China (see Table 9.1.)

The total cost of each *set* of units is

$$nW k_n = nW kn^{-\gamma} = Wkn^{1-\gamma}, \tag{2}$$

Table 9.3

Simulation of costs under alternative choices of technological diversity in stage 1

Variable	Definition	Unit	Equation	Number of Technologies			
				1	2	4	8
n	Number of units in a set			8	4	2	1
d	Diversity			0.125	0.250	0.500	1.000
$k(n)$	Construction cost per MW	$/kW	1	$1,949	$2,089	$2,239	$2,400
K	Total capital cost	$B	3	$14	$15	$16	$17
K/MWh	Capital cost/MWh	$/MWh		$22.98	$24.63	$26.40	$28.30
C_2	Realized operating cost	$/MWh	5	$31.68	$34.45	$37.23	$40.00
$/MWh	Average Generation I cost	$/MWh		$54.67	$59.09	$63.63	$68.30
TC_2	Total operating cost in stage 2	$B	6	$2.0	$2.2	$2.3	$2.5
PV_2	Present value of TC_2	$B	7	$38	$41	$45	$48
k_3	Average K cost in Generation II	$/kW		$1,464	$1,570	$1,682	$1,803
k_3/MWh	Capital cost/MWh	$/MWh		$17.27	$18.51	$19.83	$21.26
C_3	Realized C in Generation II	$/MWh	9	$27.68	$28.80	$29.23	$28.69
$/MWh	Average Generation II cost	$/MWh		$44.95	$47.30	$49.06	$49.94
K_3	Discounted total K in Generation II	$B		$30	$32	$34	$37
TC_3	Annual C per stage in Generation II	$B		$1.7	$1.8	$1.8	$1.8
PVC_3	Present value of TC_3	$B	10	$60	$62	$63	$62
PV_3	Expected costs in Generation II	$B		$89	$94	$97	$98
$PV*$	**Present value of total costs**	**$B**	**11**	**$71**	**$76**	**$80**	**$83**

Note: See text for derivation of values.

where W is the size of each unit in MW. The total cost (K) of building all N plants, assuming all units are the same size, is

$$K = M(Wkn^{1-\gamma}) = MWk(N/M)^{1-\gamma} = NWk(M/N)^{\gamma} = NWkd^{\gamma}. \quad (3)$$

For example, for a program of eight 900 (net) MW units with first-of-a-kind costs of \$2,400/kW and $\gamma = 0.10$ yields a total cost of \$17 billion (B) with total diversity $(d = 1.0)$ and \$14B with total standardization $(d = 0.125)$; that is, cost increases with diversity (Table 9.3, line 4). With a thirty-year life and a *real* cost of capital of 7 percent,[5] the capital recovery factor would be 8 percent.[6] With an 80 percent capacity factor (see Rothwell 1998) the capital cost per megawatt-hour (MWh) would be \$28/MWh with total diversity and \$23/MWh with total standardization (Table 9.3, line 5).[7]

Stage 2: Operations and Incremental Learning

In Stage 2 of Generation I the focus is on minimizing the cost of generating electricity at units built in Stage 1. Generating costs per MWh are composed of two parts: a capital (construction) cost and an annual operations cost.[8] The capital cost per MW is kd^{γ}. The annual cost reflects an initial cost (c) minus a cost saving (cs), anticipated and optimized in Stage 1 and thus realized from the beginning of Stage 2. Assume that the initial operations cost, c_j, is equal to an average c for all types. However, for each level of diversity the cost savings component (cs_j) varies with differences in learning-by-using: cs_j is a function of the number of units constructed of each type. Operation yields learning opportunities that generate a distribution of attainable cost savings. A larger number of units of a particular type leads to more experience and to an increase in the probability of discovering the *least cost* method of producing electricity *in a particular context* (such as in China): $\partial F(cs_j)/\partial n > 0$, where $F(cs_j)$ is the cumulative distribution function of attaining the *maximum* cost savings for each technology.

If cost savings cs_j are distributed with mean μ_j and variance σ_j^2, the expected *maximum* cost savings for units of type j is $E(cs_j^{\max} \mid n)$. What is the relationship between $cs_j^{\max}$ and n? Making use of a general result regarding extreme value distributions, the expected extreme value $(cs_j^{\max})$ is a positive function of the mean and the standard deviation, when such samples are drawn from a unimodal distribution (see Gumbel 1958). Also, the expected extreme value is a positive concave function of the sample size (n): The standard deviation of the underlying distribution increases with the sample size.[9] Assuming normality, the expected maximum improvement from experienced-based learning for each type can be modeled as:[10]

$$E(cs^{max} \mid n) = \mu + \sigma(\log n), \quad \text{for } n \geq 1. \tag{4}$$

Assume that $\mu = 0$ for all types (the mean cost savings is absorbed into c at the beginning of Stage 2). Then the annual cost and realized cost savings in Stage 2 per MWh are

$$C_2 = c - \mu - \sigma \log n = c - \sigma \log (N/M)$$
$$= c - \sigma (-\log (M/N)) = c + \sigma \log d. \tag{5}$$

For N units of capacity W the total operations cost per year is NWC_2h, where h is the hours per year, usually 8,760. For example, assume that $N = 8$, $W = 900$, $c = \$40/\text{MWh}$, and $\sigma = \$4/\text{MWh}$. With total diversity, $C_2 = \$40/\text{MWh}$ and total Generation I operating costs are \$2.5B per year. With total standardization, $C_2 = \$32/\text{MWh}$ and total operating costs are \$2.0B per year (Table 9.3, line 6). Under these assumptions, total cost per MWh would be \$55 with total standardization and \$68 with total diversity (Table 9.3, line 7). This is similar to the price of power from Daya Bay at \$68/MWh (Hibbs 1999a).

These costs are discounted to the beginning of Stage 2 by $\delta_2(r, \tau_2)$, where δ_2 is a uniform series, present-value factor that depends on the cost of capital, r, and the life of the nuclear unit, τ_2.[11] The present value of costs at the beginning of Stage 2 (PV_2) for the N plants is

$$PV_2 = NW\{kd^\gamma + \delta_2 h[c + \sigma \log d]\}. \tag{6}$$

With a thirty-year life and a 7 percent *real* cost of capital, $\delta_2(r, \tau_2) = 12.10$. PV_2 is \$48 billion with total diversity, but PV_2 is only \$38 billion with total standardization (Table 9.3, line 9). Diversity drives up expected costs during Generation I: $\partial PV_2/\partial d > 0$. Therefore, total costs decline with standardization. What is the value of diversity? Under what circumstances would diversity in Generation I be beneficial for a second generation?

3.2. GENERATION II: CONSTRUCTION AND OPERATION

After learning from the construction and operation of the first generation, a second generation of plants could be built. Generation II could start at any time after Stage 1 of Generation I. For example, Generation II could start five years into Stage 2 (for example, after a single five-year plan). Define the start of Generation II to be τ_4 years since the start of Stage 1 (for example, ten years after the start of Stage 1 in 1995). In Generation II, assume the following.

1. $(X \cdot N)$ standardized units are built at a rate of N units per stage with X stages in Generation II every τ years (for example, eight units every five years).

2. Construction costs for all units in each stage of Generation II are equal to the previous generation's "Nth-of-a-kind" costs, where N is the number of units completed through the end of the previous stage and the rate of learning is the same as in Generation I.

3. Opportunities to observe different nuclear power plant types in Generation I make it possible to select the best design suited to the local industrial structure, the abilities and training of local engineers and scientists, and local transmission networks.

4. Operation of the type of plant selected for standardization yields the same distribution of potential cost reductions with the expected maximum improvement exceeding that available in the second stage of Generation I only if there was more than one technology type built in the first stage of Generation I.

Corresponding to assumptions (1) and (2), the construction costs per MW for N units of a single type built in each stage of Generation II would be

$$k_x(N \mid m) = (kd^\gamma)(xN)^{-\gamma}, \tag{7}$$

where $x = 1, \ldots, X$ and $(xN)^{-\gamma}$ represents learning in constructing units of a single type. For example, if $\gamma = 0.1$, $k_2 = \$2,089/kW$ in Stage 1, and 32 units $(X = 4)$ are built in Generation II, the *average* cost per unit would be $\$1,570/kW$ (Table 9.3, line 10). With an 80 percent capacity factor the average capital cost per MWh would be \$21/MWh with total diversity and \$17/MWh with total standardization (Table 9.3, line 11).

Corresponding to assumptions 3 and 4, the selection of the type of plant with the largest expected (single plant) cost reduction can be represented as a draw from the extreme value distribution. The expected mean cost savings is:[12]

$$E(cs_3^{max} \mid M) = \mu + \sigma M^\alpha, \quad 0 < \alpha < 1, \tag{8}$$

where α is a measure of learning from diversity in operating many types of Generation I plants. Here, diversity during Stages 1 and 2 permits more learning, reducing operating costs during Generation II: in developing a standardized Chinese nuclear generating station, more diversity would be beneficial in Stage 1. Unlike in Generation I, where $\mu = 0$, in Generation II cost savings cumulate from Generation I, so $\mu = -\sigma \log d$ and annual cost per MWh is

$$C_3 = c + \sigma \log d - \sigma M^\alpha. \tag{9}$$

For example, assume $c = \$40/MWh$, $\sigma = \$4/MWh$, and $\alpha = 0.5$. With total standardization in Generation I, $C_3 = \$28/MWh$. With total diversity in Generation I, $C_3 = \$29/MWh$. Under these assumptions, total cost would be \$45/MWh with total standardization in Generation I and \$50/MWh with total diversity. These are similar to the cost of electricity from new coal plants (see May, Heller, and Zhang 1999) and are under the Chinese goal of \$55–\$60/MWh (Hibbs 1999a).

These costs are discounted to the beginning of Generation II by the factor $\delta_3(r, \tau_3)$. For example, as in Generation I, assuming a thirty-year life and a 7 percent *real* cost of capital, $\delta_3(r, \tau_3) = 12.10$. The expected present value *at the beginning* of Generation II, PV_3, for the $X \cdot N$ plants is

$$PV_3 = \Sigma e^{-rx\tau} NW \{(kd^\gamma)(xN)^{-\gamma} + \delta_3 h [c + \sigma \log d - \sigma M^\alpha]\} \tag{10}$$

for $x = 1, \ldots X$. For example, with parameter values equal to those in Table 9.2 with total diversity in Generation I, $PV_3 = \$98B$ and with total standardization $PV_3 = \$89B$ (Table 9.3, line 17). With these parameter values, early standardization is the least-cost option for this multistage program. This depends on the scale parameter γ and the learning parameter α. The next section explores optimal diversity as a function of γ and α.

3.3. OPTIMAL DIVERSITY

Again, what is the cost-minimizing value of $M(M^*)$, the number of different plant types to build in Stage I? To answer this question, define continuous-compounding discount factors: $\delta_1 = e^{-r\tau}$ that translates second-stage Generation I costs to the start of the program, and $\delta_4 = e^{-r\tau_4}$ that translates start of Generation II costs to start of program present-value equivalents. Expressing all costs at the beginning of the program (see equations 6 and 10),

$$PV^*(N \mid M) = \delta_1 NW\{kd^\gamma + \delta_2 h[c + \sigma \log d]\} + \delta_4 \Sigma e^{-r\times\tau}NW$$
$$\times \{(kd^\gamma)(xN)^{-\gamma} + \delta_3 h[c + \sigma \log d - \sigma M^\alpha]\}. \qquad (11)$$

The last line of Table 9.3 gives values for these costs in the simulation. In this case, it can be seen that maximum standardization yields the lowest present value of total costs. More generally, the total cost formula can be used to derive M^* and thus the cost-minimizing diversity of technologies as a function of the parameters. It can be shown (see Rothwell 2002) that there are two main cases and two subcases:

- **Case 1:** $(\gamma - \alpha) \leq 0$ implies there is no interior cost-minimizing value for M. Under these conditions there are two subcases.
  - **Case 1a** in which the lowest costs are achieved where only one type of plant is built from the outset: $M = 1$ and $d = 1/N$.
  - **Case 1b** in which maximum diversity is cost minimizing: $M = N$ and $d = 1$.
- **Case 2:** $(\gamma - \alpha) > 0$ is necessary, but not sufficient, for the existence of an interior optimum for the value of M.

First, considering Case 1, is there an α such that the present value of total program costs could be minimized with total diversity? With the parameter values in Table 9.2, at $\alpha = 0.82$ the present value of program costs is equal for total standardization and total diversity. With $\alpha > 0.82$ *total diversity* yields a lower present value of costs. The relationship between total costs and diversity for different values of the learning parameter α is shown in Figure 9.2. Clearly, with $(\gamma - \alpha) \leq 0$, the coefficient of learning during operations must be *very high* for diversity to be the optimal strategy.

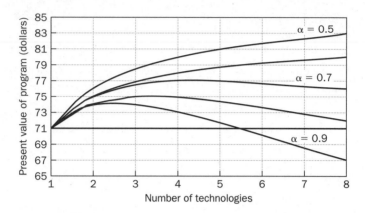

Figure 9.2 The influence of the learning parameter in operations on present value

Next, consider Case 2 in which $(\gamma - \alpha) > 0$ satisfies the necessary condition for the PV^* to be strictly minimized by selecting some initial level of design diversity—that is, $M > 1$. However, for a strict minimum, $(\gamma - \alpha) > 0$ is not sufficient. The second-order condition must be satisfied. Are there values for α that can satisfy this condition? Given $0 \leq \gamma \leq 1$ and $0 < \alpha < 1$, the least restrictive value of γ for evaluating α would be $\gamma = 1$. However even with $\gamma = 1$, there are no values where the second-order condition for Case 2 are satisfied.

With reasonable parameter values, there is no interior optimum value for M. The optimum is either **Case 1a:** complete standardization in both Generations I and II, or **Case 1b:** complete diversity in Generation I with standardization in Generation II. The optimality of complete diversity (**Case 1b**) depends on *unrealistically high* values for α—that is, an expectation that diversity in Generation I will yield a *large* reduction in cost in Generation II. So **Case 1a,** early standardization, is the likely optimal strategy under the assumptions in Table 9.2.

4. POLICY CONCLUSIONS AND FURTHER RESEARCH

Two sets of conclusions flow from this analysis. The first concerns standardization, diversity, and learning in China's commercial nuclear power program. The second concerns the applicability of the model in David and Rothwell (1996b) to industrial policy.

As in most economic analyses of industrial policy, I assume that the objective of the nuclear power planners in China is to *maximize Chinese social welfare*. This involves minimizing the price of electricity, maximizing the profitability of the enterprises involved with the industry, and encouraging industrial development in China. All of these goals should coincide with policies that lead to an efficient long-run allocation of resources.

The interpretation of these objectives by state planners in China has led to the following policies: (1) minimize the investment of Chinese capital in building nuclear power plants, (2) minimize state subsidies to Chinese enterprises in nuclear power, (3) increase local content and technology transfer with each new contract with an international supplier, and (4) encourage international competition by building a variety of nuclear power plants.

This has resulted in a nuclear power industry with a Chinese prototype (Qinshan 1 and 2), a Chinese-French hybrid (Daya Bay and Ling'ao), and competing international designs (Qinshan 3 and Tianwan). Presently, the stated long-run goal of the Chinese National Nuclear Corporation (Hibbs 2000b) is to develop a 1,000 MW Chinese standard Nuclear Plant (CNP-1000).[13] For 20,000 MW of capacity by 2010, *at least* four new units should be started in the Tenth Five-Year Plan to avoid equipment and personnel bottlenecks in building eight more units in the Eleventh Five-Year Plan (2006–10). Of course, fewer units could be built, missing the 2010 goal.

While the construction cost per kilowatt has been declining for the French-Chinese hybrid, Chinese electricity consumers will pay dearly (in present-value terms) for this program unless the CNP can be developed at minimum cost with maximum learning. The model discussed here demonstrates that initial standardization would be cheaper than initial diversity unless there is tremendous learning from the Generation I plants. The model has focused on learning from diversity in operations. A model with learning from diversity in engineering design and construction would likely lead to the same conclusions.

Unfortunately, there is a conflict between (1) the goal of developing a CNP that relies on learning through *cooperation* and (2) a strategy that minimizes cost through *competition* (for example, minimizing Chinese capital by encouraging competition among international suppliers to provide financing or lower project cost). This conflict is present in many research and development programs. Given the diversity and competition in the Chinese nuclear power program, how can learning now be maximized (that is, how can the value of α be increased)?

First, the Chinese should recognize the experimental nature of their situation and treat the Generation I as a scientific program, not simply a commercial one; that is, they should use scientific and engineering standards of evaluation, as well as profitability. The standard design should include a standardized construction program with modularization and virtual construction. These aspects of the program can be learned from construction at all NPP sites in China.

Second, the Chinese should develop standards for acquiring and analyzing information on *all* aspects of construction, operation, and regulation, including problems encountered, possible solutions considered, the process of determining the solution to each problem, and the success of each chosen solution. For example, IAEA (1999) outlines a method of studying management practices at nuclear power plants (see the "Wolsong Case Study" in IAEA 1999). Similar studies should be conducted on construction management (including equipment acquisition, scheduling, and human resources), operation (including equipment quality and reliability), and regulation (including probability risk assessment and risk-informed regulation; see Rothwell 2000a). This information can be used to integrate standardized building, training, operating, and licensing procedures.

Third, the Chinese should develop a long-term plan for a standardized design that specifies equipment and services that can be provided by *more than one* supplier domestically or internationally and subject to competitive bidding. A standard design that relies only on monopoly suppliers will not be able to compete with other forms of electricity generation either because construction costs will not decline with scale or because operating costs will not improve (for example, through increases in productivity).

Fourth, the Chinese should consider (1) building more plants similar to those already completed or under construction and (2) operating those under construction before choosing a Generation II standard. In particular, before developing the indigenous three-loop CNP-1000, the two-loop, two-unit

Qinshan 2 should be operated through the initial fuel cycle before CNP engineering is finalized. This could imply that nonindigenous three-loop units should be built during the Tenth Five-Year Plan, postponing the CNP-1000 to the Eleventh Five-Year Plan. (The French built thirty-four three-loop units in France in association with Westinghouse before developing their indigenous four-loop 1300 MW PWR. Daya Bay and Ling'ao use the French three-loop design.)

The second purpose of this chapter was to test the applicability of the model in David and Rothwell (1996b) to industrial policy. While the model successfully captured many aspects of the problem of designing a present-value-minimizing industrial policy, its focus on tractability reduced its ability to represent China's nuclear power program. Therefore, future research should address the following issues.[14] First, sensitivity analysis should be conducted and simplifications made to improve tractability and realism. Second, the model of "learning-by-using" in operations relies on extreme value statistics. Therefore, the model should be embedded in a probabilistic framework: (1) probability distributions should be specified for key variables and parameters and (2) Monte Carlo simulations should be done to determine the robustness of the conclusion regarding optimal diversity in Generation I. Third, the Chinese program has been hampered by capital constraints. The implicit assumption here has been perfect capital markets. The model should incorporate financing constraints and be solved using constrained optimization techniques. Fourth, the model should be embedded in an industrial organization framework where the incentives of international technology suppliers are incorporated and the observed outcome can be interpreted as an equilibrium between Chinese planners and international interests. These features will provide a more realistic model in which to evaluate standardization, diversity, and learning in the evolution of technologies such as commercial nuclear power in China.

Notes

Acknowledgments: This chapter was presented at "History Matters: Economic Growth, Technology, and Population—A Conference in Honor of Paul David," Stanford University, June 2–3, 2000. It is based on David and Rothwell, "Standardization, Diversity, and Learning: Strategies for the Coevolution of Technology and Industrial Capacity," *International Journal of Industrial Organization* (1996). I thank C. Braun, J. S. Choi, R. Crow, P. David, E. Fei, R. Hagen, D. Hale, S. Kondo, L. Langlois, M. May, K. Matsui, K. Nagano, C. Perin, W. Sailor, D. Shen, C. Siddayao, J. Sinton, J. Stewart, W. Sundstrom, T. Tyborowski, Y. Yang, M. Yajima, and C. Zhang for their comments, data, or encouragement. I also thank participants in the Lawrence Livermore National Laboratory's "Nuclear Cooperation Meeting on Spent Fuel and High-Level Waste Storage and Disposal," Las Vegas, Nevada, March 7–9, 2000. Of course, any errors are my own.

1. The Qinshan 1 unit is similar to the first unit in Pakistan's Chashma Nuclear Power Project (Chasnupp 1) that started commercial operation in September 2000. The primary difference between the two plants is that the Qinshan reactor vessel was manufactured in Japan, but because of nonproliferation concerns the Chashma reactor vessel was manufactured in China. In August 2001, Pakistan invited Chinese cooperation in building units similar to Qinshan 2.

2. Although General Electric (GE Nuclear) is now building two 1,350 MW Advanced Boiling Water Reactors in Taiwan (see Liaw and Lee 1998), it is reluctant to do business in China without a stronger nuclear liability and insurance program (see Winston and McManamy 1997).

3. The current version of the Tenth Five-Year Plan does not specify nuclear power plants to be started during the plan. However, at least three provinces have applied for permission to build nuclear power plants: Guangdong (the location of Daya Bay and Ling'ao), Zhejiang (the location of the three Qinshan plants), and Shandong (Hibbs 2001b). Site preparation has begun at Zhejiang. The Tianwan site in Jiangsu province has been prepared for two more units, but it is unlikely that these units would be started before 2005.

4. In David and Rothwell (1996a), HHI is a weighted average of diversity of (1) reactor vendor, (2) turbine-generator manufacturer, and (3) architect-engineer. This leads to a lower HHI.

5. The assumption of a 7 percent real cost of capital is from Sinton 1998 (p. 73), which discusses the terms of financing for Ling'ao.

6. The capital recovery factor is equal to $[r(1 + r)^t]/[(1 + r)^t - 1]$, where r is the cost of capital and t is the life of the nuclear power plant. In the model a continuous time version is used. It is equal to $[e^{rt}(e^r - 1)]/(e^{rt} - 1)$.

7. The capacity factor is equal to $Q/(W \cdot h)$, where Q is annual output in megawatt-hours, W is megawatts, and h is the number of hours per year (see Rothwell 1998).

8. This analysis assumes that all operation costs are fixed during a year. This is true for most operation and maintenance costs at nuclear power plants (Rothwell 2000b).

9. Here I focus on operating costs. A more rigorous model would consider the mean and variance of capital costs (construction and postconstruction additions) under diversity and standardization. While early standardization lowers capital cost, it might increase its variance owing to the lack of learning from a diversity of plant designs. Further, standardization includes the possibility that a design flaw could affect many plants and that this design flaw might not be discovered until after many years of operation.

10. In David and Rothwell (1996b), this equation is equivalent to $E(cs^{\max} \mid n) = \mu + B\sigma(\log n)^{\beta}$. Here, I assume that both B and β are equal to 1.

11. The uniform series, present-value factor is equal to $[(1 + r)^t - 1]/[r(1 + r)^t]$, the inverse of the capital recovery factor. The continuous time version is used in the model.

12. In David and Rothwell (1996b), this equation is equivalent to $E(cs_3^{\max} \mid M) = \mu + A\theta M^{\alpha}$. Here, I assume that $A = 1$ and $\theta = \sigma$.

13. This is similar to the development of the Korean standard nuclear plant, of which six units are currently operating and two units are under construction (Park 1998). On the Chinese standard nuclear plants (a three–loop 1000 MW PWR), see MacLachlan (2000); Hibbs (2001a).

14. This model has been adapted to the selection of a portfolio of new nuclear power technologies (Rothwell 2001).

References

David, P. A., and G. S. Rothwell. 1996a. "Measuring Standardization: An Application to the American and French Nuclear Power Industries." *European Journal of Political Economy* 12: 291–308.

———. 1996b. "Standardization, Diversity, and Learning: Strategies for the Coevolution of Technology and Industrial Capacity." *International Journal of Industrial Organization* 14: 181–201.

Gumbel, E. J. 1958. *Statistics of Extremes.* New York: Columbia University Press.

Hibbs, M. 1999a. "Cost of Nuclear Electricity Must Come Down, Beijing Says." *Nucleonics Week* (May 27).

———. 1999b. "With Demand Below Projections, China May Drop Nuclear Projects." *Nucleonics Week* (March 4).

———. 2000a. "Beijing Orders Nuclear Sector to Revamp PWR Development Plan." *Nucleonics Week* (January 6).

———. 2000b. "Foreign Vendors Say They Expect China in 2001 to Plan 4–6 Units." *Nucleonics Week* (March 30).

———. 2001a. "China May Be Still Further Away from Decision on PWR Cooperation." *Nucleonics Week* (April 19).

———. 2001b. "Shandong PWR Project Beset by Problems That May Impact Bids." *Nucleonics Week* (April 5).

IAEA (International Atomic Energy Agency). 1999. *Evaluating and Improving Nuclear Power Plant Operating Performance.* G. S. Rothwell, ed. Vienna: IAEA. IAEA-TECDOC-1098.

———. 2000. *MicroPRIS.* Vienna: IAEA. *www.iaea.or.at*

Liaw, B. D., and G. C. Lee. 1998. "Commercial Nuclear Power Development in Taiwan: A Review." *Pacific and Asian Journal of Energy* 8: 103–15.

MacLachlan, A. 2000. "French Industry Cheered by Chinese Three-Loop Decision." *Nucleonics Week* (January 6).

May, M., T. Heller, and C. Zhang. 1999. "Electricity Choices and Carbon Emissions in Guangdong Province." Paper presented at Stanford University (November 17).

Park, S. D. 1998. "Current Development of Nuclear Power in Korea." *Pacific and Asian Journal of Energy* 8: 92–102.

Rothwell, G. S. 1998. "Comparing Asian Nuclear Power Plant Performance." *Pacific and Asian Journal of Energy* 8: 51–64.

———. 2000a. "Profitability Risk Assessment at Nuclear Power Plants under Electricity Deregulation." *The Impact of Competition*. Montgomery Research and PricewaterhouseCoopers, October.

———. 2000b. "The Risk of Early Retirement of U.S. Nuclear Power Plants under Electricity Deregulation and Carbon Dioxide Emission Reductions." *The Energy Journal* 21.

———. 2001. "Choosing the Optimal Number of New Nuclear Power Technologies." Paper presented at "New Energy Technologies: A Policy Framework for Micro-Nuclear Technology," James A. Baker III Institute for Public Policy, Rice University, March 19–20.

———. 2002. "Optimal Diversity in China's Nuclear Power Program." Stanford Institute for Economic Policy Research Discussion Paper. *http://siepr.stanford.edu*

Sinton, J. E. 1998. "Nuclear Power Industry Development in China." *Pacific and Asian Journal of Energy* 8: 67–76.

Suttmeier, R. P., and P. C. Evans. 1996. "China Goes Nuclear." *The China Business Review* (September–October).

Winston, S., and R. McManamy. 1997. "Nuclear Pact Opens Export Doors." *Engineering News Record* (November 10).

Zhu Rongji. 2001. "Report on the Outline of the Tenth Five-Year Plan for National Economic and Social Development." Presented at the Fourth Session of the Ninth National People's Congress, March 5.

III CONTEXT MATTERS: THE INFLUENCE OF CULTURE, GEOGRAPHY, AND POLITICAL INSTITUTIONS ON ECONOMIES AND POLICIES

10

INCENTIVES, INFORMATION, AND WELFARE: ENGLAND'S NEW POOR LAW AND THE WORKHOUSE TEST

Timothy Besley, Stephen Coate, and Timothy W. Guinnane

1. INTRODUCTION

In 1834 England adopted a set of reforms to its poor-relief system that sought to overturn a system dating back to the time of Elizabeth I. Local parishes under the old system granted outdoor relief to a wide class of persons, including able-bodied workers, and did so in many forms, including in-kind grants, cash, and several forms of wage supplements. The 1834 reforms, collectively referred to as the New Poor Law, established large administrative units beholden to a central authority and attempted to abolish outdoor relief for the able-bodied. Central to the New Poor Law was the workhouse test. Relief officials could not refuse to grant relief to a poor person, but they could "offer the house," which meant requiring that the applicant enter the workhouse to obtain relief. Since those in the workhouse were maintained in deliberately unpleasant conditions, this was not an attractive option.

This essay offers a new interpretation of the role of the workhouse test in the New Poor Law. Our interpretation rests on two key premises, the first of which concerns the objective of policy makers. They divided the poor at a point in time into two categories: the needy and the non-needy. The former are those who require public support in order to achieve an acceptable minimum standard of living, while the latter are those who, owing to superior labor market opportunities, more savings, richer families, and other advantages, have access to sufficient resources to be self-supporting. Among the needy poor, there are two further categories: the deserving and undeserving. The deserving are those who are needy through no fault of their own, while the undeserving are needy because of some vice such as drinking or sloth. Our first premise is that the objective of policy makers was to assist only the deserving.

Our second premise concerns changes in the constraints faced by policy makers. To implement a system of poor relief that assists only the deserving requires a considerable amount of information. Officials must be able to observe individuals' current access to resources (thereby distinguishing the needy from the non-needy), and they must also know their past behavior (thereby distinguishing the deserving from the undeserving). We argue that the violent economic and social changes that characterized the late eighteenth and early nineteenth centuries in England meant that obtaining such information became increasingly difficult.

Given the objective of assisting only the deserving poor, the workhouse test, we argue, was a natural response to the new informational constraints confronting policy makers. First, it ensured that only the needy would apply for relief. Any poor person who had an alternative source of support would rather utilize this than have to live in the workhouse. Following Besley and Coate (1992), we call this the screening role of the workhouse test. In addition, the workhouse test ensured that those who were needy were deserving. Any individual who could avoid getting into poverty would have every incentive to do so to escape the workhouse. Again following Besley and Coate, we refer to this as the deterrent role of the workhouse test.

There are other tests that administrators could impose on recipients. They could, for example, require recipients to undertake hard manual labor in public works projects. Indeed, this was the alternative chosen by British administrators in some of the colonies. Why did reformers in Britain want to erect new institutions rather than use labor tests? We argue that the workhouse was a potent signal to the poor of a change from the more generous Old Poor Law. Such a signal was essential for the deterrent role to be effective. All of this notwithstanding, the workhouse test was not without its drawbacks, and we point these out below.

Our interpretation differs from those previously advanced in the literature in its emphasis on informational changes and the informational role of the workhouse test. Existing interpretations focus largely on changes in attitudes toward the poor. Our interpretation does not rule this out, but offers an additional consideration that we believe to be important. At the very least, our interpretation of the workhouse test explains what is otherwise a puzzling fact: the workhouse was more expensive per pauper than outdoor relief. The only way it could reduce costs was to reduce the total number of paupers relieved by a great deal. Just why did reformers think that the workhouse could accomplish this?

In the next section we provide some brief background on the Poor Law and the adoption of the system. Section 3 discusses the changes in informational constraints facing administrators and the screening and deterrence roles of the workhouse test. Section 4 explains why the workhouse test was chosen rather than some other type of self-acting test. Section 5 discusses some drawbacks to the workhouse test. Section 6 discusses how our interpretation relates to the existing literature, and section 7 concludes.

2. HISTORICAL BACKGROUND

The Old Poor Law

The Old Poor Law was based on two principles: the administrative basis of relief was local, and those making decisions about poor relief had broad latitude in the amounts and types of relief to advance. Poor relief was a statutory right for any pauper who was deemed to be deserving. Relief was administered by some 15,000 parishes ranging in size from thirty acres to thirty square miles, and in population from several dozen to many thousands of persons (Blaug 1963, pp. 156–57). Some parishes before 1834 used institutions resembling the later workhouses, but by the early nineteenth century most relied primarily on grants of food and other necessities, cash, and wage subsidies and employment guarantees. The Speenhamland system common in many southern English parishes during the early nineteenth century used elaborate bread-price scales to determine relief (Blaug 1963, pp. 161–62).

Poor relief became extremely costly during the Napoleonic Wars of the late eighteenth and early nineteenth centuries. Costs continued to climb even after the peace. Poor rates rose on average by 62 percent from 1802–03 to 1832–33. These tax increases far outstripped the gross rentals from farmland on which poor relief assessments primarily fell; rentals increased by only 25 percent over the same period (Digby 1982, p. 9). Some contemporaries traced these high relief costs to abuses of the system: farmers in rural areas, some argued, used the relief system to support their workers in the slack agricultural season. Others alleged that relief was given in the forms most likely to return to the pockets of shopkeepers and publicans.[1]

The New Poor Law was not a pure break with the past. The late eighteenth and early nineteenth centuries was a period of experimentation in relief practices, and the "obstinate diversity of parochial practice" led in some cases to relief based heavily on workhouses (Digby 1982, p. 7). Some parishes erected workhouses on their own while others amalgamated for the purpose of constructing a workhouse, taking advantage of provisions in Gilbert's Act (1782).[2] Opposition to the New Poor Law, as we shall see, also led to the continuation of some old practices long after 1834.

The New Poor Law

Concern about the Old Poor Law led Parliament to appoint several bodies to inquire into its workings during the early nineteenth century. The most famous, the Royal Commission on the Poor Laws, was appointed in 1832, and its recommendations formed the basis for the 1834 act. The New Poor Law changed both the role of local authorities and the form of poor relief. The 1834 act established a Poor Law Board consisting of three commissioners with great powers over the operation of local relief systems. The act also established Poor Law Unions administered by elected officials called guardians. Unions were large local units formed by combining parishes; eventually the 15,000 parishes of England were combined into some 600 Poor Law Unions. Unlike the parish vestries, the Boards of Guardians could be compelled, at least in theory, to adhere to the dictates of the Poor Law Board. At the administrative level, then, the New Poor Law brought about a radical degree of centralization, at both the local and the national level. The New Poor Law also attempted to restrict outdoor relief to the sick and the aged; the Royal Commission's second major recommendation was that the able-bodied and their families be henceforth granted poor relief only in workhouses, under conditions "less eligible" than the working poor. The notion of less eligibility meant to contemporaries that life in the workhouse would be less pleasant than life as a nonpauper member of the working class.[3]

Neither the original Poor Law Commission nor its successors, the Poor Law Board (1847) and the Local Government Board (1871), succeeded in gaining full compliance with the edicts of the central authority. The poor, not surprisingly, resisted the New Poor Law virtually everywhere in England, perceiving it quite rightly as a radical departure from the system under which they had been raised. The Poor Law Board and later the Local Government Board also encountered serious resistance from some Poor Law guardians. Many unions refused to reform their old workhouse or construct a new one because they were unwilling to spend additional money. In industrial areas such as the West Riding (Yorkshire), Poor Law Unions resisted workhouse construction on the grounds that their relief system had to deal primarily with unemployment caused by cyclical depressions, a point to which we return below. Guardians retained sufficient autonomy and knowledge of loopholes to grant outdoor relief when they wished, taking advantage, for example, of their ability to grant outdoor relief to any "sick" pauper.

Table 10.1 summarizes the numbers on relief and costs of relief for the period between 1840 and World War I. The Poor Law Board did eventually succeed in reducing outdoor relief considerably, but never abolished it. Moreover, as critics often pointed out, the New Poor Law did not reduce the overall

Table 10.1

English poor relief, 1840–1914

	Number on Relief per 1,000 Population		Index of (Nominal) Expenditures (1840 = 100)		
Year	Indoor Relief[a]	Outdoor Relief	Indoor Relief	Outdoor Relief	Per Capita
1840	11.0	66.0	100	100	100
1850	7.0	50.4	113	108	103
1860	5.1	35.3	113	98	93
1870	6.4	37.7	186	124	118
1880	6.3	22.9	218	92	107
1890	5.8	18.7	235	84	115
1900	5.9	15.7	315	92	123
1910	7.8	15.2	416	114	140
1914	7.0	10.6	432	83	139

SOURCE: Official sources, after Williams (1981, Appendix A, B).

[a]Indoor relief expenditures *exclude* construction costs and staff salaries. Williams emphasizes a number of definitional ambiguities and inconsistencies. See MacKinnon (1988) for detailed discussion of Poor Law statistics.

costs of the system.[4] In 1865 Parliament strengthened the role of the Poor Law Union by introducing union chargeability, which meant that all poor rates were levied on the Poor Law Union as a whole. Before 1865 each parish within a union paid for the relief of its own paupers plus a share of the workhouse maintenance costs that was based on the number of paupers it had in the past (Brundage 1878, p. 184). MacKinnon (1987) argues that union chargeability was an important underlying cause of the Crusade Against Outrelief, an effort led by the Charity Organization Society (COS) and other private groups to abolish outdoor relief—to return to the "principles of 1834." As the table shows, the New Poor Law's intentions came closer to realization after this episode than they had before.

The Poor Law remained in force in theory until the 1920s, but it gradually lost its functions to other programs and bodies. During the late nineteenth century medical relief and the care of the insane became increasingly distinct from the Poor Law. Later acts supplanted parts of the relief system with social insurance schemes.[5] Social insurance programs differed from poor relief in that the benefits were not invested with stigma, and benefits were conditioned on tests of means (as with the Old Age Pension) or situation (for unemployment or health benefits) rather than on past behavior.

3. WORKHOUSES AND THE WORKHOUSE TEST

The Information Environment

The Industrial Revolution of the late eighteenth century and earlier changes in the organization of agriculture had dramatically altered the structure of labor markets and the social connections between employer and worker. As in Karl Polanyi's famous account of the "Great Transformation," paternal relations between master and servant, farmer and laborer, were replaced by the impersonal market relations of capitalist and wage-laborer. Stated differently, society underwent "the displacement of 'moral economy' by political economy. The traditional rights of the poor were being eroded, and a humane relationship between men of different status and income was often replaced by a narrower cash nexus" (Digby 1982, p. 10). Enclosures reduced employment in agriculture and forced many of the rural poor to migrate to find work. And urban industrial work had none of the close personal contact that had characterized the countryside: "there is far less *personal* communication between the master cotton spinner and his workmen, the calico printer and his blue-handed boys, between the master tailor and his apprentices, than there is between the Duke of Wellington and the humblest laborer on his estate."[6] The Elizabethan system of poor relief was based on localized, discretionary relief and presupposed that the relief applicant's circumstances and past were well known to the locals who ran the parish relief system. As society became increasingly anonymous and market relations supplanted personal relations, the Elizabethan system became increasingly impractical. The relief system had to devise new institutions to contend with underlying social and economic changes.

Reformers also wanted to shift administration of relief to larger units, in large measure to equalize tax burdens. But officials of the new system's much larger Poor Law Unions could not hope to have personal knowledge of those who applied for relief. Thus for two distinct reasons—the violent social change that characterized the late eighteenth and early nineteenth centuries, and the independent desire to abandon parishes in favor of larger units—the Poor Law required a mechanism that could substitute for direct information about the poor. A central difference between the Old and New Poor Laws, and the main incentive argument for the workhouse test, thus turns on the problem of collecting information on the poor. Both the old and new systems had, in theory, the same objective: to provide relief at least cost to those who were both needy and deserving, but to deny it to all others.[7] However, as we argued above, cost-minimization requires identifying the needy and the deserving. The more anonymous system of relief envisaged by the New Poor Law needed to rely on broader incentive-based tests rather than assessment of each case after detailed investigation.

As we would expect, the problem of information is central to the 1832 report. The Royal Commission on the Poor Laws notes that investigating applications to identify who was needy under the Old Poor Law was often a thankless task. Applicants resented intruding questions and the official knew that in most cases the applicant did his or her best to hide some assets or other important details. And, explicitly or implicitly, the time spent on investigating relief claims was costly. Just *how* costly, however, depends on the social context of the relief apparatus. In a parish of several hundred people the poor are likely to be well known to those in charge of the relief systems. Members of the vestry know who does and does not have employment, who cannot work and who is simply lazy, and other personal details.

Identifying the deserving was also important. The Old Poor Law operated on the implicit presumption that a reliable life history of each relief applicant was available to the authorities; close proximity and life-long residence made each potential pauper's habits clear to all. Relief officials could then apply simple rules based on past and current behavior to determine who did and did not deserve relief. Those who drank would be denied relief. Those who, on the other hand, fell into poverty through sickness, widowhood, or other conditions beyond their control would be granted the amounts and types of relief required to ameliorate their condition. Some opposition to the centralization implicit in the New Poor Law was based on this loss of local information.[8] Low-cost information might also be suspect, as the Royal Commission emphasized. Those who knew the poor well could profit from abuse of the Poor Law:[9]

> What our evidence does show is, that where the administration of relief is brought nearer to the door of the pauper, little advantage arises from increasing knowledge on the part of the distributors, and great evil from their increased liability to every sort of pernicious influence. It brings tradesmen within the influence of their customers, small farmers within that of their relations and connexions, and not infrequently of those who have been their fellow workmen. (Royal Commission 1834, pp. 276–77)

Information about the poor either is costly or, when not, should be viewed with suspicion.

What Was the Workhouse Test?

The New Poor Law, like the Old Poor Law, did not deny the needy and deserving poor their statutory right to relief. An applicant could be offered outdoor relief if the guardians thought it warranted (and if, in theory, the individual fell within the class of those for whom outdoor relief was not prohibited). Alternatively, the guardians could offer an applicant "the house." If the applicant

declined to enter the workhouse, the union had discharged its statutory obligation to relieve the poor. An applicant willing to enter the workhouse could be
denied poor relief only if there was some clear evidence that he was not actually poor, such as an offer of a job. The Royal Commission saw this "self-acting
test" as an effective substitute for information:

> If, then, regulations were established and enforced with the degree of strictness
> that has been attained in the dispauperized parishes, the workhouse doors might
> be thrown open to all who would enter them, and conform to the regulations . . .
> [and] no agency for contending against fraudulent rapacity and perjury, no stages
> of appeal, (vexatious to the appellants and painful to the magistrates,) [would] be
> requisite to keep the able-bodied from the parish. (Royal Commission 1834, p. 264)

Polanyi agreed with this interpretation, although he viewed its operation as
less benign: "It was now left to the applicant to decide whether he was so utterly
destitute of all means that he would voluntarily repair to a shelter which was
deliberately made into a place of horror" (Polanyi 1944, pp. 101–2).

Workhouses were large, centralized institutions, built and maintained by
the Poor Law Union and staffed with more or less professional employees.
Workhouse advocates wanted to ensure that the pauper had a less enjoyable
life (was "less eligible") than another poor person who was not receiving relief.
Less eligibility was accomplished not only by making workhouse inmates
labor, but by enforcing a strict regime of waking hours, limiting inmates to a
monotonous diet, and forbidding small pleasures such as tobacco. The idea
was to provide for basic material needs while nonetheless making a self-
supporting life outside the workhouse preferable to the working poor: "The
cruelty of the workhouse did not reside in its material deprivation but in its
psychological harshness. Indeed, the Poor Law commissioners themselves
appreciated that it was through psychological rather than material deterrence
that the workhouse test would operate" (Digby 1982, p. 17).

An important component of workhouse administration, at least as advocated by the Poor Law Board, was the "classification" or separation of paupers
by age, sex, and health status. This separation was held to improve workhouse
functioning and to reduce the chance of "immoral" behavior within the institution. Separation also advanced the cause of less eligibility by effectively

denying family members contact with one another. The poor saw this classification as one of the chief horrors of the workhouse. One historian quotes a petition presented to Parliament in 1836 by laborers who were "dismayed and disgusted beyond anything they can describe, with the idea of being shut up in one part of a prison and their wives and children in other separate parts because they are poor through no fault of their own" (Digby 1982, p. 17).

Workhouse advocates usually saw labor as part of the discipline of the institution rather than as a means to reduce relief costs, although some Unions made heavy use of inmate labor for running the institution. The Poor Law commissioners themselves were ambivalent on the subject of inmate labor. Using labor as punishment for workhouse inmates would inculcate the wrong attitude toward work in those who, after all, were supposed to one day leave the institution and become self-supporting workers (Crowther 1981, pp. 196–97).

Per-pauper costs for outdoor relief were much lower than for indoor relief. Outdoor relief grants were normally not given unless the person had other resources; that is, they were not intended to be the pauper's entire support. In addition, the workhouse was a large, permanent institution, implying construction and maintenance costs as well as a staff. The difference between per-pauper outdoor and indoor relief costs varied over time and from place to place. Rent and wages being large components of workhouse costs, they were especially expensive in cities. MacKinnon estimates that outdoor relief costs in the late 1860s averaged £2.5 to £5.5 per pauper per year, while indoor relief costs (*excluding* salaries and other fixed costs of running the workhouse) averaged £5.5 to £20 per pauper per year (MacKinnon 1987, p. 608). She and others have emphasized that the Poor Law statistics before the 1860s are very sketchy, but what is available shows similar differences in the costs of outdoor and indoor relief. In 1840, for example, each indoor pauper cost between 1.7 and 3.4 times as much as each outdoor pauper.[10]

The Workhouse Test: Deterrence

In using the phrase "deterrent workhouse" the historiography of the New Poor Law usually means simply that a more harsh poor relief system would lead to fewer applicants for relief. We use the term here in a narrower sense.

Deterrence refers here only to the effect on behavior of potential paupers who increase their attempts to avoid poverty because of the workhouse test. The difference in the well-being of an independent laborer and an indoor pauper is a measure of the incentive to avoid ending up in the position of the latter. This use of the term accords with that of the authors of the 1832 Report and leaders of the later Crusade Against Outrelief: if individuals become poor at least in part because of decisions they make with respect to poverty-reducing investments such as savings and work skills (and Chadwick, Senior, and others clearly thought this was so), then the number of paupers at any one time reflects, in part, the generosity of relief. As the Royal Commission put it: "Wherever inquiries have been made as to the previous condition of the able-bodied individuals who live in such numbers on the town parishes, it has been found that the pauperism of the greatest number has originated in indolence, improvidence, or vice, and might have been averted by ordinary care and industry" (Royal Commission 1834, p. 264). By tailoring relief to give the poor better incentives to avoid poverty, the New Poor Law could actually *reduce* the incidence of poverty.

Deterrence is a *dynamic* concept: the workhouse test would reduce pauperism only by inducing the poor to change their behavior and so reduce their *future* dependence on the poor relief system. Thus to the extent that the New Poor Law reduced pauperism in its first few years, the reduction may have little to do with deterrence in our sense. Not surprisingly, much debate about the efficacy of the workhouse test in practice turns on disagreements over how well it served as a deterrent in our sense.

Central to the deterrent function of the test was the idea that relief officials could not be certain whether a given applicant had tried hard to avoid poverty. Distinguishing the deserving from the undeserving applicant required knowing whether he or she had in the past exercised ordinary care and industry. Rather than attempt complete life histories of each applicant, the workhouse test simply gave the working poor a strong incentive to increase their efforts to avoid poverty. Two implications of this view are developed and illustrated below.

Deterrence via the workhouse was not an ideal solution. First, the work-house had a cost insofar as it reduced the ability of resident paupers to search for a self-supporting opportunity. This implies a poverty trap; the form of relief made it more difficult to escape from poverty. Second, directly reducing the level of poor relief—simply cutting outdoor relief grants—would have been a more cost-effective way to affect incentives to invest in poverty-reducing investments. This was not possible, given the implicit constraint that no person be allowed to starve, a constraint that also explains the New Poor Law's emphasis on making the workhouse *psychologically* unpleasant. The workhouse's peculiar genius was its ability to keep people alive but make them wish they were elsewhere. Third, the workhouse test was inferior to one that was sensitive to the attempts individuals made to avoid destitution. A blanket application of the workhouse test makes sense only when information about such individual efforts is not available. The New Poor Law initially recognized this fact when it spared widows and the infirm from the workhouse test, recognizing that poverty in this case was unlikely to be related to some past investment that was not undertaken.[11]

The Workhouse Test: Screening

A second function of the workhouse test was to screen the "truly needy" from those who simply did not want to work or who wanted to enjoy a higher living standard at the community's expense. The workhouse's advocates clearly viewed the test as a screen that was preferable to actually investigating the histories of relief applicants.

> The offer of relief on the principle suggested by us would be a self-acting test of the claim of the applicant.
>
> By the means which we propose, the line between those who do, and those who do not, need relief is drawn, and drawn perfectly. If the claimant does not comply with the terms on which relief is given to the destitute, he gets nothing; and if he does comply, the compliance proves the truth of the claim, namely, his destitution. (Royal Commission 1834, p. 264)

Screening, in contrast to deterrence, is essentially *static*. The workhouse test distinguishes those who are needy from those who are not needy *at a point in time* and does not, therefore, pertain to the Poor Law's efforts to alter the characteristics of the working poor. In the first few years after the New Poor Law's enactment, most of the reduction in applications should be traced to the screening function (since the non-needy now knew they stood no chance of outdoor relief) rather than to deterrence in the sense outlined above. The same applies to the reductions in outdoor pauperism achieved immediately after the Crusade Against Outrelief.

Screening is necessary only because obtaining information on the state of the poor required costly and potentially acrimonious and fraudulent investigation. The workhouse test dispensed with all investigation. By accepting or declining the workhouse, the applicant in effect told the guardians whether he or she was needy. This might be particularly important in cases where the relevant information was actually beyond the knowledge of the applicant. Asking a pauper's relatives whether they were willing to support him or her might bring a predictable response; but putting such a person in the workhouse would bring forth a more honest reply:

> It is, I believe, within the experience of many Boards of Guardians, that there are persons who, while in prosperous circumstances, readily permit their aged relatives to receive out-relief, an offer of in-door relief is frequently found to put pressure upon them to rescue themselves, if not their relatives, from the discredit incident to the residence of the latter in the Workhouse. (Royal Commission 1834, p. 188)

4. WHY THE WORKHOUSE TEST?

On its face the workhouse test appears to be a rather cumbersome instrument for accomplishing its objectives of providing sufficiently for all deserving paupers. First, the workhouse test required a huge investment in infrastructure before the program could be properly implemented. Second, as MacKinnon (1988) has shown, it was more expensive (per pauper) than granting outdoor relief. Third, it would seem more cost effective to provide incentives to avoid poverty by reducing the generosity of the relief granted rather than imposing the test. British colonial administrators relied on rural public works without the formal structure of workhouses to provide famine relief. Why was this option not pursued at home?

The workhouse had one simple advantage over other forms of tests, and over simply reducing the generosity of relief grants. Since its unpleasantness was primarily psychological, as noted above, the workhouse was both consistent with the harsh treatment of paupers *and* a policy designed to make reliance on relief undesirable. That is, only through a device such as the workhouse test could the Poor Law both be harsh and accomplish its basic function, preventing starvation.

There are, however, several additional reasons why building imposing workhouse structures was important to the objectives of the New Poor Law. They stem from the need to convince the population that the policy regime ushered in by the New Poor Law was really different. Workhouses were not only expensive to build and staff; each pauper in them cost more than the typical outdoor relief grant. Some of that cost might be recouped in screening from the day the system was established, but much of the deterrent benefit would come in the future, if at all. The government might find it worthwhile to threaten a future draconian policy toward the poor in order to reap the advantages of deterrence today, but then not actually implement the program and so save its additional cost. In other words, the government faced an important time-consistency problem.

The introduction of the New Poor Law caused riots and other forms of civil disturbance in much of England.[12] The working classes argued in effect that the old system was one of their rights, and they resisted the deprivation they saw in the new system. The violent reaction to this change reflects one of the dynamic problems inherent in the deterrent function of the workhouse test. The workhouse test was intended to alter some day-to-day behavior, such as willingness to work. This aspect of the deterrent function takes effect quickly; there is no reason why a lazy man cannot commence work upon denial of outdoor relief. But much of the behavior the workhouse test sought to deter was, by the admission of even the new system's advocates, life-long. A relief policy might be able to deter a twenty-year-old from marrying young and from not saving. But for a fifty-year-old the change in rules amounts to punishment for behavior he cannot now change. Thus much of the deterrent function was lost on those beyond early adulthood at the time of the New Poor Law's introduction. What these older people experienced instead was a pure reduction in their well-being. On the other hand, the authorities could hardly treat middle-aged workers in 1834 with relative kindness and still expect the younger workers, those whose behavior they hoped to alter, to believe that the system had changed. Henry Longley, a Poor Law inspector and influential figure in the Crusade Against Outrelief, was well aware of the problems associated with such regime shifts:

> It has always appeared to me that the poor have good reason to complain when, having been induced, and, as it were, educated, by the practices of a Board of Guardians, to rely unduly upon Poor Law relief, a sudden and abrupt change of practice alters the position in which they have been placed . . . due warning should be given of an change in the rules on which relief is administered. (Longley 1874, pp. 146–47)

This, more generally, represents a dilemma. When a new policy regime is introduced that requires credibility to function, then it may be difficult to grandfather the policy so as to protect those whose behavior and expectations were shaped by an earlier regime.

This problem suggests a signaling argument for why the workhouse test could enhance credibility.[13] By building a workhouse, the government could demonstrate to the poor that it was, in fact, serious about a new regime in poor relief. *Tough* governments that are really committed to reform of the poor law find it worthwhile to offer the house; *weak* governments do not. Tough governments may then want to distinguish themselves from weak governments by constructing workhouses. For workhouse construction to serve as a signaling device, it must be true that weak governments find their construction costlier at the margin than tough ones.[14] This might be true because workhouse construction crowds out other government programs, for a given budget, which are valued more by the weak governments. Apfel and Dunkley make precisely this argument in their study of the Poor Law in Bedfordshire: "Bedfordshire's spanking-new workhouses, dotting the landscape with their 'immense size,' stood as highly visible monuments to the frustrations of ratepayers with the social-legal obligation of public charity and to the resolve of authority (in its various forms) to maintain social discipline"(Apfel and Dunkley 1985, p. 53).

The signaling argument also explains why reformers rejected the use of buildings that existed before the implementation of the New Poor law. After the amalgamation of parishes, many Poor Law Unions had at their disposal several older buildings that could have housed the poor. But the Poor Law commissioners, after some initial indecision, insisted on constructing a large, new, central workhouse that would house *all* indoor paupers in the union. The central institution was at some level counterproductive, since the Poor Law also wanted to physically separate different classes of persons within the institution. Yet a new edifice would more effectively signal the government's toughness:

> It was plain that one building would be a more potent symbol of the new law than a series of familiar parish poorhouses. The essence of the single workhouse was its novelty, its mystery, and its formidable appearance . . . . This new construction, which in many rural Unions would be the largest public building, was bound to have a powerful effect on the local population. Thus the Commissioners accepted that the large *single* building was itself an essential part of deterrence. (Crowther 1981, p. 40; emphasis in original)

The signaling argument also explains in part why the Royal Commission did not favor other "tests," such as the labor test in use in some parishes at the time of the report. Forcing paupers to pick oakum or break stones to receive their relief was a form of less eligibility, but it did not involve any large, obvious expenditures that enabled the government to signal a regime change: there was no reason why one Poor Law administrator could not impose the labor test today and another administrator revoke it tomorrow. The investment in workhouses, while second best, signals a change in Poor Law policy, encourages poverty reducing investments, and reduces the cost of poor relief.[15]

5. PROBLEMS WITH THE NEW POOR LAW AND THE WORKHOUSE TEST

Few opponents doubted the efficacy of the workhouse test to screen the needy from the non-needy or to encourage poverty-reducing investments in theory. Debate over the workhouse focused on several potential limitations. The first was the magnitude of the relevant elasticities. How much could *any* Poor Law affect savings behavior, or drinking? The deterrent abilities of poor relief programs are an inherently empirical question, one that lies today at the heart of many efforts to reform welfare programs.[16] The debate was particularly active during the Crusade Against Outrelief in the 1860s. A second important problem with the workhouse test concerned the identity of those whose behavior the Poor Law sought to change versus those who would suffer because of the new policy. Longley advocated the workhouse test for nearly *everyone*. Consider his opposition to outdoor relief for widows with children. The widows themselves could be prodded to work, he claimed. And if married men knew the Poor Law would provide for their families, they would be less likely to take constructive steps themselves, such as buying insurance or joining benefit societies (Longley 1874, pp. 183, 185). Longley makes a similar deterrent argument against outdoor relief for deserted wives: "The habitual grant of outrelief to applicants of this class, especially among the Irish residents in London, is very generally believed to encourage and facilitate the desertion of their wives and families by husbands" (ibid., p. 187). Deterrence related to families and family-formation behavior can amount to punishment of some who have no say in the behavior of those whose behavior is supposedly subject to deterrence.[17]

A third limitation to deterrence formed the focus of much opposition to the New Poor Law in its early years. Poor Law Unions in some northern industrial regions refused to build workhouses. Relief authorities there contended that poverty in their areas was due to recurring trade depressions and not to laziness or drink on the part of their workers. In normal times few would apply for relief; and in cyclical downturns large numbers of workers would be out of jobs and applying for relief. How would the workhouse test function in these circumstances? If trade depressions really were the cause of poverty, and if these depressions really were beyond the power of English workers, then the workhouse test would have little deterrent effect.[18] The observation that much urban poverty was caused by unemployment and not by the behaviors the New Poor Law sought to deter was a sustained and intellectually coherent basis of opposition to the rigid application of the workhouse test.

A fourth problem is the obverse of the workhouse's efficiency in imposing unpleasantness: it could run up against a fundamental tenet of the English relief system, which was voluntary participation by the poor. If the workhouse is sufficiently awful to screen out most of the lazy, it be may be so awful as to lead some of the more proud or more independent to prefer death by starvation.

The starvation of paupers unwilling to enter workhouses became, in fact, a stock anecdote in many attacks on the New Poor Law.[19] Although many such instances might have been imagined, some doubtless occurred, and they underscore the limits of screening in a legal environment that did not support the idea of forcing the poor to accept relief.

A fifth problem with the new system turns on the credibility issue. The New Poor Law appeared to be hamstrung by the need to rigidly interpret its rules. The idea that rigid rules may serve a role in the face of time-consistency problems is due to Kydland and Prescott (1977). The New Poor Law did indeed lay down a centrally administered collection of regulations with inflexible rules for Guardians to follow and insisted that the Poor Law Guardians always and visibly adhere to these rules. In Longley's words,

> It is one of the main objects of Poor Law administration to discourage the formation by the poor of improvident habits. This work must be gradual, and its success must mainly depend upon the general conception which the poor form of the attitude towards them of the administrators of the law. This attitude receives expression from, and is formulated by the enunciation of rules of practice, which convey to the poor with clearness, with precision, and, above all, with certainty, the measure of their relations with the Poor Law.
>
> The general, and what may be termed the *anticipatory* reliance of the poor upon legal relief, will, I believe, be found to vary in direct proportion to the uncertainty which is permitted to prevail among them as to the terms on which it may be obtained. That which an applicant does not know certainly that he will not get, he readily persuades himself, if he wishes for it, that he will get; and the poor, to whom any inducement is held out to regard an application for relief as a sort of gambling speculation, in which, though many fail, some will succeed, will, like other gamblers, reckon upon their own success. (Longley 1874, p. 144; emphasis in original)

This concern to establish and protect a reputation underlies some of the fanatical opposition to outdoor relief evidenced during the Crusade Against Outrelief. Only if *no* Poor Law Union granted outdoor relief would all poor people truly believe that the system had been changed for good.

Credibility problems also explain the desire to administer the system from London. This degree of centralization was radical for its day. Few other domestic government functions in mid-nineteenth century England were effectively run from London. Some parishes resisted the formation of Poor Law Unions, and some unions resisted construction of a workhouse and other actions required under the new law. Many Poor Law Unions, however, went ahead and built their workhouses without complaint. We have seen that even before the New Poor Law some unions had been formed under Gilbert's Act. Was the central Poor Law authority redundant in such cases, simply telling locals to do what they would have done otherwise? No; the national legislation and authority backing the workhouse test added to the credibility of the commitment each local union had made to its poor. In theory, should any Board of Guardians begin to grant outdoor relief to the able-bodied, the national authority had the right to compel it to mend its ways. The power of the central authority stripped local officials of their power but enabled them to carry out a dramatic reform:

> A few landlords insisted on their right to discretion in the administration
> of relief . . . but the vast majority were content *not* to have this discretion. . . . Time
> and again, the landlord chairing a Board of Guardians would call on the central
> commission to enforce a uniform rule on his refractory colleagues. Some would
> go so far as to bludgeon their subordinate Guardians into *thanking* the central
> commission for overruling them. Many a Board passed resolutions congratulating
> the commission for freeing them from "local prejudice"; that is, for freeing them
> from self-determination by means of a national and uniform rule. (Mandler 1987,
> p. 156)

By giving up some of their power, local reformers obtained the ability to make a commitment to the new system.

6. OUR MODEL AND THE HISTORIOGRAPHY OF THE NEW POOR LAW

As we argued at the outset, our interpretation of the new poor law focuses on a change in the environment precipitated by a change in the underlying production relations.[20] An alternative view is that the New Poor Law was a symptom of changing attitudes toward the poor. Several historians have taken this route, although in different ways (for example, Himmelfarb 1984; Thompson

1963). According to this view, society's tastes for supporting the poor changed in ways that were eventually reflected in poor law legislation. This view may well explain the desire for some type of reform, probably harsher on the poor; but it does *not* explain the selection of the workhouse test as the centerpiece of the reform. Our view explains the selection of the new administrative system in a way the historiography has not.

Our information-based argument also accords well with discussions of the New Poor Law's political economy. Many accounts of the New Poor Law treat the creation of Poor Law Unions and the workhouse test as logically distinct innovations. They were not, as we have argued; simply moving to the large Poor Law Union in the 1830s reduced the amount of information available about the poor. Understanding the close connection between union and workhouse supports Mandler's interpretation of the New Poor Law as driven by landlords who wanted to assert control over local affairs (Mandler 1987). Mandler emphasizes essentially social and political reasons for landlord interest in poor reform. There was also a direct fiscal reason. Poor rates were levied on buildings and land and were paid by the occupier rather than the owner of such property. Landlords, as suppliers of the least elastic factor of production, would almost certainly bear the brunt of the poor rates' *final* incidence. There were several reasons to create unions, including the need for a larger rating basis for the new workhouses and the desire to equalize ratings across wealthier and poorer parishes. Yet Mandler's analysis suggests a more subtle reason for amalgamation. A large English estate could encompass several dozen parishes. Few landlords could sit on each parish vestry, and few would want to incur the expense of sending a representative to each meeting of each parish: "The fact is that country gentlemen—substantial proprietors—did not have much to do with the administration of relief under the old poor law. The unit of administration, the parish, was too small to concern them, and the case-by-case scrutiny usual in the dispensing of relief made the job of overseeing of the poor too tedious even for their more respectable tenants" (Mandler 1987, p. 133). Keeping an eye on the Old Poor Law would require great efforts from a wealthy landlord. Yet reliance on unions meant giving up the detailed knowledge of the poor and their condition that came with close contact between the poor and those on the parish vestry. The methods of the Old Poor Law were only consistent with parochial administration. The New Poor Law could not have reduced local autonomy and enhanced landlord influence without the adoption of the workhouse test.

7. CONCLUSIONS

The Poor Law lost most of its functions during the early twentieth century and was formally abolished shortly after World War II. In its place arose a vast welfare state. The transition from poor relief to social insurance and the welfare state doubtless reflects many changes in social attitudes, and perhaps the nature of poverty itself. Yet our argument suggests a component in this shift that has received little attention in the historiography: information about those seeking benefits. The New Poor Law was designed to do away with the need to undertake expensive, intrusive, and unreliable investigations of a pauper's condition and background. Later, social insurance schemes took advantage of the fact that with changes in the organization of work, in methods of saving, and in the family, among others, most conditions directly relevant to an individual's economic status (such as a work history or contributions to an insurance fund) can be documented at relatively low cost.

The New Poor Law's creation and demise thus reflect two transformations in English society and the English economy. The Old Poor Law became impractical to administer when having adequate information about the poor entailed keeping poor relief at a parochial level subject to abuse and fraught with large differences in wealth and levels of pauperism. As English society became more anonymous—or to adopt Polanyi's language, as market relations replaced personal relations—the basis of Poor Law administration had to become a device so impersonal that it could be operated by officials who did not even know the pauper in question. The New Poor Law, a relatively short-lived program between parochial relief and the welfare state, can be explained as economizing on the need for information during a period when the information was no longer available on a personal or local basis, and not yet available on a bureaucratic basis.

NOTES AND REFERENCES

Notes

Acknowledgments: We thank Mary MacKinnon and Peter Mandler for helpful comments on an earlier draft. This paper was revised while Guinnane was a visiting scholar at the Russell Sage Foundation.

1. Digby points out that relief costs per capita actually fell between 1816–19 and the early 1830s (Digby 1982, p. 9). Recent research supports the view that farmers used the relief system to supplement their workers' wages (Boyer 1985).

2. Gilbert's Act permitted parishes to form unions for the purpose of constructing a workhouse, bearing obvious resemblance to the 1834 reform.

3. This legislation did not extend to Scotland or Ireland. Ireland's Poor Law, first established in 1838, was very similar to England's New Poor Law. Guinnane (1993) discusses the Irish Poor law.

4. The New Poor Law's defenders noted, however, that the appropriate question to ask was what relief costs would have been in 1900 had the *old* system remained in place.

5. These innovations included the Workmen's Compensation Acts (1897 and 1906); the Unemployed Workmen Act (1905); the Old Age Pensions Act (1908 and 1911); and health insurance (1911).

6. Hobsbawm (1968, p. 87), quoting a clergyman's description of Manchester.

7. Historians have stressed other objectives, including regulation of the labor market. Cost-minimization may not be at variance with these other aims; at the least, cost-minimization is a useful maintained hypothesis.

8. Some opponents feared the New Poor Law was the first step toward a national relief system and objected to it on the grounds that a national system could not take advantage of local information on the poor (Rose 1976, p. 42).

9. This same sentiment is echoed later in connection with the Crusade Against Outrelief (Chance 1895, pp. 21–23).

10. Calculations from official Poor Law statistics as reported by Williams (1981, tables 4.5 and 4.6). The lower-bound figure comes from treating the cost of indoor relief as "in-maintenance" only. The upper-bound figure adds to this cost, for indoor paupers, the costs of salaries for workhouse officials, charges for workhouse

construction and maintenance, and so forth. Neither figure is exact because of reporting deficiencies and because the upper-bound figure necessarily includes charges for the maintenance of mentally ill persons and other items that are not strictly indoor relief. Given the available figures, no more refined estimates for England and Wales as a whole are possible.

11. Peter Mandler has pointed out that however much the Royal Commission might have believed in deterrence in this form, there were others who did not believe the Poor Law could have any effect on the working poor. To them, the workhouse was simply a way to keep paupers alive and to separate them from the rest of society.

12. Worker resistance to the New Poor Law often focused on the workhouse structure itself. Efforts to burn the new workhouse were a common form of anti–Poor Law violence (Snell 1985, pp. 135–36). Often the Poor Law Guardians had to provide guards for the structure both during and after construction; for examples, see Digby (1978), p. 220.

13. There is a second argument based on the idea of capital as commitment so that government incentives are altered ex post (see, for example, Dixit 1979). Workhouse construction entailed at least some sunk cost; each building was designed specially for this use and would require substantial modification to be used for commercial, industrial, or residential purposes should the Poor Law authorities decide to sell it. If incurring this sunk cost made the marginal cost of indoor relief less than the marginal cost of outdoor relief, then workhouse construction itself would have made the New Poor Law credible simply by changing the Poor Law officials' ex post incentives to grant indoor relief. Perhaps this is what D. G. Adey, the first assistant Poor Law commissioner for the county of Bedfordshire, had in mind when he claimed in 1835 that "the 'mere extent' of accommodation in union workhouses was sufficient to intimidate the labouring poor." As MacKinnon has shown, however, the marginal cost of indoor relief was higher than the cost of outdoor relief. The workhouse could not have enhanced credibility in this way. In fact MacKinnon's estimates are not strictly marginal cost, which is the figure of interest to this argument. Her "in-maintenance costs" per pauper include all workhouse costs other than buildings and salaries and so are, strictly speaking, a portion of average variable costs. Marginal cost would probably be less, but it is doubtful that it could be any less than the £.05–.1 per week typical of outdoor relief grants at mid-century.

14. See, for example, Kreps (1990), chap. 17, for an account of the formal structure of such models.

15. Labor tests also suffer from an unrelated drawback: they cannot be used to screen the non-able-bodied who might have assets. This was not an issue with the original New Poor law, since the outdoor relief restrictions were aimed at the able-bodied and their families only. But during the Crusade Against Outrelief the workhouse test was applied to aged and disabled people with the intention of forcing them to reveal assets or to get their relatives to care for them.

16. See, for example, the discussion of the impact of workfare programs on teenage child-bearing in Ellwood and Summers (1986).

17. Similar logic applies to Malthus's famous complaint that the Old Poor Law encouraged "early and improvident marriage" by providing laborers' allotments and child allowances. Boyer provides econometric evidence that these policies actually did serve to increase birthrates in the English counties that had relatively generous allowances (Boyer 1989).

18. This aspect of the discussion turns on the question of whether there is true involuntary unemployment. If so, then the only deterrent effect would be if workers were induced to save more to tide them over through bad periods, or to migrate. Industrial employers did not want their workers emigrating from the area whenever there was a downturn in the economy.

19. Snell (1985, p. 133) discusses some examples related to aged paupers.

20. We are not directly concerned with attacking or defending any of the different positions historians have taken on the reasons for and consequences of the New Poor Law (see, for example, Brundage 1978; Crowther 1981; Digby 1972, 1982; Williams 1981; Snell 1985; Mandler 1987).

References

Apfel, W., and P. Dunkley. 1985. "English Rural Society and the New Poor Law: Bedfordshire, 1834–47." *Social History* 10: 37–68.

Besley, T., and S. Coate. 1992. "Workfare vs. Welfare: Incentive Arguments for Work Requirements in Poverty Alleviation Programs." *American Economic Review* 82: 249–61.

Blaug, Mark. 1963. "The Myth of the Old Poor Law and the Making of the New." *Journal of Economic History* 23: 151–84.

Boyer, George. 1985. "An Economic Model of the English Poor Law circa 1780–1834." *Explorations in Economic History* 22: 129–67.

————. 1989. "Malthus Was Right after All: Poor Relief and Birth Rates in Southeastern England." *Journal of Political Economy* 97: 93–114.

Brundage, Anthony. 1978. *The Making of the New Poor Law: The Politics of Inquiry, Enactment, and Implementation, 1832–1839.* New Brunswick, N.J.: Rutgers University Press.

Chance, W. 1895. *The Better Administration of the Poor Law.* London.

Crowther, M. A. 1981. *The Workhouse System 1834–1929.* Athens: University of Georgia Press.

Digby, Anne. 1978. *Pauper Palaces.* London: Routledge and Kegan Paul.

————. 1982. *The Poor Law in Nineteenth-Century England and Wales.* London: The Historical Association.

Dixit, Avinash. 1979. "The Role of Investment in Entry Deterrence." *Economic Journal* 90: 95–106.

Ellwood, David, and Laurence Summers. 1986. "Poverty in America: Is Welfare the Answer to the Problem?" In Sheldon Danziger and D. Weinberg, eds., *Fighting Poverty: What Works and What Doesn't,* pp. 78–105. Cambridge, Mass.: Harvard University Press.

Guinnane, Timothy W. 1993. "The Poor Law and Pensions in Ireland." *Journal of Interdisciplinary History* 34: 271–91.

Himmelfarb, Gertrude. 1984. *The Idea of Poverty.* New York: Knopf.

Hobsbawm, Eric. 1968. *Industry and Empire.* Harmondsworth, England: Penguin.

Hunt, E. H. 1981. *British Labour History 1815–1914.* Atlantic Highlands, N.J.: Humanities Press.

Kreps, David. 1990. *A Course in Microeconomic Theory.* Princeton, N.J.: Princeton University Press.

Kydland, F., and E. Prescott. 1977. "Rules Rather Than Discretion: The Inconsistency of Optimal Plans." *Journal of Political Economy* 85: 473–91.

Longley, H. 1874. "Report to the Local Government Board on Poor Law Administration in London." *House of Commons Sessional Papers,* vol. 25.

MacKinnon, M. 1987. "English Poor Law Policy and the Crusade against Outrelief." *Journal of Economic History* 47: 603–25.

————. 1988. "The Use and Misuse of Poor Law Statistics, 1857 to 1912." *Historical Methods* 21: 5–19.

Mandler, Peter. 1987. "The Making of the New Poor Law Redivivis." *Past and Present* 117: 131–57.

————. 1990. "Tories and Paupers: Christian Political Economy and the Making of the New Poor Law." *The Historical Journal* 33: 81–103.

McCloskey, D. N. 1973. "New Perspectives on the Old Poor Law." *Explorations in Economic History* 10.

McDowell, R. B. 1964. *The Irish Administration 1801–1914.* London: Routledge and Kegan Paul.

Polanyi, K. 1944. *The Great Transformation.* New York.

Rose, M. E. 1971. *The English Poor Law 1780–1930.* New York: Barnes and Noble.

————. 1976. "Settlement, Removal, and the New Poor Law." In D. Fraser, ed. *The New Poor Law in the Nineteenth Century.* London.

Royal Commission. 1834. "Report from His Majesty's Commissioners for Inquiring into the Administration and Practical Operation of the Poor Laws." London: Fellowes, 1834.

Snell, K. D. M. 1985. *Annals of the Labouring Poor.* Cambridge, England: Cambridge University Press.

Thompson, E. P. 1963. *The Making of the English Working Class.* London: Victor Gollancz.

Williams, K. 1981. *From Pauperism to Poverty.* London: Routledge and Kegan Paul.

11

FAMILY MATTERS: THE LIFE-CYCLE TRANSITION AND THE ANTEBELLUM AMERICAN FERTILITY DECLINE

Susan B. Carter, Roger L. Ransom, and Richard Sutch

An enduring puzzle, which has occupied the attention of demographers and economic historians for decades, is the early and rapid decline in American fertility. From an extraordinarily high level around 1800, white female fertility plummeted by more than half over the course of the next hundred years (Coale and Zelnik 1963). Figure 11.1 presents the long-run picture of American fertility decline as measured by the total fertility rate of white women. The total fertility rate is the standard measure of completed family size.[1] The data for 1800 through 1920 come from Warren Sanderson (1976, 1979). These data suggest that in 1800 the average American woman who survived to the end of her reproductive life would have given birth to 8.02 children! Because some women never marry and others are infertile or develop secondary infertility, eight children per woman is close to the biological maximum for a large, heterogeneous population such as that of the United States in 1800. From this high level, the series shows a continuous and rather steady decline for the next 120 years. The figure also illustrates the dip in fertility during the Great Depression of the 1930s and World War II and the rebound in the late 1940s and early 1950s, commonly known as the Baby Boom.

In what follows we define fertility not by the total rate, but by the child-woman ratio. The child-woman ratio, variously defined, is the standard used in studies of antebellum fertility patterns. For our purposes we define the child-woman ratio as the number of children aged 0 to 4 per 1,000 women aged 15 to 44. This measure, which we shall refer to as the CRS Fertility Index,

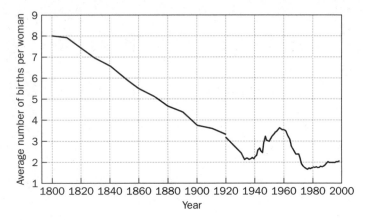

Figure 11.1   Total fertility rate of white women, 1800–2000
SOURCE: Sanderson (1979), Carter et al. (2004).

is introduced because, unlike total fertility, it can be easily calculated from published age distributions based on the decennial U.S. censuses. The required detailed age distributions are available for individual states and counties from published census data.[2] We require geographically disaggregated measures of fertility for the empirical analysis described in this chapter. It is reassuring to note that our measure of fertility closely follows the same downward path as that shown by the total fertility rate shown in Figure 11.1, a point that has been affirmed in more sophisticated tests (Bogue and Palmore 1964; Sundstrom and David 1986, Appendix II).

One of the interesting features of the American fertility decline is that it was a rural phenomenon. It is true that fertility was substantially lower in urban than in rural places throughout the nineteenth century and also that the urban population increased more rapidly than the rural population over that time, owing to a strong rural-urban migration. Yet even by 1860 the fraction of the total population living in towns and cities was still so small that the relative rise of the urban population had only a small impact on the national fertility rate. The fertility decline in the United States was driven by the rural fertility decline.

The overall picture of a sustained decline in white rural fertility beginning around 1800–15 has long been known and has perplexed demographers for at least seventy years (for example, see Thompson and Whelpton 1933, p. 263). There are three questions.

- Why was fertility so high in 1800? The crude birth rate (births per thousand population) around 1800, by both contemporary (Blodget 1806: 58) and modern estimates put the number for the white population in the range of fifty to fifty-five.[3] By any standards a birth rate over fifty per thousand is enormously high—as high, indeed, as the birth rate in any country in the world today and considerably higher than the birth rates in western Europe at the outset of the nineteenth century.[4]

- Why did the decline begin circa 1800–15? This date is well in advance of any measured decline in infant or childhood mortality and therefore departs from the stylized model of the "demographic transition" in which mortality decline precedes or occurs simultaneously with fertility decline. Mortality did not begin to fall in the United States until sometime after 1880, at least two generations after the onset of the fertility decline. If anything, mortality rates were increasing in the eighteenth and early nineteenth centuries (Haines 2000, 2001a).

- Why was there any fertility decline at all before the late nineteenth century? Throughout the nineteenth century America was primarily an agricultural economy, and the continent's European settlers and their descendants enjoyed the continuous availability of new and productive agricultural land. The Malthusian argument for a fertility decline based on population growth bearing down on scarce resources cannot straightforwardly explain the American case.

This chapter is an effort to answer all three puzzles. It also represents the continuation and elaboration of our long and always interesting discussion of these issues with Paul David and his collaborators, most notably Warren Sanderson and William Sundstrom. This dialog had its origins in 1984 when David and Sundstrom circulated a formal cooperative game model that linked fertility decisions of couples to a life-cycle strategy to secure support for their old age. This was one of the first papers from David's highly important "Stanford Project on the History of Fertility Control" (David and Sundstrom 1984). Influenced by this work, Ransom and Sutch presented two papers on the decline in antebellum fertility to the All-UC Group in Economic History at its conference in Laguna Beach in May of 1986 (Ransom and Sutch 1986a, 1986c). A few days later Susan Carter presented two papers connecting the fertility decline with the rise of school attendance at the 1986 Cliometrics Conference in Oxford, Ohio (Carter 1986a, 1986b). At the same two conferences, Sundstrom and David presented an early version of a paper on farm-family fertility in the antebellum era that was subsequently published and has since enjoyed considerable attention (1986, 1988). In this chapter we return to these issues and offer a more general account of the antebellum fertility decline, one that embraces factors described in all six papers.

Our story is a public policy story as well. In addition to explaining the otherwise anomalous behavior of the time trend in American antebellum fertility, it contains a message for today's policy makers. That message is that: family matters. Where children directly provide for their parents' old-age, fertility will be high—perhaps too high to allow for economic development. Where physical and financial assets—perhaps together with credible governmental pledges—secure parents' old-age, fertility will be low and parents will invest in their children's education and other nurturing that enhances their adult productivity.

1. CURRENT STATE OF THE DISCUSSION[5]

The 1988 Sundstrom-David article and the 1984 theoretical paper on which it was based were ingenious efforts to explain the early onset of the rural white fertility transition in America. They suggested that the high demand for children in the early years was motivated by parents' desire to provide for their own old-age security. By having a large number of children and by offering these children a portion of the farm family's wealth as a potential inheritance in exchange for their continuing support, parents could ensure for themselves a comfortable and secure flow of goods and services even after their own ability to support themselves was diminished by poor health or old age. More children were better than few for providing old-age security for two reasons. With many children, the parents' bargaining power would be enhanced and the threat of disinheritance made more salient. Moreover, the more children who cooperated in the support of their aged parents, the smaller would be the burden on any one of them. That factor, too, enhanced the security of the arrangement. The resulting bequests passed at death to obedient children and were established out of strategic rather than altruistic considerations.

This model of intergenerational bargaining over old-age support and the distribution of the family wealth at the parents' death also helps Sundstrom and David explain the timing and motivation for an early rural fertility decline. According to their argument, the old-age security motive for having many children would have weakened substantially when opportunities outside of agriculture began to improve sometime in the early nineteenth century. The bargaining position of parents would weaken with the growth of alternative employment opportunities away from the parental farmstead. The importance of inheriting farmland would be diminished. Sundstrom and David focused on the growth of nonagricultural employment as the lever of change in antebellum America. Testing their model using state-level data for 1840, they concluded that nonagricultural labor market opportunities had a large negative effect on rural white fertility.

An additional contribution of the Sundstrom-David article was to demonstrate that the inclusion of measured nonagricultural labor market opportunities in the statistical analysis eliminated the explanatory power of the most widely cited alternative explanation for temporal and spatial variations in the fertility of the rural white population: the decreasing availability of cheap farmland with the progress of settlement. This competing hypothesis is associated with Richard Easterlin's proposal that American farmers had a strong target-bequest motive, which persisted throughout the nineteenth century.[6] The farmer's goal, according to this argument, was to leave each son and daughter a farm that was at least as productive as the one the farmer had received with his own inheritance. Despite the general availability of land in nineteenth-century America, Easterlin argued that land became "scarce" in any given agricultural community as its population grew and the number of suitable farm sites in the vicinity declined.

Cross-Section Evidence on the Target-Bequest Model

At the time that the Sundstrom-David (1988) paper appeared, the most widely accepted explanation for the anomalous pattern of American fertility decline focused on the role of change in local land availability. That focus was first inspired by an 1843 observation by George Tucker that fertility was lower in the relatively densely populated areas of southern New England, eastern New York and Pennsylvania, New Jersey, Delaware, and Maryland than in the newly and still sparsely settled regions to the west of the Appalachian Mountains (Tucker 1855). Figure 11.2 illustrates this geographic pattern by displaying county-level values of our fertility index in 1840 for each of the counties in existence at that time.[7] The map illustrates the strong regional character of fertility variation at that time. In 1840, only southern New England, southeastern New York, northern New Jersey, and the portions of Pennsylvania, Maryland, and Virginia east of the Appalachian Mountains exhibited low fertility: under 800 children per thousand women. Other counties, especially those in the western states,

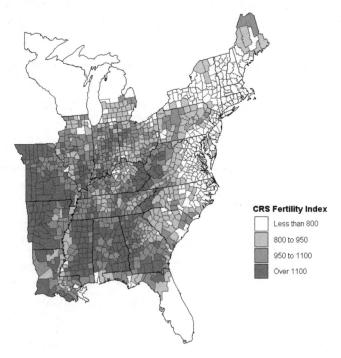

CRS Fertility Index

☐ Less than 800
▨ 800 to 950
▨ 950 to 1100
■ Over 1100

Figure 11.2   White fertility in the United States, 1840

experienced relatively high fertility. Counties in the southern states also exhibited a rising east-west fertility gradient, although the *level* of the white fertility index was generally higher in the South than in the North.[8] Detailed study of county-level census data—not shown here—reveals that the geographic patterns of fertility variation seen in 1840 were also present across the entire period from 1800 to 1860. To illustrate this point, Figure 11.3 provides the same information as Figure 11.2, but this time for 1850.[9] Both the East-West fertility gradient and the North-South fertility differential are still evident, though the overall fertility level was lower across the board in 1850. Figure 11.3 (studied in conjunction with Figure 11.2) suggests an expansion of low fertility behavior out of the East and into the West. One way to view the national fertility decline, then, is to see it as the adoption of northeastern low-fertility behaviors progressively westward and southward into the rest of the country.

To aid comparison, Figures 11.2 and 11.3 use shading based on the quartile ranges of the 1840 fertility index. However, fertility fell so much between 1840

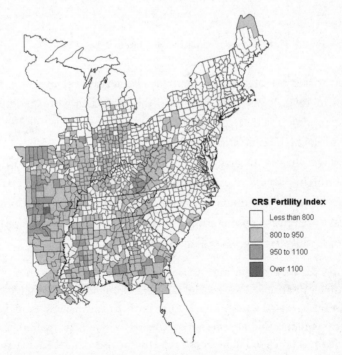

Figure 11.3   White fertility in the United States, 1850

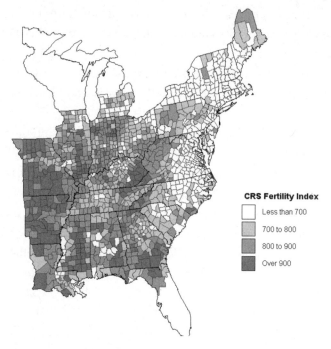

Figure 11.4 White fertility in the United States, 1850

and 1850 that most of the country had CRS fertility of less than 950 per thousand in 1850. Figure 11.4 redisplays the 1850 data with shading ranges more appropriate for that year. The regional patterns clearly visible in 1840 remained intact ten years later.

Yasuba was the first to suggest, in 1962, that the availability of easily accessible land might provide an explanation for the robust East-West fertility gradient that drew the comment of so many observers. Yasuba proposed that East-West differences in population density could account for the geographic pattern of fertility. Here is his explanation.

> [A]s time passed, the acquisition of new land in the settled areas became increasingly difficult and costlier and the average distance from the settled to the new areas where land was plentiful became further. Consequently, fertility in the older communities may have been reduced directly in response to the decreased demand for children or indirectly as a result of the rise in the age at marriage and the fall in the incidence of marriage. (Yasuba 1962: 159)

Easterlin recast this argument in a compelling format that was an ingenious attempt to salvage the Malthusian relationship between resource abundance and fertility from the dilemma posed by the declining American fertility rate. Easterlin and his students suggested that parents had an altruistic motive to preserve and augment the family's wealth—primarily the land and capital required for farming—and to pass those assets on to their children when they died.[10] Young couples, with target bequests for their future children in mind, would anticipate difficulty in providing an inheritance of land for their off-spring and would take steps to limit their family size accordingly. Over time, fertility would decline because, in any given community, land would become increasingly scarce, more expensive, and more difficult to acquire. In Easterlin's model there is no period of Malthusian stress or economic hard-ship because parents would foresee the developing problem of land scarcity and take effective birth control measures to protect the living standards of their children.

Rather than test this hypothesis about the link between declining local land availability and the decline in rural fertility by tracking developments in a given community, Easterlin and his followers viewed the cross-sectional vari-ation in fertility displayed in Figure 11.2 as a synthetic time trend. Regions of high fertility in 1840 were at an early stage in a transition process, while those with low fertility had advanced further. Thus cross-section analysis of the geographic pattern of fertility could reveal the forces that would act over time to reduce fertility in any given region. Because the 1840 census was the first to include agricultural variables, and because that date seems to capture the fertility decline in mid-transition when the cross-sectional variation was high, empirical work has focused almost exclusively on state-level data for 1840 (and to some extent for 1850).[11]

Scholars have proposed a variety of measures of fertility and of local land availability. The most important finding within this literature is the robust positive correlation between local land availability and female fertility, regard-less of the way in which either variable is measured. This would appear to give strong support to the local land–availability model. However the Sundstrom-David paper reported that when measures of nonagricultural employment opportunities are added to the local land–availability model, land availability

Table 11.1
Sequence of tests of the land-availability hypothesis: Adjusted R^2
cross-section ordinary least square linear regressions
for twenty-seven states, 1840[a]

		Dependent Variable[b]	
Measure of Land Availability	Reference	Yasuba Index	Rural Yasuba Index
Persons per square mile	Tucker[c]	0.637	0.573
Persons per 1,000 arable acres	Yasuba[d]	0.545	0.496
Adults, 1830, per farm, 1860	Forster et al.[e]	0.744	0.675
Value of average farm, 1860	Vinovskis[f]	0.270	0.163
Density of rural settlement	Schapiro[g]	0.538	0.527
Mean of the dependent variable		1579	1695
Standard deviation		347	380

SOURCE: Roger L. Ransom and Richard Sutch. "Did Rising Out-Migration Cause Fertility to Decline in Antebellum New England? A Life-Cycle Perspective on Old-Age Security Motives, Child Default, and Farm-Family Fertility." California Institute of Technology Social Science Working Papers no. 610. Pasadena (April 1986): 42–44.

[a]The twenty-seven states included in these tests are Alabama, Arkansas, Connecticut, Delaware, Florida Territory, Georgia, Illinois, Indiana, Kentucky, Louisiana, Maine, Maryland, Massachusetts, Michigan, Mississippi, Missouri, New Hampshire, New Jersey, New York, North Carolina, Ohio, Pennsylvania, Rhode Island, South Carolina, Tennessee, Vermont, and Virginia.

[b]The Yasuba index of white fertility is the number of children under age 10 per thousand women aged 16 to 44. Yasukichi Yasuba, *Birth Rates of the White Population in the United States, 1800–1860* (The Johns Hopkins University Press, 1962): table II-7, pp. 61–62. The rural Yasuba index is defined using the white rural population of each state and has been standardized to correct for the effect of the age distribution of the women. Our source is Colin Forster, G. S. L. Tucker, and Helen Bridges, *Economic Opportunity and White American Fertility Ratios, 1800–1860* (New Haven, Yale University Press, 1972): table 6, pp. 40–41.

[c]George Tucker, *Progress of the United States in Population and Wealth in Fifty Years* (Press of Hunt's Merchant's Magazine, 1855), first observed the relationship between fertility and persons per square mile. We have used the population density per square mile for 1840 given in U.S. Bureau of the Census, *Historical Statistics of the United States* (U.S. Government Printing Office, 1975): I, Series A196.

[d]Yasuba's measure of the availability of land is the number of persons per thousand acres of cropland in 1949. Our source is Yasuba, *Birth Rates*, table V-9, pp. 163–64.

[e]Forster et al. use a measure of economic opportunity they call the "adult-farm ratio." The white population over the age of 15 in 1830 is divided by the number of farms in 1860 (see Forster, Tucker, and Bridges, *Economic Opportunity*, pp. 11–12, 19–21, and 41, for an explanation of this variable). We have calculated this ratio using the population data in U.S. Census Office, Fifth Census (1830), *Fifth Census or Enumeration of the Inhabitants of the United States, 1830,* and the number of farms for each state reported in U.S. Bureau of the Census, *Historical Statistics of the United States, Colonial Times to 1970, Bicentennial Edition* (Washington, 1975), Series K20-K63.

[f]Maris A. Vinovskis, "Socioeconomic Determinants of Interstate Fertility Differentials in the United States in 1850 and 1860," *Journal of Interdisciplinary History* 6 (Winter 1976), used the average value of farms as a measure of the relative cost of obtaining a working farm (p. 381). He entered the 1850 average value into a regression explaining the Yasuba index for 1850. The average value of a farm is not available from the census of 1840. As a rough substitute we have entered the 1850 value into our 1840 regression. This procedure may perhaps be justified by suggesting that the expected cost of a farm fifteen to twenty years in the future should be relevant to the child-bearing decisions of the 1830s. The R^2 for a linear regression with the 1850 Yasuba index as the dependent variable and the 1850 average farm value (27 observations) was 0.268. The rural Yasuba index is not available for 1850. Our data on the average value of a farm in 1850 is taken from U.S. Census, *Historical Statistics*, Series K20-K63.

[g]The density of rural settlement is a measure designed by Morton Owen Schapiro, "Land Availability and

exhibits a *negative* rather than the expected positive effect on fertility. This suggests that the anomalous behavior of nineteenth-century American fertility may not have been due to declining land availability at all, but rather to some other force positively (and perhaps spuriously) correlated with it.

At the same time, other empirical work was also undermining the credibility of local land availability as the proximate cause of the early American fertility decline. In Table 11.1 we display the results of ten ordinary least-squares regressions that we ran in 1986 using 1840 state-level data (Ransom and Sutch 1986a). These regressions were designed to explore the robustness of the connection between land availability and fertility when measured in the variety of ways that appear in the literature. We constructed five different proxies for local land availability and two different indexes of rural fertility. The ten equations result from pairing each of the fertility measures with each of the land availability measures. All ten equations were estimated using the same data set so that differences in the outcomes are due entirely to differences in the definitions.[12] We take the R^2 values from the regressions as our measure of the success of each linear model—the higher the R^2 the more successful we judge the model.

What we find is that the more conceptually appropriate the proxy for local land availability, the poorer its performance. This is not what a proponent of the target-bequest hypothesis would have expected, and this finding suggests that the correlation between land scarcity and fertility may be spurious. To reach this conclusion, first compare the results of measuring rural fertility according to the fertility index for the state as a whole versus defining it to apply to the rural population only. Clearly the latter is a more appropriate measure of rural fertility. Nonetheless, each and every one of the five measures of local land availability does a better job of explaining total fertility than it does rural fertility.

Fertility in the United States, 1760–1870," *Journal of Economic History* 42 (September 1982). It is defined as the rural population of the state in 1840 divided by the local maximum rural population observed for that state (pp. 586–87 and table 1, p. 589). We used the variant of the Schapiro measure advocated by William A. Sundstrom and Paul A. David, "Old-Age Security Motives, Labor Markets, and Farm Family Fertility in Antebellum America," Stanford Project on the History of Fertility Control Working Paper no. 17R (February 1986): 47–48. This replaces the "first clear peak" in rural population with the maximum rural population observed between 1790 and 1940. For this variable the data on rural populations come from *Historical Statistics*, Series A203.

Next consider the five measures of local land availability. The first, persons per square mile, is the measure that caught the eye of George Tucker in the 1840s and motivated him to propose a negative relationship between land availability and fertility. Yasuba (1962) developed a more refined measure of land availability by limiting the numerator to potentially arable cropland, which he defined as cropland in 1949. Schapiro (1982) developed a "potential farmland" measure that was more robust in the face of rural population decline by defining the potential in terms of the first "clear peak" in rural population. Vinovskis (1976) sought to incorporate the productivity of the farm by measuring land availability in terms of average farm value. In all three cases, these conceptually superior measures of land availability perform more poorly than the crude index employed by Tucker. The only measure whose performance is superior to that of Tucker is the one developed by Forster, Tucker, and Bridge, who calculated the "adult-farm ratio," which they defined as the ratio of the adult white population to the number of farms existing at a future date arbitrarily chosen to reflect "full settlement." They experimented with both 1860 and 1880 as the target; the 1860 measure proved to be the superior predictor of rural fertility in 1840 (Forster, Tucker, and Bridge 1972, pp. 19–21, 41). Maris Vinovskis was critical of the adult-farm ratio and proposed, we think correctly, that the average value of a farm is a more direct and conceptually superior measure of the cost of assisting one's children in establishing a household of their own (Vinovskis 1976). In other words, the better the proxy for local land availability, the poorer the performance of the measure.

Time-Series Evidence on the Target-Bequest Model

In addition to the somewhat technical objections to the local land–availability model, we have at least three a priori problems with the Easterlin target-bequest model's time-trend predictions:

- First, acceptance of the land-scarcity argument as an explanation of the fertility decline requires the view that families found it increasingly difficult to provide farms for their children throughout the nineteenth century. In fact, improvements in transportation and communication, the continuing release of the public domain at land auctions, and rising agricultural incomes should have made it easier, at the margin, to purchase a farm.

- Second, the land-scarcity model has difficulty explaining why fertility was so high in the late eighteenth century and why the onset of the fertility decline occurred when it did. Fertility began to fall at precisely the time American land policy changed, opening up vast expanses of public domain to settlement. Relatively speaking, the threat of land scarcity must have appeared much greater in 1800 than at any time during the period between 1815 and 1840. The land-scarcity model would also predict that the fertility decline should halt shortly after a community had reached its peak population density, yet states such as Vermont and Delaware continued to show fertility declines long after their rural populations had ceased to grow.

- Third, the land-scarcity model does not easily provide an explanation for the case of the deep South. That region began its fertility decline later than the North and exhibited a more gradual decline in white fertility despite a settlement history not unlike that of the states of the old Northwest. Despite this challenge to his model, Easterlin concentrated his attention upon the northern farm areas in his empirical work "because of the more plentiful supply of data for this region, and the fairly homogeneous structure of agricultural organization." However, he suggested that the land-scarcity model ought to fit the American South and called for research on the subject (Easterlin 1976b, pp. 46, 73).[13]

2. CROSS-SECTION EVIDENCE ON THE INTERGENERATIONAL BARGAINING MODEL

In their 1988 paper, Sundstrom and David demonstrated using ordinary-least-squares regression analysis that interstate differences in nonagricultural employment opportunities could account for interstate differences in rural white fertility in 1840. Their dependent variable was a variant of the child-woman ratio for whites (the ratio of children under age 10 to women 16 to 45). Their independent variables included two different measures of the relative attractiveness of nonfarm employment: the relative employment share of nonagricultural to agricultural labor in 1840 and the relative wage, measured as the ratio of the daily common labor wage to the monthly farm labor wage, both with board. These wage data are available for 1850, but not 1840. Sundstrom and David point out that the anticipated wage a decade later "might be more appropriate on expectational grounds" (p. 187). The greater the nonagricultural employment opportunities relative to the total employment in the state and the higher were common laborers' wages relative to wages for agricultural labor, the stronger would be children's bargaining power and the weaker would be that of their parents.

To capture cross-state differences in the marital status of the female population, Sundstrom and David include a measure of the relative share of males in the rural white population aged 10 and older. Where this ratio was unusually low, marriage opportunities for adult females would be limited and thus the child-woman ratio would be depressed. Finally, to measure the power of the alternative, target-bequest hypothesis, Sundstrom and David included a measure of the density of rural settlement, defined in the spirit of Schapiro (1982) as the ratio of the state's rural population in 1840 divided by the state's maximum rural population over the period 1790 through 1940. All of the variables were log-transformed.

Sundstrom and David estimated their model for the country as a whole and for the North and South separately. In the presence of the variables measuring the nonagricultural employment opportunities, the scarcity of local land no longer appeared to reduce fertility. In fact, the opposite was the case. Rural fertility was highest where rural settlement was most dense, though the magnitude of this relationship was not large and the effect was not measured with precision. A second striking finding was that nonagricultural employment opportunities explained rural fertility differentials not only in the North but also in the South, as well as in the regression for the country as a whole. This finding led Sundstrom and David to speculate on the demographic implications of the institution of southern slavery. "If only Emancipation had occurred in 1789 or before," they write,

> rural white fertility in the South might well have followed a course during the first half of the 19th century which hewed more closely to that taken by the northern section of the country. . . . We would say that a more precipitate decline in Southern fertility levels would have ensued, not as a consequence of intensified agricultural settlement in the absence of slavery, but rather, as a result of a

difference in the path of development both with regard to the growth of commerce and industry, and the penetration of those activities into the economic life of the region's rural population. (Sundstrom and David 1988, pp. 192–93)

Sundstrom and David relied on state-level data to test their model. Given the heterogeneity of economic opportunities for young people within states in 1840, this is really too high a level of aggregation. For example, we would expect that the nonagricultural employment opportunities of young adults in upstate New York were quite different from those who lived in or near New York City. The state-level aggregation provided only twenty-nine observations for their countrywide estimating equation and only sixteen and thirteen observations, respectively, for their northern and southern state equations. Because of the small number of observations their coefficient estimates are necessarily imprecise. Recognizing these shortcomings, Sundstrom and David conclude by advocating "further empirical studies based upon disaggregated data" (ibid., p. 193).

We respond to their call by developing a data set based on county-level aggregates and estimating a regression model designed to explain cross-county fertility differences with a specification designed to embrace the spirit of their model. Table 11.2 presents summary statistics from our tests of the Sundstrom-David model using county-level data for the 1840s. (All of the county-level variables are defined and described in appendix tables 11.A1 and 11.A2.) Our findings confirm the robustness and predictions of their cross-section estimating model. They are also consistent with important implications of the model that they themselves were not able to test with the state-level data available to them.

Table 11.2 reports the results of seven separate cross-sectional regressions designed to explain cross-county variations in white fertility in 1840. We use as our index of fertility the white child-woman ratio, which we call the CRS Fertility Index. Using the number of children aged 0 to 4 rather the number aged 0 to 9 is, we believe, a better index of local fertility—one less distorted by the interstate migration of women. The dependent variable in these regressions is the natural logarithm of the CRS index since, as Sundstrom and David pointed out, the relationship between the fertility and its economic and social determinants cannot be strictly linear (ibid., pp. 54–55).

Table 11.2

Determinants of the white child–woman ratio in the spirit of Sundstrom-David (1988): Cross-sectional weighted median (MAR) regressions, county-level data, 1840. Dependent variable: natural logarithm of the CRS Fertility Index[a]

Variable[b]	0 All Rural Counties	1 All Rural Counties	2 Northern Rural Counties	3 Southern Rural Counties	4 All Rural Counties	5 All Rural Counties	6 All Counties	7 All Counties
NON-AG JOBS	—	-1.40 (0.055)	-1.30 (0.161)	-0.95 (0.057)	-0.99 (0.053)	-0.83 (0.107)	-0.67 (0.035)	-0.50 (0.022)
Ln [MEN SCARCE]	—	0.75 (0.186)	2.32 (1.051)	1.05 (0.149)	1.11 (0.167)	1.12 (0.323)	1.54 (0.159)	1.41 (0.087)
WOMEN SCARCE	—	0.019 (0.016)	-0.013 (0.044)	0.021 (0.014)	0.031 (0.014)	0.034 (0.027)	0.015 (0.010)	0.034 (0.005)
Ln [LAND ABUNDANCE]	0.0012 (.0170)	-0.126 (0.0110)	-0.264 (0.0510)	-0.151 (0.0089)	-0.166 (0.0104)	-0.143 (0.0204)	-0.049 (0.0035)	-0.038 (0.0019)
SOUTH	—	—	—	—	0.192 (0.0134)	0.143 (0.0275)	0.097 (0.0094)	0.101 (0.005)
RAIL	—	—	—	—	—	-0.098 (0.0259)	-0.169 (0.0079)	-0.137 (0.0043)
WATER	—	—	—	—	—	-0.035 (0.0230)	-0.047 (0.075)	-0.048 (0.0041)
TOWNS	—	—	—	—	—	—	—	-0.095 (0.0075)
Constant	-0.140	0.295	0.315	0.325	0.162	0.175	0.006	-0.050
n	1,016	984	320	664	984	984	1,079	1,079
Pseudo R^2 from MAR	0.000	0.243	0.170	0.401	0.306	0.334	0.445	0.456
R^2 from OLS	0.001	0.361	0.296	0.567	0.489	0.546	0.666	0.675

SOURCE: Authors' calculations from county-level data published by the U.S. Census (1830, 1840, and 1850) and corrected and compiled by Michael Haines, "Historical Demographic, Economic and Social Data: The United States, 1790–1970," Department of Economics, Colgate University, Computer File, 2001. The RAIL and WATER data are based on maps consulted by Lee A. Craig, Raymond B. Palmquist, and Thomas Weiss, "Transportation Improvements and Land Values in the Antebellum United States: A Hedonic Approach," Journal of Real Estate Finance and Economics (March 1998): 173–89.

[a] Standard errors in parentheses. The observations in each regression are weighted by the number of women aged 15 to 44 (CRS MOMS). "Rural Counties" are defined as those with no reported urban place with 2,500 persons or more. Ln(.) denotes a natural logarithm.

Before discussing tests of the Sundstrom-David strategic-bequest model, we make a final test of the Easterlin target-bequest model at the county level using variables that are available to us. For that we need some measure of local-land availability. The Sundstrom-David measure—the ratio of the 1840 rural population to the maximum rural population of the state during the period 1790–1940—is not practical to calculate on the county level given the many county boundary changes that occurred over this long time span. As an alternative we use the natural logarithm of improved acres of farmland per rural white resident in 1850 (*LAND ABUNDANCE*).[14] It is not unlike the measure constructed by Yasuba (1962) and Forster, Tucker, and Bridge (1972) and has the advantage of being easy to calculate with the data at hand. The target-bequest hypothesis would predict that this variable should appear with a positive coefficient. The more acreage available in the county per capita, the larger the number of children parents could safely provide for. Equation zero, listed in the first column of data, is a regression with the logarithm of the CRS Index as the dependent variable and the logarithm of the acreage per capita as the independent variable.[15] It is comparable to the regressions reported in Table 11.1, but with over 1,000 county-level observations rather than twenty-seven state-level observations. Interestingly, the coefficient on *LAND ABUNDANCE* at the county level turns out to be quantitatively insignificant. Here again an attempt to improve the specification of the target-bequest model, in this instance by disaggregating to the county level, makes the fit worse rather than better. The R^2 value is reduced to zero.

Equations 1 through 7 in Table 11.2 are our attempt to replicate with county-level data the intergenerational bargaining model specified in the spirit of Sundstrom and David. We are able to measure nonagricultural employment opportunities at the county level in a way that is similar to the measure that Sundstrom and David used. As we pointed out, use of county-level data should sharpen the measure of nonagricultural opportunities by reducing the heterogeneity observed across a large and economically diverse state such as New York. On the other hand, the draw of nonfarm jobs might in some cases have extended across county boundaries. We explore this possibility later in the chapter by introducing measures of transportation links among counties. For 1840, we have total county employment by sector. We used these data to construct an index of opportunities outside of agriculture (*NON-AG JOBS*) by dividing nonagricultural by total employment.[16] The other Sundstrom-David measure of the attractiveness of nonagricultural employment—the relative wage in nonagricultural versus agricultural employment—is not available at the county level and we cannot incorporate it into our analysis.

Sundstrom and David included a measure of the male-female ratio for the rural population 10 years of age and older in the state as another independent variable. They argued for its inclusion by noting that a high ratio of men to women raises the proportion of women at every age who are married and at risk of pregnancy. This would be the case in frontier settlements. We feel that it is at least equally important to put the argument the other way around: where women of marriageable age outnumber men, the chance of marriage is reduced. This would be the typical case in regions experiencing extensive out-migration of their young male populations. We calculate the male-female ratio as the number of men aged 15 to 49 relative to the number of women aged 15 to 44. We suspect, however, that there is a limit to the extent to which very high male-female ratios could increase fertility. Once all or most marriageable women have a spouse, further increases in the male-female ratio would have little effect. Since the weighted mean across counties and the median county value of the male-female ratio defined in this way are both close to 1.1 (1.11 and 1.09 respectively), we have introduced the male-female ratio in such a way to have an influence only at values below 1.1.[17] For reasons discussed in the text that follows, we are concerned about introducing a spurious correlation through the introduction of the male-female ratio, but we retain it here to keep our county-level replication of the intergenerational bargaining model as faithful to Sundstrom and David as possible.

Our data set includes one observation per county in 1840. However, we excluded some areas that were newly and very thinly settled in 1840.[18] Altogether this left a data set with 1,112 counties. In addition, we had to omit thirty-three counties because they failed to report data on employment, a key variable in the Sundstrom-David analysis. Thus the regressions were limited to 1,079 observations. Of those, 984 were strictly rural counties. Because the counties varied greatly in size, we weighted the observations by the number of women aged 15 to 44 (*CRS MOMS*). This gives each woman of childbearing age an equal weight in the final result.

Because of the possibility of errors and other discrepancies in the underlying census data, we used the median regression technique rather than ordinary least squares (OLS). Median regression is more robust to the presence of anomalous outliers in the data.[19] This procedure estimates the median of the dependent variable by minimizing the sum of absolute residuals (MAR) rather than estimating the mean of the dependent variable by minimizing the sum of the squared residuals as in ordinary regression. By definition, MAR will produce a lower R^2 measure of fit than would OLS. In the table we present the coefficients as estimated by MAR, which we believe are more accurately measured, and we present both the "pseudo" R^2 from MAR and the R^2 from an OLS estimate of the same model. In no case did the OLS coefficients deviate in a disturbing way from their MAR counterparts. This gives us confidence that the results are not a spurious product of poor or corrupt data.

Equations 1, 2, and 3 in Table 11.2 are our effort to re-estimate the Sundstrom-David equations. Following Sundstrom and David, we first estimate the equation for the country as a whole (equation 1) and then conduct separate estimates for the North and the South (equations 2 and 3). We also report equation 4, which pertains to the country as a whole but includes a dichotomous variable that takes the value of "1" for counties in southern states. Taken as a whole, the results of our equations 1 through 4 are testimony to the robustness of the Sundstrom-David findings. The overall goodness-of-fit measures reported in the bottom row seem excellent for cross-section regressions with hundreds of observations. The variable standing in for the intergenerational bequest hypothesis, NON-*AG JOBS,* has the appropriate negative sign. The natural logarithm of *MEN SCARCE* enters with a positive coefficient, as Sundstrom and David would predict based on the argument that low male-female ratios would put fewer women at risk of pregnancy. Also of significance is the fact that our measure of land availability, the natural logarithm of *LAND ABUNDANCE,* displays a negative sign, just as it did in Sundstrom and David's regression. This is the opposite of the positive sign predicted by the target-bequest model.

One difference between our findings and Sundstrom-David's is a much larger negative response of rural fertility to nonagricultural employment opportunities in the North than in the South. This North-South difference shows up in another way in equation 4. There the coefficient on the dichotomous variable for counties in southern states, *SOUTH,* is large and positive, suggesting that the relative paucity of nonagricultural opportunities, ceteris paribus, is not enough to account for the higher level of rural white fertility in the South. North-South labor market conditions leave a substantial share of North-South fertility differences unexplained. We return to this point later in the chapter.

Our county-level data provide us with opportunities to test several logical extensions of the Sundstrom-David model that they themselves could not test with state-level data. One intriguing extension has to do with the implications of "internal improvements," that is, the building of canals and railroads that reduced the cost of the movement of goods and people among regions. Presumably the new facilities opened up nonagricultural employment opportunities. There would be both a direct effect as workers were hired onto railroad and canal construction projects and an indirect effect from improved information and reduced travel costs to employment opportunities in other counties. We expect that variables indicating access to transportation would indicate counties served by the transportation network and would therefore indicate the impact of those internal improvements on rural fertility. In equation 5 we include all of the independent variables included in earlier equations together with two dichotomous variables, one indicating the presence of a railroad (*RAIL*) and the other indicating access to either the seacoast or an inland waterway (*WATER*). Because many coastal areas did not have seaports and many rivers and lakes were not navigable year around, we expect the average impact of water access to be smaller than that of railroads. Both the railroad and waterway variables were measured in 1850 rather than 1840 to crudely capture both the impact of railroad construction and the anticipation of railroad and canal services on the fertility decisions of couples in the period 1836 to 1840.[20] Both variables have a powerful impact and work in the expected direction of reducing fertility. Railroads display a more powerful impact than the water variable.

Finally, our county-level data allows us to explore the generalizability of the Sundstrom-David hypothesis for urban as well as rural regions. Sundstrom and David estimated their state-level regressions using the rural population of each state. Because we did not have the age distributions for each and every town with a population of 2,500 or more, we restricted our equations 0 through 5 to counties that had no towns of that size or larger. In equation 6 we re-estimate Equation 5 by expanding the universe to all counties. It is interesting that the predictive power of the model is actually improved when the urban counties are added. It is improved again by adding a categorical variable to indicate that the county has a town (*TOWN* in equation 7). That dichotomous variable has an estimated coefficient that is both large and negative. It would seem that the appearance of nonagricultural employment opportunities had an even more geographically widespread impact on fertility than Sundstrom and David proposed.

3. TIME-SERIES EVIDENCE ON THE INTERGENERATIONAL BARGAINING MODEL

While Sundstrom and David confined their empirical analysis to a cross-section of states in 1840, their objective was to shed light on the change in fertility across time. We have three reservations about the applicability of their intergenerational bargaining model to explain the decline of fertility in the United States during the nineteenth century.

- First, the fertility decline began as early as 1800, and although the change was modest between 1800 and 1810, it was well under way by 1820. Yet the rise of manufactures is traditionally dated several decades later, not beginning in earnest until after 1830. Most historians of the period suggest there was a severe contraction of manufacturing and other nonagricultural employment opportunities following the end of war in 1815 and that the recovery from the postwar setback was slow (Engerman and Sokoloff 2000). This account is consistent with Thomas Weiss's (1992) estimates of the growth of nonagricultural employment as a share of the total between 1800 and 1860. In Figure 11.5 we display three plots of fertility against nonagricultural employment. The monotonic fall in fertility and rise in nonagricultural employment over time is shown in the line marked "U.S. time trend," which connects data for the successive decennial years 1800 through 1860. Note that the very large fall in national fertility rates between 1810 and 1830 (from 944 per thousand to 836) was accompanied by only a modest increase in the fraction of the labor force working in nonagricultural occupations (from 28 to 30 percent). We have also plotted on the same figure the

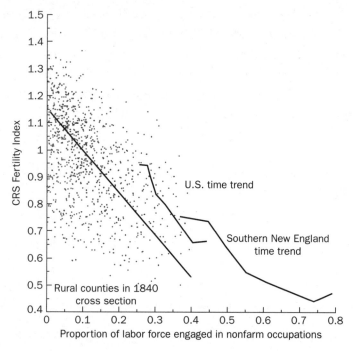

Figure 11.5 Fertility and employment opportunities: cross section in 1840 and two time series

SOURCE: Weiss (1992) and authors' calculations.

time trend for the states of Massachusetts, Rhode Island, and Connecticut for the same years, marking this "Southern New England time trend." Even in southern New England, which by all accounts was the locus of manufacturing and commercial development in the early decades of the century, it is difficult to relate the decline in rural fertility between 1810 and 1830 to the expansion of nonagricultural opportunities for young adults. The failure of the county-level data on nonfarm employment to fully explain higher fertility in the South also suggests that a richer model is required to explain both the cross-section pattern in 1840 and the decline in fertility between 1800 and 1860.

- Second, a powerful explanatory variable in the Sundstrom-David regression analysis was the adult male-female ratio. Sundstrom and David justified their inclusion of this variable as a measure of the marital status of women. In our county-level replications we used a refined version of this variable, *MEN SCARCE,* that ought to make the variable an even better measure of women's marital status. Despite these improvements, we are concerned about this variable's interpretation. We know that intercounty migrants tended to be young adult males, and there is a substantial correlation between the male-female ratio in 1840 and the rate of in-migration between 1830 and 1840. Counties with a male-female ratio substantially below 1.1 were counties that had experienced out-migration. If out-migration itself exerted an independent, negative influence on fertility, that effect would be confounded with that of marriage rates. For reasons described below, we think that out-migration should have a negative impact on fertility. To test for this possibility we require an independent measure of out-migration.

- Finally, the Sundstrom-David model is a static one in which the impact of nonagricultural employment opportunities is potentially reversible. While Sundstrom and David discussed their model in terms of the growth in opportunities off the farm, the logic of the model also predicted that a setback which reduced nonfarm opportunities should lead to an increase in fertility. We find this implausible. We suspect that the shift in rural "mentalité" was irreversible and cannot be captured with a static model. In other words, the historical process was path dependent.

Our point can be demonstrated by comparing the cross-sectional relationship between fertility and employment opportunities with the time-series evidence. In Figure 11.5 we plot our measure of fertility (CRS Fertility Index) on the vertical axis against the proportion of the labor force in nonfarm occupations (*NON-AG JOBS*) on the horizontal axis. There is a point on the scatter diagram for every rural county in 1840. This scatter can be compared to the two time trends discussed earlier.[21] The interesting conclusion is that in 1840 most rural counties with high levels of nonagricultural occupations experienced lower fertility than would be predicted using U.S. or New England time-series data. Consider a young couple that left their parents in southern

New England and moved to the frontier. They would face *fewer* nonagricultural opportunities in their new home than if they had stayed in New England. While fertility on the frontier was higher than in New England, it was not as high as we would predict from the static model and the time-series data. That suggests that the generation who moved to the frontier did not replicate the fertility patterns of their parents' generation when they faced roughly comparable nonfarm opportunities. Instead, they reduced their fertility to a level below that of their parents.

We address these three concerns about the intergenerational bargaining model by offering three contributions. First, we provide a historical framework that ties the development of nonagricultural opportunities to the same set of forces that explain the fertility decline. In our dynamic model we connect fertility decline, the rise of manufacturing, and the forces that led to the rise of manufacturing to a public policy initiative—the opening of western lands. We argue that the subsequent westward migration triggered *both* the fertility decline and the rise of manufacturing. Our historical model not only accounts for intercounty differences in fertility at some point in time, but also allows us to explain why the fertility transition took place when it did—something that the intergenerational bargaining model cannot. Moreover, it allows us to explain why fertility continued to decline even after the rural population ceased growing—something that the target-bequest hypothesis cannot. Second, we further develop our 1840 county-level data by linking it to values in 1830. The 1830–40 linkage allows us to measure the magnitude of out-migration and to take account of its impact on fertility. And third, we bring slavery into the story of white fertility change.

4. THE LIFE-CYCLE MODEL OF THE FERTILITY TRANSITION

Our story begins in much the same way as that of Sundstrom and David, with the eighteenth-century American family-owned, family-operated, self-sufficient farm economy. The fertility of the population inhabiting those farms was extremely high, close to a biological maximum. The high level of fertility and the large families it produced were desirable to parents for at least three reasons.

- First, grown children provided economic security for their parents' old age. As the children grew up, the workload of the family farm could be gradually shifted from the older to the younger generation, and parents could rely upon their children to care for them in the case of sickness or infirmity. Thus children were economic assets in this family-based system. At a time when markets for financial and liquid physical assets either did not exist or were unreliable, intertemporal reallocations of income were accomplished by relying upon reciprocity and implicit contracting with family members.

- Second, land abundance created opportunities for economies of scale in farming. Hired, nonfamily labor was scarce and expensive. Outside of the slave South, the number of family workers limited the effective size of a farm (Wright 1978, pp. 44–55). For this reason, children were assets (Craig 1993, pp. 74–75). Large families permitted an expansion of the scale of the farm and perhaps led to an increase in per capita output.

- Third, a large family with many sons vying for the inheritance was easier to control. The glue that held this system together was patriarchy. A large family was like money in the bank—provided the children remained nearby and could be relied upon or coerced to live up to their family responsibilities. In an environment where land was abundant, it was possible for parents to acquire and improve sufficient land to promise that each son might eventually inherit a farm of his own. The multi-geniture inheritance system was the father's club. Children who abrogated their responsibilities to the family could be disowned and deprived of the inheritance of land necessary to maintain their economic well-being and their social position within the community.

Thus self-sufficient farming and large patriarchal families were mutually reinforcing institutions. Self-sufficiency meant an absence of well-developed markets that, in turn, required reliance upon family-based mechanisms of reciprocity to provide farm labor and old-age security. Large families supplied the needed labor during the seasonal peaks of agricultural work, but they also offered a surplus of labor in the off-season. This energy was employed in the home manufacturing of textiles, tools, and the like. The low opportunity cost of off-peak labor, in turn, inhibited the rise of urban manufacturing and retarded the development of markets (Clark 1979; Hymer and Resnick 1969). The absence of an urban alternative to agriculture ensured that the primary emphasis of parents would be to raise their children to continue the tradition of family farming. With a tradition of self-sufficient farming there was little demand for education beyond the rudiments of literacy, and that primarily for religious reasons. This lack of more advanced schooling in the population at large inhibited entrepreneurship, long-distance commerce, and the spread of new technologies.

Given the self-reinforcing nature of the self-sufficient farming–high fertility nexus, it might seem that a regime of high fertility and self-sufficient family farming should have continued in America far into the nineteenth century. After all, the entire century was characterized by the continuous availability and gradual exploitation of large tracts of underpopulated land. Many eighteenth-century observers predicted just that. Thomas Jefferson, for example, foresaw an agrarian democracy populated by independent yeomen. With equal foresight he predicted a continuing high rate of natural increase.[22] In a letter dated July 1787, he wrote: "A century's experience has shewn that we double our numbers every twenty or twenty-five years. No circumstance can be foreseen at this moment which will lessen our rate of multiplication for centuries to come" (Jefferson 1787).

But as we have seen, Jefferson was wrong about the birth rate. At about the beginning of the nineteenth century, a long-sustained decline in fertility began. Fertility fell from the biological maximum of about eight children per woman to fewer than four children in about two generations. This dramatic demographic development coincided with an equally dramatic transition to commercial farming, the development of cities, and the appearance of banks, schools, manufacturing, and a transportation infrastructure.

What we see in the early national period of American history is a population fundamentally and irreversibly altering its approach to life. Young adults freed themselves from patriarchal control and began to choose their own marriage partners and time their marriages to suit themselves (Smith 1973; Folbre 1985). Children were sent to school, and less work was expected of them on the farm (Fishlow 1966; Lindert 1978; Kaestle and Vinovskis 1980).

Prohibitions against the distribution of birth control information were relaxed (Reed 1978; Folbre 1983). Inheritance patterns changed toward more equality and less sexism (Morris 1927; Alston and Schapiro 1984). Savings banks arose to collect the assets of savers, saving rates rose over the course of the nineteenth century until they stood at over 25 percent by the century's end (Ransom and Sutch 1995, 2001, fig. 2). Planned, self-financed retirement came to be a common phenomenon (Ransom and Sutch 1986b; Ransom, Sutch, and Williamson 1993; Carter and Sutch 1996). Geographic and social mobility increased (McClelland and Zeckhauser 1982; Wells 1982). The dramatic decline in fertility coincided with a shift from family to individual attitudes and values.

Ransom and Sutch (1986) and Sutch (1991) suggest that the decline in fertility, the appearance of individualism, and the revolution in American family values were a response to a public policy initiative that inadvertently led to a failure of the family-based income-transfer mechanism. That public policy initiative was the opening of new lands west of the Appalachian Mountains (Degler 1980; Vinovskis 1981, chap. 8; Wells 1982; Bellah, Madsen, Sullivan, Swidler, and Tipton 1985).

Trans-Appalachian settlement had long been a goal of the American revolutionaries and was viewed as essential to securing American claims to western lands against the counterclaims of the Indian Confederacy (established by the Fort Stanwix agreement with the British in 1768), the Spanish (who at the time held both the Louisiana Territory and the Floridas), and the Canadians (who occupied some lands south of the Great Lakes). Settlement had been held back first by the ineffectiveness of the land acts passed during the period of the Confederacy and then by the land policies of Alexander Hamilton implemented by the Federalists. It was the triumph of Jefferson that set in process a sequence of events that eventually triggered the western migration: the Land Ordinance of 1787 (based on Jefferson's plan), the suppression of Indian resistance at Fallen Timbers (1794) and the Treaty of Fort Greenville (1795), the Louisiana Purchase (1803), the treaty with the Sauks and the Foxes (1804), military incursions against hostile Indian communities during the War of 1812 (the defeat and death of Tecumseh, 1813, and the Creek War, 1813–14), and the implementation of land acts that provided for the sale of land in family farm–sized lots in 1817 and 1820 (Sheehan 1973; McCoy 1980). The construction of the Erie Canal (begun in 1816, completed in 1823) added considerable impetus to the westward movement of the population.

Each of these developments removed obstacles to westward migration into the lands of western New York, western Pennsylvania, and the Ohio Valley. Although halted temporarily by the 1812–15 War with England, the migration quickly resumed once peace was restored and was greatly stimulated by the fact that many who fought had been paid in part with script redeemable for western land. This bounty script was transferable, so those who did not wish to move could sell their rights to others (Oberly 1990).

While the aggregate data are far from perfect, estimates of interregional migration based on calculations by Peter McClelland and Richard Zeckhauser (1982) suggest that, overall, 5 to 6 percent of the population departed the region between 1800 and 1810, and another 7 to 8 percent left in the second decade of the century.[23] Since this migration was highly selective of those in the 15–to–34–year–old age group, the clear implication is that many young adults left their parents behind when they left New England.[24]

The impending departure of this young cohort provoked considerable tension and anxiety in their parents' families. The increasing incidence and constant threat of "child default" put such stress on the traditional familial system that it initiated a search for a more reliable strategy of securing old age.[25] The new strategy that emerged was based on saving. Henceforth, parents would attempt to save from current income during the peak earning years of their lives. They would invest these savings by accumulating assets (bank accounts, insurance policies, and stock shares, as well as farms, houses, and furnishings) and then, late in life, as their productivity declined, they would draw upon those assets for support. Grown children would no longer be needed or expected to support their aging parents.

If the parents happened to live to an old age, they might in this way exhaust the entire stock of wealth they had accumulated. In that case, there would be no inheritance left for the children. However, in the new scheme of things, this was not a crippling blow. Parents provided for their children by preparing them for independence, not with an inheritance. Growing children were relieved from much of the on-farm labor extracted in the old system, thus freeing their time for schooling and skill acquisition. The parents gave up other income from unpaid child labor and "invested" it in their education. Education equipped the next generation for the richer set of opportunities that was beginning to appear in the towns and cities. The new strategy required a new ethic: avoiding the "shame of being a burden to one's children." The old ethic of avoiding the "shame of squandering the family estate" gave way. In the process, the modernization of values was accelerated.

Because large families were no longer needed to secure old age or to labor on the family farm, and because large families impeded the ability of the parents to save, fertility fell. Because families were smaller, the rate of population growth was reduced and the need for extensive land clearing and farm building was correspondingly diminished. This freed resources to be used in the creation of capital for manufacturing. With small families, less home production was possible and the demand for manufactures increased. Because parents were saving and depositing money in banks, a pool of loanable funds was created from which manufacturing development could be financed. The transition to a manufacturing-based economy was propelled and accelerated as new institutions, asset markets, common schools, savings banks, life insurance companies, and factories took hold.

The post-transition household had a demand for fewer children. Three reasons parallel, but reverse, the three we suggested explained the high fertility of the colonial era:

- First, parents could no longer rely upon their children during old age because the children might move away. The promise of an inheritance of land was, in any event, becoming a less important and less credible reward. The household's accumulated assets became its new source of security. Once parents were no longer obligated by family conventions and expectations to pass the family farm intact to their heirs, even land could serve as a life-cycle asset. In this context a large family with its consequent consumption requirements actually became a threat to old-age security.

- Second, parents could no longer rely upon their grown children to provide faithful labor on the family farm. At one time, parents had used the promise of an inheritance as an incentive to be obedient and work hard. The loss of this bargaining chip undermined patriarchal authority. Contributing to the reduced value of child labor on the farm was a reduction in their relative productivity. New crops, the rise of animal husbandry, and agricultural developments such as the introduction of crop rotations evened out the farm's seasonal labor requirements. At about the same time, the rise of urban manufacturing provided commercial substitutes for home manufactures.

- Third, the spirit of individualism and independence favored quality rather than quantity when it came to establishing the posterity of descendants. The new ethic placed the children in school rather than in the field.

5. AN EMPIRICAL MODEL OF LIFE-CYCLE FERTILITY

Our argument postulates a diffusion of "modern" values governing intergenerational responsibilities and behavior with respect to saving, labor force participation, and fertility. Further we have suggested that it was a policy decision to open the trans-Appalachian West to settlement that triggered the revolution in family values. At the empirical level, we follow the lead of other researchers by presuming that this transition was at a different stage of completion at different geographic locations in 1840.

"Family values" are not tangible items subject to measurement or enumeration. The challenge at this point is to find indicators or "proxy variables" that would signal the appearance of modern views and that can plausibly be associated with the life-cycle transition in the cross-section data. Models that rely upon proxy variables begin with an inherent disadvantage. Any empirical test that can be designed will necessarily be a simultaneous test of two hypotheses: in our case, the hypothesis about the fertility decline *and* the hypothesis that the proxies chosen are adequate measures of the extent to which life-cycle behavior has been adopted by the child-bearing population.

These difficulties are unavoidable. We attempt to deal with them here by proposing several distinct proxy variables for life-cycle behavior and testing each separately. We hope thereby to demonstrate the consistent superiority of the life-cycle fertility model and to take some comfort in that consistency. The proxies we propose are designed to measure:

- the rate of out-migration of the 1830 population,
- the presence of nonagricultural employment opportunities, and
- the educational commitment of the adult population.

Since none of these variables may be a self-evident indicator of the county's stage in its life-cycle transition, we shall discuss each in turn, sketching out the secondary hypothesis that, in our view, links it to life-cycle modes of behavior.

Out-Migration and Child Default

We have suggested that rising out-migration may have caused fertility to decline, since the departure of young adults left parents less secure about their support in old age. The evident risk of child default would have encouraged others in the community to attempt fertility control and to adopt life-cycle strategies of wealth accumulation. An obvious candidate for a quantitative index of this effect would be a measure of the volume of out-migration, particularly the out-migration of teenagers and young adults. It is not clear, however, how such an index should be used in a cross-section analysis. Child default, we suspect, was more of a catalyst to the life-cycle transition than an ingredient. In that case, the magnitude of the rate of out-migration may not be particularly relevant. Perhaps only the direction of migration should be measured. Moreover, the hypothesis applies directly only to regions experiencing out-migration. Would married women living in states experiencing an in-migration be oblivious to the threat of child default, or would the newcomers import life-cycle values and strategies from their home states?[26]

Even if these questions are resolved, there remains the problem of measurement. There are no comprehensive data on interstate migration. Investigators have been forced to infer the migration flows between states using a technique known as the "census survival method," for which detailed age breakdowns of the population at two census dates are required. If the number of people of a given age residing in a state at the second census exceeds the number that can be expected to have survived from that age cohort as measured at the first of the two censuses, it is assumed that the increase was produced by in-migration. If fewer people remain in the cohort than would be expected after taking account of normal mortality, it is presumed that those missing have left the state.[27]

Despite the conceptual and methodological difficulties of designing an appropriate test of the link between out-migration and fertility, we have undertaken a crude experiment. As a rough index of the magnitude of net migration we have calculated the ratio of the rural white population age 10 and older in 1840 to the rural white population of all ages in 1830. Since the children younger than 10 years of age are excluded from the 1840 population for the purposes of this calculation, this growth ratio is unaffected by county differences in fertility. In a hypothetical case where the mortality rate applicable to the 1830 population can be assumed to have been constant across counties, regardless of the age and gender distribution of the population, then the growth ratio will order counties by the magnitude of the net migration flows.[28] A high value suggests that the county experienced a net in-migration and a low value suggests an out-migration. The geographic pattern of this measure is displayed in Figure 11.6.

Because our theory suggests that only out-migration generates the child default that would catalyze fertility reduction, we parse our growth index into three separate independent variables that jointly measure the migration rate. The first variable, "Ln(*DECLINE*)," is the natural logarithm of the growth ratio, top-coded at 1. It measures the rate of decline of populations that shrank between 1830 and 1840. The second, *GROW,* signals in-migration. It is a dichotomous variable that takes the value of 1 (and 0 otherwise) for counties where our growth ratio is greater than one. The third, *FRONTIER,* is defined equal to 1 (and 0 otherwise) for 1840 counties that reported no white population at all in 1830. The logic here is that we might expect fertility to be higher in frontier regions because of the high value of child labor in self-sufficient frontier economies.

As might be anticipated from the earlier discussion, the southern states have a higher fertility ratio than the northern states even after the relative magnitude of the out-migration is taken into consideration. We take account of this by including the variable, *SOUTH,* which takes on the value of 1 for the slave states and the value 0 for the northern states.[29]

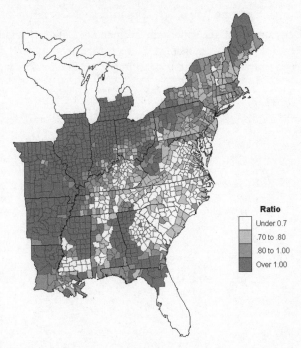

Figure 11.6 Ratio of the population aged 10 and over in 1840 to the total population in 1830

We jointly estimate the impacts of the three measures of migration on rural white fertility in a cross section of 984 rural counties using the weighted median regression technique.[30] The weights are equal to the number of white women 15 to 44 years of age, *CRS MOMS*. The dependent variable is the natural logarithm of the CRS Fertility Index for whites. The result is shown in column 1 of Table 11.3. The regression experiment is quite successful. Out-migration is positively associated with fertility decline: the greater the out-migration during the decade of the 1830s, the lower is fertility in 1840. The experience of *in*-migration into settled counties is associated with a child-woman ratio 11.7 percent higher than that for the sample as a whole. The weighted median growth ratio for counties experiencing out-migration was 0.82. In the neighborhood of that value, a 1 percent change in the out-migration rate is associated with a decline in fertility of about four children per 1,000 women. Contrary to our expectations, frontier conditions appear to have had no additional measurable effect on fertility when compared with

Table 11.3
Determinants of the white child–woman ratio, life-cycle model:
Cross-sectional weighted median (MAR) regressions, county-level data, 1840.
Dependent variable: Natural logarithm of the CRS Fertility Index[a]

Variable[b]	1 Rural Counties	2 All Counties	3 All Counties	4 All Counties	5 All Counties	6 All Counties	7 All Counties
Ln(DECLINE)	0.465	0.295	0.229	—	—	0.158	0.125
	(0.079)	(0.054)	(0.033)			(0.003)	(0.011)
GROW	0.082	0.137	0.149	—	—	0.071	0.077
	(0.031)	(.021)	(0.013)			(0.001)	(0.004)
FRONTIER	0.001	0.017	0.020	—	—	0.090	0.097
	(0.043)	(0.027)	(0.016)			(0.002)	(0.006)
SOUTH	0.276	0.221	0.235	0.047	−0.024	−0.005	0.036
	(0.021)	(0.013)	(0.009)	(0.007)	(0.009)	(0.001)	(0.005)
TOWNS	—	−0.121	−0.134	−0.143	−0.108	−0.067	−0.070
		(0.031)	(0.016)	(0.014)	(0.015)	(0.002)	(0.005)
URBAN	—	−0.435	−0.139	0.162	−0.346	−0.170	−0.136
		(0.078)	(0.034)	(0.034)	(0.032)	(0.004)	(0.014)
Ln(MEN SCARCE)	—	—	0.977	—	—	0.867	0.834
			(0.159)			(0.017)	(0.053)
WOMEN SCARCE	—	—	−0.019	—	—	0.015	0.025
			(0.011)			(0.001)	(0.004)
NON-AG JOBS	—	—	—	−0.463	—	−0.230	−0.273
				(0.032)		(0.004)	(0.012)
RAIL	—	—	—	−0.189	—	−0.063	−0.059
				(0.007)		(0.001)	(0.003)
WATER	—	—	—	−0.020	—	−0.025	−0.024
				(0.007)		(0.001)	(0.002)
SCH RATE	—	—	—	—	−0.247	−0.340	−0.349
					(0.017)	(0.002)	(0.006)
ILLIT	—	—	—	—	0.350	0.291	0.249
					(0.025)	(0.003)	(0.010)
SLAVES	—	—	—	—	—	—	−0.159
							(0.009)
Constant	−0.209	−0.226	−0.309	0.007	−0.038	0.035	−0.031
n	984	1,079	1,079	1,079	1,079	1,079	1,079
Pseudo R^2 from MAR	0.254	0.422	0.443	0.394	0.467	0.614	0.617
R^2 from OLS	0.432	0.613	0.649	0.587	0.656	0.817	0.818

SOURCE: Authors' calculations from county-level data published by the U.S. Census (1830, 1840, and 1850) and corrected and compiled by Michael Haines, "Historical Demographic, Economic and Social Data: The United States, 1790–1970," Department of Economics, Colgate University, Computer File, 2001. The RAIL and WATER data are based on maps consulted by Lee A. Craig, Raymond B. Palmquist, and Thomas Weiss, "Transportation Improvements and Land Values in the Antebellum United States: A Hedonic Approach," *Journal of Real Estate Finance and Economics* (March 1998): 173–89.

[a]Standard errors in parentheses. The observations in each regression are weighted by the number of women aged 15 to 44 (CRS MOMS). "Rural Counties" are defined as those with no reported urban place with 2,500 persons or more. Ln(.) denotes a natural logarithm.

[b]Variables are defined in Tables 11.A1 and 11.A2.

other growing regions. We find a strong North-South difference in rural white fertility that cannot be explained by regional differences in intercounty migration rates.

Next, we expand the universe of counties included to all counties, including those with towns and cities. At the same time, we add a categorical variable to indicate the presence of one or more settlements with populations of 2,500 or more (*TOWNS*) and a measure of the proportion of the total county population living in urban areas (*URBAN*). We report our findings in equation 2 of Table 11.3. This generalization of the life-cycle transition model to the entire population does not reduce the explanatory power of the out-migration variables, although it does reduce the magnitude of the coefficient on the logarithm of the growth ratio. Our measures of urban settlement, *TOWNS* and *URBAN*, have the expected negative effect on fertility, and we still observe higher levels of fertility among whites living in southern states. The explanatory power of the equation as a whole is improved by the inclusion of urban areas. We draw this conclusion after observing a substantial increase in the pseudo R^2 from the MAR and from the R^2 from the OLS in moving from equation 1 to equation 2.

In equation 3 we add the two joint variables that measure the adult male-female ratio, *MEN SCARCE* and *WOMEN SCARCE*, to the regression in order to examine the independent effect of differential marriage opportunities on intercounty fertility differentials in the presence of our growth variables. Recall that we suspected that Sundstrom and David's male-female ratio was in part picking up some of the effects of out-migration and child default on fertility. Counties that had experienced high rates of in-migration in the previous decade tended to have high male-female ratios and vice versa. In those counties where men were scarce, the natural logarithm of the male-female ratio is positively associated with fertility. That is, the more men per women, the higher would be nuptuality and thus the higher is fertility.

In our equations 3, 6, and 7, the coefficient on *WOMEN SCARCE* is of inconsequential size. Significantly, the overall improvement as measured by the goodness-of-fit tests in the bottom row is not great and the coefficients of the growth variables remain relatively undisturbed. This supports our conjecture that the male-female ratio is an alternative proxy for out-migration.[31]

We conclude that our first candidate as a proxy for life-cycle attitudes does very well. The goodness-of-fit tests for equation 3 indicate a fit approximately as good as that achieved by the augmented Sundstrom-David model displayed in equations 6 and 7 of Table 11.2.

The Nonagricultural Labor Market and Child Default

The expansion of nonagricultural occupations as manufacturing and commerce developed in the years after 1815 was a major threat to the stability of the traditional farm-family economy. Young men, and increasingly young women, were tempted by the opportunities promised by such employment to leave their parents' farms. So we might suppose that a rough indicator of the threat of child default and hence of the degree to which families were beginning to adopt life-cycle attitudes would be the relative size of the nonagricultural sector in the region. This is one of the areas where Sundstrom and David's intergenerational bargaining model and our life-cycle transition model yield the same prediction. Sundstrom and David's justification for including the relative employment share in a cross-state model of fertility was the same as ours: "This variable is designed to take account of the fact that ... the development of more ubiquitous employment openings in construction, trade and manufacturing industries would influence perceptions of the potential attraction such outside opportunities would exert upon the farm family's young" (Sundstrom and David 1988, p. 56).

As before, we measure nonfarm employment options as the nonagricultural share of total employment (*NON-AG JOBS*). We also include the two dichotomous variables indicating access to a railhead (*RAIL*) or to a waterway (*WATER*). Equation 4 in Table 11.3 displays the success of these life-cycle transition indicators in explaining rural fertility differentials. All three measures of nonfarm employment options for young adults perform as predicted by the model. That is, all three are associated with lower levels of fertility. Equation 4 can be thought of as a Sundstrom-David equation stripped of the male-female ratio variables that we now believe were, in part, indicating child default. We note for the record that this equation, which accounts for differences in nonfarm opportunities, cannot explain the higher white rural fertility in southern than in northern counties.

The Rise of Education and the Life-Cycle Transition

Once families found alternatives to patriarchal dominance as a means of providing old-age security, the life-cycle model predicts that parents would no longer feel compelled to postpone until old age or death their bequests to their children. Once the life-cycle transition was under way, parents would transfer resources to their children at much earlier points in their lives. In many cases this meant that parents helped children establish themselves on a farm or in some other occupation when the children were still in their early twenties. Such help might take the form of an outright gift or, more typically, parents would offer their children a loan on favorable terms. Such a loan is, of course, a life-cycle asset from the perspective of the parents.

Perhaps the most far-reaching change in the pattern of intergenerational transfers produced by the life-cycle transition had to do with the choice between child labor and schooling. In the traditional farm family, children were expected to work year-round on their parents' farms. The historical record is unclear about the age when children were put to work and what sorts of tasks they assumed at tender ages, but the opinion of scholars is unanimous on one point. Before the nineteenth century, children as young as 4 or 5 years of age were seen as miniature adults with corresponding expectations regarding their responsibilities for the support of the family economy (Beales 1985; Morgan 1944). Boys helped in the fields. Girls tended to younger siblings and assisted with garden plots and poultry and engaged in home manufactures. Children's labor was an integral part of the household economy, and its loss was seen as too dear a price to pay for extensive schooling.[32] Parents, perhaps, felt that their children would have little need for more than a rudimentary education since traditional family farming did not require the sorts of skills taught in early nineteenth-century schools.

After the life-cycle transition, child labor and schooling were viewed quite differently. Children were no longer seen as an "investment" in old-age security. The "consumption" motive for having children came to the fore. With the decision to have children driven by anticipation of the enjoyment they would bring, parental focus shifted toward a desire to offer their children the opportunity to develop themselves and to improve their options in the larger world. The idea that parents should put their children to full-time labor and thus compel them to contribute to the family income became unfashionable. Parents began to excuse children from year-round labor and to enroll them in school. In effect, parents made transfers when their children were still young, and the children received this form of inheritance well before their parents died.[33] The life-cycle transition enhanced the freedom of both generations. The new ethic gave children the freedom to leave home, escape parental control, and establish their own households while they were still young. It gave parents freedom to manage their assets (including the farm) to suit themselves. The increase in the educational attainment of the population was an important consequence of this profound shift.

As a proxy indicating the extent to which parents had adopted these new attitudes about children, we introduce a variable measuring enrollment in schools.[34] The variable is based on the census returns for 1840. The number of students who were enrolled in academies and grammar schools and the number enrolled in primary and common schools at any time during the preceding year was recorded in the 1840 census.[35] We divided the total enrollment by the white population aged 5 to 19 to provide a rough index of enrollment rates.[36] The school attendance rate, thus defined, is called the *SCH RATE*. Our interpretation of schooling rates is the same as John Caldwell's, whose work on less-developed countries today has emphasized the importance of the change in the direction and timing of intergenerational income transfers on fertility rates in those countries (1982). Caldwell took the parents' decision to send a child to school as evidence of their willingness to transfer resources to their children while still alive, and consequently as evidence that they no longer relied upon children to provide old-age security.

We also include a measure of the education of the parents themselves. This is the white adult illiteracy rate, or *ILLIT*. We include it in order to test a widespread assertion in the literature that education is a powerful correlate of modern values after the life-cycle transition—especially of attitudes toward one's children. Educated parents are more likely to educate their own children. Early adopters of the life-cycle transition supported public education and encouraged neighbors to adopt the same set of values. The illiteracy rate is defined as the number of whites 20 years of age and older who are unable to read and write divided by the number of whites 20 and older in the population.

The result of the experiment with this third proxy indicator of the life-cycle transition is reported as equation 5 in Table 11.3. The variables perform remarkably well. The fit of the equation is the best yet. Perhaps this is not surprising since the schooling ratio measures the extent of life-cycle behavior directly, while the out-migration and employment opportunity variables are intended to capture the child-default catalytic effect and thus are only indirect measures of the life-cycle transition. In any case, both of the educational intensity variables have large coefficients and both are associated with fertility as we predicted. Higher school attendance rates are associated with lower fertility. Higher levels of adult illiteracy are associated with higher fertility. Of great significance, which we shall return to below, is the fact that in the presence of these educational variables the coefficient on the dummy variable SOUTH becomes insignificantly small (it even has a negative sign in equation 5). It would appear that what makes the South different is its reduced commitment to education. An examination of Figure 11.7 reveals a sharp North-South difference in the schooling ratio.

We are not the first to enter an educational variable into cross-state fertility regressions. Maris Vinovskis demonstrated that the illiteracy rate for those over 20 "was the single best predictor of fertility differentials among the states in 1850 and 1860" (1976: 393).[37] Vinovskis clearly intended the illiteracy rate to capture the direct impact of their own education on the parents' desire or ability to control fertility (1976: 381). Elsewhere Vinovskis interpreted measures of adults' educational attainment as indexes of "modernization" (1981: 118–29). If Vinovskis's idea of a "modern cultural outlook" means nothing more or less than what we mean by life-cycle modes of behavior or what Caldwell means by a regime that favors intergenerational transfers from parents to children when the children are young, then we have no disagreement about the interpretation of an educational variable in fertility models.

A Multivariate Test of the Life-Cycle Fertility Model

The battery of tests with life-cycle proxies has been remarkably successful. In each case the proxy tested was significantly correlated with the rural fertility index.[38] Given this success, it might seem appropriate to combine all of the life-cycle proxies into a single regression with multiple independent variables.

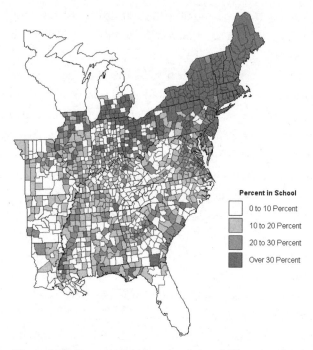

Percent in School

☐ 0 to 10 Percent

▨ 10 to 20 Percent

▩ 20 to 30 Percent

▦ Over 30 Percent

Figure 11.7 Percent of white school-age children in school in the United States, 1840

There is, of course, considerable multi-collinearity between these variables, so it would be remarkable if each one proved to contain unique information. The experiment is reported as equation 6 in Table 11.3. We regard the results as highly favorable. All of the proxy variables have the appropriate sign and are substantively significant and precisely measured. The magnitude of the coefficients on the growth ratio, the urban population share, the nonfarm employment share, and the railroad variable are attenuated in the multivariate version. This is to be expected since the various proxies are alternative attempts to capture the presence of life-cycle strategies. It is remarkable, however, that all of these variables nevertheless retain individual explanatory power in the presence of other measures. The schooling ratio is even more powerful in equation 6 than in equation 5. The dummy variable indicating a slave state has no effect and enters equation 6 with a perverse sign.

6. THE ANOMALOUS SOUTH? SLAVERY AND WHITE FERTILITY

As we have noted, the life-cycle hypothesis ought to be applicable to the white population of the slave states.[39] Higher fertility in the South was the consequence of a delayed and perhaps incomplete transition to life-cycle behavior. For the minority of whites who were slave owners, the threat of child default would be minimized by the presence of slave servants and field hands. This effect of slavery was reflected in the empirical tests that employed the growth ratio as an independent variable (equations 1–3 in Table 11.3) and those that measured nonagricultural employment opportunities (equation 4). Those proxies were independent attempts to quantify the potential threat of child default. Not surprisingly, the regressions were improved by the inclusion of a dummy variable, SOUTH, designed to shift the constant of the equation for the slave states. Child default seems to have been a less powerful catalyst in the South because slaves to some extent could substitute for children to provide security in old age.

The third life-cycle proxy, the school enrollment ratio, measures the extent of the life-cycle transition directly. In the regression containing the educational intensity variables (equation 5) the relationship between fertility and the life-cycle variables was not different for the southern than for the northern states. In this sense then, white fertility is not inexplicably high in the South; it was high because the South lagged behind the North in adopting modern values. This does mean that the institution of slavery was not relevant to the story. An indirect effect of slavery, reflected through the other variables in the equation (primarily schooling and nonagricultural labor opportunities), was responsible for the high fertility actually observed.

It would also be our prediction that the presence of slavery should have had the direct effect of lowering white fertility among slave masters. Slave-owning families would have had less reason to depend upon children for old-age security or farm labor. To test for this possibility we introduce a final variable, the proportion of the total population of the county that was enslaved, SLAVES. We conjecture that the higher the proportion of slaves, the greater would be the fraction of the white population that was part of the slave-owning class.

Equation 7 in Table 11.3 repeats the multivariate specification of equation 6 with the addition of the *SLAVES* variable. The negative sign on this indicator confirms our prediction, while the return of the positive sign on *SOUTH* balances the negative pull of the proportion of slaves.[40] The anomaly of southern white fertility seems to be adequately explained by the life-cycle fertility hypothesis.

7. THREE CONCLUSIONS

This chapter proposes an explanation for the decline in American fertility based on the idea that life-cycle determinants of fertility gradually came to dominate the traditional old-age security motive for high fertility. This was part of a more general development, which we have called the life-cycle transition, initiated by the rising out-migration of young adults.

We asserted that a satisfactory model of the American fertility decline should be able to pass three tests. It should explain the time trend of the decline, and particularly the onset of the decline shortly after 1800. It should be able to explain the pattern of regional fertility differences that existed in an intermediate year such as 1840. It should be able to explain the special case of white fertility in the slave states. We have assembled evidence to demonstrate that our life-cycle transition model successfully passes all three tests.

Finally, we believe we can draw three specific conclusions:

- Child default was the catalyst that triggered the American fertility decline. As the public domain was opened to settlement and as the nonagricultural labor market expanded, children frequently left home to take up new opportunities. This reduced the value of children as "assets" who could provide old-age security for their parents.

- The target-bequest model specified with land-availability variables intended to be applicable to the fertility decisions of a nineteenth-century rural population is rejected. That model, first introduced by Richard Easterlin, is difficult to reconcile with the time-series evidence on fertility, performs poorly in cross-section tests, and consistently fails in the presence of alternative variables suggested by the life-cycle model of fertility proposed in this chapter.

- The David-Sundstrom model of intergenerational bargaining is best interpreted if it is embedded into an explicitly path-dependent story of the adoption of life-cycle behavior.

Table 11.A1
Definitions, means, and deviations of continuous variables:
county-level data, 1840, 1,079 observations

Variable Name	Variable Definition	Mean Value	Standard Deviation
CRS Fertility Index	The number of white children under age 5 divided by number of white women aged 15 to 44	0.9365	0.1900
CRS KIDS	The number of white children under age 5	2,162	2,690
CRS MOMS	The number of white women aged 15 to 44	2,736	4,600
LAND ABUNDANCE	The number of improved acres reported in farms in 1850 divided by the rural white population in that year	9.01	7.45
Growth Ratio	The white population aged 10 and over in 1840 divided by the total white population in 1830	1.199	1.312
DECLINE	The growth ratio top coded at the value of one	0.836	0.154
URBAN	The proportion of the population of the country residing in towns or cities with populations over 2,500 persons	0.0285	0.1143
Male-Female Ratio	The number of white males aged 15 to 49 divided by the number of white females aged 15 to 44	1.157	0.198
MEN SCARCE	The male-female ratio top coded at the value of 1.1	1.069	0.048
NON-AG JOBS	Employment in mining, commerce, manufactures, hand trades, navigation of the ocean, navigation of canals, lakes, and rivers, and those engaged in the learned professions or as engineers divided by total employment, which includes all of the above plus agriculture	0.1519	0.1557
SCH RATE	The number of students enrolled in academies and grammar schools and the number of scholars enrolled in primary and common schools at any time during the year preceding the date of the 1840 census divided by the white population aged 5 to 19	0.2419	0.2381
ILLIT	The number of whites 20 years of age and older unable to read and write divided by the number of whites 20 and older in the population	0.1569	0.1465
SLAVES	The number of slaves divided by the total population of the country	0.1992	0.2182

SOURCE: Authors' calculations from county-level data published by the U.S. Census (1830, 1840, and 1850) and corrected and compiled by Michael Haines, "Historical Demographic, Economic and Social Data: The United States, 1790–1970," Department of Economics, Colgate University, Computer File, 2001.

Table 11.A2
Definitions of dichotomous variables:
county-level data, 1840, 1,079 observations

Variable Name	Variable Is Zero or Equal to One If:	Number of Observations Equal to One
GROW	The *Growth Ratio* is equal to or greater than one	387
FRONTIER	The population in 1830 was equal to zero	44
SOUTH	The county is located in Maryland, Virginia, Delaware, North Carolina, South Carolina, Georgia, Mississippi, Alabama, Louisiana, Arkansas, Tennessee, Kentucky, or Missouri	694
TOWNS	The county has a town or city with at least 2,500 persons in 1840	95
WOMEN SCARCE	The *Male-Female Ratio* is greater than or equal to 1.1	588
RAIL	The county had a railhead in 1850	320
WATER	The county is located on a coastal or inland waterway in 1850	585

SOURCE: Authors' calculations from county-level data published by the U.S. Census (1830, 1840, and 1850) and corrected and compiled by Michael Haines, "Historical Demographic, Economic and Social Data: The United States, 1790–1970," Department of Economics, Colgate University, Computer File, 2001. The *RAIL* and *WATER* data are based on maps consulted by Lee A. Craig, Raymond B. Palmquist, and Thomas Weiss, "Transportation Improvements and Land Values in the Antebellum United States: A Hedonic Approach," *Journal of Real Estate Finance and Economics* (March 1998): 173–89.

Notes

Acknowledgments: The authors acknowledge the helpful comments of Paul A. David, Alex Field, Sheila Johansson, Naomi Lamoreaux, Thomas Mroz, and William Sundstrom. Data assembled by and generously made available to us by Michael Haines and Thomas Weiss made our task easier.

1. The total fertility rate is calculated as the sum of the age-specific birth rates across the entire reproductive span. This rate specifies how many children each woman would bear if she lived to the end of her reproductive life and experienced the age-specific fertility rates for the year specified throughout. See Bogue (1985).

2. We calculate the CRS fertility index using the revised U.S. census data in Haines (2001a). At some census dates interpolations are required to calculate the numerator or denominator of our index since the age categories used for the published data do not always break at 5, 15, and 44. McClelland and Zeckhauser introduced the method of interpolation that we have employed (1982, pp. 23–25).

3. See McClelland and Zeckhauser (1982, tables C-14, C-15, and C-19, pp. 156, 158); Haines (2000, table 4.3, pp. 158, 144; Haines (2001b, table 8.2, p. 308). Blodget's 1806 estimate of the crude birth rate for the period 1790 to 1803 ranged between 52 and 53 per thousand. See our discussion in Ransom and Sutch (1986a, pp. 16–22).

4. The only place in the world today with a comparably high reported crude birth rate is sub-Saharan Africa: Mali (49.2), Niger (51.5), and Chad (48.8). Five other crude birth rates above 46 per 1,000 reported by the U.S. Census Bureau in its "International Data Base" as of May 10, 2000, were also in Africa (Uganda, Kinshasa [Congo], Angola, Liberia, and Somalia). The highest birth rates in Europe around 1800 were in Lombardy (40–45), Iceland (39.8), and Finland (38–40). See Cipolla (1965, p. 576); Jónsson and Magnússon (1997, p. 51); and Gille (1949, p. 63).

5. In this chapter we focus on our discussion with Paul David; for a more extensive review of the literature see Lee A. Craig (1993, Chap. 1).

6. Easterlin (1971, 1976a, 1976b); Easterlin, Alter, and Condran (1978). Sundstrom and David's assault on the Easterlin hypothesis has relevance to the

much larger debate in economics over the relative power of life-cycle versus target-bequest models to explain saving behavior.

7. The CRS fertility index is the children (0–4) to women (15–44) ratio described earlier. The quartile ranges plotted in Figure 11.2 are quoted as the number of children per *thousand* women. It should be noted that in 1840 Wisconsin Territory (spelled at that time "Wiskonsin") included what is now eastern Minnesota. The blank areas on the maps in Wisconsin, northern Michigan, and southern Florida were largely unpopulated in 1840.

8. Maine fits the general pattern since it was sparsely settled when it became a state in 1820. Eastern Louisiana (the parishes around New Orleans and north along the Mississippi River) also fits the pattern. It was settled territory by 1840 and might be properly regarded as similar in this respect to the seaboard east of the Appalachians.

9. To facilitate comparison between the two maps, the CRS Index is plotted using the 1840 county boundaries for both years.

10. See Easterlin (1976a, 1976b); Easterlin, Alter, and Condran (1978); Leet (1976, 1977); and Schapiro (1982). In addition to the contributions of Tucker and Yasuba mentioned in the text, the Easterlin hypothesis had antecedents in the work of Forster, Tucker, and Bridge (1972) and Leet (1975), but none of these authors attributed the relationship between fertility and land scarcity to target-bequest behavior.

11. There was a serious cholera epidemic in 1849, which would distort the fertility indexes calculated for some states from the 1850 census (Vinovskis 1978); Rosenberg 1987: pt. 2). Other variables to be introduced below are not available before 1840.

12. The dependent variable of these regressions is the version of the child-woman ratio introduced by Yasuba. It employs a different definition and interpolation technique than the CRS index we use below in our analysis, but we employ it here since the Yasuba index is the variant used by those researchers referred to in the table.

13. The southern case seems not to have been pursued by the other supporters of the target-bequest hypothesis. Leet (1975, 1976, 1977) confined his examination to Ohio, and Morton Schapiro specifically excluded the southern states from his analysis because of their "idiosyncratic economic and social structures." As he put it, "slavery played an important role" in the South (Schapiro 1982, pp. 585–86). Schapiro did not, however, offer a comment on how or why slavery

should affect white fertility rates. Steckel (1977) took up Easterlin's challenge to test his model with southern data but reported that in his regression analysis the "measure of population pressure [was] statistically insignificant or [had] a sign unfavorable to the population pressure hypothesis" (pp. 15, 170–76).

14. To move the data from 1850 back to 1840, we made several adjustments to reflect county boundary changes between those two dates. To do so we combined counties into "super counties" that represented the smallest contiguous geographic region whose 1840 and 1850 boundaries remained substantially unchanged. Because of the not-infrequent subdivisions of large counties or unorganized regions between 1840 and 1850, most of these super counties were aggregations of contiguous 1850 counties to match the 1840 boundaries. We then calculated the per capita acreage figure for 1850 for each of these super counties and applied that figure to each of the counties in 1840 that coincided with the super county. Our guide to this process was the invaluable *Map Guide* of Thorndale and Dollarhide (1987).

15. For the regression experiments, the CRS Fertility Index is entered as a child-woman ratio and is not converted to children per thousand women. This keeps the dependent variable scaled to the same order of magnitude as the various independent variables.

16. For each county the census reported the industry of employment in seven categories: mining; agriculture; commerce; manufactures and [hand] trades; navigation of the ocean; navigation of canals, lakes, and rivers; and the learned professions and engineers. Sundstrom and David used the figures on nonagricultural employment from Easterlin (1960, pp. 126–32), which are based on the same 1840 census figures that we use. Easterlin, however, made two adjustments that we have not made. First, he excluded the learned professions and engineers. Second he made estimates for counties that reported no labor force statistics and revised the data for several counties with very low labor force estimates. In our regressions thirty-three counties without occupational data were simply dropped from the analysis. Because employment in some counties is *only* in agriculture, nonagricultural employment ratios in those cases are zero. Since the natural logarithm is not defined for zero, the purely agricultural counties would drop out of the analysis if we followed Sundstrom and David precisely and took a logarithmic transformation. Because fertility behavior in purely agricultural counties is an important part of the overall story, we do not want to exclude them from the analysis. For this reason, we entered this variable as a proportion.

17. We define two variables. One is equal to the male-female ratio for the county, if and only if that ratio is less than 1.1. This we call *MEN SCARCE* in the table. For all counties with a calculated male-female ratio of 1.1 or greater, this first variable is set equal to 1.1. The second variable is a dichotomous dummy variable equal to zero for counties with below median male-female ratios and equal to one for those with a ratio of 1.1 or higher. This variable we label as *WOMEN SCARCE*.

18. Excluded were the territories of Florida, Wisconsin, and Iowa (regions that were not states in that year). In addition we excluded most of northern Michigan, northern Illinois and Indiana, and one adjoining county in Ohio (Van Wert) and portions of southwest and far western Arkansas.

19. The regressions were performed with the software package Stata 7.0. In Stata median regressions are run with the command "qreg."

20. These variables were constructed and first used by Craig, Palmquist, and Weiss (1998) and were included in the data set assembled by Haines (2001a).

21. The time-series data on the labor force come from Weiss (1992, pp. 37, 51).

22. Benjamin Franklin and Adam Smith also explained the high American birth rate by the abundance of land and on that basis predicted the continuation of high birth rates for many generations (Franklin 1751; Smith 1776, pp. 70, 392). Had they foreseen the American acquisition of the trans-Mississippi territory or the coming transportation revolution, it would have only strengthened their confidence in the argument.

23. There is no comparable data for the colonial period, though what evidence we have suggests a much lower rate of geographic mobility.

24. A good discussion of the out-migration from New England and the seaboard states during this period can be found in Rohrbough (1978, pp. 81–87, 157–61). Stilwell (1948) provides a detailed portrayal of the migration from Vermont.

25. The term "child default" is used by Williamson (1985) to suggest that children were previously viewed as a type of "asset" by their parents. Because the departing young rarely—almost never—returned, and because remittances of money to family members who remained behind were also rare, these departures of the young were tantamount to a default on the parents' investment in their children. "If children were viewed as assets by their parents, and if the returns to those assets dropped as children fled . . . ," Williamson asks, "wouldn't parents have had fewer children, seeking alternative ways to accumulate for old age?"

26. We suspect that the new arrivals who came to take up land in the western states would be likely to exhibit life-cycle saving and fertility behavior. After all, they would be well aware of the possibility (even likelihood) of child default and of the potent lure of newly open lands. Thus, in the two decades following their migration, we should expect to observe relatively low fertility rates in these regions. In other words, fertility should be lower in the West in 1850 and 1860 than it was in 1840. This is, in fact, what we observe. See the county-level maps of the CRS Fertility Index for 1840 and 1850 (Figures 11.2 and 11.3).

27. The census survival method measures *net* migration, the balance of inflows and outflows. This variable may understate the impact of child default for counties in states such as New York and Massachusetts that experienced considerable immigration from abroad during the 1830s. For a more detailed discussion of the possibilities and limitations of the census survival method, see Carter and Sutch (1996).

28. For the U.S. white population as a whole, the national ratio according to the census is 0.92, reflecting the decline due to mortality and the increase due to net international migration. The average of the ratio across counties retained in our sample, weighted by the number of women 15 to 44 years of age, is 1.04. This value indicates that the included counties experienced a level of net in-migration that slightly offset mortality experienced by the 1830 population over the decade of the 1830s.

29. This is the same variable *SOUTH* that was introduced in Table 11.2. The southern states in our analysis are states where slavery was legal in 1840: Maryland, Virginia, Delaware, North Carolina, South Carolina, Georgia, Mississippi, Alabama, Louisiana, Arkansas, Tennessee, Kentucky, and Missouri.

30. These are the same counties included in equations 1 through 5 of Table 11.2.

31. When we rerun equation 3 without the three growth ratio variables, the pseudo R^2 is substantially below that of equation 2, suggesting that the growth ratio is a better proxy for the impact of child default than the male-female ratio.

32. We do not mean to suggest that most children in eighteenth-century New England grew up illiterate. Literacy was encouraged for religious reasons, and literacy rates were quite high. Formal schooling beyond the point of acquiring an ability to read the Bible, however, did not become common until the early decades of the nineteenth century (Carlton 1908, chap. 1; Kaestle 1983, chap. 1).

33. The cost to parents of permitting their children to attend school should not be underestimated. The major component of that cost was the forgone labor of the children. But there were tuition expenses as well. Before the 1840s even the public schools were not free. In New York parents were charged user fees called "rate bills," and those who did not pay could not send their children to school. In Massachusetts only a short regular session was provided at public expense; parental fees were charged to lengthen the term (Kaestle and Vinovskis 1980, p. 16).

34. Carter (1986a) estimated a simultaneous system of equations for schooling and fertility in the antebellum United States using county-level census data for 1840 and 1850 and two-stage estimation procedures.

35. Fishlow (1966, pp. 66–67) deemed these data from the 1840 census to be reliable indicators of enrollment.

36. The index is rough because the numerator represents the cumulative enrollment over the preceding year whereas the denominator counts the population at the time of the census. The measure will thus overstate the average enrollment rate and may be distorted in unpredictable ways by the impact of migration. See Kaestle (1980, pp. 13–14, 29–31).

37. Vinovskis's (1976) other variables included the sex ratio, the percentage of the free population that was foreign-born, the degree of urbanization, and the value of an average farm. Despite the fact that school enrollment rates and the illiteracy rates of those over 20 are highly correlated (the correlation coefficient between the respective weighted logarithms of the two measures in 1840 is minus 0.5), the two variables measure very different phenomena. The schooling rate refers to children between the ages of 5 and 19; illiteracy rates for adults say something about those children's parents.

38. Using state-level data, Steckel (1977) also showed the strong impact of the existence of banks in a fertility regression. This too would be a proxy for the life-cycle transition, a point that Steckel explicitly uses to motivate his model.

39. The fertility history of slaves is an entirely different issue. There is abundant evidence that slave fertility was, at least in part, subject to the influence of the slave owners, and in any case, the problems of old-age security and the accumulation of a bequest were hardly ones to trouble or motivate slaves. On the subject of slave breeding, see Sutch (1975, 1986). See Steckel (1977) on slave fertility.

40. Carter (1986a, p. 14) was the first to report a significant negative effect of slavery on white fertility.

References

Alston, Lee J., and Morton Owen Schapiro. 1984. "Inheritance Laws across Colonies: Causes and Consequences." *Journal of Economic History* 44: 277–87.

Beales, Ross W. 1985. "In Search of the Historical Child: Miniature Adulthood and Youth in Colonial New England." In R. Hiner and J. M. Hawes, eds., *Growing Up in America: Children in Historical Perspective*, pp. 7–26. Urbana: University of Illinois Press.

Bellah, Robert N., Richard Madsen, William M. Sullivan, Ann Swidler, and Steven M. Tipton. 1985. *Habits of the Heart: Individualism and Commitment in American Life*. Berkeley: University of California Press.

Blodget, Samuel. [1806] 1964. *Economica: A Statistical Manual for the United States of America*. Reprint of original 1806 edition, New York: Augustus Kelly.

Bogue, Donald J. 1985. *The Population of the United States: Historical Trends and Future Projections*. New York: Free Press.

Bogue, Donald J., and James A. Palmore. 1964. "Some Empirical and Analytic Relations among Demographic Fertility Measures with Regression Models for Fertility Estimation." *Demography* 1: 316–38.

Caldwell, John C. 1982. *Theory of Fertility Decline*. New York: Academic Press.

Carlton, Frank Tracy. 1908. *Economic Influences Upon Educational Progress in the United States, 1820–1850*. Madison: University of Wisconsin Press.

Carter, Susan B. 1986a. "Schooling and Fertility in Antebellum America." Paper presented at the NSF Cliometrics Conference, May 1986, Oxford, Ohio.

———. 1986b. "Which Came First, Students or Schools? Educational Expansion in Antebellum America." Paper presented at the NSF Cliometrics Conference, May 1986, Oxford, Ohio.

Carter, Susan B., Scott S. Gartner, Michael R. Haines, Alan L. Olmstead, Richard Sutch, and Gavin Wright, eds. 2004. *Historical Statistics of the United States, Millennial Edition*. New York: Cambridge University Press, forthcoming.

Carter, Susan B., and Richard Sutch. 1996. "Myth of the Industrial Scrap Heap: A Revisionist View of Turn-of-the-Century American Retirement." *Journal of Economic History*: 5–38.

Cipolla, Carlo M. 1965. "Four Centuries of Italian Demographic Development." In D. V. Glass and D. E. C. Eversley, eds., *Population in History: Essays in Historical Demography*. New York: Edward Arnold.

Clark, Christopher. 1979. "Household Economy, Market Exchange and the Rise of Capitalism in the Connecticut Valley, 1800–1860." *Journal of Social History* 13: 169–89.

Coale, Ansley J., and Melvin Zelnik. 1963. *New Estimates of Fertility and Population in the United States: A Study of Annual White Births from 1855 to 1960 and of the Completeness of Enumeration in the Censuses from 1880 to 1960.* Princeton, N.J.: Princeton University Press.

Craig, Lee A. 1993. *To Sow One Acre More: Childbearing and Farm Productivity in the Antebellum North.* Baltimore: The Johns Hopkins University Press.

Craig, Lee A., Raymond B. Palmquist, and Thomas Weiss. 1998. "Transportation Improvements and Land Values in the Antebellum United States: A Hedonic Approach." *Journal of Real Estate Finance and Economics* (March): 173–89.

David, Paul A., and Warren C. Sanderson. 1986. "Rudimentary Contraceptive Methods and the American Transition to Marital Fertility Control, 1855–1915." In Stanley L. Engerman and Robert E. Gallman, eds., *Long Term Factors in American Economic Growth*, pp. 307–79. Studies in Income and Wealth, Vol. 51. Chicago: University of Chicago Press.

David, Paul A., and William A. Sundstrom. 1984. "Bargains, Bequests, and Births." Stanford Project on the History of Fertility Control, Working Paper No-12-R. Stanford: Stanford University.

Degler, Carl N. 1980. *At Odds: Women and the Family in America from the Revolution to the Present.* New York: Oxford University Press.

Easterlin, Richard A. 1960. "Interregional Differences in per Capita Income, Population, and Total Income: 1840–1950." In *Trends in the American Economy in the Nineteenth Century*, pp. 73–140. Vol. 24, *Studies in Income and Wealth.* Princeton: Princeton University Press.

———. 1971. "Does Human Fertility Adjust to the Environment?" *American Economic Review* 64: 399–407.

———. 1976a. "Factors in the Decline of Farm Family Fertility in the United States: Some Preliminary Research Results." *Journal of American History* 63: 600–14.

———. 1976b. "Population Change and Farm Settlement in the Northern United States." *Journal of Economic History* 36: 45–83.

Easterlin, Richard A., George Alter, and Gretchen A. Condran. 1978. "Farms and Farm Families in Old and New Areas: The Northern States in 1860." In Tamara K. Hareven and Maris A. Vinovskis, eds. *Family and Population in Nineteenth-Century America, pp. 22–84.* Princeton: Princeton University Press.

Engerman, Stanley L., and Kenneth L. Sokoloff. 2000. "Technology and Industrialization, 1790–1914." In Stanley L. Engerman and Robert E. Gallman, eds.,

The Cambridge Economic History of the United States. Vol. II, *The Long Nineteenth Century,* pp. 367–401, 909–14. New York: Cambridge University Press.

Fishlow, Albert. 1966. "The American Common School Revival: Fact or Fancy?" In Henry Rosovsky, ed., *Industrialization in Two Systems: Essays in Honor of Alexander Gerschenkron,* pp. 40–67. New York: John Wiley and Sons.

Folbre, Nancy R. 1983. "Of Patriarchy Born: The Political Economy of Fertility Decisions." *Feminist Studies* 9: 261–84.

———. 1985. "The Wealth of Patriarchs: Deerfield, Massachusetts, 1760–1840." *Journal of Interdisciplinary History* 16: 199–220.

Forster, Colin, G. S. L. Tucker, and Helen Bridge. 1972. *Economic Opportunity and White American Fertility Ratios, 1800–1860.* New Haven: Yale University Press.

Franklin, Benjamin. 1751. "Observations Concerning the Increase of Mankind, Peopling of Countries, &c." In L. W. Labaree and Whitfield J. Bell, eds., *The Papers of Benjamin Franklin,* Vol. 4, pp. 225–34. New Haven: Yale University Press, 1961.

Gille, H. 1949. "The Demographic History of the Northern European Countries in the Eighteenth Century." *Population Studies* 3: 3–65.

Haines, Michael R. 2000. "The Population of the United States, 1790–1920." In Stanley L. Engerman and Robert E. Gallman, eds., *The Cambridge Economic History of the United States.* Vol. II, *The Long Nineteenth Century,* pp. 143–206. New York: Cambridge University Press.

———. 2001a. "Historical Demographic, Economic and Social Data: The United States, 1790–1970." Hamilton, N.Y.: Department of Economics, Colgate University, Computer File.

———. 2001b. "The White Population of the United States, 1790–1920." In Michael R. Haines and Richard Steckel, eds., *A Population History of North America,* pp. 305–69. New York: Cambridge University Press.

Hymer, Stephen, and Stephen Resnick. 1969. "A Model of an Agrarian Economy with Nonagricultural Activities." *American Economic Review* 59: 493–506.

Jefferson, Thomas. 1787. "Letter to Count de Montmorin [July 23, 1787]." In Julian P. Boyd, Mina R. Bryan, and Frederick Aandahl, eds., *The Papers of Thomas Jefferson,* Vol. 11, pp. 614–18. Princeton, N.J.: Princeton University Press, 1955.

Jónsson, Guómundur, and Magnús S. Magnússon, eds. 1997. *Hagskinna: Sögulegar hagtölur um Ídland* [Icelandic Historical Statistics]. Reykjavik: Hagstofa Ísland, 1997.

Kaestle, Carl F. 1983. *Pillars of the Republic: Common Schools and American Society, 1780–1860.* New York: Hill and Wang.

Kaestle, Carl F., and Maris A. Vinovskis. 1980. *Education and Social Change in Nineteenth-Century Massachusetts.* New York: Cambridge University Press.

Leet, Don R. 1975. "Human Fertility and Agricultural Opportunities in Ohio Counties: From Frontier to Maturity, 1810–60." In David C. Klingaman and Richard K. Vedder, eds., *Essays in Nineteenth Century Economic History: The Old Northwest,* pp. 138–58. Athens: Ohio University Press.

———. 1976. "The Determinants of the Fertility Transition in Antebellum Ohio." *Journal of Economic History* 36: 359–78.

———. 1977. "Interrelations of Population Density, Urbanization, Literacy, and Fertility." *Explorations in Economic History* 14: 388–401.

Lindert, Peter H. 1978. *Fertility and Scarcity in America.* Princeton: Princeton University Press.

McClelland, Peter D., and Richard J. Zeckhauser. 1982. *Demographic Dimensions of the New Republic: American Interregional Migration, Vital Statistics, and Manumissions, 1800–1860.* New York: Cambridge University Press.

McCoy, Drew R. 1980. *The Elusive Republic: Political Economy in Jeffersonian America.* Chapel Hill: University of North Carolina Press.

Morgan, Edmund S. 1944. *The Puritan Family: Religion and Domestic Relations in Seventeenth-Century New England.* Boston: The Public Library.

Morris, Richard B. 1927. "Primogeniture and Entailed Estates in America." *Columbia Law Review* 27: 24–51.

Oberly, James W. 1990. *Sixty Million Acres: American Veterans and the Public Lands before the Civil War.* Kent, Ohio: Kent State University Press.

Ransom, Roger L., and Richard Sutch. 1986a. "Did Rising Out-Migration Cause Fertility to Decline in Antebellum New England? A Life-Cycle Perspective on Old-Age Security Motives, Child Default, and Farm-Family Fertility." California Institute of Technology Social Science Working Papers No. 610 (April 1986). Pasadena: California Institute of Technology.

———. 1986b. "The Labor of Older Americans: Retirement of Men on and off the Job, 1870–1937." *Journal of Economic History* 46: 1–30.

———. 1986c. "The Life-Cycle Transition: A Preliminary Report on Wealth Holding in America." In *Income and Wealth Distribution in Historical Perspective.* Utrecht: University of Utrecht.

————. 1995. "The Impact of Aging on the Employment of Men in Working Class Communities at the End of the Nineteenth Century: A Cross-Section Analysis of Surveys from Maine, New Jersey, California, Michigan, and Kansas." In David I. Kertzer and Peter Laslett, eds., *Aging in the Past: Demography, Society, and Old Age,* pp. 303–27. Berkeley: University of California Press.

————. 2001. "Conflicting Visions: The American Civil War as a Revolutionary Conflict." *Research in Economic History* 20: 249–301.

Ransom, Roger L., Richard Sutch, and Samuel H. Williamson. 1993. "Inventing Pensions: Age Discrimination, and the Search for Old-Age Security in Industrial America, 1900–1940." In K. Warner Schaie and W. Andrew Achenbaum, eds., *Societal Impact on Aging: Historical Perspectives,* pp. 1–44. New York: Springer.

Reed, James. 1978. *From Private Vice to Public Virtue: The Birth Control Movement and American Society since 1830.* New York: Basic Books.

Rohrbough, Malcolm. 1978. *The Trans-Appalachian Frontier: People, Societies, and Institutions, 1775–1850.* New York: Oxford University Press.

Rosenberg, Charles E. 1987. *The Cholera Years: The United States in 1832, 1849, and 1866.* Chicago: University of Chicago Press.

Sanderson, Warren C. 1976. "New Estimates and Interpretations of the Decline in Fertility of White Women in the United States, 1800–1920." Stanford Project on the History of Contraceptive Technology Working Paper (November 1976). Stanford: Stanford University.

————. 1979. "Quantitative Aspects of Marriage, Fertility and Family Limitation in Nineteenth Century America: Another Application of the Coale Specifications." *Demography* 16: 339–58.

Schapiro, Morton Owen. 1982. "Land Availability and Fertility in the United States, 1860–1870." *Journal of Economic History* 42: 577–600.

Sheehan, Bernard W. 1973. *Seeds of Extinction: Jeffersonian Philanthropy and the American Indian.* Chapel Hill: University of North Carolina Press.

Smith, Adam. [1776] 1937. *An Inquiry into the Nature and Causes of the Wealth of Nations.* 2 vols. Reprint, New York: Random House.

Smith, Daniel Scott. 1972. "The Demographic History of Colonial New England." *Journal of Economic History* 32: 165–83.

————. 1973. "Parental Power and Marriage Patterns: An Analysis of Historical Trends in Hingham, Massachusetts." *Journal of Marriage and the Family* 35: 419–28.

———. 1983. "Migration of American Colonial Militiamen, A Comparative Note." *Social Science History* 7: 475–80.

Steckel, Richard H. 1977. *The Economics of U.S. Slave and Southern White Fertility.* Ph.D. dissertation, University of Chicago. Reprint, New York: Garland, 1985.

Stilwell, Lewis D. 1948. *Migration from Vermont.* Montpelier: Vermont Historical Society.

Sundstrom, William A., and Paul A. David. 1986. "Old-Age Security Motives, Labor Markets, and Farm Family Fertility in Antebellum America." Stanford Project on the History of Fertility Control Working Paper, No. 17R (February 1986). Stanford: Stanford University.

———. 1988. "Old-Age Security Motives, Labor Markets, and Farm Family Fertility in Antebellum America." *Explorations in Economic History* 25: 164–97.

Sutch, Richard. 1975. "The Breeding of Slaves for Sale and the Westward Expansion of Slavery, 1850–1860." In Stanley L. Engerman and Eugene Genovese, eds., *Race and Slavery in the Western Hemisphere: Quantitative Studies.* Princeton: Princeton University Press: 173–210.

———. 1986. "Slave Breeding." In Randall M. Miller and John David Smith, eds., *Dictionary of Afro-American Slavery,* updated ed., pp. 82–86. Westport, Conn.: Pager, 1997.

———. 1991. "All Things Reconsidered: The Life Cycle Perspective and the Third Task of Economic History." *Journal of Economic History* 51: 1–18.

Thompson, Warren S., and P. K. Whelpton. [1933] 1969. *Population Trends in the United States.* Reprint, New York: Gordon and Breach.

Thorndale, William, and William Dollarhide. 1987. *Map Guide to the U.S. Federal Censuses, 1790–1920.* Baltimore: Genealogical Publishing.

Tucker, George. [1843] 1964. *Progress of the United States in Population and Wealth in Fifty Years, with an Appendix Containing an Abstract of the Census of 1850.* Press of Hunt's Merchant's Magazine, 1855. Reprint, New York: Augustus M. Kelley.

Vinovskis, Maris A. 1972. "Mortality Rates and Trends in Massachusetts before 1860." *Journal of Economic History* 32: 184–213.

———. 1976. "Socioeconomic Determinants of Interstate Fertility Differentials in the United States in 1850 and 1860." *Journal of Interdisciplinary History* 6: 375–96.

———. 1978. "The Jacobson Life Table of 1850: A Critical Reexamination from a Massachusetts Perspective." *Journal of Interdisciplinary History* 8: 703–24.

————. 1981. *Fertility in Massachusetts from the Revolution to the Civil War.* New York: Academic Press.

Weiss, Thomas. 1992. "U.S. Labor Force Estimates and Economic Growth, 1800–1860." In Robert E. Gallman and John J. Wallis, eds., *American Economic Growth and Standards of Living before the Civil War.* Chicago: University of Chicago Press: 19–78.

Wells, Robert V. 1982. *Revolutions in Americans' Lives: A Demographic Perspective on the History of Americans, Their Families, and Their Society.* New York: Greenwood Press.

Williamson, Jeffrey G. 1985. "Did Rising Emigration Cause Fertility to Decline in 19th Century Rural England? Child Costs, Old Age Pensions, and Child Default." Harvard Institute for Economic Research Discussion Paper (August 1985). Cambridge: Harvard University.

Wright, Gavin. 1978. *The Political Economy of the Cotton South: Households, Markets, and Wealth in the Nineteenth Century.* New York: W. W. Norton.

Yasuba, Yasukichi. 1962. *Birth Rates of the White Population in the United States, 1800–1860: An Economic Study.* Baltimore: The Johns Hopkins University Press.

12 | BUILDING "UNIVERSAL SERVICE" IN THE EARLY BELL SYSTEM: THE COEVOLUTION OF REGIONAL URBAN SYSTEMS AND LONG-DISTANCE TELEPHONE NETWORKS

David F. Weiman

In 1907, at the dawn of an earlier technological epoch, Theodore Vail pronounced AT&T's ambition to build a seamless electronic communications network of continental proportion and, I should add, under Bell control. Vail's ambitious goal, what he termed "universal service," would require vast investments in AT&T's long lines plant and fundamental innovations, especially in transmission technology.[1] Although his vision would not be realized until the 1930s, Vail insisted that the Bell System had "assimilated itself into and in fact become the nervous system" of American business.[2]

Vail's claim could be readily dismissed as mere hype, echoing the pretensions of earlier and later entrepreneurs promoting new electronic communications and information technologies (see, for example, Tarr et al. 1987, p. 54; Gates 1999). Yet it contains an important kernel of truth. In the interim between his reigns over AT&T, Bell managers and engineers had built a more integrated transregional telephone network that followed and reinforced the maturing U.S. urban system.[3] Organized into a hierarchy of hubs and spokes, Bell's long-distance telephone network paralleled the spatial organization of cities within metropolitan regions. Moreover, it bolstered the locational advantage of metropolitan centers by providing them with more efficient and reliable connections to cities in their hinterland as well as to other metropolises.

When viewed from this perspective, Vail—as well as key AT&T managers and engineers—recognized the coevolution of regional telephone networks and urban systems and ultimately their common impulse in the dynamics of wholesale trade.[4] I elaborate this point through an analytical rendition of their strategies and insights during the formative period of the AT&T Company, from 1887 and 1914. The argument unfolds in four parts. The first section reviews the basic technology of early telephone service and Bell's traffic studies, which suggest an affinity between long-distance telephone service and wholesale trade. Sections two and three explain the hierarchical organization of regional long-distance telephone networks by the "natural" flows of long-distance telephone traffic and ultimately increasing returns to long-distance telephone service. I conclude by specifying the spatial-economic, not technical, sources of increasing returns, which correspond to the very conditions fostering metropolitan or regional urban system development.

1. WHOLESALE TRADE AND EARLY LONG-DISTANCE TELEPHONE SERVICE

The parallel between regional urban systems and long-distance telephone networks is not incidental, a mere correlation. By substituting for direct face-to-face contact, the telephone carried the very economic transactions vital to metropolitan intermediaries—open-ended negotiations and nonstandardized information. Moreover, because of the novelty and expense of long-distance telephone service during this formative period, it was used for little else.[5]

In 1887, Edward J. Hall, then general manager of the newly formed AT&T Company, clearly envisioned this potential market for long-distance service. Responding to the very pressing question of why customers would purchase more costly long-distance telephone instead of telegraph service, Hall specified its "separate and distinct" demand or market segment.[6] "When the nature of the business requires personal communication, question and answer, the railroad or the telephone line must be used, and this is our field: quick communication with instantaneous replies and prolonged personal interviews." In other words, he observed, "If the long-distance telephone competes with anything, it is with the railroad," not the telegraph. Once "people learn its uses," he predicted, long-distance telephone service will become "the most important factor in the transaction of business between distant points."

As a corollary, Hall envisioned regional long-distance networks in terms of a hierarchy of hub-and-spoke systems, each anchored by a commercial center and bound by the city's trade area. Writing to the president of AT&T's parent company, American Bell Telephone, in 1888, he recommended the construction of two regional networks, centered on New York and Chicago. "Included within each of these two great circles," he elaborated, "would be a host of smaller ones centering at the various large cities from which the business of a state or section radiates." In his plan, regional and local toll centers would mediate calls within and between their territory and so constitute a more seamless network—that is, "universal service."

Universal service would enable telephone customers, regardless of their location, to communicate directly by efficiently channeling their calls through interlocking complementary networks. At the local level, a city or district of a large metropolitan center, the exchange network connected the telephones of residential and business customers to a central office, which housed the switching equipment. Toll and long-distance trunk lines, in turn, linked central offices within and between the territories of telephone operating companies and thereby formed larger geographic networks. Local toll networks embraced economically and geographically proximate centers, and in turn were joined by toll and long-distance trunk lines, typically between the largest centers, to form regional and transregional (for example, national) networks.

The distinct domains of local exchange and toll and long-distance service suggest an obvious parallel to the differences between retail and wholesale trade. Paralleling their trips to the grocer or drug store, households tended to restrict their telephone calling to the immediate vicinity, often only to the neighborhood level. As historical studies of its use have clearly demonstrated, the telephone did not directly expand households' geographic horizons, but instead merely cemented their local ties.[7] Moreover, exchange service satisfied the spontaneous demand for local interactions by completing these connections almost instantaneously—that is, in less than a minute or while the caller remained on the line.[8] Subscribers gained prompt access because their telephones were directly wired or looped into the central office switchboard, and in most cases the same operator could complete the entire transaction.[9]

Like wholesaling, toll and long-distance service mediated transactions over greater distances, within and between operating company territories respectively. These far-flung interactions were more complex, often following indirect routes, and so demanded additional steps and time. Even under the best of circumstances, operators could require almost ten minutes to make the desired connection.[10] Consequently, when customers contacted a toll operator, they in effect issued an order to be fulfilled at a later, specified time and so simply reserved a time slot on toll trunk lines. In turn, by accumulating these demands, toll centers coordinated the flow of traffic to and from, as well as within, their territory.

Toll service required greater mediation because of the hierarchical design and operation of the network. Unlike in an urban exchange, subscribers acquired access to the toll network indirectly through a limited number of trunk lines connecting exchange and toll switchboards.[11] To complete a toll transaction, the exchange operator funneled the call to a toll operator, who recorded the desired connection and directed the call along the appropriate route to its final destination. The speed of service depended on the number of intermediate switches necessary to reach the end point and the available trunk line circuits at each step along the way. Excess demand for toll circuits at any juncture caused the formation of queues and delays. Thus the efficient organization of the toll network operated according to the principles of pooling bulk transactions analogous to those in wholesale trade.

Despite the potential geographic scope of telephone connections, the vast majority of traffic before 1930 was local, restricted to the domain of the local exchange. Between 1890 and 1920 toll and long-distance calls accounted for 2 to 3 percent of all telephone calls in the United States (see Figure 12.1). Their share barely exceeded 4 percent by 1929 despite the rapid growth of long-distance service in the 1920s. Nonetheless, the utilization of the toll network served as a keen barometer of aggregate economic activity. The volume of toll calls tracked the seasonal flows of trade and credit and the peaks and troughs of the business cycle (as evidenced by the sharp relative decline in toll calling during the Great Depressions of the 1890s and 1930s).[12]

Correlation in this case corresponds to causation because of the selective demand for toll and long-distance telephone service. Local exchange service

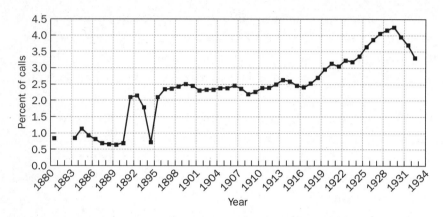

Figure 12.1 Share of toll and long-distance messages, 1880–1932

mediated both business and personal interactions and so issued mixed signals. By contrast, toll and long-distance services were an "economic instrument," carrying almost exclusively transactions within and between business enterprises (Richter 1925). Even toll and long-distance calls made from residences or vacation resorts, while ostensibly personal, were often for business purposes, as managers used the convenience of the telephone to keep tabs on their distant operations.

Business demand for toll connections can be ascertained quantitatively from traffic studies of Bell operating companies, which indicate the frequency of toll calls by type of customer—residential versus business—and even by "class" of business. An early report from the Bell exchange in Buffalo provides such a detailed breakdown of outward toll traffic in 1891. Residential customers, including doctors, accounted for almost a quarter of exchange subscribers and approximately 10 percent of local calls. Yet only 17 percent of these households called beyond the local level and made on average only two toll calls per month (see Table 12.1).

Businesses, by contrast, utilized telephone service more intensively, including the toll and long-distance networks. Over half of all business customers placed at least one nonlocal call a month, although most firms did not call frequently. The largest users of toll and long-distance services were firms

Table 12.1
Telephone traffic by business class: Buffalo, N.Y., 1891

| Business Class | Stations | Local Calls | Calls/ Station | Toll and Long Distance | | | |
				Stations	% Toll	Calls	Calls/ Station
Business	1,412	203,490	144.1	737	52.2	2,694	3.66
Wholesale	405	93,068	229.8	237	58.5	1,349	5.69
Other	1,007	110,422	109.7	500	49.7	1,345	2.69
Residential	433	20,076	46.4	73	16.9	153	2.10
Professionals	144	5,966	41.4	20	13.9	34	1.70
Other	289	14,110	48.8	53	18.3	119	2.25
Public Stations	5	351	70.2	5	100.0	246	49.20
Total	1,850	223,917	121.0	815	44.1	3,093	3.80

SOURCE: AT&T Archives Book Collection, Telephone Switchboard Conference, March 15–18, 1892.
Notes: A station is a telephone unit. % Toll equals the percentage of exchange subscribers making toll calls. Public stations are telephones located in public places, such as stores.

that figured significantly in the nexus of wholesale trade: hotels, telegraph companies, commission merchants, specialized wholesalers, banks, and shippers (see Table 12.1). Firms in retail trade (such as carting, stationery supplies, and dry goods) made fewer toll calls because they conducted transactions on a more local (exchange) level.[13]

The pattern of use in Table 12.2, based on a smaller exchange in upstate New York, shows an even sharper disparity in business and residential demand for local and toll services. Households accounted for 44 percent of all exchange customers, but only a third used toll service during the month. Of those who did, only 5 percent placed more than five toll calls.

Businesses obviously constituted the principal source of demand for toll service. Almost two-thirds of business subscribers used the toll network, and their calls represented nearly 90 percent of the toll traffic originating from subscriber telephones (see Table 12.2). Although these data do not identify the actual source of toll traffic, they do show the avid demand for long-distance connections by a small segment of the business community. Half of all business users made fewer than ten calls per month. At the opposite end of the spectrum, the largest 5 percent made at least twenty toll calls per month and

Table 12.2
Toll calls in an upstate New York exchange, July 1900

A. Toll Calls by Type of Customer

| | Subscribers | Toll Users | Toll Calls | | Toll Calls per: | |
			All	Subscribers	Subscriber	Toll User
Business	275	176	1,165	1,165	4.24	6.62
% of total	56.1	70.4	72.5	88.3		
Residential	215	74	155	155	0.72	2.09
% of total	43.9	29.6	9.6	11.7		
Public Stations	2		288			
% of total			17.9			
Total	490	250	1,608	1,320		

B. Size Distribution of Toll Calls

| | Business | | Residential | |
Number of Calls	% Subscribers	% Calls	% Subscribers	% Calls
0	36.0	0.0	65.6	0.0
1–5	42.9	21.5	32.6	73.5
6–10	11.3	20.6	0.9	11.6
11–20	5.1	17.5	0.9	14.8
20+	4.7	40.3		

SOURCE: AT&T Archives, Box 1330, AT&T Co., Toll Line Service, 1901, Doolittle–Cochrane 1/16/1901.

accounted for 40 percent of toll calls by businesses and over a third of all toll calls in the district.

Finally, Table 12.3 lists the largest users of toll and long-distance services in New York City in the mid-1920s and so further specifies some of the principal sources of business demand. With a few exceptions, two types of enterprises predominate. The first are hotels. Without discounting their tourist trade, hotels, then as today, furnished business executives and sales agents with lodging and vital services during their routine trips to the nation's economic center. The second set of establishments included the corporate offices, often headquarter facilities, of national and multinational firms. In both cases, toll connections were essential to conduct wholesale trade, whether to reach retail customers in the trade area or to keep close contact with distant

Table 12.3
Largest users of long-distance service, New York City, 1926

Name	Business Class	Messages per Business Day
Pennsylvania Hotel	Hotel	197
Commodore Hotel	Hotel	156
Biltmore Hotel	Hotel	93
McAlpin Hotel	Hotel	89
Waldorf-Astoria Hotel	Hotel	87
Astor Hotel	Hotel	69
Roosevelt Hotel	Hotel	62
Vanderbilt Hotel	Hotel	49
Belmont Hotel	Hotel	45
Chelsea Bro. and Robbins Inc.	Fish	35
Coleman and Reitze	Bankers	30
Shelton Hotel	Hotel	29
Prince George Hotel	Hotel	27
McAlpin Annex Hotel	Hotel	26
Imperial Hotel	Hotel	23
Ford Motor Co. of Delaware	Automobile	23
Standard Oil Co. of New York	Oil	22
United States Rubber	Rubber	22
First National Corp. of Boston	Bankers	18
Times Square Hotel	Hotel	18
General Electric	Electric	18
Woodstock Hotel	Hotel	18
Ambassador Hotel	Hotel	17
Barrett Company	Roofing materials	17
Alamac Hotel	Hotel	17
Breslin Hotel	Hotel	16
Bethlehem Steel Co.	Steel	16
Yale Club of New York	Club	15
Debevoise Anderson Co., Inc.	Iron	15
W. J. Rainey, Inc.	Coal	15
Langham Hotel	Hotel	15

SOURCE: AT&T Co., *Proceedings of the Bell System Educational Conference, June 21–25, 1926* (New York: AT&T Co., 1926), p. 60.

production facilities and distribution centers. Notably missing on the list are intermediaries in New York's financial and wholesale trade districts. As Bell's head of marketing noted, his tabulation would most likely exclude these firms, because their intensive demand for long-distance connections justified the leasing of toll lines directly from AT&T.[14]

2. THE BELL STANDARD: THE DESIGN AND OPERATION OF REGIONAL TOLL NETWORKS

Under Vail's predecessor, Frederick P. Fish, AT&T's Engineering Department launched a thorough reorganization of Bell's operating divisions and long-distance networks. In 1904 it circulated a manual on the proper design and operation of regional toll networks.[15] Prepared by Thomas Doolittle, head of the Toll Traffic Studies Division, these guidelines would forge a hierarchical regional network, differentiating centers according to their network accessibility and functions. The hierarchical organization, Doolittle insisted, would ensure efficient, uninterrupted toll service because it would "follow the natural trend of the business within its territory." In other words, when designed and operated according to Bell standards, the hierarchy of centers would reflect the patterns of wholesaling and so the regional urban system.

In the geography of networks, accessibility (or nodality) conveys the sense of "being close," a general proximity to any other center, not just one or two. Proximity, of course, is a deceptively simple term. In explaining the efficient routing of traffic, Doolittle initially stressed the "shortest and best route" and so used "circuit mileage" as the sole criterion. In explicating this rule, however, he subtly shifted tone and replaced physical distance with a metric rooted in the very structure of the network. An efficient path, he continued, required the "least number of [intermediate] switches," and in the case of a tie, the "best route" was furnished "with the greater number of circuits."

Proximity in the second sense means connectivity, the "complications and cost" of linking two points in the network, and depends on the number of direct pathways or circuits joining them.[16] By avoiding relays at intermediate points, direct lines with multiple circuits minimized the time required to complete connections, the likelihood of errors, and the risk of congestion delays along the way. Also, fewer switches diminished the attenuation and distortion of the voice signal and so enhanced the clarity of the message.[17] In addition, direct lines to multiple locations afforded efficient secondary routes in case of congestion or service interruptions on primary ones.

Thus a nodal center would ensure immediate connections to any destination in the network because it provided more direct circuits to a wider range of points, especially other pivotal nodes. Doolittle's case study—a small regional

network redesigned according to Bell standards—neatly illustrates this principle. Of the twenty-four exchanges (labeled A through X), A and D were more
nodal centers than I and J, even though the latter were more centrally located.
A simple measure of their accessibility is the average number of switches or
routes connecting each center to any other point in the territory (see column 2
in Table 12.4, panel A). Following the primary or most efficient routes as desig-
nated by Doolittle, traffic to or from centers A and D required on average less

Table 12.4
Traffic patterns in a regional toll network

A. Patterns of Calls by Center

| Center | No. of Calls | Average No. of Switches | Alternative Routes | | Concentration of Call (%) |
			2d(%)	3d(%)	
A	7,947	0.83	87.0	56.5	57.5
D	5,536	0.70	87.0	39.1	60.4
I	1,920	1.43	87.0	26.1	73.5
J	3,306	1.04	100.0	78.3	72.9

B. Patterns of Calls by Type of Route

Center	Type of Route	%	Average No. of Calls	% of Calls
A	Direct	34.8	850.8	85.6
	One	47.8	83.5	11.6
	Two+	17.4	55.5	2.8
D	Direct	39.1	555.6	90.3
	One	52.2	42.5	9.2
	Two+	8.7	13.0	0.5
J	Direct	21.7	524.6	79.3
	One	52.2	53.8	19.5
	Two+	26.1	6.3	1.1
I	Direct	17.4	335.5	69.9
	One	26.1	85.2	26.6
	Two+	56.5	5.2	3.5

SOURCE: AT&T Archives, Box 1057, T. B. Doolittle, Toll Lines, 1904.
Notes: Number of calls is the volume of monthly traffic. Average switches is the average number of relays required to
reach any destination in the network. Alternative routes is the percentage of destinations furnished with a secondary
(2d) and tertiary (3d) route. Concentration of calls is the share of traffic on the largest four routes. Type of route
indicates the number of switches: direct or none, one intermediate switch, and at least two switches.

than one intermediate switch (0.83 and 0.70 respectively). By contrast, routes connecting J and I to other points in the network were more roundabout, averaging 1.04 and 1.43 intermediate switches.

This index abstracts from the quality of toll connections in relation to the spatial patterns of traffic and so understates the greater accessibility of exchanges A and D (see Table 12.4, panel B). Exchanges A and D were furnished with direct circuits to almost twice as many destinations in the network as exchanges J and I (35 and 40 percent of all centers versus 22 and 17 percent), and the bulk of their traffic (between 86 and 90 percent of total calls) flowed along these uninterrupted routes.[18] Moreover, these exchanges were furnished with multiple circuits along the most heavily traveled lines, which greatly enhanced transmission capacity and hence the reliability and speed of service. Finally, with one exception, the more nodal centers afforded a greater range of auxiliary routes (see columns 3 and 4 in Table 12.4, panel A).[19] The anomaly, exchange J, illustrates a potential benefit of its central location at the crossroads of routes connecting other centers.

The design and organization of the network also illustrates the dual relationship between accessibility and functionality. Dominant exchanges like A and D housed toll operators, who were responsible for routing calls through the network and financial accounting. Conversely, more marginal centers reached other network points indirectly through dominant centers and so were rendered tributary to them. Thus the accessibility of centers defined their spatial range, the scope of network traffic they mediated, or equivalently the number and location of places in their hinterland.

Network design such as routing instructions imposed a similar hierarchy among toll centers. Following Doolittle's "simple" rule, they specified the most efficient paths between all points in the network and tended to channel traffic through more nodal toll centers. Elaborating Doolittle's guidelines, for example, the toll center plan of New England Telephone consolidated control and coordination functions in the company's seventy-nine largest toll centers, as compared to its early plan of delegating one center to each of its 730 exchanges.[20]

Following his most fundamental tenet, Doolittle organized the network in accordance with the "trend of traffic." The implied relationship between accessibility, functionality, and traffic patterns reflects the influence of in-creasing returns that imposed demand thresholds on the construction of toll facilities. For a toll exchange, the volume of traffic was expected to cover fixed and quasi-fixed costs, including depreciation and maintenance of the plant and employment of full-time operators and supervisory personnel. If mar-kets were too small to support an exchange, they could be furnished with toll stations, wired into an adjacent exchange by lower-quality circuits. Acquiring even this limited access depended on whether projected revenues exceeded break-even levels, determined by the overhead costs of the physical plant.

Doolittle did admit one exception. "It is sometimes advisable," he coun-seled, "to build lines that do not promise an immediate return, in order to round out a system."[21] Although he did not elaborate this criterion, it suggests extending the network to nearby towns, regardless of the expected volume or trend of traffic. At the very least, the incremental cost of building these lines would be small because of the short distances involved. Yet, as shown in the concluding section, he implicitly offered an alternative interpretation, consis-tent with his principle relating network design to the spatial-economic pat-terns of toll traffic.

In examples taken from the case study, Doolittle decided to add (or remove) a direct circuit between two centers based on the total flow of traffic between them, equal to their "own" traffic—calls between parties in each district—and relay traffic destined for other points. The inclusion of the latter element implies that the nodality of a center could simply derive from its designation as a switching point for traffic to and from other places. In other words, accessibility would depend on Doolittle's instructions for routing traf-fic, not vice versa.

A closer inspection of his method for designing the network resolves the dilemma. Instead of circular reasoning, his procedures imply a self-reinforcing mechanism that gives priority to a center's own traffic—its inward and out-ward calls. In every instance, this component accounted for the majority of its traffic and therefore made the largest contribution to achieving the necessary demand thresholds. Moreover, Doolittle determined the routing instructions and thus the volume of relay traffic sequentially. He initially furnished centers with a sufficient number of direct circuits to handle their own traffic, and then ascertained the most efficient paths for relaying calls through the network. Consequently, the flow of relay traffic favored routes through more dominant centers, based on the scale and scope of their own traffic, and so augmented, not offset, the flows of their own traffic.

Thus, Doolittle's analysis specified, at least implicitly, the "trend of traffic" by the matrix of inward and outward calls for each center and so yields an alternative criterion for determining the hierarchy of centers. For example, the dominant position of centers A and D ultimately derived from the larger volume and greater diversity of their inward and outward traffic (see the first and last columns in Table 12.4, panel A). These centers supported 200 to 300 calls daily, and the four largest routes accounted for only 60 percent of the total flow. By contrast, the more marginal position of exchanges I and J accorded with their narrower niches in the network. Both exchanges supported a significantly lower volume of traffic, only 74 and 127 calls daily. Equally important, the bulk of their traffic was confined to neighboring centers.

This simple case vividly illustrates Jacob Price's thesis, explaining the formation of entrepots or metropolises by the "complexity of trade."[22] In fact, his notion corresponds precisely to the source of accessibility in toll networks, for, as shown in the previous section, the size and scope of a center's own traffic stemmed from and so mirrored the wholesale trade of its district. Just as in the Chesapeake colonies, the sheer volume of toll calls was not a sufficient condition to elevate centers to nodal points, controlling and coordinating traffic through the network. A large number of calls, restricted to only one or two routes, relegated centers to a tributary position, because their simple, bilateral transactions could be conducted at distance. A pivotal node or higher-order center, just as the term connotes, required more generalized contacts; its interactions, in other words, could not be so readily confined.

3. INCREASING RETURNS IN TOLL NETWORKS

The hierarchical organization of regional telephone networks, as suggested above, ultimately depended on the sources of increasing returns, which created and reinforced the initial advantage of larger, more dominant centers. Hall, for one, clearly perceived these systemic processes and their influence.

"Developing fully a good system of terminal and branch feeding lines," he observed, ". . . will not only pay in themselves but will add to the business of the main trunk lines, and every gain in business requiring additional trunk wires means a large gain in profit."[23] Increasing returns, he implies, derived from economies of scale and interdependent demands. Scale-dependent processes yielded greater efficiencies (the "gain[s] in profit") from concentrating traffic through larger toll centers and the trunk lines connecting them. At the same, extending the network to encompass interdependent users, those bound by a strong "community of interest," enlarged the demand for toll services, especially the utilization of trunk lines.[24] A properly designed network would tap these complementary demands and generate substantial externalities, the unintended or synergistic benefits from their mutual interaction.

Although Bell engineers had regarded these forces mechanistically—that is, as inherent properties of the technology—key officials eventually comprehended the necessary market conditions to realize fully the telephone's economic potential. Harnessing these market forces influenced the design of all facets of the network—plant technology, operating methods, and spatial structure. Thus, when properly conceived, the processes underlying the development of the toll network are more aptly termed "eco-technic" and exemplify the opposing but mutually reinforcing tendencies of centralization and dispersion that propel the development of metropolitan regions.[25]

Economies of Scale

Building toll lines required large, indivisible investments in transmission capacity. Telephone companies could economize on these outlays in numerous ways by reducing the number of circuits on a line and increasing the spacing between poles.[26] Still, even the most rudimentary connections imposed truly fixed costs on operating budgets, such as leasing and maintaining rights of way. In turn, the growing volume of traffic increased capacity utilization and lowered unit costs.

On more heavily traveled routes, additional investments in transmission capacity, including the adoption of new technologies, yielded even greater economies and improvements in service quality.[27] Stringing more miles of wire on existing pole lines, for example, spread fixed costs over a larger number of circuits and so reduced the unit overhead charges on each. Moreover, through practice and theoretical analysis, AT&T engineers discovered that larger circuit groups—trunk lines furnished with multiple circuits—yielded genuine economies of scale. Doolittle's 1904 bulletin indicated the actual magnitude of these efficiency gains.[28] Under "ordinary conditions," a line equipped with a single circuit could carry an average load of 30 calls per day. The same line, furnished with five circuits, could transmit 200 to 225 calls daily or an average of 40 to 45 calls per circuit. In other words, enlarging the circuit group by a factor of five enhanced the effective capacity or load of each circuit by 33 to 50 percent.

Around the same time, Bell engineers embarked on a program of theoretical research, which explained the source of and limits to these efficiencies. The reasoning is essentially probabilistic, an instance of the law of large numbers. Under "normal" conditions, pooling diverse sources of traffic at a single large center and along larger circuit groups would smooth out random variations in the timing and duration of individual calls.[29] Consequently, plant managers could predict more accurately average loads over time (such as a day, week, or a year) and plan network capacity accordingly. In turn, because demands would exceed plant capacity on an incidental or irregular basis, individual circuits could carry, on average, higher daily loads without increasing the risk of congestion and so reducing service quality.[30]

Concentrating traffic through larger toll centers also initiated a Smithian dynamic of technological and organizational change. Denser, more differentiated traffic patterns warranted the construction of switching and transmission facilities tapered to distinct market segments. In turn, Bell engineers refined operating methods that exploited more fully the economic potential of these specialized facilities. Despite the greater outlays of fixed capital and employment of overhead personnel, these innovations magnified the productivity of switchboard operators and the rate of "throughput" of the toll plant by standardizing and speeding up manual operations.[31] The centralization of more specialized equipment and personnel also enabled Bell companies to offer new services, extending the economic scope of its fixed plant and overhead staff.

An important instance was the evolution of toll operating methods within metropolitan regions. The greater volume of intraregional traffic justified the construction of direct circuits, which greatly enhanced the speed of service and circuit loads. In turn, on denser routes furnished with multiple circuits, Bell engineers exploited the greater transmission capacity to improve operating methods. An 1898 memorandum from Doolittle to American Bell President Hudson described such innovations, the "recording" and "call wire" systems developed by Joseph Carty of New York Telephone.[32] In the former, specialized toll operators divided the tasks of recording information on and overseeing the desired connection. "Recording" operators relieved local operators of clerical tasks and ensured a more thorough accounting of outgoing toll calls. "Line" operators, responsible for a limited number of trunk lines and destinations, completed connections more quickly and monitored them more carefully.

Bell engineers further refined these procedures for traffic ranging from 50 to 100 kilometers.[33] Its "two-number" system approximated the switching methods used in urban exchanges. Toll calls were routed through a separate "two-number" operator, who could complete connections to any destination in the territory. As a result, connections were made instantaneously—that is, while customers remained on the line.

This method depended on the publication of a regional telephone directory, which enabled customers to request connections without the assistance of information operators and greatly simplified the task of receiving operators.[34] The larger, more regular flow of intraregional traffic justified the investment in compiling a directory of frequently called numbers. On the flip side, the greater density of the metropolitan market offered firms an inducement to purchase a listing and so to advertise in the telephone company's classified directory.

In a similar fashion, the "single-ticket" method rationalized the routing of long-haul traffic between metropolitan centers. Operators at the point of origin assumed full control over recording and routing toll connections— preparing tickets for billing customers and issuing routing instructions to operators at intermediate and destination points. The greater centralization of control substantially reduced the time and cost required to make long-distance connections, as well as potential operator error. More rapid, reliable service translated into higher levels of capacity utilization as operators required less time for signaling.

Like other innovations, this method was initially adopted on more densely trafficked routes between large metropolitan centers such as New York and Chicago. Equipped with high-gauge wires and loading coils, these lines afforded clearer voice transmission over longer distances. Also, because of their tighter integration, the respective Bell operating companies had adopted uniform technological and operational standards, which allowed effective communication among operators.

Interdependent Demands and Network Externalities

Alongside the technological and organizational processes fostering centralization, Bell officials and engineers also recognized an opposing tendency to extend the network geographically. Characteristic of other communications and transport networks, this centrifugal force derived from the interdependent demands for telephone service. As Doolittle repeatedly claimed, a vaster network, connecting more people over a wider area, would increase the potential use of the telephone and hence its value to customers. Despite this initial abstract formulation, Doolittle would elaborate Hall's original insight and conceive this principle in terms of the complementary demands for toll service within urban regions.

Interdependent demands, Doolittle explained, depended on the geographic range of economic and social relationships. Within urban centers, the highly localized nature of social interactions tended to restrict the systemic benefits of widening telephone networks. Residential customers called frequently within their immediate vicinity, but except for occasional transactions requiring connections to business districts, they rarely contacted subscribers in other neighborhoods. By way of explanation, Doolittle offered a quaint analogy to the impact of urban annexations: "The individual use of the telephone is quite similar to the individual use of the streets; each [person] has his particular route and rarely deviates from it and would not if the city were many times greater."[35] Thus, enlarging exchange networks to incorporate new districts would add subscribers, but not notably increase the demand for service by existing ones.

The toll network, by contrast, mediated more far-flung relationships and therefore was governed by an opposing principle. After a decade's experience,

Doolittle wrote to Joseph Davis, head of the Engineering Department: "Our records show that the larger the number of places connected, the larger will be the percentage of people interested in the toll lines."[36] He illustrated these interdependent demands through a schematic model, showing the mutual interaction between the short- and long-haul traffic of commercial centers. In the model the construction of toll lines to hinterland cities literally multiplies the volume of traffic between metropolitan centers and thereby yields scale economies on long-haul trunk lines.

Doolittle intended the simple model to promote local network development by Bell operating companies. Ignoring the systemic benefits from a more extensive network, they often devoted too few resources to building complementary toll lines in their territory. Even if tributary lines were not profitable when reckoned on a stand-alone basis, the model showed, they would induce greater utilization of the entire network, especially trunk lines, and so enhance aggregate earnings. In effect, he advocated subsidizing the construction of tributary connections to smaller centers with the greater earnings on trunk lines between larger cities.[37]

Moreover, as his model implies, these internal transfers of funds are not truly subsidies. Rather, they reflect the spatial separation between the source and realization of the network externalities: the investments in tributary connections on the one hand and the greater profits on more heavily utilized trunk lines on the other. In the absence of a rate structure based on value of service, accounting for and thus realizing these systemic benefits would demand a more extensive, vertically integrated network. In turn, this vital relationship specified the integral components of areal networks and so delineated their spatial boundaries systemically—that is, in terms of the geographic scope of these reciprocal demands.[38]

An ambitious program of network development, proposed by New England Telephone, exemplifies Doolittle's model and concretely demonstrates the potential benefits from expanded toll connections.[39] The company would furnish smaller cities and towns with rudimentary exchanges, offering limited local service. These centers, it was acknowledged, would generate few outgoing calls, the basis upon which Bell companies charged customers and so reckoned the revenues and net earnings of toll lines. They would, however, attract a substantial volume of incoming traffic from larger commercial centers and thereby increase the overall utilization of the network and aggregate revenues. To determine prospective sites, then, Doolittle projected their contribution to toll revenues in both directions.

AT&T's Key Town Sales Plan also illustrates the interdependent demands of business users for toll services.[40] The plan integrated the telephone into the annual routine of sales agents. At the principal center of each territory, sales agents reached customers in tributary towns more easily and inexpensively through the toll network. Relying on telephone contact for routine transactions such as collecting orders, they reserved occasional, longer business trips for more complex deals, negotiating price schedules or the introduction of new products. Using this method, sales agents "covered larger territories and did more business," but their "costs in relation to sales were extremely low" (Whitcomb 1929, p. 52; Richter 1925, p. 293).

To assist sales agents, AT&T and its operating companies prepared maps of trade territories and their key towns or "calling points" that followed the contours of the regional urban system. In addition, Bell designed programs that facilitated these transactions. To reduce delays in securing connections and to routinize their planning, sales agents could submit, in advance, sequenced lists of periodically called numbers. Before embarking on their trip, agents would reserve space at toll centers by notifying the chief operator when they would arrive. Bell also offered a credit plan that billed toll charges to the sales office. Finally, its classified business directories furnished sales agents with vital information on potential customers and new market areas.

Bell also promoted toll service to rural merchants, who occupied the lowest rung in the mercantile hierarchy. In response to competition from mail-order catalogues, Bell managers combined the toll network and the postal delivery system to furnish the equivalent of fast freight service to farm households.[41] Through telephone calls, rural merchants could maintain more regular contact with their customers, and use "carriers on [rural] routes to act as expressmen . . . [to] guarantee quick delivery."

In the other direction, toll service expedited transactions between rural merchants and their wholesale suppliers. By ordering over the telephone, rural merchants could restock their shelves in response to consumers' demands and so economize on their inventory holdings. This system of "hand-to-mouth" purchasing availed retailers of the larger, more diverse stores of wholesalers, while it enabled the latter to exploit economies of bulk purchasing and distribution.

4. MARKET SOURCES OF INCREASING RETURNS

Like the systemic processes of urban systems development, increasing returns in the telephone network were the product of economies of coordination and specialization. The former correspond to the benefits from pooling traffic at nodal centers in the network, and the latter to the agglomeration effects of vertical disintegration and new market development. Specifying these market processes reinforces and elaborates the conclusion of section two. The nodality and hierarchy of centers depended on the "*quality* of economic activity" in their trade area and resulting greater "complexity of trade," and not simply on the volume of exports of a single staple product (Price 1974, pp. 129, 142).

Through experience, traffic engineers not only detected scale economies on denser trunk lines, but also specified conditions necessary to realize them. In particular, they found that average costs, or conversely, normal circuit capacity depended critically on seasonal fluctuations in demands or loads. As Frank Fowle, a regular contributor to *Telephony*, observed, for a given grade of service (for example, speed in completing connections and risk of congestion delays), capacity utilization varied inversely with the load factor—the ratio of daily average-to-peak demands.[42] Other things being equal, "an uneven load curve with prominent peaks and large, abrupt changes in demand" would either reduce the average speed of service or the unit capacity of circuits.

The assumptions underlying the theoretical analysis of traffic flows, referred to above, offered a sharper formulation of these conditions. Larger circuit groups yielded the predicted economies, when the probability of congestion delays was small and when demands during the relevant interval were uncorrelated with each other and so could be regarded as essentially "random" events.[43] The latter is best illustrated by the opposite case of perfectly synchronized calling patterns. If the same event triggered large numbers of users to place toll calls simultaneously, then centers would be flooded with demand,

and congestion delays would mount. Such extreme events are uncommon, occurring usually during a holiday or in the aftermath of a disaster.

Yet under less extraordinary circumstances, calls could still exhibit high degrees of correlation over time because of the seasonality of economic activity. For example, in a specialized agricultural region, the daily volume of traffic multiplied during the harvest season, as farmers and intermediaries used toll lines to negotiate the sale and movement of crops. The resulting peak loads during busy periods of the day (typically mid-morning and early afternoon) severely strained the operation of toll centers.[44] To minimize congestion delays at these busy times, centers would mostly likely be burdened with excessive capacity during the rest of the year and charge higher rates. Alternatively, furnished with fewer circuits, they would experience large excess demand at peak periods, which violated both conditions. Similar strains would arise in regions dominated by a few very large users, such as a company town, where demand patterns reflected a single firm's specific production schedules or the seasonality of its purchases and sales.[45]

Realizing the benefits of pooling traffic, therefore, depended on the very structure of demand for toll service and hence of the regional economy. Demands approximated the theoretical ideal in more densely developed regions embracing specialized, interdependent economic sectors. Under these spatial economic conditions, no single industry or firm would thoroughly dominate the use of toll lines and so impose its seasonal demands on aggregate levels. Moreover, the presence of many and varied sources of demand, each following distinctive but complementary seasonal patterns, would ensure a smoother distribution of calls over time.[46]

Obviously, no area completely avoided seasonal influences; however, the resulting overflow traffic was less disruptive where centers were furnished with numerous, efficient alternate routes. The availability of such secondary paths, as noted earlier, depended on both the scale and geographic scope of a center's own traffic, the diverse sources and destinations of its inward and outward calls. Like the initial one, this condition too was only satisfied in more developed diversified regional economies and derived ultimately from its more varied economic base.

In other words, the realization of these interdependent demands, and hence of increasing returns, depended on the extent of metropolitan or urban systems development. The planned extension of the network by New England Telephone clearly hinged on the dense volume of trade between metropolitan and hinterland centers in its territory. Unlike in Doolittle's schematic model, however, the company expected trade to flow from *large to small centers* along feeder lines, and not vice versa. This trend suggests that users in the former, not the latter, valued more highly the greater range of toll connections and, in turn, more strongly advocated the extension of the network.

A later report by AT&T engineers stressed this very point. "Unless . . . complete facilities [are] provided in towns of all kinds and characteristics, the value of telephone service in places of *higher commercial activity* will be materially lessened because of the absence of exchanges in towns of smaller activity."[47] Significantly, the predicted asymmetric flow of traffic from centers of "higher" to "lower" commercial activity correspond to the spatial range of their mercantile functions and hierarchical order in the urban system.[48]

Doolittle's very analysis of interdependent demands depended on these spatial-economic relationships, even though his own formulations often obscured the connection. In his analogy to pedestrian traffic, for example, he incorrectly attributed interdependent demands to a particular geographic network. In fact, it only showed how the use of the telephone by residential subscribers paralleled the highly circumscribed fields of personal economic and social interactions. By contrast, business customers, especially intermediaries in larger commercial centers, demanded the most extensive range of telephone connections both within and beyond city limits. In local markets with dual service these core users typically subscribed to the competing telephone companies to gain access to all points. In addition, to obtain toll connections to nearby cities and towns, they willingly accepted hefty rate increases for extended Bell service, and if necessary even committed resources to establish their own independent telephone companies.[49]

In other words, interdependent demands characterized both exchange and toll networks, but were more visible in the latter, whose use was dominated by core business customers. Through the telephone, wholesale merchants and other intermediaries could maintain closer contact with clients in their trade area. Substituting more frequent telephone calls for costly, time-consuming business trips, they could offer more prompt and responsive service. Also, by lowering transactions costs and amplifying the channels along which information flowed, telephone service potentially deepened and widened trade areas and so enabled merchants in one center to encroach on the markets of another. Consequently, the telephone became a potent weapon in recurrent rivalries between urban centers.[50]

Similarly, Doolittle often insisted on a simple, almost linear relationship between city size and effective demand for toll service, despite his own evidence, which showed a weak empirical regularity at best.[51] In a different context, Bell engineers vehemently denied this correlation and instead focused on the "the class and general prosperity of the population" and "business conditions" as more fundamental determinants of demand.[52] Like urban geographers, it seems, Doolittle used population as a shorthand to gauge the economic functions of a center and in turn its potential economic interactions with other centers. Significantly, in his comprehensive reviews of territorial networks, he consulted "Dun's Reference Book," and not simply the census of population, to identify "the most promising places" to extend the network.[53] From this source, he gleaned information on their economic structure: the number, size, and type of banks; "rated" manufacturing and mercantile establishments; and the size distribution of firms by net worth.

These data identified the likely sources of demand for toll service in each city, as well as the likely recipients of toll calls from other centers. Unlike population aggregates, they measured more accurately a center's total contribution to the growth of the regional toll market. From this perspective, Doolittle's criterion of building lines "to round out a system" takes on a rather different meaning. It implies completing the nexus of economic relationships within urban regions, and not simply the physical connections between proximate centers. Like Hall, he recognized that expanding linkages between metropolitan centers and the cities and towns in their hinterland would enhance traffic flows through the entire network, not only on adjacent lines, and so generate substantial externalities.[54]

To reinforce the point, Bell's marketing strategies for long-distance service depended on complementary transport networks and business services, not just on efficient toll facilities. Key towns, for example, were chosen because of their "railroad facilities, hotel accommodations, etc." (Whitcomb 1929, pp. 52–53). Their location at nodal points in the rail network facilitated scheduling trips and, if necessary, arranging the shipment and storage of orders. Similarly, hotels offered business travelers lodging and even auxiliary telephone services. Likewise, the anticipated efficiencies in rural merchandising and hence the value of toll connections to rural merchants and their suppliers critically depended on frequent, reliable transport services to ensure "just-in-time" deliveries (Richter 1925, p. 291). Merchants, obviously, derived little additional benefit from ordering over the telephone, if the resulting deliveries were delayed because of inefficient or infrequent transport services.

Thus, to engage the systemic processes that fueled increasing returns, long-distance telephone networks required a suitable economic environment, one that embraced a wide range of specialized but complementary economic activities and in particular related wholesale, transport, and communications networks. The economic interdependencies among these spatially proximate sectors render in a concrete and recognizable form the more abstract notion of a "community of interest," underlying the reciprocal demands for toll service. A highly developed regional spatial division of labor mediated by interlocking networks of transport and communications engendered the complex seasonal and spatial patterns of transactions that furthered the cumulative development of regional long-distance networks. In turn, the resulting hierarchical organization of regional telephone networks followed and reinforced metropolitan or urban system development.

Notes

Acknowledgments: For helpful suggestions and discussions, I would like to thank Bill Brainard, David Gabel, Stanley Engerman, Albert Hirschman, Daniel Koditschek, Sumner La Croix, Margaret Levenstein, Richard Levin, Kenneth Lipartito, David Pearce, Jean-Laurent Rosenthal, Matthew Shapiro, Ross Thomson, and participants in the Columbia University and University of Michigan Economic History Seminars. Funding from the Yale University Social Science Research Fund and the National Endowment of the Humanities through a fellowship from the Institute for Advance Study is gratefully acknowledged.

1. In 1907, Vail emphasized the "universality" of service furnished by the Bell System. By 1909 he articulated his full vision of "One System, One Policy, Universal Service." See Annual Reports of the AT&T Co., 1907, p. 28; 1909, pp. 18–19. On the differences between the original and modern notions of "universal service," see Mueller (1997, chap. 1).

2. Annual Report of the AT&T Co., 1908, p. 22. According to H. C. Osborne, Vail's vision would finally be realized around 1935 with the implementation of Bell's General Toll Switching Plan (Osborne 1930, pp. 429–47; 1936, pp. 58–65); Gherardi and Jewett (1930, pp. 61–62). The General Switching Plan forged a truly national telephone network through the establishment of additional regional centers—in Atlanta, Dallas, Denver, San Francisco, and Los Angeles—to mediate intra- and interregional traffic.

3. On the maturing U.S. urban system, see Conzen (1977, pp. 88–108) and Duncan and Lieberson (1970).

4. On the relationship between the geography of wholesaling and regional urban systems, see Vance (1970, pp. 149–50) and Meyer (1980, pp. 121–22).

5. In similar fashion, Wheeler and Mitchelson (1989) use Federal Express shipments to delineate the hierarchy of metropolitan centers in the early 1980s. The diffusion of the World Wide Web reveals a similar spatial bias; see Moss and Townsend (1998) and Wheeler and O'Kelly (1999, pp. 327–39).

6. AT&T Archives, box 1259, AT&T Co., E. J. Hall, Long Distance Telephone Work, 1887. To justify their proposed acquisition of Western Union, Bell officials

elaborated the complementarity between telegraph and telephone service; AT&T, *Annual Reports*, 1909, pp. 31–32; 1910, pp. 49–53; and 1911, pp. 41–43.

7. Moyer (1977, pp. 357–61) and Fischer (1992, esp. chap. 7) document the narrow scope of telephone communications before 1940. Even in the 1970s, telephone use by residential customers exhibits the same spatial patterns; see Simmons (1972, pp. 203–6) and Fischer (1992, pp. 225–26).

8. In the mid-1920s the time to complete local connections varied from nineteen seconds in smaller cities to twenty-nine seconds in larger ones; AT&T Company, *Proceedings of the Bell Educational Conference, June 21–25, 1926* (New York: AT&T Co., 1926), p. 55; Gherardi and Jewett (1930, p. 7); U.S. Bureau of the Census (1910, p. 84). Bell estimates indicate that the longest component was the time spent waiting for the desired party to answer the call.

9. This scenario fits all urban exchanges except those located in the largest cities, which were served by multiple central offices and switchboards connected by trunk lines. In the latter settings technology and operating methods more closely resembled those of toll service. It also presumes the adoption of the common battery system, whose central power source automatically signaled operators of the demand for and termination of a connection. For an excellent description of urban exchange technology and switching methods, see Mueller (1989a) and Lipartito (1994). Fagen et al. (1975) provide a comprehensive overview of Bell technology and operating methods during this period.

10. AT&T Company, *Annual Report*, 1907, p. 22; *Bell System Educational Conference*, p. 59; Gherardi and Jewett (1930, p. 34); and Fagen et al. (1975, pp. 619–22). In 1926 the average speed of toll service varied from thirty-five seconds for calls to nearby central offices with direct trunk connections to more than twelve minutes for long-haul traffic over 250 miles. For "regular" toll board service, the average was seven minutes.

11. The hierarchical design and operation of the toll plant derived from two sources: the greater technological sophistication and cost of switching and transmission equipment, and the limited scope of demand—the infrequent use of toll service by most customers and shorter duration of calls; Valentine (1911: July 15, p. 76). These points are discussed more fully in sections two and three.

12. Traffic exceeded average monthly levels during the fall harvest season and was below average during the summer months (Fowle 1908: December 19, p. 638). Recognizing the connection between aggregate economic activity and toll service, Bell's Commercial Engineering Department devoted considerable

resources to analyzing and forecasting aggregate trends; Helmle (1925) and Valentine (1926).

13. Levings (1909, p. 306) observed that small retailers often purchased limited service or dispensed with telephone service entirely. Similarly, in New Orleans, retailers, grocers, and druggists favored dual or competitive service, even if it fragmented the urban market; "The Telephone Situation in New Orleans," *American Daily Telephone* 17 (May 12, 1908), p. 406.

14. AT&T Co., *Bell System Educational Conference,* p. 59. Fowle (1908: December 19, p. 636) made a similar point: "Leased wires are used extensively by stock and grain brokers, packing companies, press associations and large industrial concerns." See also Field (1998).

15. AT&T Archives, box 1057, AT&T Co., T. B. Doolittle, Toll Lines, 1904. The analysis in this section draws mainly on Doolittle's manual. Subsequent quotations and references, unless noted otherwise, are to this document. Before Vail's return to the helm of AT&T, the efforts to achieve this goal were frustrated by the myopic vision of managers of the parent company and its licensed operating companies. For example, Doolittle's "procedure" was first adopted by a Bell operating company—the Missouri and Kansas—in 1905, and as late as July 1906 he was writing to the head of the engineering department on ways to interest the other operating companies in adopting Bell standards; AT&T Archives, box 2020, Thomas B. Doolittle, *Annual Reports,* 1903, 1906–08, Doolittle–Fish, January 14, 1907. See Garnet (1985, pp. 113–25, 131–46); Lipartito (1989, pp. 158–67); and Galambos (1992).

16. AT&T Co., *Annual Report,* 1907, pp. 22–23. From this perspective, distance is an economic concept and is more accurately gauged by the facility of communications, such as the average number of paths connecting two places or the speed of service between them; see Abler et al. (1971, pp. 257–63); Simmons (1972, pp. 212–15); Puffert (1991, p. 33); and Irwin and Kasarda (1991, p. 528).

17. The commercial application of loading and repeating (or amplification) technology in the 1920s obviated this problem; see Gherardi and Jewett (1930, pp. 33–34); Osborne (1930, pp. 13–22); and Fagen et al. (1975, pp. 251–56).

18. This comment amounts to altering the index by weighting the number of switches for each route by its share of the center's total traffic. As inspection of Table 12.4, panel B, clearly indicates, this modification would reinforce the nodality of exchanges A and D.

19. Selecting auxiliary routes involved a tradeoff between the additional time required for sending calls along more roundabout paths and the waiting time for

a clear circuit on the primary route. A second path offered a real alternative when primary circuits were busy; a tertiary path was used only in case of an emergency, such as damage to primary lines. All exchanges had practically the same range of second routes, but the availability of a third route depended critically on a center's nodality.

20. Valentine (1911: July 1, pp. 26–27; July 8, pp. 47–48; July 15, pp. 75–76; July 22, pp. 105–6). The resulting design clearly anticipated the top-down structure of Bell's General Switching Plan introduced in the late 1930s.

21. AT&T Archives, box 1057, AT&T Co., T. B. Doolittle, Toll Lines, 1904; and box 2020, Thomas B. Doolittle, Annual Reports, 1903, 1906–08, Doolittle–Fish, March 7, 1904.

22. Price (1974, pp. 129–30). For a similar notion of entrepots as an "intelligence complex" or control and coordination center, see Vance (1970, pp. 149–50) and Meyer (1980, pp. 121–22).

23. AT&T Archives, box 1011, AT&T Co., Building of Early Long Distance Lines, Hall–Hudson, January 21, 1888.

24. Rohlfs (1975, pp. 30–31), uses the term "community of interest groups" to characterize interdependent demands for telephone service.

25. I have borrowed the term *eco-technic* from Thomson (1984), who emphasizes the dialectic between technology and the market in the process of innovation. For similar notions, see Hughes (1987) and Lazonick (1991). I am grateful to Kenneth Lipartito, who cautioned against reifying the economic relationships embodied in complex technological systems, like the telephone network, into the very instruments or "artifacts" themselves.

26. They could also reduce circuit quality by using lower-gauge copper wire or even by substituting iron for copper; see, for example, Southern Bell Telephone and Telegraph Co. (SBT&T), *Annual Report,* 1907 (Atlanta: n.p., n.d.), Pickernell–Hall, February 21, 1908 (appended to 1907 *Annual Report*). Circuits made of lower-gauge copper and iron were effective only on low-density, short-haul routes; see Osborne (1930, pp. 443–44) and Fagen et al. (1975, p. 343).

27. AT&T Archives, box 1309, Relation between Population and Rates, 1906, Ford–Fish, May 24, 1906; Fowle (1909: January 9, p. 41). For example, increasing the number of circuits from four to five reduced the "average annual charges" *per circuit mile* from $36.2 to $30.2, or by 16.6 percent.

28. These figures refer to feasible loads during peak periods—that is, the maximum number of calls subject to tolerable levels of congestion or uncompleted connections because of busy circuits; AT&T Archives, box 1057, AT&T Co., T. B.

Doolittle, Toll Lines, 1904; and Wilkinson (1956a, pp. 796–98). See also Fowle
(1909: January 2, p. 9) and Gann (1909, p. 206). According to Wilkinson, Bell engineers drafted "the first 'comprehensive' traffic engineering" study in 1903, which
demonstrated these "objective efficiencies" empirically.

29. Molina (1927); see also Wilkinson (1956a, pp. 796–803). The "normal"
conditions, necessary to realize these economies, are discussed more fully in note
30 and in the text. The same principles apply to wholesale trade and explain the
rationale for bulk transactions—the accumulation of orders and shipments over
time and space.

30. A simple example, taken from Feller (1968, pp. 191–92), illustrates the
point. A city is divided into two equal districts, each served by separate toll centers
furnished with same number of circuits, k. The likelihood that a caller will encounter a busy signal depends on whether demand at either center exceeds circuit
capacity, or $Prob(X_1 > k \text{ or } X_2 > k)$, where X_1, X_2 = the demand for toll calls at
centers 1, 2 respectively. If the demand for calls in the two districts is essentially
uncorrelated, then it is far less likely that both centers would encounter capacity
constraints at the same time, or $Prob(X_1 > k \text{ and } X_2 > k) \ll Prob(X_1 > k \text{ or }$
$X_2 > k)$. Therefore, when one center experienced excess demand, the other, most
likely, would have excess capacity—unutilized circuits that could handle the overflow traffic. By consolidating the two centers into one or enlarging the circuit
group to $2k$, the company could either improve the grade of service (that is, reduce
the risk of congestion delays) or increase average circuit loads.

31. See Chandler (1990, pp. 21–31).

32. AT&T Archives, box 1285, Toll Line Service, 1896–98, Doolittle–Hudson,
May 25, 1898. I am grateful to David Gabel for bringing this document to my
attention.

33. The editors of *Telephony* were particularly interested in improving toll
operating methods and ran a series of articles describing these innovations and
their economic benefits; see "Development of Long Distance Business," *Telephony*
13 (May 1907), pp. 305–6; "Improving Toll Line Service," *Telephony* 13
(May 1907), pp. 311–12; "Efficiency in Toll Operating Methods" *Telephony* 16
(October 31, 1908), pp. 433–34; Fowle (1908: December 12, pp. 612–14; 1909:
January 2, pp. 8–9); Gann (1909, pp. 205–7); "Methods of Securing High
Efficiency in the Operation of a Toll Line System," *Telephony* 60 (May 6, 1911),
pp. 557–58; and Valentine (1911). See also Gherardi and Jewett (1930, pp. 35–36);
Osborne (1930, pp. 35–40); Fagen et al. (1975, pp. 618–24).

34. See, for example, "What the Two-Number System Is—A Toll Operating Method for Concentrated Business Traffic," *Telephony* 61 (September 9, 1911), p. 308.

35. AT&T Archives, box 1285, AT&T Co., Toll Line Service, 1892–96, Doolittle–Davis, June 4, 1896.

36. AT&T Archives, box 1285, AT&T Co., Toll Line Service, 1892–96, Doolittle–Davis, June 4, 1896 (diagram); box 1330, AT&T Co., Toll Line Service, 1900, Doolittle–Hudson, June 20, 1900; AT&T Co., Toll Line Service, 1903–04, Doolittle–Hudson, March 22, 1904; and box 2020, AT&T Co., Thomas B. Doolittle, *Annual Reports,* 1903, 1906–08, Doolittle–Fish, March 7, 1904.

37. AT&T Archives, Box 1285, AT&T Co., Toll Line Service, 1892–96, Doolittle–Davis, June 4, 1896; Doolittle–Davis, July 7, 1896; box 1309, AT&T Co., Relation between Population and Rates, 1906, Ford–Fish, May 24, 1906; and box 1330, AT&T Co., Toll Line Service, 1903–04, Doolittle–Hudson, March 22, 1904.

38. This point is developed more fully in a companion paper (Weiman 1996).

39. AT&T Archives, box 1285, AT&T Co., Toll Line Service, 1897–98, Doolittle–Hudson, June 14, 1898.

40. Whitcomb (1929, p. 52). Other examples include the use of the telephone in facilitating the purchase and sale of standard commodities, like coal and other materials, and in dispatching trains; see "My Partner, the Telephone—Using Modern Methods," *Telephony* 60 (April 22, 1911), pp. 490–22; Heyer (1911, pp. 19–21); and Richter (1925, pp. 286–90).

41. AT&T Archives, box 1342, AT&T Co., Rural Telephone Service, 1903–04, Allen–Fish, August 12, 1903. Toll service also transformed how farmers marketed their crops. According to one observer, "The rural telephones and rural mail routes . . . put the street grain broker out of business completely," as farmers negotiated the sale of their crops over the telephone before they carted them to town; "The Rural Telephone and the Grain Market," *Telephony* 16 (September 19, 1908), pp. 263–64.

42. Fowle (1909: January 2, p. 9); AT&T Archives, box 1309, AT&T Co., Relation between Population and Rates, 1906, Wray–Hibbert, May 14, 1906, and Ford–Fish, May 24, 1906. Specifically, where demands are correlated, "but not fully coincident . . . it is possible to exploit . . . economies of scope"; Mitchell and Vogelsang (1991, p. 11).

43. Molina (1927, pp. 467–68) and Wilkinson (1956a, pp. 800–801). Referring to the simple example in note 30, these conditions ensure that the probability of

congestion is much smaller in the case of consolidation; that is, $Prob(X_1 > k$ or $X_2 > k) = Prob(X_1 > k) + Prob(X_2 > k) - Prob(X_1 > k) \times Prob(X_2 > k) \approx Prob(X_1 > k) + Prob(X_2 > k) = 2Prob(X_1 > k) > Prob(X_1 + X_2 > 2k)$.

44. Wilkinson (1956b, pp. 443–46). See also Joel et al. (1982, pp. 95–100) and Hills (1979, chap. 4).

45. Fowle (1908: December 19, p. 638).

46. For example, local processing industries not only enhanced the value of farm produce, but also operated during the nonpeak seasons in agriculture, when the network's capacity was otherwise underutilized. In addition, improved communications networks fostered the spatial dispersion of processing facilities nearer to sources of supply and so contributed to the formation of these regional complexes. Under these conditions, Berry's entropy model of urbanization implies a uniform rank-size distribution; see Berry (1964, pp. 147–49) and Richardson (1973, p. 244). My formulation also satisfies the criticism of Berry's model by Higgs (1970, p. 253).

47. AT&T Archives, box 1309, Relation between Population and Rates, Ford–Fish, May 24, 1906 (emphasis added).

48. In fact, geographers use this very evidence to delineate urban systems and the trade areas of higher-order centers; see Borchert and Adams (1963) and Abler (1977). According to Abler et al. (1971, pp. 265–66), a more nodal or dominant center sends its greatest flow of traffic to a smaller city, where size is measured by population.

49. Weiman and Levin (1994); see also Langdale (1978); Lipartito (1987, pp. 82–100); Mueller (1989a, pp. 177–81); and Gabel (1994).

50. The threat of competition from merchants in nearby towns frequently prompted merchants to demand greater toll connections; see AT&T Archives, box 1214, AT&T Co., Rural Telephone Service, 1899–1902, President of Nebraska Telephone–Fish, April 14, 1902.

51. To be fair, Doolittle was making a different point; toll traffic depended more on the *total population* of a center than on the number of *exchange subscribers*. Managers, he worried, myopically focused on the latter, and so underestimated the potential toll traffic in their territory, especially where competition was strong. Still, his empirical evidence shows that toll receipts per capita varied from a minimum of $0.262 in a city of 4,703 people to $1.610 in a town of 1,342; AT&T Archives, box 1057, T. B. Doolittle, Toll Lines, 1904. Also, in an earlier document, he offered an important qualification: "It is fair to presume that there should be some relation in the amount of receipts per inhabitant, provided that the toll

facilities are of like character, and adequate"; AT&T Archives, box 1285, AT&T Co., Toll Line Service, 1897–98, Doolittle–Hudson, June 3, 1898.

52. AT&T Archives, box 1309, AT&T Co., Relation between Population and Rates, 1906, Wray–Hubbard, May 14, 1906 (quotation); Ford–Fish, May 24, 1906.

53. AT&T Archives, box 1285, AT&T Co., Toll Line Service, 1892–96, Doolittle–Davis, July 8, 1896; AT&T Co., Toll Line Service, 1897–98, Doolittle–Hudson, June 14, 1898; box 2020, AT&T Co., Thomas B. Doolittle, *Annual Reports,* 1903, 1906–08, Doolittle–Fish, January 4, 1907; box 2026, SBT&T Co., Toll Traffic Matters, 1909, Doolittle–Carty, July 14, 1909. Geographers define the hierarchical order of a center by the number and geographic range of its economic functions; it is often highly correlated with population. See, for example, Berry (1967, pp. 14–18, 35–40).

54. AT&T Archives, box 2020, AT&T Co., Thomas B. Doolittle, *Annual Reports,* 1903, 1906–08, Doolittle–Fish, March 7, 1904.

References

Abler, Ronald. 1977. "The Telephone and the Evolution of the American Urban System." In Ithiel de Sola Pool, ed., *The Social Impact of the Telephone,* pp. 318–41. Cambridge, Mass.: MIT Press.

Abler, Ronald, John S. Adams, and Peter Gould. 1971. *Spatial Organization: The Geographer's View of the World.* Englewood Cliffs, N.J.: Prentice-Hall.

Berry, Brian J. L. 1964. "City Size Distribution and Economic Development." In John Friedmann and William Alonso, eds., *Regional Development and Planning: A Reader,* pp. 138–52. Cambridge, Mass.: MIT Press.

———. 1967. *Geography of Market Centers and Retail Distribution.* Englewood Cliffs, N.J.: Prentice-Hall.

Borchert, John R., and Russell B. Adams. 1963. "Trade Centers and Trade Areas of the Upper Midwest." *Upper Midwest Economic Study,* Urban Report no. 3.

Chandler, Alfred D., Jr. 1990. *Scale and Scope: The Dynamics of Industrial Capitalism.* Cambridge, Mass.: Harvard University Press.

Conzen, Michael P. 1977. "The Maturing Urban System in the United States, 1840–1910." *Annals of the Association of American Geographers* 67: 88–108.

Duncan, Beverly, and Stanley Lieberson. 1970. *Metropolis and Region in Transition.* Beverly Hills, Calif.: Sage.

Fagen, M. D., et al. 1975. *A History of Engineering and Science in the Bell System, The Early Years (1875–1925).* Warren, N.J.: Bell Telephone Laboratories.

Feller, William. 1968. *An Introduction to Probability Theory and Its Applications.* Vol. 1. New York: John Wiley.

Field, Alexander J. 1998. "The Telegraphic Transmission of Financial Asset Prices and Orders to Trade: Implications for Economic Growth, Trading Volume, and Securities Market Regulation." *Research in Economic History* 18: 145–84.

Fischer, Claude S. 1992. *America Calling: A Social History of the Telephone to 1940.* Berkeley: University of California Press.

Fowle, Frank F. 1908–09. "Economical Development of Toll Territory." *Telephony* 17, various issues.

Gabel, David. 1994. "Competition in a Network Industry: The Telephone Industry, 1894–1910." *Journal of Economic History* 54: 543–72.

Galambos, Louis. 1992. "Theodore N. Vail and the Role of Innovation in the Modern Bell System." *Business History Review* 60: 95–126.

Gann, George K. 1909. "Handling Long Distance Traffic." *Telephony* 18 (August 28): 204–6.

Garnet, Robert W. 1985. *The Telephone Enterprise: The Evolution of the Bell System's Horizontal Structure, 1876–1909.* Baltimore, Md.: The Johns Hopkins University Press.

Gates, Bill. 1999. *Business @ the Speed of Light: Using a Digital Nervous System.* New York: Warner Books.

Gherardi, Bancroft, and F. B. Jewett. 1930. "Telephone Communication System of the United States." *Bell System Technical Journal* 9: 1–100.

Helmle, W. C. 1925. "The Relation between Telephone Development and Growth and General Economic Conditions." *Bell System Quarterly* 4: 8–21.

Heyer, G. K. 1911. "Telephone Economy in Railway Service." *Telephony* 61 (January 1): 19–21.

Higgs, Robert. 1970. "Central Place Theory and Regional Urban Hierarchies: An Empirical Note." *Journal of Regional Science* 10: 253–55.

Hills, M. T. 1979. *Telecommunications Switching Principles.* Sydney: George Allen and Unwin.

Hughes, Thomas P. 1987. "The Evolution of Large Technological Systems." In Wiebe E. Bijker, Thomas P. Hughes, and Tevor J. Pinch, eds., *The Social Construction of Technological Systems: New Directions in the Sociology and History of Technology,* pp. 51–82. Cambridge, Mass.: MIT Press.

Irwin, Michael D., and John D. Kasarda. 1991. "Air Passenger Linkages and Employment Growth in U.S. Metropolitan Areas." *American Sociological Review* 56: 524–37.

Joel, A. E., Jr., et al. 1982. *A History of Engineering and Science in the Bell System: Switching Technology (1925–75).* Warren, N.J.: Bell Laboratories.

Langdale, John V. 1978. "The Growth of Long-Distance Telephony in the Bell System, 1875–1907." *Journal of Historical Geography* 4: 145–59.

Lazonick, William. 1991. *Business Organization and the Myth of the Market.* New York: Cambridge University Press.

Levings, S. D. 1909. "The Development Study." *Telephony* 17 (March 13): 306.

Lipartito, Kenneth. 1989. *The Bell System and Regional Business: The Telephone in the South, 1877–1920.* Baltimore, Md.: Johns Hopkins University Press.

———. 1994. "When Women Were Switches: Technology, Work, and Gender in the Telephone Industry, 1890–1920." *American Historical Review* 99: 1075–1111.

Meyer, David R. 1980. "A Dynamic Model of the Integration of Frontier Urban Places into the United States System of Cities." *Economic Geography* 56: 120–40.

Mitchell, Bridger M., and Ingo Vogelsang. 1991. *Telecommunications Pricing: Theory and Practice.* New York: Cambridge University Press.

Molina, Edward C. 1927. "Application of the Theory of Probability to Telephone Trunking Problems." *Bell System Technical Journal* 6: 461–94.

Moss, Mitchell L., and Anthony M. Townsend. 1998. "Spatial Analysis of the Internet in U.S. Cities and States." Unpublished manuscript, New York University.

Moyer, Alan J. 1977. "Urban Growth and the Development of the Telephone: Some Relationships at the Turn of the Century." In Ithiel de Sola Pool, ed., *The Social Impact of the Telephone,* pp. 342–69. Cambridge, Mass.: MIT Press.

Mueller, Milton L. 1989a. "The Switchboard Problem: Scale, Signaling, and Organization in Manual Telephone Switching, 1877–1897." *Technology and Culture* 30: 534–60.

———. 1989b. "The Telephone War: Interconnection, Competition, and Monopoly in the Making of Universal Telephone Service, 1894–1920." Ph.D. dissertation, University of Pennsylvania.

———. 1997. *Universal Service: Competition, Interconnection, and Monopoly in the Making of the American Telephone System.* Cambridge, Mass.: MIT Press.

Osborne, H. C. 1930. "A General Switching Plan for Telephone Toll Service." *Bell System Technical Journal* 9: 429–47.

———. 1936. "Technical Developments Underlying the Toll Service of the Bell System." *Bell System Technical Journal* 15 (Supplement to July): pp. 1–80.

Price, Jacob. 1974. "Economic Function and the Growth of American Port Towns." *Perspectives in American History* 8: 123–84.

Puffert, Douglas. 1991. *The Economics of Spatial Network Externalities and the Dynamics of Railway Gauge Standardization.* Ph.D. dissertation, Stanford University.

Richardson, Harry W. 1973. "Theory of the Distribution of City Sizes: Review and Prospects." *Regional Studies* 7: 239–51.

Richter, F. E. 1925. "The Telephone as an Economic Instrument." *Bell System Quarterly* 4: 281–95.

Rohlfs, Jeffrey. 1975. "A Theory of Interdependent Demand for a Communications Service." *Bell Journal of Economics and Management Science* 5: 16–37.

Simmons, J. W. 1972. "Interaction among the Cities of Ontario and Quebec." In L. S. Bourne and R. D. McKinnon, eds., *Urban Systems Development in Central Canada: Selected Papers,* pp. 198–219. Toronto: University of Toronto Press.

Tarr, Joel A., et al. 1987. "The City and the Telegraph: Urban Telecommunications in the Pre-Telephone Era." *Journal of Urban History* 14: 38–80.

Thomson, Ross. 1984. "The Eco-Technic Process and the Development of the Sewing Machine." In Gavin Wright and Gary Saxonhouse, eds., *Technique, Spirit, and Form in the Making of Modern Economies: Essays in Honor of William N. Parker,* pp. 243–69. Greenwich, Conn.: JAI Press.

U.S. Bureau of the Census. 1910. *Special Report, Telephones: 1907.* Washington, D.C.: U.S. Government Printing Office.

Valentine, F. P. 1911. "Problems in Telephone Traffic Engineering." *Telephony* 61, various issues.

———. 1926. "Some Phases of the Commercial Job." *Bell System Quarterly* 5: 34–43.

Vance, James E., Jr. 1970. *The Merchant's World: The Geography of Wholesaling.* Englewood Cliffs, N.J.: Prentice-Hall.

Weiman, David F. 1996. "Systemic Limits to a National Telephone Network: The Anomaly of the Deep South." Unpublished manuscript, Queens College.

Weiman, David F., and Richard C. Levin. 1994. "Preying for Monopoly? The Case of Southern Bell Telephone Company, 1894–1912." *Journal of Political Economy* 102: 103–26.

Wheeler, David C., and Morton E. O'Kelly. 1999. "Network Topology and City Accessibility of the Commercial Internet." *Professional Geographer* 51: 327–39.

Wheeler, James A., and Ronald L. Mitchelson. 1989. "Information Flows among Major Metropolitan Areas in the United States." *Annals of the American Association of Geographers* 79: 523–43.

Wilkinson, R. I. 1956a. "Beginnings of Switching Theory in the United States." *Electrical Engineering* 75: 796–803.

———. 1956b. "Theories of Toll Traffic Engineering in the U.S.A." *Bell System Technical Journal* 35: 421–514.

Whitcomb, Richard. 1929. "The Key Town Plan of Selling by Telephone." *Bell System Quarterly* 8: 47–58.

13

INTERNATIONAL COMPETITION FOR TECHNOLOGY INVESTMENTS: DOES NATIONAL OWNERSHIP MATTER?

Trond E. Olsen

1. INTRODUCTION

With increased international mobility of capital and other productive re-sources, governments have adopted policies to attract and maintain favorable investments from firms to their national economies. Investments in advanced technology with potentials for positive spillover effects on the national econ-omy appear especially attractive. Such investments are most often controlled by multinational enterprises (MNEs),[1] and individual governments have incentives to offer favorable conditions for local investments. Foreign direct investments have been increasing, and empirical research shows that effective tax rates are important for the localization decisions of multinationals.[2] Tax policy, broadly defined, can thus be an effective instrument for national governments. The broad definition includes not only statutory corporate tax rates, but also other measures that influence effective tax rates, such as depreciation rates, tax holidays, and subsidized land. The present chapter discusses this kind of international competition, with an emphasis on spillovers and the relevance of national ownership. Many countries attempt to secure minimum national ownership stakes in firms that invest locally, for example, by indigenization requirements. The rationale and the implica-tions of such policies are not well understood. The analysis presented here contributes to an understanding of the national ownership issue by show-ing how such ownership might matter in this setting and how firms and governments then might want to affect ownership structure in order to further their respective interests.

In their dealings with technologically advanced firms, governments are likely to be constrained by information asymmetries; a firm is likely to be better informed about its technology than are the national governments that it relates to. The model presented here captures this aspect by assuming that the firm has private information about its operating profits and productivity. It is also assumed to have superior information about the positive spillovers that its activity may generate. As a part of a bargaining strategy the firm may then have incentives to misrepresent its earning potential and the extent of spillovers in each individual country. Also, having investment opportunities in several countries, the firm may try to reduce taxes or increase explicit or implicit subsidies by an implicit threat of directing a larger fraction of its investments to another country. The model, which frames the governments as principals and the firm as an agent, shows that competition among the governments may in this setting lead to severe misallocations relative to a cooperatively optimal solution. Such competition among the countries may also harm the firm. Investment allocations, profits, and welfare are shown to depend on the firm's ownership structure, and we discuss what structure would be optimal from the point of view of the firm, and from the perspective of the societies at large, respectively.

This chapter draws on previous work by Olsen and Osmundsen (2001a, 1999, 2003). This research shows, among other things, that competition among the countries to attract valuable investments results, for some ownership configurations, in excessive amounts of investments being made in one country, and insufficient amounts being made in the other. Such results are in contrast with tax competition models with symmetric information, in which competition to attract real investments invariably causes source taxes to fall and investments to rise (see, for example, Zodrow and Mieszkowski 1986). Our focus is on ownership and private information about spillover effects and productivity; that is, we do not specifically address issues of intrafirm trade and transfer pricing (for an analysis of transfer pricing regulation see, for example, Bond and Gresik 1996). Huizinga and Nielsen (1997) consider implications of foreign ownership on tax policies, but in a setting with symmetric information, a small open economy, and exogenous constraints on the government's ability to capture rents. Tax implications of national ownership have also been addressed in analyses of irreversible investments (see Konrad and Lommerud 2001). Local ownership may protect a multinational firm from the hold-up problem in foreign direct investment: since the host country's government cares about its citizens' income from portfolio investment, the government is less willing to use distortive taxes to extract the firm's net revenues. Our approach is complementary and focuses on a different link between ownership and government policy.

The model is also related to Laussel and Lebreton (1995), who analyze taxation of a large investor that possesses an exogenous amount of capital that it may allocate in two locations.[3] We extend this analysis by allowing for spillover effects and national ownership, which affects the qualitative results by introducing equity externalities.[4] A different, yet related multi-principal regulatory problem is analyzed by Mezzetti (1997), who considers a case where an agent has private information about his *relative* productivity in the tasks he performs for two principals. In contrast, our focus is on private information about the *absolute* efficiency level. Also, we introduce spillover effects. Another difference is that we address a case of substitutes, whereas in Mezzetti's model there is complementarity between the agent's tasks.

2. THE SETTING

The model follows Olsen and Osmundsen (2001a, 2001b) and depicts a bargaining situation between a unique, large MNE (agent) and two independent countries (principals).[5] There is strategic tax competition between the two countries where the firm is located, which is captured by a common agency framework. The MNE invests K_1 in country 1 and K_2 in country 2, yielding global profits (before taxes) $\Pi(K_1, K_2, \theta)$, where θ is an efficiency parameter.[6] Investments are substitutes: $\partial^2\Pi/\partial K_1 \partial K_2 < 0$. There are various reasons for assuming substitutability. First, there may be interaction effects in terms of joint costs, so that an increase in investments in one of the countries implies a higher marginal joint cost, and thus lower marginal (global) profits from investments in the other country. Also, instead of—or in addition to—interaction effects from joint costs, there may in the case of imperfect competition be interaction effects in terms of market power. For example, if the two affiliates sell their output on the same market (for example in a third country), their activities are substitutes: high investments (and output) in affiliate 1 reduce the price obtained by affiliate 2. Last, but not least, an important case of a market interaction effect arises when K_1 and K_2 are investments in R&D; the marginal payoff on R&D activities of affiliate 1 are then often lower the higher is the R&D activity of affiliate 2, for example, owing to a race to develop a new product or process.[7]

The countries compete to attract scarce real investments from the MNE and design their respective tax systems with a view to this competitive situation. Letting R_1 and R_2 denote, respectively, the taxes paid to the two countries, the post-tax global profits of the firm are given by

$$\pi = \Pi(K_1, K_2, \theta) - R_1 - R_2. \tag{1}$$

The firm has private information about θ. It is presumed that if the firm is efficient in one country it is also an efficient operator in the other country; for reasons of tractability we assume that the firm has the same efficiency in the two countries. The efficiency types are distributed on an interval $[\underline{\theta}, \overline{\theta}]$ according to a cumulative distribution function $F(\theta)$, with density $f(\theta) > 0$, where $\underline{\theta}$ denotes the least and $\overline{\theta}$ the most efficient type. The probability distribution satisfies the monotone hazard rate condition. Efficient types have higher net profits than less efficient types, both on average and at the margin: $\partial\Pi/\partial\theta > 0$ and $\partial^2\Pi/\partial\theta\partial K_j > 0$, $j = 1, 2$. The joint return function has sufficiently decreasing marginal returns on capital so that it is optimal for the firm to invest in both countries.

The firm's investments contribute some positive spillovers/externalities $\tilde{E}_j(K_j, \theta)$ to each country. The magnitudes of these externalities are known by the firm, but not by the authorities. We thus consider the case where the firm, owing to its superior knowledge regarding the specific technology, has better information than the local governments about the spillovers that this technology is likely to generate.[8] Spillovers are further assumed to be positively correlated with the firm's productivity; so $\partial\tilde{E}_j(K_j, \theta)/\partial\theta > 0$. Domestic consumer surpluses in the two countries are assumed to be unaffected by changes in the MNE's production level, since the firm is assumed to be a price taker or its market is outside the two countries. The governments have utilitarian objective functions: the social domestic welfare generated by an MNE of efficiency type θ is given by a weighted sum of the domestic taxes paid by the firm, the positive spillovers that it generates (for other domestic firms), and the MNE's global profits: $W_j = (1 + \lambda_j)R_j + \tilde{E}_j(K_j, \theta) + \alpha_j \pi$, $j = 1, 2$, where λ_j is the general equilibrium shadow cost of public funds in country j, and α_j is the owner share of country j in the MNE. By inserting for equation 1, the social welfare function for country 1 can be restated as

$$W_1 = (1 + \lambda_1)(\Pi(K_1, K_2, \theta) - R_2 + E_1(K_1, \theta)) - (1 + \lambda_1 - \alpha_1)\pi, \quad (2)$$

where $E_j(K_j, \theta) = \frac{1}{1 + \lambda_1} \tilde{E}_j(K_j, \theta)$. The social welfare consists of two terms. The first term is the domestic welfare we would obtain if the government had full information and were able to tax away all the residual income of the MNE. The government's revenue is in this case given by the MNE's net operating profits minus foreign source tax, plus the "adjusted" value of spillovers, and is multiplied by $(1 + \lambda_1)$ to obtain a welfare measure. The second term of the welfare function corrects for the loss of social welfare that stems from private information—that is, the welfare loss to the country caused by the MNE's keeping parts of the rent. The loss caused by imperfect rent extraction is equal to the MNE's global rent multiplied by the difference between the welfare weights for income accruing to the MNE and the national government. The social welfare function for country 2 is analogous. Assuming that $\lambda_1 = \lambda_2 = \lambda$, the cooperative welfare function $W = W_1 + W_2$ takes the form

$$W = (1 + \lambda)(\Pi(K_1, K_2, \theta) + E_1(K_1, \theta) + E_2(K_2, \theta)) - (1 + \lambda - \alpha_1 - \alpha_2)\pi.$$
$$(3)$$

Inserting $\pi(\theta) = 0$ in equation 3 and maximizing with respect to K_1 and K_2, we obtain *the first-best global allocation,* given by

$$\frac{\partial \Pi}{\partial K_1} + \frac{\partial E_1}{\partial K_1} = \frac{\partial \Pi}{\partial K_2} + \frac{\partial E_2}{\partial K_2} = 0. \quad (4)$$

This allocation is obtained in the case of cooperating principals and symmetric information. The solution can be attained by imposing type-dependent taxes that correct for the externalities and at the same time extract the firm's rents. Such taxes are obviously not feasible when the firm's type is private information.

3. INTERNATIONAL COOPERATION

We consider first the case where there is international cooperation among the governments. When the agent has private information and the principals cooperate, they seek to maximize the joint welfare given by equation 3, subject to incentive compatibility and participation constraints. A more efficient firm can always mimic a less efficient one and by that obtain additional profits relative to the latter. The profit differential will correspond to the firm's technological advantage; so if a firm of type $\theta + d\theta$ mimics a less efficient type θ the profit differential will be $d\pi = \frac{\partial \Pi}{\partial \theta} d\theta$. To avoid such behavior the principal must allow for these differentials in the tax scheme. Incentive compatibility thus implies that the profit (information rent) for a firm of type θ must satisfy

$$\pi'(\theta) = \frac{\partial \Pi}{\partial \theta}(K_1(\theta), K_2(\theta), \theta). \tag{5}$$

Leaving rents to the firm is costly for the governments because of the costs of raising public funds ($\lambda > 0$) and the fact that some profits may accrue to owners residing outside the two countries. This leads to a tradeoff between efficiency and rents, and optimal investments are then distorted relative to their first-best levels.

To derive the optimal distortions, consider a tax change that induces all firms with efficiency types in $(\theta, \theta + d\theta)$ to increase investments marginally in country j. The production surplus in country j then increases by $(\frac{\partial E_j}{\partial K_j} + \frac{\partial \Pi}{\partial K_j})f(\theta)d\theta$, while the rents to type $\theta + d\theta$ increase by $\frac{\partial}{\partial K_j}\frac{\partial \Pi}{\partial \theta} d\theta$. In order to preserve incentive compatibility the same rent increase must be given to all types that are more efficient—that is, to a fraction $1 - F(\theta)$ of the possible types. This rent increase is costly and must be weighted against the production surplus. Taking account of the appropriate welfare weights—which reflect the costs of raising public funds and the costs of leaving rents to foreign owners (see equation 3)—we see that the tradeoff between production efficiency and rents yields the following optimality condition:[9]

$$(1 + \lambda)\left(\frac{\partial E_j}{\partial K_j} + \frac{\partial \Pi}{\partial K_j}\right) = (1 + \lambda - \alpha_1 - \alpha_2)\frac{\partial^2 \Pi}{\partial \theta \partial K_j}\frac{1 - F(\theta)}{f(\theta)}, j = 1, 2. \tag{6}$$

Compared with the first-best global optimum, the information asymmetry generates the additional right hand sides of equation 6, which represent marginal information costs. The investment portfolios are distorted in order to enhance the governments' rent extraction from the firm, and the distortions entail reductions of investment levels in both countries for all types except the most efficient one. The tax scheme that implements these optimal investments balances the concerns to induce production efficiency and to extract rents from the firm. The first calls for negative tax rates (subsidies) to correct for positive external spillovers, the second for positive tax rates to reduce investments and thereby facilitate rent extraction. The optimality conditions show that there are no distortions from the first-best "at the top" (for type $\bar{\theta}$), and it follows that marginal tax rates are negative for such a firm. These marginal subsidies induce an efficient firm—which by assumption also generates high spillovers—to increase its investments beyond what would otherwise have been privately optimal. In order to extract rents from the firm, less efficient types should be induced to invest less, and marginal taxes may for that reason be positive for lower investment levels.

We see that the firm's ownership structure influences the cooperative solution, but only via the total owner shares that belong to residents of the two countries ($\alpha_1 + \alpha_2$). The distribution of ownership between the two cooperating countries is of no importance in this setting.

4. INTERNATIONAL TAX COMPETITION

Consider now the case where the governments of the two countries compete to attract the firm's investments. The MNE then relates to each government separately. The governments act noncooperatively; each country seeks to maximize expected domestic welfare, subject to incentive compatibility and participation constraints for the firm and given the strategy of the other country. In this setting it is natural to assume that each country offers a tax/subsidy schedule, specifying the firm's net tax payments to that country as a function of its investments there. So we are looking for an equilibrium in tax schedules (or menus) $R_1(K_1)$, $R_2(K_2)$. To interpret these tax schedules, we can envision the countries keeping the statutory corporate income tax rates fixed and offering nonlinear depreciation schedules and tax exemptions to attract investments from the MNE.

We have assumed that the firm has private information about its efficiency, whereas its investment levels have been assumed to be subject to symmetric information. Profits may to a large extent be observable for purely domestic firms and be captured by a traditional corporate income tax. For multinational firms, transfer pricing may make any attempt to measure profits difficult, so that countries are forced to estimate profits based on what is observable. Our assumption is that investments are the key such observable variable, and the tax schemes derived are made contingent on the national investment levels.

In designing a nonlinear corporate income tax scheme for internationally mobile firms, each country takes the tax schedules of the other country as given. However, each country must take into account that its choice of strategy (tax schedule) may cause investment externalities: a change in the contract of country 1 may affect the firm's investments in country 2 and thereby make it deviate from the investment level intended for it by country 2.

Consider the strategic problem for country 1; that of country 2 is similar. Incentive compatibility requires that the firm's equilibrium profits (rents) must increase in accordance with equation 5 in the noncooperative case as well. In addition to this constraint regarding the firm's rents, country 1 must also take into account that the firm's investments in the other country are given by

$$\frac{\partial \Pi}{\partial K_2} (K_1(\theta), K_2(\theta), \theta) - R_2'(K_2(\theta)) = 0. \tag{7}$$

Via its tax policy the government of country 1 is able to directly affect the MNE's "domestic" investment K_1. But the firm will react to this change by also adjusting its "foreign" investment K_2, and country 1 must take this reaction into account when it designs its domestic tax policy. From equation 7 we see that the change in the MNE's foreign investments induced by a change in domestic investments depends on the foreign country's tax policy and is given by $\frac{\partial K_2}{\partial K_1} = \frac{\Pi_{12}}{R_2'' - \Pi_{11}}$ (the Π_{ij}'s denote second-order partials). Formally, the tax design problem of country 1 can then be seen as maximizing domestic welfare subject to this constraint (or equivalently the constraint in equation 7), and the constraints that secure incentive compatibility (in equation 5) and voluntary participation by the firm.

This problem again entails a tradeoff between efficiency and rent extraction. From the point of view of country j, the tradeoff leads to the following optimality condition for domestic investments:

$$(1 + \lambda)\left(\frac{\partial E_j}{\partial K_j} + \frac{\partial \Pi}{\partial K_j}\right) = (1 + \lambda - \alpha_j)\left[\frac{\partial^2 \Pi}{\partial \theta \partial K_j} + \frac{\partial^2 \Pi}{\partial \theta \partial K_i}\frac{\partial K_i}{\partial K_j}\right]\frac{1 - F(\theta)}{f(\theta)}. \quad (8)$$

The left-hand side of this relation accounts for the marginal effects on the domestic production surplus in country j, while the terms on the right-hand side account for the marginal effects on rents for that country. There are now two components of the rent effect; the first is a conventional (direct) one, just as in the cooperative case; the second is a strategic effect, working through the change in foreign investments ($\frac{\partial K_i}{\partial K_j}$) induced by a change in domestic investments. This is a fiscal externality that is due to the ability of government j—via a strategic tax policy—to affect the investment made by the MNE in the other country i.

We saw that the strategic effect for country 1—that is, the firm's investment response $\frac{\partial K_2}{\partial K_1}$—depends on the tax policy in country 2. In equilibrium both countries' tax policies are endogenously determined. We return to this point below, but note here that if investments are substitutes, increasing in both countries and commonly implementable, the strategic effect will be negative. The firm will then to some degree compensate reduced domestic investments by increased foreign ones. This implies that reduced domestic investment is now a less effective means for each government to extract rents from the firm. The strategic effect works against the direct conventional effect and calls as such for *increasing* the investment levels for all firms but the most efficient one. To illustrate this point for an extreme case, suppose the operating profit function is symmetric and that the strategic effect is $\frac{\partial K_i}{\partial K_j} = -1$.[10] Reduced domestic investments will then have *no effect* on the firm's rents; the strategic effect completely offsets the conventional effect. (The terms on the right-hand side of equation 8 vanish.) Any tax-induced reduction dK_j of domestic investments will be met by the firm by an offsetting change of foreign investments ($dK_i = -dK_j$), and this will leave the firm's rents unaltered. Unilateral tax-induced distortions of domestic investments are thus completely ineffective as a means for country j to capture rents from the firm. In less extreme cases the strategic effect will be weaker, and some distortions will then be desirable from each country's point of view.

The magnitudes of the strategic effects are determined endogenously. To see how, note that the first-order condition (equation 7) for "foreign" investment must hold as an identity in θ in equilibrium. By differentiating this relation with respect to θ, and substituting for the terms involving the "foreign" tax scheme (here R_2'') in the expression found previously for the strategic effect, we find that this effect can be written as follows (for $i = 2, j = 1$):

$$\frac{\partial K_i}{\partial K_j} = \frac{\Pi_{ij} K'_i(\theta)}{\Pi_{\theta i} + \Pi_{ij} K'_j(\theta)}.$$

This relation and relation 8 now constitute a set of equilibrium conditions that determines equilibrium investment allocations.[11]

Apart from differences due to the strategic effect (the fiscal externality), the cooperative and noncooperative solutions also differ because in the latter case neither of the governments internalizes the profits that accrue to investors in the other country (equity externalities). For this reason the motive to extract rents is always stronger in the latter case $(1 + \lambda - \alpha_j > 1 + \lambda - \alpha_j - \alpha_i)$. This is reflected in the different weights that appear on the right-hand sides of equations 6 and 8. The equity externalities lead to more aggressive rent collection by the governments, which implies higher distortions (lower investments) than in the cooperative case. Olsen and Osmundsen (2003) showed that this underinvestment effect will dominate when both λ and the firm's outside-owner share $(1 - \alpha_1 - \alpha_2)$ are small, while the overinvestment effect associated with the strategic effect may dominate otherwise, such as when spillovers are small and the investments K_1, K_2 are close substitutes for the firm. In the former case one thus finds that *competition for the firm's investments and rents may actually reduce investments relative to the cooperative solution.* Since lower investments imply lower marginal profits and hence lower absolute profits for the firm—see equation 5—it follows that *competition between the countries may also reduce the firm's profits relative to its profits in a regime where the governments cooperate.*

5. IMPLICATIONS OF NATIONAL OWNERSHIP

From the equilibrium conditions it is clear that the pattern of ownership will have implications for the equilibrium allocation of resources. In particular, the equity externalities discussed above depend very much on this pattern. In this respect it is of importance both how ownership is distributed between the two countries and to what extent it is distributed to investors outside the two countries. In the cooperative case only the latter aspect is of importance for the outcome. In this section we examine some of these consequences.

We focus on variations in owner shares between the two countries. For a fixed outside-owner share, such variations will not affect the cooperative outcome. Among other things, this implies that if technologies are symmetric between the two countries, the investment profiles will in the cooperative case also be symmetric, irrespective of how ownership is distributed between the countries. Not so in the case of tax competition. If owner shares are asymmetric, the governments will have different views on the importance of extracting the firm's rents, and this will lead to asymmetric tax schedules and hence asymmetric investment patterns. Comparing this asymmetric pattern under competition to the symmetric pattern under coordination, it is perhaps not so surprising that the former may entail higher investments in one country and lower investments in the other. What is perhaps more surprising, at least at a first glance, is that the outcome under tax competition may yield overinvestment in one country compared to the first-best (symmetric information) global optimum.[12]

Proposition 1 *Suppose technologies (including spillovers) are symmetric between the two countries. Then the first-best as well as the second-best allocation under international cooperation are symmetric, and the latter always exhibits lower investments than the former. These allocations are not influenced by the distribution of ownership between the two countries. The equilibrium under international competition is, however, influenced by this ownership distribution, and the equilibrium may entail overinvestment relative to the first-best allocation in one country. This is the case for country j if the marginal cost of public funds λ is sufficiently small and that country has a sufficiently large owner share.*

375 INTERNATIONAL COMPETITION FOR TECHNOLOGY INVESTMENTS

The first part of the proposition is straightforward. The economic intuition for the overinvestment result is as follows. The country that holds a large equity stake in the MNE—for example, country 1—has low incentives to extract rents from the firm, since a large fraction of profits are repatriated to national investors. Absent strategic effects, this country will thus not induce much of a (downward) distortion of investments (which also reduce before-tax profits) in its tax policy. Second, country 2—on the other hand—imposes high distortions due to a low equity stake in the firm. Low K_2 implies low marginal joint costs, which by substitution imply higher K_1 (the strategic effect). Thus there is for country 1 a strong investment-increasing strategic effect and a weak investment-reducing direct effect. For a sufficiently high α_1 the former may dominate, and we may then have K_1 higher than in the first-best case.[13]

We turn now to an analysis of the consequences of variations in owner shares. Keeping the outside owner share fixed, we examine for the noncooperative tax regime how profits and welfare respond to variations in the distribution of owner shares between the two countries. Olsen and Osmundsen (2001) considered this problem for the case with no spillovers ($E_1 = E_2 = 0$) and showed that for symmetric technologies a balanced ownership structure is optimal for the firm as well as for the two countries at large. This structure protects the firm against highly distortive taxes in the two countries and thus reduces the costs of asymmetric information, which is beneficial both for the firm and for the governments. The balanced-ownership result remains valid for the case of positive and symmetric spillovers. When we subsequently consider asymmetric technologies, we will see that optimal owner shares are asymmetric (and sometimes highly so) and that the firm's preferred share distribution is not the distribution that is optimal for the societies at large.

The symmetric case is illustrated in Figure 13.1. To every owner-share combination (α_1, α_2) there corresponds an equilibrium investment outcome K_1, K_2. The lower curve in the figure represents, for a given type θ, the set of equilibrium investment combinations K_1, K_2 generated as the firm's owner shares vary, subject to $\alpha_1 + \alpha_2 = 1$. (We assume here a zero outside-owner share.) When the owner share of country 1 is high ($\alpha_1 > \alpha_2$), equilibrium investments are high in that country and low in country 2 ($K_1 > K_2$): the country with the higher owner share is less eager to extract rents and hence less inclined to induce

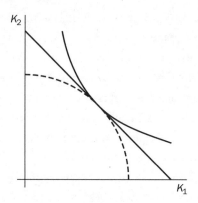

Welfare contour (top), marginal profits contour (middle),
and equilibrium set (bottom).

Figure 13.1 Optimal investment and owner shares
in the symmetric case

downward distortions of domestic investments. The curve representing equilibrium investment combinations K_1, K_2 therefore falls as α_1 increases; higher α_1 yields higher K_1 and lower K_2 in equilibrium. Moreover, the symmetry assumptions imply that the curve must be symmetric around the 45-degree line.

The firm would like to have in place the owner combination that maximizes its equilibrium rents. These rents are implicitly determined by equilibrium investments; this follows because incentive compatibility implies that marginal rents are given by $\frac{\partial \Pi}{\partial \theta}(K_1(\theta), K_2(\theta), \theta)$ (see equation 5). The middle curve in Figure 13.1 represents a set of investment combinations that yield constant marginal rents for the given type of firm; the curve is defined by $\frac{\partial \Pi}{\partial \theta}(K_1, K_2, \theta)$ = *const.* The symmetry assumptions imply that any such marginal rents contour must also be symmetric around the 45-degree line. Since marginal rents are increasing with more investments—this follows from $\frac{\partial^2 \Pi}{\partial \theta \partial K_j} > 0$—we see that, among all the feasible equilibrium investment combinations, the symmetric one yields the highest marginal rents for the firm.[14] This is true for every type of firm, and since the symmetric owner-share combination thus yields uniformly the highest marginal rents, it will also yield the highest absolute rents. Symmetric owner shares are therefore optimal for the firm.

The upper curve in Figure 13.1 is a contour for the aggregate welfare of the two countries, also corresponding to the given type θ. For $\lambda = 0$ this is a contour for the aggregate surplus $E_1 + E_2 + \Pi$, see (3), for $\lambda > 0$ this surplus must be adjusted for rents. Since that contour is also symmetric, we see that the owner-share distribution that generates the most favorable investment combination for the firm is also the distribution that generates the highest welfare. This argument can be formalized in a way similar to the formal analysis in Olsen and Osmundsen (2001); here we just state the result.

Proposition 2 *Suppose there is tax competition and that technologies (including spillovers) are symmetric between the two countries. Keeping the outside owner share fixed, the firm's equilibrium profits are maximal when ownership is equally distributed between the two countries. The aggregate welfare for the two societies is also maximal for this ownership structure.*

The discussion here has been confined to symmetric technologies. Olsen and Osmundsen (2003) examine some of these issues when technologies are asymmetric. For tractability reasons it is then found necessary to introduce special functional forms. The analysis complements Proposition 2 by showing, among other things, that the owner shares that are optimal from the firm's point of view are not generally optimal from the point of view of the two societies at large. The last result indicates that the alignment of interests for the firm and the two societies with regard to the distribution of ownership is a special case, closely tied to the assumption of symmetric technologies. It is not so difficult to see why. In the general case, all the curves in Figure 13.1 will be asymmetric, and the firm's optimum will occur for $K_1 \neq K_2$. At such a point it will not generally be the case that the welfare contour and the profits contour have equal slopes. Hence there appears in the general (asymmetric) case to be a conflict of interests between the firm and the societies with respect to how the firm's owner shares should be distributed.

By assuming specific functions, explicit regulatory mechanisms may be derived. Olsen and Osmundsen (2001b) solve for the case of quadratic/linear functions and a uniform distribution. Specifically, all second-order derivatives of the firm's operating profit function (Π_{ij}, $i, j = 1, 2, \theta$) are assumed to be constant, spillovers are assumed to be given by

$$E_j(K_j, \theta) = e_j \theta K_j,$$

and the efficiency parameter θ is assumed to be uniform on $[0, 1]$. To focus sharply on the effects of different degrees of spillovers in the two countries, it is further assumed that *the firm's private returns (given by $\Pi(K_1, K_2, \theta)$) are symmetric* with respect to investments in the two countries.

With the specified functional forms the noncooperative equilibrium can be explicitly characterized, and it then becomes possible to examine how the firm's rents vary with its ownership distribution. Note that if the firm is partly owned by investors outside the two countries where it operates, the two countries' motives for rent extraction will be stronger than if the firm has no such outside owners. From the firm's point of view it is therefore clearly advantageous (with respect to maximizing its rents) to have all its owners inside the two countries. In the following we consider only this case; that is, we assume throughout that $\alpha_1 + \alpha_2 = 1$.

The equilibrium, and hence the optimal ownership pattern for the firm, will depend on the parameters that characterize spillovers and the firm's private investment returns. Keeping the latter fixed, one finds that the owner shares that maximize the firm's equilibrium rents $\pi(\theta)$ depend on the extent of spillovers in each country in a way such that *equal owner shares ($\alpha_1 = \alpha_2$) are optimal only when spillovers are symmetric. Otherwise, the optimal owner share in country j is increasing in domestic spillovers (e_j) and decreasing in foreign spillovers (e_i).*

We see that if spillovers are not symmetric between the two countries ($e_1 \neq e_2$), the firm will prefer an uneven distribution of its owner shares. From the point of view of the firm, the country where spillovers are largest is the most favorable. If the firm has a larger owner share in that country, its government will be more eager to attract investments, and this will increase the firm's profits.

In the symmetric case we saw that the ownership pattern most preferred by the firm was also the best one from a social point of view. As we have indicated, this is no longer true when spillovers are asymmetric. For the specified model we can also say something about the direction in which the firm will bias its ownership. Olsen and Osmundsen (2003) show that *the ownership pattern (α_1, α_2) that maximizes the firm's equilibrium rents will also maximize the (equilibrium) total surplus $W = W_1 + W_2$ if and only if $\alpha_1 = \alpha_2 = \frac{1}{2}$. If the firm prefers* *an unbalanced ownership, with say $\alpha_2 > \frac{1}{2}$, then a more balanced ownership (smaller α_2) would be better from a social point of view.*

To get some intuition for this result, suppose technologies are symmetric except for larger spillovers in country $2(e_2 > e_1)$. The firm prefers the owner distribution that maximizes its rents, which entails a larger owner share and consequently larger equilibrium investments in country $2(\alpha_2 > \alpha_1$ and $K_2 > K_1)$. The optimum for the firm is characterized by tangency between the "equilibrium locus" and the marginal profits contour. (See the discussion related to Figure 13.1, but note that all curves are now asymmetric.) The point is now that for $K_2 > K_1$ one can show that the slope of the welfare contour is steeper than the slope of the marginal profit contour. The welfare contour is therefore at this investment combination also steeper than the equilibrium locus, and welfare will thus increase if we increase K_1 at the expense of K_2 along the latter locus. This is precisely what will take place if the owner share α_1 is increased. Hence we see that the owner share α_1 that is most preferred by the firm is in this case too low from a social point of view.

6. CONCLUDING COMMENTS

We have considered a situation where two jurisdictions compete to attract shares of the investment budget of a large multinational enterprise whose investments confer positive spillovers on national firms. The firm contributes to local welfare by spillovers, by tax payments, and by dividends paid to local investors. In our context any profits accruing to the MNE are then part of the national welfare to the extent that the country has an equity share in the firm. This assignment of positive welfare weights to profits implies, among other things, that under some owner configurations investments are lower in both countries when the governments compete than when they cooperate. Moreover, not only can aggregate investment fall with tax competition with domestic ownership, but this reduced investment may be misallocated across the two countries relative to the cooperative choice, causing a further fall in efficiency. Under other owner configurations, investments can be higher when the countries compete than when they cooperate. In fact, we may get *overinvestment* (compared with the first-best global optimum) in one country in equilibrium.

This occurs for example, if one country has a large owner share in the MNE and the countries are otherwise symmetric. Furthermore, we examined how the MNE's profits depend on the ownership structure, in particular on how the MNE's equity is distributed between the two countries. Unlike the symmetric information case and the case of cooperating principals, ownership matters. We analyzed the optimal ownership structure seen from the perspective of the MNE and the governments, and pointed to a conflict of interests between these parties regarding this issue.

In practice the ownership structure can be most easily affected for nonlisted firms. The initial owners may then select its investors, and this may allow them to obtain the preferred ownership configuration. A stable ownership structure can further be promoted by initially approaching long-term investors. For listed companies such a policy is to some extent restricted by liquidity requirements imposed by stock exchanges, but the trading requirements are generally not large, giving room for long-term ownership for a large fraction of the shares. Moreover, as a means to induce an even distribution of ownership among investors in the two countries, the MNE may also want to be listed on the stock exchanges of both countries. As for the governments, the national distribution of equity shares may be affected by regulations, by personal income tax design, or by direct government equity acquisitions or sales. With respect to regulations, some countries have imposed ownership restrictions— for example, on foreign ownership of financial institutions. Many countries attempt to secure a minimum national ownership stake in firms that invest locally. Targeted policies in use include indigenization requirements, meaning that the host government requires an investor to share ownership of an affiliate with residents in the host country (see Katrak 1983).

An obvious shortcoming of the analysis in this chapter is the lack of consideration of intertemporal issues. The model is static and neglects dynamic aspects of information as well as technology. In reality, current policies will be influenced by expectations about future technological developments and growth, and also be conditioned on the current state of affairs, determined by history. In situations with asymmetric information there is also the particular informational aspect that if an agent's current private information is relevant for his own and other players' decisions in the future, he may be very reluctant to reveal this information. Information may then be revealed only slowly over time, and each stage of this process can only be understood by realizing that agents choose current actions conditional on history and with a view to the future.[15] In short, history matters, and it is a challenge for future research in the area studied in this chapter to better incorporate such aspects in the analysis.

NOTES AND REFERENCES

Notes

Acknowledgments: The paper draws on joint work with Petter Osmundsen. I thank Paul David and a referee for constructive comments on an earlier draft. Financial support from the Norwegian Research Council is gratefully acknowledged.

1. MNEs tend to be important in industries and firms that are characterized by high levels of research and development (R&D) relative to sales, a high value of intangible assets, a large share of professional and technical workers in their work force, products that are new or technically complex, and high levels of product differentiation and advertising (Markusen 1995).

2. See, for example, Devereux and Freeman (1995).

3. A similar setup is found in Haaparanta (1996), but under perfect information. Haaparanta analyzes a subsidy game where two governments, maximizing the net wage income, compete to attract investments of a single firm.

4. Our model is also somewhat related to Biglaiser and Mezzetti (1993), in which two principals compete for the exclusive services of an agent that has private information about his or her effort and productivity. Whereas we focus on a multinational enterprise that divides its activities between several countries, Biglaiser and Mezzetti analyze a case where a worker must work full-time for a single company.

5. Alternatively, the model can be interpreted as describing multi-principal regulation of an internationally mobile industry with a continuum of small firms with different efficiency types for investments in the two countries and with different extent of local spillovers.

6. In addition, there may be sunk investments in both countries.

7. Olsen (1993) analyzes single-principal regulation of independent units and emphasizes the role of research activities as substitutes.

8. Other informational distributions are clearly possible. If the extent of spillovers depends more on local conditions than on the specific technology, a local government might be better informed than the firm about the relevant externality effects.

9. For a technical survey of single-principal regulation theory, see Guesnerie and Laffont (1984).

10. This is an extreme case, since implementability conditions typically will imply that the strategic investment effects are less than 1 in absolute value.

11. After substitution for the strategic effects relation 8 constitutes a system of differential equations, and if this system defines a pair of nondecreasing investment schedules $\{K_1(\theta), K_2(\theta)\}$, and those schedules in addition satisfy a set of implementability conditions, they constitute a differentiable equilibrium outcome for the common agency game; see for example, Stole (1992) and Martimort (1992, 1996).

12. Although there may be overinvestment in one country, simulations with parametric functions indicate that total investments will be lower than in the first-best case.

13. To prove this, consider the extreme case where $\lambda = 0$ and $\alpha_1 = 1$. The equilibrium conditions will then imply $\frac{\partial E}{\partial K_i} + \frac{\partial \Pi}{\partial K_i} = 0$ and $\frac{\partial E}{\partial K_2} + \frac{\partial \Pi}{\partial K_2} > 0$, and hence $K_1 \geq K_2$. Since the first-best investment levels K_{jF} (where $K_{1F} = K_{2F}$) are given by $\frac{\partial E}{\partial K_j} + \frac{\partial \Pi}{\partial K_j} = 0$, and since $\Pi_{12} < 0$, it then follows that $K_1 > K_{1F}$ and $K_2 < K_{2F}$. Since the inequalities are strict, they will continue to hold when λ and $1 - \alpha_1$ are positive but small.

14. The argument implicitly assumes that the curve representing equilibrium investments is more concave than the marginal profits contour. Formal conditions can be formulated as in Olsen and Osmundsen (2001a). These conditions hold for the quadratic-uniform case considered below, where the marginal profits contour is linear.

15. For dynamic aspects of principal-agent relationships with hidden information, see, for example, Laffont and Tirole (1993), chaps. 9–10. Olsen and Torsvik (1995) study such aspects in common agency.

References

Biglaiser, G., and C. Mezzetti. 1993. "Principals Competing for an Agent in the Presence of Adverse Selection and Moral Hazard." *Journal of Economic Theory* 61: 302–30.

Bond, E. W., and T. A. Gresik. 1996. "Regulation of Multinational Firms with Two Active Governments: A Common Agency Approach." *Journal of Public Economics* 59: 33–53.

Devereux, M. P., and H. Freeman. 1995. "The Impact of Tax on Foreign Direct Investment: Empirical Evidence and the Implications for Tax Integration Schemes." *International Tax and Public Finance* 2: 85–106.

Guesnerie, R., and J. J. Laffont. 1984. "A Complete Solution to a Class of Principal-Agent Problems with an Application to the Control of a Self-Managed Firm." *Journal of Public Economics* 25: 329–69.

Haaparanta, P. 1996. "Competition for Foreign Direct Investments." *Journal of Public Economics* 63: 141–53.

Huizinga, H., and S. B. Nielsen. 1997. "Capital Income and Profit Taxation with Foreign Ownership of Firms." *Journal of International Economics* 42: 149–65.

Katrak, H. 1983. "Multinational Firms' Global Strategies, Host Country Indigenisation of Ownership and Welfare. "*Journal of Development Economics* 13: 331–48.

Konrad, K. A., and K. E. Lommerud. 2001. "Foreign Direct Investment, Intra-Firm Trade and Ownership Structure." *European Economic Review* 45: 475–94.

Laffont, J.-J., and J. Tirole. 1993. *A Theory of Incentives in Procurement and Regulation.* Cambridge, Mass.: MIT Press.

Laussel, D., and M. Lebreton. 1995. "On the Tax Schedule Nash Equilibria of a Fiscal Competition Game II: The Large Investor's Case." Unpublished note, LEQUAM, University of Aix-Marseilles 2.

Markusen, J. R. 1995. "The Boundaries of Multinational Enterprises and the Theory of International Trade." *Journal of Economic Perspectives* 9: 169–89.

Martimort, D. 1992. "Multi-Principaux avec Anti-Selection." *Annales D' Économie et de Statistique* 28: 1–37.

———. 1996. "The Multiprincipal Nature of Government." *European Economic Review* 40: 3–5, 673–85.

Mezzetti, C. 1997. "Common Agency with Horizontally Differentiated Principals." *Rand Journal of Economics* 28: 325–45.

Olsen, T. E. 1993. "Regulation of Multiagent Research and Development." *Rand Journal of Economics* 24: 529–41.

Olsen, T. E., and P. Osmundsen. 1999. "Common Agency with Outside Options; The Case of International Taxation of an MNE." Discussion Paper 2/99, Department of Finance and Management Science, Norwegian School of Economics and Business Administration.

————. 2001. "Strategic Tax Competition: Implications of National Ownership." *Journal of Public Economics* 81: 253–77.

————. 2003. "Spillovers and International Competition for Investments." *Journal of International Economics* 59: 211–38.

Olsen, T. E., and G. Torsvik. 1995. "Intertemporal Common Agency and Organizational Design: How Much Decentralization?" *European Economic Review* 39: 1405–28.

Osmundsen, P., K. P. Hagen, and G. Schjelderup. 1998. "Internationally Mobile Firms and Tax Policy." *Journal of International Economics* 45: 97–113.

Stole, L. 1992. "Mechanism Design under Common Agency." Working paper, University of Chicago.

Zodrow, G. R., and P. Mieszkowski. 1986. "Pigou, Tiebout, Property Taxation, and the Underprovision of Local Public Goods." *Journal of Urban Economics* 19: 356–70.

IV

EVIDENCE MATTERS: MEASURING
HISTORICAL ECONOMIC GROWTH
AND DEMOGRAPHIC CHANGE

14

CONJECTURAL ESTIMATES OF ECONOMIC GROWTH IN THE LOWER SOUTH, 1720 TO 1800

Peter C. Mancall, Joshua L. Rosenbloom, and Thomas Weiss

The economy of the British North American mainland colonies, so history and economics textbooks tell us, was a great success. Enterprising Europeans arrived in North America and, through hard work and the availability of land, created a prosperous economy based on the export of agricultural staples. Yet despite wide acceptance of such a notion, scholars remain divided about the actual rate of growth in the colonies.[1] The range of opinion on the speed of economic growth reflects the relative paucity of quantifiable data for the period before 1800, and past efforts to measure colonial economic performance have relied heavily on the behavior of exports. Recently, Mancall and Weiss (1999) employed the controlled conjectural method, an approach brought to the fore by Paul David (1967), to shift the focus of attention from exports to the far more dominant activities related to agricultural production for the domestic market.[2] As David demonstrated, the conjectural approach requires a minimum of information and is thus well suited to dealing with historical periods that may appropriately be described as a statistical dark age.

Subjected to such analysis, the early American economy no longer looks so successful. Based on the limited information available in published documents, Mancall and Weiss (1999) concluded that there was little likelihood of economic growth in colonial America over the course of the eighteenth century. The rate of growth of GDP per capita was certainly less than 0.5 percent per year, and more likely was very sluggish, perhaps zero. Although Mancall and Weiss sought to present a picture of the most likely course of economic progress before 1800, their primary purpose was to shift the focus of attention to the domestic economy and lay out a way of approaching its measurement, not to present the final word on the subject.[3]

One way in which those estimates could be improved upon is to apply their method of estimation to subsets of the colonies and then sum up the parts to obtain the aggregate figures for the colonies as a whole. Here we present the results of our examination of one of those regions, the Lower South.[4] Since this region was more heavily dependent on the export trade than any other region in the mainland colonies, historians have used exports as the key indicator of the success of the economy of South Carolina and its neighbors.[5] But we need to set these assessments in a larger context by viewing the performance from the domestic side as well. When this is done, the region's growth record does not appear quite so successful.

We have measured the performance of the region's economy by estimating real gross domestic product (GDP) per capita at four benchmark dates: 1720, 1740, 1770, and 1800.[6] Our findings demonstrate the impact of a large but relatively unprogressive domestic farm sector on the overall pace of economic growth. We find that during the colonial period, from 1720 to 1770, GDP per capita was virtually unchanged. The rate of growth varied within that time period. From 1740 to 1770, the economy performed somewhat better as GDP per capita rose slightly, but in the heyday of export success, 1720 to 1740, when exports grew by 6 percent per year in the aggregate, the per capita value of GDP declined slightly, from $60 to $58. And in the period from 1770 to 1800, when exports per capita declined at 2.1 percent per year, GDP per capita rose ever so slightly. The region's performance over the longer period from 1720 to 1800 was about the same as Mancall and Weiss found for the colonies as a whole. The greater reliance on exports did not stimulate the region's growth of GDP per capita; exports were not always and everywhere as powerful an engine of growth as some scholars have suggested.

1. AN OVERVIEW OF THE LOWER SOUTH'S ECONOMIC DEVELOPMENT

A generation of scholars has concluded that the Lower South and the Chesapeake were the most economically successful regions of British mainland North

America. Both regions made extensive use of slave labor, had apparently successful staple-export sectors, and by 1774 had the highest levels of private wealth per capita in the colonies.[7] Until recently, however, our knowledge about the Lower South did not go much beyond this. Writing in 1985, McCusker and Menard (1985, chap. 8) decried the lack of knowledge about this region. Since then, Peter Coclanis (1989), Joyce Chaplin (1993), Marc Egnal (1998), and others have broadened our knowledge, but they continue to focus on the export sector. When they revealed that not everyone lived in the low country, not everyone was a planter, and not everyone was engaged in foreign trade, they did not pursue the consequences of these observations for the region's growth implied by the wide variations in economic performance across these different spheres.

The conventional economic history of the Lower South has focused heavily on South Carolina, and especially the low country, for most of the eighteenth century.[8] Such a focus makes some sense given the fact that colonists there were more heavily involved in international trade and the low country was home to some of the wealthiest British colonists in the Western hemisphere. North Carolina was more populous than South Carolina, but had far fewer slaves for most of the eighteenth century.[9] Georgia, which was not established until 1732 and prohibited slavery until 1749, was a relative latecomer and contained only a small fraction of the region's population.

The economic history of South Carolina, and indeed of the region, consists of two distinct stories: one for the low country and a second for the back country. Historians, however, have focused predominantly on the development of staple agricultural production, which was confined primarily to the low country until the introduction of short-staple cotton in the mid-1790s. To be sure, exports—especially of rice—were substantial.[10] In 1700, rice exports totaled only 450,000 pounds, but by 1720 they amounted to 6.5 million pounds and continued to climb, reaching a temporary peak of 43 million pounds in 1740. This initial period of expansion was brought to a sudden end in 1740 by international conflicts that raised shipping and insurance costs and restricted the market for rice. The depressed conditions persisted for most of the decade, during which time planters experimented with other crops, including indigo, which emerged as an important complement to rice.[11] With the return of peace in the late 1740s, rice prices recovered along with exports. Both exports and prices fluctuated without trend for the next decade, but beginning in the early 1760s and continuing until the American Revolution, rice prices and exports both increased steadily (Nash 1992, p. 692; Dethloff 1982, p. 235). During this upsurge in exports, planters expanded rice cultivation into Georgia and the Cape Fear region of North Carolina. But despite the expansion, South Carolina remained by far the largest producer.

The upward trajectory of rice exports came to an end with the American Revolution. Material losses during the war were substantial owing to the sustained conflict in the region.[12] The devastation caused by the war is apparent in the low levels of exports in the immediate postwar period. Exports rose rapidly in the second half of the 1780s, but even at their peak in 1793, Charleston's postwar exports were well below the level of the early 1770s (Gray 1958, pp. 1020–23).

The robust, export-based growth of the low country in the decades before the Revolution coincided with the rapid expansion of settlement into the interior of the region. For the most part, the settlement of the back country was by small independent farmers who possessed few if any slaves and produced only small quantities of marketable crops (Hughes 1985; Johnson 1997, pp. 40–60; Klein 1990, pp. 10–27). As late as 1770, only 6,000 (8.7 percent) of South Carolina's 76,000 slaves lived in the back country. In contrast, 30,000 (61 percent) of the colony's 49,066 free inhabitants resided in this region, and they were virtually unconnected to the export trade dominated by the low country.[13] Over the next twenty years, the back country's share of both free and slave population increased, the latter having risen by nearly 400 percent to slightly more than 29,000 by 1790 and accounting for 27 percent of the state's slave population.[14] Although this shift of the population set the stage for the ascendance of cotton at the end of the century, rice planters remained the dominant employer of slaves.

In contrast to South Carolina, the economic histories of Georgia and North Carolina remain relatively unexplored. Georgia got a late start, and a disappointing one to its founders, but after the prohibition on slavery was lifted its economy grew more quickly. Its success paralleled that of South Carolina, and by the end of the colonial period it too could boast of being home to some of the wealthiest colonists in British America (Chaplin 1993; Egnal 1998, p. 99). Unlike its southern neighbors, North Carolina had only a small export sector.

Although the colony exported some naval stores, tobacco, and wheat, for the most part its economy resembled that of the back country of South Carolina (Egnal 1998, pp. 114–17).

Although the disparities between colonies and regions have been pointed out by other scholars (see, for example, Chaplin 1993, pp. 4–8 and chap. 8; Coclanis 1989, pp. 75–76; Egnal 1998, p. 117), their implications for the course of economic growth have not been pursued in previous discussions of the region's economic history. Exports benefited only a minority of the region's population. Slaves never reaped any of the fruits of this success, of course, but export-based success also escaped the majority of the free population. To understand the performance of the entire economy, we need to look beyond the low country's rice exports. We need, that is, to assess the contributions of every sector of the southern economy, including the nonstaple agricultural segments.

2. THE METHOD

The measurement of a nation's or a region's aggregate output, such as gross domestic product, is one way in which all aspects of the economy can be taken into account. Such statistics add up the output of the dynamic sectors as well as the sluggish ones and present a composite view of the economic activities. There are no such national income statistics available for the colonies, nor is there enough evidence to compile the sort of national income accounts that have been prepared for the nineteenth century. To circumvent this paucity of data, we have used the controlled conjectural method of estimation to produce approximations of the Lower South's gross domestic product.[15] GDP, as commonly defined, measures the value of output produced within the domestic economy regardless of the ethnic background or nationality of the people involved in producing it.[16] Because we are interested in gauging the importance of the economic activity of Native Americans, and because their residences were located more widely and changed more often than those of the colonists and their slaves, we have defined the region broadly to include Tennessee, where many Cherokee resided.

Like the conjectures about the early nineteenth century by David (1967) and Weiss (1992, 1994), those we report here should not be given the same status as estimates prepared today by national income accountants or the extensions backward into the nineteenth century by Kuznets (1946) and Gallman (1966). Our work is best viewed as a quantitative experiment about the likely course of economic progress, rather than as a precise estimate of the course of real aggregate product. In order to generate estimates of aggregate output we have had to resort to using some average figures and stylized facts. The values selected for some variables may not have occurred in the specific year to which we refer, perhaps not in any year, but should represent what likely occurred, on average, around the time of each benchmark date. Those likely values enable us to establish a baseline performance for the region that can not only represent the best estimate of economic growth but can also be used to conduct experiments using other values for selected variables.

We have generated separate estimates of output produced by the Native Americans and output produced by the colonists and their slaves. The latter figure is more akin to the measure that has been used in previous discussions of the period and is the chief focus of our empirical work. The estimate of production by Native Americans is more experimental but provides illuminating results, especially when combined with the estimate for the non-Indian population. As Mancall and Weiss did in an earlier work, we refer to this more comprehensive figure as a "multicultural" estimate.[17] Because of the difficulty of disentangling some economic activity of Native Americans from that of the colonists, we believe this multicultural estimate may be a more reliable gauge of aggregate production than either of the separate estimates.

We report here on the estimates of GDP per capita that exclude the value of home manufacturing and farm improvements.[18] GDP is the sum of the conjectured values of the output produced in three sectors: agriculture, housing, and nonagricultural industries.[19] Because the estimation proceeds backward in time—that is, we take the values available for each of the components in the base year of 1800 (1770 in some cases) and then extrapolate them backward to earlier years—the base year figures take on added significance.[20] It is these known pieces of information that set bounds on the growth that could have occurred over the preceding century.[21] These base-year values are summarized in Table 14.1 and compared to values for the nation as a whole.

In order to extrapolate the 1800 value of GDP per capita to earlier years, we followed the method espoused by Paul David. Output per person (GDP/P) in any year equals the product of the labor force participation rate (LF/P) and output per worker. Output per worker in turn can be written as a weighted average of output per worker in agriculture (a) and nonagriculture (n), where the weights are each sector's share of the labor force.[22]

$$GDP/P = (LF/P)[S_a(O/LF)_a + S_n(O/LF)_n] \qquad (1)$$

In the absence of time-series evidence on output per worker in the nonagricultural industries, David assumed that productivity there grew at the same rate that it did in agriculture. As a result, at any point in time $(O/LF)_n = k(O/LF)_a$, where k is the ratio of sectoral productivities in some given year. With that modification, and the fact that $S_n = (1 - S_a)$, the equation becomes:

$$GDP/P = (LF/P)[S_a(O/LF)_a + (1 - S_a)k(O/LF)_a]. \qquad (2)$$

As can be seen, very little information is needed and changes in GDP per capita arise from only three things: changes in the participation rate, changes in agricultural output per worker, and shifts in the distribution of the labor force out of agriculture.

We have modified this equation in one way in order to make our baseline estimates.[23] We have treated shelter as an independent sector rather than subsume it in either agriculture or nonagriculture. We have done so because we did not want the value of shelter output to influence the calculation of output per worker in either of the other sectors. Although shelter output arose in both agriculture and nonagriculture, in neither case was it produced directly by labor. Our estimating equation is:

$$GDP/P = (LF/P)[S_a(O/LF)_a + (1 - S_a)k(O/LF)_a] + O_s/P \quad (3)$$

In order to solve this equation for each of our benchmark years we need information on four items: the population; the labor force and its distribution between agriculture and nonagriculture; the values of agricultural output, including exports; and the value of k. David had available to him estimates for

Table 14.1
Estimates of GDP and components in the base year of 1800: United States and Lower South (U.S. dollars, prices of 1840)

	United States: Non-Indian Population		Lower South: Non-Indian Population		Ratio of per Capita Values: Lower South to United States
	Totals ($000s)	Per Capita ($)	Totals ($000s)	Per Capita ($)	
GDP, narrowly defined ($)	351,522	66.24	64,362	58.98	0.89
Agricultural Output					
Food (consumption)	158,653	29.37	30,185	27.66	0.94
less intrastate food imports	—	—	1,146	1.05	NA
Food production	158,653	29.37	29,039	26.61	0.92
Firewood	35,258	6.64	6,662	6.10	0.92
Agricultural exports abroad	17,806	3.36	6,309	5.76	1.71
Agricultural exports to other states	—	0.00	1,637	1.50	NA
Nonagricultural Output					
Shelter	29,187	5.50	3,758	3.44	0.63
Nonagricultural output (residual)	113,410	21.37	16,990	15.77	0.74
Labor Force (000s)	1,713		428		0.25
Agricultural	1,262		344		0.27
Nonagricultural	451		84		0.19
Output per Worker ($)					
Agricultural	168		127		0.76
Nonagricultural	251		202		0.80
Ratio of Output per Worker:					
non-agricultural to agricultural (k)	1.50		1.59		1.06

Notes: Population figures for the United States and the Lower South are from U.S. Bureau of the Census, 1975, series A-7. The population of the Lower South includes that in Georgia, North Carolina, South Carolina, and Tennessee. The figures for GDP and its components for the United States in 1800 were taken from Mancall and Weiss (1999).

Easterlin (1960) estimated that per capita income for the Lower South in 1840 was equal to between 81 and 89 percent of the per capita figure for the nation, when GDP is measured exclusive of the value of home manufacturing and farm improvements. We used the higher of these ratios in order to maximize the possibility of economic growth in the century leading up to 1800.

The per capita food figures for free adults (those aged 10 and over) and free children (aged 0–9) in the Lower South in 1800 were assumed to equal the average of the national figures for those population groups in 1839, 1849, and 1859. The latter figures were calculated from data in Gallman (1960), table, A-2, and U.S. Census Bureau (1975, series U-215 and 216). See Mancall, Rosenbloom, and Weiss (2002a) for further details.

The value of firewood per person for the nation was taken from U.S. Department of Agriculture (1942), table 2. We used the reported figures on firewood consumed for the South Atlantic (North Carolina, South Carolina, and Virginia) for the periods 1790–99 and 1800–1809 to calculate a per capita figure for the Lower South. We further assumed that slaves consumed one-half the quantity consumed by free persons.

The export figure is explained in the notes to Table 14.2.

Food imports from other states in 1800 were assumed to equal that for 1770 (see Table 14.2). For exports to other states in 1800, we used the evidence on interregional shipments in the period 1840 to 1860 compiled by Fishlow (1964) to put the figure at $1.50 per person in 1800.

The value of shelter services equals 22 percent of the value of the stock of dwellings in 1798 adjusted for omitted each of these, although he did make some improvements and modifications to them.[24] We have had to construct each of these series, except that for total population.[25]

Labor Force Estimates

The labor force series was derived by using the procedures set out by Lebergott (1966) and Weiss (1992) to produce estimates for the nineteenth century. The total labor force is the sum of the estimates of the number of free male workers, free female workers, male and female slave workers, and male and female Native American Indian workers, all aged 10 and over.[26] The labor force in each population category is the product of the estimated population in that category and an assumed labor force participation rate.[27] We estimated the agricultural labor force as the product of the rural population aged 10 and over and a specified rural agricultural participation rate plus a similar estimate for the urban population. The rural agricultural participation rates were based on the evidence for the nineteenth century. We assumed that those rates declined for all workers over the course of the eighteenth century at the same rate that they changed for free workers in the first half of the nineteenth century. Although this rate of decline was slow, 0.09 percent per year, we believe this imparts some slight bias to the changes in the agricultural labor force, in effect slowing down the growth of the farm labor force, which in turn biases upward our measured growth in output per worker and thus output per capita as well. As we show below, the impact of this bias is not large and suggests our best estimates are robust with regard to this specification.

---

values (Weiss 1992, table 1.2; Pitkin 1967; Soltow 1989; and Soltow and Land 1980). The flow was revalued in prices of 1840 by using the deflator for the gross rental value of farm dwellings estimated by Towne and Rasmussen (1960) to obtain a per capita figure for free persons of $4.80. We assumed that the value of slave dwellings was equal to the value of dwellings located in rural areas and valued at less than $100, which amounted to only $2.77 per person. Using a service flow of 22 percent we obtain the annual value of shelter of $0.60 per slave.

The residual nonagricultural output is the difference between the total GDP and the estimates of all the other components. This residual encompasses all nonagricultural output, except shelter. Thus it includes the output of manufacturing, mining, construction, final services flowing to consumers, the value of government services, and investment spending.

The labor force figures are from Weiss (1992), modified as follows. Weiss's earlier estimates assumed that the share of the slave population aged 10 and over in 1800 (and 1810) was equal to that for 1820, namely 65 percent. The evidence we have compiled in the current research indicates that the 65 percent figure is too low. We derived an alternative value (68 percent) by interpolating between the shares found for the colonial period and the 1820 figure.

Agricultural Output

We estimated the value of agricultural output as the sum of food that was produced for consumption within the colonies (f), firewood (w), and those agricultural products that were exported (x). The food produced for consumption
within the region (f) equals the food consumed (c) less the value of any imports
of food (m). Agricultural exports can be divided into those shipped abroad (x_f)
and those shipped to other colonies (x_c). We treat all this agricultural output as
though it were marketed in order to place a value on it and to make our estimates
comparable in scope to those for the early part of the nineteenth century.

The dominant component of agricultural output in the colonies was food,
and regrettably there are no time-series data on this item for the eighteenth
century. Its production can be approximated, however, by the value of consumption if allowance is made for the import and export of food items.
Although there is no time-series evidence on consumption, we believe there is
enough information about the diets of colonists and slaves to permit a reasonable approximation of the likely values of food consumed.

Existing documents provide evidence on the diet or its components, and on
the value of providing a specified diet for a number of different groups in the
population: free settlers, soldiers, slaves, prisoners, charity cases, and so on.
The evidence comes from a variety of sources, such as official colonial records,
court cases, committee hearings, travelers' accounts, plantation records, and
vestry minutes. The records of the Trustees of Georgia, for example, contain
well-documented evidence on the monthly costs of maintaining those persons
sent over to the Colony, and reported as well the standard provisions for maintenance of settlers (Candler 1904–16, vol. 3). The specified diet included beef
or pork, rice, peas, flour, beer, molasses, cheese, butter, spice, sugar, vinegar,
and salt. Moreover, the different quantities of each were specified for adult
males, adult females, children, and servants.[28] The colonial records for Georgia
and South Carolina also reported expenditures on provisions for troops,
including in some instances slaves and Indians.[29] The evidence from South
Carolina indicates that the value of provisions provided to soldiers declined
over the period from 1734 to 1756.[30]

Vestry minutes are another rich source of evidence on weekly, monthly,
and annual maintenance and in some cases cover a long span of time.[31] The

minutes from St. Paul's Parish in North Carolina, for example, contain over 200 entries about the provision of maintenance between 1727 and 1776. The assortment of evidence indicates there was very little change in the average allowance.[32] The evidence also indicates that the allowance for children ran between one-half and two-thirds that of an adult.

Information about the slave diet is scarcer, making assessments about changes in the diet over time especially uncertain.[33] It may very well be that there was little change in the slave diet. After all, it was not highly varied in the nineteenth century, and the quantities of food planters provided had to be sufficient to provide the calories and protein necessary to carry out the arduous work of producing rice or indigo. In the nineteenth century, the value of a slave's diet equaled about 75 percent that of a free person. The information we have found for the colonial period would put the relative value anywhere between 20 percent and 75 percent.[34] In other words, the value of the slave diet may have risen substantially or remained constant over the eighteenth century.

Based on this variety of evidence, we have assumed in our baseline conjecture that the value of an adult colonist's diet rose from 1720 to 1800 at an annual average rate of 0.25 percent per year. The diet surely had its ups and downs with the state of the harvest and with the booms and busts of the economy, but the underlying trend value was likely rather steady.[35] The evidence is more clear that the diet of a slave differed from that of a colonist, and that of an adult colonist differed from that of a child. We have assumed that the value of a child's diet remained at 50 percent of an adult's diet for the entire century.[36] In estimating the diet of a slave, we assume that its value increased from around 50 percent of a colonist's diet in 1700 to 75 percent in 1800.[37] With these assumptions we have calculated the value of food consumed at each benchmark date.

Although international trade data are more abundant, as would be expected given the nature of the relationship between the colonies and Great Britain, the coverage is not comprehensive for the earlier years of the colonial era or for the period from 1772 through 1790. Moreover, we wanted a series on only domestically produced agricultural exports, not one that included re-exports.[38] The notes to Tables 14.1 and 14.2 explain how we constructed the

Table 14.2

Per capita value of agricultural output for colonists and slaves in the Lower South, 1720–1800

| Year | Food Production ($) | | | | Agricultural Exports ($) | | | Agricultural Output |
	Food Consumed	Less Food Imported	Food Produced	Firewood	Abroad	To Other Colonies	Total	
1720	22.69	0.76	21.94	4.12	13.15	2.55	15.70	41.75
1740	23.12	2.80	20.31	4.11	15.11	1.87	16.98	41.40
1770	24.84	1.05	23.80	5.74	10.97	1.41	12.37	41.92
1800	27.66	1.05	26.61	6.10	5.76	1.50	7.26	39.97
			Average Annual Rate of Change (%)					
1720–1770	0.18	0.64	0.16	0.67	-0.36	-1.18	-0.47	0.01
1720–1800	0.25	0.41	0.24	0.49	-1.03	-0.66	-0.96	-0.05
1720–1740	0.09	6.78	-0.38	-0.01	0.70	-1.54	0.39	-0.04
1740–1770	0.24	-3.25	0.53	1.12	-1.06	-0.94	-1.05	0.04
1770–1800	0.36	0.03	0.37	0.20	-2.12	0.21	-1.76	-0.16

Notes: The value of food consumed per capita is a weighted average of the value consumed by the colonists and that consumed by the slaves, and the average for the colonists is a weighted average of that consumed by an adult and that consumed by a child, where the weights are their respective shares of the population. Children are those under the age of 10. We assumed that the per capita consumption figure for free adult colonists increased at an average annual rate of 0.25 percent per year between 1720 and 1800. The per capita figure for slaves was assumed to equal 75 percent that of a colonist in 1800. Based on Kahn's (1992) estimate of the least-cost diet for slaves, we set the 1700 figure at 75 percent of our 1800 figure and assumed that the value increased at a constant rate between 1700 and 1800. See Mancall, Rosenbloom and Weiss (2002b) for further details.

The estimate of food imports from and agricultural exports to other colonies for 1770 comes from Shepherd and Williamson (1992, table 2). We used statistics on tonnage entering and clearing Charleston (Clowse 1981, table C-11) to estimate the value of food imported from and the value of agricultural exports to other colonies at eight dates between 1717 and 1768–72. We assumed that the real value of intracolonial shipments comprised the same share of all shipments (foreign and coastal) at each of those dates that they did in 1770. In order to obtain the value for any specific benchmark date we interpolated between the nearest years for which we had estimates.

Agricultural exports abroad includes only those exports produced domestically. We first established a benchmark figure for agricultural exports from the Lower South to all countries in 1770 by multiplying the quantities of seven major exports reported by Shepherd and Walton (1972, pp. 210–227) by the 1840 prices of each and then inflating those figures to cover all exports. The seven items are rice, indigo, naval stores, cotton, deerskins, tobacco, and wood products, which combined accounted for 88 percent of all exports from the Lower South in 1768–72. We then extrapolated that benchmark figure forward to 1800 based on changes in the constant dollar value of those same major exports and extrapolated it backward to 1720 using a volume index based on the export of rice, deerskins, indigo, and naval stores (see Nash 1992, table 6; and Mancall, Rosenbloom and Weiss 2001a and 2002b).

desired series of export values in constant prices as well as the methods we used to estimate food imports from and agricultural exports to other colonies, the value of firewood produced, and the value of shelter provided.

3. EMPIRICAL RESULTS

The results of our conjectures are shown in Table 14.3. We have focused on the period beginning in 1720 because that date seems to best divide the region's history into an early period of experimentation and adjustment and the subsequent period based on rice exports, and because we have more reliable and complete statistics on some of the key variables that make up our conjectures. We have presented statistics for only four benchmark dates and focus on the likely trend values to avoid the impression that we have constructed a complete series on colonial GDP. Even with only these four points the results are very illuminating.

The most noteworthy result is that the conjectured trend in real GDP per capita (narrowly defined) reveals no growth over the colonial period (1720–70) or over the entire period 1720 to 1800. Instead, GDP per capita declined by about $1.00 over the eighty years.[39]

Within the colonial period the region experienced some positive success between 1740 and 1770, when GDP per capita rose at 0.06 percent per year, a result that appears to owe more to the domestic sector than to export growth. Exports in total rose over the period at 2.8 percent per year, but this was slower than population growth, with the result that the per capita value of exports abroad declined by 1.06 percent per year (see Table 14.2). Shipments of agricultural products to other colonies also did not change much on a per capita basis over that period. In that time period, GDP per capita was boosted by the domestic sector—that is, by the production of food and firewood. The former rose by $3.50 per capita and the latter by $1.60. Food production increased to some extent because the region substituted domestic production for importation from other colonies. We estimate that the value of food imported from other colonies declined by $1.75 between 1740 and 1770.

That performance contrasts sharply with the record of the previous twenty years. Between 1720 and 1740, exports abroad surged upward by 5.9 percent in

Table 14.3
Controlled conjectural estimation of GDP per capita, 1720–1800

Year	Ratio of Labor Force to Population	Output per Worker	Intersectoral Shift Effect	Value of Nonshelter GDP per Capita	Value of Shelter per Capita	GDP per Capita
Estimated Value						
1720	0.487	$106	1.12	$57.62	$2.30	$59.92
1740	0.491	102	1.11	55.65	2.38	58.02
1770	0.477	107	1.11	56.44	2.57	59.01
1800	0.392	127	1.12	55.54	3.44	58.98
Index Value (1720 = 1.00)						
1720	1.00	1.00	1.00	1.00	1.00	1.00
1740	1.01	0.96	0.99	0.97	1.03	0.97
1770	0.98	1.01	0.99	0.98	1.12	0.98
1800	0.81	1.19	1.00	0.96	1.50	0.98
Average Annual Rate of Change (%)						
1720–1770	−0.04	0.01	0.02	−0.04	0.22	−0.03
1720–1800	−0.27	0.22	0.00	−0.05	0.51	−0.02
1720–1740	0.05	−0.18	0.04	−0.17	0.17	−0.16
1740–1770	−0.10	0.14	0.00	0.05	0.26	0.06
1770–1800	−0.65	0.57	0.03	−0.05	0.98	0.00

Notes: The labor force was estimated as the product of the population aged 10 and over times the labor force participation rates, with separate estimates being made for slaves and free persons. The participation rates are those for 1800 (Weiss 1992). The agricultural labor force is the sum of the rural and urban agricultural labor forces. The agricultural participation rates were assumed to change over time at the same rate that they did in the period 1800 to 1860 (see Weiss 1992). Agricultural output used to calculate the output per worker is from Table 14.2. The intersectoral shift effect measures the impact of changes in the distribution of the labor force between agriculture and nonagriculture and equals $S_a + (1 - S_a)k$.

The three input values (cols. 1–3) are multiplied to produce the extrapolated value of GDP per capita. The independent estimate of the value of shelter is then added to the extrapolated value to obtain the full measure of GDP, narrowly defined (excluding home manufactures and farm improvements). The indexes are calculated from the input values reported in panel A.

Per capita values of shelter in 1800 of $4.80 for free persons and $0.60 for slaves are from Table 14.1. We used an index of change in the stock of dwellings to extrapolate the 1800 figure backward to 1700. We based the index on Jones's (1980, p. 78) estimate of the rate of growth of wealth per capita between 1700 and 1725, 1725 and 1750, and 1750 and 1774, and Gallman's (1992, p. 95) estimate of the rate of growth of the real value of structures between 1774 and 1799.

the aggregate and 0.7 percent per year on a per capita basis. In this period, however, GDP per capita declined at a rate of 0.16 percent per year, held in check by the slow growth of the food- and firewood-producing sector. The latter did not change on a per capita basis, while the former declined by about

$1.50. The lower per capita food production is attributable to the combined effects of the increase in the slave share of the population, which lowered per capita food consumption and increased imports of food consumed in the region. The per capita value of food imports from other colonies rose by $2 between 1720 and 1740. Thus some of the growth of exports abroad appears to have been accomplished by shifting resources out of the production of food for the local market.

The performance in that period of great export success indicates the extent to which the slower-growing food- and firewood-producing part of the agricultural sector could influence the overall rate of growth. In subsequent years the food-producing sector was less of a drag, whereas the export sector was unable to maintain its rapid pace of growth. Export growth slowed so much that the per capita value of exports grew very little between 1740 and 1770 and then declined after 1770. In those circumstances the region was fortunate to have had the larger, slower-growing food- and firewood-producing sector, which plowed ahead steadily.[40]

Clearly, any picture of colonial success that rests on the performance of the export sector alone is likely to misrepresent the true course of change. This should not be too surprising. Exports were a relatively small part of the economy. They have received a great deal of attention because they were the raison d'etre for British colonization, they were at the heart of political debate, and statistics have been readily available. Moreover, exports from the region grew quite rapidly in the aggregate—3.2 percent per year between 1720 and 1800— so that sector would appear to have been dynamic and capable of generating sustained growth. Population, however, was simply growing more quickly, in excess of 4.0 percent per year for the entire period.

Lying behind the growth in GDP per capita that had occurred were increases in output per worker. Over the longer term our estimates of agricultural output and the labor force engaged therein yield growth of output per worker of 0.22 percent per year for the entire period 1720 to 1800, but only 0.01 percent for the colonial period.[41] In the post-1770 period, output per worker surged ahead by 0.57 percent per year. By assumption, the rates of growth of nonagricultural productivity were the same. These rates of advance, especially the rate after 1770, but even the longer-term rate of 0.22, are quite rapid in comparison with what took place in the nineteenth century. Over the first half of the nineteenth century agricultural output per worker rose at an annual rate of 0.24 percent. The late antebellum period showed a higher rate, 0.57 percent per year between 1840 and 1860, but in the opening twenty years of the century the rate was only 0.14 percent per year (Weiss 1993, table 2).

The reason why these fairly high rates of productivity growth did not translate into more rapid growth of output per person is that the labor force was declining relative to the population, especially after 1770. This reflects three things: the changing importance of the slave population and its labor force, whose workers were employed more heavily in agriculture than were free workers; an increase in the share of the slave population under the age of 10; and an increase in the share of the free population made up of women and children, whose participation rates were lower than that of adult males. Before 1740 the slave share of the population had been rising, and its favorable effect on the participation rate largely offset the influence of the other shifts in the composition of the population. After 1770 all these forces worked in the same direction to lower the overall participation rate.

4. SENSITIVITY OF THE RESULTS

In order to construct our conjectures we made a number of assumptions that influence the results. The most noteworthy of these is our assumption that the value of the colonists' diet rose over the entire period at a rate of 0.25 percent per year. In the following text we discuss the implications of altering this and several other assumptions on which our estimates rest. Some of the assumptions may seem arbitrary, but we believe we have chosen a reasonable approximation in each case. In two cases, those involving the relative growth of nonagricultural productivity and the rate of decline in the share of the rural population engaged in agriculture, we chose the middle road of several alternatives. In a third case, we chose to allow the value of the slave diet to rise over the period, which seemed reasonable but has the effect of raising the estimated rates of growth.

Our assumption that nonagricultural output per worker grew at the same rate as that in agriculture is based on the evidence available for the period 1800 to 1860, or perhaps we should say on the conflicting and ambiguous evidence for that period. Modern-day intuition may suggest that nonagricultural productivity grows faster than agricultural, but such intuition is not always a good guide to past performance. The evidence for the nineteenth century indicates that nonagricultural productivity did not always increase faster than agricultural.[42] Within the period 1800 to 1860, there were twenty-year periods in which the ratio rose and twenty-year periods in which it fell, so we chose to assume no change and thus put the trend between those two conflicting values.[43] Had we instead assumed that the value of k had increased at 0.21 percent per year, as it did between 1820 and 1840, GDP per capita would have risen by 0.03 percent per year between 1720 and 1800, not much above our baseline estimate of -0.02 percent. Or, had we assumed that the value of k declined by 0.24 percent per year, as occurred between 1840 and 1860, GDP per capita would have declined at 0.09 percent per year.

Our best estimates also rest on the assumption that the share of the rural population, both free and slave, engaged in agriculture declined over time at the same rate that the share of the free population engaged in agriculture declined in the first half of the nineteenth century. No doubt one can argue that the share declined faster or more slowly than this. For one thing, the fraction of the free rural male population aged 16 and over declined faster between 1800 and 1860, at 0.16 percent per year, roughly twice the rate that we have assumed.[44] On the other hand, it seems unlikely that the entire rural labor force shifted out of agriculture at the same speed that the free population did in the nineteenth century, and especially unlikely that the slave labor force did so. The decline in the shares over the eighteenth century might have been slower than in the nineteenth century for two reasons. First, the rate of productivity growth in agriculture was likely slower in the eighteenth century than in the nineteenth and would have brought about a more gradual shift of the labor force out of agriculture for any given growth in demand. Second, because incomes were higher and growing more rapidly in the nineteenth century, the higher income elasticity of demand for nonfarm products would have induced a more rapid shift in the composition of output away from farming. Moreover, the evidence we have from probate samples for the colonial period indicates no decline in the relative importance of agricultural occupations between the 1720s and the 1760s.[45]

Our assumptions about the speed of movement out of the agricultural labor force have two implications for productivity growth. First, this estimate influences the rate at which the nonagricultural labor force increased. If the rate of growth of the nonagricultural labor force is biased upward, this gives an upward bias to the estimates of GDP growth because it increases the weight of the sector with the relatively higher average productivity.[46] Second, a too rapid rate of shift out of agriculture biases upward agricultural productivity growth and simultaneously biases upward the growth of nonagricultural productivity.

Despite this dual importance, the empirical consequences were not that great. If we had allowed the rural agricultural participation rate to decline at the faster rate found for free males aged 16 and over, GDP per capita would have risen at 0.07 percent between 1720 and 1800 rather than declined at the 0.02 percent we estimate. Had we assumed there was no change in the rural agricultural participation rate, then GDP per capita would have declined by 0.14 percent per year between 1720 and 1800.

A third assumption underlying our best estimates is that the value of the slave diet rose by 25 percent over the period, or at an annual rate of 0.29 percent. There seems no possibility that the slaves' diet could have increased any faster than this. Our assumed rate is based on the diet in 1720 being the minimum-cost diet necessary to provide the calories and protein needed for the slaves to carry out their tasks. The initial year's value could not have been any lower, while the ending year value for 1800 seems quite reliable because it rests on the more extensive literature about the treatment of slaves in the antebellum period. If anything, the slave diet may have increased more slowly because the initial year's value may have been higher than the minimum diet, and the 1800 figure may have been lower than the figure we have specified, which described the diet in the late antebellum period. If we had assumed that there was no change in the value of the slave diet, then GDP per capita would have declined by 0.08 percent per year from 1720 to 1800, and by 0.22 percent per year in the colonial period from 1720 to 1770.

Estimates of the value of food consumed by the colonists are the crux of the matter, and so our assumptions about those items are critical. We have assumed in our baseline case that the value of the colonists' diet rose over the century at 0.25 percent per year. That rate is based on a comparison of the value of the diet specified for an adult by the Rules for Georgia for 1735 with the figure we estimated for 1800. Those figures of $31 in 1735 and nearly $37 in 1800 imply the average annual increase of 0.25 percent we have assumed in our baseline case. This is a healthy advance in the value of the diet considering that it does not reflect any increase in the costs of distribution. Moreover, such an increase is likely too great for all the region's free inhabitants. The diet specified in the Rules for Georgia was for those charity cases being transported to the colony. Their diet is likely to have been inferior to the average diet of colonists residing in the longer-established and wealthier colonies of Carolina. Thus we think that our assumed rate in the baseline case is an upper bound on the growth of the diet.

The sensitivity of the results to changes in the rate of growth of the diet can be seen if we make an alternative assumption that the diet did not change over the period. In this instance, GDP per capita would have declined by 0.12 percent per year between 1720 and 1800. This alternative scenario about food consumption and production yields rates of growth of agricultural output per worker that seem more plausible than those in the baseline calculation. The baseline results showed rates of growth of output per worker that were equal to those for much of the nineteenth century. In light of the fact that the nineteenth century witnessed a greater degree of mechanization, economies of scale associated with the westward movement, and improvements in yields resulting from scientific advances in agriculture, it seems unlikely that output per worker could have risen as fast in the colonial period as it did in the first half of the nineteenth century.[47] With the value of the diet unchanged, the implied rates of productivity growth seem more plausible. Between 1720 and 1800, output per worker would have advanced at 0.12 percent per year, about half the rate found in the baseline case.[48]

5. THE INDIAN EXPERIMENT

We have also produced estimates of GDP and its components for the Native American Indian population and for the combined population. These are reported in Table 14.4. This effort is more of a hypothetical experiment than the conjectural estimates for the colonists and their slaves because there are so

Table 14.4
GDP per capita for colonists and slaves, Native Americans, and the combined population

Year	Colonists and Slaves ($)	Native American Indians		Combined Values (variant I):		Combined Values (variant II):	
		Population (variant I) ($)	Population (variant II) ($)	Indian Share of Population	Combined GDP per Capita ($)	Indian Share of Population	Combined GDP per Capita ($)
1720	60	27	27	0.30	51	0.54	44
1740	58	29	29	0.12	55	0.26	51
1770	59	33	32	0.04	58	0.10	57
1800	59	33	33	0.01	59	0.04	58
Average Annual Rate of Change (%)							
1720–1770	−0.03	0.38	0.30	−3.9	0.27	−3.3	0.52
1720–1800	−0.02	0.23	0.23	−3.7	0.18	−3.3	0.36
1720–1740	−0.16	0.34	0.24	−4.5	0.40	−3.6	0.81
1740–1770	0.06	0.40	0.34	−3.4	0.19	−3.1	0.34
1770–1800	0.00	−0.01	0.11	−3.4	0.04	−3.3	0.09

Notes: Figures for colonists and slaves are from Table 14.3. The assumptions used to make the conjectures for Native Americans are described in the text and in Mancall, Rosenbloom and Weiss (2002a). The per capita value for Indians differs from variant I to variant II because the same value of deerskin exports is distributed over a different size population. The combined values are weighted averages of the per capita values for colonists and slaves and values for Indians, the weights being population shares. The Indian population figures underlying the calculations are from Wood (1989, table 1). We have interpolated where necessary by assuming constant rates of growth between figures reported by Wood. The figures used in variant I included those Indians in North Carolina and South Carolina east of the mountains plus the Creeks in Georgia and Alabama. The variant II figures include those in variant I plus the Cherokee, Choctaw, and Chickasaw. We have put the share of the Indian population aged 10 and over at 76 percent in all years, that share being the average of figures reported for 1703, 1708, and 1725 (Greene and Harrington 1932, p. 173; Klingberg 1939, p. 496).

few statistics about the economic activity of Native Americans. To carry out the exercise we have had to resort to making a number of assumptions about how much Native Americans consumed, how productive they were, and how their labor was divided between agricultural and nonagricultural work. Nevertheless, the quantitative importance of the Native American population, especially at the beginning of the period, when they accounted for somewhere between 30 and 55 percent of the region's population, and the fact that many Indians regularly engaged in commercial relations with colonists, justifies the experiment.[49]

We have made the following assumptions about the Native Americans. First, their consumption of food was equal to 75 percent of that of a free colonist at each benchmark date.[50] Second, their consumption of shelter was equal to that of slaves in 1800 and remained constant over time.[51] Third, deerskins were the only agricultural export Indians produced, and Indians received 40 percent of the value of those exports.[52] Fourth, the labor force participation rate and the agricultural share of the labor force were the same for males and females, were equal to the 1800 rates for slaves, and remained constant over time.[53] Fifth, the ratio of nonagricultural to agricultural productivity in the base year of 1800 was the same as that for the colonists and slaves (see Table 14.3).[54] Sixth, non-agricultural productivity changed at the same rate as that for agriculture.

The combination of these assumptions yields an output per capita for Native Americans that rose slowly over time, reflecting primarily that the value of their diet was assumed to have risen at the same rate as that for the free colonists. The levels of GDP per capita and changes in the value differed slightly with differences in the scope of the Indian population, but in general Indian GDP per capita ran between $27 and $33. The figures rose from around 45 percent of the value of GDP per capita for the colonists and their slaves in 1720 to around 56 percent in 1800. The more noteworthy effect of including Native Americans shows up in our multicultural estimate of the value of output per capita for the combined populations. That figure increased noticeably over the course of the period, from $51 in 1720 to $59 in 1800 using the smaller Indian population figure, and from $44 to $58 using the more comprehensive measure of the Indian population. These results are, of course, a manifestation of the relative decline in the importance of the Native American population and the role of food consumption in our method of estimation. Native Americans were a much larger portion of the population in 1720 than in 1800, and their consumption standard was a fraction of the non-Indian population. Their inclusion pulls down the weighted average consumption per capita in 1720 but has little effect on the 1800 figure, making for an increase in food consumption for the entire population of $6.00. This increase in food production to meet this consumption in turn contributed to the positive rate of productivity advance in agriculture and helped push up GDP per capita. The rates of growth of GDP per capita for this combined population ran between 0.2 and 0.4 percent per year over the full period 1720 to 1800, and 0.3 to 0.5 percent during the colonial era. The latter rates resemble closely the rates of growth postulated for the colonies by McCusker and Menard and others.

6. CONCLUSIONS

Our conjectures about growth of output per capita in the Lower South indicate that the region did not advance over the course of the eighteenth century, and may even have declined slightly. The region clearly did not measure up to the rates of advance McCusker and Menard (1985) postulated for the colonies as a whole. If the Lower South's economy were the most export-oriented and one of the most successful in British America, then it seems unlikely that the growth of GDP per person for the entire British mainland colonies could have been as high as 0.5 percent per year, or even above 0.3 percent per year.

This conjectural exercise does not provide much support for the traditional and widely held view that export success led to economic growth more generally. In the period 1740 to 1770 the growth of exports combined with other favorable developments to nudge GDP per capita for the region upward. But as good a performance as exports exhibited, this period also serves to demonstrate the impact of the domestically oriented part of agriculture on the entire economy. In those years, production for the domestic sector was the more positive force. The weight of the domestic sector is even more evident in the period 1720–40. Even with export growth surging upward at 6 percent per year, the food-producing sector held the entire economy back. Had export growth continued at that high rate, the economy might have fared better in subsequent years when the domestic sector was not such a drag. Export growth did not continue at that high rate, however. Instead of pushing up output per capita to ever greater heights, exports appear to have contributed some degree of volatility to the region's economy.

These results make clear how important it is to take into account all parts of the economy. The emphasis in previous research on South Carolina, and in particular the low country's export and economic success, has fostered a misleading view of the performance of the entire region. The low country was only a portion of the region, and in demographic terms a dwindling one at that. The economic activity taking place in the more populous North Carolina and in the rapidly growing back country of South Carolina played a large role in shaping the region's economic performance.

Our conjectures have focused on the per capita value of GDP because of its relationship to the standard of living. Only if the per capita value rises can we know that the expansion of the economy has made its members better off *on average*. But our focus on the per capita figures may downplay the region's success. The region's aggregate economy and population were growing rapidly in the eighteenth century. Colonists had more children because they felt they could afford to and because the children would eventually become productive workers; others migrated there because the economy looked attractive to them. These responses are signs of a successful economy. Indeed, the fact that the region's economy could forge ahead in the wake of such population increases attests to its capabilities.

Part of the reason why the per capita figure rose so slowly, or not at all, is because the population was growing rapidly and in ways that held growth in check. Throughout the period the share of the population under the age of 10 was increasing; after 1770 the free share of the population was increasing and that of slaves was decreasing. These shifts served to hold down and indeed decrease the labor force participation rate; the number of dependents was rapidly increasing. The population was growing by adding people who were not as productive as full-time workers. As a consequence, even though workers were becoming more productive, the impact of the improvement in productivity was muted because of the decline in labor inputs per capita due to the demographic shifts.

The region's economy included others besides colonists and slaves. Though these newcomers became a majority of the population, at the beginning of the colonial period they were but a minority. The economy created by the colonists and slaves had innumerable connections to the economy of Native American Indians, and not only in the deerskin trade; as we have argued elsewhere, Indians' participation in clearing land, preserving peace, and provisioning traders, among other activities, renders incomplete any measure of the region's economy that does not take into account Indians' varied economic activities (Mancall, Rosenbloom, and Weiss 1999b). If the impact of the Native Americans is taken into account, the performance of the colony looks a bit better. This of course reflects the assumptions underlying our conjectures about the Indians' economic performance, and the actual picture could have been much different. Still, however different the economic performance of the Indians might have been, their numbers were initially so large and the demographic shift so pronounced that the colony's economy had to have been affected. Our conjectures highlight the dimensions of this contribution.

The favorable impact of this momentous demographic shift, however, highlights the shortcomings of relying on a measure of tangible output such as GDP to gauge the progress of a society. Progress in this case was purchased at the expense of a large segment of the society. The measured increases in GDP per capita were obtained in effect by removing some of the capitas, not by making everyone better off in some average sense. This is clearly not what Kuznets and others had in mind when they developed national income statistics. These estimates of GDP per capita for the multiethnic population—that which includes the Native Americans—are not a good measure of improvement for that society. Rather, they serve to highlight the ways and extent to which the colonists may have benefited from being part of this society, and from becoming the dominant portion of it.

Notes

1. McCusker and Menard (1985, pp. 52–57) argue that output per capita increased between 0.3 and 0.6 percent per year. The lower rate was achieved by England, which they argue set the lower bound for the colonies; the higher rate reflected their view that because the colonies had started out far behind they likely grew faster than the mother country. Egnal (1975, pp. 191–222) puts the growth at 0.5 percent per year between 1720 and 1775, while Jones (1980, p. 78) puts it around 0.4 percent per year. Taylor (1964, pp. 427–44), however, asserts a much faster rate of 1.0 percent per year.

2. David's controlled conjectural technique was based on the work of Kuznets (1952) and has been extended by Weiss (1992).

3. The impetus for this shift was the 1995 conference "The Economy of Early British America: The Domestic Sector," organized by John McCusker.

4. For the colonial period this region is conventionally defined as including what would become the states of Georgia, North Carolina, and South Carolina. Because one of our goals is to incorporate into our conjectures the economic activity of American Indians, we also include what came to be Tennessee. Its inclusion has little impact on any of our results.

5. See Coclanis (1989) and Egnal (1998), among others.

6. All figures are real dollars expressed in 1840 prices. These estimates are similar in concept to the earlier conjectures made by David (1967), Weiss (1992 and 1994), and Mancall and Weiss (1999) in that the scope of coverage is consistent regarding the extent to which marketed and nonmarketed output is measured.

7. Much of their wealth was in the form of slaves. If measured by nonhuman wealth, these regions were about equal to the rest of the colonies; see Jones (1980, p. 54).

8. McCusker and Menard devote almost their entire discussion on the Lower South to South Carolina and mention North Carolina and Georgia only in passing (1985, chap. 8).

9. North Carolina's share of total regional population fell from around 65 percent in 1700 to about 50 percent at the end of the century, while South Carolina's

share of regional population rose from 35 percent in 1700 to a peak of 50 percent in 1730, before falling back to around 35 percent at the end of the century. Slaves, however, made up a much larger share of South Carolina's population— constituting a majority for most of the eighteenth century. As a result, South Carolina contained 85 percent of the region's slave population in 1700, and although the numbers of slaves in Georgia and North Carolina grew more rapidly than those in South Carolina, at the end of the century South Carolina still accounted for 43 percent of the region's slaves (U.S. Bureau of the Census 1975, Series A-7, and Z-1–19).

10. Cattle raising, production of naval stores, and the deerskin trade were also important activities (Menard 1996, p. 275; Dethloff 1982, p. 233; Clifton 1981, p. 274; Nash 1992, pp. 679–81).

11. British bounties made the indigo crop commercially attractive, and because it was less bulky than rice it was less affected by the wartime rise in shipping costs. Moreover, since it could be grown on lands not suited to rice cultivation and its peak labor demands did not coincide with those of rice cultivation, planters could add indigo without substantially reducing their commitment to rice (Gray 1958, p. 289).

12. Perhaps the most important effect was the reduction in the slave population occasioned by the war. The conflict interrupted the importation of slaves and resulted in significant losses to the existing slave population. Although data are imprecise, it is estimated that approximately 25,000 slaves died, ran away, or were carried off by the British during the war (Morgan 1983, p. 111; Gray 1958, p. 596).

13. In 1768–72, average annual exports per capita in Carolina's low country averaged £3.7 for the entire population, and a whopping £17.1 for the white population. The back-country figure was a mere £0.5 (Coclanis 1989, p. 75).

14. The rapid expansion of cotton cultivation beginning in the early 1790s perpetuated this shift, so that close to 44 percent of the state's slaves were living in the back country in 1810.

15. An alternative measure would be gross national product. The difference between domestic product and national product amounts to the net balance of factor payments to and from foreign nationals, which for most of American history has not been very large. For the colonial era the differences are likely to have been larger, and their size would depend on which population was thought of as the national one. The value of either measure would depend to a large extent on how one treated Indians and their output, and because Indians made up a much

larger portion of the population in 1700 than in 1800, the divergence between domestic and national product would have been larger at the earlier date.

16. The "economy" is commonly defined by the geographic boundaries of the country, but it is subject to other interpretations and has been applied differently in some instances. See, for example, Metzer (1995) and Butlin (1986). For the colonial period it is difficult to speak strictly of domestic or national product because geographic boundaries were ambiguous and fluid, and the British and Indian populations resident in the Lower South were citizens of other nations.

17. Butlin (1986) coined this the term to describe the estimates he prepared for Australia.

18. The exclusion of these unconventional items is not as serious a matter as it might appear. We have not excluded these items because they were unimportant, but rather because they were likely more important in 1720 than in 1800. Their inclusion would raise the level of GDP in all years, but more so in 1720, and would thus bias downward the estimated rate of economic growth.

19. Nonagricultural output, other than the value of shelter, encompasses a wide variety of items: the value of manufactured goods (including those exported); investment; and services, including the value of government services.

20. These 1800 figures are in effect *known* values. They are not known with the precision or completeness of official statistics, but they were taken from existing work and were not generated by our conjectures.

21. The GDP per capita figures in 1800 for the region were based on the national estimates by Weiss (1992, table 1.4). David's (1967) estimates for 1800 are lower than Weiss's and would thus dictate less growth for the preceding century. In both cases, the figures were conjectured in ways that leave the 1800 figures unbiased by business-cycle influences that may have occurred.

22. David used the input values to calculate an index of output per capita in each benchmark year that was then used to extrapolate the base year's (1800) dollar value of GDP per capita to each of the earlier years, but one can solve the equations directly.

23. In our sensitivity analysis we also allow nonagricultural productivity to increase faster than agricultural productivity; that is, we allow the value of k to rise over the period.

24. David had evidence on three of the four, and for lack of time-series evidence on sectoral productivities assumed a constant value of k based on the evidence for 1840.

25. The free and slave population figures were available in U.S. Bureau of the Census, *Historical Statistics,* series Z15–19; McCusker and Menard 1985, p. 182; and Coclanis 1989, p. 64; the Native American population figures come from Wood 1989, pp. 38–39. We had to estimate the age and sex distributions. The evidence we have found for the colonies of the Lower South indicates that the share of the free and slave population that was aged 10 and over, and thus more likely in the labor force, declined over time: from around 69 percent in 1720 to 63 percent in 1800 for the free population and from 79 percent to 68 percent for slaves. The share of Native American Indians aged 10 and over appears to have been constant. See Chaplin 1993; Klingberg 1939; Menard 1995; Morgan 1983; Wood 1974; and Weiss 1992.

26. The figures for 1800 included separate estimates for free males and females aged 10–15 and those aged 16 and over (Weiss 1992).

27. The participation rates were those specific to the Lower South in 1800 (Weiss 1992). Although we assume that these rates were constant over time for each population component, because the rates differed across the components, the average for the entire population changed over time.

28. We have calculated the value of this diet to equal $31 per adult male in prices of 1840. The diet for women and children aged 12 and over was calculated to be 83 percent that of a male; that for children aged seven to twelve was specified be half that for those aged 12 and over; and that for those aged two to seven was one-third. Apparently no provisions were provided for those under two years of age (Candler 1904–16, vol. 3, pp. 408–09).

29. See, for example, the expenditures for Oglethorpe's siege of St. Augustine (Candler 1904–16, vol. 2, pp. 159–202. Gallman (1971, pp. 71–78) argued that military rations seem like a reasonable proxy for food consumption by the colonists.

30. The figures, converted to dollars and valued in 1840 prices, were $32 in 1734 and $22 in 1756. It may be that the soldiers were expected to obtain some of their provisions by hunting and fishing, and perhaps increasingly so over time as suggested by the decline in the allotment after 1736 (CRSC, vols. 1, 2, 7, and 14).

31. Vestry minutes are the records of the church parishes. Parishes had the primary responsibility for the care of the poor and could levy taxes to finance their activities (Brown 1928; Watson 1977). The expenses reported for maintaining wards of the church reflect the deliberations of those on the scene familiar with the standard of living in the vicinity and the costs of providing for it (Salley 1919; Fouts 1999).

32. This was most evident in allowances made for terms of six months or longer. Mancall, Rosenbloom, and Weiss (2002b) discuss this evidence further.

33. Morgan (1998, pp. 135–43) argues there were differences in slave diets across regions, and slaves in the low country produced more food on their own time than did those in the Chesapeake. His evidence, however, does not suggest much about changes over time.

34. CRSC, vol. 2, p. 493, and CRSC, vol. 3, p. 377. The relative value of 20 percent seems too low. The figures lying behind that ratio imply annual values of $46 for a free person and $9 for a slave (in prices of 1840). The value seems very low for slaves and high for free persons, thus yielding much too low a relative figure for slaves.

35. We think this is the upper bound on the rate of growth in the diet. See Mancall, Rosenbloom, and Weiss (2002b).

36. If instead we had assumed that the child's diet equaled 75 percent of an adult's, food consumption and production per capita would have been $3 to $4 higher in each year, but growth would have been about the same.

37. We based this beginning year value on Kahn's estimate for the "least-cost diet with minimum fat requirements" using the medium price of pork (Kahn 1992, table 25.5, p. 532). That estimate equaled approximately 75 percent of the cost of the diet specified by Fogel and Engerman or Sutch, which in turn was equal to 75 percent of the cost of a free person's diet. Thus we assumed that the value of the slave diet in 1800 equaled 75 percent that of a free person, and the value in 1700 equaled 75 percent of the 1800 figure—that is, 56 percent of a free person's diet—and that it changed at a constant rate between those two dates.

38. Re-exports were especially large from 1793–1806 and were not reported by state or region, so we estimated the values of domestically produced exports using a volume index of change in the seven most important components of the region's exports. See the notes to Table 14.2 and Mancall, Rosenbloom, and Weiss (2001a) for further details.

39. We have constructed a terms of trade index and used it to calculate a trade-adjusted GDP series, which shows about the same amount of change as the unadjusted series over the entire period 1720 to 1800.

40. Changes in the value of food exports to and imports from other colonies appear to have had little bearing on the long-term rate of economic growth, but fluctuations in those values, especially in the import of food from northern colonies, affected the pace of growth in specific subperiods. Clearly the role of intracoastal trade deserves further investigation.

41. These high rates of productivity growth stem in part from our assumption that the rural labor force (slaves as well as free) shifted out of agriculture at the same rate that it did in the nineteenth century.

42. See Gallman (1971), Engerman and Gallman (1981), and Weiss (1994). The specific figures discussed in the text come from the worksheets underlying Weiss (1992 and 1994).

43. The rate of change over the entire 1800 to 1860 period was 0.06 percent per year—virtually unchanged.

44. Specifically we have assumed that the fraction of the *rural* population engaged in agriculture declined at 0.09 percent per year.

45. Bentley's (1977) summary of probate inventory data shows that the share of farmers and planters rose from 44 percent of all decedents in 1722–26 to 53 percent in 1757–62. If those decedents whose occupation was listed by Bentley as "other" were primarily agricultural workers, however, then the proportion of agricultural occupations would be 89 percent in 1722–26 and 93 percent in 1757–62.

46. As shown in Table 14.1, we estimate that nonagricultural productivity was 59 percent higher than agricultural in the Lower South.

47. Moreover, the rates of productivity growth implied by our conjectures are noticeably higher than those derived from other independent evidence about the pace of productivity change in agriculture in the Lower South (see Mancall, Rosenbloom, and Weiss 2002a).

48. The advance between 1770 and 1800 is a bit more plausible than the base case rate, but is still high at 0.48 percent per year.

49. Recent work by Baron, Hood, and Izard (1996) indicates more frequent and greater integration than previously believed. The interaction of course varied over time and across regions. For more discussion of these issues, see Mancall, Rosenbloom, and Weiss (1999b).

50. Evidence from Oglethorpe's expedition against St. Augustine indicates that the value of an Indian diet may have been as low as 30 percent that of a male colonist (CRSC, vol. 2, pp. 175–201). We think this is too low, perhaps because Indians on expeditions were expected to have foraged for much of their food. We have instead put the relative value at 75 percent in all years, assuming thereby that the Indians' diet was no less valuable than that of slaves.

51. It is possible, perhaps likely, that Indian housing was more valuable than that of slaves, but there is little evidence to suggest that it improved over the eighteenth century. See Williams (1989) and Waselkov and Braund (1995).

52. See Brown (1975, p. 123) and Murphy (1998, pp. 153–55). The proportion of the final price of deerskin exports that the Indians may have received appears to have been around 40 percent in the early 1700s. It may have risen to a peak near the middle of the century and then fallen back. For our initial conjectures we have assumed the 40 percent figure was the long-term trend value.

53. The average labor force participation rate for all male and female Native Americans and the industrial composition of that employment is unlikely to ever be known with great accuracy because there was variation across tribes in the extent to which men and women engaged in the different tasks and because there are no statistical compilations of their economic activities. There is little question that agriculture engaged most of the workers, especially when agriculture is defined to include hunting and fishing, as it is in our conjectures. In most tribes there was a clear sexual division of labor: women were the predominant workers in crop agriculture, while men helped with the clearing of land and were engaged primarily in hunting and fishing. We have assumed that the agricultural share of the labor force was 86 percent, the same share as that for slaves in 1800. See for example Brown (1995); Bonvillain (1989, pp. 1–28); Cronon (1983, pp. 40, 44–48); and Mancall, Rosenbloom, and Weiss (1999a).

54. The level of productivity differed, with productivity of Indians ranging between 35 and 45 percent that of colonists and slaves.

References

Baron, Donna, Edward J. Hood, and Holly V. Izard. 1996. "They Were Here All Along: The Native American Presence in Lower-Central New England in the Eighteenth and Nineteenth Centuries." *William and Mary Quarterly*, 3d ser., 53: 561–86.

Bentley, William George. 1977. "Wealth Distribution in Colonial South Carolina." Ph.D. dissertation, Georgia State University.

Bonvillain, Nancy. 1989. "Gender Relations in Native North America." *American Indian Culture and Research Journal* 19.

Brown, Kathleen. 1995. "The Anglo-Algonquian Gender Frontier." In Nancy Shoemaker, ed., *Negotiators of Change: Historical Perspectives on Native American Women.* New York: Routledge.

Brown, Philip M. 1975. "Early Indian Trade in the Development of South Carolina." *South Carolina Historical Magazine* 76: 118–28.

Butlin, N. G. 1986. "Contours of the Australian Economy." *Australian Economic History Review* 26: 96–147.

Candler, Allen D. 1904–16. *The Colonial Records of the State of Georgia.* Compilations of transcripts of records in the Public Record Office begun by Allen D. Candler and completed by William J. Northen and Lucian Lamar Knight.

Chaplin, Joyce E. 1993. *An Anxious Pursuit: Agricultural Innovation and Modernity in the Lower South, 1730–1815.* Chapel Hill: University of North Carolina Press.

Clifton, James M. 1981. "The Rice Industry in Colonial America." *Agricultural History* 55: 266–83.

Coclanis, Peter. 1989. *The Shadow of a Dream.* New York: Oxford University Press.

Cronon, William. 1983. *Changes In the Land: Indians, Colonists, and the Ecology of New England.* New York: Hill and Wang.

Crouse, Maurice A. 1977. *The Public Treasury of Colonial South Carolina.* Columbia: University of South Carolina Press for the South Carolina Tricentennial Commission.

CRSC (Colonial Records of South Carolina). 1959–89. *Journals of the Commons House of Assembly.* 14 vols. J. H. Easterby et al. Columbia: South Carolina Department of Archives and History.

David, Paul. 1967. "The Growth of Real Product in the United States before 1840: New Evidence, Controlled Conjectures." *Journal of Economic History* 27: 151–97.

Dethloff, Henry C. 1982. "The Colonial Rice Trade." *Agricultural History* 56: 231–43.

Easterlin, Richard A. 1960. "Interregional Differences in per Capita Income, Population and Total Economy." In William Parker, ed., *Trends in the American Economy,* Studies in Income and Wealth, vol. 24. Princeton, N.J.: Princeton University Press.

Egnal, Marc. 1975. "The Economic Development of the Thirteen Continental Colonies, 1720 to 1775." *William and Mary Quarterly,* 3d ser., 32: 191–222.
————. 1998. *New World Economies.* New York: Oxford University Press.

Engerman, Stanley, and Robert Gallman. 1981. "Economic Growth 1783 to 1860." *Research in Economic History* 8: 1–46.

Fishlow, Albert. 1964. "Antebellum Interregional Trade Reconsidered." *American Economic Review* 54: 352–64.

Fouts, Raymond Parker. 1999. *Vestry Minutes of St. Paul's Parish Chowan County, North Carolina, 1701–1776*. 2d ed. Cocoa, Fla.: GenRec Books.

Gallman, Robert. 1966. "Gross National Product in the United States, 1834–1909." In Dorothy Brady, ed., *Output, Employment and Productivity in the United States after 1800*. Studies in Income and Wealth, vol. 30. New York: National Bureau of Economic Research.

———. 1971. "The Statistical Approach: Fundamental Concepts Applied to History." In G. R. Taylor and L. F. Ellsworth, eds. *Approaches to American Economic History*. Charlottesville: The University Press of Virginia.

———. 1992. "American Economic Growth before the Civil War." In R. Gallman and J. Wallis, *American Economic Growth and Standards of Living before the Civil War*. Chicago: University of Chicago Press.

Gray, Lewis C. 1958. *History of Agriculture in the Southern United States to 1860*. Gloucester, Mass.: Peter Smith.

Gray, Ralph, and Betty Wood. 1976. "The Transition from Indentured to Involuntary Servitude in Colonial Georgia." *Explorations in Economic History* 13: 353–70.

Hughes, Kaylene. 1985. "Populating the Back Country: The Demographic and Social Characteristics of the Colonial South Carolina Frontier, 1730–1760." Ph.D. dissertation, Florida State University.

Johnson, George Lloyd, Jr. 1997. *The Frontier in the Colonial South: South Carolina Backcountry, 1736–1800*. Contributions in American History, no. 175. Westport, Conn.: Greenwood Press.

Jones, Alice Hanson. 1980. *Wealth of a Nation to Be*. New York: Columbia University Press.

Kahn, Charles. 1992. "A Linear Programming Solution to the Slave Diet." In Robert Fogel and Stanley Engerman, eds., *Without Consent or Contract*. Technical papers, vol. 3, pp. 522–35. New York: W. W. Norton.

Klepp, Susan. 1994. "Seasoning and Society: Racial Differences in Mortality in Eighteenth-Century Philadelphia." *William and Mary Quarterly*, 3d ser., 51: 481–82.

Klein, Rachel N. 1990. *Unification of a Slave State: The Rise of the Planter Class in the South Carolina Backcountry, 1760–1808*. Chapel Hill: University of North Carolina Press.

Klingberg, Frank J. 1939. "The Indian Frontier in South Carolina," *Journal of Southern History* 5: 479–500.

_____. 1941. *An Appraisal of the Negro in Colonial South Carolina.* Washington, D.C.: Associated Publishers.

Kuznets, Simon. 1946. *National Product since 1869.* New York: National Bureau of Economic Research.

_____. 1952. "Long Term Changes in the National Income of the United States of America since 1870." In *Income and Wealth of the United States, Trends and Structure.* International Association for Research in Income and Wealth, Income and Wealth Series II. Baltimore, Md.: The Johns Hopkins University Press.

Lebergott, Stanley. 1966. "Labor Force and Employment, 1800–1960." In Dorothy Brady, ed., *Output, Employment and Productivity in the United States after 1800.* Studies in Income and Wealth, no. 30. New York: National Bureau of Economic Research.

Mancall, Peter C., and Thomas Weiss. 1999. "Was Economic Growth Likely in Colonial British North America?" *Journal of Economic History* 59: 17–40.

Mancall, Peter C., Joshua L. Rosenbloom, and Thomas Weiss. 1999a. "Economic Activity of Native Americans." Paper presented at the meetings of the Economic History Association, Baltimore.

_____. 1999b. "Indians and the Economy of Eighteenth-Century Carolina." Paper presented at the Emergence of the Atlantic Economy Conference, Charleston, October 1999. Forthcoming in Peter Coclanis, ed., *The Emergence of the Atlantic Economy.* Charleston: University of South Carolina Press.

_____. 2001a. "Economic Growth in the Lower South, 1720 to 1800: The Role of Exports versus the Domestic Sector. Paper presented at the Social Science History Association, Chicago.

_____. 2001b. "Slave Prices and the Economy of South Carolina, 1722–1809." *Journal of Economic History,* 62: 616–39.

_____. 2002a. "Agricultural Labor Productivity in the Lower South, 1720–1800." Photocopy, University of Kansas.

_____. 2002b. "Estimates of Deerskin Exports from the Lower South, 1700 to 1800." Photocopy, University of Kansas.

_____. 2002c. "The Value of the Diet in the Lower South in the Eighteenth Century." Photocopy, University of Kansas.

McCusker, John J. 1992. *How Much Is That in Real Money? A Historical Price Index for Use as a Deflator of Money Values in the Economy of the United States.* Worcester, Mass.: American Antiquarian Society.

McCusker, John, and Russell Menard. 1985. *The Economy of British America, 1607–1789.* Chapel Hill: University of North Carolina Press.

Menard, Russell R. 1995. "Slave Demography in the Lowcountry, 1670–1740: From Frontier to Plantation Region." *South Carolina Historical Magazine* 96.

_____. 1996. "Economic and Social Development of the South." In Stanley L. Engerman and Robert E. Gallman, eds., *The Cambridge Economic History of the United States.* Vol. 1: *The Colonial Era.* Cambridge, England: Cambridge University Press.

Metzer, Jacob. 1995. "Two Peoples in One Country: A Comparative Look at the Economic Record and Socio-Economic Profile of Mandatory Palestine." Paper presented at the International Economic Association Eleventh World Congress, Tunis, December.

Morgan, Philip D. 1983. "Black Society in the Lowcountry, 1760–1810." In Ira Berlin and Ronald Hoffman, eds., *Slavery and Freedom in the Age of the American Revolution.* Charlottesville: University of Virginia Press.

_____. 1998. *Slave Counterpoint: Black Culture in the Eighteenth-Century Chesapeake and Lowcountry.* Chapel Hill: University of North Carolina Press for the Omohundro Institute of Early American History and Culture.

Murphy, Edward. 1998. "The Eighteenth Century Southeastern American Indian Economy: Subsistence vs. Trade and Growth." In Linda Barrington, ed., *The Other Side of the Frontier: Economic Explorations into Native American History.* Boulder, Colo.: Westview Press.

Nash, R. C. 1992. "South Carolina and the Atlantic Economy in the Late Seventeenth and Eighteenth Centuries." *Economic History Review* 45: 677–701.

Pitkin, Timothy. [1816] 1967. *A Statistical View of the Commerce of the United States.* Reprint, New York: Augustus Kelley.

Salley, A. S., Jr., ed. 1919. *Minutes of the Vestry of St. Helena's Parish, South Carolina, 1726–1812.* Columbia: Historical Commission of South Carolina.

Shepherd, James, and Gary Walton. 1972. *Shipping, Maritime Trade and the Economic Development of Colonial North America.* Cambridge, England: Cambridge University Press.

Shepherd, James, and Samuel Williamson. 1972. "The Coastal Trade of the British North American Colonies, 1768–1772." *Journal of Economic History* 32: 783–810.

Soltow, Lee. 1989. *Distribution of Wealth and Income in the United States in 1798.* Pittsburgh, Penn.: University of Pittsburgh Press.

Soltow, Lee, and Aubrey Land. 1980. "Housing and Social Standing in Georgia, 1798." *The Georgia Historical Quarterly* 64: 448–58.

Taylor, George R. 1964. "American Economic Growth before 1840: An Exploratory Essay." *Journal of Economic History* 24: 427–44.

Towne, Marvin, and Wayne Rasmussen. 1960. "Farm Gross Product and Gross Investment in the Nineteenth Century." In William Parker, ed., *Trends in the American Economy*. Studies in Income and Wealth, vol. 24. Princeton, N.J.: Princeton University Press.

U.S. Bureau of the Census. 1975. *Historical Statistics of the United States*. Washington D.C.: U.S. Government Printing Office.

U.S. Department of Agriculture. 1942. "Fuel Wood Used in the United States, 1630–1930." Circular no. 641. Washington, D.C.: U.S. Government Printing Office.

Waselkov, Gregory A., and Kathryn E. Braund. 1995. *William Bartram on the Southeastern Indians*. Lincoln: University of Nebraska Press.

Weiss, Thomas. 1992. "U.S. Labor Force Estimates and Economic Growth, 1800 to 1860." In R. Gallman and J. Wallis, eds., *American Economic Growth and Standards of Living before the Civil War*. Chicago: University of Chicago Press.

———. 1993. "Long Term Changes in U.S. Agricultural Output per Worker, 1800–1900." *Economic History Review* 46: 324–41.

———.1994. "Economic Growth before 1860: Revised Conjectures." In Thomas Weiss and Donald Schaefer, eds., *American Economic Development in Historical Perspective*. Stanford, Calif.: Stanford University Press.

Williams, Michael. 1989. *Americans and Their Forests: A Historical Geography*. Cambridge, England: Cambridge University Press.

Wood, Peter H. 1974. *Black Majority: Negroes in Colonial South Carolina from 1670 through the Stono Rebellion*. New York: Knopf.

———.1989. "The Changing Population of the Colonial South: An Overview by Race and Region, 1685–1790." In Peter H. Wood, Gregory A. Waselkov, and Thomas M. Hatley, eds., *Powhatan's Mantle*. Lincoln: University of Nebraska Press.

15

THE VALUE-ADDED APPROACH TO THE MEASUREMENT OF ECONOMIC GROWTH

Mark Thomas and Charles Feinstein

I

Problems of measurement lie at the heart of two of the most lively debates in British economic historiography: how far economic growth accelerated at the end of the eighteenth century, and how far it slowed down at the end of the nineteenth. The pace and timing of any changes in the rate of industrial growth are central to our interpretation of the meaning of the Industrial Revolution.[1] Likewise, accurate measurement of the nature and timing of changes in the dominant industrial sector is vital if there is to be an accurate assessment of the extent and sources of Britain's relative economic decline in the late Victorian and Edwardian periods.[2]

This chapter represents a preliminary investigation of some crucial aspects of the measurement of production in past periods. We hope the results will in due course enable us to make a contribution to both debates about economic growth in the United Kingdom. After 1850 real GNP in Britain can be measured using all three variants of the national income procedure—the income, expenditure, and value-added approaches. Unfortunately, there are some marked inconsistencies between the different estimates, most notably in the period from the mid-1890s to World War I, during which the income-based estimates point to a striking slowdown in the progress of real incomes. This is strongly supported by other indicators, such as the abnormally high level of industrial unrest and other signs of social and political discontent. Nothing comparable is evident in the output series, and it has not been possible to reconcile the discrepancies by reference to factors such as a redistribution of income in favor of capital or an adverse movement in the international terms of trade.[3] One possible explanation is that there are deficiencies in the output indices, and this issue needs investigation.

Before 1850 the sources of information are more limited, and growth rate estimates must effectively rely on the output approach. The results can to some extent be checked against series for real wages (Feinstein 1998) and also—as in the dual approach adopted by Antràs and Voth (2003)—by data on factor prices. Nevertheless, the absence of suitable information on income or expenditure means that it is vital that the accuracy of the output series is not compromised by imperfect procedures if we are to fully understand the growth record during British industrialization.

In order to improve the estimates of real product derived from the output side it is necessary to have better procedures and/or better sources both for (a) the measurement of real value added in the individual sectors and subsectors that make up the aggregate GDP index, and for (b) the value-added weights by which these components are combined. In the present chapter we wish to investigate both these topics, though our primary concern is with the former. This is, in some sense, a more fundamental issue, because it affects the way in which the component value-added series are constructed. It is, however, a less well known issue, at least among historians, who have focused a good deal recently on matters of weighting (especially with regard to the question of growth during early industrialization).[4]

II

The standard view among official statistical agencies and national income accountants is that net output should be measured at constant prices by revaluing both the current value of gross output and the current value of the inputs of materials, fuel, etc., and subtracting the latter from the former. This is known as "double deflation," or the Fabricant-Geary approach (Fabricant 1940; Geary 1944). If the value of output for any sector is $P_Q Q$, and the value of the inputs is $P_M M$, where P_Q and P_M are the respective prices and Q and M

the respective quantities, then double deflation provides a measure of the real value of net output, V_d, where:

$$V_d = (P_Q Q/P_Q - P_M M/P_M) = Q - M \qquad (1)$$

However, it is equally widely agreed that the method is difficult to apply in practice because it requires so much data. Furthermore, because V_d is derived as the difference between two other series, it will also be very sensitive to errors in the measurement of those series, particularly if value added is small relative to Q and M. Thus, after describing the computation of ideal indexes of physical output, Fabricant concluded that the construction of "indexes of net physical output . . . was impossible with the available data. Therefore we have followed what appeared to be the next best procedure: we have combined the indexes of gross physical output for individual industries, with value added as the weight, to measure the output of major groups and total manufacturing output" (1940, p. 33).

In the United Kingdom the typical response to the problems of double deflation has been to rely—as Fabricant did—on some measure of the movement in real *gross* output, and to assume that this provides an acceptable measure of real *net* output (see Office for National Statistics, 1988). This measure might be a direct indicator of physical output, such as yards of cloth or gallons of beer produced, or a series for the nominal value of gross output (for example, the value of deliveries) deflated by an appropriate price index. Failing that, some physical measure of material inputs (pounds of raw cotton, bushels of malt) could be used as a proxy or, in the last resort, numbers employed (adjusted if possible for hours worked) or the use of electric power.

This has been the most common approach in historical research in the UK. The classic analysis of British industrial production, by Hoffmann (1955), used such indicator methods throughout, as did the later study by W. Arthur Lewis (1978). GNP estimates on this basis are published annually by the Office for National Statistics for the economy as a whole, and historical series were compiled by Feinstein (1972).

In the United States a similar procedure using series for gross output was adopted for the industrial sector by Edwin Frickey (1947) for 1860–1914 and—as already noted—it also underlies the estimates of manufacturing output by Fabricant (1940) for 1899–1937. For the modern period, an index running from 1919 to the present time is compiled by the Federal Reserve Board (see, for example, 1985). However this methodology has not been extended to other sectors of the economy, and both the historical and the contemporary estimates of real GNP for the United States are estimated from the expenditure side, using either the output of final products for consumption and capital formation deflated by appropriate price indices or the corresponding quantities valued at base year prices; or alternatively series for real GNP are derived by deflation of total incomes.[5]

For estimates made in the modern period, the use of gross output indicators as a substitute for measurement of real value added may work reasonably well, because the base years are updated at frequent intervals and there is little scope for any marked discrepancies between gross and net output to emerge. However, historical estimates typically cover very much longer periods without a change in the base year; for example, both Lewis and Frickey have only one base year for indices covering fifty or more years.

The issue of how best to measure real value added in production sectors was carefully considered in the initial phase of national income accounting, but there has been little reference to the problems in more recent historical analysis, and we think it is now timely to consider how far the existing measurements might be defective on this account. There is also another reason why this is an appropriate topic for this volume. Although we have said that the double-deflation procedure was widely recommended during the formative period during which national income conventions were laid down, there was not universal agreement on this matter. Almost forty years ago Paul David, then a young assistant professor at Stanford, published a paper written while he was a Fellow of Alexander Gerschenkron's Economic History Workshop at Harvard (David 1962). David criticized double-deflation methods on the grounds that they may produce the nonsense result of negative value added, noting that this problem arises whenever "the relative product and material prices in any given year reflect a particular technological nexus between the quantity of input and output which is not appropriate to the production situation of another year" (David 1962, p. 153).[6]

In order to deal with the "potentially nasty index number problems raised by the residual deflation procedure," David (1962, p. 154) initially recommended that the net output of individual sectors of the economy be deflated by an index "reflecting the prices which the factors of that industry paid in making their final demand purchases." The particular attraction of this solution to the national income accountant is that it produces a result that is consistent with the expenditure deflation procedure used to produce real national product at factor cost. However, although David suggested a possible short-cut by assigning separate expenditure deflators to "property-income receivers and service-income receivers" respectively, and then combining these according to their weights in each sector's value added, he recognized the serious statistical limitations of this solution. Indeed, in a later paper, David (1966) noted that, by recommending that the Fabricant-Geary method be abandoned with no definitive empirical replacement for calculating real value added, he had thrown the baby out with the bath water.

David originally rejected the application of industry gross output deflators because it implicitly treats the payments to the factors as "being made in the commodities they produce, valued in the prices of the base year" (1962, p. 155). However, his further reflection on the subject led him to conclude that the best means to "retrieve the lost child" of real net output was to deflate "the industry's current dollar value added (or gross income originating) directly by an index of the industry's final product price" (1966, p. 420). In what Bent Hansen subsequently described as "impeccable" logic (1974, p. 415), David derived this solution from the first-order conditions for profit maximization in a perfectly competitive environment with constant returns to scale. In such a situation, the final price of the industry product will be precisely equal to the weighted average of the marginal products of the factor inputs—that is, the real price of value added. This second solution is elegant and, moreover, can never produce negative measurements of real net output, thus overcoming the peculiar problem of double deflation that motivated David's first contribution.

David's two essays stimulated a flurry of papers approaching the problem of real value added from the production side, out of which a consensus finally emerged.[7] The substance of the consensus is that there is an ideal measure of real value added, which is consistent not only with the theoretical precepts of production function analysis, but also with the national accounting requirement that the estimate of real GNP should be the same whether measured by deflation of net output or of final expenditure.[8]

III

The ideal measure may be derived from a simple production function, in which there are three factors, labor (L), capital (K), and materials (M), which combine to produce gross output (Q). The form of the production function may be written as:

$$Q = f(K, L, M), \tag{2}$$

which we assume to be well-behaved, twice-differentiable, and linearly homogeneous.[9] Differentiation of the function yields:

$$dQ = F_L\, dL + F_K\, dK + F_M\, dM \tag{3}$$

or

$$\frac{dQ}{Q} = \frac{F_L L}{F} \frac{dL}{L} + \frac{F_K K}{F} \frac{dK}{K} + \frac{F_M M}{F} \frac{dM}{M}, \tag{4}$$

where dQ/Q is the weighted sum of the rates of change in individual products within the industry (which we will henceforth write in rate of change form as $\dot{q}$) and likewise for the elements on the right-hand side.

By applying the economic assumption that $F_M = P_M/P_Q$, etc. (that is, that factor demands are governed by relative prices), we may rewrite equation 4 in rate-of-change form as:

$$\dot{q} = s_l\dot{l} + s_k\dot{k} + s_m\dot{m}, \tag{5}$$

where $s_i (i = l, k, m)$ indicates the output elasticities (value shares) of the three factors.

The ideal index of real value added may in turn be derived by defining value added as the contribution of primary factors (labor and capital) to total output. Thus,

$$\dot{v} = \frac{s_l\dot{l} + s_k\dot{k}}{s_l + s_k}. \tag{6}$$

This demonstrates that changes in real net output should be measured as the weighted sum of capital and labor inputs, where the weights are established by the marginal productivity conditions.

If it is further assumed that the production function is homogeneous to degree one (constant returns), the value shares sum to one, and substituting equation 5 into equation 6 produces:

$$\dot{v} = \frac{\dot{q} - s_m \dot{m}}{1 - s_m} = \frac{\dot{q} - s_m \dot{m}}{s_v} \tag{7}$$

which indicates that real value added may be calculated from the difference between changes in gross output and material inputs, appropriately weighted.[10] This is the Divisia index of real value added.

The same result may be approached from the accounting side. Define value added as the difference between the value of gross output and the cost of materials or intermediate inputs and value it in nominal terms. Thus,

$$P_V V = P_Q Q - P_M M. \tag{8}$$

Differentiation of (8) yields:

$$P_V \, dV = P_Q \, dQ - P_M \, dM, \tag{9}$$

which may be rewritten as:

$$P_V V \frac{dV}{V} = P_Q Q \frac{dQ}{Q} - P_M M \frac{dM}{M}. \tag{10}$$

After simple manipulation and conversion to rate-of-change form, this may be expressed as:

$$\dot{v} = \frac{\dot{q} - s_m \dot{m}}{s_v}, \tag{11}$$

which is identical to equation 7.

The Divisia index is thus the "ideal" measure of real value added, whether approached in terms of national income criteria or by applying production theory. It has the distinct advantage over conventional double deflation that it cannot produce negative value added.

The David strategy of deflating nominal value added by the industry's output price is also immune to negative outcomes, so on this basis there is no reason to prefer the Divisia to the David index. But it is important to recognize that these two methods differ in their treatment of changes in the prices of materials relative to final products and are thus essentially measuring different concepts of real product. This can be seen by defining David's single-deflated value added (V_S) from the accounting side as:

$$V_S = \frac{P_Q Q - P_M M}{P_Q}. \tag{12}$$

Differentiating equation 12 yields:

$$dV_S = dQ - (P_M/P_Q)\, dM - M d(P_M/P_Q), \tag{13}$$

which may be rewritten in rate-of-change form as:

$$\dot{v}_s = \frac{\dot{q} - s_m \dot{m}}{s_v} - \frac{s_m}{s_v}\left(\frac{p_m}{p_q}\right). \tag{14}$$

This differs from equation 11 because of the second term, which captures the effect of any change in the relative price of materials on the single-deflated measure of real net output. This terms-of-trade factor is entirely relevant when dealing with the overall effect of changing prices on real value added as a welfare concept, but should not be incorporated in a measure of the physical productivity effects.[11] For this reason, Hansen recommends David's deflator for calculations of gross national income based on net output, but advocates excluding the terms-of-trade effect when measuring gross domestic output from the production side. These relative price effects are absent from both Fabricant-Geary and Divisia indices.

The Divisia index also avoids the problem inherent in double deflation, that results calculated with early-year weights can differ significantly from those calculated with late-year weights. In this context, however, the standard index number result is reversed: under normal market conditions, double-deflated value added will show a slower rate of growth when measured in early-year prices than in late-year prices.[12] If, for example, the prices of inputs rise relative to those of final output, there will be an incentive for firms to reduce the quantity of inputs used. Since the early-year prices are lower for materials (relative to the final product prices) than the late-year prices, they will give a lower weight to the relative decline in material inputs and will thus understate the growth of real value added. Conversely, if late-year prices are used the growth of real value added will be overestimated.

The two versions of the Laspeyres methodology thus bracket the true figure. The Divisia index, by continuously revaluing the prices, instead produces an exact application of the double-deflation method. While the Divisia index may represent the ideal index, continuous revaluation is unfortunately a purely theoretical concept that cannot be applied in practice, and its empirical implementation is normally approximated by a discrete (Törnqvist) index. The Fisher ideal index may also be a reasonable approximation if the period of time over which the indices are calculated is not too long and the movements in relative prices and quantities are not too large.

Single-value deflation is also vulnerable to index number problems, because the index used to deflate value added will itself normally be a weighted index of the prices of the various final products produced by the sector. If these are weighted with early-year prices the increase in the index will be an overestimate and the change in real value added will be correspondingly underestimated, while an index compiled with late-year prices will generate an overestimate of the growth of real value added.

A further advantage of the Divisia index is that, as noted by Sato (1976, p. 435), it is not sensitive to the level of aggregation or sectoral integration. By contrast, the results obtained by single deflation will vary according to the way in which the component sectors are defined. Thus if the cotton industry is treated as an integrated activity with cotton cloth as the final output, the measurement of real value added will be different from when it is disaggregated into yarn production and cloth production respectively. Over time, the different definitions will generate different profiles of real value added, unless the relative prices of yarn and cloth remain constant.[13]

The discussion has thus highlighted five major differences between the Divisia index and the two alternatives of double deflation and single deflation of value added, and these are summarized for convenience in Table 15.1.

IV

In this section, we extend the insights of the debate over using double- and single-deflation methods to measure real value added to the use of data on gross output (or inputs) as a substitute for the ideal Divisia index. We apply a

Table 15.1
Attributes of three measures of real value added

	1 Divisia Index	2 Double Deflation	3 Single Deflation Using Final Product Prices
Identical to real expenditure	Yes	Yes	No
Only nonnegative real value added	Yes	No	Yes
Consistent aggregation	Yes	Yes	No
Excludes effects of changes in terms of trade between input and final product prices	Yes	Yes	No
Eliminates index number problems	Yes	No	No

specific form of production function with weak separability of materials and factors.[14] This allows us to be more precise in our evaluation of the nature and direction of the bias introduced by applying either these indicators or the double-deflation or single-deflation methods rather than the preferred Divisia method.

The general form of the production form is thus:

$$Q = f(K, L, M) = g(v(K, L), M) \qquad (15)$$

where the nested form indicates a separate value-added production function within the overall production process. Following Bruno and Sachs (1985), we model this two-step process using the CES (constant elasticity of substitution) production function. In rate of change form, the production function may be represented as:

$$\dot{q} = s_v \dot{v} + s_m \dot{m} \qquad (16)$$

which is identical to equation 11, but with the added requirement that $\dot{v}$ is separable and has its own functional form, $\dot{v} = v(\dot{l}, \dot{k})$.

In the CES formulation, the product elasticities are equivalent to the shares of the each factor in total product; if we assume constant returns,[15] the sum of the shares exhausts the product. Thus, $s_v = (1 - s_m)$ and equation 16 reduces to

$$\dot{q} = s_v \dot{v} + s_m \dot{m} = (1 - s_m)\dot{v} + s_m \dot{m} \qquad (17)$$

We can extend the basic model to allow for the possibility of materials-saving technical progress. The factor demand curve for materials, derived from the augmented CES function, is:

$$\dot{m} = \dot{q} - \sigma\dot{\pi} - \dot{\lambda} \qquad (18)$$

where σ represents the elasticity of substitution between materials and factors (value-added), $\dot{\pi}$ is the rate-of-change form of Π, the ratio of the prices of materials and final output, and $\dot{\lambda}$ represents the rate of materials-saving technical progress. Since σ already captures changes in the ratio of materials to output induced by movements in relative prices, $\dot{\lambda}$ is defined as materials saving initiated for all other reasons.

Combining equations 17 and 18 permits us to restate the Divisia measure of value-added in terms of key parameters as follows:

$$\dot{v} = \dot{q} + \frac{s_m(\sigma\dot{\pi} + \dot{\lambda})}{1 - s_m}. \qquad (19)^{16}$$

This formulation may be used to judge the biases introduced by adopting one of the alternative procedures. In what follows, we examine the use of double-deflated value added (DDVA), single-deflated value added (SDVA), gross output indicators, and material input indicators as proxies for the ideal, Divisia real value-added function.[17]

Double Deflation

For double-deflated value added (V_d), we have, following equation 1 above, $V_d = Q - M$ (assuming $\Pi = 1$ at $t = 0$). By logarithmic time differentiation:

$$\dot{v}_d = \frac{Q\dot{q} - M\dot{m}}{Q - M}. \qquad (20)$$

Invoking equation 18, this can be reduced to:

$$\dot{v}_d = \dot{q} + \frac{M\sigma\dot{\pi}}{Q - M}. \qquad (21)$$

Since $Q = \dfrac{\Pi M}{s_m}$, and, therefore, $\dfrac{M}{Q - M} = \dfrac{s_m}{\Pi - s_m}$, equation 21 may be rewritten as:

$$\dot{v}_d = \dot{q} + \frac{s_m(\sigma \dot{\pi} + \lambda)}{\Pi - s_m} \qquad (22)$$

The direction and intensity of bias in using double deflation methods to capture the movement of real value added is the difference between equations 22 and 19:

$$\dot{v}_d - \dot{v} = \frac{s_m}{(1 - s_m)} \frac{(-\sigma \dot{\pi} - \lambda)(\Pi - 1)}{\Pi - s_m} \qquad (23)$$

Double deflation will only be unbiased if there is no technical progress ($\dot{\lambda} = 0$) *and* there are either fixed proportions ($\sigma = 0$) or stable relative materials prices ($\dot{\pi} = 0$). The extent of bias will approach zero as the share of materials in gross output approaches zero ($s_m \, \text{Æ} \, 0$).

In the absence of technical progress, the degree of bias is unaffected by the direction of change in relative prices. If the deflation is undertaken using early-year prices, the bias is always negative (note that $\dot{\pi}$ and $\Delta\Pi$ share the same sign). Thus, $\dot{v}_d < \dot{v}$, no matter whether materials are becoming cheaper or more expensive relative to final product prices. Moreover, the longer the time period over which the DDVA calculation is carried out, the larger the error (assuming monotonicity in relative price movements). Thus, using double-deflation methods with beginning-year prices ($t = 0$) will always understate the degree of value-added growth. Conversely, if the deflation is undertaken using end-year prices ($t = n$), the bias is always positive ($\dot{v}_d > \dot{v}$).

If $\dot{\lambda}$ is non-zero, the entire matter becomes more complicated. If we can assume that technical progress is materials-saving, such that $\dot{\lambda} > 0$, rising relative materials prices will invariably produce a negative bias in beginning-year double-deflation and a positive bias in end-year calculations. However, the bias arising from falling prices will depend on the relative strengths of technical change and the terms-of-trade effect. Technical progress diminishes the extent of bias in beginning- and end-year calculations; if it is large enough, it may neutralize or even counteract the terms-of-trade effects. Clearly, the probability of this effect increases, the smaller are σ and $\dot{\pi}$.

A comparison of equations 22 and 19 reveals that they are identical if $\Pi = 1$, regardless of the state of technical change. This would occur if the base-year were revised in each year, and a chained index of (double-deflated) value added was calculated (this is equivalent to an annualized Törnqvist approximation to the Divisia index). In practice, of course, it may not be possible to construct a chain-index; the need for continuous reweighting is equivalent to requiring annual input-output tables. It is likely that new sources of error would be introduced by stretching most historical data sources this far. However, since beginning- and end-year relative prices bracket the real-value added product, the use of a Fisher ideal index (the geometric mean of the two estimates) is a good first approximation to the desired figure. Obviously, occasional re-weighting is preferred to none at all, since the accuracy of the Fisher ideal deteriorates, the longer the time over which it is estimated.

Single-Deflation Value Added

In single deflation of value added (SDVA), both gross output and material inputs are deflated by the price of the final product. Thus,

$$\dot{v}_s = \frac{P_Q Q - P_M M}{P_Q} = Q - \Pi M, \tag{24}$$

since $\Pi = P_M / P_Q$.

Thus,

$$\dot{v}_s = \frac{Q\dot{q} - \Pi M \dot{m} - \Pi M \dot{\pi}}{Q - \Pi M}, \tag{25}$$

which reduces to:

$$\dot{v}_s = \dot{q} + \frac{s_m}{1 - s_m}[\dot{\lambda} + \dot{\pi}_m(\sigma - 1)]. \tag{26}$$

The bias in SDVA relative to the Divisia ideal can be captured by comparing equation 26 with equation 19:

$$\dot{v}_s - \dot{v} = -\frac{\dot{\pi} s_m}{1 - s_m}. \tag{27}$$

The error in applying SDVA methods for the measurement of physical productivity derives, as noted previously, from the change in the relative price of materials and final product prices over time. The degree of bias will be larger, the longer the time period over which single-deflation is employed (assuming monotonicity of relative price movements), and the larger the share of materials in total product. The direction of bias is opposite from the direction of change in relative prices (thus, if materials prices rise faster than product prices, SDVA methods will tend to understate real value added, that is, $\dot{v} > \dot{v}_s$, and vice versa). The bias in single-value deflation is inherent and cannot be removed by continuous reweighting of the factor shares. It is also unaffected by $\dot{\lambda}$, the rate of materials-saving technical progress.

Indicator Approaches

The indicator approach is, as we have suggested, the most common form of industrial production index measurement applied by historians. It is therefore important to understand the biases and limitations inherent in the use of indices of final output and material inputs.

If real gross output is used as a proxy for real value added, the bias is:

$$\dot{q} - \dot{v} = \frac{(-\sigma\dot{\pi} - \dot{\lambda})s_m}{1 - s_m}. \tag{28}$$

If an input indicator is used, the bias is:

$$\dot{m} - \dot{v} = \frac{-\sigma\dot{\pi} - \dot{\lambda}}{1 - s_m}. \tag{29}$$

In both cases, there is no bias if there is no technical change ($\dot{\lambda} = 0$) *and* either relative prices remain stable ($\dot{\pi} = 0$) or factor proportions do not change ($\sigma = 0$); in the case of gross output, the bias will tend to zero as the share of materials tends to zero ($s_m \,\text{\AE}\, 0$), regardless of the state of technical change.

The extent and direction of bias will be determined by the interaction of technical progress and relative prices. If $\dot{\lambda} = 0$, the direction depends entirely on the direction of relative prices: as materials prices fall (rise) relative to product prices, both indices will over- (under-) state changes in real value added. The extent of bias will cumulate over time, assuming relative prices move in the same direction. Technical progress in the utilization of materials will exacerbate the bias in both indicators if materials prices rise relative to output prices; it will counteract the influence of falling relative materials prices.

If the extent of technical progress is large enough, it may even reverse the direction of bias—such that a decline in P_m/P_Q could produce a negative bias ($\dot{m} - \dot{v} < 0$). The likelihood of such a bias reversal is increased the smaller are σ and $\dot{\pi}$.

Clearly, the exact nature of the biases involved in applying these alternatives to the Divisia index will depend on the size and signs of the various parameters, s_m, $\dot{\lambda}$, $\dot{\pi}$, and σ. Before we turn to a discussion of how large these biases might be in practice, there is one further finding that emerges from the preceding analysis and that it is worthwhile to mention explicitly.

We have so far been concerned solely with the correct measurement of the changes in real value added in individual sectors of the economy, but—as noted at the outset—the output approach also requires accurate measurement of the value-added weights that are used to combine these components into indices of industrial production or larger aggregates. Where a detailed census of production has been taken, the necessary information on the nominal value of gross output and on the materials, fuel, and other inputs can be obtained for a benchmark year. The absence of a census for the United Kingdom before 1907 forced Arthur Lewis (1978) to rely on a single base year for the entire period (1852–1913) covered by his index of industrial production. This not only assumes constant relationships between gross and net output for each sector over more than half a century, it is also a year that occurs almost at the very end of the period and is thus a striking example of a Laspeyres index calculated with late-year weights.

Motivated in part by the desire to obtain reliable value-added weights for an earlier year, one of us is attempting to obtain the required data for the United Kingdom in 1851 by constructing a detailed input-output table. In the absence of any form of census for either agriculture or industry, it is necessarily a highly questionable exercise, but an input-output table imposes stern discipline on one's conjectures, and the provisional (and still unpublished) outcome is thought—at least by the author—to provide a broadly reliable set of estimates. One of a number of checks that can be made is to extrapolate the estimates of value added in each industry from 1851 to 1907 and then to compare the result with the 1907 values. If this can be done successfully, the procedure can also be applied to extrapolate the estimates backward from

1851 to earlier years in order to obtain suitable weights for the construction of indices over the period of the Industrial Revolution.

The important conclusion that emerges from the previous analysis is that such extrapolation of value added cannot be done—as is sometimes suggested—simply by using indices for the quantity and price of the output produced by the sector. Assuming that the indicator of gross output ($\dot{q}$) is used to measure the change in real value added, then the correct calculation of nominal value added in the second period is the product of (a) the change in the gross output indicator, (b) the change in the final product price, and (c) the gain or loss from the change in the terms of trade implied by the ratio of the value of the single-deflated measure of real value added to the change in gross output. Calculations that exclude the third element, (c), will introduce errors in the forecasted level of value added.

V

In the previous section we have identified the parameters s_m, $\dot{\lambda}$, $\dot{\pi}$, and σ as the crucial determinants of the bias caused by measuring changes in real value added by SDVA, DDVA, or indicator methods rather than by a Divisia index. It remains to consider what the values of these key parameters are likely to have been for nineteenth-century Britain, and thus to assess the potential extent of the bias in the existing estimates.

The parameter for which we have most information, from both the 1907 census and the provisional input-output table for 1851, is s_m, the share of materials in value added. At one extreme, this can take values as low as 0.15 in extractive industries such as coal and iron ore in which the only purchased materials are ancillary items such as pit props and repairs to machinery. At the other end of the range, values of 0.8 and 0.9 are found in materials-intensive industries such as sugar refining, flour milling and non-ferrous metal production. For the majority of industries s_m falls between 0.4 and 0.7, and both mean and median are close to 0.6.

For $\dot{\lambda}$, the rate of materials-saving technical progress other than that undertaken in response to changes in relative prices, we have to think of two distinct cases. In the first, such technical advances may be both large and concentrated in a relatively short period of time. Notable examples include the coal-saving improvements in the iron industry in the 1830s following the introduction of Nielsen's hot blast (Hyde 1977, pp. 150–53), the adoption by the chemical industry of the Solvay process for the manufacture of alkalis in place of the Leblanc process in the 1850s, and the general economies in material costs at the end of the century following the growth of electricity as a source of power. In the second case, the main scope for saving materials lies in the reduction in waste: for example, the economies achieved by the British cotton industry during the American Civil War, more efficient cutting of leather or cloth, or better utilization of waste as a source for wool. The scale of such economies was clearly more limited, though it might occur more continuously. We might take values for $\dot{\lambda}$ of 0.5 percent per year to represent the case of a brief, dramatic, one-off change, and 0.1 percent per year to represent the alternative of slower but more sustained movement.

$\dot{\pi}$, the rate of change in the price of materials relative to final product prices, is potentially very volatile and can cover a wide range of possibilities, with either positive (materials relatively more expensive) or negative movements in the terms of trade. To illustrate the scope of such movements, as shown by nineteenth-century British experience, price ratios were calculated for six major industries, taking in each case only the principal raw material used. Ratios for coal and pig iron, wheat and flour, flour and bread, raw cotton and cotton yarn, cotton yarn and cotton cloth, and raw wool and woolen yarn, were calculated for five-year periods centered on 1830, 1850, 1870, 1890, and 1910 (see Table 15.2). Positive or negative rates of change between these benchmarks are typically between 0.5 and 1.5 percent per year, with occasional movements appreciably larger than this. For illustrative purposes we will use +1.0 percent per year, zero, and −1.0 percent per year.

The final parameter is σ, the elasticity of substitution between materials and the factors of production. We have no direct empirical evidence on this, though we can expect that the higher is s_m, the smaller is the potential for price-induced substitution of factors for materials. Overall, it seems reasonable to assume that the possibility of substituting labor or capital for materials was very limited, and for the purposes of the present exercises we use estimates of 0.1 and 0.5.[18]

Table 15.2
Rates of change of the price of materials relative to final product prices,
selected industries, 1830–1910 (percent, per year)

	1 Coal and Pig Iron[a]	2 Wheat and Flour[b]	3 Flour and Bread[c]	4 Raw Cotton and Cotton Yarn[d]	5 Cotton Yarn and Cotton Cloth[e]	6 Raw Wool and Woolen Yarn[f]
1830–1850	3.8	0.6	−0.7	1.0	0.4	—
1850–1870	−0.4	−0.6	0.6	0.4	1.5	0.7
1870–1890	0.8	1.5	−2.2	−0.6	−0.8	−1.2
1890–1910	1.1	−0.5	0.9	−0.3	1.2	−0.2

SOURCES: [a]Average pit-mouth value of coal in Scotland and price of Scottish pig iron (Mitchell 1988, pp. 751 and 763).
[b]Average price of wheat in England and Wales (Mitchell 1988, p. 756) and contract price of wheat flour (Board of Trade 1903, p. 99), extrapolated by retail cost of flour in London (Board of Trade 1915, p. 103).
[c]Flour as above and average price of bread in London (Mitchell 1988, p. 770).
[d]Raw cotton (Mitchell 1988, p. 760) and cotton yarn (Board of Trade 1903, p. 46), extrapolated by average export values (Great Britain 1914–16, pp. 302–3).
[e]Cotton yarn as above and gray cloth (Sandberg 1974, pp. 239–41).
[f]Raw wool (Mitchell 1988, pp. 767–68) and woolen yarn (Board of Trade 1903, p. 60), extrapolated by average export values (Great Britain 1914–16, pp. 304–5).

Table 15.3 illustrates the extent of the bias inherent in using each of the substitutes for the ideal Divisia index, applying values for the crucial parameters that reflect the historical realities of the British economy in the nineteenth century. Thus we have set s_m at the median level of 0.6, λ at 0.1 and 0.5 percent per year, σ at 0.1, and $\ddot{\pi}$ at either +1.0 percent per year, −1.0 percent per year, or zero. This produces six possible results for each measure of real value-added growth. Annual growth rates are calculated for the Divisia index (applying the Törnqvist discrete approximation), for three variants of DDVA (beginning-year weights, end-year weights, and the Fisher geometric average), for SDVA, and for the output and input indicators. In each case, it is assumed that exogenous demand conditions generated a growth in output of 2.0 percent per year and that output prices rose by 3 percent per year;[19] the demand for inputs and the price of materials are endogenously determined, according to the parameter values in the system. Table 15.3 reports the results for each measure, calculated over five-year and twenty-year periods. The table indicates that altering the period of analysis has little effect on the comparisons between measures.

Table 15.3
Rates of growth of real value added (percent per year)

	Divisia Index	Year 1 Prices	Double Deflation End-Year Prices	Fisher Index	Single Deflation	Indicators Gross Output	Input
I. Five-Year Period							
(i) $\lambda = 0.1$ *percent per year*							
$\dot\pi = +1.0$	2.32	2.31	2.35	2.33	0.73	2.00	1.79
$\dot\pi = 0$	2.15	2.15	2.15	2.15	2.15	2.00	1.90
$\dot\pi = -1.0$	2.00	2.00	2.00	2.00	3.46	2.00	2.00
(i) $\lambda = 0.5$ *percent per year*							
$\dot\pi = +1.0$	2.94	2.89	3.01	2.95	1.38	2.00	1.38
$\dot\pi = 0$	2.74	2.74	2.74	2.74	2.74	2.00	1.49
$\dot\pi = -1.0$	2.56	2.60	2.53	2.57	4.00	2.00	1.59
II. Twenty-Year Period							
(i) $\lambda = 0.1$ *percent per year*							
$\dot\pi = +1.0$	2.40	2.30	2.54	2.42	0.51	2.00	1.79
$\dot\pi = 0$	2.15	2.15	2.15	2.15	2.15	2.00	1.90
$\dot\pi = -1.0$	2.01	2.01	2.01	2.01	3.25	2.00	1.99
(i) $\lambda = 0.5$ *percent per year*							
$\dot\pi = +1.0$	3.03	2.81	3.40	3.10	1.35	2.00	1.38
$\dot\pi = 0$	2.68	2.68	2.68	2.68	2.68	2.00	1.49
$\dot\pi = -1.0$	2.46	2.57	2.37	2.47	3.61	2.00	1.59

Note: All growth rates are calculated with $s_m = 0.6$, $\sigma = 0.1$, the rate of growth of final product = 2.0 percent per year, and the rate of growth of final product prices = 3.0 percent per year.

Certain conclusions are readily apparent. On a positive note, double defla-tion produces reasonable approximations to the Divisia ideal index, at least in the short run. Clearly, the faster the rate of materials-saving technical progress, the larger the error in applying either early or late weights. However, the Fisher geometric average comes very close to the Divisia, even for quite long periods of analysis. The cumulative error of using the Fisher index over a twenty-year period when technical progress is rapid ($\lambda = 0.5$ percent per year) and relative materials prices are rising at 1.0 percent a year is only 1.5 percent as compared with the Divisia baseline (in the twentieth year, the Divisia and Fisher indices measure 181.60 and 184.29 respectively, relative to 100 in the first year).[20]

The other measures fare much less well. Single-deflation methods perform particularly poorly. Only in the case where relative prices of materials and final output remain static over the period of analysis will SDVA methods produce appropriate results. As Table 15.2 makes clear, this was not the pattern for the staple industries of Victorian Britain. Indeed, a comparison of Tables 15.2 and 15.3 indicates that SDVA methods would produce quite significant distortions to the measured rate of growth in the British economy of the nineteenth century. Thus when relative materials prices rise by 1 percent a year and λ is set at 0.1 percent a year, the cumulative error in using single-deflated value added after twenty years is over 45 percent (110.6 vs. 160.68). Similarly, when the terms of trade fall by 1 percent a year and λ is set at 0.5, the cumulative error over twenty years is in excess of 25 percent (203.5 for SDVA vs. 162.62 for Divisia).

Although the indicator approach is certainly superior to SDVA methods, it is nonetheless liable to produce substantial errors. An important finding from Table 15.3 is that the direction of the errors is consistent for all cases: both output and input measures understate the rate of economic growth.[21] The more rapid the rate of materials-saving technical progress, the larger the understatement. Although this is intuitively obvious for indicators that use material inputs to proxy real value added, it also extends (albeit to a lesser extent) to output indicators.

But we should be careful not to generalize too readily from the results of Table 15.3. This is especially true of the bias inherent in applying the indicator approach. The consistent understatement of $\dot{q}$ and $\dot{m}$ relative to $\dot{v}$ in the two panels arises because of the assumption that λ is positive. If λ were negative (such that an industry experienced materials-using technical change),[22] the direction of bias would depend on the strength of the technical impetus compared with the substitution effect generated by changing relative prices of materials and factors. In the absence of technical progress ($\lambda = 0$), both output and input indicators would understate the rate of growth of real value added if the terms-of-trade effects were positive and overstate it if materials prices rose more rapidly than output prices. A similar outcome could also result from a higher value of σ, if, in combination with the terms of trade, it generated a substitution effect large enough to offset a positive λ.

These caveats indicate the limitation of tabular representation of the extent (and even the direction) of bias when there are a number of parameters that

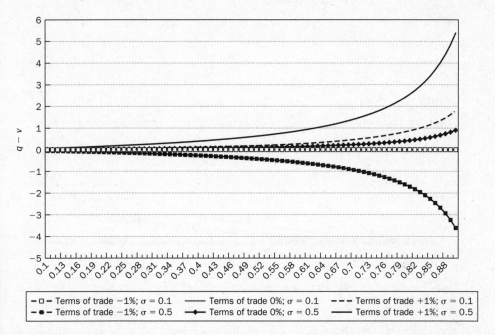

Figure 15.1 Difference between Divisia and indicator (output) measures of economic growth: $\dot{\lambda} = 0.1$

can change simultaneously. Table 15.3, for simplification, deals not only with only one value of σ, but also with a single value of s_m. The materials share in Table 15.3 was chosen to represent the median case for nineteenth-century British industry, but we have noted that there was substantial range around the value of 0.6. Moreover, the bias equations of section IV emphasize that rising values of s_m create an accelerating magnification effect, since the expression $s_m/(1 - s_m)$ tends toward ∞ as $s_m \text{Æ} 1.0$.

For these reasons, we supplement the tabular analysis with a diagrammatic representation of the bias from using physical output measures to proxy real value added. Figures 15.1 and 15.2 illustrate the impact of changes in s_m and σ on the extent of bias ($\dot{q} - \dot{v}$), given certain levels of movement in the terms of trade. The impact of changes in the share of materials in gross output is indicated along the horizontal axis, which shows values of s_m from 0.10 to 0.90.[23] The vertical axis measures the difference between $\dot{q}$ and $\dot{v}$, derived by the application of equation 28 with appropriate parameters. Of these parameters,

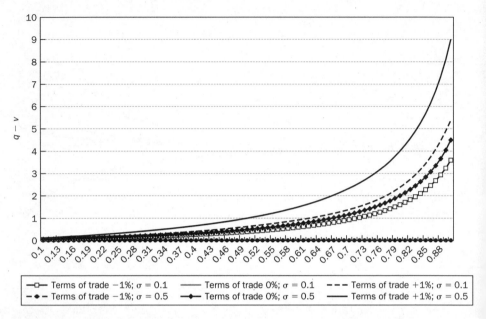

Figure 15.2 Difference between Divisia and indicator (output) measures of economic growth: $\dot{\lambda} = 0.5$

the impact of different values of σ is captured by a pair of lines that indicate the degree of bias when σ is at 0.1 and 0.5 respectively. Intermediate values of σ will produce levels of bias that fall symmetrically within these bounds. There are two such pairs of lines in Figures 15.1 and 15.2, each of which reflects a different rate of relative price movement of materials and final output. The top pair represents the impact on the bias when relative materials prices are rising at 1 percent a year. The bottom pair represents the impact on $(\dot{q} - \dot{v})$ of a decline of 1 percent a year in the terms of trade. The middle line represents the situation when relative prices of inputs and outputs remain constant. Since changing σ has no impact on the extent of bias with fixed relative prices, there is only one line for this case.[24] Finally, we accommodate different rates of materials-saving technical progress by producing separate diagrams for the cases in which $\dot{\lambda}$ equals 0.1 percent per year and 0.5 percent per year respectively.

In Figure 15.1, in which $\dot{\lambda}$ equals 0.1, there is a certain symmetry to the curves charting the effects of rising and falling terms of trade (the symmetry would be complete had $\dot{\lambda}$ been set equal to zero). The direction of bias is consistent with Table 15.3. The growth of real gross output is less than the growth of real value added if relative prices are stable or rising. The one case in which output overstates value-added growth is when the elasticity of substitution is sufficiently high (0.5) that, in combination with falling terms of trade, it overwhelms the effect of the weak materials-saving technical change implicit in the choice of $\dot{\lambda}$. The diagram makes it clear that this latter result will be replicated with values of σ above 0.1, in conjunction with declining relative materials prices at $\dot{\pi} = -1.0$ percent per year (note also that the curve will also become negative if σ is smaller than 0.1, but the terms-of-trade effect is stronger than -1.0). The impact of a higher σ is also apparent in cases when the materials are becoming relatively more expensive than final output. The upper pair of curves in the diagram show the increasing distorting effect of using output to proxy value added as σ rises.

Figure 15.1 also shows the magnification effect of s_m at work. As the materials share rises, the bias increases exponentially. Thus, for $\sigma = 0.5$, increasing s_m from 0.6 to 0.75, ceteris paribus, doubles the bias associated with a rising terms of trade of 1 percent a year (from 0.9 to 1.8 percent per year); at $s_m = 0.9$, the bias becomes 5.4 percent per year. To some extent the upper reaches of the top curve in Figure 15.1 are fiction. As previously noted, it is likely that s_m and σ will be negatively correlated, since the materials-intensive sectors have limited scope to substitute factors for inputs. But the same general effect is apparent for lower values of σ; indeed, even if there are fixed proportions ($\sigma = 0$), the negative effect of technical progress slowly rises with s_m, reaching close to 1.0 percent a year at $s_m = 0.9$.[25]

In Figure 15.2, in which $\dot{\lambda} = 0.5$ percent per year, the indicator approach systematically understates true value-added growth. The limiting case is where σ equals 0.5 and the terms of trade decline by 1 percent per year, in which case the downward bias becomes zero. Only if $\sigma > 0.5$ or $\dot{\pi} > 1$ percent per year (or some combination of these two conditions) will $\dot{q} > \dot{v}$. The higher rate of technical progress raises the level of the bias for all parameter values, although the divergence between different levels of σ for any given terms-of-trade effect is the same, no matter the rate of technical progress. Once again, it is important to think about the extent to which a single industry is likely to have been characterized by a high value of σ, a high value of λ, and a high value of s_m;

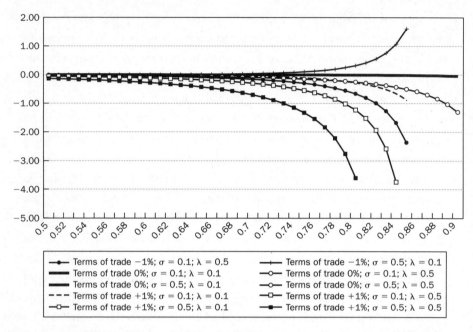

Figure 15.3 Difference between Divisia and Fisher measures of economic growth: 20-year period

nonetheless, the diagram makes clear the potential for serious discrepancies between $\dot{q}$ and $\dot{v}$, even with quite modest values of these parameters.[26]

By contrast, Table 15.3 implies that the Fisher geometric average of beginning- and end-period double-deflated value added provides a close approximation to the ideal Divisia index. But does this result hold more generally? Once again, a graphical approach is called for.

In Figures 15.3 and 15.4, we reproduce the bias between the two measures $(\dot{v}_d^F - \dot{v})$, applying the same parameter combinations as in Figures 15.1 and 15.2. Once again, the bias is measured on the vertical axis, while the horizontal axis shows values of s_m. Since the Fisher index produces measures of growth that are time-dependent, we calculate the bias for twenty and fifty years respectively. In each case, we show ten of the twelve possible combinations of the parameter values for σ, $\dot{\lambda}$, and $\dot{\pi}$. We have excluded those cases in which materials-saving technical change is fully offset by substitution of materials for factors,[27] in which case the bias between the Fisher and Divisia measures is

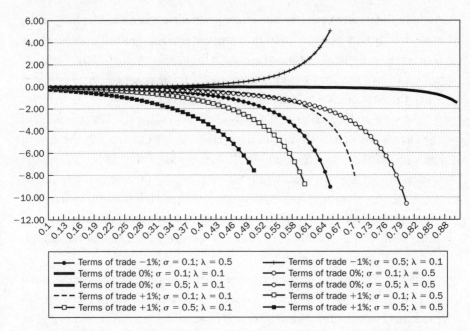

Figure 15.4 Difference between Divisia and Fisher measures of economic growth: 50-year period

zero for all values of s_m. Note also that certain of the curves are superimposed on each other; this occurs when the combined effect of the parameters produces the same difference between the growth rates of materials and final output $(\dot{q} - \dot{m})$.[28] Such cases are represented by the same line format (for example, both dotted or solid).

Figures 15.3 and 15.4 illustrate the strengths and weaknesses of using the Fisher index as a substitute for the preferred Divisia procedure. Figure 15.3 confirms the finding of Table 15.3, namely that the two indices produce very similar results for levels of s_m at or below 0.6 over a twenty-year period, even for higher levels of λ(note that the figure excludes values of s_m below 0.5, for which the difference is trivial).[29] The bias inherent in using the Fisher index becomes larger, however, as the size of s_m increases. Yet, for short periods, the error in applying the Fisher method remains low at even higher levels of s_m, other than in cases where the rate of materials-saving technical change and the elasticity of substitution of materials and value added are simultaneously high. In the twenty-year case, the errors generally remain small as long as the materials share is below 0.75. In the fifty-year case, by contrast, the errors are large even for moderate values of s_m, except in cases in which the terms of trade are stable and the rate of materials-saving technical change is small—that is, when the ratio of materials to output is largely fixed.

The scale and direction of the bias inherent in using the Fisher instead of the Divisia are directly (if nonlinearly) related to the difference in the growth rates of materials and final output. If $\dot{q} > \dot{m}$, the Fisher index will always understate the growth of real value added; if $\dot{m} > \dot{q}$, the bias is reversed. The larger the gap between $\dot{q}$ and $\dot{m}$, the greater the bias; if $\dot{q} = \dot{m}$, the two indices are identical. Thus, even if there is no knowledge of the technical coefficients, some sense of the potential errors can be gauged by examining the relative growth of inputs and outputs.

Finally, the graphs provide more evidence relating to the fundamental objection raised by Paul David to double deflation, namely the tendency to produce negative value added. If there is negative value added in either end or beginning periods, the Fisher index cannot be calculated. These situations show up in Figures 15.3 and 15.4 when the bias curves peter out at levels of s_m below 0.9. Clearly this becomes a more severe problem the longer the time period between the two periods. In very short periods (such as the five-year case), it does not present a problem; it matters only in the twenty-year case if s_m is above 0.8. In the fifty-year case, however, the problem is endemic, except once again if $\dot{q} = \dot{m}$.

VI

This chapter has, we hope, made it clear that the decision as to how to measure historical economic growth needs closer attention than is usually given. The theory and the empirical analysis demonstrate that the choice of index matters. There are circumstances in which this is not true, for example if relative prices of materials and factors stay the same over the period of analysis or there are fixed proportions in production in the short run, as well as an absence of materials-saving (or -using) technical change. But we find these situations uninteresting from both a theoretical and a historical perspective. It is certainly the case that researchers ought to consider the consequences of their choice of index before reporting their results.

In the particular case of Britain in the nineteenth century, the analysis of section IV suggests that the indicator approach is an especially brittle tool for measuring growth in a period of sizable movements in the terms of trade and in the rate of technical change. The implication of Table 15.3 is that measuring growth on the basis of output or input indicators is liable to understate the rate of economic growth. Were that true, it would suggest that the recent revisionism of growth in the Industrial Revolution is premature, based as it is on the behavior of physical proxies for value added; it would also suggest some further reconsideration of the extent of any slowdown in British growth over the later nineteenth century.

Of course, we recognize that the results embedded in Table 15.3, as well as in Figures 15.1 and 15.2, are due to the choice of parameters, especially of λ and σ. As we have discussed in the text, our collective knowledge of these parameters is relatively limited. Our estimates are little better than educated guesses. We are on much firmer ground in considering the other key elements in the bias formulae, namely s_m and $\dot{\pi}$. Nonetheless, we have been careful to suggest that the selection of parameters cannot be made in isolation from each other; they are part of a system and it is important to recognize the constraints in assigning specific combinations of λ and σ, s_m and $\dot{\pi}$.

But it is not our intention simply to suggest that researchers and critics exercise a healthy skepticism in evaluating measures of economic growth that rely on indicators or single-deflated value added. One other aspect of Table 15.3 that we would emphasize is the resilience of the Fisher ideal index as a substitute for the Divisia index. Whereas neither beginning-year nor end-year weighted double deflation produces very satisfactory estimates of growth, they bracket the true figure, and the geometric average of the two is a very close approximation of the Divisia ideal. This is not always true, of course, and Figures 15.3 and 15.4 illustrate the limitations of using the Fisher approach instead of the Divisia. The primary problem is not, however, as is commonly suggested, the proclivity of double-deflation procedures to generate negative value added. Rather it is the tendency for the bias in the measured growth rate to escalate as the period of analysis lengthens. But even here, we can conclude with some optimism. It is not necessary to recalibrate value-added for every industry at five- or even ten-year intervals. For most industries, the Fisher method comes close to the Divisia for periods as long as twenty years. Only if the materials share is high (above 0.75) and there is indication of substantial materials-saving behavior via technical change or price-induced substitution is the application of Fisher methods liable to produce a significant bias.

Notes

1. For a summary of the debate from the vantage point of industrial production statistics, see Crafts, Leybourne, and Mills (1991), and later contributions by Berg and Hudson (1992) and Crafts and Harley (1992).

2. For an introduction to this debate, see Thomas (1988).

3. For further discussion, see Feinstein (1990).

4. We are thinking here especially of the contributions of Harley (1982), Crafts (1985), Jackson (1992), and Crafts and Harley (1992).

5. The final product procedure was adopted in the classic studies by Kuznets (1946) and Shaw (1947), and in their historical counterpart by Gallman (1966).

6. Negative value added can occur either because of large changes in the relative prices of inputs and outputs, or because of large changes in the ratio of inputs to output due to technical change or substitution.

7. See Arrow (1974); Bruno (1978); Diewert (1978); Fenoaltea (1976); Hansen (1974, 1975); Sims (1969, 1977); and especially Sato (1976). This consensus among the theoreticians has had relatively little impact on national accounting practice, though there is now greater recognition of the problems that can arise with double deflation and the standard alternatives; see, in particular, the discussion and recommendations in United Nations et al. (1993, pp. 390–93).

8. Note, however, that the national income condition will hold only if both expenditure and value-added deflators are calculated using the same index number procedure, whether Divisia, Laspeyres, or Paasche.

9. For ease of exposition, we have removed the industry subscripts, i. However, the analysis that follows should be interpreted as applying to industry-level production functions. The implications for aggregation across all industries of this and other procedures for measurement of real output are considered later in the chapter.

10. Sato (1976) observes that constant returns are not a necessary precondition for the Divisia index. If returns to scale are nonconstant, however, the "true" Divisia index must incorporate the economies of scale.

11. David (1962, p. 154, n. 22) recognized the need to exclude terms-of-trade effects when calculating industry productivity estimates that are consistent with national productivity.

12. The reason for the reversal is that in this case the index number is based on the subtraction of one item from the other, rather than the addition of two or more items as, for example, when compiling standard volume or price indices of consumer goods.

13. As Fenoaltea (1977, p. 128) notes, "Since any ordinary industry can be disaggregated into almost as many successive steps as one chooses to contemplate, [SDVA methods generate] a whole family of indices."

14. Formally, weak separability of materials asserts that the marginal rate of technical substitution between the components of value added (capital and labor) depends only on K/L and is not affected by changes in M (materials inputs). In essence, it states that the shape of the isoquant in capital labor space is unaffected by changes in the ratio of materials to output. By duality, weak separability in inputs implies weak separability in prices; the factor price frontier is likewise immune from changes in relative prices of materials.

15. In the discussion that follows, the method does not depend on the assumption of constant returns.

16. Note that if the rate of materials-saving technical progress is zero, this equation collapses to equations 7 and 11.

17. The analysis of the bias from DDVA methods is adapted from Bruno and Sachs (1985, pp. 57–58); the extensions to SDVA and indicator biases are our own.

18. Bruno and Sachs (1985, p. 257) estimate the average elasticity of substitution between materials and value added across all manufacturing sectors for a sample of 10 OECD countries in the postwar period at 0.32.

19. The comparisons across the various measures are not affected by the choice of these variables.

20. The oddity of the case in which the terms of trade deteriorate by 1 percent a year and the rate of materials-saving technical progress is 1 percent a year (note that the Divisia and all DDVA measures coincide) is due to the selection of parameters, in which the fall in $\dot{\pi}$ is precisely compensated by the rise in $\dot{\lambda}$.

21. The exception, once again, is when $\dot{\pi} = \dot{\lambda} = 1$ percent per year, when $\dot{q} = \dot{m} = \dot{v}$.

22. An example of materials-using technical change in the British case may be found in the switch from sail to steam in transoceanic shipping (Harley, 1971), in

which coal was substituted for labor. But this is certainly an unusual case for Britain in the nineteenth century when materials-saving was more commonly characteristic of new technology.

23. In each case, the value of s_m is the Törnqvist discrete approximation to the Divisia valuation.

24. Or, more pedantically, there are two lines but they are superimposed on each other.

25. Of course, for an industry with fully fixed proportions (both σ and $\dot{\lambda} = 0$), the bias from using an output indicator will entirely disappear.

26. The text has referred exclusively to the bias involved in using an output proxy for value added; we have also generated diagrams that show the bias involved in using an input proxy. Essentially, as Table 15.3 would suggest, the general curves look much the same for $(\dot{m} - \dot{v})$ as for $(\dot{q} - \dot{v})$, save that the levels of bias are considerably higher. The worksheets and diagrams for these cases are available on request.

27. Thus, when $\dot{\pi} = -1, \sigma = 0.1,$ and $\dot{\lambda} = 0.1$; and when $\dot{\pi} = -1, \sigma = 0.5,$ and $\dot{\lambda} = 0.5$.

28. For example, $\dot{\pi} = 1, \sigma = 0.1,$ and $\dot{\lambda} = 0.5$ and $\dot{\pi} = 1, \sigma = 0.5,$ and $\dot{\lambda} = 0.1$.

29. A similar diagram for the five-year case indicates that this finding holds a fortiori for shorter periods.

References

Antràs, Pol, and Hans-Joachim Voth. 2003. "Productivity Growth during the English Industrial Revolution: A Dual Approach." *Explorations in Economic History* 40: 52–77.

Arrow, K. J. 1974. "The Measurement of Real Value Added." In P. A. David and M. W. Reder, eds., *Nations and Households in Economic Growth*, pp. 3–19. New York: Academic Press.

Berg, Maxine, and Pat Hudson. 1992. "Rehabilitating the Industrial Revolution." *Economic History Review* 45: 24–50.

Board of Trade. 1903. *Report on Wholesale and Retail Prices in the United Kingdom in 1903, with Comparative Statistical Tables for a Series of Years.* British Parliamentary Papers, HC 321.

———. 1915. *Abstract of Labour Statistics of the United Kingdom.* 17th ed. British Parliamentary Papers.

Bruno, M. 1978. "Duality, Intermediate Inputs and Value Added." In M. Fuss and D. McFadden, eds., *Production Economics: A Dual Approach to Theory and Applications.* Vol. 2: *Applications of the Theory of Production,* pp. 3–16. Amsterdam: North-Holland.

Bruno, Michael, and Jeffrey Sachs. 1985. *Economics of Worldwide Stagflation.* Cambridge, Mass.: Harvard University Press.

Crafts, N. F. R. 1985. *British Economic Growth during the Industrial Revolution.* Oxford: Oxford University Press.

Crafts, N. F. R., and C. K. Harley. 1992. "Output Growth and the British Industrial Revolution: A Restatement of the Crafts-Harley View." *Economic History Review* 45: 703–30.

Crafts, N. F. R., S. J. Leybourne, and T. C. Mills. 1991. "Britain." In R. Sylla and G. Toniolo, eds., *Patterns of European Industrialization: The Nineteenth Century,* pp. 109–52. London: Routledge.

David, Paul A. 1962. "The Deflation of Value Added." *Review of Economics and Statistics* 44: 148–55.

———. 1966. "Measuring Real Net Output: A Proposed Index." *Review of Economics and Statistics* 48: 419–25.

Diewert, W. Erwin. 1978. "Hicks' Aggregation Theorem and the Existence of a Real Value-Added Function." In Melvyn Fuss and Daniel McFadden, eds., *Production Economics: A Dual Approach to Theory and Applications.* Vol. 2: *Applications of the Theory of Production,* pp. 17–51. Amsterdam: North-Holland.

Fabricant, S. 1940. *The Output of Manufacturing Industries 1899–1937.* Princeton, N.J.: National Bureau of Economic Research.

Federal Reserve Board. 1985. "A Revision of the Index of Industrial Production." *Federal Reserve Bulletin* 71: 487–501.

Feinstein, Charles H. 1972. *National Income, Expenditure and Output of the United Kingdom, 1855–1964.* Cambridge, England: Cambridge University Press.

———. 1990. "What Really Happened to Real Wages? Trends in Wages, Prices and Productivity in the United Kingdom, 1880–1913." *Economic History Review* 43: 329–55.

———. 1998. "Wage-Earnings in Great Britain during the Industrial Revolution." In S. G. B. Henry and I. Begg, eds., *Applied Economics and Public Policy,* pp. 181–209. Cambridge, England: Cambridge University Press.

Fenoaltea, S. 1976. "Real Value Added and the Measurement of Industrial Production." *Annals of Economic and Social Measurement* 5: 111–38.

Frickey, Edwin. 1947. *Production in the United States 1860–1914.* Cambridge, Mass.: Harvard University Press.

Gallman, Robert E. 1966. "Gross National Product in the United States 1834–1909." In D. S. Brady, ed., *Output, Employment and Productivity in the United States after 1800.* Princeton, N.J.: National Bureau of Economic Research.

Geary, R. C. 1944. "The Concept of Net Volume of Output, with Special Reference to Irish Data." *Journal of the Royal Statistical Society* 107: 251–59.

Great Britain. 1914–16. *Statistical Abstract for the United Kingdom.* British Parliamentary Papers, Cd. 8128.

Hansen, Bent. 1974. "A Proposed Real Net Output Index: A Comment." *Review of Economics and Statistics* 56: 415–16.

———. 1975. "Double Deflation and the Value Added Product: Comment." *Review of Economics and Statistics* 57: 382–83.

Harley, C. K. 1982. "British Industrialization before 1841: Evidence of Slower Growth during the Industrial Revolution." *Journal of Economic History* 42: 267–89.

Hoffmann, Walther G. 1955. *British Industry, 1700–1950.* Trans. W. O. Henderson and W. H. Chaloner. Oxford: Blackwell.

Hyde, Charles K. 1977. *Technological Change and the British Iron Industry, 1700–1870.* Princeton, N.J.: Princeton University Press.

Jackson, R. V. 1992. "Rates of Industrial Growth during the Industrial Revolution." *Economic History Review* 45: 1–23.

Kuznets, Simon. 1946. *National Product since 1869.* New York: National Bureau of Economic Research.

Lewis, W. Arthur. 1978. *Growth and Fluctuations, 1870–1913.* London: Allen and Unwin.

Office for National Statistics. 1998. *United Kingdom National Accounts, Concepts, Sources and Methods.* London: H.M.S.O.

Sandberg, Lars. 1974. *Lancashire in Decline.* Columbus: Ohio State University.

Sato, Kazuo. 1976. "The Meaning and Measurement of the Real Value Added Index." *Review of Economics and Statistics* 58: 434–42.

Shaw, William H. 1947. *The Value of Commodity Output since 1869.* New York: National Bureau of Economic Research.

Sims, Christopher A. 1969. "Theoretical Basis for a Double Deflated Index of Real Value Added." *Review of Economics and Statistics* 51: 470–71.

———. 1977. "Remarks on Value Added." *Annals of Economic and Social Measurement* 6: 127–31.

Thomas, Mark. 1988. "Slowdown in the Pre–World War One Economy." *Oxford Review of Economic Policy* 4: 14–24.

United Nations et al. 1993. *System of National Accounts.* Washington, D.C.: United Nations.

16

A USER'S GUIDE TO THE JOYS AND PITFALLS OF COHORT PARITY ANALYSIS

Warren C. Sanderson

1. INTRODUCTION

Cohort parity analysis (CPA) is an analytic method for determining the extent of fertility control from data on the distribution of women by the number of children they have borne.[1] It was designed to provide insight into the nature of historical fertility transitions. CPA is a tool, and like every other tool it can cause accidents. A hammer misused can smash a finger. CPA misapplied can damage a reputation. The goal of this chapter is to guide the user so that, when all is said and done, his or her digits are all in the right place.

CPA has three distinct parts. The first is a target parity distribution, a distribution of continuously married women by the number of children they have borne, cross-classified by age at marriage and duration of marriage.[2] The target parity distribution is the object of study. One goal of CPA is to provide upper and lower bounds on the proportion of the target population who controlled their fertility. CPA determines the bounds by comparing the target parity distribution with a model parity distribution. The model parity distribution, the second part of CPA, comes from a population like the target population except without the influence of fertility control. The third part of CPA is the methodology by which inferences are made from those two parity distributions.

The first application of CPA was to Ireland in 1911. This case provided a fortuitous triple coincidence. First, with a little arithmetic, the 1911 Census of Ireland provided the requisite parity distributions for rural and urban areas of the country. Second, rural Ireland in 1911 was widely believed to be home to a population that did not practice fertility control. Finally, it seemed that the rural Irish would be close enough to the urban Irish in all other fertility determinants to make them the perfect model for testing for the existence of control in urban Ireland. What CPA showed was striking. In 1911 a considerable fraction of the urban Irish population was practicing family limitation (see David et al. 1988; David and Sanderson 1988).

Problems arise in the application of CPA because of the use of inappropriate model parity distributions. Okun (1994) criticized CPA in general and the urban Irish findings in particular. On the basis of results from a microsimulation model of fertility (Barrett 1971), she suggested that CPA is worthless as a tool because model parity distributions are extremely sensitive to the determinants of uncontrolled fertility that can never be accurately measured in historical data. On the basis of this she claimed that the urban Irish of 1911 did not practice fertility control and that what CPA registered as control was nothing more than a difference in one of those determinants.

Okun, Trussell, and Vaughan (1996) noted that one potential source of model parity distributions for a country consists of early parity distributions from a time at which fertility control was not widespread. If the earliest usable observation for the country includes some controllers, then the employment of those parity distributions as a model would cause biases in CPA measures. They claimed that these biases would be sufficiently large as to make the utilization of the earlier parity distributions pointless.

CPA needs a user's guide because there are real pitfalls. Without proper guidance it is possible to use inappropriate model and target parity distributions and obtain incorrect results. This chapter shows that avoiding those pitfalls is not only generally possible, but in many cases quite easy.

Section 2 contains a full description of the problems that the user needs to avoid. We delineate three of them: (1) the natural fertility pitfall, (2) the unnatural fertility pitfall, and (3) the supernatural fertility pitfall. The natural fertility pitfall occurs when the CPA practitioner uses parity distributions from one noncontrolling (natural fertility) population as a model and the parity distributions from another natural fertility population as a target. Okun (1994) claims that Paul and I fell into this pitfall with respect to our analysis of 1911 Ireland. The unnatural fertility pitfall is the use of a population with some control as the model for a similar population with more control. This is the problem discussed in Okun, Trussell, and Vaughan (1996). The supernatural fertility pitfall is the analysis of a target population using a non-controlling population as a model, which has even higher fertility than the true model population.

We begin our guide in section 3 with an important but hitherto unobserved feature of the demographic landscape. Applying the same microsimulation model of fertility used in Okun (1994), we show that, in noncontrolling populations, the logits of parity progression rates for women married for ten to fourteen years are almost perfectly linear. The logits derived from the 1911 rural Irish parity distributions are nearly linear as well, confirming the microsimulation result. In section 4 we show how this linearity can be used as part of a procedure to help users avoid the natural fertility pitfall. We test this procedure on the 1911 urban Irish and show that Okun's claim that urban Irish population in 1911 did not exhibit control is soundly rejected.

In section 5 we discuss the unnatural fertility pitfall. We present explicit CPA formulae for the magnitude of the biases that arise when there is control in the model population. Among other things, we show there that: (1) we can still obtain a lower bound on the true extent of control, (2) that the upward bias in the measured increase in control is bounded from above by the true extent of control in the model population, and (3) that the upward bias in the measure of the increase in control diminishes as the extent of control in the target population increases. We conclude that the use of model parity distributions from populations with a small proportion of controllers can provide very informative results.

We discuss how to avoid the supernatural fertility pitfall in section 6. Again we provide explicit CPA formulae. We show that the bias in the measures of control are bounded from above by the amount of (false) control that we would find using the true lower-fertility natural fertility population as the target and the wrong higher-fertility natural fertility population as the model.

We also demonstrate that this bias diminishes as the true extent of control in the target population increases. CPA is most sensitive to the supernatural fertility pitfall, when the true extent of control in the target population is small. Fortunately, this is exactly the situation where the linearity of the logits of target population's parity progression rates can come to our aid.

We conclude our user's guide in section 7. CPA does provide us with the pleasure of seeing the dynamics of historical fertility transitions more clearly, but we can only do this if we avoid the pitfalls.

2. THE OKUN CRITICISMS

Okun (1994) employed a modified fertility microsimulation program, originally written by Barrett (see Barrett 1971), to produce parity distributions that could be used to study CPA's estimates of fertility control. The main components of the model are: the Coale and McNeil (1972) age-at-first-marriage function, the Lesthaeghe and Page (1980) model of amenorrhea, a beta distribution of fecundability, the Pittenger (1973) exponential model of sterility, an infant mortality rate, and an assumption about how fecundability evolves with age.[3]

First, Okun took a set of parameters that she said were appropriate for historical European populations and used them to compute a baseline set of parity distributions for a noncontrolling population. Second, she produced other parity distributions, some of noncontrolling populations with different fertility determinants, some of controlling populations with the same fertility determinants. Finally, she computed upper and lower bounds on the extent of control using CPA and compared the results with the known control proportions.

In order to understand Okun's results more fully, it is useful to discuss two of the specifications that she used in computing her baseline parity distributions. The Lesthaeghe and Page model of amenorrhea is a logit relational model. Standard proportions of women who remain amenorrheic by month after giving birth are transformed into logits. Let $LGTSTD(j)$ be the logit of the standard proportion of women who remain amenorrheic j months after giving birth. Predicted distributions of proportions who remain amenorrheic are derived from logits, which are linear transformations of the logits of the standard proportions. In other words,

$$LGTPRED(j) = \alpha + \beta \cdot LGTSTD(j), \tag{1}$$

where $LGTPRED(j)$ is the predicted logit of the proportion still amenorrheic j months after the birth of her child, and where α and β are the two parameters that can be modified to produce different sets of predicted proportions still amenorrheic by month since giving birth.

Fecundability, the monthly probability of conception, is specified to have a beta distribution. We use the standard notation and call the two parameters of this beta distribution a and b.

Table 16.1 shows the results most critical of CPA. In Table 16.1, Population A, in which there is truly no control, is used as a target population. Two different noncontrolling populations are used as models. Population B was produced with exactly the same parameters as Population A, except that the median duration of amenorrhea in Population B is 0.7 months shorter, 4.9 months rather than 5.6 months. Population C is the same as Population A except that the monthly probability of conception is greater: 0.25 for Popoulation B and

Table 16.1
Cohort Parity Analysis (CPA) bounds on the proportions controlling their fertility

	CPA Lower Bound	CPA Upper Bound
Model Population B. Target Population A.	0.08	0.18
Model Population C. Target Population A.	0.19	0.31

SOURCE: Okun (1994), table 5, p. 217, and table 6, p. 218.

Notes: All populations refer to women married at ages 20–24 and observed on their thirty-fifth birthdays. These women were married for ten to fourteen years at the time of observation. We retain the population names in Okun (1994). Population A is generated with Lesthaeghe and Page amenorrhea parameters $\alpha = -1.1$, $\beta = 1$. This implies that the median duration of amenorrhea is 5.6 months. The mean monthly probability of conception is generated from a beta distribution with parameters $a = 2$, $b = 8$. These parameters produce a mean proportion conceiving of 0.20 per lunar month. Population B is generated with amenorrhea parameters $\alpha = -1.2$, $\beta = 1$, (median duration of amenorrhea of 4.9 months) and the same beta distribution parameters as Population A. Population C is generated with the same amenorrhea parameters as Population A, but with fecundability parameters $a = 2$, $b = 6$. This implies a mean monthly probability of conception of 0.25. In Population A, the cutoff parameter, k, in CPA was the upper eighth percentile of the parity distribution.

0.20 for Population A. This is a clear example of the natural fertility pitfall. Here the parity distributions from one natural fertility population are used as the targets and the parity distributions from another natural fertility population are used as the models.

Table 16.1 shows the kinds of misinterpretations that are possible if the natural fertility pitfall is not avoided. A small change in the median duration of amenorrhea can be incorrectly read as the presence of fertility control. The difference in mean monthly probability of conception from 0.20 to 0.25 is a large one. It is not nearly as surprising that it produces the appearance of a significant amount of control.

While it is possible to take issue with the details of figures in Table 16.1, the point remains that if both the target and model parity distributions are derived from noncontrolling populations, the model with higher fertility and the target with lower fertility, CPA would report the existence of the family limitation where there was none. Thus CPA practitioners need some way of differentiating parity progression rates generated by a controlling population from those produced by a noncontrolling population.

The Okun, Trussell, and Vaughan (1996) criticism of CPA is somewhat different. One possible approach to applying CPA is to use parity distributions for a given country at an earlier point in time as models and parity distributions observed later as targets. They found that this approach could be implemented for thirty-two developing countries where earlier and later fertility surveys existed. Although there are no tables in the paper to support the claim, the authors write that "CPA consistently overestimated the increase in the proportion of ever-users." On the basis of this and a proof that I supplied to them they concluded that "*model populations that contain a significant proportion of controllers cannot be used to estimate reliably the difference between the proportions of controllers in the model and target populations*" (Okun, Trussell, and Vaughan 1996, p. 166, italics in original).

Okun, Trussell, and Vaughan (1996) provide a statement of the unnatural fertility pitfall. The use of parity distributions from a controlling population does indeed cause CPA results to be biased. In order to use CPA effectively, practitioners need to be aware of the existence, magnitude, and direction of those biases.

Okun (1994) and Okun, Trussell, and Vaughan (1996) have drawn our attention to real pitfalls. Fortunately, there are ways to avoid those pitfalls. The remainder of the paper is a guide to how to do it.

3. THE LINEARITY OF LOGITS OF NATURAL FERTILITY PARITY PROGRESSION RATES

We consider the linearity of the logits of natural fertility parity progression rates from two different perspectives: (1) simulated natural fertility parity progression rates from the Barrett/Okun microdemographic simulation program, and (2) observed parity progression rates of the rural Irish population in 1911.

Logits of Parity Progression Rates Simulated Using the Barrett/Okun Program

When there is no fertility control, the Barrett/Okun simulation model produces parity progression rates for women married for ten to fourteen years whose logits are remarkably linear.[4] The same tendency is also evident for women married five to nine years, fifteen to nineteen years, and twenty to twenty-four years, but because the linearity is even more striking for those married ten to fourteen years, we focus on this group here.

Figure 16.1 shows the logits of the parity progression rates produced by the Barrett/Okun microsimulation model for women married ten to fourteen years for two age-at-marriage groups, those aged 15–19 and those aged 30–34, and straight lines fit to them using ordinary least squares.[5] In what follows, we only show graphs for women married at ages 15–19 and 30–34. In all respects, the conclusions from women married at ages 20–24 and 25–29 are identical. Whenever we present results from the Barrett/Okun simulation model, we specify two numbers: the median duration of amenorrhea and the mean monthly probability of conception. Those numbers are determined by two parameters, α and β for the duration of amenorrhea distribution and a and b for the distribution of monthly probabilities of conception. All the other parameters and specifications are those used in Okun (1994).[6] In Figure 16.1, the fecundity parameters are $a = 2$, $b = 8$ (mean monthly probability of

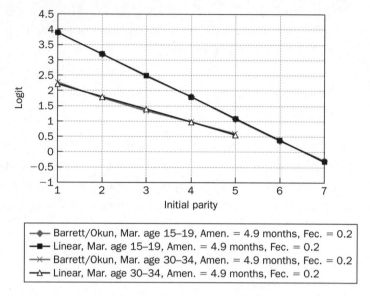

Figure 16.1 Logits of simulated parity progression rates and best fitting straight line (duration of marriage 10–14 years)

conception is 0.20) and the amenorrhea parameters are $\alpha = -1.2$, $\beta = 1$ (median duration of amenorrhea is 4.9 months).

Figure 16.1 contains four lines. Two are logits of the parity progression rates for women married at different ages,[7] and two are straight lines fit to them using ordinary least squares. In these figures and all that come after, the first parity progression rate that we consider is the transition from parity 1 to parity 2.[8] The last parity progression rate shown is from the $(k-1)$th to the kth birth, where k is the cutoff parity. In CPA, the cutoff parity is the lowest parity that is rarely reached by controllers. In David and Sanderson (1988), we recommended that k be set as close to the upper twentieth percentile of the model parity distribution as possible. We follow that recommendation here.

In Figure 16.1 the simulated logits and the straight lines fit to them are so close as to be practically indistinguishable. For age at marriage of 15–19, the two curves fit so closely that there is no room visible between them. For women married at 30–34, the differences between the curves are visible, but very slight. We have computed over 100 tests of the linearity of the logits of parity progression rates like the ones in Figure 16.1 by varying the values of the

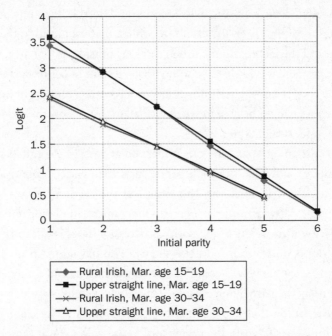

Figure 16.2   Logits of parity progression rates of 1911 rural Irish and the closest straight lines lying above them (duration of marriage 10–14 years)

parameters of the amenorrhea and fecundity distributions. Without exception, they all appear very similar.[9]

Logits of the 1911 Rural Irish Parity Progression Rates

The question that motivates this subsection is whether the logits of the 1911 rural Irish parity progression rates show the same linearity that we see in the simulated data. The logits of the rural Irish parity progression rates for women married at ages 15–19 and 30–34 and married for ten to fourteen years in 1911 are shown in Figure 16.2. We do not follow the example of the previous section here and fit straight lines to those numbers using ordinary least squares. Instead we fit a straight line that both minimizes the sum of squared deviations from the data *and* lies nowhere below the observed curve.

We show the upper straight line here because of an element of the oral tradition of CPA. Paul David and I used the terms "urban Irish" and "rural Irish" as shorthand to denote those who lived inside and outside of county boroughs in 1911 respectively. Given the extent of control that we found in the county boroughs and the fact that some urban areas lay outside of that area, we conjectured that there was likely to be some small amount of control evident outside of the county boroughs. If this conjecture is correct and the linear model holds, then we should be able to see that small extent of control as deviations from the upper straight line.

Figure 16.2 and graphs for women married at ages 20–24 and 25–29 (not included here) show that the logits of the rural Irish parity progression rates come quite close to being linear. This empirical observation confirms the theoretical result derived from the Barrett/Okun microsimulation model. The near linearity of the logits of the parity progression rates is a feature of both this real-world observation and the theory. The deviations from linearity in Figure 16.2 are small and could be due to the existence of a tiny extent of control among the Irish living outside of county boroughs.

The observation that logits of parity progression rates are close to being linear in initial parity gives us a strong tool to use with CPA. It can help keep us from falling into the error of analyzing one natural fertility parity distribution with another.

4. AVOIDING THE NATURAL FERTILITY PITFALL

In the following subsection we provide two easily applied criteria that can be used to avoid the natural fertility pitfall. In the next subsection, we use those criteria to test whether the urban Irish in 1911 were a noncontrolling population.

The Theory

In Figures 16.3 and 16.4, we show examples of the patterns that we would expect to see in the case of the natural fertility pitfall. We begin with a baseline simulation, using the fecundability parameters $a = 2$, $b = 11$ (mean monthly probability of conception of 0.15) and the amenorrhea parameters $\alpha = -1$, $\beta = 1$ (median duration of amenorrhea of 6.2 months), for women married

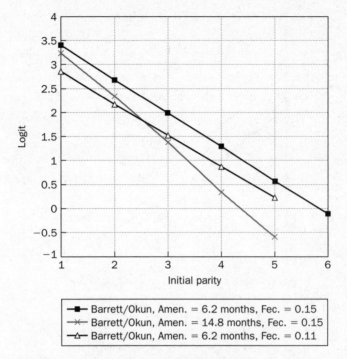

Figure 16.3 Logits of parity progression rates generated by Barrett/Okun program with various fertility determinants (duration of marriage 10–14 years, age at marriage 15–19)

ten to fourteen years at observation. These parameters produce logits of parity progression rates for women married at age 20–24 that are almost identical to those of the 1911 rural Irish.

In addition to the simulation for the baseline natural fertility population, each graph contains two additional curves, one for a natural fertility population with a longer average duration of amenorrhea and one for a natural fertility population with lower fecundability. The parity progression rates of the noncontrolling population with a longer duration of amenorrhea were generated using the parameters $\alpha = 0$ and $\beta = 1$ (median duration of amenorrhea of 14.8 months). The other curve is based on parity progression rates from a simulated noncontrolling population with lower fecundability, $a = 2$, $b = 16$ (mean monthly probability of conception of 0.11).

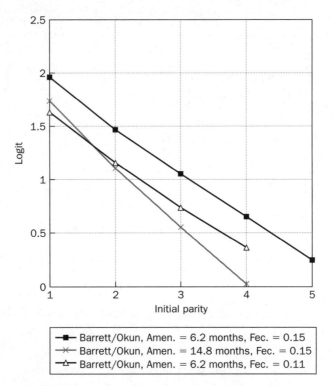

Figure 16.4 Logits of parity progression rates generated by Barrett/Okun program with various fertility determinants (duration of marriage 10–14 years, age at marriage 30–34)

Figure 16.3 shows the relationships for women married at age 15–19; Figure 16.4 shows the relationships for those married at age 30–34. The natural fertility pitfall arises from analyzing the parity progression rates from either the noncontrolling population with a longer duration of amenorrhea or the noncontrolling population with lower fecundability using the baseline population as the model.

When one noncontrolling population has the same microdemographic fertility determinants as another except that it has longer average duration of amenorrhea, the logits of their parity progression rates have a clear relationship to one another. The logits from the population with the longer average duration of amenorrhea (1) are always below those of the population with the shorter average duration, (2) always have a more negative slope, and (3) at initial parity 1 deviate increasingly from those of the population with the shorter average duration as age at marriage increases.

When one noncontrolling population has the same microdemographic fertility determinants as another except that it has lower average fecundability, the logits of their parity progression rates have a different relationship to one another. The logits from the population with the lower average fecundability are also always below those of the population with the higher average fecundability, but the slope can be either more or less negative depending on the other parameters.

These observations suggest that there are tests to avoid the natural fertility pitfall in cases where the existence of fertility control in the target population is in question. Plot the logits of parity progression rates of the target and the model populations for all available ages at marriage. First, inspect the graphs for linearity. If the logits from the target and the model populations are linear and those from the target population are always below those of the model population, this may well be a case of the natural fertility pitfall. Second, the graphs should be inspected for consistency. If patterns similar to those in Figures 16.3 and 16.4 are evident, then there is a strong suspicion that the target population is another natural fertility population and the analysis should end there. If linearity is observed but there are inconsistent relationships between the lines, then more analysis is required. It could be that this is evidence for some sort of fertility control or for some biological difference that we do not understand yet.

An Example from 1911 Urban Ireland

Figure 16.5 shows logits of rural and urban Irish parity progression rates in 1911 for women married for ten to fourteen years who were married at age 15–19. Figure 16.6 shows the analogous rates for women married at age 30–34. In Figure 16.5, the logits of the urban Irish are identical to those for the rural Irish at initial parity 4, but lower at every other initial parity. This is inconsistent with the hypothesis that the urban Irish differ from the rural Irish on some fertility determinants such as length of amenorrhea or fecundability. If this were the case, we would expect the urban Irish curve to lie below the rural Irish curve everywhere. Although the urban Irish curve is based on 3,667 women

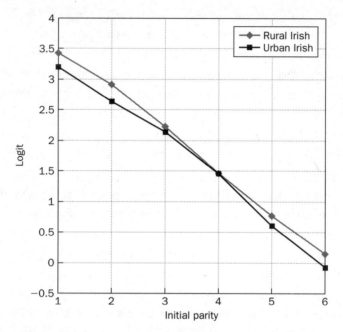

Figure 16.5 Logits of 1911 rural and urban Irish parity progression rates (duration of marriage 10–14 years, age at marriage 15–19)

and the rural curve on even more, it is possible to argue that there is not enough nonlinearity in the logits of the urban population in Figure 16.5 to provide convincing evidence for fertility control in urban Ireland.

Figure 16.6, taken together with Figure 16.5, however, provides over-whelming evidence for control. First, the pattern of the logits in Figure 16.6 is distinctly nonlinear.[10] This by itself clearly indicates the presence of control. Second, Figures 16.5 and 16.6 taken together are inconsistent with the hypothesis that the urban Irish were just a different natural fertility population. If for a moment we accepted the hypothesis suggested by Figure 16.5 that the parity progression rates in the urban population were like those in the rural population, we would expect to see the rural and urban curves in Figure 16.6 close to one another. This is observably not the case. By applying the criteria of linearity and consistency, we can easily avoid the natural fertility pitfall, even in the previously controversial case of urban Ireland in 1911.

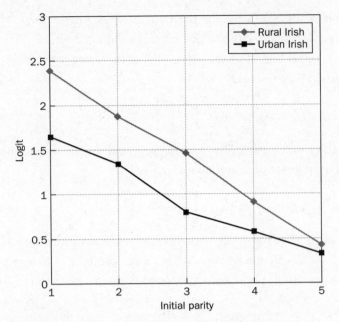

Figure 16.6   Logits of 1911 rural and urban Irish parity progression rates (duration of marriage 10–14 years, age at marriage 30–34)

5. AVOIDING THE UNNATURAL FERTILITY PITFALL

The natural fertility pitfall exists when the target population is, inappropriately, a noncontrolling population. The unnatural fertility pitfall exists when the model population is suitable for the analysis of the target population except that it contains some controllers.

We will deal with the unnatural fertility pitfall analytically and then give some examples. In standard CPA notation $t(j)$ is the proportion of the target population observed at parity j, and $T(j)$ is the proportion of the target population with j or more children. Similarly $n(j)$ is the proportion of model (noncontrolling) population observed at parity j, and $N(j)$ is the proportion of the model (noncontrolling) population with j or more children.[11] In some cases we might not observe the true model population, only another population with less control than the target. Let $s(j)$ be the proportion of the population in this intermediate population observed at parity j and $S(j)$ be the proportion of that population with j or more children.

The true upper bound on the proportion of the target population controlling at parity j is $c_u^t(j)$ where

$$c_u^t(j) = t(j) - n(j) \cdot \left[\frac{T(k)}{N(k)} \right], \tag{2}$$

and k is the cutoff parity. The true upper bound on the proportion of the intermediate population controlling at parity j is

$$c_u^s(j) = s(j) - n(j) \cdot \left[\frac{S(k)}{N(k)} \right]. \tag{3}$$

We cannot compute the upper bounds indicated in equations 2 or 3 because the $n(j)$ and $N(k)$ are unobserved. What we can compute is an upper-bound measure based on the population that already contains some controllers,

$$c_u^o(j) = t(j) - s(j) \cdot \left[\frac{T(k)}{S(k)} \right], \tag{4}$$

where the superscript o indicates that the equation is written in terms of observed quantities. Substituting the expression for $t(j)$ that can be derived from equation 2 and the expression for $s(j)$ that can be derived from equation 3 into equation 4, we obtain an expression that relates the measured upper bound to the true upper bound on the extent of control in the intermediate and target populations,

$$c_u^o(j) = c_u^t(j) - c_u^s(j) \cdot \left[\frac{T(k)}{S(k)} \right] \tag{5}$$

Taking equation 5 and summing over all parities from 0 to $k - 1$,[12] we obtain the expression that relates the aggregate upper bound measures,

$$C_u^o = C_u^t - C_u^s \cdot \left[\frac{T(k)}{S(k)} \right], \tag{6}$$

where the upper-case C's refer to sums over all the eligible parities. Since the target population exhibits more control than the intermediate population, we know that the ratio $T(k)/S(k)$ in equation 6 is less than 1.0.

When we use a population with some control as our model instead of a noncontrolling population, the measured upper bound on the extent of control of course understates the true upper bound on the extent of control, $C_u^o < C_u^t$. One interesting feature of equation 6 is that the magnitude of the understatement decreases as the extent of control in the target population increases, holding the amount of control in the intermediate population constant. This happens because the ratio $T(k)/S(k)$ decreases as the extent of control in the target population increases (holding the extent of control in the intermediate population constant).

Imagine a target population where the true upper bound on the extent of control is 50 percent and where the upper bound on the extent of control in the intermediate population is 10 percent. CPA tells us that the true upper bound on the extent of control in the target population can be written as $1 - T(k)/N(k)$ and that the true upper bound on the extent of control in the intermediate population can be written as $1 - S(k)/N(k)$. Given the assumptions above $T(k)/N(k) = 0.5$, $S(k)/N(k) = 0.9$, and therefore $T(k)/S(k) = 0.56$. We can see from equation 6 that when the true extent of control is 50 percent and we incorrectly use as our model population one in which the upper bound on the extent of control is 10 percent, we do not obtain a measured upper bound of 40 percent. Instead we compute a measured upper bound of 44.4 percent (50 percent minus 0.56 times 10 percent). When we use as our model population one in which there is some control, the upper bound that we calculate is not an upper bound on the true extent of control in the target population, but some lower figure. Still it is informative. For example, it would be interesting to know that the true upper bound on the extent of control was more than 44.4 percent.

The lower-bound story is basically the same, but not quite as neat. We begin with the three equations:

$$c_L^t(j) = t(j) - n(j) \cdot \left[\frac{T(j+1)}{N(j+1)} \right], \tag{7}$$

$$c_L^s(j) = s(j) - n(j) \cdot \left[\frac{S(j+1)}{N(j+1)} \right], \tag{8}$$

and

$$c_L^o(j) = t(j) - s(j) \cdot \left[\frac{T(j+1)}{S(j+1)} \right], \tag{9}$$

where the subscript L refers to the lower bound. From these we can derive the analog to equation (5):

$$c_L^o(j) = c_L^t(j) - c_L^s(j) \cdot \left[\frac{T(j+1)}{S(j+1)}\right]. \qquad (10)$$

Since there is more control in the target population than in the intermediate population, $T(j+1)/S(j+1)$ is always less than unity.

Summing over all the parities from 0 through $k-1$, we obtain

$$C_L^o = C_L^t - \sum_{j=0}^{k-1} c_L^s(j) \cdot \left[\frac{T(j+1)}{S(j+1)}\right]. \qquad (11)$$

Clearly C_L^o is less than C_L^t and therefore is a lower bound, although not the highest possible lower bound. Since $T(j+1)/S(j+1)$ decreases as the extent of control in the target population increases, holding control in the intermediate population constant, the downward bias in C_L^o also decreases, just as in the case of the upper bound.

In summary, if we incorrectly use a population in which there is some control as a model population, both the measured upper and lower bounds will lie below the true upper and lower bounds. Both of the measured bounds are informative. The measured lower bound is a lower bound, and we know that the highest possible lower bound is somewhat higher. The measured upper bound is not an upper bound, but it is still interesting that the lowest possible upper bound lies above it. It is important that the magnitude of the downward bias is never as large as the true extent of control in the intermediate population and that it diminishes as the extent of control in the target population increases, holding control in the intermediate population constant. So long as we understand what we are doing, using a similar population with some control in it as a model in CPA can still produce informative results.

6. AVOIDING THE SUPERNATURAL FERTILITY PITFALL

The supernatural fertility pitfall occurs when we use the wrong natural fertility population. In particular, the wrong natural fertility population must be one with higher fertility than the true one. If we use a natural fertility population where the parity progression rates are below those of the true model population, the equations are identical to those in section 5 with suitable renaming. The supernatural fertility pitfall causes the measured bounds on the extent of control to be biased upward.

To see what this case looks like analytically, let there be a true model population and a target population. We use the same notation for them as above: n and N refer to the model population and t and T to the target population. Suppose now that we do not observe the true model population, but an inappropriate noncontrolling population with higher parity progression rates. We use the notation m and M to refer to this population.

Again, let us deal with the upper bound first. The true upper bound on the extent of control at each parity is the same expression as equation 2,

$$c_u^t(j) = t(j) - n(j) \cdot \left[\frac{T(k)}{N(k)} \right]. \tag{12}$$

If we were to analyze the noncontrolling population with lower parity progression rates using the noncontrolling population with the higher parity progression rates as the model, we would be falling into the natural fertility pitfall. We would calculate control where there was none. The amount of *false control* at each parity would be

$$c_u^m(j) = n(j) - m(j) \cdot \left[\frac{N(k)}{M(k)} \right]. \tag{13}$$

The observed control at each parity is determined from the equation

$$c_u^o(j) = t(j) - m(j) \cdot \left[\frac{T(k)}{M(k)} \right]. \tag{14}$$

With a little algebraic manipulation as above we obtain

$$c_u^o(j) = c_u^t(j) + c_u^m(j) \cdot \left[\frac{T(k)}{N(k)} \right]. \tag{15}$$

After summing over the parities 0 through $k - 1$, equation 15 becomes

$$C_u^o = C_u^t + C_u^m \cdot \left[\frac{T(k)}{N(k)} \right]. \tag{16}$$

Since $T(k)/N(k) = 1 - C_u^t$, we can rewrite equation 16 as

$$C_u^o = C_u^t + C_u^m \cdot (1 - C_u^t) \tag{17}$$

Equation 17 tells us that the full amount of the false control, C_u^m is not added to the true amount of control. If the true upper bound on the proportion controlling were 40 percent, then the observed upper bound would be the true upper bound plus 60 percent of the amount of false control. As the true upper bound increases, the upward bias in the observed upper bound decreases.

By the same reasoning, the version of equation 17 for the lower-bound measure can be written

$$C_L^o = C_L^t + \sum_{j=0}^{k-1} c_L^m(j) \cdot \left[\frac{T(j+1)}{N(j+1)} \right]. \tag{18}$$

The observed lower bound is larger than the true lower bound, and the bias decreases as the extent of control in the target population increases.

The most important problem caused by the supernatural fertility pitfall occurs when the extent of control in the target population is small, and we believe that the model parity distribution exhibits higher parity progression rates than the true model population. The first step in this case is to ensure that there is control in the target population. This means finding either non-linearity in the logits or inconsistent relationships with the model across ages at marriage. If it is not clear that there is control in the target population, then we cannot proceed further without risking the natural fertility pitfall.

The second step is to investigate the relationships between the logits of the model and target parity progression rates. If there is just a small amount of control in the target population and the model is appropriate, then the logits of the parity progression rates of the target population will be almost linear and lie close to those of the model. If the model is inappropriate, the logits of the target population will still be almost linear but will not lie close to those of the model. Still, the relationships between the two sets of logits should be consistent.

If the model is in question, there is an easy procedure to use that produces a lower-bound estimate, which is guaranteed to be below the maximum possible lower bound. Simply produce the upper straight line, as I did in section 3, and employ it as the model. This approach could produce lower-bound estimates that are significantly below the maximum possible lower bound, but it could still be useful in cases where you are searching for clear evidence that some fertility control was being practiced.

7. CONCLUSIONS

CPA is not foolproof. It has real pitfalls that need to be avoided. In this chapter, we have shown concretely how to do that. Our methods of avoiding the pitfalls involve the use of a previously unrecognized regularity; in a noncontrolling population the logits of the parity progression rates of women married for ten to fourteen years are nearly linear. This is also the case for women married for fifteen to nineteen and twenty to twenty-four years, but the linearity is not quite as pronounced.

The future of CPA is bright. Combining early survey data from developing countries where the extent of fertility control is low with the knowledge that the logits of natural fertility parity progression rates are linear, we can estimate appropriate natural fertility parity distributions for most of the twenty-three countries studied in Okun, Trussell, and Vaughan (1996). In addition, more and more historical European data are becoming available. CPA's greatest potential contribution lies in the analysis of these data.

The linearity of the logits of the parity progression rate is a surprising result. Another is the fact that I could find no parameterization of the Barrett/Okun simulation model that is consistent with the 1911 rural Irish parity progression rates either across marriage ages, holding duration of marriage constant, or across durations of marriage, holding age at marriage constant. There are three possibilities here. First, it is possible that there is a parameterization that makes the two consistent and I have not found it yet. The second possibility is that there is something wrong with the Barrett/Okun model. In either event, if we could make the Barrett/Okun model consistent with the rural Irish and other natural fertility parity distributions, it would be a wonderful addition to the CPA toolkit.

The most intriguing possibility is that there is something wrong with the 1911 rural Irish, in the sense that they did not exhibit the consistent noncontrolling behavior that has been expected of them. For example, based on the Barrett/Okun model, rural Irish women who married at age 30–34 had higher monthly probabilities of conception than those married at age 20–24. If this is indeed the case, then natural fertility might be a much more complex set of behaviors than scholars have thought.

CPA has already generated some surprising findings. This chapter suggests that there may be more to come.

Notes

1. Paul David invented the term "cohort parity analysis." He and I were co-authors on four papers that developed and used the technique: David and Sanderson (1987), David et al. (1988), David and Sanderson (1988), and David and Sanderson (1990).

2. It is also possible to use parity distributions cross-classified by current age and duration of marriage. The analysis in this case is more complex. See David and Sanderson (1987) for an example of how it can be done.

3. Fecundability is a demographic term for the probability that a woman in a heterosexual union, who is not controlling her fertility, becomes pregnant during a given menstrual cycle.

4. Okun generously gave us a copy of her modification of the Barrett program in 1993. All the simulations done with the Barrett/Okun model in this chapter used that copy of the program. The program is in Fortran. It produces the same results as were published in Okun (1994).

5. The simulated parity distributions for those married at 15–19 (30–34) are based on 165,975 (93,231) trials. An analogous graph for women married at 20–24, and 25–29 (not shown here because of space limitations) display logits of parity progression rates that are indistinguishable from straight lines.

6. In the baseline version of the Barrett/Okun model fecundability is assumed to be constant until age 36, at which time it declines quadratically until the randomly determined age of sterility. The mean age at first marriage is 25.0 and its standard deviation is 6.0.

7. Logits are normally defined as $0.5 * \frac{\ln(ppr)}{[1 - \ln(ppr)]}$, where ppr is a parity progression rate. In this paper, for simplicity, we have omitted the multiplicative factor 0.5.

8. The transition from parity 0 to parity 1 is dominated by the primary sterility and therefore has fundamentally different determinants from the higher order transitions.

9. The version of this paper presented at the "History Matters" conference in honor of Paul David contained many more figures than this one. For a copy of that paper, please write the author at wsanderson@notes.cc.sunysb.edu.

10. The urban Irish parity progression rates in Figure 16.6 are based on 1,575 observations. Therefore the nonlinearities are not due to small sample problems.

11. See David et al. (1988) for a presentation of CPA notation and the development of the basic upper- and lower-bound formulae.

12. One CPA assumption is that k is set so that there are an inconsequential number of controllers at that parity or above.

References

Barrett, J. 1971. "Use of a Fertility Simulation Model to Refine Measurement Techniques." *Demography* 8: 481–90.

Bongaarts, J., and J. Potter. 1983. *Fertility, Biology, and Behavior: An Analysis of Proximate Determinants.* New York: Academic Press.

Coale, A. J., and D. McNeil. 1972. "The Distributions by Age of the Frequency of First Marriage in a Female Cohort." *Journal of the American Statistical Association* 67: 743–49.

David, P., and W. Sanderson. 1987. "The Emergence of a Two-Child Norm among American Birth Controllers." *Population and Development Review* 13: 1–41.

———. 1988. "Measuring Marital Fertility Control with CPA." *Population Index* 54: 691–713.

———. 1990. "Cohort Parity Analysis and Fertility Transition Dynamics: Reconstructing Historical Trends in Fertility Control from a Single Census." *Population Studies* 44: 421–45.

David, P., T. Mroz, W. Sanderson, K. Wachter, and D. Weir. 1988. "Cohort Parity Analysis: Statistical Estimates of the Extent of Fertility Control." *Demography* 25: 163–88.

Lesthaeghe, R., and H. Page. 1980. "The Post Partum Non-Susceptible Period: Development and Application of Model Schedules." *Population Studies* 34: 143–69.

Okun, B. S. 1994. "Evaluating Methods for Detecting Fertility Control: Coale and Trussell's Model and Cohort Parity Analysis." *Population Studies* 48: 193–222.

Okun, B. S., J. Trussell, and B. Vaughan. 1996. "Using Fertility Surveys to Evaluate an Indirect Method for Detecting Fertility Control." *Population Studies* 50: 161–71.

Pittenger, D. 1973. "An Exponential Model of Female Sterility." *Demography* 10: 113–21.

17 | STOCHASTIC DYNAMIC OPTIMIZATION MODELS WITH RANDOM EFFECTS IN PARAMETERS: AN APPLICATION TO AGE AT MARRIAGE AND LIFE-CYCLE FERTILITY CONTROL IN FRANCE UNDER THE OLD REGIME

Thomas A. Mroz and David R. Weir

The three key characteristics of France's unique early fertility transition can be easily summarized. The overall level of fertility declined nearly simultaneously and proportionately to the decline in infant and child mortality, resulting in nearly constant surviving family sizes. By contrast, the rest of Western Europe experienced rapid population growth over the nineteenth century when mortality fell and overall fertility did not. Overall fertility in historical Europe was composed of two primary behavioral components: nuptiality (age at marriage and proportions marrying) and marital fertility (age-specific fertility rates of married women). In the prototypical demographic transition, it is the beginning of sustained declines in marital fertility that marks the onset of the fertility transition (Coale 1973). In France, aggregate statistics point to the 1790s, during the French Revolution, as such a starting point (Weir 1994). Overall fertility began declining sooner than that, however, and there is some localized evidence of marital fertility decline before the Revolution (Bideau and Bardet 1988). This second key characteristic, the timing of change, leads us to focus on the behavior of mid-to-late eighteenth-century families.

A third key issue concerns the relationship between the two major behavioral determinants of fertility: marriage timing and fertility within marriage. The well-known European marriage pattern of late marriage and high rates of permanent celibacy substantially reduced total fertility for most of Europe's recorded demographic history (Hajnal 1965). Time-series variation in nuptiality in England has been linked to economic conditions (Lee 1981; Smith 1981; Wrigley and Schofield 1981). In the early stages of France's fertility transition, nuptiality and marital fertility complemented one another: age at marriage rose while marital fertility fell (Weir 1994). Later in the nineteenth century the trends in nuptiality reversed while overall fertility continued to fall. Despite the powerful influence of marriage on completed fertility, little attention has been paid to whether cross-sectional or time-series differences in age at marriage were exogenous to fertility decisions or instead reflected different preferences for numbers of surviving children.

Our previous work focused on the first key characteristic of the French transition and sought to measure the response of fertility within marriage to the number of surviving children (David, Mroz, and Wachter 1987; Mroz and Weir 1990). A primary goal of this chapter is to integrate the timing of marriage into a model of life-cycle fertility to test whether it acted simply as an exogenously imposed constraint on decisions about marital fertility or whether instead it appears to share the influence of preferences for number of surviving children.

We examine this issue with an estimation strategy that approximates and follows directly from a stochastic dynamic optimization framework.[1] The empirical approach is based upon a "nonparametric" regression framework that does not require the researcher to specify explicit functional forms for the utility function or the agent's expectations about the future. This approach can readily be expanded to incorporate complex interactions of state and decision variables. It can easily accommodate controls for unobservable factors that influence an agent's decisions over time; the approach controls for the possible statistical endogeneity of state variables and allows researchers to assess accurately the impact of state variables on decisions.

The approach described here can easily incorporate complex interactions among unobservables and state and decision variables. The estimated models can include random coefficients that are correlated with endogenous variables. Preliminary empirical analyses suggest that modeling such variations in tastes across agents does significantly improve the explanatory power of the models. We find that the effects of some "dynamic" variables without behavioral justifications become small and insignificant after allowing for such interactions.

While this approach clearly expands the complexity of problems that researchers can examine empirically, it cannot replace more explicit structural approaches; many important policy issues can only be addressed through formal, completely specified models. Nevertheless, a wide range of interesting economic and policy questions can be addressed in this simple empirical framework, and it can suggest which of the many possible complex interactions should be incorporated into the more explicit modeling approaches. The approximation approach also can be combined with a more formal dynamic optimization approach to help one uncover all of the structural parameters of interest that could be estimated by structural dynamic estimation procedures. By combining these two approaches, one can relax empirically many strong assumptions in formal optimization models while reducing computational burdens.

This paper has five sections. The next section uses Bellman's principle to set up a stochastic dynamic optimization problem and discusses several approaches for estimating and identifying the impacts of current state variables and expectations on agents' actions. Section 2 presents a brief overview of identification issues in stochastic process models with persistent unobservable determinants. Section 3 describes the data and our econometric approach. Section 4 presents estimates of an approximation to the life-cycle optimization problem governing contraceptive choices by rural French women born during the period 1720–50. Section 5 summarizes the main findings from this analysis.

1. EMPIRICAL MODELS OF LIFE-CYCLE DECISIONS UNDER UNCERTAINTY

A simple empirical model of decisions made at a particular point in time during the life cycle might incorporate the impacts of the current state variables (and possibly expectations) on an agent's actions at that point in time. In a job search or welfare dependence analysis, for example, one might model the propensity to exit the state as a function of the duration of time in the state, state contingent income, and local labor market characteristics. In a study of contraceptive use, one might specify that contraception is determined in part by the age of the mother, the mother's age at marriage, her education, and the number of children in the family at that point in time. Most researchers would consider such simple empirical models of these outcomes (for example, dichotomous probit or logit) as approximations to some true functions determining the outcomes of interest.

This type of modeling approach has many features similar to a reduced-form specification. The approach, however, includes as explanatory variables previous outcomes and behaviors that can have a direct impact on a person's current behavior. Most researchers would consider these "predetermined" explanatory variables to be partially determined by many of the same unmeasured characteristics that affect the current outcome. These previous outcomes are potentially endogenous, so the approach differs from a standard reduced-form approach in a fundamental way. This simple modeling approach is, in many aspects, more like a structural model than a reduced-form specification.

Including these previous outcomes as explanatory variables, rather than specifying a "true" reduced form, serves two purposes. First, it can provide more information about actual behaviors than a pure reduced-form approach. A government program that increases educational opportunities, for example, may increase the ages of women at marriage. Yet it may have no impact on completed fertility. To assess this possibility, one would like to know how the demand for children, as represented through birth timing and spacing, varies with age at marriage. Late marriers, for instance, might increase their pace of childbearing, so the education policy might have no impact on population growth. If one could disentangle these two effects, however, it may be possible to develop better policies for achieving the government's goals.

Such aggregate effects could, in principle, be captured in a strict reduced-form model. The reduced form, however, has two major shortcomings. First, one would not be able to uncover exactly how the women changed their behaviors in response to the increased educational opportunities. One may be able to assess the program's impact, but the analysis would provide little information about how to devise better programs. Second, the true reduced form of a nonlinear dynamic model may be quite complex with a wide range of interactions among time-varying and age-dated exogenous variables. Attempts to approximate this could entail the estimation of a large number of parameters with little precision in the estimators. The second purpose of the modeling strategy proposed here is to help obtain more precise estimates by incorporating directly some of the paths through which the programs could have their impacts.

One can consider this type of empirical model as an approximation to more formally derived models of behavior over the life cycle, such as those considered by Wolpin (1984), Newman (1984), Montgomery (1987), and Hotz and Miller (1989). It is an approximation because it does not incorporate directly the explicit structure of the underlying preference function and the processes generating expectations of the future. In general, an approximating model cannot uncover estimates of the utility function parameters needed to simulate predictions of behavioral responses to changing environments. As discussed in the text that follows, however, it may be possible to identify many interesting functions of the fundamental parameters while imposing fewer restrictions on the data-generating process than are used in more formal models.

Many substantive questions can be answered without being able to identify utility function parameters. To estimate the impact of a change in infant mortality rates on life-cycle fertility, for example, one needs only to know how variations in mortality rates influence jointly the current marginal utility of contraceptive effort and the parents' expectations about future demographic events. The combination of these effects can, in some instances, be estimated without one's being able to identify separately the impact of mortality rates on contemporaneous utility and on expectations about the future.

To illustrate this point, consider the following discrete-time stochastic-programming problem governing a couple's choice of fertility control over the life cycle. David, Mroz, and Wachter (1987) present a dynamic model quite similar to the one presented here and provide some simple comparative dynamics from it. This illustrative model assumes that one month is the relevant decision-making period for the household, it imposes time separability on the life-cycle utility function, and it assumes a one-month gestation period. The model also abstracts from an intertemporal budget constraint and ignores possible corner solutions and multiple births. These more realistic features would add little additional content to the discussion.

Let contraceptive activities, h_t, be costly in either monetary or psychic terms. Contraceptive activities are measured in terms of the probability of conception. Define the vector $D_t = D(i_t, o_t, p_t)$ as the demographic composition of the household at the woman's age t, where i is an indicator of a (just born) infant in the household, o represents the age structure of older children in the household, and p indicates the parents' ages all at time t. D_t clearly depends on the outcomes of all previous household decisions and is influenced by the aging of its members and age-specific forces of mortality. As of age t, D_t is the state variable for the maximization process, and h_t measures the amount of control the household exerts over the accumulation of children.

At each age t, the household will maximize

$$V_t(h_t, i_t, o_t, p_t) = U(h_t, i_t, o_t, p_t) + E_t W_{t+1}(i_{t+1}, o_{t+1}, p_{t+1}) \quad (1)$$

with respect to the level of contraceptive activity h_t, where W_t is the maximized value function at time t. Since the birth of a child is a discrete event, this maximization problem is equivalent to

$$\underset{\text{w.r.t. } h_t}{Max}\ V_t(h_t, i_t, o_t, p_t) = U(h_t, i_t, o_t, p_t) + h_t E_t[W_{t+1}(1, o_{t+1}, p_{t+1})]$$
$$+ (1 - h_t)E_t[W_{t+1}(0, o_{t+1}, p_{t+1})], \quad (2)$$

provided that current contraceptive activity influences only future D_t's through the *event* of an infant's being born at the start of the next period. The function $W_t(.)$ is free to vary with respect to the components of D_t. The presence of an infant, for example, could easily influence the survival probabilities of older children in the household.

The first-order conditions for a maximum imply

$$\frac{\partial U_t}{\partial h_t} = E_t W_{t+1}(1, o_{t+1}, p_{t+1}) - E_t W_{t+1}(0, o_{t+1}, p_{t+1}). \quad (3)$$

This condition has the familiar interpretation that at time t the couple will incur costs of contraception up to the point where the costs equal the expected future value of not having an infant in the household at the start of period $t + 1$. The second-order conditions can be satisfied by a concavity assumption on the utility function U, concave preferences over the number of children surviving at the end of the couple's reproductive lifetime, and moderate discount rates.

To simplify the exposition, suppose that the marginal utility function is multiplicatively separable in contraceptive effort and household composition and that the utility function is strictly concave, as would be the case in a Cobb-Douglas specification. The primary purpose of these assumptions is to provide a simple and easily interpretable behavioral relationship. The marginal utility of contraceptive activity in equation 3 becomes

$$\frac{\partial U_t}{\partial h_t} = g^{-1}(h_t)[C(D_t)]^{-1}. \tag{4}$$

Substituting equation 4 into the first-order conditions 3 and solving for the optimal level of contraceptive activity yields

$$h_t = g[C(D_t)K(I_t)], \tag{5}$$

where the function K is the difference of the expectation terms in equation 3. Note that these expectations are functions only of the information set available at time t, I_t. Part of this discussion assumes that the function $g(.)$ is known, but many of the nonparametric identification results do not rely on this assumption.

The difficulties in implementing such a model in an empirical analysis are well known, and the major problem stems from the specification of the expected value functions summarized in the function $K(.)$. Two basic approaches have been used in the literature. Both make functional form assumptions for the contemporaneous utility function, $U(h_t, D_t)$; they differ in how they specify the expectations of the value functions.

The first approach exploits the explicit dynamic programming aspects of the economic model. It assumes that the researcher has exact knowledge of the stochastic processes governing all future events, as well as knowledge about the contemporaneous utility function for all future time periods. Rust (1987a, 1987b), Wolpin (1984), Montgomery (1987), and Berkovec and Stern (1991) use this technique in a variety of dynamic stochastic models. In general, such an approach requires that the researcher's assumptions coincide exactly with those of the agents. The researcher then explicitly solves each agent's stochastic optimization problem to uncover the difference in the expected value functions. This approach can accommodate unobserved differences among the agents, and such extensions let one control for statistically endogenous behaviors. Identification of the impact of the explanatory variables in these models typically follows from the nonlinearities implicit in the life-cycle optimization problem.[2]

This approach has at least two attractive features. First, the empirical specification follows directly from the economic model, so the estimates correspond to well-defined economic concepts. Second, the estimates can be used to simulate the impacts of changes in the environment on behaviors. The drawback of the approach is that all inferences depend crucially on the researcher's ability to specify correctly the entire stochastic optimization problem faced by the household. This correct specification is required for consistent estimation of the utility function parameters. For simulations of the impact of a change in the environment on behaviors, the researcher must also be able to specify precisely how the entire expectations process changes in response to the change in the environment.

The second approach, applied by Hotz and Miller (1989) and Altug and Miller (1991), uses observations on the "future" outcomes of "identical" agents to help determine the expected value functions. This is in some aspects more general than the explicit dynamic programming approach, for it does not rely on the researcher's being able to specify perfectly the entire optimization problem facing the household. In particular, it does not require a priori specification of the agent's subjective distribution function for the probabilities of future random events. Instead, it infers these conditional probabilities of future states of the world by seeing what happened to identical agents (as of age t) in the future.

From this knowledge of the conditional probabilities of all future states and an assumed functional form for the utility function in all future states and time periods, the expectation of each value function at age t can be expressed as a weighted (and discounted) sum of all possible future utilities. This approach requires the researcher to identify a set of households nearly identical to a household when determining that household's expectations. With interrupted family histories as would be obtained from a census, one frequently must assume away the existence of cohort effects. Unobserved differences across households, such as unobserved "heterogeneity," cannot be accommodated in this approach because one cannot identify the "type" of family when calculating the conditional probabilities of all future states.

The formulation in equation 5 pinpoints the exact source of identification of the utility function parameters. The dynamic programming approach implicitly constructs a complicated function of the current state vector, the fundamental parameters of the utility function, and the current information set to stand for the function $K(.)$. Nonlinearities, in essence, let the researcher separate the effects of the current state vector on the current marginal utility of contraceptive effort and on the expected value functions. The Hotz and Miller formulation replaces the function $K(.)$ with the difference of probability-weighted sums of all possible future utilities. The assumption that one can infer perfectly the probabilities of future states, as well as the maintained functional form for the utility function in all future time periods, lets the researcher separate out the contemporaneous effects of the current state vector from its impacts on the expected value functions. Note that the expectations of the value functions are functions only of the current state vector, the fundamental utility function parameters, and the current information set available to the household at age t. Like the dynamic-programming approach, the Hotz-Miller approach exploits the implicit nonlinearities in the expectations to secure identification.

Consider the case where a researcher is unwilling to take a stand on either the period-specific marginal utility function or the process generating the expectations. An immediately obvious drawback of this approach is that it will, in general, be impossible to identify separately the functions $C(.)$ and $K(.)$ without strong assumptions. At best, one will only be able to identify the two functions up to a scalar multiple and intercept shift. In certain circumstances, the researcher may impose either functional form restrictions or exclusion restrictions to help identify particular parameters of the utility function.

Exclusion restrictions alone can provide some information about the parameters of the utility function with only weak assumptions on the functional forms of the marginal utility function and the expectations of future utility.

Suppose that two variables, say x_{1t} and x_{2t}, are assumed to influence the current marginal utility and not to enter the household's information set. This assumption is quite restrictive in practice, for it requires that everything in the agent's information set that is unobserved by the researcher to be independent of x_{1t} and x_{2t}. Consider using nonparametric methods to estimate

$$h_t = N(x_{1t}, x_{2t}, D_t, I_t) = g[C(x_{1t}, x_{2t}, D_t)K(I_t)]. \tag{6}$$

Under fairly general assumptions, one can obtain estimates of the partial derivatives of $N(.)$ with respect to x_{1t} and x_{2t}. The ratio of these partial derivatives yields an estimate of the ratio of the current marginal utilities (that is, $(\partial C_t/\partial x_{1t})/(\partial C_t/\partial x_{2t})$), even if the function $g(.)$ is unknown. If one chooses a functional form for the contemporaneous utility function [that is, the $g(.)$ and $C(.)$ functions], then it may be possible to make some assessment of the validity of this functional form assumption and obtain more informative estimates of some of the parameters of the utility function.

In a similar fashion, one could use exclusion restrictions to identify the relative effects of variables on the household's future expectations. It is much easier to think of variables that influence expectations that do not influence current utility (for example, variations in mortality rates across regions) than it is to specify factors that influence current marginal utility and do not impact expectations. One could, in principle, recover the relative effects on the expectations process for these excluded variables. The identification of these effects, however, does little to help recover the fundamental preference parameters. This approach does help one to assess the reliability of assumptions placed on the expectations process.

Consider using nonparametric procedures to estimate the function $A(.)$ in

$$A(D_t, I_t) = E[h_t|D_t, I_t] = E[g[C(D_t, u_{1t})K(I_t, u_{2t})]|D_t, I_t] \tag{7}$$

$$= \int\int g[C(D_t, u_{1t})K(I_t, u_{2t})]\, dG(u_{1t}, u_{2t}|D_t, I_t). \tag{8}$$

This formulation assumes that D_t and I_t are observed by the agent and the researcher and that $u_t = (u_{1t}, u_{2t})$ is observed only by the agent. $G(._.)$ is the distribution of the unobservables conditional on the researcher's observed variables.

If u_t is independent of the observed explanatory variables, then the estimated derivatives of $A(.)$ have a direct economic interpretation: they are the expectations of the change in h_t due to exogenous (for example, externally imposed) changes in the observed variables. These derivatives are analogous to the parametric wage changes MaCurdy (1981) discusses in his model of life-cycle labor supply. They measure the sum of the direct impact of a change in an explanatory variable on current behavior and the indirect effect resulting from the change in expectations elicited by the change in that explanatory variable. When u_t is not independent of the observed variables, there is a bias similar to that in the standard linear simultaneous equations model. In this case, the estimated derivatives do not measure behavioral responses to an exogenous change in the observed variables.

When u_t is independent of the observed explanatory variables, the nonparametric estimation procedure can provide sufficient information to predict the impact of an exogenous change on behavior at a point in time. There are, however, three shortcomings to this approach. First, since it is impossible to uncover utility function parameters without additional strong assumptions, one cannot confidently use these estimates to carry out welfare analyses. Second, the nonparametric estimation procedures do not let one estimate expected impacts when the set of explanatory variables is hypothesized to change in such a way that the observed data do not encompass the hypothesized change. This is exactly the problem of making out-of-sample predictions when the relationship is estimated only within sample. This type of procedure could not, for example, predict the change in retirement behavior due to raising the social security retirement age to 75. It may, however, provide a reasonable estimate of the impact of education on fertility for uneducated individuals who are quite similar to educated persons observed in the data. Third, the required independence assumption seems unreasonable when either D_t or I_t contains the outcomes of previous choices by the agent. By using unobserved heterogeneity models, however, one may be able to control for the nonindependence of the unobserved factors and the state variables.

It is possible to incorporate many of the features of this approximation approach with a more formal dynamic optimization approach and retain most of the advantageous features of each approach. Suppose, for example, that one uses an approximation approach to model empirically the expectation of the $(t+3)$ value function at time $t+2$. The identification conditions do suggest that the utility function parameters at time period $t+2$ cannot be identified when the expectation of the value function at $(t+3)$ is modeled nonparametrically. But, if one specifies parametrically the utility function and the expectation processes only for t to $t+1$, $t+1$ to $t+2$, and for $t+2$ to $t+3$, the utility function parameters and the nonparametric function describing the expectation of the value function can often be identified by estimating with data from just time periods t, $t+1$, and $t+2$. The identification conditions require that there be multiple ways to achieve identical state variables at $t+3$, and that these various ways of arriving at the same $t+3$ value function incurred different utility costs.

This approach significantly reduces the computation time required to evaluate the expectations of the value functions. At each point in time, one only need consider forecasts for three steps ahead. In particular, one could combine sequential groups of time periods of observed data (for example, $[t, t+1, t+2]$, $[t+1, t+2, t+3]$, ...) in the estimation and treat the value functions from successive "fourth periods" as "close" in a semiparametric specification. If the model is identified, then one never needs to solve the optimization problem for more than three periods ahead.

It may be possible to obtain more precision in the estimates of the utility function parameters by specifying longer horizons than four time periods. Such extensions would permit more complex single-period utility functions and expectation processes. In the limit, of course, extending the time horizon to the end of the lifetime implies that all of the model identification will be driven by only the parametric specification of the preference function and the imposed specifications of the expectation processes.

2. IDENTIFICATION

There are two important identification problems inherent in this approach. The first concerns the use of a random effects specification to capture what is inherently a fixed-effect problem with stochastic shocks. The second deals with the consistent estimation of the impacts of endogenous variables generated by the stochastic process on future outcomes of interest. This discussion does not present formal identification proofs, but it does indicate the types of assumptions and data needed to identify the impacts of interest.

Random effect models fail to capture the relevant concept in dynamic models because the individual specific effect is correlated with all variables in the information set. The problem is most obvious in nonstochastic models, for each decision made by the agent is a function of all possible outcomes of the dynamic process and of all past and future explanatory variables. In a stochastic environment many of the conceptual problems with random effects remain, but they might be mitigated because agents do not know idiosyncratic future outcomes with certainty.

Consider the case where agents' expectations at age t depend only upon (measured) current state variables and a common set of parameters describing how the state variables influence the joint distribution of future outcomes. Such assumptions are made, for example, in empirical stochastic optimization models with Markov state transition processes. Assumptions of this sort imply that the expectation function $K(I_t)$ in equation 5 could be captured by the age t variables observed by the researcher, so the fixed effect relevant for decisions at this date is absorbed by measured variables. Backdating the process from age t to age 0 (birth or some other early age) suggests that the sequence of life-cycle decisions could be represented by observable characteristics without either fixed or persistent random effects.[3]

Once one permits meaningful unobserved variables into the analysis, the interpretation of estimates becomes more problematic. If the only distinction between the agent's information set and the researcher's observed variables is a set of taste parameters independent of the agent's characteristics relevant for decisions made at date 0, then a random effects formulation like the one used in this study could provide interpretable results.[4] In this instance, one can interpret the derivatives of equation 8 as the researcher's expectation of a change in behavior elicited by a change in explanatory variables at each age,[5] holding constant the distribution of persistent tastes. Correct interpretation of these estimated expectations, however, depends crucially upon the independence of events over time after conditioning upon the assumed random effect.

The second identification issue concerns the estimation of the impact of past state variables determined by the stochastic process on current actions taken by the agents. This discussion assumes that the random effects specification can capture adequately the unobserved differences across agents. In highly non-linear models of the type used in this paper, functional form assumptions alone can provide enough information to identify these effects. Without strong a priori knowledge about functional forms, one would prefer to rely upon other types of information to secure identification.

Exclusion restrictions can provide sufficient information to secure identification of these effects, but the choice of exclusion restrictions must be guided by the structure of the behavioral model under consideration. Examination of equation 5 suggests that any lagged variables that do not directly enter the current marginal utility $(C(D_t))$ or the expectations function $(K(I_t))$ are possible candidates for valid exclusion restrictions, provided that they do help determine the endogenous current state variables. Because of the assumed time separability in the utility function, it is relatively easy to specify observed characteristics that do not directly influence current utility. Time-varying exogenous variables, such as lagged prices or other time-varying measures that are uncorrelated with the random effects, for example, satisfy this first criterion.[6]

The independence of such lagged exogenous variables and the expectation process, $K(I_t)$, is more difficult to justify. In principle, the expectation process could depend arbitrarily upon past outcomes and past exogenous variables. Without some restrictions on the expectation process it is impossible to use lagged exogenous variables to secure identification.

Perhaps the simplest way to impose restrictions on the expectation process is to assume that this process depends upon known aggregations of lagged exogenous variables. The most basic assumption would be that the parameters of the expectations process do not depend upon the past realizations of the exogenous variables. The actual expectations at age t, however, may depend upon the current state variables. One could interpret this assumption as a world where the agents have a fixed expectations process and do not update their subjective probability distribution functions in response to past changes in the exogenous variables. The commonly used stationary first-order Markov assumption falls under this definition.

Less restrictive assumptions would allow the expectations process to depend upon lagged exogenous variables, but in a restricted fashion. Finite-order moving averages of functions of the lagged exogenous variables, for example, could influence the expectations process, and one could still identify the impacts of past outcomes of the stochastic process on current actions. In practice, all one needs to impose is that the aggregates of the lagged exogenous variables used to define the expectation process do not predict perfectly any expectation of (nontrivial) functions of the previous outcomes of the stochastic process given the entire sequence of lagged exogenous variables. This requirement is similar to the rank condition in linear simultaneous equation models.

This discussion of identification issues suggests a potentially fruitful way to secure identification in these models, namely, to incorporate relevant, time-varying exogenous variables as determinants of the outcomes of the stochastic process at each point in time. If these explanatory variables do help determine the outcomes of the stochastic process, one can impose reasonable (and realistic) restrictions on how they affect the current information set. It should be possible to estimate parameters that can measure the responsiveness of the controlled stochastic process to prior realizations of the stochastic process.

3. DATA AND EMPIRICAL FORMULATIONS

The data for this analysis come from the INED national random sample of forty villages, which produced family reconstitutions for women married between 1680 and 1820 (Henry 1972; Henry and Houdaille 1973; Weir 1983). The full data set contains approximately 20,000 marriage records and over 100,000 childbirth records. In this chapter we focus on a small subset of the sample: 1,512 women born between 1730 and 1750 in fifteen northern rural villages (excluding those who first married after age 35), and their associated fertility and mortality histories.

The empirical model takes Mroz and Weir (1990) as the starting point for modeling the stochastic processes generating birth sequences. That model focused on a limited range of ages at marriage and treated age at marriage as exogenous. It modeled explicitly the hazard functions generating conceptions leading to live births, with heterogeneous fecundability, along with waiting times to resumption of ovulation following a birth and secondary sterility.

Our new model adds several important features. Most important, it explicitly models the marriage decision process jointly with the fecund birth process, allowing for the statistical endogeneity of marriage. Closely related to this type of endogeneity is the use of delayed age at marriage as a substitute for marital fertility control. Our empirical model incorporates such relationships by allowing there to be an association between marriage propensities and woman-specific variability in the response of contraceptive efforts to increased family-building pressures, as measured by the number of surviving children at each point in time. We also allow for there to be unobserved woman-specific factors affecting amenorrhea, and we introduce functional forms to minimize the attribution of substantive, life-cycle heterogeneity effects to restrictive econometric specifications. We achieve these enhancements through our treatment of heterogeneity, to which we now turn.

In an earlier work we incorporated heterogeneity only in fecundability (the probability of a successful conception in a month in which ovulation occurred). This form of heterogeneity is labeled "Permanent Birth Hazard Heterogeneity" in Table 17.1. We concluded that there were other dimensions of heterogeneity not fully captured by our model. These might reflect either additional biological differences or different fertility preferences. To accommodate these sources of unobserved variability, we therefore add three additional dimensions of heterogeneity.

First, the new model incorporates person-specific differences in the propensity to resume ovulation (labeled "Permanent Amenorrhea Hazard Heterogeneity" in Table 17.1). This could reflect either different durations of breast feeding or biological differences in the effect of breast feeding on amenorrhea.

Second, we introduce separate heterogeneity terms at each birth interval into the resumption of ovulation process ("Spell-Specific Amenorrhea Heterogeneity") and the fecund hazard process ("Spell-Specific Birth Heterogeneity"). These heterogeneities are modeled as independent draws across birth intervals and across individuals. Their simplest interpretation is that they help control for functional form mis-specification in these processes.

Table 17.1
Comparison of three models with varying levels of heterogeneity control

	Model 1	Model 2	Model 3
Estimated Parameters	35	65	74
Log Likelihood	−36008.9	−35603.0	−35575.4
Heterogeneity Mass Points (#)			
In spell-specific birth (fecund) hazard	0	2	2
In spell-specific amenorrhea hazard	0	2	2
In interval-specific common (birth and amenorrhea hazards)	0	2	2
In marriage hazard	0	6	6
In birth hazard (permanent)	0	4	4
In amenorrhea hazard (permanent)	0	3	3
For permanent common (birth, amenorrhea, marriage hazards, and surviving children effects on births)	0	0	3
Heterogeneity and age-varying effects of surviving children on births	No	No	Yes
Selected Estimates			
Interval 7 dummy	1.799	0.153	−0.111
	(0.097)	(0.210)	(0.252)
Interval 11+ dummy	3.203	0.995	0.378
	(0.1431)	(0.330)	(0.405)
Effect of age at marriage on birth hazard	0.0074	0.0071	0.0036
	(0.0004)	(0.0016)	(0.0021)
Effect of surviving children on birth hazard	0.0163	−0.103	−.258
	(0.0152)	(0.023)	(on average)

We also allow there to be birth-interval-specific correlations between the birth and ovulation processes by incorporating a birth-interval-specific common heterogeneity that influences these two processes (labeled "Interval-Specific Common Heterogeneity"). In addition, we use a heterogeneity specific to the waiting time to marriage process ("Marriage Hazard Heterogeneity") to minimize functional form influences when we introduce heterogeneity terms to control for the endogeneity of the age at marriage.

Third, in addition to the person-specific single-process heterogeneity terms in marriage, the fecund hazard, and amenorrhea processes, we add an additional person-specific heterogeneity term that influences jointly all three processes across time. This term captures possible endogeneity of marriage to the birth accumulation processes. It is unlikely that any biological characteristic simultaneously influences these three processes, so its most likely interpretation is that it captures preferences for number of children as they are reflected in age at marriage, breast-feeding durations, and birth-spacing behaviors.

Fourth, we model interactions between the person-specific multi-process heterogeneity and the impact of the number of surviving children on the propensity to become pregnant. The surviving-children coefficient is the key indicator of the extent to which fertility behavior is responsive to family-building pressures. The use of fertility control was clearly less than universal in France before the Revolution (Weir 1983), and in general appears to diffuse gradually through populations (David and Sanderson 1990). Our interaction terms allow for this variation to be linked with other endogenous behaviors.

4. RESULTS

The top panel in Table 17.1 compares likelihood function values for models with three different heterogeneity specifications, while the last panel in this table displays point estimates of a few of the parameters measuring the impact of variables on the propensity to conceive after the resumption of ovulation. Model 1 contains no heterogeneity, and model 2 adds heterogeneity that only influences the process separately through time. Model 3 allows for there to be person-specific unobservable factors that influence, marriage, amenorrhea, the fecund hazard rate, and the impact of surviving children on the fecund hazard rate.

Model 2 uses twenty variables to control for the unobserved factors listed in the second panel of the table. The log-likelihood function value increases by over 400 points from the model with no heterogeneity (p-value $<$ .000001). Model 3 adds nine additional parameters to allow for the correlation of the processes over time, and its log-likelihood is 27.6 points higher than that for Model 2 (p-value $<$ .000001). The addition of each form of heterogeneity clearly improves the fit of the statistical model to the data.

The effects of several key variables on the birth hazard rate do change appreciably with the addition of heterogeneity. The last panel in Table 17.1

displays selected regression coefficients from the three models with differing controls for heterogeneity. Each model summarized in Table 17.1 includes a set of dummy variables that capture how the hazard of conception for each birth interval differs from the second live birth interval.[7]

First, consider the impacts of birth interval order on the propensity to conceive. The estimates for model 1 indicate that the fecund hazard rates for later birth intervals are significantly higher than for the second birth interval. If the interval 2 monthly birth hazard rate were constant at 0.025 (for approximately six children in twenty years), then according to the model 1 estimates the monthly hazard of conception would be 0.13 and 0.39, respectively, for birth intervals 7 and 11 and higher. These estimates are quite extreme, with the interval 11 and higher estimate implying the average waiting time to conception after the resumption of ovulation to be less than three months. The heterogeneity controls used in model 2 significantly diminish the magnitude of the birth interval effects, with the point estimates implying monthly hazard rates of only 0.029 for interval 7 and 0.065 for intervals 11 and higher. The additional heterogeneity controls introduced in model 3 further reduce the impact of the birth intervals on the hazard of conception, with the point estimates implying monthly hazard rates of 0.022 and 0.036. Neither of these birth interval effects (that is, the deviations from birth interval 2) is statistically significant in model 3. Given that there are few compelling structural interpretations for birth interval effects after controlling for the number of surviving children, mother's age, and the onset of secondary sterility, one could conclude that model 3 does an adequate job of controlling for unobserved heterogeneity of the life cycle.

The third line of estimates listed in the lower panel of Table 17.1 measures the impact on the argument to the fecund hazard rate of having a one-month increase in the age at marriage. Neither model 1 nor model 2 controls for the possible endogeneity of the age at marriage, and their point estimates of this impact are nearly identical and quite significant. A five-year delay in marriage from the model 2 estimates, for example, implies a 50 percent increase in the monthly probability of conception over a base rate of 0.025. This estimate suggests that delaying the age at marriage might be a way for a family to substitute for marital fertility control. Model 3 controls for the endogeneity of marriage, and the estimated impact of delaying marriage on the fecund hazard rate falls by 50 percent and becomes statistically insignificant. After using these more exacting controls for heterogeneity, there is no compelling evidence of a delayed age at marriage substituting for marital fertility control in rural France during the mid 1700s.

The simple stochastic dynamic optimization model presented in David, Mroz, and Wachter (1987) implies that families desiring to limit their fertility should reduce their fecund hazard rate in response to increases in the number of surviving children in the family. The final row of estimates reported in Table 17.1 addresses this issue by measuring the impact of the number of surviving children on the fecund hazard rate. In model 1, with no heterogeneity controls except for birth interval dummies, there appears to be no such response to family-building pressures.

Model 2 adds heterogeneity and retains the restriction that the response to family building pressures is constant across families. The estimates from this model indicate that there was a statistically significant reduction in the fecund hazard rate in response to increases in the number of surviving children in the family. These estimates of the responsiveness of fertility control for model 1 and model 2 are quantitatively quite similar to those in similarly specified empirical models that were presented in Mroz and Weir (1990).

The econometric formulation used in model 3 allows the impact of children ever born on the fecund hazard to vary with the age of the mother and unobserved heterogeneity. To obtain an average effect, we integrate across ages by assuming a uniform distribution for ages from 20 to 45, and we integrate with respect to heterogeneity by using the estimated distribution for the heterogeneity that is common to the marriage, fecund hazard, amenorrhea hazard functions, and the surviving children effects. This average effect is more than 150 percent higher than the simple effect estimated with model 2.

These estimates of the interaction between the number of children alive and the person-specific heterogeneity are graphed in Figure 17.1. Using the estimated heterogeneity distribution, about 39 percent of the population did not respond to family-building pressures, about 9 percent had quite large responses, and the remaining 52 percent had a large response that diminished with age. For this third group, each additional child led to a 30 percent reduction

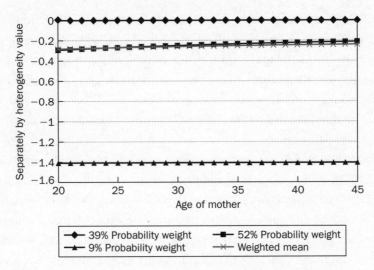

Figure 17.1 Impact on fecund hazard argument of an additional child

in the monthly probability of a conception at age 20, and this tapered off to a 21 percent reduction by age 45.

To obtain a more exacting interpretation of these effects, we assumed that there is no age variation in the response to the number of children alive (held fixed at its mean value for each value of the heterogeneity) and simulated out completed family sizes under the various mass points estimated for the un-observed heterogeneity distribution. We assumed twenty-five years at risk of childbearing, with a ten-month gestation period and no child mortality, and used 1,000 simulations to calculate these effects. For the base case (39 percent), where there appeared to be no fertility control in response to the number of surviving children, expected completed family size was 5.06 children. For those with moderate responses of the fecund hazard to the surviving stock of children, expected family size fell to 3.53 children. For those with extreme responses to the number of surviving children (9 percent), the expected com-pleted family size was 1.81.

In general, one should not interpret estimates from these discrete hetero-geneity distributions as we just have, namely to make statements about how various subsets of the population were responding. The problem is that there is no identifying information that allows one to categorize individuals into particular "types." In principle, all we may have estimated is a discrete approximation to an underlying continuous distribution, and such an approximation need not accurately reflect responses over intervals of the support of the distribution. We can, however, compare the average of these estimates of responses to those implied by the constant effect as estimated in models without the random parameters.

Without random parameters, there does appear to be a significant response to family-building pressures as indicated in the estimates for model 2. But the random parameter models suggest that the estimates without the random parameters severely underestimate the responsiveness of many couples to family-size pressures on average. If one fails to recognize the differences between couples in their desires to limit fertility in response to the accumulation of children, then the statistical model appears to compensate by reducing substantially the estimate of the impact of the number of children on the desire to have additional children.

Empirically, this effect seems to operate in the following fashion. Only those women who have little desire to limit fertility end up having a large number of children. This implies that those with a large number of children at some point in time are those who tend to have little desire to limit fertility. This introduces a strong negative correlation between the endogenous explanatory variable (number of live children) and the random parameter, and this correlation cannot be captured by simple, noninteractive forms of unobservable variables. Even a small proportion of "noncontrollers" appears to have a dramatic impact on the estimates of the responsiveness of couples to family-building pressure. We suspect that random parameter effects could be important to model in a wide variety of dynamic optimization models.

We also explored the impact of several community-level variables on the propensity to marry. We found that women in villages farther away from markets were older at marriage. A one standard deviation increase in the market distance for a 24-year-old woman, for example, lowers the hazard rate of marriage to the level of a woman about three months younger; at age 20 the implied reduction in the hazard rate from being farther from a market brings the hazard rate down to the level of a woman four or five months younger.

These effects are statistically significant at the 0.01 percent level. Increases in local life expectancy also imply statistically significant ($p < 0.0001$) reductions in the propensity to marry. An increase of one standard deviation in expected remaining lifetime at age 30 implies changes in the marriage hazard rate nearly twice as large as those described above for an increase of one standard deviation in the distance to a market. The impact of village size on the marriage rate was small and insignificant, with the estimates implying that an increase of one standard deviation in village population had only half the impact of an increase of one standard deviation in distance to a market.

5. CONCLUSIONS

This empirical model of the determinants of the timing of marriage and marital fertility provides key information about the beginnings of the fertility transition in rural France. Nearly all of the women in our sample had completed their fecund lifetimes before the French Revolution, yet we uncovered important variability in how their marital fertility changed in response to births and deaths in the family. We interpret these variations to indicate that many of these women were practicing fertility control, with the amount of the control depending on demographic pressures in the family.

Marriage patterns appear to have responded to regional variations in life expectancy and to the proximity of a market. Those women residing closer to markets married at earlier ages, and this effect does not appear to be due to the size of the population in their villages. Those living in areas with lower life expectancy also appeared to marry at younger ages.

The impact of age at marriage on marital fertility is harder to describe. Without controls for unobserved heterogeneity that influenced both the propensity to marry and marital fertility, a later age at marriage was associated with higher conception rates and shorter birth intervals. One might be tempted to interpret this effect as meaning that delays in marriage could substitute for marital fertility control. However, it is important to recognize that the empirical model holds constant the main indicators of the need to regulate fertility, namely, the woman's current age and the number of children in the family at each point in time.

The empirical model controlling for heterogeneity that affects marital fertility and marriage (model 3) reveals that the age-at-marriage effect uncovered by the simpler models might be spurious. The magnitude of the effect falls by about 50 percent, and it becomes statistically insignificant. A Hausman test of whether the marriage-age-effects on fertility are the same in the two models containing heterogeneity rejects the hypothesis. The less-detailed models significantly overestimate the impact of age at marriage on fertility.

These estimates also reveal possible reasons why the simpler models uncovered a spurious impact of delayed marriage age leading to higher conception rates. The estimates of the common heterogeneity distribution indicate that unobserved factors causing a lower age at marriage are associated with smaller fertility responses to the number of surviving children and with a higher level of fecundity. Apparently, women who wanted more children and felt less need to try to limit their fertility tended to marry at a younger age, and those desiring fewer children married later and practiced more parity-dependent fertility control.

Notes

1. See Eckstein and Wolpin (1989) for an excellent survey of the specification and estimation of stochastic discrete choice models.

2. The term *nonlinearities* is ambiguous. In this paper, it means that the functions $C(.)$ and $K(.)$ are sufficiently different so that one can identify (parts of) them separately when one only observes their product. Suppose $I_t = D_t$ and $C(D_t)$ and $K(D_t)$ are linear functions of D_t. Then, it will be impossible to identify the separate impacts of D_t on $C(.)$ and D_t on $K(.)$. If $C(D_t)$ is linear and $K(D_t) = \exp\{b_0 + b_1'D_t\}$, then one can identify the parameters b_1 and the relative impacts of the variables in D_t on the function $C(.)$. Because of the functional form restrictions, this latter example has sufficient "nonlinearities" for identification of many of the parameters of interest.

3. This could be estimated, for example, by a nonparametric "probit" procedure. The outcome is whether or not the woman conceived in month t, and the explanatory variables are x_{1t}, x_{2t}, D_t, I_t.

4. The evolution of the random effects in the empirical model over time could be modeled as dependent upon past outcomes of the stochastic processes.

5. This expectation is analogous to the average derivative across agents.

6. This type of variation can be used to calculate particular types of local average treatment effects and some types of effects of treatment on the treated from estimates obtained with these approximation models.

7. Complete sets of estimates are available from the authors on request.

References

Altug, S., and R. A. Miller. 1991. "Human Capital Aggregate Shocks and Panel Data Estimation." Economic Research Center/NORC Discussion Paper Series, no. 91-1. Chicago.

Becker, G. 1981. *A Treatise on the Family*. Cambridge, Mass.: Harvard University Press.

Berkovec, J., and S. Stern. 1991. "Job Exit Behavior of Older Men." *Econometrica* 59: 189–210.

Bideau, Alain, and Jean-Pierre Bardet. 1988. "Fluctuations Chronologiques ou Début de la Révolution Contraceptive?" In Jacques Dupâquier, ed. *Histoire de la Population Française*, vol. 2, pp. 373–98. Paris: Presses Universitaires de la France.

Coale, Ansley J. 1973. "The Demographic Transition Reconsidered." In *International Population Conference, Liège, 1973*, vol. 1, pp. 53–72.

David, P. A., and T. A. Mroz. 1989. "Evidence of Fertility Regulation among Rural French Villagers, 1749–1789: A Sequential Econometric Model of Birth-Spacing Behavior." *European Journal of Population* Part 1, 5(1): 1–16; Part 2, 1(2): 173–206.

David, P., T. Mroz, and K. Wachter. 1987. "Fertility Control in Natural Fertility Populations." Unpublished manuscript, Stanford University.

David, Paul A., and Warren C. Sanderson. 1990. "Cohort Parity Analysis and Fertility Transition Dynamics: Reconstructing Historical Trends in Fertility Control from a Single Census." *Population Studies* 44: 421–45.

Gritz, M. 1987. *An Empirical Analysis of the Effect of Training Programs on Employment*. Ph.D. dissertation, Stanford University.

Guilkey, D. K., and T. A. Mroz. 1992. "An Evaluation of Discrete Factor Models in Simultaneous Equations with Both Discrete and Continuous Outcomes." Unpublished manuscript.

Hajnal, J. 1965. "European Marriage Patterns in Perspective." In D. Glass and D. Eversley, eds., *Population in History*, pp. 101–43. London: Edward Arnold.

Heckman, J. J., and B. E. Honoré. 1990. "The Empirical Content of the Roy Model." *Econometrica* 58: 1121–49.

Heckman, J. J., and B. Singer. 1984a. "Econometric Duration Analysis." *Journal of Econometrics* 24: 63–122.

———. 1984b. "A Method for Minimizing the Impact of Distributional Assumptions in Econometric Models for Duration Data." *Econometrica* 52: 271–320.

Heckman, J. J., and J. R. Walker. 1990. "The Relationship between Wages and Income and the Timing and Spacing of Births: Evidence from Swedish Longitudinal Data." *Econometrica* 58: 1411–41.

Heckman, J., and R. Willis. 1975. "Estimation of a Stochastic Model of Reproduction: An Econometric Approach." In Nestor Terleckyj, ed., *Household Production and Consumption*, pp. 99–138. New York: Columbia University Press.

Henry, Louis. 1972. "Fécondité des mariages dans le quart sud-ouest de la France de 1720 à 1829." *Annales: ESC* 3: 612–40.

Henry, Louis, and Jacques Houdaille. 1973. "Fécondité des mariages dans le quart nord-ouest de la France de 1670 à 1829." *Population* 28: 873–924.

Hotz, V. J., and R. A. Miller. 1985. "The Economics of Family Planning." Carnegie Mellon University Working Paper no. 14-84–85.

————. 1989. "Conditional Choice Probabilities and the Estimation of Dynamic Models." Carnegie Mellon University, GSIA Working Paper no. 88–89-10.

Kochar, A. 1991. "An Empirical Investigation of Rationing Constraints in Rural Credit Markets in India." Ph.D. dissertation, University of Chicago.

Lee, Ronald D. 1981. "Short-Term Variation: Vital Rates, Prices, and Weather," In E. A. Wrigley and Roger Schofield, eds., *The Population History of England, 1541–1871*, pp. 356–401. Cambridge, Mass.: Harvard University Press.

MaCurdy, T. E. 1981. "An Empirical Model of Labor Supply in a Life-Cycle Setting." *Journal of Political Economy* 89: 1054–85.

Montgomery, M. R. 1987. "Lifetime Fertility as a Controlled Stochastic Process: An Application of Rust's Estimation Method." Unpublished manuscript, Department of Economics, SUNY-Stonybrook.

Mroz, T. A., and D. R. Weir. 1990. "Structural Change in Life Cycle Fertility during the Fertility Transition: France before and after the Revolution of 1789." *Population Studies* 44: 61–87.

Newman, J. L. 1984. "A Stochastic Dynamic Model of Fertility." Tulane University Working Paper.

Olsen, R. J. 1980. "Estimating the Effects of Child Mortality on the Number of Births." *Demography* 17: 429–43.

Rust, J. 1987a. "A Dynamic Programming Model of Retirement Behavior." National Bureau of Economic Research Working Paper no. 2470.

————. 1987b. "Optimal Replacement of GMC Bus Engines: An Empirical Model of Harold Zurcher." *Econometrica* 55: 999–1034.

Smith, Richard M. 1981. "Fertility, Economy, and Household Formation in England over Three Centuries." *Population and Development Review* 7: 595–622.

Walker, J. R. 1986. *An Empirical Investigation of the Timing and Spacing of Births in Sweden: The Effects of Changing Economic Conditions.* Ph.D. dissertation, University of Chicago.

Weir, David R. 1983. "Fertility Transition in Rural France, 1740–1829." Ph.D. dissertation, Stanford University.

————. 1994. "New Estimates of Nuptiality and Marital Fertility in France, 1740–1911." *Population Studies* 48: 307–31.

Wolpin, K. 1984. "An Estimated Dynamic Model of Fertility and Child Mortality." *Journal of Political Economy* 92: 852–74.

Wrigley, E. A., and Roger Schofield. 1981. *The Population History of England, 1541–1871.* Cambridge, Mass.: Harvard University Press.